To Mary Ellen
from someone who
loves & admires you,
Carol

LOVE
A BOOK OF DAYS

Edited by
Roy Finamore and Sarah Longacre

STEWART, TABORI & CHANG
NEW YORK

Published in 1989 by
Stewart, Tabori & Chang, Inc.
740 Broadway, New York, New York 10003

ISBN: 1-55670-100-4

Distributed in the U.S. by Workman Publishing,
708 Broadway, New York, New York 10003
Distributed in Canada by Canadian Manda Group,
P.O. Box 920 Station U, Toronto, Ontario M8Z 5P9
Distributed in all other territories by Little, Brown
and Company, International Division, 34 Beacon
Street, Boston, Massachusetts 02108

Printed in Italy
10 9 8 7 6 5 4 3 2 1

Page 1: Marc Chagall (1887–1985), *The Equestrian.*

Page 2: Baron François Gérard (1770–1837), *Amor and Psyche*, also known as *Psyche Receiving the First Kiss of Love.*

Jean-Honoré Fragonard (1732–1806), *Stolen Kiss*.

JANUARY

Jean Auguste Dominique Ingres (1780–1867), *Venus Anadyomene* (detail)

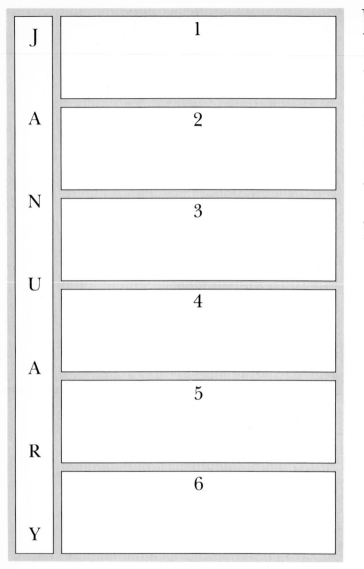

JANUARY

J	1
A	2
N	3
U	4
A	5
R	
Y	6

Had I the heavens' embroidered cloths,
Enwrought with golden and silver light,
The blue and the dim and the dark cloths
Of night and light and half-light,
I would spread the cloths under your feet:
But I, being poor, have only my dreams;
I have spread my dreams under your feet;
Tread softly because you tread on my dreams.

William Butler Yeats (1865–1939),
"He Wishes for the Cloths of Heaven"

Pablo Picasso (1881–1973),
The Country Dance

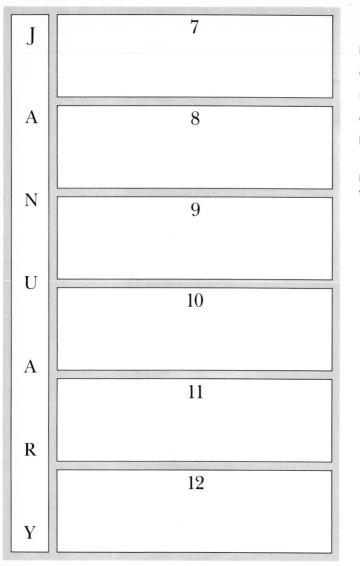

J	7
A	8
N	9
U	10
A	11
R	
Y	12

A great part of all the pleasure of love begins, continues and sometimes ends with conversation. A real, enduring love-affair, in marriage and out of it, is an extremely exclusive club of which the entire membership is two co-equal Perpetual Presidents.

Robertson Davies (b. 1913),
from "The Pleasures of Love"

Kees van Dongen (1877–1968),
Couple

William Hogarth (1697–1764), *The Lady's Last Stake*

ABSOLUTE Ah! my soul, what a life will we then live! Love shall be our idol and support! We will worship him with a monastic strictness; abjuring all worldly toys, to centre every thought and action there.—Proud of calamity, we will enjoy the wreck of wealth; while the surrounding gloom of adversity shall make the flame of our pure love show doubly bright.— By heav'ns! I would fling all goods of fortune from me with a prodigal hand, to enjoy the scene where I might clasp my Lydia to my bosom, and say, the world affords no smile to me—but here. [*Embracing her.*]—[*Aside.*] If she holds out now the devil is in it!

Richard Sheridan (1751–1816),
from *The Rivals*

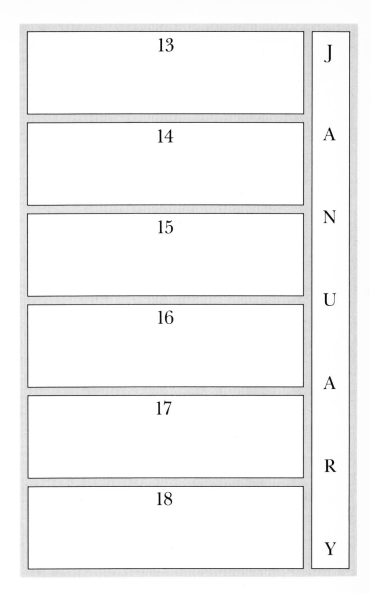

13

14

15

16

17

18

J A N U A R Y

Where are you going, winsome maid,
Through deepest, darkest night? (he said.)
I go to him whom love has made
Dearer to me than life (she said.)
Ah, girl, and are you not afraid,
For you are all alone? (he said.)
The god of love shall be mine aid,
Arrows of love fly true (she said).

Bhartrihari (−651),
"The Arrows of Love"

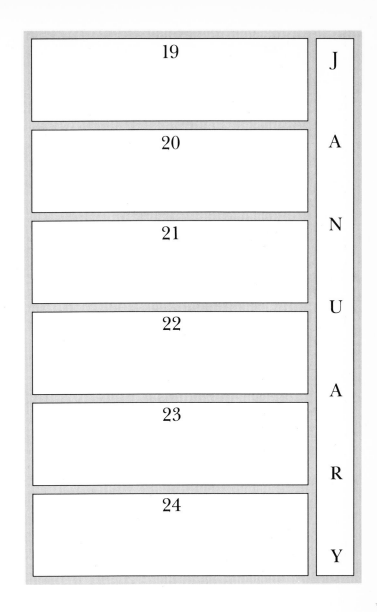

19

20

21

22

23

24

J
A
N
U
A
R
Y

Claude Monet (1840−1926),
Bazille and Camille

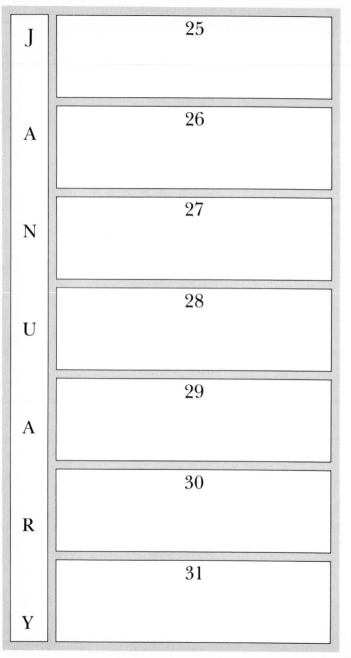

J	25
A	26
N	27
U	28
A	29
R	30
Y	31

To make a final conquest of all me,
Love did compose so sweet an Enemy,
In whom both Beauties to my death agree,
Joyning themselves in fatal Harmony;
That while she with her Eyes my Heart does
      bind,
She with her Voice might captivate my Mind.

I could have fled from One but singly fair:
My dis-intangled Soul it self might save,
Breaking the curled trammels of her hair.
But how should I avoid to be her Slave,
Whose subtile Art invisibly can wreath
My Fetters of the very Air I breath?

It had been easie fighting in some plain,
Where Victory might hang in equal choice,
But all resistance against her is vain,
Who has th' advantages both of Eyes and
      Voice,
And all my Forces needs must be undone,
She having gained both the Wind and Sun.

Andrew Marvell (1621–1678),
"The Fair Singer"

Jean Auguste Dominique Ingres (1780–1867),
Venus Anadyomene

FEBRUARY

Henri Rousseau (1844–1910), *Carnival Evening* (detail)

I took her hand in mine, and we went out of the ruined place; and, as the morning mists had risen long ago when I first left the forge, so, the evening mists were rising now, and in all the broad expanse of tranquil light they showed to me, I saw no shadow of another parting from her.

Charles Dickens (1812–1870),
from *Great Expectations*

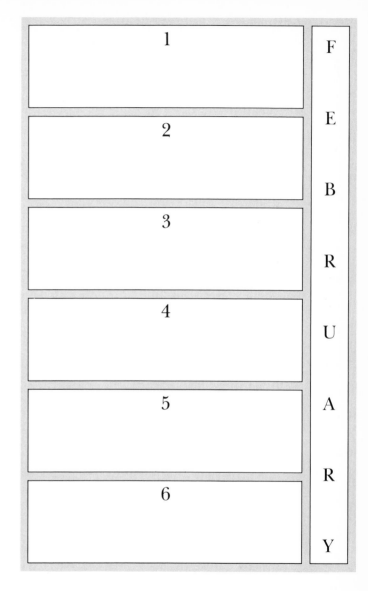

1

2

3

4

5

6

F

E

B

R

U

A

R

Y

Henri Rousseau (1844–1910),
Carnival Evening

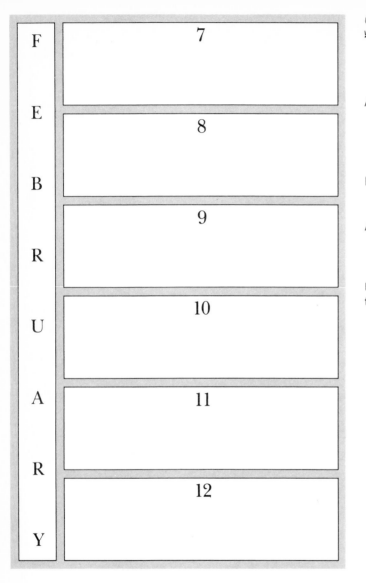

F
E
B
R
U
A
R
Y

7

8

9

10

11

12

Sigh, heart, and break not; rest, lark, and
wake not!
Day I hear coming to draw my Love away.
As mere-waves whisper, and clouds grow
crisper,
Ah, like a rose he will waken up with day.

In moon-light lonely, he is my Love only,
I share with none when Luna rides in grey.
As dawn-beams quicken, my rivals thicken,
The light and deed and turmoil of the day.

Baron de Tabley (1835–1895),
from "Nuptial Song"

Henri Marie Raymond de Toulouse-Lautrec (1864–1901), *The Bed*

By what device shall I my soul prevent
From touching thine? My soul how shall I lift
To other things above thee? Great
Indeed is my desire to have it pent
In something lost in some still spot, and let it
    mate
With darkness which thy gladness shall not
    rift,
And which shall not with thy own deeps
    vibrate.

But all that touches us,
Takes us together, thee and me, as does
A fiddle-bow one voice prolong
Out of two chords. Upon what instrument
Then are we stretched? What master's face is
    o'er us bent?
O sweet song.

Rainer Maria Rilke (1875–1926),
"Love-Song"

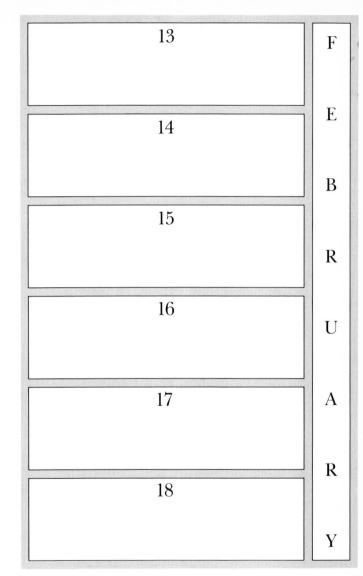

Pablo Picasso (1881–1973),
The Embrace

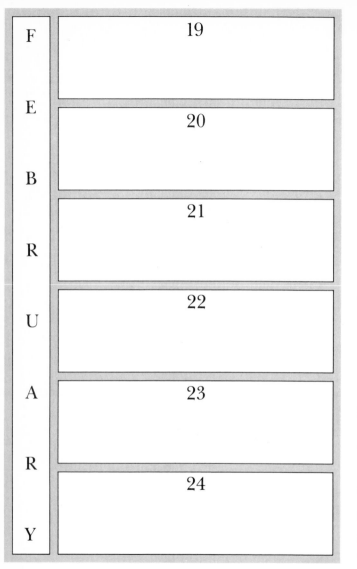

F	19
E	20
B	21
R	
U	22
A	23
R	
Y	24

I want to show you
the maple leaves
growing. I want
to be there and watch
your eyes wake
as the time
cleaves and you can see
through it: two winged seeds,
the young leaves.

I want to hear you
speak for hours about
the world beginning,
about dust pollen and
time's insane ashes,
bloodroots and promises.

I won't be visible,
if you prefer.
I can avoid
presences and words.
I can walk in shades
that don't reflect color.
I can be a person
of no body or mind.

We can meet in
solitude.
You don't even
have to remember.

**Marylin Krepf,
"I Love You"**

René Magritte (1898–1967), *The Lovers*

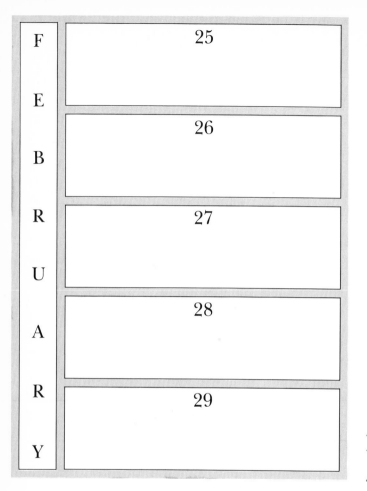

F	25
E	
B	26
R	27
U	
A	28
R	29
Y	

What do I care if you are wise?
Be beautiful and sad! For tears
Add an enchantment to the eyes
Just as a river mirrors skies;
A storm revives the flowers.

I love you most when happiness
Deserts your countenance o'ercast;
When terrors do your heart oppress;
When, overhead, and ominous,
There spreads the dark cloud of the past.

I love you when your eyes let fall
A rain of tears as warm as blood;
When, though my hands caress and lull,
Your pain is irresistible,
Like moaning at infinitude.

I love, divine felicity!
Anthem profound and exquisite!
Your sobs, your heartfelt misery,
And think your heart shines brilliantly
With pearls shed by your eyes so bright!

Charles-Pierre Baudelaire (1821–1867),
from "Sad Madrigal"

Sandro Botticelli (c. 1445–1510),
Pallas Subduing a Centaur

MARCH

Jean-Honoré Fragonard (1732–1806), *A Kiss Won* (detail)

William Dyce (1806–1864), *Paolo and Francesca*

But my heart is brighter
   Than all of the many
Stars in the sky,
   For it sparkles with Annie—
It glows with the light
   Of the love of my Annie—
With the thought of the light
   Of the eyes of my Annie.

Edgar Allan Poe (1809–1849),
from "For Annie"

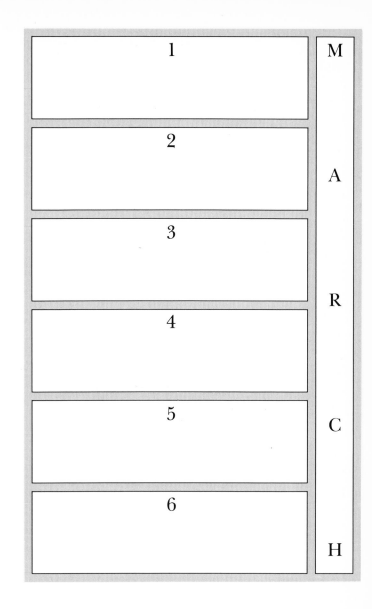

The Princess was silent, then suddenly exclaimed in a low voice: "Try to have a secret with him. Something that, in the whole world, only you and he know of. You will be feeling, then, that he is you and you are he."

Isak Dinesen (1885–1962),
from *Ehrengard*

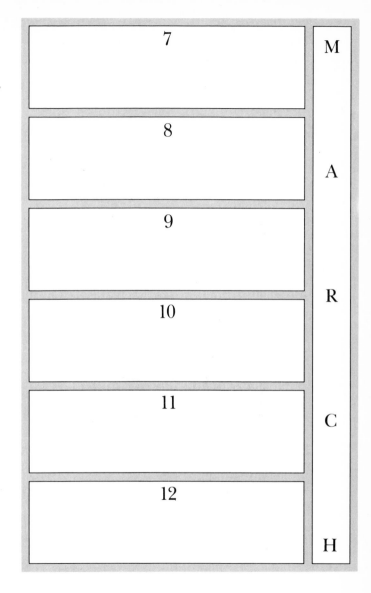

Emil Hansen Nolde (1867–1956),
Portrait of the Artist and his Wife

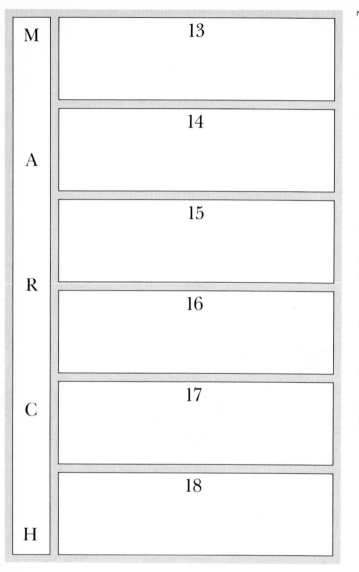

M	13
A	14
R	15
	16
C	17
H	18

The dazzling whiteness of my first love
At the sweet, sad sound of reveille!
What celestial joy was it that opened those
    oriental gardens
To my youthful soul, that morning?
It was a holiday. All pallid sorrow died out
In the green of false springtime;
Everything was charged with laughter, with
    flowers.
The ground was rushes, the air was pennons.
And that sweet blue night, on that bench,
Under the doubled shadow of the drooping
    acacia,
While the moon gave its white flax to the
    world,
She said she had loved me all her life long.

Juan Ramón Jiménez (1881–1958),
from "Elegies"

Gustav Klimt (1862–1918),
Love

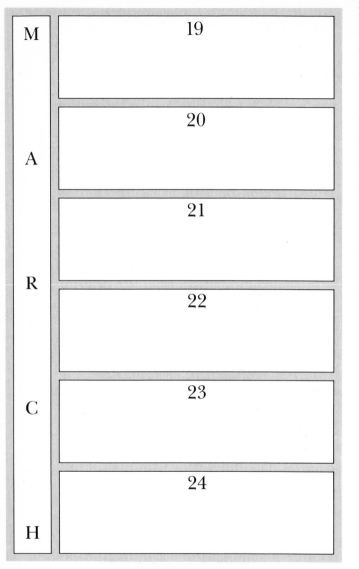

<table>
<tr><td>M</td><td>19</td></tr>
<tr><td>A</td><td>20</td></tr>
<tr><td>R</td><td>21</td></tr>
<tr><td></td><td>22</td></tr>
<tr><td>C</td><td>23</td></tr>
<tr><td>H</td><td>24</td></tr>
</table>

I am a draper mad with love. I love you more than all the flannelette and calico, candlewick, dimity, crash and merino, tussore, cretonne, crépon, muslin, poplin, ticking and twill in the whole Cloth Hall of the world. I have come to take you away to my Emporium on the hill, where the change hums on wires. Throw away your little bedsocks and your Welsh wool knitted jacket, I will warm the sheets like an electric toaster, I will lie by your side like the Sunday roast.

Dylan Thomas (1914–1953), from *Under Milk Wood*

Jean-Honoré Fragonard (1732–1806), *A Kiss Won*

Sir Edward Coley Burne-Jones (1833–1898), *The Love Song*

COUNTESS It's three hours since you've met and known and loved each other. Kiss each other quickly. [*Pierre hesitates.*] Look at him. He hesitates. He trembles. Happiness frightens him. . . . How like a man! Oh, Irma, kiss him, kiss him! If two people who love each other let a single instant wedge itself between them, it grows—it becomes a month, a year, a century; it becomes too late. Kiss him, Irma, kiss him while there is time, or in a moment his hair will be white and there will be another madwoman in Paris. Oh, make her kiss him, all of you!

Jean Giraudoux (1882–1944),
from *The Madwoman of Chaillot*

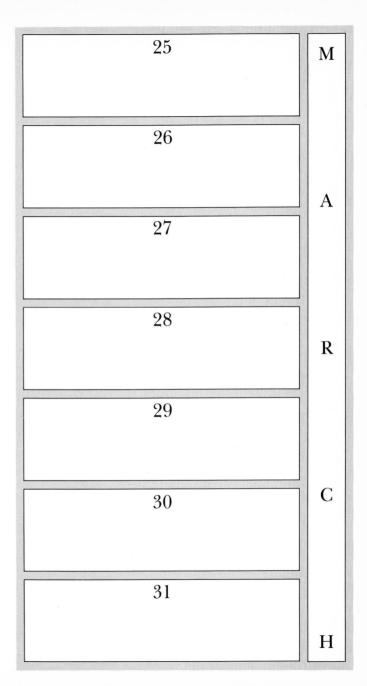

APRIL

Pierre Auguste Renoir (1841–1919), *Dance at Bougival* (detail)

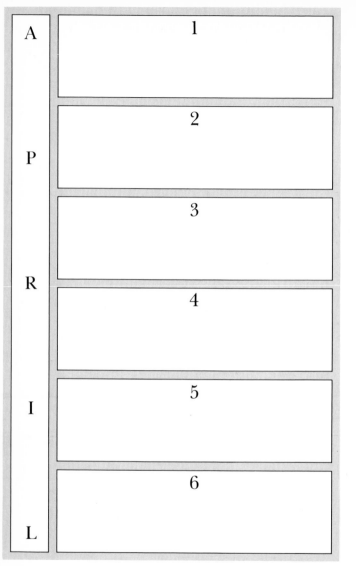

A
P
R
I
L

1
2
3
4
5
6

How do I love thee? Let me count the
    ways.
I love thee to the depth and breadth and
    height
My soul can reach, when feeling out of sight
For the ends of Being and ideal Grace.
I love thee to the level of everyday's
Most quiet need, by sun and candle-light.
I love thee freely, as men strive for Right;
I love thee purely, as they turn from Praise.
I love thee with the passion put to use
In my old griefs, and with my childhood's faith.
I love thee with a love I seemed to lose
With my lost saints,—I love thee with the
    breath,
Smiles, tears, of all my life!—and, if God
    choose,
I shall but love thee better after death.

Elizabeth Barrett Browning (1806–1861),
Sonnets from the Portuguese, No. 43

Angelica Kauffmann (1741–1807),
Venus and Adonis

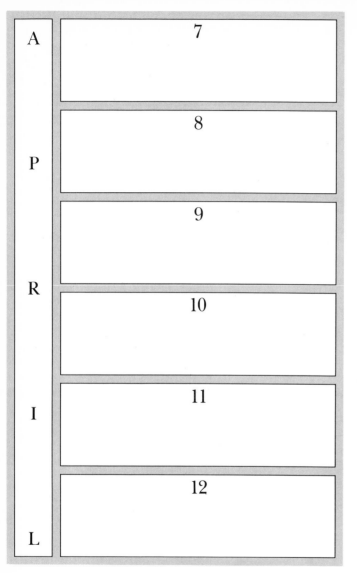

A	7
P	8
	9
R	10
I	11
L	12

At twenty she loved Z., at twenty-four she married N. not because she loved him, but because she thought him a good, wise, ideal man. The couple lived happily; every one envies them, and indeed their life passes smoothly and placidly; she is satisfied, and, when people discuss love, she says that for family life not love nor passion is wanted, but affection. But once the music played suddenly, and, inside her heart, everything broke up like ice in spring: she remembered Z. and her love for him, and she thought with despair that her life was ruined, spoilt for ever, and that she was unhappy. Then it happened to her with the New Year greetings; when people wished her "New Happiness," she indeed longed for new happiness.

Anton Chekhov (1860–1904),
from *Notebook of Anton Chekhov*

David Hockney (b. 1937), *The Second Marriage*

Charles Willson Peale (1741–1827), *Benjamin and Eleanor Ridgely Laming*

Let me not to the marriage of true minds

Admit impediments. Love is not love

Which alters when it alteration finds,

Or bends with the remover to remove:

O no! it is an ever-fixéd mark

That looks on tempests, and is never shaken;

It is the star to every wandering bark,

Whose worth's unknown, although his height

be taken.

Love's not Time's fool, though rosy lips and

cheeks

Within his bending sickle's compass come;

Love alters not with his brief hours and

weeks,

But bears it out ev'n to the edge of doom:—

If this be error, and upon me proved,

I never writ, nor no man ever loved.

William Shakespeare (1564–1616),
Sonnet 116

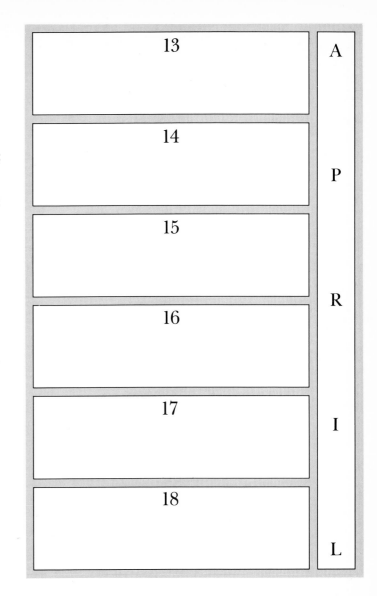

Let us dance!

Surpassingly I loved her eyes,
Clearer than the starry skies;
I loved their swift surprise.

Let us dance!

She had such wild ways, truly
A sweetheart most unruly;
And she took life so coolly.

Let us dance!

But beyond these memories start
The kisses her flower-lips dart. . . .
Since she is dead to my heart.

Let us dance!

I recall, still I recall
Pensive hours at evenfall:
And they are best of all.
Let us dance!

**Paul Verlaine (1844–1896),
"Streets"**

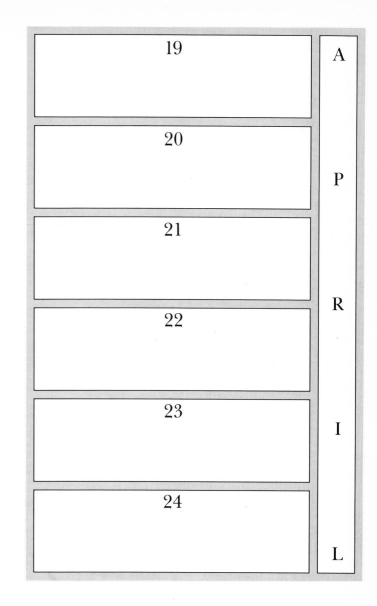

19

20

21

22

23

24

A

P

R

I

L

Pierre Auguste Renoir (1841–1919),
Dance at Bougival

Ben Shahn (1898–1969), *Spring*

Riches this youthful pair will possess—but what is gold? May they be rich in each other's society, in each other's love! May they—I can wish them no greater joy—be as happy in their married life as my—my—as Miss Sylvester and I 'ave been in ours!

Arthur Wing Pinero (1855–1934), from *Trelawny of the "Wells"*

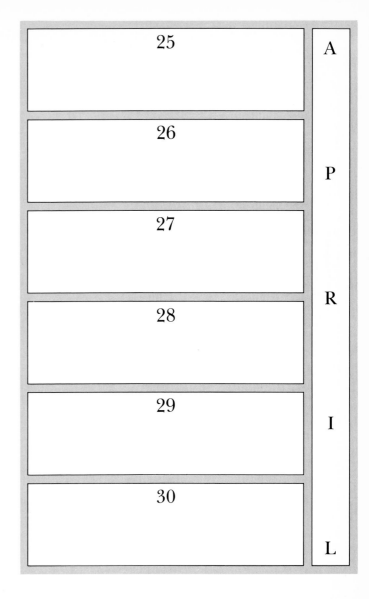

MAY

Sir Lawrence Alma-Tadema (1836–1912), *Welcome Footsteps* (detail)

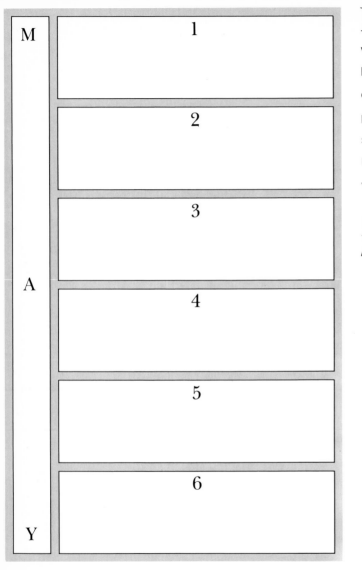

M

A

Y

1

2

3

4

5

6

But then, can I describe what it was like when we were first together? It just had to be. What others find in other ways, the oneness with all that lives and breathes, the peace of all peace, it does pass all under-standing, that was between us, never to be lost completely. Love can be such a little thing with little meaning, then it can be a big one.

Frieda Lawrence (1879–1956),
from *Frieda Lawrence:
Memoirs and Correspondence*

Jane Fasse (b. 1952),
Blue Is for Boys, Pink Is for Girls

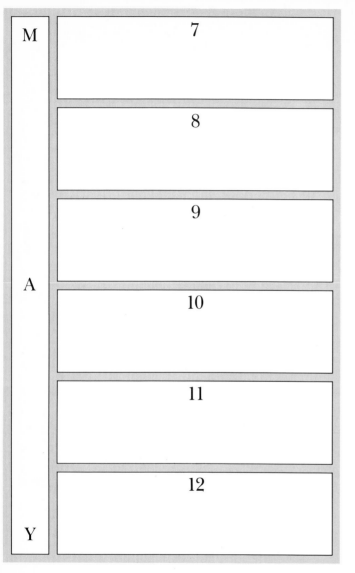

M	7
	8
	9
A	10
	11
Y	12

More than a catbird hates a cat,
Or a criminal hates a clue,
Or the Axis hates the United States,
That's how much I love you.

I love you more than a duck can swim,
And more than a grapefruit squirts,
I love you more than gin rummy is a bore,
And more than a toothache hurts.

As a shipwrecked sailor hates the sea,
Or a juggler hates a shove,
As a hostess detests unexpected guests,
That's how much you I love.

I love you more than a wasp can sting,
And more than the subway jerks,
I love you as much as a beggar needs a
        crutch,
And more than a hangnail irks.

I swear to you by the stars above,
And below, if such there be,
As the High Court loathes perjurious oaths,
That's how you're loved by me.

Ogden Nash (1902–1971),
"To My Valentine"

Marc Chagall (1887–1985), *Birthday*

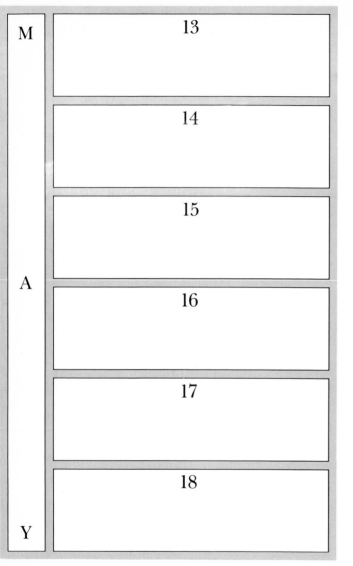

M

A

Y

13

14

15

16

17

18

Love not me for comely grace,
For my pleasing eye or face,
Nor for any outward part,
No, nor for my constant heart,—
  For those may fail, or turn to ill,
    So thou and I shall sever:
Keep therefore a true woman's eye,
And love me still, but know not why—
    So hast thou the same reason still
      To doat upon me ever!

Anonymous

Georges Antoine Rochegrosse (1859–1938), *The Knight of the Roses*

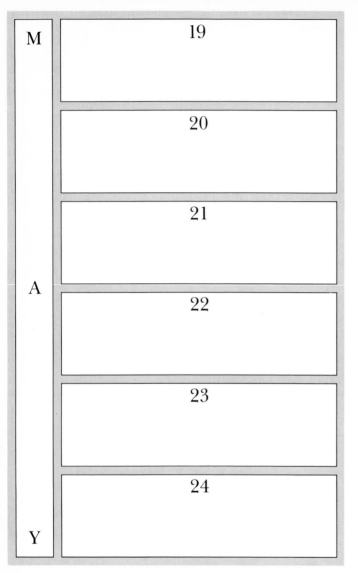

M	19
	20
	21
A	22
	23
Y	24

Deare, if you change, Ile never chuse
againe,
Sweete, if you shrinke, Ile never think of love;
Fayre, if you faile, Ile judge all beauty vaine,
Wise, if to weake, my wits Ile never prove.
Deare, sweete, fayre, wise; change,
shrinke nor be not weake,
And on my faith, my faith shall never
breake.

Earth with her flowers shall sooner heav'n
adorne,
Heaven her bright stars through earths dim
globe shall move,
Fire heate shall loose and frosts of flames be
borne,
Ayre made to shine as blacke as hell shall
prove;
Earth, heaven, fire, ayre, the world transform'd shall view,
E're I prove false to faith, or strange to you.

Anonymous

Edwin Austin Abbey (1852–1911), *May Day Morning*

Sir Lawrence Alma-Tadema (1836–1912), *Welcome Footsteps*

My heart is like a singing bird

   Whose nest is in a watered shoot;

My heart is like an apple-tree

   Whose boughs are bent with thickset fruit;

My heart is like a rainbow shell

   That paddles in a halcyon sea;

My heart is gladder than all these

   Because my love is come to me.

Christina Rossetti (1830–1894),
from "A Birthday"

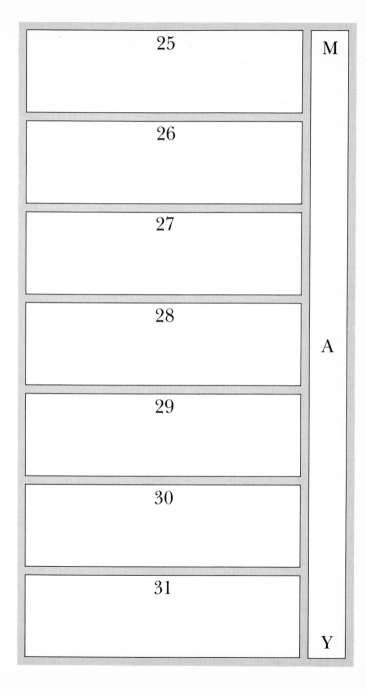

M

25

26

27

28

A

29

30

31

Y

JUNE

François Boucher (1703–1770), *Pastoral Scene*

W here, like a pillow on a bed,
    A pregnant bank swell'd up, to rest
The violet's reclining head,
    Sat we two, one another's best.

Our hands were firmly cemented
    With a fast balm, which thence did spring;
Our eye-beams twisted, and did thread
    Our eyes upon one double string:

So to intergraft our hands, as yet
    Was all our means to make us one,
And pictures on our eyes to get
    Was all our propagation.

As, 'twixt two equal armies, Fate
    Suspends uncertain victory,
Our souls (which to advance their state
    Were gone out) hung 'twixt her, and me.

And whilst our souls negotiate there,
    We like sepulchral statues lay;
All day, the same our postures were,
    And we said nothing, all the day.

John Donne (1573–1631),
from "The Ecstasy"

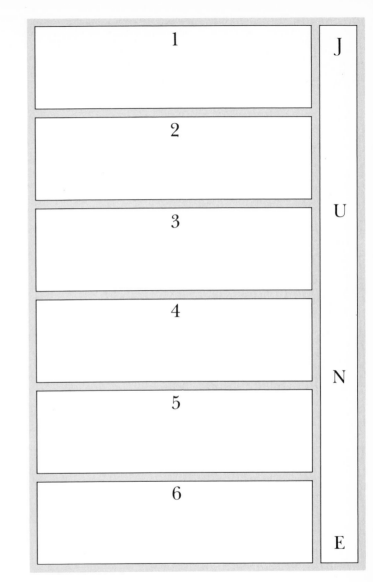

Give me the splendid silent sun with all his
  beams full-dazzling,
Give me juicy autumnal fruit ripe and red from
  the orchard,
Give me a field where the unmow'd grass
  grows,
Give me an arbor, give me the trellis'd grape,
Give me fresh corn and wheat, give me
  serene-moving animals teaching
  content,
Give me nights perfectly quiet as on high
  plateaus west of the Mississippi, and I
  looking up at the stars,
Give me odorous at sunrise a garden of
  beautiful flowers where I can walk
  undisturb'd,
Give me for.marriage a sweet-breath'd
  woman of whom I should never tire.

Walt Whitman (1819–1892),
from "Give Me the Splendid Silent Sun"

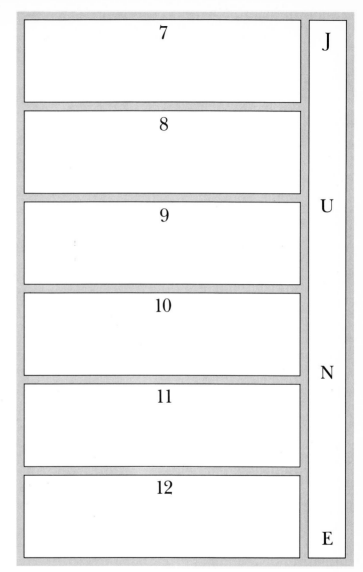

Jean Léon Gérôme (1824–1904),
Pygmalion and Galatea

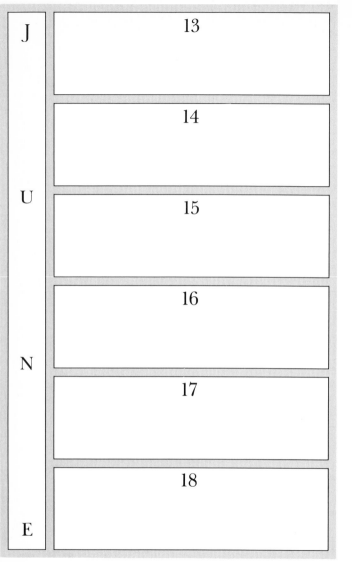

J
U
N
E

13
14
15
16
17
18

And now good morrow to our waking
    soules,
Which watch not one another out of feare;
For love, all love of other sights controules,
And makes one little roome, an every where.
Let sea-discoverers to new worlds have gone,
Let Maps to other, worlds on worlds have
    showne,
Let us possesse one world, each hath one,
    and is one.

John Donne (1572–1631),
from "The Good-Morrow"

Vincent van Gogh (1853–1890), *Undergrowth with Two Figures*

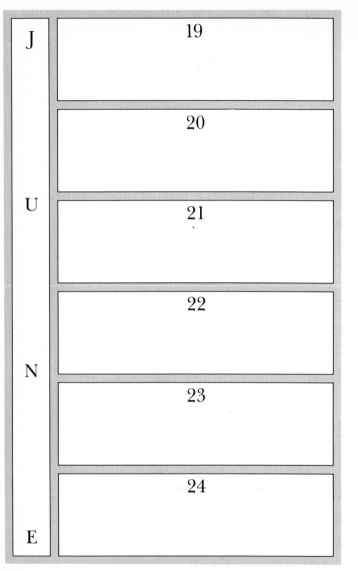

J	19
	20
U	21
	22
N	23
E	24

O my Luve's like a red, red rose
  That's newly sprung in June:
O my Luve's like the melodie
  That's sweetly play'd in tune.

As fair art thou, my bonnie lass,
  So deep in luve am I:
And I will luve thee still, my dear,
  Till a' the seas gang dry:

Till a' the seas gang dry, my dear,
  And the rocks melt wi' the sun;
I will luve thee still, my dear,
  While the sands o' life shall run.

Robert Burns (1759–1796),
"A Red, Red Rose"

Adrien Moreau (1843–1906), *The Proposal*

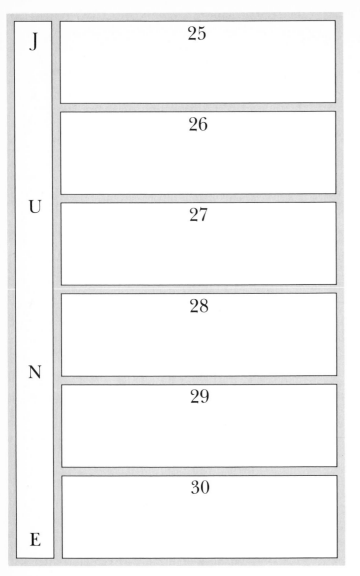

J

U

N

E

25

26

27

28

29

30

I know where I'm going.
I know who's going with me,
I know who I love,
But the dear knows who I'll marry.

I'll have stockings of silk,
Shoes of fine green leather,
Combs to buckle my braid,
And a ring for every finger.

Feather beds are soft,
Painted rooms are bonny;
But I'd leave them all
To go with my love Johnny.

Some say he's dark,
I say he's bonny.
He's the flower of them all,
My handsome, coaxing Johnny.

I know where I'm going.
I know who's going with me,
I know who I love,
But the dear knows who I'll marry.

**Anonymous,
"I Know Where I'm Going"**

Henry Koerner (b. 1915), *June Night*

JULY

Egon Schiele (1890–1918), *The Embrace* (detail)

Winslow Homer (1836–1910), *Scene at Houghton Farm*

Oh! the days are gone when Beauty bright

    My heart's chain wove!

When my dream of life, from morn till night,

    Was love, still love,

    New hope may bloom,

    And days may come

   Of milder, calmer beam,

But there's nothing half so sweet in life

    As Love's young dream!

Oh! there's nothing half so sweet in life

    As Love's young dream!

Thomas Moore (1779–1852),
"Love's Young Dream"

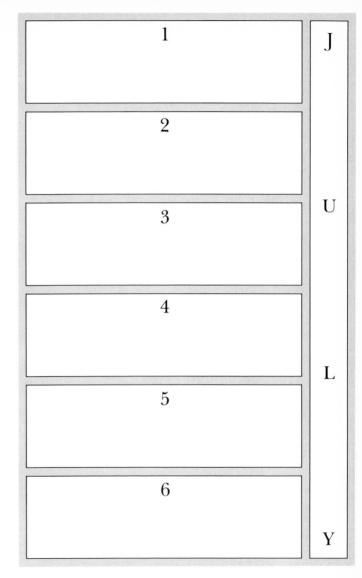

Let others freeze with angling reeds,
And cut their legs with shells and weeds,
Or treacherously poor fish beset,
With strangling snare, or windowy net:

Let coarse bold hands, from slimy nest
The bedded fish in banks out-wrest;
Or curious traitors, sleave-silk flies,
Bewitch poor fishes' wand'ring eyes.

For thee, thou need'st no such deceit,
For thou thyself art thine own bait;
That fish, that is not catch'd thereby,
Alas, is wiser far than I.

John Donne (1572–1631),
from "The Bait"

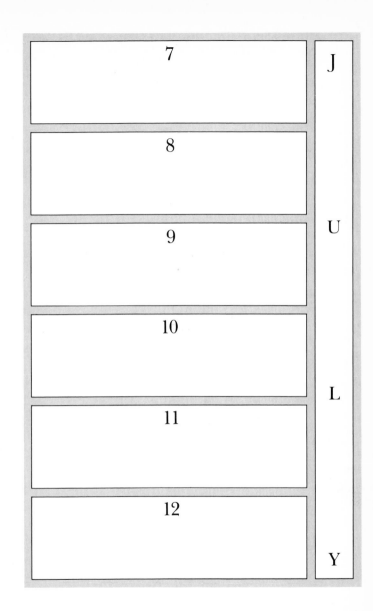

Édouard Manet (1832–1883),
Argenteuil

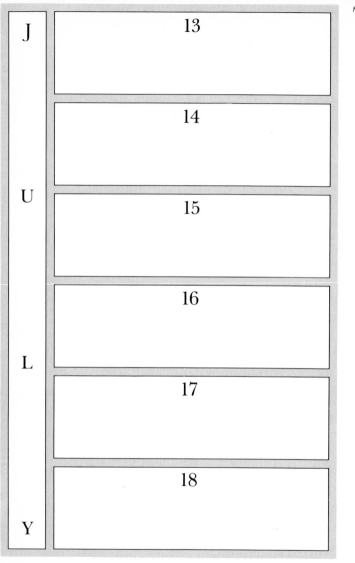

J

U

L

Y

13

14

15

16

17

18

Thy husband is thy lord, thy life, thy keeper,
Thy head, thy sovereign; one that cares for
thee
And for thy maintenance; commits his body
To painful labour both by sea and land,
To watch the night in storms, the day in cold,
Whilst thou liest warm at home, secure and
safe;
And craves no other tribute at thy hands
But love, fair looks, and true obedience,—
Too little payment for so great a debt!
Such duty as the subject owes the prince,
Even such a woman oweth to her husband;
And when she is froward, peevish, sullen,
sour,
And not obedient to his honest will,
What is she but a foul contending rebel,
And graceless traitor to her loving lord?—

William Shakespeare (1564–1616),
from *The Taming of the Shrew*

Rembrandt van Rijn (1606–1669),
Lady and Gentleman in Black

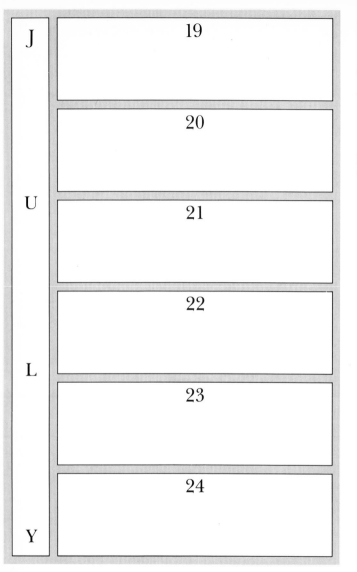

My love I call her, and she loves me well:
But I love her as in the maelstrom's cup
The whirled stone loves the leaf inseparable
That clings to it round all the circling swell,
And that the same last eddy swallows up.

**Dante Gabriel Rossetti (1828–1882),
from "The Orchard-pit"**

Egon Schiele (1890–1918), *The Embrace*

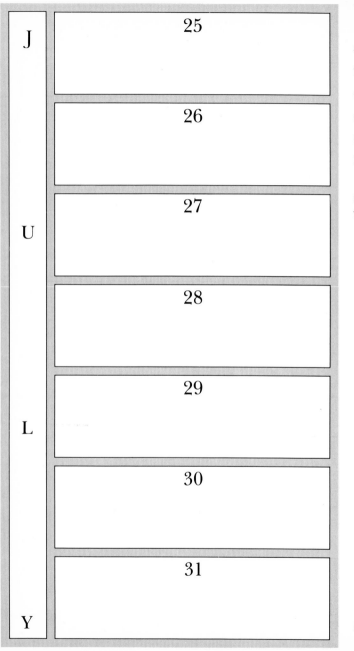

J

U

L

Y

25

26

27

28

29

30

31

Physical Love. You are hunting; you come across a handsome young peasant girl who takes to her heels through the woods. Everyone knows the love that springs from this kind of pleasure, and however desiccated and miserable you may be, this is where your love-life begins at sixteen.

Stendahl (1783–1842),
from *Love*

Pierre August Cot (1837–1883),
The Storm

AUGUST

John Singer Sargent (1856–1925), *Paul Helleu Sketching with his Wife* (detail)

C ome away, come sweet Love,

The golden morning breakes:

All the earth, all the ayre,

Of love and pleasure speakes.

Teach thine armes then to embrace,

And sweet Rosie lips to kisse:

And mix our soules in mutuall blisse.

Eyes were made for beauties grace,

Viewing, ruing Loves long paine:

Procur'd by beauties rude disdaine.

Anonymous

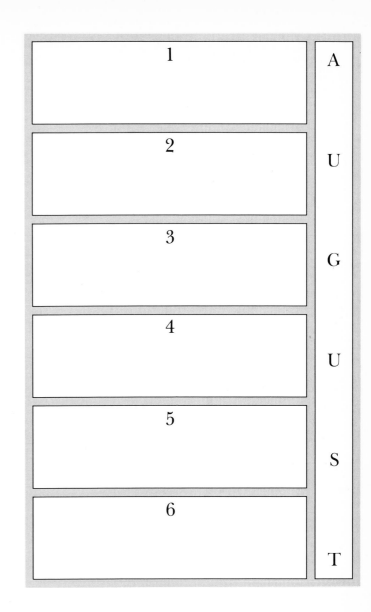

John Rae (b. 1961),
Man and Woman

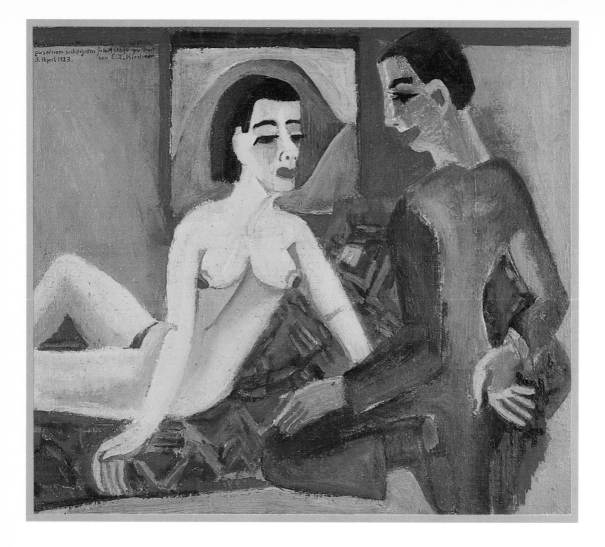

Ernst Ludwig Kirchner (1880–1938), *The Couple*

. . . yes when I put the rose in my hair like the Andalusian girls used or shall I wear a red yes and how he kissed me under the Moorish wall and I thought well as well him as another and then I asked him with my eyes to ask again yes and then he asked me would I yes to say yes my mountain flower and first I put my arms around him yes and drew him down to me so he could feel my breasts all perfume yes and his heart was going like mad and yes I said yes I will Yes.

James Joyce (1882–1941),
from *Ulysses*

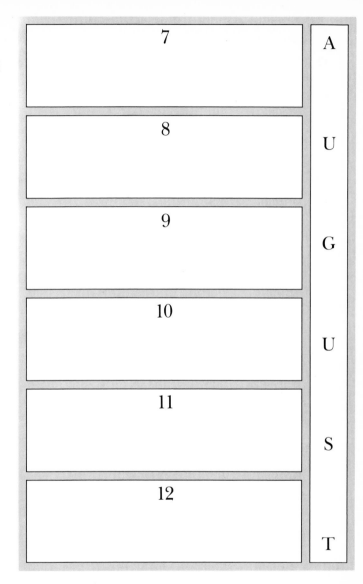

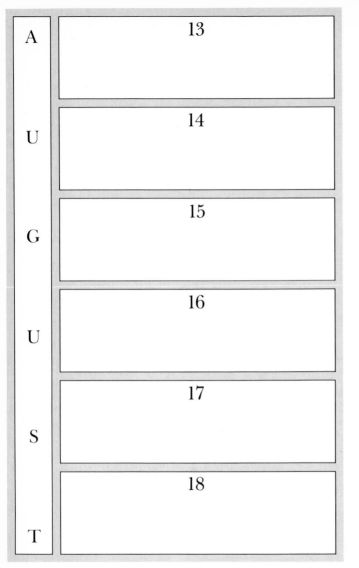

A	13
U	14
G	15
U	16
S	17
T	18

I knew that Gilbert was falling in love with me. I watched it happen. And Gilbert knew that I was falling in love with him. We thought we had been fated for one another, but actually we were only getting used to good romantic luck. It is not so often that well-matched people meet. My being in love with Gilbert was accompanied by a sense of rightness I had never felt before, and we decided that we would marry within a year.

Laurie Colwin (b. 1944),
from *The Lone Pilgrim*

John Singer Sargent (1856–1925), *Paul Helleu Sketching with his Wife*

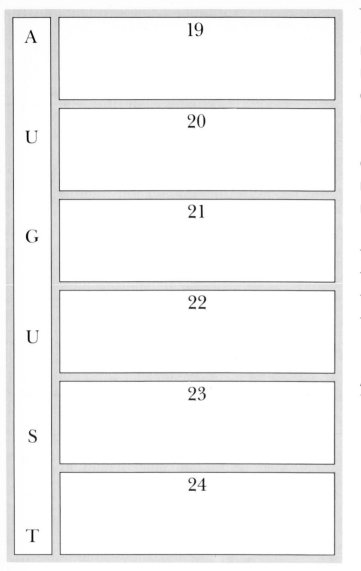

A	19
	20
U	
G	21
	22
U	
	23
S	
	24
T	

If ever two were one, then surely we,
If ever man were lov'd by wife, then thee.
If ever wife was happy in a man,
Compare with me, ye women, if you can.
I prize thy love more than whole Mines of
    gold,
Or all the riches that the East doth hold.
My love is such that Rivers cannot quench,
Nor ought but love from thee give
    recompence.
Thy love is such I can no way repay;
The heavens reward thee manifold I pray.
Then while we live, in love lets so persever,
That when we live no more, we may live
    ever.

Anne Bradstreet (c. 1612–1672),
"To my Dear and Loving Husband"

Thomas Hart Benton (1889–1975),
Romance

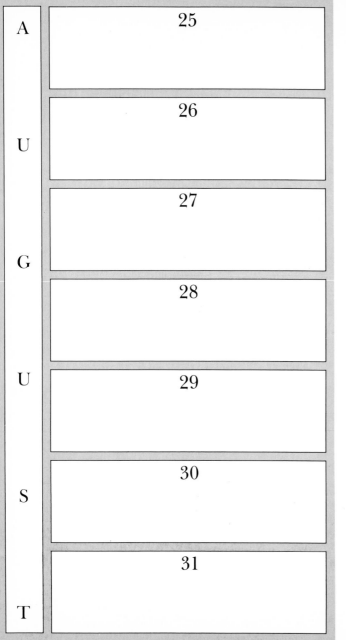

A	25
U	26
G	27
U	28
S	29
	30
T	31

Then I cried out upon him: Cease,
Leave me in peace;
Fear not that I should crave
Aught thou mayst have.
Leave me in peace, yea trouble me no more,
Lest I arise and chase thee from my door.
What, shall I not be let
Alone, that thou dost vex me yet?

Christina Rossetti (1830–1894),
from "Despised and Rejected"

Anna Lee Merritt (1844–1930),
Love Locked Out

SEPTEMBER

John J. Lee (active 1850–1860), *Sweethearts and Wives* (detail)

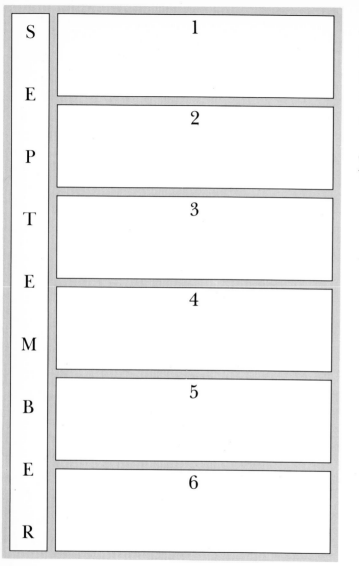

1

2

3

4

5

6

A lover is easily found, but someone who is everything at once and who would leave you an orphan, a widow, and friendless, if he left you, would be a miracle. You are that miracle—I adore you!

Colette (1873–1954),
from *Young Lady of Paris*

John J. Lee (active 1850–1860),
Sweethearts and Wives

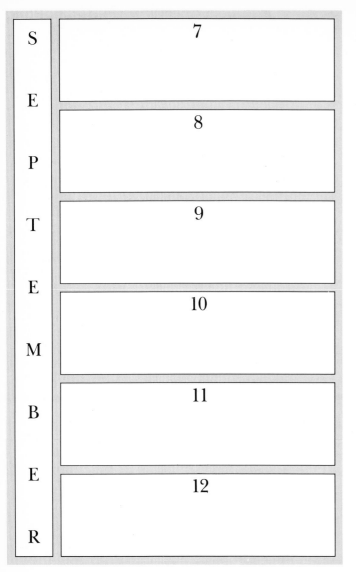

S	7
E	
P	8
T	9
E	
M	10
B	11
E	
R	12

If you hear her snore
It is not before you love her
You love her so that to be her beau is very
lovely
She is sweetly there and her curly hair is
very lovely
She is sweetly here and I am very near and
that is very lovely.
She is my tender sweet and her little feet
are stretched out well which is a treat
and very lovely
Her little tender nose is between her little
eyes which close and are very lovely.
She is very lovely and mine which is very
lovely.

Gertrude Stein (1874–1946),
from "A Valentine for Sherwood Anderson"

Pablo Picasso (1881–1973), *Sleeping Peasants*

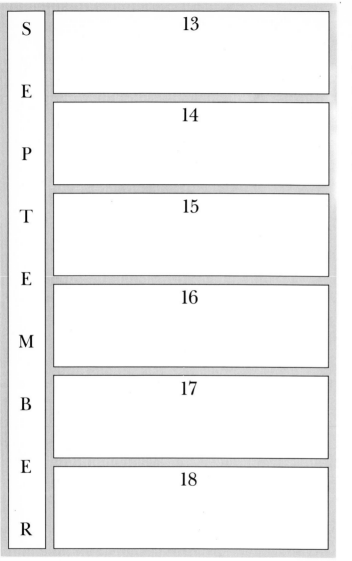

S
E
P
T
E
M
B
E
R

13

14

15

16

17

18

Therefore I shall speak to you of love. Speak in the night. Speak before both night and love are gone—and the eye of day looks upon my sorrow and my shame; upon my blackened face; upon my burnt-up heart."

Joseph Conrad (1857–1924),
from "The Lagoon"

Jean Auguste Dominique Ingres (1780–1867),
Francesca of Rimini and Paolo Malatesta

PEGEEN [*looking at him playfully*] And it's that kind of a poacher's love you'd make, Christy Mahon, on the sides of Neifin, when the night is down?

CHRISTY It's little you'll think if my love's a poacher's or an earl's itself when you'll feel my two hands stretched around you, and I squeezing kisses on your puckered lips till I'd feel a kind of pity for the Lord God is all ages sitting lonesome in his golden chair.

John Millington Synge (1871–1909),
from *Playboy of the Western World*

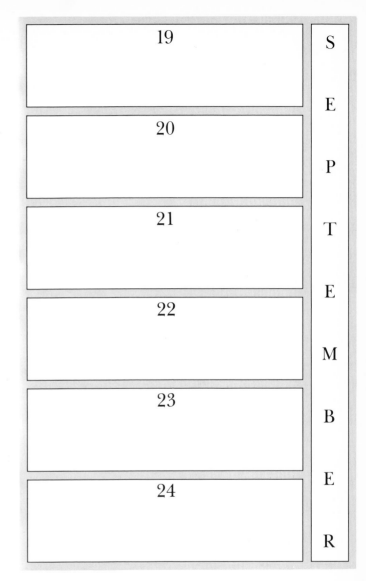

19	S
20	E
	P
21	T
22	E
	M
23	B
	E
24	R

Frans van Mieris (1635–1681),
The Officer and the Light-O'-Love

Philip R. Goodwin

F or when the storms of time have moved
Waves on that cheek that was beloved,
When a fair lady's face is pined
And yellow spread where red once shined,
When beauty, youth and all sweets leave her,
Love may return, but lovers never.

Oh, love me then, and now begin it,
Let us not lose this present minute.

Thomas Carew (1595?–1639?),
from "Persuasions to Love"

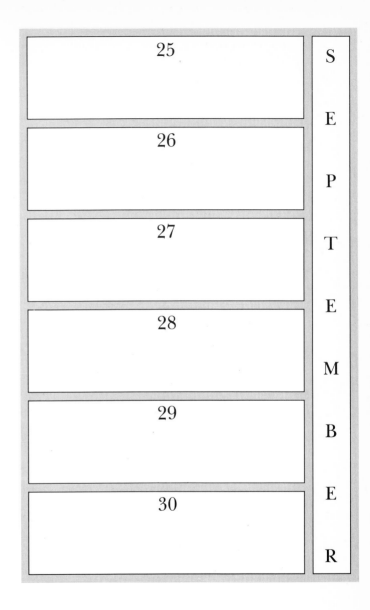

	SEPTEMBER
25	
26	
27	
28	
29	
30	

Philip R. Goodwin (1882–1935),
Seeking Shelter from the Rain

OCTOBER

Fernando Botero (b. 1932), *Dancing in Colombia* (detail)

Haynes King (1831–1904), *Jealousy and Flirtation*

Oh, the sweet lies lurk in kisses!
  Oh, the charm of make-believe!
Oh, to be deceived sweet bliss is,
  Bliss still sweeter to deceive!

What thou'lt grant, I know, my fairest,
  Vowing, "Nay, I never must!"
I will trust whate'er thou swearest,
  I will swear what thou wilt trust.

Heinrich Heine (1797–1856),
"Oh, the Sweet Lies Lurk in Kisses!"

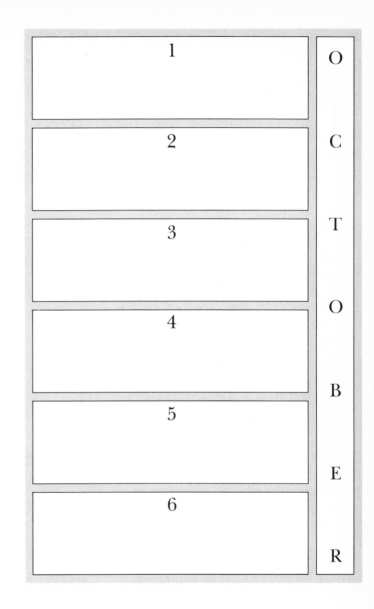

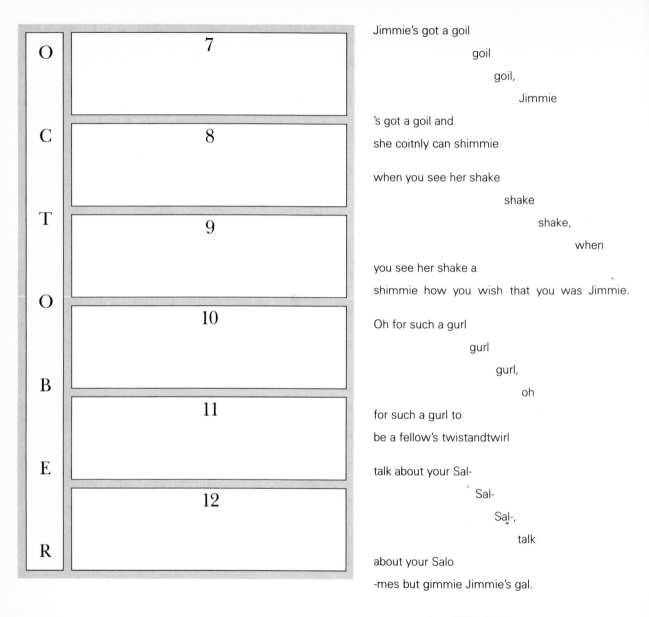

Jimmie's got a goil
            goil
              goil,
                Jimmie
's got a goil and
she coitnly can shimmie

when you see her shake
                shake
                  shake,
                    when
you see her shake a
shimmie how you wish that you was Jimmie.

Oh for such a gurl
              gurl
                gurl,
                  oh
for such a gurl to
be a fellow's twistandtwirl

talk about your Sal-
              Sal-
                Sal-,
                  talk
about your Salo
-mes but gimmie Jimmie's gal.

e. e. cummings (1894–1962),
is 5, VI

Fernando Botero (b. 1932), *Dancing in Colombia*

First of all, love is a joint experience between two persons—but the fact that it is a joint experience does not mean that it is a similar experience to the two people involved. There are the lover and the beloved, but these two come from different countries. Often the beloved is only a stimulus for all the stored-up love which has lain quiet within the lover for a long time hitherto. And somehow every lover knows this. He feels in his soul that his love is a solitary thing. He comes to know a new, strange loneliness and it is this knowledge which makes him suffer. So there is only one thing for the lover to do. He must house his love within himself as best he can; he must create for himself a whole new inward world—a world intense and strange, complete in himself. Let it be added here that this lover about whom we speak need not necessarily be a young man saving for a wedding ring—this lover can be man, woman, child, or indeed any human creature on this earth.

Carson McCullers (1917–1967),
from *The Ballad of the Sad Café*

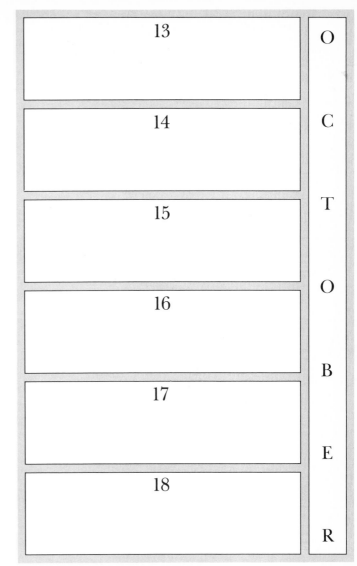

OCTOBER

Gabriel Metsu (1629–1667), *Lady and Cavalryman*

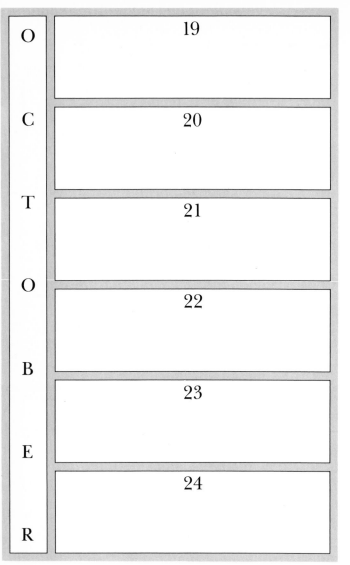

OCTOBER

O	19
C	20
T	21
O	22
B	23
E	24
R	

She opened the door of the West to me,
    With its loud sea-lashings
    And cliff-side clashings
Of waters rife with revelry.

She opened the door of Romance to me,
    The door from a cell
    I had known too well,
Too long, till then, and was fain to flee.

She opened the door of a Love to me,
    That passed the wry
    World-welters by
As far as the arching blue the lea.

She opens the door of the Past to me,
    Its magic lights,
    Its heavenly heights,
When forward little is to see!

**Thomas Hardy (1840–1928),
"She Opened the Door"**

Edvard Munch (1863–1944), *Adam and Eve*

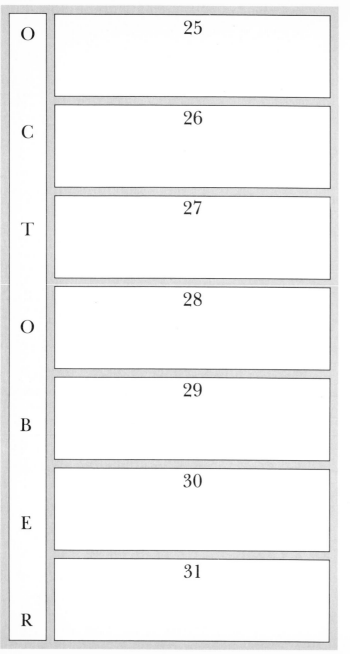

O	25
C	26
T	27
O	28
B	29
E	30
R	31

Ah, love, let us be true
To one another! for the world, which seems
To lie before us like a land of dreams,
So various, so beautiful, so new,
Hath really neither joy, nor love, nor light,
Nor certitude, nor peace, nor help for pain;
And we are here as on a darkling plain
Swept with confused alarms of struggle and
     flight,
Where ignorant armies clash by night.

**Matthew Arnold (1882–1888),
from "Dover Beach"**

Titian (Tiziano Vecellio) (c. 1487–1576), *Venus and Adonis*

NOVEMBER

Michelangelo Merisi da Caravaggio (1571–1610), *The Fortune Teller* (detail)

Let him kiss me with the kisses of his mouth: for thy love *is* better than wine.

Song of Solomon 1:2

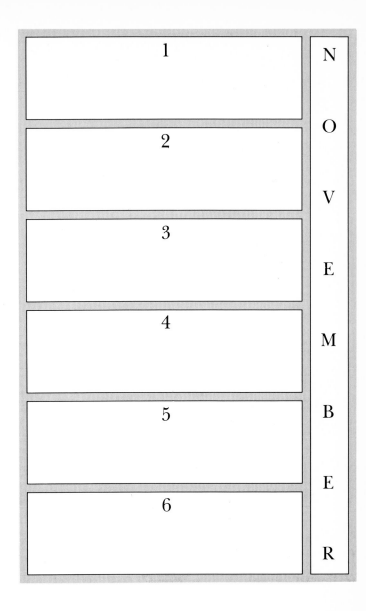

N
O
V
E
M
B
E
R

1

2

3

4

5

6

Francesco Hayez (1791–1882),
The Kiss

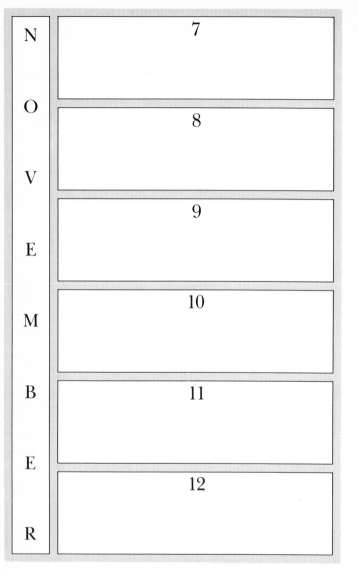

N	7
O	
V	8
E	
	9
M	
	10
B	
E	11
R	12

I will not go when she calls
even if she says I love you,
especially that,
even though she swears
and promises nothing
but love love.

The light in this room
covers every
thing equally;
my arm throws no shadow even,
it too is consumed with light.

But this word *love*—
this word grows dark, grows
heavy and shakes itself
and begins to eat
through this paper.
Listen.

Raymond Carver (1938–1988),
"This Word *Love*"

Michelangelo Merisi da Caravaggio (1571–1610), *The Fortune Teller*

Isidro Nonell y Monturiol (1873–1911), *Woe*

I love you, May," he'd say, kissing her forehead or her hair. He never wanted to make love on Sunday afternoons. Only to hold her in the stillness for half an hour or more until it seemed to May that a spell came over them, a heavy sense of peace, as if the whole of life had swept away from them in a great wave and they'd become as motionless and changeless as the rocking chair beside the window, the tall white dresser and the row of pictures on the flowered wall that grew more dim and less distinct each minute in the dusky room. She would imagine the darkness grow-ing in the house, filling up the unlit rooms downstairs, the empty kitchen growing deso-late and grey and disappearing, until she'd suddenly jump up from the dark bed and with a beating heart she'd hurry like a child from room to room snapping the lights on, her face urgent and serious, as if she were preventing a great death.

Ellen Wilbur,
from "Sundays"

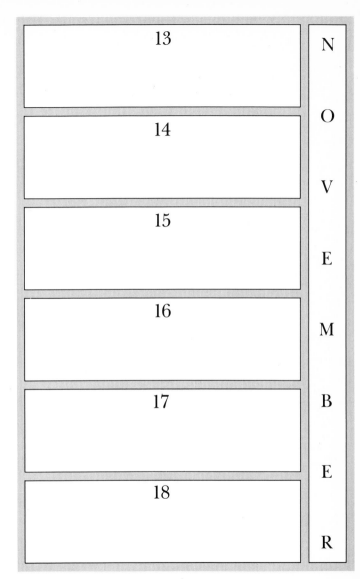

13

14

15

16

17

18

N
O
V
E
M
B
E
R

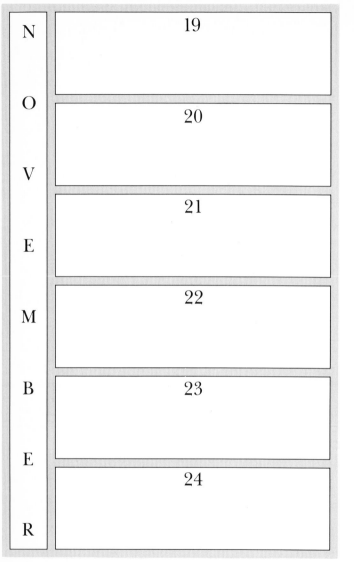

N
O
V
E
M
B
E
R

19

20

21

22

23

24

Love, the fisher, casts his woman-hook
 Into the sea of lust and fond desire,
And just as soon as greedy men-fish look
 And snap the red bait, lips so sweet, so
  dire:
Then he is quick to catch them and to cook
 The hungry wretches over passion's fire.

Bhartrihari (−651),
"Love, the Fisher"

Peter Paul Rubens (1577−1640),
A Shepherd Embracing a Woman

Love is born. To love is to enjoy seeing, touching, and sensing with all the senses, as closely as possible, a lovable object which loves in return.

Stendahl (1783–1842),
from *Love*

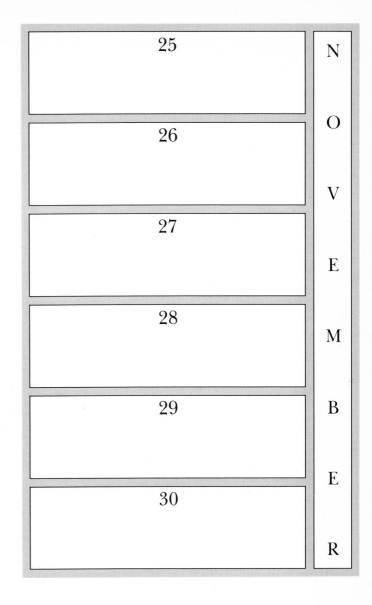

25	N
26	O
27	V
28	E
29	M
30	B
	E
	R

Niccolò dell'Abbate (c. 1512–1571),
Eros and Psyche

DECEMBER

Paolo Veronese (c. 1528–1588), *Mars and Venus* (detail)

Jean-Honoré Fragonard (1732–1806), *The Bolt*

A sweet disorder in the dress

Kindles in clothes a wantonness:—

A lawn about the shoulders thrown

Into a fine distraction,—

An erring lace, which here and there

Enthrals the crimson stomacher,—

A cuff neglectful, and thereby

Ribbands to flow confusedly,—

A winning wave, deserving note,

In the tempestuous petticoat,—

A careless shoe-string, in whose tie

I see a wild civility,—

Do more bewitch me, than when art

Is too precise in every part.

Robert Herrick (1591–1674),
"Delight in Disorder"

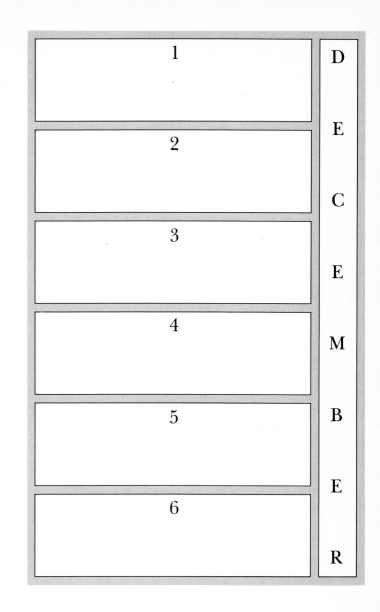

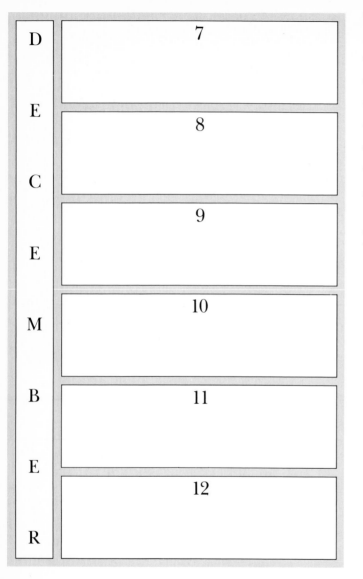

D E C E M B E R

7

8

9

10

11

12

We've been so close for so long that it is only in flashes that I see him aging, and I have one of these as he comes toward me. How gray he is now! There are wrinkles around his eyes. It must be the same with me, although I don't really see it. In another twenty years, if we are lucky, we will both be old. I ask him about his day.

Joanne Greenberg (b. 1932),
from "Days of Awe"

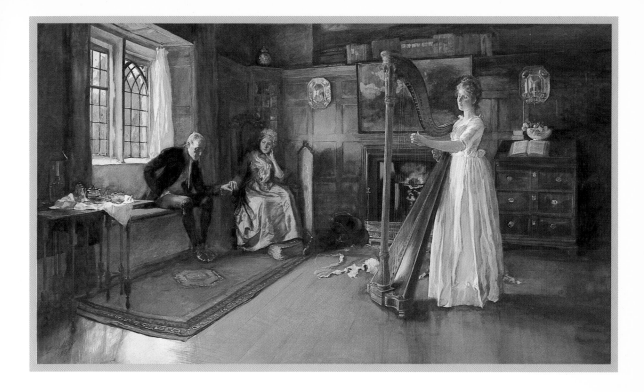

Edwin Austin Abbey (1852–1911), *An Old Song*

In what ideal world or part of heaven
    Did Nature find the model of that face
    And form, so fraught with loveliness and
        grace,
In which to our creation she has given
Her prime proof of creative power above?
What fountain nymph or goddess ever let
    Such lovely tresses float of gold refined
    Upon the breeze, or in a single mind
Where have so many virtues ever met,
E'en though those charms have slain my
        bosom's weal?
    He knows not love, who has not seen her
        eyes
    Turn when she sweetly speaks, or smiles,
        or sighs,
Or how the power of love can hurt or heal.

Francesco Petrarca (1304–1374),
from "Sonnets to Laura"

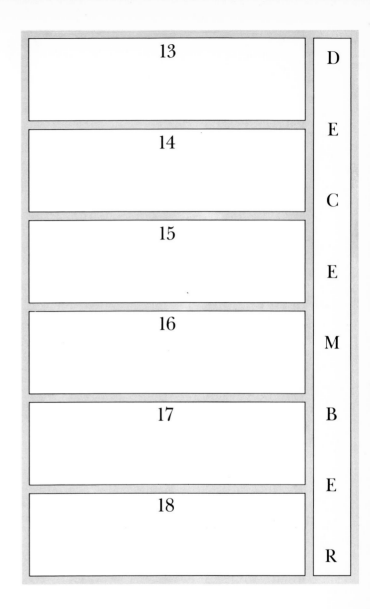

Paolo Veronese (c. 1528–1588),
Mars and Venus

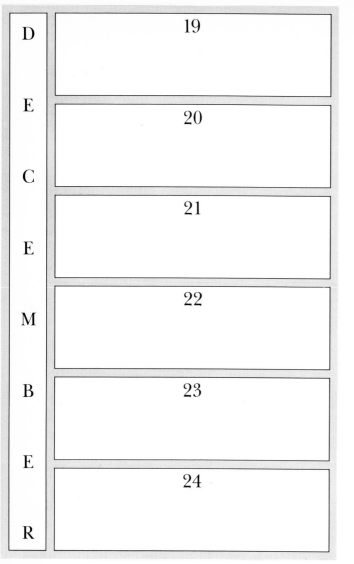

DECEMBER

19

20

21

22

23

24

Oh, what toil it is
loving you as I love you!

For the love of you, the air,
my heart
and this hat pain me.

Who would buy from me
this ribbon that I have
and this white thread
of sadness, to make handkerchiefs?

Oh, what toil it is
loving you as I love you!

Federico García Lorca (1898–1936),
"It Is True"

Peppino Mangravite (1896–1978),
Young Couple Drinking

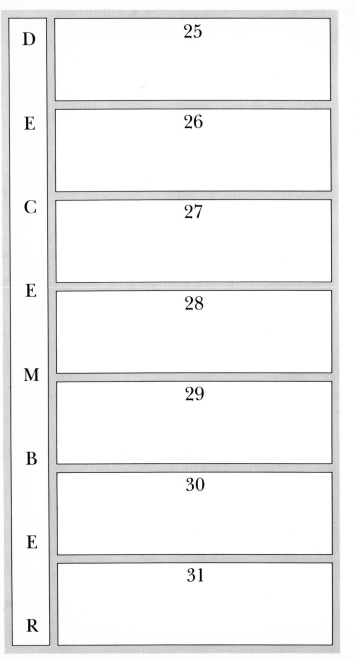

What is love? 'tis not hereafter;
Present mirth hath present laughter;
What's to come is still unsure:
In delay there lies no plenty;
Then come kiss me, sweet and twenty,
Youth's a stuff will not endure.

**William Shakespeare (1564–1616),
from** *Twelfth Night*

Edvard Munch (1863–1944), *The Kiss on the Beach*

SOURCES

Art

Cover (detail), page 1: Marc Chagall (1887–1985), *The Equestrian.* Stedelijk Museum, Amsterdam.

Page 2: Baron François Gérard (1770–1837), *Amor and Psyche*, also known as *Psyche Receiving the First Kiss of Love.* Scala/Art Resource, New York.

Page 5: Jean Honoré Fragonard (1732–1806), *Stolen Kiss* (cat. no. 461). The Hermitage, Leningrad.

Page 6 (detail), page 17: Jean Auguste Dominique Ingres (1780–1867), *Venus Anadyomene.* Giraudon/Art Resource, New York.

Page 9: Pablo Picasso (1881–1973), *The Country Dance.* Giraudon/Art Resource, New York.

Page 11: Kees Van Dongen (1877–1968), *Couple.* SEF/Art Resource, New York.

Page 12: William Hogarth (1697–1764), *The Lady's Last Stake* (1759, oil on canvas, 36″ × 41½″). Albright-Knox Art Gallery, Buffalo, New York. Gift of Seymour H. Knox, 1945.

Page 14: Claude Monet (1840–1926), *Bazille and Camille.* National Gallery of Art, Washington, D.C. Ailsa Mellon Bruce Collection.

Page 18 (detail), page 20: Henri Rousseau (1844–1910), *Carnival Evening.* Philadelphia Museum of Art. Louis E. Stern Collection.

Page 23: Henri Marie Raymond de Toulouse-Lautrec (1864–1901), *The Bed.* Giraudon/Art Resource, New York.

Page 24: Pablo Picasso (1881–1973), *The Embrace.* Giraudon/Art Resource, New York.

Page 27: René Magritte (1898–1967), *The Lovers.* Richard S. Zeisler Collection, New York.

Page 29: Sandro Botticelli (c. 1445–1510), *Pallas Subduing a Centaur.* Scala/Art Resource, New York.

Page 30 (detail), page 39: Jean-Honoré Fragonard (1732–1806), *A Kiss Won* (cat. no. 459). The Hermitage, Leningrad.

Page 32: William Dyce (1806–1864), *Paolo and Francesca.* National Gallery of Scotland.

Page 34: Emil Hansen Nolde (German, 1867–1956), *Portrait of the Artist and his Wife.* (20th-century watercolor, 20¾″ × 14⅛″, acc. no. 70.323). © The Detroit Institute of Arts. Bequest of Robert H. Tannahill.

Page 37: Gustav Klimt (1862–1918), *Love.* Bridgeman/Art Resource, New York.

Page 40: Sir Edward Coley Burne-Jones (1833–1898), *The Love Song.* The Metropolitan Museum of Art. The Alfred N. Punnett Endowment Fund, 1947. (47.26)

Page 42 (detail), page 50: Pierre Auguste Renoir (French, 1841–1919), *Dance at Bougival* (oil on canvas, 71⅝″ × 38⅝″, 37.375). Courtesy Museum of Fine Arts, Boston, Picture Fund.

Page 45: Angelica Kauffmann (1741–1807), *Venus and Adonis.* Collection, Bayly Art Museum of the University of Virginia, Charlottesville.

Page 47: David Hockney (British, b. 1937), *The Second Marriage* (1963, oil and wallpaper on shaped canvas, 77¾″ × 90″). National Gallery of Victoria, Melbourne. Presented by the Contemporary Arts Society, London, 1965.

Page 48: Charles Wilson Peale (1741–1842), *Benjamin and Eleanor Ridgely Laming.* National Gallery of Art, Washington, D.C. Gift of Morris Schapiro.

Page 52: Ben Shahn (1898–1969), *Spring* (1947, tempera on masonite, 17″ × 30″). Albright-Knox Art Gallery, Buffalo, New York. Room of Contemporary Art Fund, 1948.

Page 54 (detail), page 64: Sir Lawrence Alma-Tadema (1836–1912), *Welcome Footsteps.* Bridgeman/Art Resource, New York.

Page 57: Jane Fasse (b. 1952), *Blue Is for Boys, Pink Is for Girls.* Courtesy of the Ann Campbell Collection, New York.

Page 59: Marc Chagall (1887–1985), *Birthday* (1915, oil on cardboard, 31¾″ × 39¼″). Collection, The Museum of Modern Art, New York. Acquired through the Lillie P. Bliss Bequest.

Page 61: Georges Antoine Rochegrosse (1859–1938), *The Knight of the Roses.* Musée d'Orsay/Service Photographique de la Réunion des Musées Nationaux, S.P.A.D.E.M.

Page 63: Edwin Austin Abbey (1852–1911), *May Day Morning.* Yale University Art Gallery. The Edwin Austin Abbey Memorial Collection.

Page 66 (detail), page 70: Jean Léon Gérôme (1824–1904), *Pygmalion and Galatea.* The Metropolitan Museum of Art. Gift of Louis C. Raegner, 1927. (27.200)

Page 68: François Boucher (1703–1770), *Pastoral Scene* (cat. no. 257). The Hermitage, Leningrad.

Page 73: Vincent Van Gogh (1853–1890), *Undergrowth with Two Figures.* Cincinatti Art Museum. Bequest of Mary E. Johnson.

Page 75: Adrien Moreau (1843–1906), *The Proposal.* The Sterling and Francine Clark Art Institute, Williamstown, Massachusetts. Gift of the children of Mrs. E. Parmalee Prentice.

Page 77: Henry Koerner (b. 1915), *June Night.* Dallas Museum of Art, Foundation for the Arts Collection. Gift of Joshua L. Logan.

Page 78 (detail), page 87: Egon Schiele (1890–1918), *The Embrace.* Österreichische Galerie, Vienna.

Page 80: Winslow Homer (1836–1910), *Scene at Houghton Farm.* Art Resource, New York.

Page 82: Édouard Manet (1832–1883), *Argenteuil.* Scala/Art Resource, New York.

Page 85: Rembrandt van Rijn (1606–1669), *Lady and Gentleman in Black.* Isabella Stewart Gardner Museum/Art Resource, New York.

Page 89: Pierre Auguste Cot (1837–1883), *The Storm.* The Metropolitan Museum of Art. Bequest of Catherine Lorillard Wolfe, 1887. Catherine Lorillard Wolfe Collection. (87.15.134)

Page 90 (detail), page 97: John Singer Sargent (1856–1925), *Paul Helleu Sketching with his Wife* (1889). The Brooklyn Museum. Museum Collection Fund. (20.640)

Page 92: John Rae (b. 1961), *Man and Woman.* Collection of the artist, New York.

Page 94: Ernst Ludwig Kirchner (1880–1938), *The Couple.* SEF/Art Resource, New York.

Page 99: Thomas Hart Benton (1889–1975), *Romance.* Archer M. Huntington Art Gallery, The University of Texas at Austin. Lent by Mari and James A. Michener.

Page 101: Anna Lee Merritt (1844–1930), *Love Locked Out.* The Tate Gallery, London.

Page 102 (detail), page 105: John J. Lee (active 1850–1860), *Sweethearts and Wives.* Bridgeman/Art Resource, New York.

Page 107: Pablo Picasso (1881–1973), *Sleeping Peasants* (1919, tempera, watercolor, and pencil, 12¼″ × 19¼″). Collection, The Museum of Modern Art, New York. Abby Aldrich Rockefeller Fund.

Page 109: Jean Auguste Dominique Ingres (1780–1867), *Francesca of Rimini and Paolo Malatesta.* Giraudon/Art Resource, New York.

Page 110: Frans van Mieris (1635–1681), *The Officer and the Light-O'-Love.* Mauritshuis, The Hague.

Page 112: Philip R. Goodwin (1882–1935), *Seeking Shelter from the Rain.* Art Resource/New York.

Page 114 (detail), page 119: Fernando Botero (b. 1932), *Dancing in Colombia.* The Metropolitan Museum of Art. Anonymous gift, 1983. (1983.251)

Page 116: Haynes King (1831–1904), *Jealousy and Flirtation.* By Courtesy of the Board of Trustees of the Victoria and Albert Museum, London.

Page 120: Gabriel Metsu (1629–1667), *Lady and Cavalryman.* Scala/Art Resource, New York.

Page 123: Edvard Munch (1863–1944), *Adam and Eve.* Scala/Art Resource, New York.

Page 125: Titian (Tiziano Vecellio) (c. 1487–1576), *Venus and Adonis.* National Gallery of Art, Washington, D.C. Widener Collection.

Page 126 (detail), page 131: Michelangelo Merisi da Caravaggio (1571–1610), *The Fortune Teller.* Scala/Art Resource, New York.

Page 128: Francesco Hayez (1791–1882), *The Kiss.* Scala/Art Resource, New York.

Page 132: Isidro Nonell y Monturiol (1873–1911), *Woe.* Scala/Art Resource, New York.

Page 135: Peter Paul Rubens (1577–1640), *A Shepherd Embracing a Woman.* Bayerische Staatsgemäldesammlungen, Munich.

Page 136: Niccolò dell'Abbate, (Italian, c. 1512–1571), *Eros and Psyche* (16th-century, oil on canvas, 39¼″ × 36½″, acc. no. 65.347). © The Detroit Institute of Arts. Founders Society Purchase, Robert H. Tannahill Fund.

Page 138 (detail), page 144: Paolo Veronese (c. 1528–1588), *Mars and Venus.* National Gallery of Scotland, Edinburgh.

Page 140: Jean-Honoré Fragonard (1732–1806), *The Bolt.* Scala/Art Resource, New York.

Page 143: Edwin Austin Abbey (1852–1911), *An Old Song.* Yale University Art Gallery. The Edwin Austin Abbey Memorial Collection.

Page 147: Peppino Mangravite (American, 1896–1978), *Young Couple Drinking* (1937, oil on canvas, 24″ × 20″). Munson-Williams-Proctor Institute Museum of Art, Utica, New York. Edward W. Root Bequest.

Page 149: Edvard Munch (1863–1944), *The Kiss on the Beach.* Oslo Kommunes Kunstsamlinger. Munch Museet.

Literature

Page 26: "I Love You" is reprinted by kind permission of the author.

Page 58: "To My Valentine" is reprinted by permission of Curtis Brown, Ltd. Copyright © 1942 by Ogden Nash.

Page 106: The selection from "A Valentine to Sherwood Anderson" is reprinted by kind permission of the estate of Gertrude Stein and Peter Owen Ltd., Publishers.

Page 118: "Jimmie's got a goil/goil/goil,/Jimmie" is reprinted from *is 5* poems by E. E. Cummings, edited by George James Firmage, by permission of Liveright Publishing Corporation and Grafton Books, a division of William Collins & Sons. Copyright © 1985 by E. E. Cummings Trust. Copyright © 1926 by Horace Liveright. Copyright © 1954 by E. E. Cummings. Copyright © 1985 by George James Firmage.

Page 130: "This Word *Love*" is reprinted from *At Night the Salmon Move*. Copyright © 1976 by Raymond Carver. Reprinted by permission of Capra Press, Santa Barbara.

Page 146: The translation of "It Is True" is reprinted by kind permission of Jose Pouso.

We have endeavored to obtain necessary permissions to reprint the works of art and literature in this volume and to provide proper copyright acknowledgement. We welcome information on any oversight, which will be corrected in subsequent printings.

Designed by Jeff Batzli
Composed by Trufont Typographers, Inc., Hicksville, New York.
Printed and bound by Amilcare Pizzi s.p.a.—arti grafiche, Milan, Italy.

A Chanticleer Press Edition

National Audubon Society®
Field Guide to Fishes

National Audubon Society®
Field Guide to Fishes
Revised Edition

North America

Saltwater Fishes
Carter R. Gilbert
Curator Emeritus of Fishes
Florida Museum of Natural History

Freshwater Fishes
James D. Williams
Research Associate
Florida Museum of Natural History

Alfred A. Knopf, New York

This is a Borzoi Book
Published by Alfred A. Knopf

Copyright ©2002 by Chanticleer Press, Inc. All rights
reserved. Published in the United States by Alfred A.
Knopf, a division of Penguin Random House LLC,
New York, and distributed in Canada by Random
House
of Canada, a division of Penguin Random House Ltd.,
Toronto.

www.aaknopf.com

Prepared and produced by Fieldstone Publishing, Inc.
for Chanticleer Press, Inc. New York.

Printed and bound by
Toppan Leefung Printing Limited, China.

Published November 1983
Second edition, fully revised, April 2002
Eleventh printing, May 2018

Library of Congress Cataloging-in-Publication Number:
2002020773
ISBN: 978-0-375-41224-0

CONTENTS

SPECIES ACCOUNTS

APPENDICES

NATIONAL AUDUBON SOCIETY

The mission of NATIONAL AUDUBON SOCIETY, *founded in 1905, is to conserve and restore natural ecosystems, focusing on birds, other wildlife, and their habitats for the benefit of humanity and the earth's biological diversity.*

One of the largest, most effective environmental organizations, AUDUBON has nearly 550,000 members, numerous state offices and nature centers, and 500+ chapters in the United States and Latin America, plus a professional staff of scientists, educators, and policy analysts. Through its nationwide sanctuary system AUDUBON manages 160,000 acres of critical wildlife habitat and unique natural areas for birds, wild animals, and rare plant life.

The award-winning *Audubon* magazine, which is sent to all members, carries outstanding articles and color photography on wildlife, nature, environmental issues, and conservation news. AUDUBON also publishes *Audubon Adventures,* a children's newsletter reaching 450,000 students. Through its ecology camps and workshops in Maine, Connecticut, and Wyoming, AUDUBON offers nature education for teachers, families, and children; through *Audubon Expedition Institute* in Belfast, Maine, AUDUBON offers unique, traveling undergraduate and graduate degree programs in Environmental Education.

AUDUBON sponsors books and on-line nature activities, plus travel programs to exotic places like Antarctica, Africa, Baja California, the Galápagos Islands, and Patagonia. For information about how to become an AUDUBON member, subscribe to *Audubon Adventures,* or to learn more about any of our programs, please contact:

AUDUBON
225 Varick Street, 7th Floor
New York, NY 10014
(212) 979-3000
(800) 274-4201
www.audubon.org

THE AUTHORS

Carter R. Gilbert is Curator Emeritus of Fishes, Florida Museum of Natural History, and Professor Emeritus of Zoology, University of Florida, having served on the faculty of that institution for 37 years. Previously, he was a research associate at the National Museum of Natural History, Smithsonian Institution, Washington, D.C., where he was employed on a grant from the Office of Navy Research. He received Bachelor's and Master's degrees from Ohio State University, and the degree of Doctor of Philosophy from the University of Michigan. He is the author or coauthor of more than 80 scientific publications, mostly involving freshwater and marine fishes of the southeastern United States and the tropical western Atlantic. He has been a member of the American Society of Ichthyologists and Herpetologists since 1954, serving as Secretary (1982–1989) and President (1993), as well as in a number of other capacities. He is also a member of the American Fisheries Society and several foreign ichthyological societies. Dr. Gilbert has described more than two dozen new species of marine and freshwater fishes, and is currently a member of the joint American Fisheries Society–American Society of Ichthyologists and Herpetologists committee on common and scientific names of North American fishes. He lives in Gainesville, Florida.

James D. Williams is a Research Associate at the Florida Museum of Natural History. He has conducted research on the conservation and biology of freshwater fishes and mussels with the Department of the Interior for more than 25 years. Prior to joining the Department of the Interior, he taught at several colleges and universities in the southeastern United States. His initial work with the Department of the Interior was in the U.S. Fish and Wildlife Service's Office of Endangered Species in Washington, D.C., where he researched freshwater fishes and prepared documentation for listing species as endangered or threatened and determining their critical habitat. In 1987, Dr. Williams moved to the U.S. Fish and Wildlife Service's National Fisheries Research Center in Gainesville, Florida (currently the U.S. Geological Survey–Florida Caribbean Science Center), where he conducted research on the distribution and biology of nonnative fishes and the conservation of freshwater fishes and mussels and served as Chief of the Biodiversity Branch. During his career, Dr. Williams has described more than a dozen new species of freshwater fishes and mussels and coauthored the *National Audubon Society Field Guide to North American Fishes, Whales, and Dolphins* (Alfred A. Knopf, Inc., 1983), *Vanishing Fishes of North America* (Stone Wall Press, 1983), and *Nonindigenous Fishes Introduced into Inland Waters of the United States* (American Fisheries Society, 1999). He lives in Gainesville, Florida.

ACKNOWLEDGMENTS

We wish to acknowledge the many ichthyologists and aquatic biologists whose works provided the background literature for the preparation of this guide. Unfortunately, there are too many to mention here. We would like to express our sincere appreciation to our fellow members of the American Fisheries Society and American Society of Ichthyologists and Herpetologists Names of Fishes Committee—Joseph S. Nelson (Chairman), Edwin J. Crossman, Héctor Espinosa-Pérez, Lloyd T. Findley, and Robert N. Lea —who made valuable contributions to our effort. We would like to thank the International Game Fish Association for use of the maximum weights of fishes from the all-tackle records in the 2001 World Record Game Fishes.

Many people helped in the preparation of this book. We are particularly grateful to the consultant, Dr. C. Lavett Smith, who carefully reviewed the revised manuscript.

Our special thanks go to George Scott, editor-in-chief, and the staff of Chanticleer Press. Particular thanks are due to Lisa R. Lester, project editor, who patiently edited the text. We agree that Lisa—very thorough, persistent, and always pleasant—is one of the best editors that we have ever worked with. Thanks also go to Drew Stevens, art director, who supervised the art and layout; John Norton, who created the fish illustrations; Gary Antonetti, who prepared the distribution maps; and Laura Russo, assistant photo editor, who, often with great difficulty, located and secured the photographs used in this guide. In addition, Dr. Rudy Arndt reviewed the initial submission of fish photographs. We also appreciate the entire staff of Chanticleer Press for their patience, assistance, and careful attention to detail.

Dr. Williams wishes to thank his mentor, Dr. Herbert T. Boschung, who stimulated his interest in ichthyology and guided him through his graduate career, and continues to provide support and encouragement.

Carter R. Gilbert
James D. Williams

INTRODUCTION

Fishes have nourished and fascinated humans for millennia. The importance of fishes in history and culture has been reflected throughout the ages in paintings, sculpture, and tapestries. Depictions of these mysterious animals that live and breathe underwater abound in the rock carvings left by North American Indians and in frescoes made by the ancient Minoans, dating from the second millennium B.C. An abundant source of food, it is not surprising that fish are prominently displayed in primitive paintings and are an important subject in man-made artifacts. Almost every known culture, ancient and modern, has made use of them, and today they remain an important source of protein for the ever-increasing human population.

Although other animal groups are also very important economically (particularly certain mammals and birds), those almost entirely comprise domesticated stocks that have been morphologically modified by humans for hundreds, or even thousands, of years. Fishes are unique in this regard in that (with a few exceptions, such as domesticated Goldfish and Koi) the economic benefits are based on wild populations.

Many species of fishes are attractive and have interesting habits and behavior. Because people find them fascinating, they are popular subjects for recreational scuba diving, and many of the smaller species are maintained in public or home aquariums. In addition, fishing is a tremendously important and popular form of recreation.

The Introduction consists of three sections. Biology of Fishes discusses the classification, anatomy, and life history of fishes; this section, which includes detailed illustrations and instructions on how to identify fish species, provides the user with the information needed to understand the written species descriptions. Organization of the Guide explains how the guide works and gives a breakdown of what the user will find in the color plate section and the species accounts. Notes from the Authors, which includes informa-

tion on conservation, introduced species, and dangerous
fishes, concludes the Introduction.

BIOLOGY OF FISHES

Fishes are cold-blooded vertebrates that have evolved for an
aquatic existence. Their gills extract dissolved oxygen from
water, and their streamlined shapes allow them to slip easily through the water. Fishes typically move by the action of
both their fins and their bodies. As a fish swims, the body is
thrown into a series of curves that move rearward as waves,
propelling the fish forward. The fins also propel the fish by
a series of wave-like and paddle-like motions.

Undulation of the rear part of the body, combined with
lateral movement of the caudal fin, is the most characteristic swimming motion, but there are many other alternative
modes of locomotion. For example, sharks move entirely by
undulation of the rear part of the body (propelled by the
caudal fin); the other fins are completely rigid and function
only in body equilibrium and stabilization. Skates and rays
move by an undulating or flapping movement of the lateral
extensions of the body. Eels move by undulating the entire
body, the fins having no function in locomotion. Parrotfishes and wrasses propel themselves with sculling movements of the pectoral fins and do not use the tail for
locomotion. Pipefishes and seahorses rely entirely on undulating movements of the dorsal fin as they propel themselves
both backward and forward.

Classification of Fishes

There is some disagreement over the classification of living
fishes, but they are generally divided into three major
groups: the jawless fishes (hagfishes and lampreys), the cartilaginous fishes (sharks, skates, rays, and related fishes), and
the ray-finned fishes (also called bony fishes). There are
about 25,000 described species worldwide, 97 percent of
which are ray-finned fishes. More than 2,500 species are
found in North American waters.

Biologists divide living organisms into major groups
called phyla (singular: phylum). Fishes belong to the large
phylum Chordata (animals having a spinal cord), and to the
subphylum Vertebrata, along with amphibians, reptiles,
birds, and land-dwelling mammals. Phyla are divided into
classes, classes into orders, orders into families, families into
genera (singular: genus), and genera into species. The
species is the basic unit of classification and is generally
what we have in mind when we talk about a "kind" of fish.

The formal definition of a species is rather difficult to understand, but in practical terms species are groups of organisms that breed successfully and produce fertile offspring.

Subspecies are populations of a species that differ from one another in some way and, most important, are completely or partly isolated geographically.

Life History of Fishes

Fishes have a wide variety of life-history patterns. Some species attach their eggs to the hard bottom and guard them until they hatch. Others carry the eggs in their mouths during the embryonic period. Some sharks give birth to live young. Most saltwater fishes, however, release eggs and sperm into the water and have nothing further to do with them; after fertilization, these free-floating eggs then become part of the plankton, carried along to remote areas by the currents.

Most saltwater fishes have a planktonic larval stage when the larvae are dispersed. Some species have larval stages that are so different from the adults that the larvae were once thought to be different species or to belong to different genera or even families.

The length of time spent as larvae is highly variable and is unknown for most species. In the post-larval stage, the fish has the shape of an adult but lacks a complete pigment pattern; next it becomes a juvenile, which may or may not resemble an adult. A fish between the juvenile and adult stage is sometimes referred to as a subadult, indicating that the adult morphology and color pattern is present but the individual has not yet reached sexual maturity. Finally, the subadult matures and is ready to reproduce. Some fishes start their reproductive life as one sex and then transform into the other, and a few species are hermaphroditic throughout their lives.

General Fish Anatomy and Coloration

Fishes vary tremendously in shape but always have three major parts: the *head,* the *body,* and the *tail.* They are generally streamlined, and the transition from head to body is imperceptible. The head is generally considered to end at the gill opening, the body at the base of the tail (usually at the anus). The surfaces of a fish are referred to as *dorsal* (the top, or back), *ventral* (the bottom, or belly), and *lateral* (the sides). The front of a fish is referred to as *anterior*, the rear as *posterior*.

Body Shapes

The body shape is the shape of a fish in profile. This book uses the following terms to describe body shapes: *fusiform* (tapering at both ends), *tapering* (narrowing toward the tail), *rectangular* (not tapering, narrowing abruptly right before the caudal peduncle), *oval, disk-shaped* (rounded), and *eel-like*.

BODY SHAPES

CROSS SECTIONS

PROPORTION

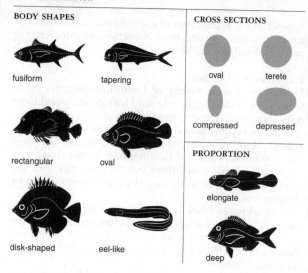

The cross section is the shape of the fish viewed head-on. Terms used in this guide to describe the cross section of a fish are *oval, terete* (the body slightly tapering at both ends and round in cross section), *compressed* (flattened from side to side), and *depressed* (flattened from top to bottom). The head can be depressed while the body is compressed.

The proportion of a fish's length (from snout to tail) to its depth (from back to belly) is also important in identification. A fish is said to be *elongate* when the depth measurement is small in comparison to the body length. A fish is considered to be *deep* when the depth measurement is large compared to the body length.

Coloration and Pattern

The majority of fishes are countershaded—dark above and paler below. In most fishes the transition is gradual, but sometimes there is a sharp line of demarcation between the dark and pale coloration.

Many fishes are quite colorful—particularly darters in freshwater habitats and marine fishes in reef habitats—and

PATTERNS

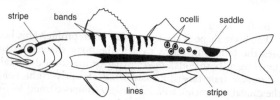

color can be very important in identification. However, color can also be misleading, as fishes can change color with age, sex, breeding period, and time of day. The coloration of certain fishes changes with the depth at which they live. In addition, some fishes undergo a color change at times of stress or while they sleep. Changes in coloration are most pronounced in temperate freshwater fishes, and usually involve a temporary seasonal enhancement of coloration in breeding males; bright colors in tropical freshwater fishes and in marine fishes are generally more permanent.

Pattern is often more diagnostic than color when identifying a fish. In general, *stripes* run lengthwise (head to tail); *lines* are narrow stripes; and *bands* or *bars* are vertical, usually extending from the back to the belly. *Spots* are distinct and sharp-edged; *blotches* are diffuse. *Saddles* are spots or blotches that extend across the back down onto the sides. *Ocelli* (singular: ocellus) are spots with an outer edge of contrasting color.

Head

The head features the eyes, nostrils, gills, and mouth. The area in front of the eyes above the mouth is called the *snout,* and the *cheek* is the area between the eye and the gills. The *nostrils* of fishes are olfactory organs, used only for smell and not in respiration. Ray-finned fishes have one or two pairs of nostrils (sometimes tubular in shape) that are usually situated ahead of the eyes. In sharks and batoids (sawfishes, skates, and rays), the nostrils are on the underside of the head in front of the mouth.

Gills are the respiratory organs of fishes. In lampreys, hagfishes, sharks, batoids, and related fishes, the gills are behind *pores* or *slits,* but in ray-finned fishes the gills are protected by a cover, called the *operculum.* This gill cover is supported by two main bones, the *opercle* and the *subopercle.* On each side of the head there is a triangular-shaped bone called the *preopercle.* The ventral and posterior edges of the preopercle meet at an angle and are usually "free" (that is, the skin folds under the edge of the bone); sometimes the edge is serrate or bears one or more *preopercular spines.*

With rare exceptions, fishes breathe by taking water in through the mouth, forcing it past the gills and out through the gill opening. The *gill membranes,* located along the edge of the operculum, serve as a valve and prevent water from entering the gill chamber through the gill openings. Ventrally, the gill membranes are supported by bony rods called *branchiostegal rays.* The gills are supported by bony *gill arches.* Usually there are four pairs of gill arches, each with two rows of gill filaments along its posterior surface; the *gill filaments,* finger-like projections that take oxygen from the water, are

THE HEAD

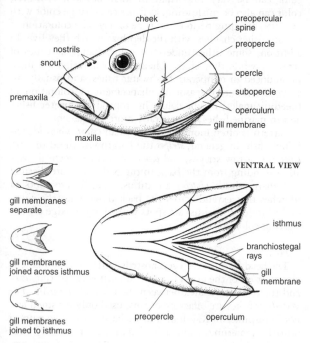

the "lungs" of the fish. In most fishes, a row of bony, finger-like *gill rakers* along the front of the gill arch protects the gills and prevents prey from escaping past the gills and out the gill opening. In some fishes, the gill rakers are long, slender, and numerous, and are used for straining plankton for food. Some species have a respiratory opening behind each eye, called a *spiracle*. Most batoids have large spiracles through which water is taken in and pumped over the gills for respiration. In most sharks, the spiracles are vestigial and not used for breathing.

GILLS: INTERIOR VIEW

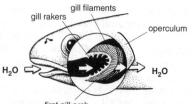

On the underside of the body, the triangular area that extends forward between the gill covers is the *isthmus*. The arrangement of the gill membranes and the isthmus varies in ray-finned fishes: In some species, the gill membranes are separate ventrally, and the isthmus is exposed; in others, the gill membranes are joined to one another across the isthmus; and in still others the gill membranes are joined to the isthmus.

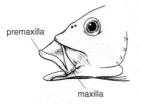

PROTRACTILE JAWS

Except for lampreys and hagfishes, fishes have two jaws: the upper jaw, consisting of the *premaxillary* and *maxillary* bones, and the lower jaw. In some ray-finned fishes, the premaxillae are capable of sliding forward and displacing the upper jaw into a sort of a tube; such jaws are said to be *protractile*.

The position of the mouth varies among species. It is described as *terminal* when it is at the very tip of the head; *superior* when the lower jaw projects beyond the upper; and *inferior* when it is under the head with the upper jaw or snout projecting (an inferior mouth is sometimes described as *subterminal* when the upper jaw projects only slightly beyond the lower). In addition, the term *oblique* is used to describe a mouth that is at an angle.

MOUTH POSITIONS

terminal   superior   inferior

Fishes can have teeth on the jaws, the tongue, the roof of the mouth, and the pharynx. There are five basic kinds: *Conical* teeth are short, pointed, and fine and are usually arranged in rows; *villiform* teeth are somewhat conical and are arranged in masses; *canine* teeth are long, conical or lance-like, and sharp; *molar-like* teeth are flattened for grinding and crushing; and *incisors* are sharp cutting teeth. Some fishes may have a combination of kinds of teeth; for example, in many sharks, the teeth in the upper and lower jaws can be quite different, and the teeth at the front of the jaw may differ from those at the sides in shape and, especially, in size.

PARTS OF A RAY-FINNED FISH

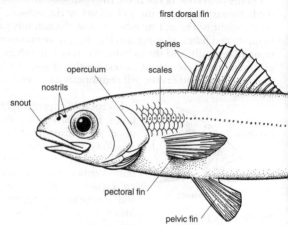

Body

The body is the part of the fish between the gill opening and the base of the tail (usually at the anus). The area just behind the operculum is called the *pectoral* or *breast* region. The *humeral* area (also called the *shoulder*) lies above the base of the pectoral fin, and the *belly* extends from the pectoral fin to the anus.

Tail

The tail is the posterior end of the fish, usually considered to begin at the anus and is composed of the *caudal peduncle* and the *caudal fin*. The caudal peduncle is the slender section of the tail that supports the caudal fin. Certain groups of fishes, such as the batoids, include species with very long and slender tails.

Fins

Fins are membranes supported by bony (or, rarely, horny) rods called *fin rays*. There are two kinds of fin rays: *spines,* which are stiff, pointed, unsegmented, and unbranched; and *soft rays,* which are flexible, usually segmented, and sometimes branched toward the tip. The fins of ray-finned fishes are often composed of both spines and soft rays. The more primitive fishes have only soft rays, while most relatively advanced fishes have spines as well as soft rays. The fins of sharks, rays, and some eel-like fishes are fleshy. When spines are present, they are nearly always at the anterior part of the fin. Sometimes one or more spines or rays are longer than the rest of the rays and extend as long filaments.

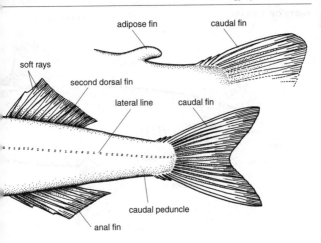

adipose fin

caudal fin

soft rays

second dorsal fin

lateral line

caudal fin

caudal peduncle

anal fin

There are two sets of *paired fins*—pelvic and pectoral—one of each on either side of the body. The *pectoral fins* are located behind the operculum, in the breast area, or on the side behind the head, and may be situated high or low on the body. The *pelvic fins* may be positioned anywhere between the throat and the abdomen.

There are usually three unpaired fins—dorsal, anal, and caudal—collectively known as the *median fins*. The *dorsal fin* is on the midline of the back. It may be divided into two (occasionally three) segments. Most sharks have two separate dorsal fins. The *anal fin* is on the underside of the body, typically just behind the anus. The *caudal fin* is at the end of the tail. Species in some families have an additional, usually small, fleshy *adipose fin* on the midline of the back behind the dorsal fin.

The part of a fin joined to the body is called the *base;* the forward-most limit of the fin base is referred to as its *origin.*

PARTS OF A FIN

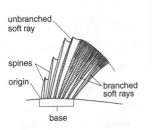

unbranched
soft ray

spines

origin

branched
soft rays

base

DORSAL FINS

dorsal fin
continuous,
no notch

dorsal fin
continuous, with
shallow notch

dorsal fin
continuous, with
deep notch

two dorsal fins

PARTS OF A SHARK

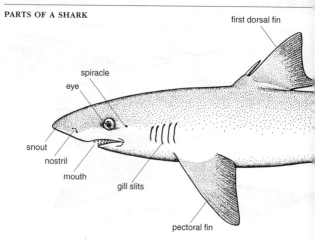

The point at which the front of a paired fin joins the body is its *insertion*. The length of a fin is the measure of the entire depressed fin itself, and the height is determined by the length of its longest rays. Thus, a fin can be described as short or long and high or low.

The arrangement of the dorsal fins is important in the identification of many types of fishes. In species with a single dorsal fin, the spiny and soft segments are connected (continuous), but there may be a deep or shallow notch between them. In species with more than one dorsal fin, the fins may be close together or widely separated.

Caudal fins come in a variety of shapes: *forked, lunate* (crescent-shaped), *emarginate* (shallowly forked), *truncate* (squared-off), *rounded,* and *pointed*. The caudal fin of most ray-finned fishes is nearly or completely symmetrical. The caudal fin of sharks and other cartilaginous fishes, as well as that of a few groups of ray-finned fishes, is asymmetrical, with a larger upper lobe (described as *heterocercal*).

TAIL SHAPES

heterocercal   forked   lunate   emarginate

truncate   rounded   pointed

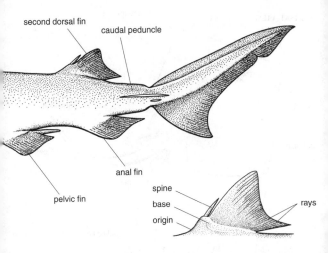

How to Count Fin Rays The number and kind of fin rays in a species is often an important identification feature. To count fin rays, first determine whether they are spines or soft rays. Distinguish between spines and soft rays when recording counts.

To count dorsal fin rays, begin counting from front to back, starting with the first well-developed ray in soft-rayed fishes, or the first spine in spiny-rayed fishes. Count rays from the base; the last two ray elements count as one (they arise from one root). For the pelvic and pectoral fins, count all spines and rays. For the caudal fin, count all branched rays and then add two.

Scales and Lateral Line

In most ray-finned fishes, the body is covered with scales. Some species have scales on only part of the body, while others lack scales entirely. Most ray-finned fishes have overlapping, disk-like scales, which are thin plates made up of

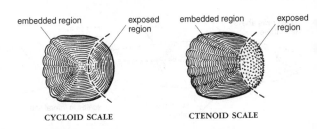

PARTS OF A BATOID

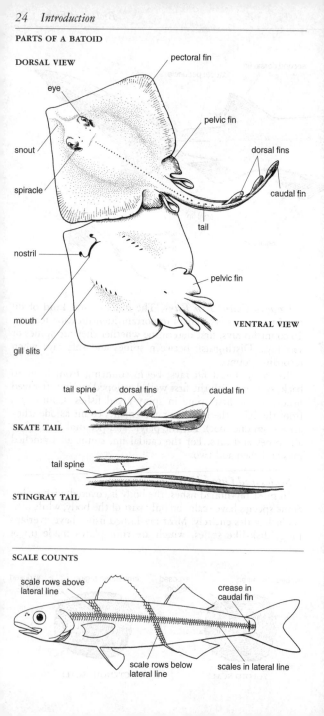

DORSAL VIEW

pectoral fin

eye

pelvic fin

snout

dorsal fins

spiracle

caudal fin

tail

nostril

pelvic fin

mouth

VENTRAL VIEW

gill slits

tail spine   dorsal fins   caudal fin

SKATE TAIL

tail spine

STINGRAY TAIL

SCALE COUNTS

scale rows above
lateral line

crease in
caudal fin

scale rows below
lateral line

scales in lateral line

concentric bony ridges embedded in flexible connective tissue. (Such scales are very different from the tooth-like scales of cartilaginous fishes.) They may either be smooth *(cycloid)* or have a spiny exposed edge *(ctenoid),* often giving the fish a rough surface texture. Some species have modified scales, such as an axillary scale, which is located at the insertion of the pectoral or pelvic fin.

A conspicuous landmark on the body of most ray-finned fishes is the lateral line, typically a tubular canal that runs along the length of the fish at mid-side just beneath the scales and usually ends at the caudal fin base or extends to the tip of the tail. Branch tubes reach the surface through the scales, where they open to the outside through small pores. Each pore leads into a canal that contains sensory nerve endings; the sensory structures record vibrations, helping the fish avoid obstacles and locate prey. These specialized pores or pored scales may form a visible lateral line. (A lateral line is considered to be complete when it runs uninterrupted from the opercle to the caudal fin base, and incomplete when it does not reach the caudal fin base.) Some species do not have a visible lateral line on the body, while a few have several lateral lines. The position of the lateral line(s) on the fish's body and the number and size of the scales in the lateral line are often important identification clues. In addition, some species have sensory pores on the head, the overall pattern of which can also be useful in identification.

How to Count Fish Scales When identifying a fish, it is often helpful to determine the number and kind of scales, including those in the lateral line. To find the lateral line, look for a dark line or ridge running along the length of the fish from the shoulder just above the operculum to the caudal fin. Each pore will appear as a small hole, or you may be able to see or feel a ridge, indicating the canal underneath. It may be helpful to lift each scale as you count, using a needle or a thin-bladed knife. The scales of some fishes are quite small and difficult to see and may require examination with a magnifying glass. Begin by counting the first scale behind the operculum and continue to the last vertebra, located at the crease made by flexing the caudal fin. For those fishes that do not have a visible lateral line, determining the number of scales in the lateral series may aid in identification; to do so, count the diagonal rows of scales between the rear edge of the upper side of the operculum and the caudal fin base.

Some additional scale counts may be necessary for identification, such as the number of rows of scales above or below the lateral line, the number of predorsal scales, and the number of caudal peduncle scales. To count the scale rows

above the lateral line, begin at the front of the first dorsal
fin and count the number of scales in a diagonal row downward and backward to the lateral line. To count the scale
rows below the lateral line, begin at the front of the anal fin
and count the number of scales in a diagonal row upward
and forward to the lateral line. To find the number of predorsal scales, count the number of scales along the midline
of the back from the back of the head to the dorsal fin origin. To determine the number of caudal peduncle scales,
count the rows of scales around the most slender region of
the body in front of the tail.

ORGANIZATION OF THE GUIDE

The body of this guide is composed of two main sections.
The first is the color plate section, which contains instructions on how to use the guide, photographs of representative North American habitats, and photographs of the fishes
discussed in the book. This is followed by the text section,
which gives written descriptions of the scientific groupings
of North American fishes and the individual species accounts. These are supplemented by the Appendices, which
include a glossary of terms used throughout the guide, an
index of the fishes, and photo credits.

Geographical Scope

This field guide covers the most common freshwater and
saltwater fishes found in North American waters north of
Mexico. The geographic scope for freshwater fishes includes
all freshwater habitats north of Mexico. The geographic
scope for saltwater fishes includes North American coastal
waters and open seas as far offshore as the continental shelf.
In the east, the guide covers saltwater fishes occurring from
Greenland south to the Gulf of Mexico and throughout the
Caribbean, including Bermuda, the Bahamas, and off the
coasts of Central and northern South America. In the west,
it covers fishes occurring from the Bering Sea south to Baja
California, including the Gulf of California.

The Color Plates

The color plate section opens with detailed instructions ex-
plaining how to use the guide to identify fishes, representative photographs of the region's freshwater and saltwater
habitats, the Family Key, and the Thumb Tab Key, and photographs of the fishes described in the book.

   This field guide presents the fishes in full-color photographs rather than more traditional paintings or drawings.
In artists' renderings the patterns and colors of fishes are
often exaggerated and idealized, whereas a good photograph

captures the true color pattern of the fish. The photographs are not only beautiful but are true to nature, presenting the fishes in their natural settings and often engaged in characteristic behavior. We have attempted to use, as much as possible, photographs of live fishes in their natural environment; in a few cases we have had to use photographs of dead specimens. Each species for which a suitable photograph was unavailable is represented in a detailed illustration that appears alongside the species account.

The photographs are divided into two habitat sections: freshwater and saltwater; species that live in both types of water or move between them appear in both sections. The habitat sections are identified at the top of each page: the blue "F" indicates fishes found in fresh water, the white "S" indicates fishes found in salt water. Within each section, the color plates are generally arranged according to shape and color, the most obvious features observed in the field.

Family Key

The chart following the habitat photographs will help you determine the family to which a fish belongs. Here, drawings of the fish families included in this guide are arranged in groups according to their most distinctive features: body shape and fin type. Choose the drawing that your fish most resembles, then turn to the page number indicated for the family description to learn the diagnostic characteristics of that family.

Thumb Tab Key

Once you've determined the family, you may use the Thumb Tab Key to locate the photographs of potential species. A silhouette of a typical member of each group appears on the left edge of each double page of color plates devoted to the group. Thumb tabs for the freshwater section are blue, and those for the saltwater section are white.

Captions

The caption under each photograph gives the plate number, the common name of the species, its maximum size, and the page number of the text description. The sex or age—male (♂), female (♀), or juvenile (juv.)—are indicated if the male and female or adult and juvenile of a species differ greatly. If the fish should be approached or handled with caution, the danger symbol △ precedes the caption. In the majority of the photographs, the measurement given is the fish's length; for rays and skates and similar fishes, the width is given in the caption and the species account.

Written Descriptions

The text is arranged phylogenetically, according to scientific classification, which reflects the general evolutionary history of fishes from the jawless hagfishes through the cartilaginous sharks and rays to the most advanced ray-finned fishes. Each grouping of fishes (superclass, class, subclass, order, and family) is introduced by a discussion of its distinctive features; when reading about a specific fish, readers are urged to review these introductions. Within each group, the orders and families are arranged in the sequence adopted by the American Fisheries Society in 2001. The arrangement of genera and species within each family is alphabetical by scientific name. The following details are given in the species accounts:

Plate Numbers

The majority of the species accounts begin with the number of the color plate on which the fish is shown; some species have more than one corresponding color plate number. Species for which a quality photograph was not available do not have a plate number; instead, a detailed illustration accompanies the written description.

Names

Next to the plate number are the fish's common and scientific names. Common names can be unreliable because the same species may be known by different common names in different areas; in addition, the same common name may be applied to more than one species. Scientific names are more precise because each species can have only one valid scientific name. However, scientific names continue to be modified as our knowledge and understanding of the biological relationships among fishes expand. The common and scientific names used in this guide are those given in *A List of Common and Scientific Names of Fishes from the United States and Canada,* published by the American Fisheries Society in 2002. Each scientific name consists of two words, usually derived from Latin or Greek. The first, always capitalized, is the name of the genus (plural: genera); the second, in lower case, is the specific epithet. For example, the scientific name of Rainbow Trout is *Oncorhynchus mykiss*. It is the only member of the genus *Oncorhynchus* that bears the specific name *mykiss*. (Scientific names for genera and species are always italicized; those for the larger groupings—such as classes, orders, and families—are not.)

Description

This section presents the basic characteristics that permit identification of a fish. Each description begins with the verified maximum total length of the adult, from the tip of the snout to the tip of the tail. Width, rather than length, is given for certain groups of fishes, such as rays and skates. For some large fishes, the maximum recorded weight is also provided. The weight measurement does not always correspond to the maximum length, and these weights are not necessarily North American records. The metric conversions of the length, width, and weight measurements are given in parentheses. (Size information should be used with caution: Fishes may keep growing throughout their lives, and occasionally an unusually large individual is encountered. The function of the sizes provided here is to give a general idea of how big the species gets; because all fish start out as tiny embryos, most of the individuals encountered will be smaller than the expected maximum lengths.) Next, the adult is described, indicating its body shape, color, distinguishing marks, and, if pertinent, the number of fins, rays, spines, and scales. If they vary greatly, males, females, and/or juveniles are described separately. The key diagnostic characteristics appear in italics. Drawings in the margin illustrate details and special features.

Habitat

Fishes can only survive in certain kinds of environments; certain species obviously have broader habitat tolerances than others, but even the most highly adapted species cannot live in every possible habitat occupied by some other fish species. Therefore, the habitats of the fishes covered by this guide are described as specifically as possible. Habitat information for saltwater fishes is often described in terms of the distance from the shore and the depth of the water.

Range

This section describes the fish's verified geographic distribution in North American waters north of Mexico. In general, the range is given from north to south and from east to west. Ichthyologists determine ranges by studying confirmed records in different areas. Records of a species are often scattered, and the range has to be estimated based on habits and habitat; thus, the range information is often most accurate if used in conjunction with the habitat description. Abbreviations are used here for northern (n), southern (s), eastern (e), and western (w), and for compounds of these words, such as northeastern (ne). Abbreviations are also used for the names of states and Canadian provinces (see the map at the beginning of the book for an abbreviation key). The North American distribution of the species is also shown on an accompanying map.

Similar Species

Many of the species accounts include this section to help distinguish between species that are physically similar. The differences among these look-alikes, which may or may not be related, are discussed here. Information on habitat and range is given only if the similar species does not have its own account in the book and if its habitat and range differ from that of the main species.

Comments

Each species account concludes with additional comments, which may include information about the fish's behavior, reproduction, diet, and use as a sport, food, or commercial fish. Alternate common names or changes in scientific classification are often noted. There may also be further information to help confirm an identification, such as color variations or a discussion of seasonal migrations. Remarks on any species that should be approached or handled with caution or that may be toxic when eaten are indicated by the danger symbol △.

NOTES FROM THE AUTHORS

Conservation

The waters of the tropical western Atlantic, the Caribbean Sea, and the Gulf of Mexico are particularly susceptible to the environmental problems that plague many marine areas: overfishing, destruction of habitat, and pollution. Fish watchers are encouraged to enter these areas with respect for the fragility and uniqueness of the ecosystems, especially the coral reefs, and the great diversity of life within them. Do as little as possible to disturb the wildlife: Do not touch live coral, avoid chasing fishes and other creatures, and do not collect specimens of plants or animals. Those who fish in the region are reminded to follow local laws regarding licensing, seasons, and catch limits. The best way to conserve marine habitats and the flora and fauna within them is to look but not touch and leave no traces behind.

Introduced Fishes

The problem of introduced nonnative species, including fishes, in North America is not new. It began with the arrival of the first European settlers more than 500 years ago and has continued at an increasing rate ever since. Many of the early introductions of plants and animals were intentional and generally viewed as welcome additions to the North American flora and fauna. Some of the first introductions were domesticated animals and plants, which offered considerable economic and recreational benefits. As the number of nonnative species increased, however, their economic and ecological costs became apparent. Today the nonindigenous species problem begs our attention to prevent further loss of our native fishes.

The definition of nonnative species has often been inconsistent, and such species have been called exotic, alien, transplanted, introduced, nonindigenous, and invasive. Political boundaries have sometimes been used to determine the status of an introduction. For example, some natural resource managers would not consider it an introduction to move a fish beyond its native range inside a state or national boundary (such as from northern to southern California, or from the East to West Coast). However, many biologists now define introduction as "the movement of a species beyond its natural or native range by humans."

The ability of nonnative fishes to alter native fish populations, aquatic community structure, and ecosystem structure and function is well known. Ecosystem-level changes that alter nutrients, energy cycles, and productivity directly impact human society. One of the major effects of invasive nonindigenous species on biodiversity is outright loss of native species. Invasive nonindigenous species should be treated as biological pollutants that can push native biota to or past the brink of extinction, especially when they occur in the presence of other forms of pollution, such as physical habitat alteration or chemical pollution.

There is no question that the introduction of nonnative species is one of the most important issues in the conservation of aquatic natural resources today. There are now more than 80 foreign fishes established in the waters of North America. An additional 210 species of North American fishes have been moved and are established beyond their native range. The U.S. Fish and Wildlife Service currently lists more than 100 native fishes as endangered or threatened, and nonindigenous species have contributed to the decline of about half of these. Of the 30 extinct fishes in the United States, nonindigenous species were a factor in the extinction process of 24. The mechanism of the extinction varied from predation and competition for food and space resources to genetic contamination through hybridization.

The effects of nonindigenous fishes on endangered species and aquatic biodiversity will probably significantly increase during the next 25 years. The basis for this prediction is the drastic increase in introduced fishes during the past 45 years. Analysis of records of introduced fishes revealed that between 1831, the date of the first known release of nonindigenous fishes, and 1950, a period of 120 years, fewer than 117 known fishes were introduced. Between 1950 and 1995, only 45 years, more than 458 fish species were introduced, but not all became established. Introductions of nonindigenous fishes were made in all states, but more were made in California, Florida, Hawaii, Nevada, and Texas than in the other states.

Nonindigenous fishes have originated from a variety of locations. Intentional introductions have been made by management agencies as part of game or forage fish stocking. However, many game fishes were illegally stocked by well-intentioned but misguided anglers. Several species, such as Grass Carp *(Ctenopharyngodon idella),* were widely introduced for biological control of aquatic plants, many of which were also introduced. Aquarium fishes represent another group of nonindigenous fishes that now occur in a variety of habitats. The tropical origin of most aquarium fishes has limited their distribution to the extreme southern portion of the United States or to thermal springs in colder areas.

Native fishes throughout the desert Southwest are in serious jeopardy from nonindigenous fishes. This region, characterized by low native fish diversity and high endemism, received the most fish introductions and suffered the greatest loss of native fishes. Species such as Bonytail *(Gila elegans)* and Razorback Sucker *(Xyrauchen texanus),* which inhabit large rivers in the Colorado basin, the Sonoran Topminnow *(Poeciliopsis occidentalis),* and several pupfishes and springfishes, inhabitants of small desert streams and springs, are directly threatened by the presence of numerous predaceous nonindigenous fishes.

Dangerous Fishes

Some fishes are poisonous or otherwise dangerous. In certain species, the fin spines are capable of producing puncture wounds into which toxins can be injected. The spines found on the head and body of some fishes are so sharp that simply touching them may result in a wound. In other fishes, the skin may be toxic or the flesh or roe poisonous when eaten. Eating certain tropical fishes may result in ciguatera poisoning, a type of poisoning caused by toxic algae eaten by fishes. Many sharks are potentially dangerous if provoked, as are some other large fishes. These large fishes are not the only ones that may bite; even a salmon can inflict a painful wound if care is not taken when removing it from a hook. All species that are known to be poisonous or otherwise dangerous to people are indicated in this book by the symbol ⚠.

ORGANIZATION OF THE COLOR PLATES

The color plate section is made up of five parts. The first, How to Identify Fishes, explains how to use this guide to identify the fishes you encounter and provides specific examples. This essay is followed by photographs of coastal, brackish or marshy, still water, and moving water habitats. The third part is the Family Key (printed on white paper), which presents silhouette illustrations of typical representatives of the families of fishes found in the region, grouped according to shape and other shared physical characteristics. The fourth part is the Thumb Tab Key (printed on black paper), a guide to the representative silhouettes that are used in the thumb tabs on the left-hand pages of the species photographs; this key also serves as a visual index to the color plates.

The final and largest part of the color plate section consists of the fish species photographs. The caption of each photograph provides the common name of the species, its maximum adult size (most often the length), and the page number on which the species is described in the text following the color plate section. If the specimen shown is a juvenile (juv.) or exhibits a particular phase of coloration, and if the sex (male ♂, female ♀) is known, that information is also noted in the caption.

The photographs are divided into freshwater and saltwater sections; species that are found in both fresh and salt water are shown in each section. These habitat sections are further subdivided into categories based on visual cues. Each subdivision is represented by a different thumb tab. Thumb tabs for the freshwater section are blue; those for the saltwater section are white. The type of habitat is also identified at the top of each page: the blue "F" indicates fishes found in fresh water, the white "S" indicates fishes found in salt water.

As you attempt to identify a fish, keep in mind that color can change in and out of the water, and that it also changes under different lighting conditions; the photographs of the fishes included in this guide may reflect these variables. In addition, many species change shape and color with age and reproductive condition. Many male fishes display brilliant breeding coloration during the spawning season. A fish that is significantly smaller than the maximum size given in the text and the caption may be a juvenile. Finally, remember that fishes may occasionally be found in habitats and ranges they do not normally frequent.

HOW TO IDENTIFY FISHES

Because fishes are so varied and abundant, their identification may at first seem difficult. The fish may dart away before you get a good look at it, or it may be a species with so many similar relatives that you are able to identify only the family or genus to which it belongs. Further complicating identification, unrelated species may share similar physical characteristics (and sometimes common names).

The most obvious characteristics of a fish are its color and shape. However, color can vary substantially with age, sex, reproductive condition, surrounding environment, water depth, and time of day. In addition, the body shape of some species, and even the shape of the fins in certain species, may change during the breeding season.

Other important identification characteristics include the shape of the fins, the number of dorsal fins, the number of spines and soft rays in each fin, and the size, shape, position, and number of scales, including those in the lateral line. (See the Introduction for instructions on how to count fin rays and scales.)

These characteristics are by no means the only ones used in the identification of fishes. Many other external (and internal) features are important in species identification, such as the number and morphology of gill rakers; the location and arrangement of spines on the head; pigmentation of the peritoneum; size, placement, arrangement, and number of teeth; and the number of branchiostegal rays. The distinguishing characteristics of each species are outlined in the written descriptions, which follow the color plate section, and all technical terms are defined in the glossary at the end of the book.

Keep in mind that individuals of a species vary. If you see a fish that is an inch longer or has more spines in the dorsal fin than the description says, that species should not necessarily be eliminated from consideration; it may be an exceptional individual.

Even the most experienced ichthyologist cannot identify every individual fish he or she sees. With practice, however, you will become familiar with many types of fishes and will learn which features and behaviors to focus on when you encounter a species unknown to you.

Using This Guide

This guide contains many features that will assist you in identifying a species of fish. The Introduction discusses fish structure and anatomy. The Family Key (on the white pages following the habitat photographs) arranges fish families by shape and other physical features and may enable you to find at a glance the family to which an individual belongs. To help you find a fish using visual cues, the photographs of the species are arranged according to overall appearance; the thumb tabs show a silhouette of a representative of each subdivision, and will help you turn quickly to the photographs of the fishes most like the one you are seeking to identify. The caption beneath each photograph gives the page number on which that species is described in the text.

The text also discusses the larger taxonomic groupings of fishes, such as order and family. These essays define the characteristics of the fishes in these groups. The individual species accounts provide detailed information on size, coloration, structural features, habitat, range, and the distinguishing features of similar species, thus narrowing your search for the correct identification. Illustrations in the margins provide close-ups of certain key features. Descriptions of the habitat and range of the species and a range map accompany each species account. In the Appendices are a glossary and an index.

Identifying a Fish

Using this guide, the first step in identifying a fish is to locate the photograph of the species most like the one you are observing. If the specimen is distinctive, you may be able to find a matching photograph by simply thumbing through the color plate section. To find the photograph of a fish that is less distinctive or completely unknown to you, refer to the Family Key and look for the closest match. You may be able to immediately identify the family to which your fish belongs; if at first you are able only to narrow it down to a few families, turn to the essays introducing each family (page numbers for the written family descriptions are given in the Family Key) and read the information there. When you think you have determined the correct family, look for the family's silhouette in the Thumb Tab Key; this visual index lists the color plate numbers on which the photographs of the family members are found. Flip through the photographs to see if you recognize your fish.

Once you have found the photograph that most closely resembles the fish you have seen, the next step is to compare your fish to the written description of the species shown in the photograph. The page number for the species account is given in the photograph's caption. Examine your fish closely, comparing the details to those described in the species account. If your fish matches the written description, check the habitat and range information and map to confirm your identification. If the diagnostic characteristics

and the habitat and range described do not all match, check
the similar species section to determine if your fish more
closely resembles the species described there (bear in mind
that information on habitat and range is given only if the
similar species does not have its own account in the book
and if its habitat and range differ from that of the main
species). You may need to go through this process more
than once before you are sure you have correctly identified
the species.

HOW TO USE THIS GUIDE

Example 1
Fish in a river in western Colorado
You catch a fish with an elongate body and dark spots on the back, sides, and fins. It has a dark olive back becoming lighter toward the belly and a bright red to reddish-orange mark on either side of the throat. It has a small rounded fin behind the larger dorsal fin and a slightly forked tail.

1. Turn to the *Freshwater families* section of the Family Key. Look for the shape that most resembles the fish you caught. From the group labeled *Small fleshy fin behind dorsal fin* you choose Trouts and Salmons, which refers you to color plates 67 and 70–86.
2. Checking the color plates you see that the photograph of Cutthroat Trout (plate 75) shows similar coloration, a small fin behind the dorsal fin, and a moderately forked tail. The caption refers you to text page 197.
3. The species account confirms that Cutthroat Trout has a bright red to reddish-orange mark on either side of the throat, an adipose fin, a moderately forked tail, and occurs in your range.

Example 2
Fish in a shallow estuary in North Carolina
You observe a silvery fish with a streamlined body and a yellowish belly. It has very small scales, one angular dorsal fin, and a deeply forked tail.

1. In the *Saltwater families* section of the Family Key you see that the group labeled *1 angular dorsal fin, forked tail* resembles your fish. Of this group, five shapes are a close match: Anchovies (plates 644–646), Herrings (plates 651–653, 678–680), Tenpounders (plates 640, 641), Tarpons (plate 643), and Bonefishes (plate 642).
2. Turning to the color plates you narrow down your choice to Ladyfish, Machete, Bonefish, and Tarpon (plates 640–643). The captions refer you to text pages 92–96.
3. Checking each fish's range text and map, you find that Machete does not occur in your area. Reading the descriptions of the three remaining fishes you learn that Bonefish has a projecting upper jaw. Tarpon has extremely large scales and a thread-like dorsal fin ray, while Ladyfish has very small scales and no thread-like dorsal fin ray. Ladyfish is also the only one of the four species described as having a yellowish belly, and thus you conclude that the fish you have seen is a Ladyfish.

1   Swan's Island, ME

2   St. Joseph Peninsula State Park, FL

3   Franklin Point, Año Nuevo State Reserve, CA

4 East Gloucester, MA

5 Cape Blanco, OR

6 Cape Alava, Olympic National Park, WA

7 Wabasha County, MN

8 Bayou de View, AR

9 Atchafalaya River Basin, LA

10   The Everglades, FL

11   Assateague Island National Seashore, VA

12   Merchants Millpond State Park, NC

13 Colorado River, Canyonlands National Park, UT

14 Lamar River, Yellowstone National Park, WY

15 Youghiogheny River, Ohiopyle State Park, PA

16 Rutland Brook, MA

17 Boreas River, Adirondack Mountains, NY

18 Little Missouri Falls, Ouachita National Forest, AR

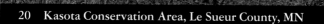

19 Big Wood River, ID

20 Kasota Conservation Area, Le Sueur County, MN

21 Big Lake, Shasta-Trinity National Forest, CA

22   Sandy Stream Pond, Baxter State Park, ME

23   Freezeout Lake, MT

24   Lake Helen, Bighorn National Forest, WY

FAMILY KEY

The silhouettes in the following key show the typical shapes of fish families that occur in North America. The silhouettes are grouped by general physical similarities, such as body shape and the size, shape, number, and placement of fins. This key is designed to help you quickly determine the family to which a particular specimen belongs. Once the family is known, you are well on your way to identifying the species.

For each family, the silhouette of a typical fish is shown; this shape is repeated next to the family description in the text that folllows the color plates. Remember that in each family some genera or species may be atypical and may not resemble the silhouettes at all. For example, although most species in a family have two separate dorsal fins, a few may have only one. Similarly, body shape sometimes varies within a family, often significantly. In addition, young fishes may differ significantly from older ones.

How to Use the Family Key

First, turn to the appropriate habitat section: *Freshwater families* (indicated by a blue "F" at the top of each page) or *Saltwater families* (indicated by a white "S"). Fishes that have very distinctive shapes are grouped first by body shape and then are further divided by characteristics such as fin shape. Other families that are not distinctively shaped are grouped mainly by fin characteristics. The scientific and common names of each family are given above the representative shape, along with the page number for the family description and the plate numbers of the family members that are shown in the photographs. Once you have found the silhouette that seems to match the shape of your fish, turn to the written family description and read it carefully to determine if you have successfully identified the family to which your fish belongs.

F Freshwater families

Eel-like body

Freshwater Eels
Anguillidae
Pl. 44, *p. 97*

Lampreys
Petromyzontidae
Pl. 39–43, *p. 36*

Elongate body, long snout

Pikes
Esocidae
Pl. 35–38, *p. 188*

Gars
Lepisosteidae
Pl. 27–29, *p. 86*

Flat body

Righteye Flounders
Pleuronectidae
Pl. 89, *p. 553*

American Soles
Achiridae
Pl. 87, *p. 559*

1 dorsal fin, spiny and soft segments joined

Cichlids
Cichlidae
Pl. 115, 116, *p. 454*

Sunfishes
Centrarchidae
Pl. 90–104, 109–112, *p. 339*

1 rounded dorsal fin, square to round tail

Pirate Perches
Aphredoderidae
Pl. 263, *p. 212*

Cavefishes
Amblyopsidae
Pl. 234–236, *p. 212*

Mudminnows
Umbridae
Pl. 246, 258, *p. 191*

Goodeids
Goodeidae
Pl. 256, *p. 262*

Elongate body, sharp pointed snout

Needlefishes
Belonidae
Pl. 25, *p. 244*

Pipefishes and Seahorses
Syngnathidae
Pl. 26, *p. 272*

Paddlefishes
Polyodontidae
Pl. 30, *p. 85*

Sturgeons
Acipenseridae
Pl. 31–34, *p. 82*

1 long dorsal fin

Labyrinth Catfishes
Clariidae
Pl. 47, *p. 184*

Bowfins
Amiidae
Pl. 46, *p. 89*

Pygmy Sunfishes
Elassomatidae
Pl. 122–125, *p. 452*

Mojarras
Gerreidae
Pl. 113, *p. 413*

Topminnows
Fundulidae
Pl. 238–245,
247–254, *p. 248*

Livebearers (male)
Poeciliidae
Pl. 262, *p. 259*

Livebearers (female)
Poeciliidae
Pl. 237, 255, 259,
p. 259

Pupfishes
Cyprinodontidae
Pl. 257, 260, 261, *p. 263*

1 angular dorsal fin, forked tail

Suckers
Catostomidae
Pl. 142–149,
151–155, 157, 168,
p. 162

Mooneyes
Hiodontidae
Pl. 171, *p. 90*

3–16 isolated spines on back

Sticklebacks
Gasterosteidae
Pl. 265, 266, *p. 270*

2 or more separate dorsal fins

Perches
Percidae
Pl. 119–121,
267–304, *p. 353*

Temperate Basses
Moronidae
Pl. 105–108, *p. 320*

2 well-separated dorsal fins, forked tail

Mullets
Mugilidae
Pl. 68, 69, *p. 237*

New World Silversides
Atherinopsidae
Pl. 185, 186, *p. 240*

Small fleshy fin behind dorsal fin

Trouts and Salmons
Salmonidae
Pl. 67, 70–86,
p. 195

Smelts
Osmeridae
Pl. 126, 127, *p. 192*

Suckermouth Armored Catfishes
Loricariidae
Pl. 65, *p. 187*

Sea Catfishes
Ariidae
Pl. 64, *p. 185*

Carps and Minnows
Cyprinidae
Pl. 128–141, 150, 156, 158, 166, 167, 169, 170, 172, 174–183, 187–233, *p. 114*

Herrings
Clupeidae
Pl. 159–165, *p. 108*

Anchovies
Engraulidae
Pl. 184, *p. 105*

Cods
Gadidae
Pl. 45, *p. 223*

Drums and Croakers
Sciaenidae
Pl. 114, *p. 425*

2 well-separated dorsal fins, rounded tail

Sleepers
Eleotridae
Pl. 117, 118, *p. 514*

North American Catfishes
Ictaluridae
Pl. 48–63, 66, *p. 174*

Characins
Characidae
Pl. 173, *p. 173*

Trout Perches
Percopsidae
Pl. 264, *p. 211*

Seahorse

**Pipefishes and
Seahorses**
Syngnathidae
Pl. 484, *p. 272*

Flat body

Righteye Flounders
Pleuronectidae
Pl. 326, 329, 332,
333, 335–337,
p. 553

Lefteye Flounders
Bothidae
Pl. 324, *p. 545*

Sand Flounders
Paralichthyidae
Pl. 325, 328, 331,
334, 338, 340,
p. 548

Kite-like body,
well-developed
tail

Angel Sharks
Squatinidae
Pl. 305, *p. 46*

Electric Rays
Narcinidae
Pl. 306, *p. 66*

Kite-like body,
long thin tail

Mantas
Mobulidae
Pl. 317, *p. 80*

Whiptail Stingrays
Dasyatidae
Pl. 312, 321, 322,
p. 73

Cownose Rays
Rhinopteridae
Pl. 318, *p. 79*

Hemispherical body, poorly developed tail

Molas
Molidae
Pl. 366, *p. 578*

American Soles
Achiridae
Pl. 327, 330,
p. 559

Tonguefishes
Cynoglossidae
Pl. 323, *p. 561*

Turbots
Scophthalmidae
Pl. 339, *p. 547*

Thornbacks
Platyrhinidae
Pl. 307, *p. 69*

Round Stingrays
Urolophidae
Pl. 310, *p. 75*

Torpedo Electric Rays
Torpedinidae
Pl. 308, 309, *p. 66*

Skates
Rajidae
Pl. 313–316, *p. 70*

Eagle Rays
Myliobatidae
Pl. 319, 320, *p. 77*

Butterfly Rays
Gymnuridae
Pl. 311, *p. 76*

S Saltwater families

Deep body, elaborate dorsal fin

Butterfishes
Stromateidae
Pl. 688, *p. 543*

Triggerfishes
Balistidae
Pl. 387, 388, *p. 563*

Filefishes
Monacanthidae
Pl. 353–355, *p. 566*

Head with "lure"

Batfishes
Ogcocephalidae
Pl. 342–344, *p. 234*

Goosefishes
Lophiidae
Pl. 341, *p. 231*

Elongate body, long snout

Sturgeons
Acipenseridae
Pl. 635, 636, *p. 82*

Gars
Lepisosteidae
Pl. 639, *p. 86*

Elongate body, sharp pointed snout

Swordfishes
Xiphiidae
Pl. 664, *p. 537*

Billfishes
Istiophoridae
Pl. 665–668, *p. 539*

Pipefishes and Seahorses
Syngnathidae
Pl. 480, 481, *p. 272*

Cornetfishes
Fistulariidae
Pl. 478, *p. 276*

Spadefishes
Ephippidae
Pl. 371, *p. 522*

Angelfishes
Pomacanthidae
Pl. 373–376, 380,
p. 444

Butterflyfishes
Chaetodontidae
Pl. 367–370, *p. 441*

Frogfishes
Antennariidae
Pl. 345, 346, *p. 232*

Needlefishes
Belonidae
Pl. 477, *p. 244*

Trumpetfishes
Aulostomidae
Pl. 482, *p. 275*

Halfbeaks
Hemiramphidae
Pl. 479, *p. 247*

Tubesnouts
Aulorhynchidae
Pl. 483, *p. 269*

Eel-like body

Cusk-Eels
Ophidiidae
Pl. 501, 516, *p. 216*

Eelpouts
Zoarcidae
Pl. 505, *p. 487*

Cutlassfishes
Trichiuridae
p. 527

Hagfishes
Myxinidae
Pl. 488–490, *p. 33*

1 long dorsal fin, square to round tail

Toadfishes
Batrachoididae
Pl. 514, 518, 519
p. 228

Clingfishes
Gobiesocidae
Pl. 350, *p. 511*

Ronquils
Bathymasteridae
Pl. 504, *p. 485*

Sand Stargazers
Dactyloscopidae
p. 498

1 long dorsal fin, mirror image of anal fin

Remoras
Echeneidae
Pl. 637, *p. 390*

Cobias
Rachycentridae
Pl. 638, *p. 391*

1 long dorsal fin, forked tail

Tilefishes
Malacanthidae
Pl. 520, 521, 676
p. 386

Dolphinfishes
Coryphaenidae
Pl. 696, *p. 392*

Morays
Muraenidae
Pl. 491–496, *p. 98*

**Snake Eels and
Worm Eels**
Ophichthidae
Pl. 497–499, *p. 102*

Freshwater Eels
Anguillidae
Pl. 500, *p. 97*

Lampreys
Petromyzontidae
Pl. 485–487, *p. 36*

Oarfishes
Regalecidae
p. 209

Pearlfishes
Carapidae
Pl. 530, *p. 215*

Pricklebacks
Stichaeidae
Pl. 502, 508, 509,
p. 488

Wolffishes
Anarhichadidae
Pl. 506, 507,
p. 492

Gunnels
Pholidae
Pl. 503, *p. 491*

Snailfishes
Liparidae
Pl. 517, *p. 316*

Sand Lances
Ammodytidae
p. 494

1 angular dorsal fin, forked tail

Anchovies
Engraulidae
Pl. 644–646,
p. 105

Herrings
Clupeidae
Pl. 651–653,
678–680, *p. 108*

Sweepers
Pempheridae
Pl. 694, *p. 440*

Flyingfishes
Exocoetidae
Pl. 695, *p. 245*

1 dorsal fin, dorsal and anal fins near tail

Porcupinefishes
Diodontidae
Pl. 347–349, 351,
352, *p. 575*

Puffers
Tetraodontidae
Pl. 360–364, *p. 571*

1 rounded dorsal fin, square to round tail

Topminnows
Fundulidae
Pl. 391, 394–397,
p. 248

Livebearers
(male)
Poeciliidae
Pl. 398, *p. 259*

2 separate dorsal fins, forked tail

Squirrelfishes
Holocentridae
Pl. 468, 470–472,
p. 266

Jacks
Carangidae
Pl. 389, 654–656,
659, 681–687, 689,
692, *p. 394*

Flying Gurnards
Dactylopteridae
Pl. 542, 543, *p. 317*

Temperate Basses
Moronidae
Pl. 588, 610, *p. 320*

Tenpounders
Elopidae
Pl. 640, 641, *p. 91*

Tarpons
Megalopidae
Pl. 643, *p. 93*

Bonefishes
Albulidae
Pl. 642, *p. 95*

Boxfishes
Ostraciidae
Pl. 356–359,
p. 568

Lumpfishes
Cyclopteridae
Pl. 365, *p. 315*

**Livebearers
(female)**
Poeciliidae
Pl. 392, *p. 259*

Pupfishes
Cyprinodontidae
Pl. 393, *p. 263*

Mackerels
Scombridae
Pl. 657, 658,
660–663, 671–674,
677, *p. 528*

Bluefishes
Pomatomidae
Pl. 675, *p. 388*

Cardinalfishes
Apogonidae
Pl. 473, 476, *p. 383*

Driftfishes
Nomeidae
Pl. 693, *p. 542*

Roosterfishes
Nematistiidae
Pl. 621, *p. 389*

S *Saltwater families*

1 dorsal fin, spiny and soft segments joined, forked tail

Bigeyes
Priacanthidae
Pl. 474, 475, *p. 381*

Snappers
Lutjanidae
Pl. 602, 603, 606, 614–616, *p. 406*

Mojarras
Gerreidae
Pl. 607, 611, 612, *p. 413*

Tripletails
Lobotidae
Pl. 624, *p. 411*

1 dorsal fin, spiny and soft segments joined, square to round tail

Cichlids
Cichlidae
Pl. 609, 622, 623, *p. 454*

Surfperches
Embiotocidae
Pl. 584–586, 589–593, *p. 458*

Wrasses
Labridae
Pl. 409–418, *p. 470*

Jawfishes
Opistognathidae
Pl. 634, *p. 338*

1 dorsal fin, spiny and soft segments notched, square to round tail

Combtooth Blennies
Blenniidae
Pl. 538–541, *p. 507*

Scorpionfishes
Scorpaenidae
Pl. 431–433, 443–445, 447, 448, 450–457, 459–461, 463–467, 469, 613, *p. 277*

Greenlings
Hexagrammidae
Pl. 424, 449, 458, *p. 301*

Porgies
Sparidae
Pl. 462, 599, 690,
691, *p. 420*

Grunts
Haemulidae
Pl. 594, 595, 601,
605, *p. 416*

Damselfishes
Pomacentridae
Pl. 372, 377–379,
381, 384, *p. 464*

Sea Chubs
Kyphosidae
Pl. 383, 600, 604,
p. 449

Surgeonfishes
Acanthuridae
Pl. 382, 385, 386,
p. 523

Parrotfishes
Scaridae
Pl. 400–408, *p. 479*

Kelp Blennies
Clinidae
Pl. 512, *p. 503*

Sea Basses
Serranidae
Pl. 587, 596, 598,
608, 617–620,
625–631, 633,
p. 325

Hawkfishes
Cirrhitidae
Pl. 597, *p. 451*

Labrisomid Blennies
Labrisomidae
Pl. 534–536, *p. 500*

2 or more separate dorsal fins, square to round tail

Sleepers
Eleotridae
Pl. 419, 420, *p. 514*

Gobies
Gobiidae
Pl. 522–528, *p. 516*

Cods
Gadidae
Pl. 515, 544, 560,
562, 564, 565,
p. 223

Phycid Hakes
Phycidae
Pl. 510, 511, *p. 219*

Dragonets
Callionymidae
Pl. 529, *p. 512*

Wreckfishes
Polyprionidae
Pl. 632, *p. 323*

2 well-separated dorsal fins, forked tail

Snooks
Centropomidae
Pl. 561, *p. 319*

Goatfishes
Mullidae
p. 439

Barracudas
Sphyraenidae
Pl. 669, 670,
p. 525

Threadfins
Polynemidae
p. 424

3–16 isolated spines on back

Sticklebacks
Gasterosteidae
Pl. 399, *p. 270*

Drums and Croakers
Sciaenidae
Pl. 390, 558, 566, 569–581, *p. 425*

Searobins
Triglidae
Pl. 426, 428–430, *p. 297*

Sculpins
Cottidae
Pl. 427, 434–437, 439, 441, 442, 446, *p. 305*

Merlucciid Hakes
Merlucciidae
Pl. 567, 568, *p. 221*

Grunt Sculpins
Rhamphocottidae
Pl. 440, *p. 304*

Searavens
Hemitripteridae
Pl. 438, *p. 313*

Stargazers
Uranoscopidae
Pl. 513, *p. 495*

Triplefins
Tripterygiidae
Pl. 533, *p. 497*

Tube Blennies
Chaenopsidae
Pl. 531, 532, 537, *p. 504*

Mullets
Mugilidae
Pl. 559, 563, *p. 237*

Sablefishes
Anoplopomatidae
Pl. 421, *p. 300*

New World Silversides
Atherinopsidae
Pl. 647, 649, 650, *p. 240*

Small fleshy fin
behind dorsal fin

**Trouts and
Salmons**
Salmonidae
Pl. 545–557, *p. 195*

Smelts
Osmeridae
Pl. 648, *p. 192*

2 separate
dorsal fins,
tapering tail

**Shortnose
Chimaeras**
Chimaeridae
Pl. 698, *p. 41*

Poachers
Agonidae
Pl. 425, *p. 313*

Shark-like,
2 dorsal fins,
long curved
upper lobe of
tail

Thresher Sharks
Alopiidae
Pl. 711, *p. 51*

Sawfishes
Pristidae
Pl. 702, *p. 68*

Shark-like,
2 dorsal fins,
notched upper
lobe of tail

**Hammerhead
Sharks**
Sphyrnidae
Pl. 700, 701, *p. 64*

Requiem Sharks
Carcharhinidae
Pl. 706, 709, 712,
714–716, *p. 59*

Hound Sharks
Triakidae
Pl. 705, 707, 708,
p. 56

Basking Sharks
Cetorhinidae
Pl. 719, *p. 52*

Shark-like,
2 dorsal fins,
squarish upper
lobe of tail

Bullhead Sharks
Heterodontidae
Pl. 697, *p. 47*

Lizardfishes
Synodontidae
Pl. 422, 423, *p. 206*

Sea Catfishes
Ariidae
Pl. 582, 583, *p. 185*

**Shark-like,
1 dorsal fin**

Cow Sharks
Hexanchidae
Pl. 720, *p. 43*

Whale Sharks
Rhincodontidae
Pl. 718, *p. 49*

Mackerel Sharks
Lamnidae
Pl. 713, 717, *p. 53*

Dogfish Sharks
Squalidae
Pl. 704, *p. 44*

Sand Tigers
Odontaspididae
Pl. 710, *p. 50*

Cat Sharks
Scyliorhinidae
Pl. 699, *p. 55*

Nurse Sharks
Ginglymostomatidae
Pl. 703, *p. 48*

THUMB TAB KEY

The table on the following pages provides a key to the photographs of the fish species covered by this guide. The photographs are divided into two main habitat sections: fresh water and salt water. (Those species that are found in both fresh and salt water are shown in both sections.) Within these sections, the photographs have been loosely grouped according to body shape and other shared physical characteristics.

One family silhouette illustration has been chosen to represent each group. These representative silhouettes appear on the thumb tabs at the left-hand edge of each double page of color plates, providing a quick and convenient index to the photographs. Thumb tabs for fishes shown in the freshwater section are blue; thumb tabs for those in the saltwater section are white.

The Thumb Tab Key itself also serves as a visual index to the color plates. In the key, the representative silhouette of the group appears in the left column of the table. The silhouettes of all the families that are included in that group are on the right, along with their common names and plate numbers. Because each family may contain atypical species, some families appear in more than one thumb tab group.

Freshwater fishes

Thumb tab	Family	
Elongate fishes with long snouts	Needlefishes Pl. 25	
	Pipefishes and Seahorses Pl. 26	
	Gars Pl. 27–29	
	Paddlefishes Pl. 30	
	Sturgeons Pl. 31–34	
	Pikes Pl. 35–38	
Eel-like fishes	Lampreys Pl. 39–43	
	Freshwater Eels Pl. 44	

Thumb tab	Family
Shads, suckers, carps, and minnow-like fishes (continued)	Suckers Pl. 142–149, 151–155, 157, 168
	Herrings Pl. 159–165
	Mooneyes Pl. 171
	Characins Pl. 173
	Anchovies Pl. 184
	New World Silversides Pl. 185, 186
Cavefishes	Cavefishes Pl. 234–236
Killifish-like fishes	Livebearers Pl. 237, 255, 259, 262
	Topminnows Pl. 238–245, 247–254
	Mudminnows Pl. 246, 258
	Goodeids Pl. 256
	Pupfishes Pl. 257, 260, 261
	Pirate Perches Pl. 263
	Trout Perches Pl. 264
Sticklebacks	Sticklebacks Pl. 265, 266
Darters	Perches Pl. 267–304

Saltwater fishes

Thumb tab	Family	
Skates and ray-like fishes	Angel Sharks Pl. 305	
	Electric Rays, Torpedo Electric Rays Pl. 306, 308, 309	
	Thornbacks Pl. 307	
	Round Stingrays Pl. 310	
	Butterfly Rays Pl. 311	
	Whiptail Stingrays Pl. 312, 321, 322	
	Skates Pl. 313–316	
	Mantas Pl. 317	
	Cownose Rays Pl. 318	
	Eagle Rays Pl. 319, 320	
Flatfishes	Tonguefishes Pl. 323	
	Lefteye Flounders Pl. 324	
	Sand Flounders Pl. 325, 328, 331, 334, 338, 340	
	Righteye Flounders Pl. 326, 327, 329 332, 333, 335–337	
	American Soles Pl. 330	
	Turbots Pl. 339	
Puffers, boxfishes, and fishes with "lures"	Goosefishes Pl. 341	
	Batfishes Pl. 342–344	
	Frogfishes Pl. 345, 346	

Thumb tab	Family	
Puffers, boxfishes, and fishes with "lures" (continued)	Porcupinefishes Pl. 347–349, 351, 352	
	Clingfishes Pl. 350	
	Filefishes Pl. 353–355	
	Boxfishes Pl. 356–359	
	Puffers Pl. 360–364	
	Lumpfishes Pl. 365	
	Molas Pl. 366	
Disk-shaped fishes	Butterflyfishes Pl. 367–370	
	Spadefishes Pl. 371	
	Damselfishes Pl. 372, 377–379, 381, 384	
	Angelfishes Pl. 373–376, 380	
	Surgeonfishes Pl. 382, 385, 386	
	Sea Chubs Pl. 383	
	Triggerfishes Pl. 387, 388	
	Jacks Pl. 389	
	Drums and Croakers Pl. 390	
Killifish-like fishes	Topminnows Pl. 391, 394–397	
	Livebearers Pl. 392, 398	
	Pupfishes Pl. 393	

Thumb tab	Family	
Sticklebacks	Sticklebacks Pl. 399	
Parrotfishes and wrasses	Parrotfishes Pl. 400–408	
	Wrasses Pl. 409–418	
Spiny-rayed fishes	Sleepers Pl. 419, 420	
	Sablefishes Pl. 421	
	Lizardfishes Pl. 422, 423	
	Greenlings Pl. 424, 449, 458	
	Poachers Pl. 425	
	Searobins Pl. 426, 428–430	
	Sculpins Pl. 427, 434–437, 439, 441, 442, 446	
	Scorpionfishes Pl. 431–433, 443–445, 447, 448, 450–457, 459–461, 463–467, 469	
	Searavens Pl. 438	
	Grunt Sculpins Pl. 440	
	Porgies Pl. 462	
	Squirrelfishes Pl. 468, 470–472	
	Cardinalfishes Pl. 473, 476	
	Bigeyes Pl. 474, 475	

Thumb tab	*Family*	
Elongate fishes with long snouts	Needlefishes Pl. 477	
	Cornetfishes Pl. 478	
	Halfbeaks Pl. 479	
	Pipefishes and Seahorses Pl. 480, 481, 484	
	Trumpetfishes Pl. 482	
	Tubesnouts Pl. 483	
Eel-like fishes	Lampreys Pl. 485–487	
	Hagfishes Pl. 488–490	
	Morays Pl. 491–496	
	Snake Eels and Worm Eels Pl. 497–499	
	Freshwater Eels Pl. 500	
Fishes with long dorsal fins	Cusk-Eels Pl. 501, 516	
	Pricklebacks Pl. 502, 508, 509	
	Gunnels Pl. 503	
	Ronquils Pl. 504	
	Eelpouts Pl. 505	
	Wolffishes Pl. 506, 507	
	Phycid Hakes Pl. 510, 511	
	Kelp Blennies Pl. 512	

Thumb tab	Family	
Fishes with long dorsal fins (continued)	Stargazers Pl. 513	
	Toadfishes Pl. 514, 518, 519	
	Cods Pl. 515	
	Snailfishes Pl. 517	
	Tilefishes Pl. 520, 521	
	Gobies Pl. 522–528	
	Dragonets Pl. 529	
	Pearlfishes Pl. 530	
	Tube Blennies Pl. 531, 532, 537	
	Triplefins Pl. 533	
	Labrisomid Blennies Pl. 534–536	
	Combtooth Blennies Pl. 538–541	
Drum-like fishes, cods, trouts, and salmons	Flying Gurnards Pl. 542, 543	
	Cods Pl. 544, 560, 562, 562, 564, 565	
	Trouts and Salmons Pl. 545–557	
	Drums and Croakers Pl. 558, 566, 569–581	
	Mullets Pl. 559, 563	
	Snooks Pl. 561	
	Merlucciid Hakes Pl. 567, 568	

Thumb tab	Family	
Sharks and shark-like fishes	Bullhead Sharks Pl. 697	
	Shortnose Chimaeras Pl. 698	
	Cat Sharks Pl. 699	
	Hammerhead Sharks Pl. 700, 701	
	Sawfishes Pl. 702	
	Nurse Sharks Pl. 703	
	Dogfish Sharks Pl. 704	
	Hound Sharks Pl. 705, 707, 708	
	Requiem Sharks Pl. 706, 709, 712, 714–716	
	Sand Tigers Pl. 710	
	Thresher Sharks Pl. 711	
	Mackerel Sharks Pl. 713, 717	
	Whale Sharks Pl. 718	
	Basking Sharks Pl. 719	
	Cow Sharks Pl. 720	

FRESHWATER FISHES

The fishes in this section are found in fresh water. Those species that also live in salt water or move between fresh and saltwater habitats appear again in the saltwater section. The thumb tabs for this section are blue.

25 Atlantic Needlefish, 25″, *p. 244*

26 Gulf Pipefish, 7″, *p. 274*

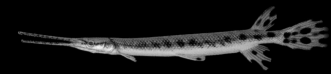

⚠ 27   Longnose Gar, 6′, *p. 88*

28   Spotted Gar, 3′, *p. 87*

29   Alligator Gar, 10′, *p. 87*

30   Paddlefish, 7′ 1″, *p. 86*

31   Lake Sturgeon, 8′, *p. 82*

32   White Sturgeon, 12′ 6″, *p. 83*

F *Elongate fishes with long snouts*

33   Atlantic Sturgeon, 14′, *p. 84*

34   Shovelnose Sturgeon, 3′, *p. 85*

35   Muskellunge, 6′, *p. 189*

36 **Chain Pickerel,** 31″, *p. 190*

37 **Redfin Pickerel,** 15″, *p. 188*

38 **Northern Pike,** 4′4″, *p. 189*

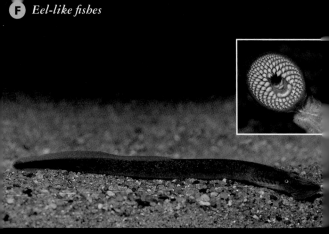

39   Chestnut Lamprey, 15″, *p. 36*

40   Southern Brook Lamprey, 7″, *p. 37*

42 Pacific Lamprey, 30″, *p. 38*

43 Sea Lamprey, 33″, *p. 39*

44 American Eel, 4′11″, *p. 97*

45 Burbot, 3′2″, *p. 225*

46 Bowfin, 34″, *p. 89*

47 Walking Catfish, 14″, *p. 184*

48 Freckled Madtom, *6″, p. 182*

49 Stonecat, *12″, p. 180*

50 Speckled Madtom, *3½″, p. 181*

🔺 51   Brindled Madtom, 5″, *p. 181*

🔺 52   Mountain Madtom, 5″, *p. 178*

🔺 53   Slender Madtom, 6″, *p. 179*

54   Tadpole Madtom, 5″, *p. 180*

55   Snail Bullhead (juv.), 12½″, *p. 174*

56   Snail Bullhead, 12½″, *p. 174*

57 **Black Bullhead**, 24″, *p. 175*

58 **Brown Bullhead**, 19″, *p. 176*

59 **Yellow Bullhead**, 18″, *p. 176*

60 White Catfish, 24″, *p. 175*

61 Channel Catfish, 3′11″, *p. 178*

62 Flathead Catfish, 5′1″, *p. 183*

63 Blue Catfish, 5′5″, *p. 177*

64 Hardhead Catfish, 24″, *p. 185*

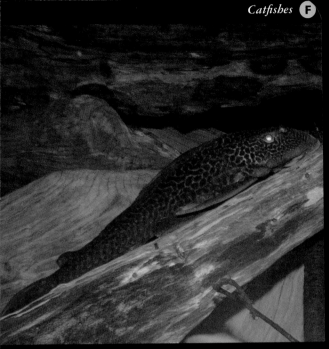

65   Orinoco Sailfin Catfish, 28″, *p. 187*

66   Widemouth Blindcat, 5½″, *p. 183*

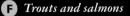

67 Cisco, 22", *p. 195*

68 Striped Mullet, 18", *p. 238*

69 White Mullet, 15", *p. 239*

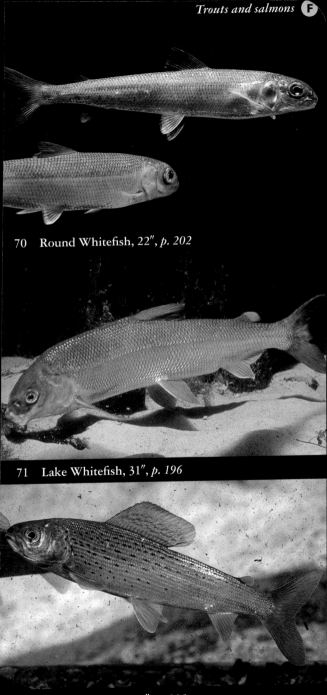

70 Round Whitefish, 22″, *p. 202*

71 Lake Whitefish, 31″, *p. 196*

72 Arctic Grayling, 30″, *p. 205*

73 Brown Trout, 3′4″, p. 203

74 Lake Trout, 4′2″, p. 205

75 Cutthroat Trout, 3′3″, p. 197

76   Apache Trout, 19¼", *p. 197*

77   Brook Trout, 28", *p. 204*

78   Rainbow Trout, 3'9", *p. 200*

79　Coho Salmon (breeding), 3′3″, *p. 199*

80　Coho Salmon (ocean phase), 3′3″, *p. 199*

81　Coho Salmon (juv.), 3′3″, *p. 199*

82   **Atlantic Salmon (juv.),** 4′ 5″, *p. 202*

83   **Pink Salmon** ♂ (breeding), 30″, *p. 198*

84   **Chinook Salmon,** 4′ 10″, *p. 201*

85   Chum Salmon (breeding), 3′4″, *p. 198*

86   Sockeye Salmon (breeding), 33″, *p. 200*

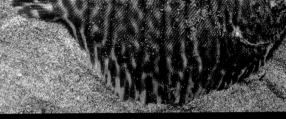

87 Hogchoker, 6″, *p. 561*

88 Gulf Flounder, 16½″ *p. 550*

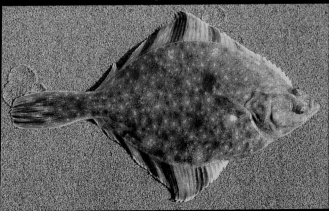

89 Starry Flounder, 3′, *p. 556*

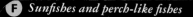

90   Pumpkinseed, 16″, *p. 344*

91   Longear Sunfish, 9″, *p. 346*

92   Redbreast Sunfish, 11″, *p. 343*

93 Green Sunfish, 12″, *p. 344*

94 Redear Sunfish, 14″, *p. 347*

95 Bluegill, 16″, *p. 345*

96   Bantam Sunfish, 3¾″, *p. 348*

97   Mud Sunfish, 10″, *p. 340*

98   Bluespotted Sunfish, 4″, *p. 342*

99 Spotted Sunfish, 6½″, *p. 347*

100 Black Crappie, 19½″, *p. 352*

101 Flier, 7¼″, *p. 343*

102   Warmouth, 12″, *p. 345*

103   Rock Bass, 17″, *p. 340*

104   Sacramento Perch, 24″, *p. 341*

105 White Bass, 18″, *p. 321*

106 Striped Bass, 6′, *p. 323*

107 Yellow Bass, 18″, *p. 322*

108   White Perch, 23″, *p. 321*

109   Spotted Bass, 24″, *p. 350*

110   Shoal Bass, 25″, *p. 349*

111   Smallmouth Bass, 27″, *p. 349*

112   Largemouth Bass, 3′2″, *p. 351*

113   Spotfin Mojarra, 8″, *p. 413*

114   Freshwater Drum, 35″, *p. 426*

115   Rio Grande Cichlid, 12″, *p. 455*

116   Mozambique Tilapia, 15″, *p. 456*

117 Fat Sleeper, 15″, *p. 514*

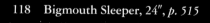

118 Bigmouth Sleeper, 24″, *p. 515*

119 Yellow Perch, 15″, *p. 371*

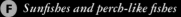

120   Sauger, 28″, *p. 380*

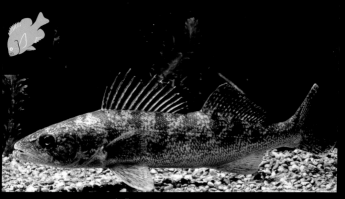

121   Walleye, 3′5″, *p. 381*

122   Banded Pygmy Sunfish, 2″, *p. 454*

123 Everglades Pygmy Sunfish, 1¼″, *p. 453*

124 Carolina Pygmy Sunfish ♂, 1¼″, *p. 453*

125 Carolina Pygmy Sunfish ♀, 1¼″, *p. 453*

126 Eulachon, 10″, *p. 194*

127 Rainbow Smelt, 13″, *p. 193*

128 Hardhead, 18″, *p. 139*

129   Leatherside Chub, *6″, p. 162*

130   Roundtail Chub, *17″, p. 127*

131   Chiselmouth, *12″, p. 114*

132 Tui Chub, 16″, *p. 126*

133 Sacramento Blackfish, 18″, *p. 149*

135 Hitch, 13″, *p. 132*

136 Colorado Pikeminnow, 5′, *p. 157*

137 Flathead Chub, 12½″, *p. 154*

138   Hornyhead Chub, 10″, *p. 139*

139   Bluehead Chub, 8″, *p. 140*

140   River Chub, 10″, *p. 141*

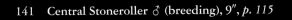

141　Central Stoneroller ♂ (breeding), 9″, *p. 115*

142　Striped Jumprock, 10″, *p. 171*

143　White Sucker, 24″, *p. 164*

144   Spotted Sucker, 20″, *p. 167*

145   Torrent Sucker, 7½″, *p. 171*

146   Razorback Sucker, 3′, *p. 172*

147   Blue Sucker, 3′4″, *p. 165*

148   Northern Hog Sucker, 24″, *p. 166*

149   Flannelmouth Sucker, 30″, *p. 164*

150   Creek Chub, 12″, *p. 161*

151   Creek Chubsucker ♂ (breeding), 11″, *p. 165*

152   Blacktail Redhorse, 18″, *p. 170*

153   Golden Redhorse, 24″, *p. 169*

154   Silver Redhorse, 25″, *p. 168*

155   River Redhorse, 30″, *p. 169*

156   Common Carp, 30″, *p. 122*

157   Quillback, 24″, *p. 163*

158   Grass Carp, 3′3″, *p. 118*

159　Alewife, 15″, *p. 109*

160　Pacific Herring, 18″, *p. 111*

161　Skipjack Herring, 21″, *p. 108*

F *Shads, suckers, carps, and minnow-like fishes*

162   American Shad, 30″, *p. 110*

163   Threadfin Shad, 9″, *p. 112*

164   Gizzard Shad, 16″, *p. 112*

165   Atlantic Thread Herring, 12″, *p. 113*

166   Golden Shiner, 12″, *p. 141*

167   Goldfish, 16″, *p. 116*

168   Smallmouth Buffalo, 3′, *p. 167*

169   Sacramento Pikeminnow, 3′, *p. 156*

170   Bonytail, 24″, *p. 126*

171   Goldeye, 20″, *p. 90*

172   Spotfin Chub, 3½″, *p. 123*

173   Mexican Tetra, 5″, *p. 173*

174   Longfin Dace, 3½″, *p. 115*

175 Southern Redbelly Dace, 3", *p. 150*

176 Rosyside Dace, 4", *p. 117*

177 Mountain Redbelly Dace, 2½", *p. 151*

178 Spikedace, 3″, *p. 138*

179 Finescale Dace, 4¼″, *p. 151*

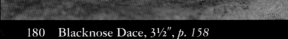

180 Blacknose Dace, 3½″, *p. 158*

181 Longnose Dace, 7″, *p. 158*

182 Little Colorado Spinedace, 4″, *p. 133*

183 Speckled Dace, 4″, *p. 159*

184 Bay Anchovy, *4″, p. 106*

185 Brook Silverside, *4″, p. 241*

186 Inland Silverside, *4″, p. 243*

187   Bigeye Chub, 3″, *p. 130*

188   Sicklefin Chub, 4″, *p. 137*

189   Silver Chub, 9″, *p. 138*

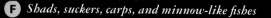

190   Slender Chub, 3¾", *p. 124*

191   Speckled Chub, 3", *p. 137*

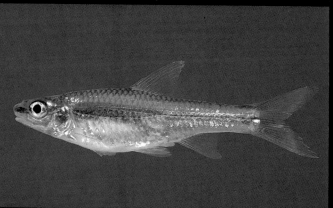

192   Pallid Shiner, 3¼", *p. 131*

193 Stargazing Minnow, 4½″, *p. 150*

194 Bluntnose Minnow, 4″, *p. 152*

195 Suckermouth Minnow, 4″, *p. 149*

196 Loach Minnow, 2½″, *p. 159*

197 Silverjaw Minnow, 3½″, *p. 143*

198 Cutlip Minnow, 5″, *p. 125*

199   Brassy Minnow, 4″, *p. 129*

200   Mississippi Silvery Minnow, 7″, *p. 129*

201   Ozark Minnow, 3″, *p. 146*

202 Pugnose Minnow, 2½″, *p. 148*

203 Roundnose Minnow, 2½″, *p. 123*

204 Emerald Shiner, 4″, *p. 142*

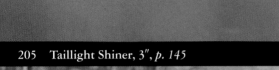

205 Taillight Shiner, 3″, *p. 145*

206 Bleeding Shiner, 4½″, *p. 135*

207 Weed Shiner, 3″, *p. 147*

208   Mimic Shiner, 3″, *p. 147*

209   Spottail Shiner, 6″, *p. 144*

210   Longnose Shiner, 2½″, *p. 144*

211   Lake Chub, 9″, *p. 117*

212   Flame Chub, 3″, *p. 128*

213   Streamline Chub, 4½″, *p. 124*

214   Warpaint Shiner, 5″, *p. 134*

215   Rosyface Shiner, 3½″, *p. 146*

216   Sailfin Shiner, 2½″, *p. 156*

217 Common Shiner, 6″, *p. 135*

218 Redside Shiner, 7″, *p. 160*

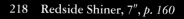

219 Bigeye Shiner, 3″, *p. 143*

220   Redfin Shiner, 3½″, *p. 136*

221   Spotfin Shiner, 4½″, *p. 121*

222   Striped Shiner, 7″, *p. 134*

223 Whitetail Shiner, 5″, *p. 119*

224 Blacktail Shiner, 7″, *p. 121*

225 Satinfin Shiner, 3½″, *p. 119*

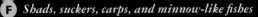

226   Red Shiner, 3½″, *p. 120*

227   Fathead Minnow, 4″, *p. 153*

228   Bluehead Shiner, 2½″, *p. 155*

229 Woundfin, 3″, *p. 153*

230 Splittail, 14″, *p. 154*

231 California Roach, 4″, *p. 128*

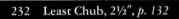

232 Least Chub, 2½", *p. 132*

233 Silver Carp, 3'3", *p. 131*

234 Spring Cavefish, 3½″, *p. 214*

235 Southern Cavefish, 3½″, *p. 214*

236 Northern Cavefish, 4¼″, *p. 213*

237   Least Killifish ♀, 1½″, *p. 260*

238   Plains Killifish, 5″, *p. 256*

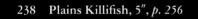

239   Rainwater Killifish, 2″, *p. 258*

240   Longnose Killifish, 6″, *p. 256*

241   Bayou Killifish, 3″, *p. 254*

242   Banded Killifish, 5″, *p. 251*

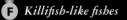

243   Pygmy Killifish, 1¼″, *p. 257*

244   Seminole Killifish, 6½″, *p. 255*

245   Bluefin Killifish, 2″, *p. 257*

246   Central Mudminnow, 5½″, *p. 192*

247   Northern Studfish, 7″, *p. 249*

248   Northern Studfish ♂ (breeding), 7″, *p. 249*

249　Golden Topminnow ♀, 3″, *p. 250*

250　Banded Topminnow, 3″, *p. 251*

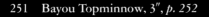

251　Bayou Topminnow, 3″, *p. 252*

252 Plains Topminnow, 2¾″, *p. 255*

253 Blackspotted Topminnow, 4″, *p. 253*

254 Gulf Killifish, 6″, *p. 252*

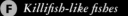

255   Gila Topminnow ♀, 2½″, *p. 261*

256   White River Springfish, 3½″, *p. 262*

257   Sheepshead Minnow, 3″, *p. 264*

258   Alaska Blackfish, 13″, *p. 191*

259   Western Mosquitofish ♀, 2½″, *p. 259*

260   Desert Pupfish, 2¾″, *p. 263*

261 Flagfish ♂, 2½", *p. 265*

262 Sailfin Molly ♂, 5", *p. 261*

263 Pirate Perch, 5½", *p. 212*

264   Trout Perch, 8″, *p. 211*

265   Brook Stickleback, 3½″, *p. 270*

266   Threespine Stickleback, 4″, *p. 271*

267   Eastern Sand Darter, 3¼″, *p. 355*

268   Western Sand Darter, 2¾″, *p. 354*

269   Crystal Darter, 6¼″, *p. 356*

270 Blackside Darter, 4″, *p. 375*

271 Swamp Darter, 2″, *p. 360*

272 Channel Darter, 2½″, *p. 373*

273   Naked Sand Darter, 2½", *p. 354*

274   Scaly Sand Darter, 3", *p. 355*

275   Glassy Darter, 2½", *p. 368*

276 River Darter, 3¼", *p. 379*

277 Johnny Darter, 2½", *p. 362*

278 Tessellated Darter, 3½", *p. 363*

279   Logperch, 7″, *p. 372*

280   Shield Darter, 3″, *p. 377*

281   Snail Darter, 3″, *p. 379*

282   Least Darter, 1¾", *p. 361*

283   Blackbanded Darter, 4", *p. 376*

284   Fantail Darter, 3", *p. 359*

285   Slenderhead Darter, 4″, *p. 377*

286   Banded Darter, 3″, *p. 370*

287   Gilt Darter, 3″, *p. 374*

288   Iowa Darter, 3″, *p. 358*

289   Striped Darter, 3″, *p. 368*

290   Bluestripe Darter, 4″, *p. 374*

291   Slackwater Darter, 2½″, *p. 357*

292   Stippled Darter, 3½″, *p. 364*

293   Greenside Darter, 6″, *p. 356*

294 Redfin Darter, 3½″, *p. 369*

295 Gulf Darter, 2½″, *p. 367*

296 Tennessee Snubnose Darter, 3″, *p. 365*

297   Speckled Darter, 2½″, *p. 366*

298   Rainbow Darter, 3″, *p. 358*

299   Orangethroat Darter, 2½″, *p. 366*

300   Tangerine Darter, 7″, *p. 372*

301   Roanoke Darter , 3″, *p. 378*

302   Redline Darter, 3½″, *p. 364*

303 Spotted Darter, 3″, *p. 361*

304 Ruffe, 10″, *p. 370*

SALTWATER FISHES

The fishes in this section are found in salt water. Those species that also live in fresh water or move between salt and freshwater habitats appear again in the freshwater section. The thumb tabs for this section are white.

305   Pacific Angel Shark, 5′, *p. 46*

306   Lesser Electric Ray, 18″, *p. 66*

307   Thornback, 3′, *p. 70*

⚠ 308   Atlantic Torpedo, 6′, *p. 67*

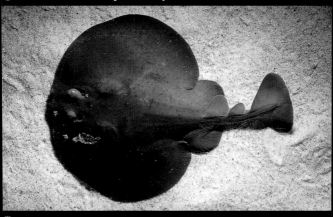

⚠ 309   Pacific Electric Ray, 4′6″, *p. 67*

⚠ 310   Round Stingray, 22″, *p. 76*

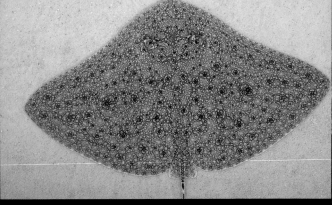

311   Smooth Butterfly Ray, 3′, *p. 77*

312   Atlantic Stingray, 24″, *p. 74*

313   Clearnose Skate, 3′1″, *p. 72*

314   Big Skate, 8′, *p. 71*

315   Roundel Skate, 24″, *p. 73*

316   Little Skate, 21″, *p. 71*

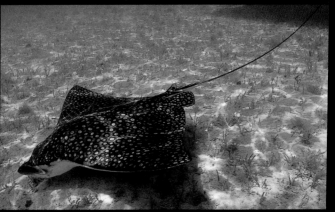

317   Atlantic Manta, 22′, *p. 80*

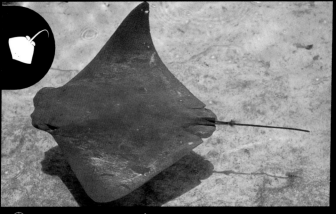

318   Cownose Ray, 3′, *p. 79*

319   Spotted Eagle Ray, 9′, *p. 78*

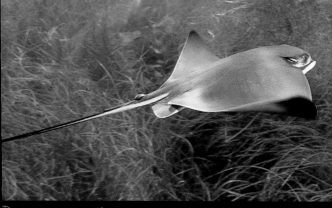

320   Bat Ray, 6', *p. 79*

321   Southern Stingray, 5', *p. 74*

322   Southern Stingray, 5', *p. 74*

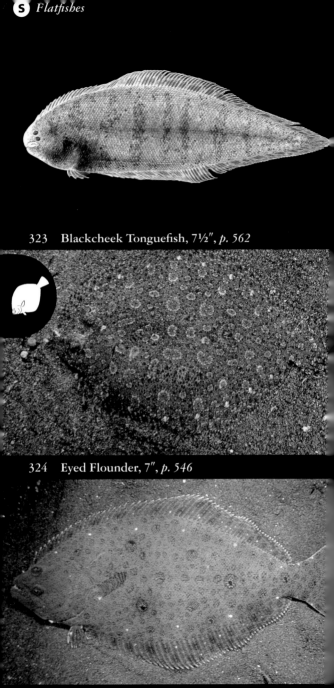

Flatfishes

323 Blackcheek Tonguefish, 7½", *p. 562*

324 Eyed Flounder, 7", *p. 546*

325 California Halibut, 5', *p. 551*

326 English Sole, 22″, *p. 555*

327 Hogchoker, 6″, *p. 561*

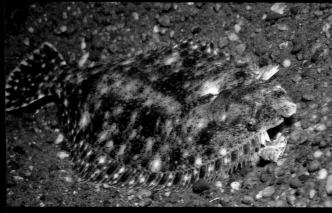

328 Summer Flounder, 3′1″, *p. 552*

329   C-O Sole, 14″, *p. 557*

330   Naked Sole, 6¼″, *p. 560*

331   Gulf Flounder, 16½″, *p. 550*

332   Winter Flounder, 23″, *p. 558*

333   Rock Sole, 24″, *p. 554*

334   Pacific Sanddab, 16″, *p. 549*

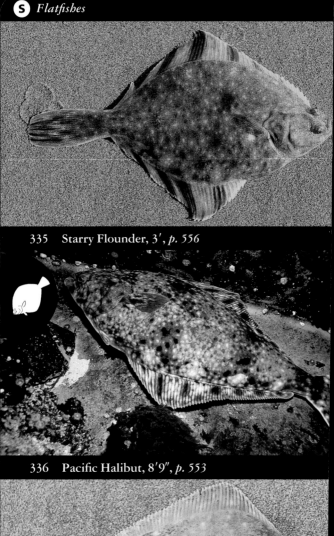

335 Starry Flounder, 3′, *p.* 556

336 Pacific Halibut, 8′9″, *p.* 553

337 Diamond Turbot, 18″, *p.* 557

338   Spotted Whiff, 6″, *p. 549*

339   Windowpane, 18″, *p. 547*

340   Three-eye Flounder, 7″, *p. 548*

341   Goosefish, 4′, *p. 231*

342   Pancake Batfish, 4″, *p. 235*

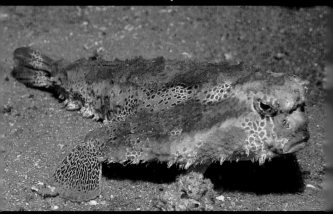

343   Polka-dot Batfish, 15″, *p. 236*

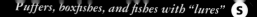

344 Roughback Batfish, 4″, *p. 235*

345 Sargassumfish, 8″, *p. 233*

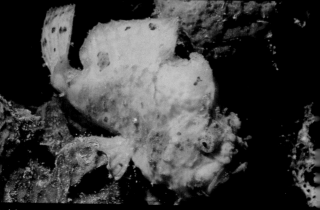

346 Longlure Frogfish, 6″, *p. 232*

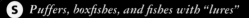

347   Striped Burrfish, 10″, *p. 576*

348   Balloonfish, 18″, *p. 577*

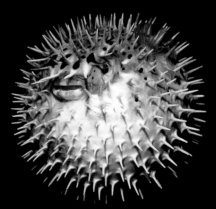

349   Balloonfish (inflated), 18″, *p. 577*

350 Skilletfish, 2¾", *p. 511*

351 Porcupinefish, 3′, *p. 577*

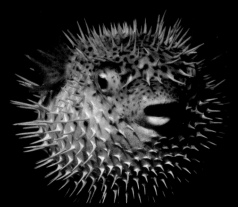

352 Porcupinefish (inflated), 3′, *p. 577*

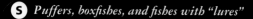

353   Scrawled Filefish, 3', *p. 567*

354   Orange Filefish, 24", *p. 566*

355   Planehead Filefish, 9", *p. 568*

356   Scrawled Cowfish, 19″, *p. 569*

357   Smooth Trunkfish, 11″, *p. 571*

358   Spotted Trunkfish, 21″, *p. 570*

359   Trunkfish, 21″, *p. 570*

360   Sharpnose Puffer, 3¾″, *p. 572*

361   Smooth Puffer, 3′3″, *p. 572*

362 Checkered Puffer, 15″, *p. 575*

363 Bandtail Puffer, 6¾″, *p. 574*

364 Northern Puffer, 10″, *p. 573*

365 Lumpfish, 24", *p. 315*

366 Ocean Sunfish, 13', *p. 579*

367   Reef Butterflyfish, 6″, *p. 443*

368   Spotfin Butterflyfish, 8″, *p. 443*

369   Foureye Butterflyfish, 6″, *p. 442*

370   Banded Butterflyfish, 6″, *p. 444*

371 Atlantic Spadefish, 3′, *p. 522*

372 Sergeant Major, 7″, *p. 465*

373 Queen Angelfish, 18″, *p. 445*

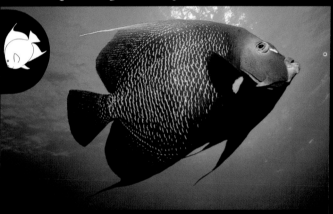

374 French Angelfish, 14″, *p. 448*

375 Gray Angelfish, 24″, *p. 447*

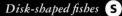

376   Rock Beauty, 14″, *p. 446*

377   Garibaldi, 14″, *p. 467*

378   Beaugregory, 4″, *p. 468*

379   Cocoa Damselfish, 4¼″, *p. 469*

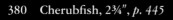

380   Cherubfish, 2¾″, *p. 445*

381   Yellowtail Damselfish, 7½″, *p. 467*

388   Black Durgon, 20″, *p. 565*

389   African Pompano, 3′6″, *p. 394*

390   Jackknife-fish, 10″, *p. 430*

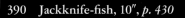

391 Rainwater Killifish, 2″, *p. 258*

392 Western Mosquitofish ♀, 2½″, *p. 259*

393 Sheepshead Minnow, 3″, *p. 264*

394 Longnose Killifish, 6″, *p. 256*

395 Bayou Killifish, 3″, *p. 254*

396 Gulf Killifish, 6″, *p. 252*

397 Diamond Killifish, 2″, *p. 249*

398 Sailfin Molly ♂, 5″, *p. 261*

399 Threespine Stickleback, 4″, *p. 271*

400   Blue Parrotfish, 4′, *p. 480*

401   Stoplight Parrotfish ♂ (terminal phase), 24″, *p. 485*

402   Stoplight Parrotfish (primary phase), 24″, *p. 485*

403 Redband Parrotfish, 11″, *p. 482*

404 Bucktooth Parrotfish (primary phase), 8″, *p. 483*

405 Yellowtail Parrotfish (primary phase), 18″, *p. 484*

406 Queen Parrotfish ♂ (terminal phase), 24″, *p. 482*

407 Princess Parrotfish ♂ (terminal phase), 13″, *p. 481*

408 Princess Parrotfish (primary phase), *p. 481*

409 Puddingwife, 20″, *p. 475*

410   Creole Wrasse, 12″, *p. 472*

411   Spanish Hogfish, 24″, *p. 471*

412   Bluehead, 6″, *p. 478*

413   California Sheephead ♂, 3′, *p. 476*

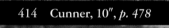

414   Cunner, 10″, *p. 478*

415   Tautog, 3′, *p. 477*

416   Señorita, 10″, *p. 476*

417   Slippery Dick, 9″, *p. 473*

418   Yellowhead Wrasse ♂, 7½″, *p. 474*

419   Fat Sleeper, 15″, *p. 514*

420   Bigmouth Sleeper, 24″, *p. 515*

421   Sablefish, 3′4″, *p. 301*

422   Inshore Lizardfish, 18″, *p. 207*

423   Sand Diver, 11″, *p. 208*

424   Lingcod, 5′, *p. 302*

425   Sturgeon Poacher, 12″, *p. 314*

426   Leopard Searobin, 10″, *p. 299*

427   Mottled Sculpin, 6″, *p. 306*

428   **Northern Searobin**, 17″, *p. 297*

429   **Bandtail Searobin**, 8″, *p. 298*

430   **Bighead Searobin**, 14″, *p. 300*

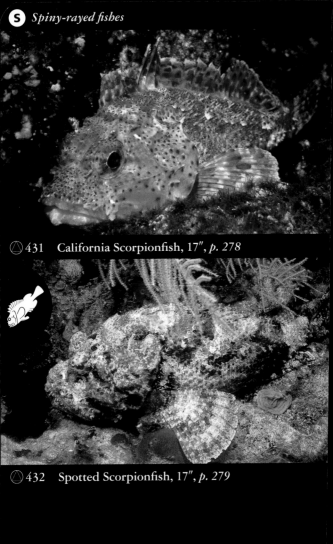

△ 431 California Scorpionfish, 17″, *p. 278*

△ 432 Spotted Scorpionfish, 17″, *p. 279*

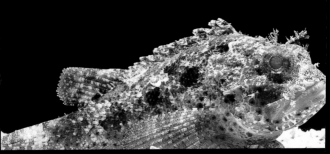

△ 433 Barbfish, 9″, *p. 278*

434 Scalyhead Sculpin, 4″, *p. 305*

435 Buffalo Sculpin, 14½″, *p. 307*

436 Snubnose Sculpin, 4″, *p. 311*

437   Lavender Sculpin, 10″, *p. 309*

438   Sailfin Sculpin, 8″, *p. 313*

439   Fluffy Sculpin, 3½″, *p. 310*

440   **Grunt Sculpin,** 3¼″, *p. 304*

441   **Longhorn Sculpin,** 18″, *p. 310*

442   **Cabezon,** 3′3″, *p. 312*

⚠ 443   China Rockfish, 17″, *p. 288*

⚠ 444   Black-and-yellow Rockfish, 15″, *p. 283*

⚠ 445   Gopher Rockfish, 15″, *p. 282*

446   Red Irish Lord, 20″, *p. 308*

447   Quillback Rockfish, 24″, *p. 286*

448   Flag Rockfish, 20″, *p. 293*

449   Kelp Greenling, 21″, *p. 302*

450   Brown Rockfish, 22″, *p . 281*

451   Black Rockfish, 24″, *p. 286*

🌙 452   Blue Rockfish, 21″, *p. 288*

🌙 453   Bocaccio, 3′, *p. 290*

🌙 454   Widow Rockfish, 21″, *p. 284*

△ 455   **Canary Rockfish,** 30″, *p. 291*

△ 456   **Yelloweye Rockfish (juv.),** 3′, *p. 292*

△ 457   **Vermilion Rockfish,** 30″, *p. 287*

458   Painted Greenling, 10″, *p. 303*

459   Tiger Rockfish, 24″, *p. 289*

460   Copper Rockfish, 22″, *p. 283*

⚠ 461   Treefish, 16″, *p. 294*

⚠ 462   Sheepshead, 3′, *p. 421*

⚠ 463   Yellowtail Rockfish, 26″, *p. 285*

464 Olive Rockfish, 24″, *p. 294*

465 Rosy Rockfish, 14″, *p. 291*

466 Honeycomb Rockfish, 10½″, *p. 295*

467 Kelp Rockfish, 17″, *p. 281*

468 Blackbar Soldierfish, 8½″, *p. 267*

469 Shortspine Thornyhead, 30″, *p. 296*

470 Squirrelfish, 14″, *p. 266*

471 Longspine Squirrelfish, 12″, *p. 267*

472 Dusky Squirrelfish, 6″, *p. 268*

473   Dusky Cardinalfish, 3″, *p. 385*

474   Short Bigeye, 10″, *p. 382*

475 Bigeye, 14½″, *p. 382*

476 Flamefish, 4″, *p. 384*

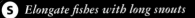

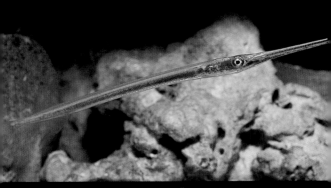

477   Atlantic Needlefish, 25″, *p. 244*

Red Cornetfish, 6′, *p. 276*

480   Bay Pipefish, 14″, *p. 273*

481   Gulf Pipefish, 7″, *p. 274*

482   Trumpetfish, 3′, *p. 275*

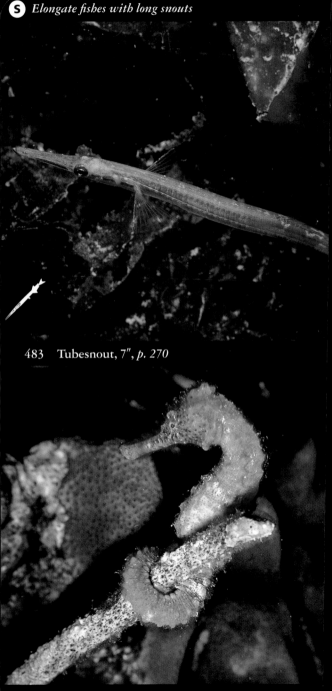

483   Tubesnout, 7″, *p. 270*

484   Lined Seahorse, 6″, *p. 272*

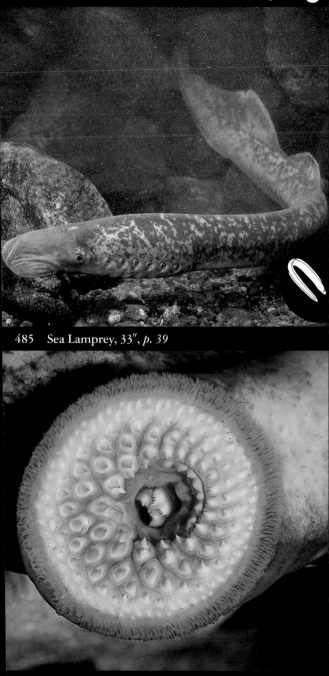

485   Sea Lamprey, 33″, *p. 39*

486   Sea Lamprey (mouth), *p. 39*

487 Pacific Lamprey, 30″, *p. 38*

488 Atlantic Hagfish, 31″, *p. 35*

489   Pacific Hagfish, 25″, *p. 34*

490   Pacific Hagfish, 25″, *p. 34*

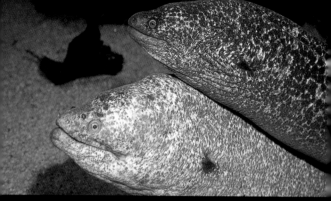

491 California Moray, 5′, *p. 100*

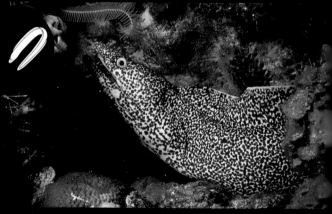

492 Spotted Moray, 3′3″, *p. 100*

493 Green Moray, 6′, *p. 99*

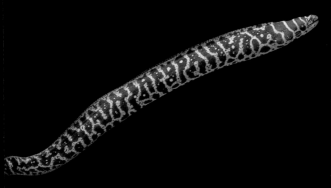

494   Honeycomb Moray, 24″, *p. 101*

495   Chain Moray, 28″, *p. 98*

496   Chain Moray, 28″, *p. 98*

497 Spotted Snake Eel, 4'7", *p. 103*

498 Goldspotted Eel, 3'7", *p. 102*

499 Speckled Worm Eel, 17", *p. 103*

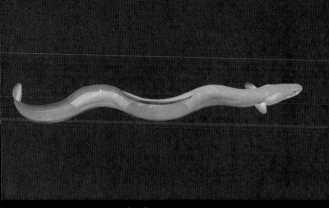

500   American Eel, 4′ 11″, *p. 97*

501   Spotted Cusk-Eel, 14″, *p. 217*

502   Snake Prickleback, 20″, *p. 490*

503   Penpoint Gunnel, 18″, *p. 491*

504   Bluebanded Ronquil, 8½″, *p. 486*

505   Ocean Pout, 3′6″, *p. 487*

🌙 506   Wolf-Eel, 6′8″, *p. 493*

🌙 507   Atlantic Wolffish, 5′, *p. 493*

508   Monkeyface Prickleback, 30″, *p. 489*

509   High Cockscomb, 7¾″, *p. 488*

510   White Hake, 4′5″, *p. 220*

511   Red Hake, 51″, *p. 219*

512   Giant Kelpfish, 24″, *p. 504*

513   Southern Stargazer, 17½″, *p. 496*

514   Oyster Toadfish, 15″, *p. 228*

515   Cusk, 3′6″, *p. 223*

516   Bank Cusk-Eel, 12″, *p. 218*

517   Tidepool Snailfish, 7″, *p. 316*

518　Plainfin Midshipman, 15″, *p. 229*

519　Atlantic Midshipman, 12½″, *p. 230*

520　Tilefish, 3′6″, *p. 386*

521   Sand Tilefish, 24″, *p. 387*

522   Highfin Goby, 8″, *p. 518*

523   Clown Goby, 2¾″, *p. 520*

524   Bridled Goby, 2¼″, *p. 517*

525   Masked Goby, 1⅜″, *p. 518*

526   Blackeye Goby, 6″, *p. 521*

527   Bluebanded Goby, 2½", *p. 520*

528   Frillfin Goby, 3", *p. 516*

529   Spotfin Dragonet, 6½", *p. 513*

530   Pearlfish, 8″, *p. 216*

531   Wrasse Blenny, 4″, *p. 506*

532   Sailfin Blenny ♂, 2″, *p. 505*

533   Redeye Triplefin, 1¼″, *p. 497*

534   Island Kelpfish, 4″, *p. 501*

535   Hairy Blenny, 8½″, *p. 501*

536　Saddled Blenny, 2½″, *p. 502*

△537　Onespot Fringehead, 9″, *p. 506*

538　Striped Blenny, 3″, *p. 508*

539 Barred Blenny, 3½″, *p. 509*

540 Feather Blenny, 4″, *p. 510*

541 Molly Miller, 4¼″, *p. 510*

542   Flying Gurnard, 18″, *p. 317*

543   Flying Gurnard, 18″, *p. 317*

544   Atlantic Cod, 4′, *p. 224*

545   Cutthroat Trout, 3′3″, *p. 197*

546   Brook Trout, 28″, *p. 204*

547 Rainbow Trout, 3'9", *p. 200*

548 Brown Trout, 3'4", *p. 203*

549 Lake Trout, 4'2", *p. 205*

550 Coho Salmon (breeding), 3′3″, *p. 199*

551 Coho Salmon (juv.), 3′3″, *p. 199*

552 Coho Salmon (ocean phase), 3′3″, *p. 199*

553 Atlantic Salmon (juv.), 4′5″, *p. 202*

554 Chum Salmon, 3′4″, *p. 198*

555 Chinook Salmon, 4′10″, *p. 201*

556 Pink Salmon, 30″, *p. 198*

557 Sockeye Salmon, 33″, *p. 200*

558 White Seabass, 5′, *p. 427*

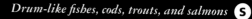

Drum-like fishes, cods, trouts, and salmons Ⓢ

559   Striped Mullet, 18″, *p. 238*

560   Pollock, 3′6″, *p. 227*

561   Snook, 4′, *p. 319*

562 Haddock, 3′8″, *p. 225*

563 White Mullet, 15″, *p. 239*

564 Pacific Tomcod, 12″, *p. 226*

565   Atlantic Tomcod, 15″, *p. 226*

566   Queenfish, 12″, *p. 437*

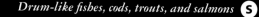

567   Pacific Hake, 3′, *p. 222*

568 Silver Hake, 30″, *p. 221*

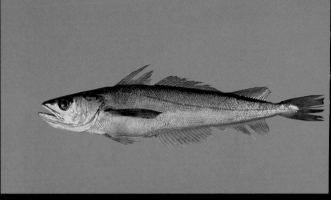

569 Northern Kingfish, 20″, *p. 432*

570 Weakfish, 35″, *p. 429*

571   Spotted Seatrout, 28″, *p. 428*

572   Silver Seatrout, 14″, *p. 429*

573   Red Drum, 5′, *p. 436*

574   Black Drum, 5′7″, *p. 435*

575   Silver Perch, 12″, *p. 427*

576   Spot, 14″, *p. 432*

577 Yellowfin Croaker, 20″, *p. 438*

578 Atlantic Croaker, 24″, *p. 433*

579 Spotfin Croaker, 27″, *p. 435*

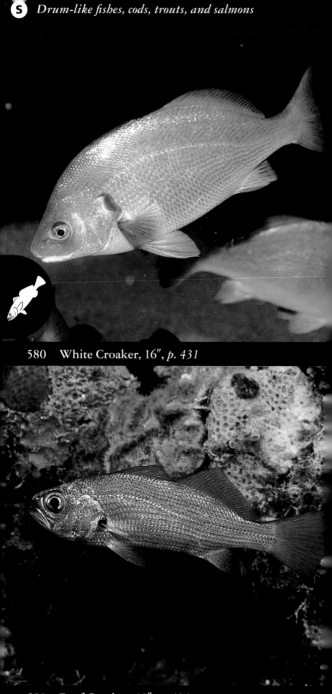

580   White Croaker, 16″, *p. 431*

581   Reef Croaker, 10″, *p. 434*

582 Gafftopsail Catfish, 3′3″, *p. 186*

583 Hardhead Catfish, 24″, *p. 185*

584 Shiner Perch (pregnant), 7″, *p. 459*

585 Kelp Perch, 8½″, *p. 459*

586 Black Perch, 15¼″, *p. 460*

587   Sand Perch, 12″, *p. 327*

588   White Perch, 23″, *p. 321*

589   Rubberlip Seaperch, 18″, *p. 463*

590   Redtail Surfperch, 16″, *p. 458*

591   Rainbow Seaperch, 12″, *p. 462*

592   Walleye Surfperch, 12″, *p. 461*

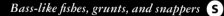

593 Sharpnose Seaperch, 12″, *p. 462*

594 French Grunt, 12″, *p. 418*

595 White Grunt, 16″, *p. 419*

596 Atlantic Creolefish, 15″, *p. 335*

597 Redspotted Hawkfish, 4″, *p. 452*

598 Tattler, 6″, *p. 336*

599 Pinfish, 15″, *p. 423*

600 Bermuda Chub, 20″, *p. 450*

601 Porkfish, 15″, *p. 417*

602 Lane Snapper, 14″, *p. 410*

603 Yellowtail Snapper, 30″, *p. 411*

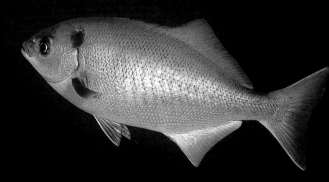

604 Half- 19″, *p. 454*

605 Tomtate, 10″, *p. 417*

606 Schoolmaster, 24″, *p. 406*

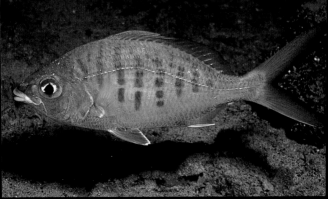

607 Yellowfin Mojarra, 16″, *p. 415*

608   Kelp Bass, 28″, *p. 334*

609   Peacock Bass, 18″, *p. 455*

610   Striped Bass, 6′, *p. 323*

611 Spotfin Mojarra, 8″, *p. 413*

612 Striped Mojarra, 12″, *p. 415*

613 Pacific Ocean Perch, 20″, *p. 280*

614   Red Snapper, 3′3″, *p. 407*

615   Gray Snapper, 3′, *p. 408*

616   Dog Snapper, 3′, *p. 409*

617 Speckled Hind, 3′7″, *p. 329*

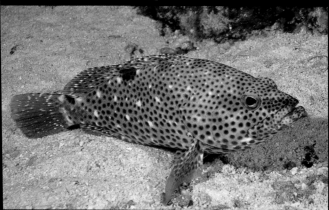

618 Rock Hind, 24″, *p. 328*

619 Red Hind, 24″, *p. 329*

620 Coney, 16", *p. 326*

621 Roosterfish, 4', *p. 389*

622 Mozambique Tilapia, 15", *p. 456*

623 Spotted Tilapia, 12″, *p. 457*

624 Atlantic Tripletail, 3′4″, *p. 412*

625 Greater Soapfish, 13″, *p. 336*

626   Belted Sandfish, 4½", *p. 337*

627   Warsaw Grouper, 6', *p. 332*

628   Black Grouper, 4', *p. 333*

629 Red Grouper, 3', *p. 331*

630 Nassau Grouper, 3'3", *p. 333*

631 Goliath Grouper, 7'10", *p. 330*

632 Giant Sea Bass, 7′5″, *p. 324*

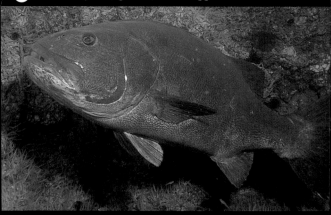

633 Black Sea Bass, 24″, *p. 325*

634 Mottled Jawfish, 5″, *p. 338*

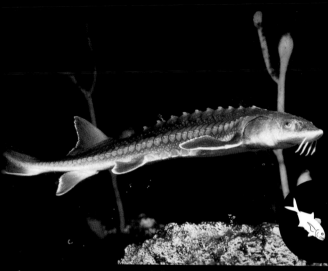

635 White Sturgeon, 12′6″, *p. 83*

636 Atlantic Sturgeon, 14′, *p. 84*

637   Sharksucker, 32″, *p. 390*

638   Cobia, 6′7″, *p. 392*

639 **Alligator Gar,** 10′, *p. 87*

640 **Ladyfish,** 3′3″, *p. 92*

641   Machete, 3′, *p. 92*

642   Bonefish, 3′, *p. 95*

643   Tarpon, 8′, *p. 93*

644   Bay Anchovy, 4″, *p. 106*

645   Striped Anchovy, 6″, *p. 106*

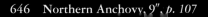

646   Northern Anchovy, 9″, *p. 107*

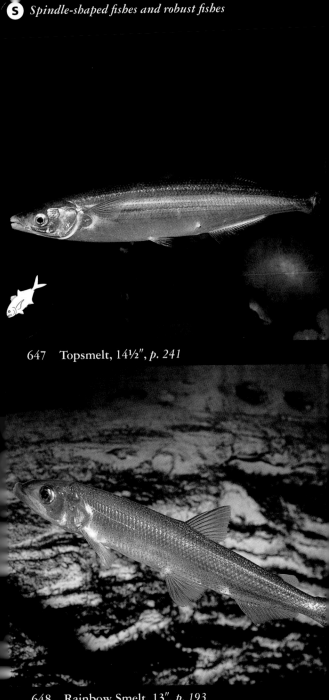

647 Topsmelt, 14½″, *p. 241*

648 Rainbow Smelt, 13″, *p. 193*

649   Inland Silverside, 4″, *p. 243*

650   California Grunion, 7½″, *p. 242*

651   Alewife, 15″, *p. 109*

652   Skipjack Herring, 21″, *p. 108*

653   Atlantic Menhaden, 18″, *p. 110*

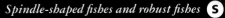

654   Bigeye Scad, 12″, *p. 399*

655   Round Scad, 8¼″, *p. 398*

656   Rainbow Runner, 4′, *p. 398*

Spindle-shaped fishes and robust fishes

657   Cero, 32″, *p. 534*

658   Atlantic Chub Mackerel, 25″, *p. 531*

659   Jack Mackerel, 32″, *p. 405*

660　Spanish Mackerel, 3′, *p. 533*

661　Atlantic Mackerel, 22″, *p. 532*

662　King Mackerel, 5′, *p. 532*

663 Atlantic Bonito, 3′, *p. 530*

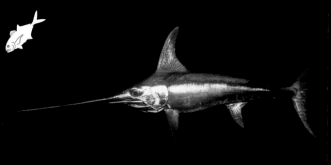

664 Swordfish, 15′, *p. 538*

665 Sailfish, 10′9″, *p. 539*

666 White Marlin, 10′, *p. 541*

667 Blue Marlin, 14′8″, *p. 540*

668 Striped Marlin, 13′5″, *p. 542*

△ 669   Great Barracuda, 6′, *p. 526*

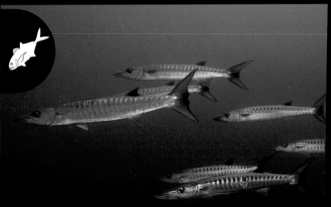

670   Pacific Barracuda, 4′, *p. 525*

671   Little Tunny, 4′, *p. 529*

672   Bluefin Tuna, 14′, *p. 536*

673   Yellowfin Tuna, 6′, *p. 536*

674   Skipjack Tuna, 3′4″, *p. 530*

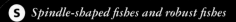

Ⓐ 675   Bluefish, 3′7″, *p. 388*

676   Ocean Whitefish, 3′4″, *p. 386*

677   Albacore, 5′, *p. 535*

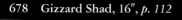

678   Gizzard Shad, 16″, *p. 112*

679   Threadfin Shad, 9″, *p. 112*

680   American Shad, 30″, *p. 110*

681 Greater Amberjack, 6′2″, *p. 401*

682 Bar Jack, 22″, *p. 397*

683 Yellowtail Jack, 5′, *p. 402*

684   Horse-eye Jack, 31″, *p. 396*

685   Crevalle Jack, 3′4″, *p. 395*

686   Florida Pompano, 25″, *p. 403*

687   Palometa, 20″, *p. 404*

688   Harvestfish, 12″, *p. 544*

689   Lookdown, 16″, *p. 401*

690   Jolthead Porgy, 27″, *p. 421*

691   Saucereye Porgy, 16″, *p. 422*

692   Atlantic Moonfish, 15″, *p. 400*

693 Man-of-War Fish, 8″, *p. 543*

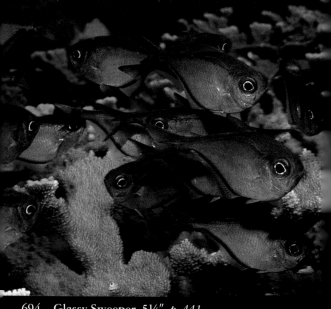

694 Glassy Sweeper, 5¼″, *p. 441*

695   Fourwing Flyingfish, 12″, *p. 246*

696   Dolphinfish, 6′6″, *p. 393*

697   Horn Shark, 4′, p. 47

698   Spotted Ratfish, 3′2″, p. 41

699   Swell Shark, 3′4″, p. 55

700 Bonnethead, 4′6″, *p. 65*

701 Scalloped Hammerhead, 13′9″, *p. 64*

702 Smalltooth Sawfish, 18′, *p. 68*

703 Nurse Shark, 14′, *p. 48*

704 Spiny Dogfish, 5′, *p. 45*

705 Soupfin Shark, 6′, *p. 56*

706   Sandbar Shark, 8′, *p. 62*

707   Smooth Dogfish, 5′, *p. 57*

708   Leopard Shark, 5′, *p. 58*

709   Blue Shark, 12′7″, *p. 63*

710   Sand Tiger, 10′, *p. 50*

711   Thresher Shark, 25′, *p. 51*

712   Blacktip Shark, 8′, *p. 60*

713   Shortfin Mako, 12′6″, *p. 54*

714   Dusky Shark, 12′, *p. 61*

△715   Tiger Shark, 18′, *p. 62*

△716   Bull Shark, 11′, *p. 59*

△717   White Shark, 21′, *p. 53*

718 Whale Shark, 45′, *p. 49*

719 Basking Shark, 45′, *p. 52*

720 Broadnose Sevengill Shark, 9′, *p. 43*

SPECIES ACCOUNTS

In the following pages, the fish species covered by this guide are given a complete description with habitat and range notes and a range map. The number preceding each species account corresponds to the number of the photograph of that species in the color plates section. The descriptions of species for which a photograph was not available are accompanied by a detailed illustration of the fish. In addition, there are a variety of drawings in the margins showing special features.

488 Atlantic Hagfish
Myxine limosa

Description: To 31″ (79 cm). Eel-like, elongate, cylindrical. Reddish brown to blackish purple. Eyes rudimentary, not visible; *6 barbels around mouth;* 5–6 gill pouches on each side; *1 exterior connection to gill pouches.* No paired fins; caudal fin slightly rounded, composed of skin fold.

Habitat: Over mud at depths of 98–3,150′ (30–960 m).

Range: Baffin Island, Canada, to NC.

Similar Species: Eastern Atlantic Hagfish *(M. glutinosa)* reaches length of about 17″ (43 cm), and is consistently grayish pink. North American hagfishes in genus *Eptatretus* have 5–14 gill pouches on each side opening independently to exterior. Sea Lamprey *(Petromyzon marinus)* also lacks paired fins and scales, but has 7 pairs of gill pouches opening to exterior, 1 nostril on top of head, and small but functional eyes.

Comments: Although most species of the genus *Myxine* live, on average, in slightly deeper water than the other genera of hagfishes, Atlantic Hagfish is exceptional in that it occasionally ventures into shallow water, within 98′ (30 m) of the surface. The intimately related Eastern Atlantic Hagfish is often considered to be the same species as Atlantic Hagfish.

Class Cephalaspidomorphi
Order Petromyzontiformes

This class contains the order Petromyzontiformes, the lampreys, plus three extinct orders. Petromyzontiformes is composed of a single family. These fishes are among the most primitive living vertebrates, with fossils dating to the Silurian period, 440 million years ago; lampreys first appeared during the Devonian period, about 410 million years ago.

LAMPREYS
Family Petromyzontidae

6 genera and 41 species worldwide; 3 genera and 18 species in North America, plus 2 species confined to Mexican waters. Lampreys occur in freshwater and marine habitats (32 species are almost exclusively freshwater), but spawn only in fresh water and die after spawning. These primitive fishes have eel-like bodies; the round, suctorial, jawless mouth is used as a suction cup to attach to prey. In adults, the mouth has varying numbers of horny teeth. Lampreys have a single nostril between the eyes (hagfishes also have a nostril on the top of the head, but it is located farther forward near the tip of the snout). There are seven pairs of gill pouches, each with a pore-like external opening. As in hagfishes, paired fins and scales are absent. The larvae are blind and lack teeth, but have a filter-feeding

filter-feeding screen in
mouth of larva

screen in the mouth. As the larvae mature, they undergo a dramatic metamorphosis during which they lose the filter-feeding apparatus; the mouth becomes round, and the fins grow larger. Adults of some species are parasitic. Lampreys have up to 168 pairs of chromosomes, the highest number known for any vertebrate species.

39   Chestnut Lamprey
Ichthyomyzon castaneus

Description: To 15″ (38 cm). Eel-like. Tan to yellowish olive above; sides, belly, and fins lighter. Eye small; mouth jawless, fringed, wider than head when expanded; teeth numerous, strong, slender; usually 4 lateral bicuspid teeth on each side of innermost row; innermost tooth plate curved, behind mouth opening, with 6–11 sharp cusps; tooth plate in front of mouth narrow, with 2–3 cusps. No paired fins; *dorsal fin long, shallowly notched. 49–56 muscle segments* between last gill opening and anus.

Habitat: Large rivers and reservoirs; ascends large creeks and small rivers to spawn. Larvae in pools and backwater areas over sand or sandy mud.

Range: Lake Winnipeg and Red River of the
North, s MB, south through MN, WI,
and Lake Michigan to e TN and nw GA,
and west to e TX.

Similar Species: Silver Lamprey (*I. unicuspis*) is grayish
brown to tan above and has teeth with 1
cusp in row surrounding mouth and
46–55 muscle segments. Ohio Lamprey
(*I. bdellium*) is grayish blue above and
has teeth with 2 cusps in row
surrounding narrower mouth and 53–62
muscle segments. Mountain Brook
Lamprey (*I. greeleyi*) is grayish brown to
olive tan and has teeth with 2 cusps in
row surrounding mouth and 55–58
muscle segments. All three species are
parasitic.

Comments: Chestnut Lamprey adults are parasitic;
they attach themselves to the side of
a fish with their suctorial mouths
and use their teeth to rasp a small
wound through which they obtain
body fluids.

40 Southern Brook Lamprey
Ichthyomyzon gagei

Description: To 7″ (18 cm). Eel-like, cylindrical.
Dark olive to brown above; lighter
below; belly olive yellow; fins yellowish.
Mouth jawless, narrower than head
when expanded; *teeth bicuspid,* in row
surrounding mouth. No paired fins;
*dorsal fin long, shallowly notched. 50–60
muscle segments* between last gill opening
and anus.

Habitat: Clear streams with moderate current and
pools with riffles over sand or gravel.
Larvae in pools with plant debris over
sand.

Range: Southeastern TN, w GA, and w FL west
to s MO and e TX.

Similar Species: Northern Brook Lamprey (*I. fossor*) has
teeth with 1 cusp in row surrounding
mouth.

Comments: The nonparasitic Southern Brook
Lamprey feeds on microscopic plants
and animals.

41 Least Brook Lamprey
Lampetra aepyptera

Description: To 6" (15 cm). Eel-like. Back dark yellowish brown, often with dark blotches; side light tan; belly and fins yellowish. Eye medium; *mouth small, usually narrower than head when expanded; teeth poorly developed.* No paired fins; *dorsal fin deeply notched, divided into 2 parts. 54–62 muscle segments* between last gill opening and anus.

Habitat: Pools and riffles of clear creeks with moderate current over sand or gravel. Larvae in pools with organic debris.

Range: Atlantic coastal plain from extreme se PA south to central NC; sw PA, s OH, and WV west to se MO and south to AL and se MS.

Similar Species: American Brook Lamprey *(L. appendix)* reaches length of 12" (30 cm), and has 63–73 muscle segments.

Comments: Both Least Brook and American Brook Lampreys are nonparasitic. The larval stage lasts two to three years.

42, 487 Pacific Lamprey
Lampetra tridentata

Description: To 30" (76 cm). Eel-like. Marine coloration: adults steel blue above, silvery below. Freshwater coloration: adults brownish red above, lighter below; larvae yellowish. Eye large; mouth jawless; *tooth plate above mouth broad, with 3 cusps; 4 pairs of lateral teeth.* No paired fins; *dorsal fin deeply notched, divided into 2 parts. 64–74 muscle segments* between last gill opening and anus.

Habitat: Coastal marine waters; large inland freshwater streams. Larvae in pools and eddies over silty mud to sand bottoms.

Range: AK to s CA.

Similar Species: River Lamprey *(L. ayresii)* reaches length of 12" (30 cm) and has 2 widely separated cusps in tooth plate above mouth and 65–70 muscle segments. Western Brook Lamprey *(L. richardsoni)* reaches length of 6″ (15 cm), and has 2 widely separated cusps in tooth plate above mouth and 58–67 muscle segments. Pacific Hagfish *(Eptatretus stoutii)* has rudimentary eyes, 10–14 pairs of gill pores, and 8 barbels.

Comments: Pacific Lamprey adults leave the ocean and ascend streams in the late spring and early summer to spawn in shallow water over gravel nests up to 24″ (61 cm) wide. They die soon after spawning. The larvae live in the stream for five to six years before entering the ocean, where they become parasitic on various fishes for one to two years. This species appears to have little impact on marine fish populations, and adults do not feed when they move into streams to spawn.

43, 485, 486 **Sea Lamprey**
Petromyzon marinus

Description: To 33″ (84 cm). Eel-like. Olive brown above; sides usually mottled yellowish brown, some individuals with shades of red, blue, and green, others blackish; pale below. Eye small; mouth jawless; *teeth numerous, rasp-like.* No paired or anal fins; *dorsal fin deeply notched, divided into 2 segments;* caudal fin rounded, spatulate. 67–74 *muscle segments* between last gill opening and anus.

Habitat: In oceans to depths of 3,000′ (915 m) or more; along coasts in estuaries and fresh water. Larvae in pools of creeks, rivers, or estuaries over silty mud to sand bottoms.

Range: Gulf of St. Lawrence to n FL and associated streams; Great Lakes.

Similar Species: Atlantic Hagfish *(Myxine limosa)* has rudimentary eyes, 5–6 gill pouches on each side, and 6 barbels.

Comments: This is the largest North American lamprey species. The adult parasitic stage in marine waters lasts two to three years. When adults reach sexual maturity they ascend coastal rivers for distances of more than 200 miles to spawn. The larvae remain in freshwater or estuarine areas for four to five years before they transform into adults and enter the ocean. The introduced population in the Great Lakes is landlocked and completes its entire life cycle in inland waters.

CARTILAGINOUS FISHES
Class Chondrichthyes

This class, which belongs to the superclass Gnathostomata, contains two subclasses: Holocephali and Elasmobranchii. Based on the current scheme of classification, there are about 846 species in this class worldwide; 122 species occur in North American inshore waters to depths of 656' (200 m), and additional species are found in Mexican waters. A number of other species are confined to deeper waters offshore.

These fishes have cartilaginous skeletons, well-developed jaws, and paired fins supported by pectoral and pelvic girdles. Each pelvic fin on the male has a clasper, which facilitates internal fertilization. The teeth are actually modified scales; the pulp cavity of each tooth-like scale is surrounded by dentine that is covered by enamel.

There are three groups of fishes in this class: chimaerids (also known as ratfishes), sharks, and batoids (which includes sawfishes, skates, and rays). There are two simple ways to distinguish sharks from batoids: The gill slits of sharks are at least partly lateral and can be viewed from the side, while the gill slits of batoids are entirely ventral; also, the pectoral fins of sharks are not attached to the gill slits, while the pectoral fins of batoids are fused to the side of the head and usually form some kind of disk-shaped body. Chimaerids are the only cartilaginous fishes that have a single gill slit on each side.

These cartilaginous fishes, unlike most bony fishes, lack a swim bladder and must move constantly or they will sink to the bottom. They have a short intestine; the surface area is increased by internal spirals or folds for the absorption of digested food.

Subclass Holocephali
Order Chimaeriformes

The subclass Holocephali is composed of a single order, the Chimaeriformes, which contains three families worldwide; two families occur in North America. All species are marine, with most occurring in deep water to depths of nearly 7,750′ (2,362 m). Only one of the 31 living species in the subclass Holocephali is found in inshore coastal waters to depths of 656′ (200 m). These fishes (called chimaerids, ratfishes, or holocephalans) share many of the characteristics of sharks and rays, including a cartilaginous skeleton, urea in the blood and tissues, and a ventral mouth. They are unique among cartilaginous fishes in having the upper jaw fused with the cranium, a single gill slit on each side, the first dorsal fin with an erectile spine, and smooth unscaled skin; another distinguishing characteristic is the club-shaped clasper organ on the head of the male.

SHORTNOSE CHIMAERAS
Family Chimaeridae

2 genera and 21 species worldwide; 1 species in North America, plus 1 genus and 4 species in deeper waters offshore. The single described North American species, found along the Pacific coast, occurs in shallower waters than any other shortnose chimaera. A second *Hydrolagus* species (probably new to science) has been found at greater depths off southern California and in the Gulf of California. The other three local members of the family occur in deep waters off eastern North America; what is believed to be a single species of the closely related family Rhinochimaeridae (longnose chimaeras), which is distinguished by an extremely long, pointed snout, occurs in deeper waters off both coasts of the western Atlantic and eastern Pacific Oceans. Shortnose chimaeras, also known as ratfishes, have short rounded snouts and long pointed caudal fins. The second dorsal fin extends from just in front of the pelvic fins almost to the base of the caudal fin.

---

698 Spotted Ratfish
Hydrolagus colliei

Description: To 3′2″ (97 cm). Elongate, tapering to slender caudal fin. Bronze above, with metallic hue; silvery below, with numerous white spots; eye green. Head large; teeth pliable, incisor-like. Males have spiny, club-shaped frontal clasper on head, sharp retracting clasping organs in front of pelvic fins, and slender claspers with expanded ends adjacent to each pelvic fin base. *1 long venomous spine in front of first dorsal fin; second dorsal with undulating outline.* Body unscaled. Lateral line wavy, with several branches on head.

Habitat: Close inshore from WA northward; southward to depths of nearly 3,000′ (915 m).

Range: Southeastern AK to Bahía Sebastián Vizcaíno, Baja California; isolated populations in upper Gulf of California.

Similar Species: A second unnamed *Hydrolagus* species has dark black coloration; occurs to depths of about 4,600′ (1,402 m).

Comments: All chimaerids deposit their eggs, which are fertilized internally, in elongate ridged brown cases. These distinctive fishes feed on clams, crabs, shrimps, and fishes. They are not sought by either sport or commercial anglers, although the liver yields an excellent machine oil. Care should be taken in handling them, as the venomous spines can cause a painful wound, and the clasping organs are quite sharp.

Subclass Elasmobranchii

This subclass includes the sharks and the batoids, or in other words, all living chondrichthyans except the members of the subclass Holocephali. According to the most recent classification scheme, the subclass contains 12 orders, with at least 46 families worldwide. Of these, 11 orders and 34 families occur in North American coastal waters to depths of 656′ (200 m); a number of other species range farther offshore in deeper waters. The elasmobranchs share important characteristics with the holocephalans, including a cartilaginous skeleton, urea in the blood and tissues, and a ventral mouth. They differ in having five to seven separate gill slits on each side, placoid scales, and the upper jaw not fused with the cranium; in addition, males do not have clasper organs on the head. Nearly all elasmobranchs are marine, although about 28 species live occasionally or permanently in fresh water. These fishes are found in a wide range of depths, from shallow waters to depths of 18,000′ (5,486 m) or more.

Order Hexanchiformes

This order is composed of two families, the Chlamydoselachidae and the Hexanchidae, both found in North America. The Chlamydoselachidae consists of a single wide-ranging species, Frill Shark *(Chlamydoselachus anguineus)*, which in North America is known only from the eastern Pacific; it is unique among living sharks in having six wrinkled ("frilled") gill covers, together with an unusually slender elongate body and a snake-like head and mouth. The eyes lack nictitating membranes. Members of this order have a spiracle and six to seven pairs of gill slits. No spines are associated with the single dorsal fin, which is located posteriorly. These sharks have anal fins.

COW SHARKS
Family Hexanchidae

3 genera and 4 species worldwide; all found in North America. The six to seven pairs of gill slits are not continuous across the throat. The lower jaw has a series of elongate, sawtooth-like teeth, each with six to nine cusps. The upper lobe of the caudal fin is elongate. Cow sharks are ovoviviparous, and the young provide for themselves from birth.

720 Broadnose Sevengill Shark
Notorynchus cepedianus

Description: To 9′ (2.7 m); 328 lb (149 kg). Elongate, rounded in cross section. Sandy gray to reddish brown, with black spots. Head depressed, moderately pointed; mouth inferior; *6 teeth on each side of lower jaw; 7 gill slits on each side;* spiracle small. Dorsal fin near caudal fin; upper lobe of caudal fin long, about one-third of total length.

Habitat: Bays over soft bottoms and off open coasts to depths of 150′ (46 m).

Range: Northern BC to Chile.

Similar Species: Sharpnose Sevengill Shark *(Heptranchias perlo)* reaches length of 7′ (2.1 m). Bluntnose Sixgill Shark *(Hexanchus griseus)* reaches length of 16′ (4.9 m), and has 6 gill slits on each side. Bigeye

Sixgill Shark *(Hexanchus nakamurai)* reaches length of 6′ (1.8 m), and has much larger eye and 5 teeth on each side of lower jaw. All occur in Atlantic and Pacific, Sharpnose Sevengill Shark to depths of 656′ (200 m).

Comments: A large female Broadnose Sevengill Shark may bear up to 85 young at one time. This big shark, widespread in the Indian and Pacific Oceans (but absent from the Atlantic), is considered a prime sport fish because of its fighting ability. It is sometimes harvested commercially. The scientific name for the North American population was originally *N. maculatus.* It was recently concluded, however, that this population does not differ taxonomically from those found elsewhere, in which case the older species name, *cepedianus,* is applicable.

Order Squaliformes

This order formerly included all sharks except those in the orders Hexanchiformes and Heterodontiformes. As now constituted, it contains eight families, five of which are found in North American inshore waters. In addition, there are five species in Mexican waters, and a number of species in deeper offshore waters. These sharks have two dorsal fins, with or without spines, and the anal fin is absent. They have a spiracle and five pairs of gill slits. The eyes lack nictitating membranes. Many squaliform sharks are small and occur in deep water; some are bioluminescent. A few are common inshore species, particularly certain members of the genus *Squalus* in the family Squalidae.

DOGFISH SHARKS
Family Squalidae

2 genera and 10 species worldwide; 2 genera and 3 species in North America, plus 1 species confined to Mexican waters. The two dorsal fins are of nearly equal size, and each has one non-grooved spine. On each side, all five gill slits are located in front of the pectoral fin insertion. There is a precaudal pit immediately in front of the upper anterior edge of the caudal fin, and the caudal peduncle has a pair of lateral keels. The teeth in the lower jaw

are not much larger than those in the upper jaw. This family was formerly much larger in size. Species removed from the family Squalidae are now included in five other families, four of which include species that have been recorded in North American inshore waters: Echinorhinidae (one genus with two species), Etmopteridae (two genera and two species), Somniosidae (two genera and three species), and Dalatiidae (one genus with one species).

---

704 Spiny Dogfish
Squalus acanthias

Description: To 5′ (1.5 m). Elongate, slender. Gray or brown above; dirty white below. Young have light spots on back. Snout long, pointed. *1 spine in front of each dorsal fin;* origin of first dorsal fin slightly behind rear of pectoral fin; origin of second dorsal fin behind rear of pelvic fin; *no anal fin;* upper lobe of caudal fin larger than lower, with rounded tip.

Habitat: Temperate coastal waters over soft bottoms to depths of 1,200′ (366 m).

Range: Atlantic coast from NF to NC; occasional stragglers south to Cuba. Pacific coast from Bering Sea to central Baja California.

Similar Species: Pacific Sleeper Shark *(Somniosus pacificus)* lacks spine in front of each dorsal fin, and origin of first dorsal fin is closer to pelvic fin insertion; occurs in deep Pacific waters. Smooth Dogfish *(Mustelus canis)* lacks spine in front of each dorsal fin and has anal fin.

Comments: The fully developed young are born in broods of two to 20 and average 8–12″ (20–30 cm) in length at birth. Tagging studies off California suggest that Spiny Dogfish is a migratory species. It is widespread in warm- to cold-temperate seas of both the Northern and Southern Hemispheres, but absent from the intervening tropical waters. Although it is an important food fish in Europe, this abundant shark is considered a pest in North America, where its main use is for instructional purposes in college anatomy classes.

ANGEL SHARKS
Order Squatiniformes
Family Squatinidae

This order consists of a single family: 1 genus with 12 species worldwide; 2 species in North America (1 Atlantic, 1 Pacific). This group was previously included in the order Squaliformes. Found in temperate and tropical waters, these bottom-dwelling sharks superficially resemble skates and rays, with whom they share a disk-like body; they differ in having the large pectoral fins separated from the head by a deep groove or notch. There are five gill slits on each side, hidden in the groove and not usually visible from above. Angel sharks have large spiracles, almost terminal mouths, and barbels. The two dorsal fins are located near the caudal fin and a row of tubercles down the center of the back. These fishes lack an anal fin.

305 Pacific Angel Shark
Squatina californica

Description: To 5′ (1.5 m). *Flat, disk-like; head separate from pelvic and pectoral fins.* Usually grayish brown above, with dark spots on back; white below. Mouth terminal; barbels and spiracle present; 5 gill slits on each side in groove behind head. Dorsal fins behind rear of pelvic fins; caudal fin lobes about equal in size.

Habitat: Near reefs over sand or mud to depths of 600′ (183 m).

Range: WA to Gulf of California; occasional stragglers north to se AK.

Similar Species: Atlantic Angel Shark *(S. dumeril)* has few reddish spots below; occurs over sand or mud in Atlantic.

Comments: Pacific Angel Shark usually lies partially buried in sand waiting for prey, such as Queenfish and California Halibut. This shark is occasionally caught by anglers, but is not highly prized as a sport fish. A small commercial gill-net fishery has recently been developed to supply fish markets.

BULLHEAD SHARKS
Order Heterodontiformes
Family Heterodontidae

This order consists of a single family: 1 genus with 8 species worldwide; 1 species in North America, plus 1 species confined to Mexican waters. These bottom-dwelling sharks occur in tropical and subtropical waters of the Pacific and Indian Oceans. They have deep, laterally compressed bodies, and are unusual in having a combination of low crushing teeth in the back of the jaws, two dorsal fins (each with a stout spine in front), and an anal fin. Bullhead sharks have a spiracle and five pairs of gill slits. The eyes lack nictitating membranes.

697 Horn Shark
Heterodontus francisci

Description: To 4' (1.2 m). Elongate, tapering, laterally compressed. Brown to gray, with *numerous dark spots.* Head large, blunt; eye lacks nictitating membrane; mouth and nostril connected by groove; front teeth small, pointed; rear teeth large, flat-surfaced; 5 gill slits on each side; spiracle present. *1 spine in front of each dorsal fin;* first dorsal fin above middle of pectoral fin, second dorsal between pelvic and anal fins; upper lobe of caudal fin with square posterior profile.

Habitat: Shallow reefs and over sand to depths of 500' (152 m); most common at 8–35' (2.4–10.5 m).

Range: Monterey Bay, CA, to n Gulf of California; not recorded from s Gulf.

Similar Species: The slimmer Spiny Dogfish (*Squalus acanthias*) has spine in front of each dorsal fin, but lacks anal fin.

Comments: No other typical shark has both an anal fin and a spine in the front of each dorsal fin. Horn Shark deposits its eggs in grenade-shaped, horny cases with spiral ridges. It feeds on fishes, mollusks, crabs, and sea urchins. Divers find this shark easy to approach and thus a good photographic subject.

Order Orectolobiformes

Previously included in the order Squaliformes, this group consists of seven families, two of which occur in North America. These sharks have an anal fin and two spineless dorsal fins. The mouth is very short, confined to the area well in front of the eyes. Specialized nostrils have prominent grooves accompanied by barbels in most species. Members of this order have a spiracle, varying in size from from small to large, usually below each eye. Most species have five small gill slits, with the fifth slit on each side often overlapping the fourth behind the insertion of the pectoral fin.

NURSE SHARKS
Family Ginglymostomatidae

3 genera and 3 species worldwide; 1 species in North America. Nurse sharks have a small spiracle below each eye. The short nostrils have short to moderately long barbels, without lobes or grooves around the outer edges. This family was formerly included in the carpet shark family (Orectolobidae).

703 Nurse Shark
Ginglymostoma cirratum

Description: To 14′ (4.3 m). Elongate. Grayish brown or yellowish; darker above than below. Snout short; *well-developed barbel attached to front of each nostril;* mouth under snout tip. Dorsal fins spineless, first dorsal fin slightly larger than second; caudal fin low in profile. Skin rough, with relatively large, closely spaced denticles.

Habitat: Inshore; often on shallow sand flats, in channels, and around coral reefs.

Range: In Atlantic from NC to Brazil, including Bermuda, Bahamas, Gulf of Mexico, and Caribbean. In Pacific from Gulf of California to Ecuador.

Comments: In North American waters, Nurse Shark is most abundant off the coasts of southern Florida. It feeds on small fishes, sea urchins, and a variety of crustaceans. This shark is thought to be harmless, but divers who grab at it often get "bitten" abrasions. It is too sluggish to be actively pursued by anglers. Although other sharks are found living in or around coral reefs, Nurse Shark is the only one that will be seen resting motionless on the bottom. No other species of shark is likely to be confused with Nurse Shark, particularly when habits and habitat are taken into consideration.

WHALE SHARKS
Family Rhincodontidae

1 species worldwide. These enormous filter-feeding sharks are usually seen on the surface far off-shore. They have a spiracle behind each eye and five pairs of gill slits. The checkered color pattern, humpback, and large lunate tail distinguish whale sharks from all other sharks.

718 Whale Shark
Rhincodon typus

Description: To 45′ (13.5 m). Very large, elongate; 3 ridges on each side from head to caudal peduncle. Dark gray to brown on back and side; much lighter below, fading to yellow or white; yellow or white spots between narrow lines of same color create *checkerboard-like pattern.* Mouth broad, near end of short snout; *gill slits very long, wide.* Pectoral fin large; pelvic, dorsal, and anal fins relatively small; dorsal fins spineless, first dorsal fin much larger than second; *caudal fin large, lunate.*

Habitat: Open seas.

Range: In Atlantic from NY to Brazil, including Gulf of Mexico; scattered records in Bermuda, Bahamas, and Caribbean. In Pacific from s CA to Ecuador.

Similar Species: Basking Shark *(Cetorhinus maximus)* lacks distinctive spotted color pattern. The dark, plankton-feeding Megamouth Shark *(Megachasma pelagios)* has bioluminescent structures inside mouth; occurs in deep Pacific waters.

Comments: This shark, the largest fish in the world, reputedly reaches a length of 60′ (18.5 m), but individuals approaching this size require verification. Whale Shark is found worldwide in tropical to warm-temperate seas. It feeds on small crustaceans and fishes, which it strains with its branchial sieve. It is unlikely that any other fish would be confused with this shark, due to its immense size and unique color pattern.

Order Lamniformes

This group of sharks, previously included in the order Squaliformes, contains seven families; six families occur in North America. The goblin shark family (Mitsukurinidae), which consists of one bizarre, deep-water species, was only recently recorded off California. The megamouth shark family (Megachasmidae), first formally described in 1983, has also been discovered off the coast of California. Members of this order have an anal fin and two spineless dorsal fins. There are five gill slits on each side; the last two are sometimes located above the pectoral fin. These fishes usually have a small spiracle behind each eye. The mouth extends well behind the eyes, which lack nictitating membranes.

SAND TIGERS
Family Odontaspididae

2 genera and 4 species worldwide; 2 genera and 3 species in North America (2 Atlantic, 1 Pacific). These sharks have five pairs of gill slits of medium length. The two dorsal fins are of about equal size, and the caudal fin is only slightly elevated. These characteristics, together with the long tricuspid teeth, distinguish sand tigers from all other sharks.

710 **Sand Tiger**
Carcharias taurus

Description: To 10′ (3 m). Elongate. Light grayish brown above, becoming paler on belly; darker spots behind pectoral fins on body and fins. *Teeth tricuspid, middle cusp very long and pointed.* Pectoral fin behind fifth gill slit; dorsal fins spineless, *about equal in size,* first dorsal fin anterior to pelvic fin; caudal fin low in profile.

Habitat: Shallow inshore waters on or near bottom.

Range: Gulf of Maine to s Brazil, w FL to TX; common north of Cape Hatteras, NC; relatively rare in Gulf of Mexico.

Similar Species: Raggedtooth Shark *(Odontaspis ferox)* reaches length of 12–13′ (3.7–4 m), and has teeth with 2 small cusps on each side of large central cusp; occurs along Pacific coast. The rare Bigeye Sand Tiger *(O. noronhai)* has larger eye and pelvic fin in more posterior position in relation to second dorsal fin.

Comments: Sand Tiger has been known to attack people. It is interesting as an example of prebirth cannibalism; a single embryo survives by obtaining nutrients from fellow embryos and yolks.

THRESHER SHARKS
Family Alopiidae

1 genus with 3 species worldwide; 2 species in North America, plus 1 species confined to Mexican waters. These distinctive sharks have an extremely long caudal fin. The large first dorsal fin is located at about mid-body; the second dorsal fin is much smaller. Thresher sharks have five gill slits on each side; the third to fifth slits are over the pectoral fin insertion.

---

711 Thresher Shark
Alopias vulpinus

Description: To 25′ (7.5 m). Elongate, greatest depth at pectoral fin. Brown, gray, or black above, on underside of snout, and on pectoral fin; white below. *Eye width about half of snout length.* Pectoral fin long, saber-like; first dorsal fin at mid-body, in front of pelvic fin; *upper lobe of caudal fin extremely long.*

Habitat: Open seas.

Range: In Atlantic from Gulf of Maine
to FL and Gulf of Mexico. In Pacific
from BC to s CA.

Similar Species: Bigeye Thresher *(A. superciliosus)*
has larger eye and rear of first dorsal
fin is over pelvic fin insertion.

Comments: Thresher Shark is viviparous; its
brood consists of two to four young.
It is found nearly worldwide in
tropical and temperate seas. It feeds
on schooling fishes, and can use its
tail to stun prey. The flesh is considered
by some to rival swordfish in taste, and
this shark is the target of a gill-net
fishery established off southern
California.

BASKING SHARKS
Family Cetorhinidae

1 species worldwide. These sharks are
found in temperate waters throughout the world. Their
general body shape is nearly identical to that of the mackerel sharks (family Lamnidae), with a distinct keel on the
caudal peduncle and caudal lobes of almost equal size. Basking sharks, in contrast to mackerel sharks, are plankton
feeders, and in association with this have a cavernous mouth
with vestigial teeth that are greatly reduced in size; long,
horny, deciduous gill rakers, for straining prey from the
water; and five very long gill slits that nearly meet under
the throat. Another difference between the families is that
adult basking sharks may develop notably elongate snouts.

719 Basking Shark
Cetorhinus maximus

Description: To 45′ (13.5 m). Fusiform. Grayish brown
to completely gray or black; occasionally
lighter below. Snout short, conical;
snout tip rounded in larger individuals,
relatively long and forming cylindrical
proboscis in smaller individuals; teeth
very small, conical; *gill slits very long,
nearly meeting under throat;* gill rakers long,
horny, united at base, sometimes absent.
First dorsal fin between insertions of
pectoral and pelvic fins; caudal fin

lunate, upper lobe slightly larger than lower. Distinct keel on caudal peduncle.

Habitat: Surface of open seas.

Range: In Atlantic from central NF to FL during winter. In Pacific from Gulf of Alaska to Gulf of California.

Similar Species: Whale Shark *(Rhincodon typus)* has distinctive checkerboard-like color pattern and shorter gill slits. The dark, plankton-feeding Megamouth Shark *(Megachasma pelagios),* previously considered a second species of Cetorhinidae but now placed in its own family (Megachasmidae), has bioluminescent structures inside mouth; occurs in deep Pacific waters.

Comments: This is one of the largest fishes in the world. Whale Shark is reputedly bigger, but the largest recorded individuals of both species are about the same size. Basking Shark uses its large combs of horny gill rakers to feed on plankton. The most benign species of shark, it has been harvested by harpoon for its oil.

MACKEREL SHARKS
Family Lamnidae

3 genera and 5 species; all found in North America. These sharks have torpedo-shaped bodies and large teeth that are used to capture prey such as fishes, squids, and marine mammals. There are five long gill slits on each side, with the fifth located in front of the pectoral fin insertion. Some species have spiracles. Similar to basking sharks (family Cetorhinidae), mackerel sharks have a distinct keel on the caudal peduncle and caudal fin lobes of almost equal size.

717 White Shark
Carcharodon carcharias

Description: To 21' (6.4 m); 2,658 lb (1,208 kg). Fusiform, elongate. Gray or brown above; dirty white below. Snout bluntly pointed; *teeth triangular, serrate. Origin of first dorsal fin above rear of pectoral fin;* anal fin beneath or behind second dorsal fin; *caudal fin lunate,* upper and lower lobes almost equal in size. Distinct keel on caudal peduncle.

Habitat: Surface of coastal waters; mostly in warm- and cold-temperate latitudes.

Range: Atlantic coast from s NF to Brazil, including Gulf of Mexico. Pacific coast from AK to Gulf of California.

Similar Species: The smaller Porbeagle *(Lamna nasus)* has smooth-edged tricuspid teeth with long slender middle cusp; occurs to depths of 480′ (146 m) in Atlantic.

Comments: This shark occurs worldwide, but is rare or absent from tropical regions. White Shark is ovoviviparous; the young are about 5′ (1.5 m) long at birth. A savage predator, it feeds on fishes, sea otters, seals, sea lions, and even crabs. This is the most dangerous North American shark; fortunately, its rarity limits the number of attacks. It is occasionally caught by commercial anglers, and the flesh is reportedly quite palatable.

713 Shortfin Mako
Isurus oxyrinchus

Description: To 12′6″ (3.8 m); 1,078 lb (490 kg). Fusiform, slender. Grayish blue to deep blue above; white below. Snout sharply pointed; *teeth large, relatively few, long, slender, smooth-edged, pointed backward, each with 1 cusp.* First dorsal fin much larger than second dorsal fin, origin behind inner corner of pectoral fin; anal fin origin behind origin of second dorsal fin. Caudal peduncle depressed, with prominent keel on each side extending onto caudal fin.

Habitat: Surface of open warm seas; often near shore.

Range: In Atlantic from Cape Cod, MA, to Argentina, including Bermuda, Bahamas, Gulf of Mexico, and Caribbean. In Pacific from mouth of Columbia River at WA–OR border to Chile, including Gulf of California.

Similar Species: Longfin Mako *(I. paucus)* is mostly dark blue or blackish below, with only small white area on belly, and has longer pectoral fin; occurs in deeper waters.

Comments: Shortfin Mako is found worldwide in tropical to warm-temperate seas. It feeds primarily on schooling fishes, such as mackerels and herrings. An active and strong swimmer, this species is famous for leaping out of the water when hooked or in pursuit of prey. It is potentially dangerous to people.

Order Carcharhiniformes

Previously included in the order Squaliformes, this group is composed of eight families, five of which occur in North American inshore waters. Other species may occur offshore in waters deeper than 656' (200 m). These sharks have two dorsal fins, without spines at the bases, and an anal fin. There are five gill slits on each side; the last one to three are located over the pectoral fin. Gill rakers are absent, and spiracles may be present. The eyes have nictitating folds or membranes.

CAT SHARKS
Family Scyliorhinidae

15 genera and at least 96 species worldwide; 6 genera and at least 5 species in North America. These fishes are found most abundantly in the western Pacific; five of the North American members of this family occur in inshore waters, and at least five other species occur in deeper offshore waters. Small and bottom-dwelling, cat sharks are among the most spectacularly marked sharks, with blotches, spotting, and vermiculations on their bodies. The fifth gill slit is located over the pectoral fin insertion. In most species the dorsal fins are far back on the body. The upper lobe of the caudal fin is longer than the lower.

699 Swell Shark
Cephaloscyllium ventriosum

Description: To 3'4" (1 m). Elongate. *Brown, with dark spots and mottling.* Head wider than deep; teeth very small, with multiple cusps. *First dorsal fin just behind pelvic fin insertion,* second directly above anal fin;

tips of dorsal and anal fins rounded; upper lobe of caudal fin elongate.

Habitat: Shallow reefs and kelp beds in caves and crevices to depths of 1,500' (458 m).

Range: Monterey Bay, CA, to Gulf of California.

Similar Species: Brown Cat Shark *(Apristurus brunneus)* has brown body and black-tipped fins; occurs in deep waters. Filetail Cat Shark *(Parmaturus xaniurus)* reaches length of 24″ (61 cm), lacks spots, and has enlarged scales on anterior edge of caudal fin; occurs in deep waters. Chain Dogfish *(Scyliorhinus retifer)* has pale brown body with strongly contrasting, chain-like reticulations; occurs at mid-depths in Atlantic.

Comments: Swell Shark is a nocturnal forager and eats decaying fishes and living organisms. It is oviparous, depositing each egg in a distinctive purse-shaped case, which is then attached to various objects by curling tendrils. This shark swells up with water when disturbed in its crevice habitat, making it difficult to remove. It will bite if provoked.

HOUND SHARKS
Family Triakidae

9 genera and 41 species worldwide; 3 genera and 8 species in North America, plus 1 species confined to Mexican waters. Relatively small, bottom-dwelling sharks of coastal waters, hound sharks are also known as smoothhounds. The jaws have moderately long labial furrows, and the anterior nasal flaps are usually not slender or barbel-like. Spiracles are present. All species are viviparous. Members of this family resemble the requiem sharks (family Carcharhinidae), and were previously included in that family. They are smaller than requiem sharks and have more numerous smaller, compact, crushing teeth; these differences, however, are by no means absolute.

705 Soupfin Shark
Galeorhinus galeus

Description: To 6′ (1.8 m). Fusiform. Dark bluish or dusky gray above; paler below; *anterior edges of dorsal fins black in adults.* Snout long, pointed, flat; teeth notched, with cusps directed toward corners of mouth; *spiracle present.* First dorsal fin origin behind rear of pectoral fin; second dorsal smaller, directly above anal fin; upper lobe of caudal fin enlarged.

Habitat: Surface waters over soft bottoms.

Range: Absent from w Atlantic. In e Pacific from n BC to Bahía San Juanico, Baja California. Also in Peru and Chile.

Similar Species: Blue Shark *(Prionace glauca)* has long pointed teeth without cusps, very long narrow pectoral fin, and first dorsal fin well behind rear of pectoral fin.

Comments: This shark is also known as Tope. Found in temperate oceans nearly worldwide, it is wide-ranging and may travel 35 miles a day. Soupfin Shark is used in sharkfin soup and is fished commercially. The eastern Pacific population was formerly recognized as *G. zyopterus.*

707 Smooth Dogfish
Mustelus canis

Description: To 5′ (1.5 m). Fusiform, relatively slender. Gray to brown. Mouth small, broadly rounded; upper labial furrow of jaws longer than lower furrow; *teeth numerous, small, crushing, compact,* in several functioning rows; spiracle present. *Dorsal fins prominent, second only slightly smaller than first; origin of second dorsal fin above a point in front of anal fin.* Shallow precaudal notch on upper part of caudal peduncle.

Habitat: Over open sand or mud; common at depths of 30–1,200′ (9–366 m).

Range: Subspecies *M. canis canis* in coastal waters from Bay of Fundy to Uruguay and Argentina; replaced by subspecies *M. canis insularis* in usually deeper waters of insular areas.

Similar Species: The two subspecies differ in number of vertebrae, height of dorsal fins, and length of caudal fin tip. The recently named Gulf Smoothhound

(*M. sinusmexicanus*) has 3-pointed scales on sides. Florida Smoothhound (*M. norrisi*) has nearly equal upper and lower labial furrows. Lemon Shark (*Negaprion brevirostris*) has blade-like teeth; occurs around coral reefs. Spiny Dogfish (*Squalus acanthias*) has stout spine in front of each dorsal fin and lacks anal fin.

Comments: Because this shark feeds primarily on commercially valued bottom-dwelling invertebrates, such as crabs and lobsters, it is often regarded as a pest by commercial anglers. In some parts of the world, hound sharks are considered an important food source and are fished commercially.

708 Leopard Shark
Triakis semifasciata

Description: Male to 5′ (1.5 m), female to 7′ (2.1 m). Fusiform, elongate. *Gray, with black spots and bars sometimes stretching across back.* Snout moderately long, pointed; fourth and fifth gill slits over pectoral fin. First dorsal fin origin above rear of pectoral fin; second dorsal fin origin in front of anal fin.

Habitat: Shallow bays over sand and mud to depths of 300′ (92 m); usually to 12′ (3.7 m).

Range: OR to Mazatlán, Mexico, including Gulf of California.

Similar Species: Gray Smoothhound (*Mustelus californicus*) lacks black spots, and midpoint of first dorsal fin is closer to pelvic fin insertion. Smooth Dogfish (*M. canis*) is gray to brown above and lacks markings on body. Brown Smoothhound (*M. henlei*) is reddish brown to bronze above, silvery below, and lacks black spots and scales on posterior dorsal fin.

Comments: The nomadic Leopard Shark feeds on fishes and crustaceans such as crabs and shrimps. It is common and very popular as a sport fish. Quite tasty, this shark forms part of the commercial shark fishery. Because Leopard Shark is attractive and easily maintained in captivity, it is often exhibited in public aquariums.

REQUIEM SHARKS
Family Carcharhinidae

12 genera and about 50 species world-wide; 5 genera and 20 species in North America, plus 2 genera and 4 species confined to Mexican waters. Until recently, the North American hound sharks (family Triakidae) and hammerhead sharks (family Sphyrnidae) were included in this group, the largest family of sharks. Although most species are pelagic, the majority of these do not regularly range beyond the limits of the continental shelf. The larger species are dangerous, but the majority are too small to be considered serious threats to people. Because they resemble one another so closely, many requiem sharks are difficult to identify, especially those in the largest genus, *Carcharhinus*. All family members have two spineless dorsal fins, with the first fin usually larger than the second; some *Carcharhinus* species have a low dermal ridge between the dorsal fins. The upper caudal fin lobe is elongate and pointed upward. There are five pairs of gill slits. The teeth are blade-like cusps, with smooth or serrate edges; it is unusual for more than one row of teeth to be functional at a time. Morphology of the teeth is important in identification, as are such characteristics as snout length and the size and position of the fins.

716 Bull Shark
Carcharhinus leucas

Description: To 11′ (3.5 m). Fusiform, relatively robust. Back grayish; belly white. Young have fins with dusky tips. *Snout short, rounded, length less than width of mouth; teeth strongly serrate; teeth in upper jaw broadly triangular; teeth in lower jaw slender;* no spiracle. Pectoral fin large, broad, with pointed tip; first dorsal fin origin in front of axil of pectoral fin; second dorsal fin much smaller, almost directly above anal fin. *No low dermal ridge between dorsal fins;* no keel on caudal peduncle.

upper and lower teeth

Habitat: Inshore, never far from land; ascends large rivers for considerable distances.

Range: In Atlantic from NY to Rio de Janeiro, Brazil, including Bermuda, Bahamas, Gulf of Mexico, and Caribbean. In Pacific from s Baja California to Peru.

Comments: Bull Shark occurs worldwide in tropical to warm-temperate seas, and occasionally in fresh water. There is a verified record from the late 1930s of an adult Bull Shark captured in the Mississippi River as far north as St. Louis, Missouri. In Florida, individuals occasionally enter the Apalachicola River. The unusual ability of this species to enter and live in fresh water is a function of its highly modified renal gland. This shark is often caught on hook and line, but it does not rise to the surface and leap as do some of the other members of the family. Several attacks on people have been reported.

712 Blacktip Shark
Carcharhinus limbatus

Description: To 8′ (2.4 m). Fusiform, moderately slender. Back gray; belly white; *pelvic fin always black-tipped,* other fin tips black but fading with age. Snout relatively long, pointed; *front teeth erect, sharp-pointed, serrate;* gill slits moderately long; no spiracle. Pectoral fin falcate; dorsal fins spineless, first dorsal fin much larger than second; anal fin almost directly below second dorsal fin. *No low dermal ridge between dorsal fins.*

upper and
lower teeth

Habitat: Coastal and offshore waters.

Range: In Atlantic from New England to s Brazil, including Bahamas, Gulf of Mexico, and Caribbean. In Pacific from Baja California and Gulf of California to Peru, including offshore islands.

Similar Species: Spinner Shark *(C. brevipinna)* has sharper snout and smooth lower teeth; occurs in Atlantic.

Comments: This species occurs worldwide in tropical to temperate seas. Blacktip and

Spinner Sharks are noted for their leaping and spinning antics; in pursuit of food or when hooked, they leap high and rotate on their long axis. These sharks often swim in small schools.

714 Dusky Shark
Carcharhinus obscurus

Description: To 12′ (3.7 m). Fusiform, moderately slender. Bluish gray or lead gray above; white below; pectoral fin grayish, darker at tips; pelvic and anal fins grayish white. Snout moderately long, length less than width of mouth, but greater than distance between inner corners of nostrils; teeth serrate, upper broadly triangular, lower with narrow cusps. *First dorsal fin relatively small, origin over inner corner of pectoral fin;* second dorsal fin directly over anal fin, origin over or in front of anal fin origin. *Low dermal ridge between dorsal fins.*

Habitat: Inshore and over outer continental shelf.
Range: In Atlantic from MA to Brazil, including Gulf of Mexico. In Pacific from Redondo Beach, CA, to Gulf of California.
Similar Species: Silky Shark *(C. falciformis)* has finer, less abrasive scales on body (hence its common name) and notably longer and more slender extension of second dorsal fin tip; occurs in Atlantic. Atlantic Sharpnose Shark *(Rhizoprionodon terraenovae)* resembles a small *Carcharhinus* species, but lacks spiracle, has smooth teeth sharply slanted backward, and second dorsal fin is well behind anal fin origin; occurs in Atlantic.
Comments: Dusky Shark is found nearly worldwide in temperate and tropical waters. It feeds primarily on bottom-dwelling fishes and smaller sharks. This shark is potentially dangerous.

706 Sandbar Shark
Carcharhinus plumbeus

upper and
lower teeth

Description: To 8′ (2.4 m). Moderately robust. Brown
to grayish brown above; lighter on side;
whitish below; no conspicuous markings
on body or fins. Snout relatively short,
broadly rounded; teeth weakly serrate;
upper teeth broadly triangular, erect,
increasingly oblique toward corners of
mouth; lower teeth erect, slender,
symmetrical. *First dorsal fin large,* origin
over axil of pectoral fin; second dorsal fin
origin directly above anal fin origin. *Low
dermal ridge between dorsal fins.*

Habitat: Inshore and over bottoms of shallow
bays and estuaries.

Range: MA to Brazil; more common north of
Cape Hatteras, NC; infrequent in Gulf
of Mexico; absent from insular areas.
Also in e Atlantic.

Similar Species: Dusky Shark *(C. obscurus)* has more
posterior dorsal fin in relation to
pectoral fin and more closely set serrate
scales.

Comments: Sandbar Shark has a more robust body
than most requiem sharks. It feeds on a
variety of mollusks, crustaceans, and
fishes. This relatively small shark is not
known to be a threat to people.
Populations in the western Atlantic
were formerly recognized as *C. milberti.*

---

715 Tiger Shark
Galeocerdo cuvier

upper and
lower teeth

Description: To 18′ (5.5 m); 1,775 lb (807 kg).
Fusiform. Gray to grayish brown; darker
above than on sides; *individuals to 6′
(1.8 m) long have prominent markings on
back, with dark spots forming bars.* Snout
short, bluntly rounded, length much less
than width of mouth; teeth alike in both
jaws, unique in shape, deeply notched
and strongly serrate, cusps low and
strongly asymmetrical; *small spiracle
behind eye.* First dorsal fin much larger
than second; caudal fin falcate. Low

dermal ridge between dorsal fins; *dermal ridge on each side of caudal peduncle.*

Habitat: Near surface of coastal and offshore waters.

Range: In Atlantic from Gulf of Maine to n Argentina, including Bermuda, Bahamas, Gulf of Mexico, and Caribbean; most common in s FL and Cuba. In Pacific from s CA to Peru.

Comments: Tiger Shark occurs worldwide in tropical to warm-temperate seas, ranging seasonally into cool-temperate waters. It is voracious and dangerous. The stomachs of captured individuals have been found to contain other fishes, porpoises, turtles, beef bones, dogs, and garbage. Due to the unique shape of its teeth, the teeth outline in shark-attack victims is often a positive clue in identifying this shark as the attacker.

709 Blue Shark
Prionace glauca

Description: To 12′7″ (3.8 m); 436 lb (198 kg). Fusiform, very slender. Dark blue above; bright blue on sides; white below; tips of pectoral, dorsal, and anal fins dusky. Snout long, narrowly rounded, length longer than width of mouth; teeth serrate, triangular and curved in upper jaw, narrower in lower jaw. *Pectoral fin very long, narrow, somewhat falcate;* dorsal fins relatively small; caudal fin falcate. No low dermal ridge between dorsal fins; weak keel on caudal peduncle.

Habitat: Common near surface of open seas; often in shallow coastal inshore waters over sand or mud.

Range: In Atlantic from NS to Gulf of Maine; rarely to Chesapeake Bay; disjunctly to Brazil. In Pacific from s AK to Chile.

Similar Species: Soupfin Shark *(Galeorhinus galeus)* has notched teeth; adults have dorsal fins with black anterior edge. Oceanic Whitetip Shark *(Carcharhinus longimanus)* has deeper and heavier body, rounded pectoral and first dorsal fins,

and usually white-tipped pelvic,
pectoral, first dorsal, and caudal fins.

Comments: The highly pelagic Blue Shark is found
worldwide. It feeds on small schooling
fishes and has been known to follow
vessels for days feeding on offal. This
shark is not considered to be dangerous.

HAMMERHEAD SHARKS
Family Sphyrnidae

1 genus with 8 species worldwide; 4
species in North America, plus 2 species confined to Mexican Pacific waters. These unusual fishes have greatly depressed and laterally expanded heads. The position of the
eyes, on the lateral expansion, gives hammerhead sharks vision in all directions and better depth perception. The patterns of the head pores (the ampullae of Lorenzini, which are
involved in the detection of electrical impulses) are taxonomically diagnostic, a characteristic unique among sharks.
The teeth are usually moderately slanted, sometimes serrate. The two dorsal fins are spineless, with the first fin usually larger than the second. The upper caudal fin lobe is
long and pointed upward. Young inhabit coastal waters,
and adults of larger species are primarily oceanic. These
sharks are voracious predators, and the biggest species are
dangerous to people.

701 Scalloped Hammerhead
Sphyrna lewini

Description: To 13′9″ (4.2 m). Elongate, compressed.
Gray above; white below. Head greatly
expanded laterally, with large eye at each
end of lateral expansion, *anterior edge
with median indentation; eye separated from
nostril by distance equal to width of eye;*
corners of mouth in front of line drawn
between rear corners of head; front of
mouth on or near line drawn between
eyes; teeth strongly slanted, not serrate.
Pelvic fin not indented on outer edge;
first dorsal fin origin above rear edge of
pectoral fin; second dorsal fin with
moderately long lobe.

Habitat: In oceans near surface; sometimes in
estuaries.

Range: In Atlantic from NJ to s Brazil,
including Bermuda, Bahamas, Gulf of
Mexico, and Caribbean. In e Pacific from
s CA to Peru.

Similar Species: Great Hammerhead *(S. mokarran)* has
head with nearly straight anterior edge,
deeply indented pelvic fin, and high
second dorsal fin with short lobe; occurs
in clear tropical waters, often around
reefs. Smooth Hammerhead *(S. zygaena)*
lacks median indentation on head, and
eye and nostril are closer together.

Comments: Scalloped Hammerhead is found
worldwide in tropical and warm-
temperate latitudes and feeds on fishes
and squids. This shark is known to
attack its own kind as well as people.

---

700 Bonnethead
Sphyrna tiburo

Description: To 4′6″ (1.4 m). Elongate. Gray to
grayish brown above; paler below. Head
depressed, slightly expanded laterally,
with eye at each end of lateral expansion,
*anterior edge without indentations and either
rounded or slightly angular at tip of snout,*
slightly concave opposite nostrils; teeth
smooth, cusps slanted in upper jaw, erect
in lower jaw, becoming flat in corners of
both jaws. First dorsal fin origin slightly
behind rear edge of pectoral fin.

Habitat: Continental waters, bays, and estuaries;
usually over sand.

Range: In Atlantic from New England to
n Argentina, including Bahamas, Cuba,
Gulf of Mexico, and s and w Caribbean.
In Pacific from s CA to Peru.

Comments: This harmless shark feeds on fishes,
crustaceans, and mollusks. It is caught
on hook and line, and sometimes eaten.

Order Torpediniformes

This order contains two families, both of which are found in
North America. These fishes have soft loose skin. A powerful electric organ, derived from branchial muscles, is located

on or near the head. The eyes are small or occasionally absent or vestigial. Members of this order have well-developed caudal fins and, when present, one or two dorsal fins.

ELECTRIC RAYS
Family Narcinidae

9 genera and about 24 species worldwide; 1 species in North America, plus 1 genus with 3 species confined to Mexican Pacific waters. These rays are often placed in the closely related torpedo electric ray family (Torpedinidae). They have disk-shaped bodies that are anteriorly rounded. The stout jaws have strong labial cartilages.

306   Lesser Electric Ray
Narcine brasiliensis

Description: To 18" (46 cm). Disk circular, *anterior profile rounded,* depressed, thick, fleshy. Grayish or brownish above, with scattered dark blotches, or rings of dark dots around blotches (especially in young); white below. Electric organ extends across head, with kidney-shaped outline visible on each side. 2 dorsal fins of about equal size and shape. Tail section thick, broad at base; caudal fin well developed, rounded posteriorly. Body unscaled, smooth.

Habitat: Over bottom in surf zone to depths of about 120' (37 m).

Range: NC to n Argentina, including Gulf of Mexico and Caribbean.

Comments: This species is reported to deliver 37 volts, but it is unlikely that the electric organ is used as an offensive weapon.

TORPEDO ELECTRIC RAYS
Family Torpedinidae

2 genera and 14 species worldwide; 1 genus with 2 species in North America (1 Atlantic, 1 Pacific). Members of this family have rounded bodies that are more or less straight across the anterior edge.

The extremely slender jaws lack labial cartilages. Dorsal and caudal fins are usually present and well developed. These rays stun their prey and protect themselves with specialized muscles, located near the head, that produce a powerful electric charge, delivering more than 200 volts. Electric rays are found in all oceans, from shallow bays to great depths.

309 Pacific Electric Ray
Torpedo californica

Description: To 4′6″ (1.4 m). Disk circular, depressed, fused with head and pectoral fins. Dark blue or grayish brown; often with black spots above; dirty white below. 2 dorsal fins, *first dorsal fin above pelvic fin,* second between caudal fin and rear of pelvic fin; caudal fin large, with nearly straight rear profile. Body unscaled, smooth.

Habitat: Shallow water over mud and sand and kelp beds to depths of 900′ (275 m).

Range: Northern BC to Bahía Sebastián Vizcaíno, Baja California.

Similar Species: Round Stingray (*Urobatis halleri*) lacks dorsal fins and has 1 long spine in front of caudal fin.

Comments: Pacific Electric Ray feeds on fishes and stuns its prey with a powerful electric charge. It has shown aggressive behavior toward divers off California and may be dangerous. Electric rays taken off Peru, Chile, and Japan may be this species.

308 Atlantic Torpedo
Torpedo nobiliana

Description: To 6′ (1.8 m). Disk circular, *slightly wider than long, truncate in front,* depressed, thick, fleshy. Brown, purplish, or slate gray to almost black above; white below. Electric organ visible as large kidney-shaped patch on each side of head. 2 dorsal fins, first larger than second, *first partly posterior to pelvic fin.* Tail section thick, broad at base; caudal fin well developed, truncate. Body unscaled, smooth.

Habitat: Over mud or sand to depths of 360′
(110 m).

Range: NS to FL and n Gulf of Mexico. Also in
e Atlantic.

Comments: The large Atlantic Torpedo can produce
220 volts of electricity, but it has not
been known to seriously injure people.

SAWFISHES
Order Pristiformes
Family Pristidae

This order consists of a single family: 2
genera and 6 species worldwide; 1 genus with 2 species in
North America. Sawfishes are shark-like fishes that have
two well-developed dorsal fins and a prominent caudal fin.
The most conspicuous feature is the saw, an extremely elongate, blade-like snout armed on both sides with large teeth
of equal size and embedded in deep sockets. All species lack
barbels. Sawfishes live close to shore, chiefly over sand or
mud and seldom in water deeper than 30′ (9 m). Certain
species are known to ascend rivers. Due partly to the mar-
keting of the saws as curios, sawfishes are often killed indiscriminately; their numbers have declined dramatically in
parts of the world. In addition, they are considered destruc-
tive nuisances by commercial anglers because they easily become entangled in fishing nets. Sawfishes are now protected
in some areas, including North America.

---

702 Smalltooth Sawfish
Pristis pectinata

Description: To 18′ (5.5 m). Moderately depressed,
shark-like. Nearly uniform mousy gray
to blackish above; paler on sides; whitish
below. Snout large, blade-like, *with at
least 24 teeth on each side.* Pectoral fin not
greatly expanded; dorsal fins of about
equal size and shape, *origin of first over
pelvic fin insertion.* Tail large; *no distinct
lower caudal fin lobe.*

Habitat: Estuaries, lower parts of large rivers, and
shallow coastal waters.

Range: Chesapeake Bay to Brazil, including
Bahamas, Gulf of Mexico, and West

Indies; rare north to NY; occasionally strays to Bermuda. Also in e Atlantic.

Similar Species: Largetooth Sawfish *(P. pristis)* has 19 teeth on each side of snout, origin of first dorsal fin well ahead of pelvic fin insertion, and tail with distinct lower caudal fin lobe.

Comments: Sawfishes slash their saw-like snout from side to side among schooling fishes in order to stun or kill them. Populations lacking a lower caudal lobe are known from the eastern Pacific and in other parts of the Indo-Pacific region, but it is unknown whether these are *P. pectinata* or a closely related species.

Order Rajiformes

Recent reclassifications have reduced this order to three families, thornbacks (Platyrhinidae), guitarfishes (Rhinobatidae), and skates (Rajidae), all of which occur in inshore and deeper North American waters and adjacent Mexican Atlantic and Pacific waters. All of these fishes have easily recognizable shapes. In skates the body is greatly depressed, with the pectoral fins expanded to form a disk. Although similar to skates, thornbacks and guitarfishes have a more robust, shark-like body posterior to the pectoral fins. The tail is usually distinct from the body. All species have a pair of spiracles and five pairs of gill slits. Members of this order usually have two dorsal fins without spines.

THORNBACKS
Family Platyrhinidae

1 genus with 5 species worldwide; 1 species in North America. These fishes are found in warm-temperate and continental shelf waters in the Pacific from California to Japan, China, and India, and are also known off western Africa. The skate-like body of thornbacks retains some of the characteristics of sharks. The portion of the body behind the pectoral fins is robust, not depressed as in skates and rays. There are five pairs of gill slits on the underside of the body. These fishes have two dorsal fins and a large caudal fin. The body shape, tail, and habits of this family are very similar to those of the related guitarfishes (family Rhinobatidae, which includes six genera and about

40 species, with two genera, *Rhinobatos* and *Zapteryx,* and three species in North America). Thornbacks, however, have a more rounded snout and one to three large hooked spines on the back and the tail. Most species are ovoviviparous.

307   Thornback
Platyrhinoidis triseriata

Description: To 3′ (91 cm). Skate-like, *disk wider than long.* Brown above; white below. Front of head rounded; gill slits on underside of disk. 3 rows of spines on back of adults. Caudal fin squarish.

Habitat: Over sand or mud to depths of 150′ (46 m).

Range: San Francisco, CA, to Thurloe Head, Baja California.

Similar Species: Shovelnose Guitarfish *(Rhinobatos productus)* has disk longer than wide and median row of spines on back. Banded Guitarfish *(Zapteryx exasperata)* has disk about as wide as long and dark transverse bands on back. Round Stingray *(Urobatis halleri)* lacks dorsal fins and rows of spines on back.

Comments: Thornbacks and guitarfishes feed on sand-dwelling worms, snails, clams, crabs, and shrimps.

SKATES
Family Rajidae

18 genera and more than 200 species worldwide; 6 genera and 24 species in North America (14 Atlantic, 10 Pacific), plus 5 species confined to Mexican waters. Four of the North American species found in the Pacific are restricted to Alaskan waters. These fishes have flat, disk-like bodies formed by large "wings" that are shaped by the pectoral fins and attached to the head and body; these wings are used for propulsion. There are usually two small spineless dorsal fins. When present, the caudal fin is rudimentary. These fishes have large thorns on the midline of the back, and males have long prominent claspers used in mating. Skates spend their time on the bottom, partially buried in the mud or sand, usually in inshore waters.

316 Little Skate
Leucoraja erinacea

Description: To 21″ (53 cm). Disk broadly rounded laterally and posteriorly, depressed, about as wide as long. Gray to dark brown above, *usually with small irregular spots;* pale below, without spots. Angle of snout about 120 degrees; upper teeth in usually fewer than 54 series (never more than 66); at least 3 rows of thorns on midline of disk between spiracle and tail. 2 dorsal fins of equal size and shape, narrowly separated, without thorns in between. Tail slightly more than half of total length, with 2 or more rows of thorns.

Habitat: Shallow inshore waters over sand or gravel to depths of about 480′ (146 m).

Range: Gulf of St. Lawrence to NC.

Similar Species: Winter Skate *(L. ocellata)* has ocelli on upper surface and usually 90–100 series of teeth in upper jaw.

Comments: Little Skate feeds on a variety of crustaceans, as well as on clams, squids, and worms. It spawns in relatively shallow water, partially burying the leathery egg case in hard sand.

314 Big Skate
Raja binoculata

Description: To 8′ (2.4 m). Disk depressed, almost rhomboid, front concave. Olive brown or gray above; whitish below; *ocellus on each side of disk.* Moderately long thorns between eyes; 1 mid-dorsal thorn behind spiracle; 1 row of mid-dorsal thorns extends to front of first dorsal fin; thorns become more apparent with age.

Habitat: Over soft bottoms at depths of 10–360′ (3–110 m).

Range: Bering Sea to Bahía de San Quintín, Baja California.

Similar Species: California Skate *(R. inornata)* has disk with slightly convex anterior edge, pointed snout, and thorns between eyes.

Sandpaper Skate *(Bathyraja interrupta)* lacks thorns between eyes and has thorn on shoulder on each side of midline in center of disk. Longnose Skate *(R. rhina)* has disk with deeply concave anterior edge and deeply notched pelvic fin. Starry Skate *(R. stellulata)* has small ocelli, both surfaces covered with thorns, and disk with convex anterior edge.

Comments: Big Skate is occasionally captured by anglers but is rarely retained. It forms a minor portion of the commercial trawl catch; only the wings are used for food.

313 Clearnose Skate
Raja eglanteria

Description: To 3'1" (94 cm). Disk rhomboid, depressed, wider than long. Light to dark brown above, with darker brown or black roundish spots and irregular bars; white below; *no ocelli on disk; sides of snout translucent.* Angle of snout about 100 degrees, snout broadly rounded posteriorly. Thorns on shoulder near eye and spiracle; 1 row of thorns along midline of disk. 2 separate dorsal fins of equal size and shape. Tail half of total length, thorny.

Habitat: Shallow inshore waters.

Range: MA to FL and n Gulf of Mexico.

Similar Species: Rosette Skate *(Leucoraja garmani)* has scattered spots forming rosette pattern and disk with broadly rounded outer corners; occurs at depths of 120–1,950' (37–595 m). Barndoor Skate *(Dipturus laevis)* reaches length of 5' (1.5 m), and has much broader disk, more sharply pointed snout, and pigmented mucous pores on lower surface; occurs to depths of 1,410' (430 m).

Comments: More common inshore during warm months, this skate moves into deeper water in the winter.

315 Roundel Skate
Raja texana

Description: To 24″ (61 cm). Disk greatly depressed, wider than long, outer corners abruptly rounded, anterior edge concave on side of snout and opposite eye and spiracle. Brownish above; *conspicuous round dark ocellus on each side of dorsal midline;* white below; sides of snout translucent. 1 row of thorns on midline of disk. 2 separate dorsal fins, *with thorns in between.*

Habitat: Shallow inshore waters over sand or mud.

Range: Western coast of FL to TX.

Similar Species: Ocellate Skate (*R. ackleyi*) has broadly rounded disk and oval ocelli.

Comments: Roundel Skate is frequently found in shrimp trawls in the Gulf of Mexico.

Order Myliobatiformes

This order includes six families, all of which are found in North America. Members of the order inhabit shallow or mid-depth waters and are mainly tropical, with relatively few species found in temperate seas. Although most are bottom dwellers, a number are pelagic. Some species enter or are confined to fresh water. Almost all species have at least one long barb on the tail, which may be accompanied by poison sacs at the base. The tail is long and whip-like, usually without a caudal fin, except in the round stingrays (family Urolophidae), which have a short stout tail and a small caudal fin. A dorsal fin is sometimes present. The body is smooth or covered with denticles and large spines. These fishes do not have electric organs. They are ovoviviparous and give birth to living young.

WHIPTAIL STINGRAYS
Family Dasyatidae

9 genera and about 70 species worldwide; 2 genera and 6 species in North America (4 Atlantic, 1 Pacific, 1 shared), plus 1 genus and 4 species confined to Mexican waters. This family previously included the round stingrays and butterfly rays, which are now placed in their own families (Urolophidae and Gymnuridae, respectively). Whiptail stingrays have greatly

depressed disks. Tubercles or prickles are present in some species, especially on the dorsal midline of the disk. The pectoral fins extend forward beyond the mouth, and the dorsal fin is absent. The long, whip-like tail is distinct from the body; it lacks an obvious caudal fin and has a poisonous spine. These stingrays can inflict wounds characterized by intense pain and slow recovery, and are therefore potentially dangerous to swimmers and waders. (To prevent an encounter, shuffle your feet as you walk through the water so you nudge the ray on the side or from underneath; it is likely to swim away.) They stir the bottom with their pectoral fins in order to dislodge worms, mussels, small crustaceans, and other prey.

321, 322 Southern Stingray
Dasyatis americana

Description: To 5′ (1.5 m) wide. Disk roughly rhomboid, *outer corners sharply rounded, anterior edges nearly straight.* Light brown, gray, or olive above, depending on surroundings; whitish below, with gray or brownish edges; ridge and skin fold of tail dark brown. Tail long, whip-like, with spine near base, skin fold on underside about as deep as tail diameter. No conspicuous tubercles on disk or tail.

Habitat: Near shore and in bays.

Range: NJ to Brazil, including Bahamas, Gulf of Mexico, and Caribbean; rare north of Cape Hatteras, NC.

Similar Species: The larger Roughtail Stingray (*D. centroura*) has conspicuous tubercles on disk and tail. Diamond Stingray (*D. dipterura*) has diamond-shaped disk; occurs in Pacific.

Comments: Southern Stingray, like most stingrays, lies partly buried in the sand with only the eyes, spiracle, and tail exposed. The tail spine of all stingrays can inflict serious wounds.

312 Atlantic Stingray
Dasyatis sabina

Description: 8–24″ (20–61 cm) wide; body length from snout tip to tail tip about one-third longer than width of disk. Disk about as long as wide, outer corners broadly rounded. Brown or yellowish brown above, becoming paler toward edge of disk; white below in small to medium individuals, sometimes edged with grayish black in larger individuals. *Snout triangular at disk apex,* length anterior to eye considerably longer than distance between spiracles. Tail short, *with well-developed longitudinal skin fold running along both upper and lower surfaces.* Disk relatively smooth, with linear row of hard tubercles running down midline of back.

Habitat: Shallow, usually inshore estuarine or fresh waters over sand or sandy mud, often near sea-grass beds; usually to depths of 8′ (2.4 m), sometimes to 70′ (21 m).

Range: Chesapeake Bay to s FL and throughout Gulf of Mexico to Bay of Campeche. Recorded well upstream in St. Johns River, FL, and Mississippi River.

Similar Species: Bluntnose Stingray *(D. say),* the only other North American stingray with longitudinal skin fold along both upper and lower surfaces of tail, has short broadly rounded snout, not pointed at tip, and disk broadly rounded at corners.

Comments: This is probably the smallest of the North American stingrays, and the only one known to enter fresh water. It is common in Florida's St. Johns River. Atlantic Stingray, Bluntnose Stingray, and Yellow Stingray *(Urobatis jamaicensis)* occur in very shallow water, and are the stingrays most likely to be involved in spine-inflicted wounds to swimmers and waders.

ROUND STINGRAYS
Family Urolophidae

2 genera and about 35 species worldwide; 1 genus with 2 species in North America (1 Atlantic, 1 Pacific), plus 7 species confined to Mexican waters. These fishes are found in warm-temperate regions of the Atlantic, Pacific, and Indian Oceans. They

resemble whiptail stingrays (family Dasyatidae), the most evident differences being that round stingrays have a slightly shorter tail with an obvious caudal fin; in addition, unlike the whiptail stingrays, some species have a dorsal fin.

310 Round Stingray
Urobatis halleri

Description: To 22" (56 cm). *Disk almost circular.* Grayish brown above, sometimes with small light spots; yellow below. No dorsal fin. Tail shorter than disk, *with long venomous spine about halfway down length of tail.*

Habitat: Shallow bays and off coast over sand or mud to depths of 70′ (21 m).

Range: Humboldt Bay, CA, to Bay of Panama.

Similar Species: Yellow Stingray *(U. jamaicensis)* has variable coloration above, including greenish or brownish vermiculations, lines, bands, or spots; occurs in Atlantic. Thornback *(Platyrhinoidis triseriata)* has 2 dorsal fins; adults have 3 rows of tubercles on back. Pacific Electric Ray *(Torpedo californica)* has 2 dorsal fins and lacks venomous spine on tail.

Comments: The venomous spines of this stingray cause painful wounds. Concentrations of Round Stingrays occasionally make some beaches in California unsafe for swimmers and waders.

BUTTERFLY RAYS
Family Gymnuridae

2 genera and about 12 species world-wide; 1 genus with 3 species in North America (2 Atlantic, 1 Pacific), plus 1 species confined to Mexican waters. Butterfly rays have an extremely flat disk, shaped like a broad rounded diamond, twice as wide as it is long; the disk is about one and one-half times wider than the length of the body from the tip of the snout to the tip of the tail. The tail is slender, whip-like, and very short (much shorter than the disk), without a caudal fin; a small spine is usually present on the tail. All species lack a dorsal fin. The mouth is small, with numerous tiny pointed teeth.

The two largest species are known to have disks to 7′ (2.1 m) wide, and there have been unconfirmed reports of individuals with disks as wide as 13′ (4 m).

---

311 Smooth Butterfly Ray
Gymnura micrura

Description: To 3′ (91 cm) wide. *Disk very broad, more than one and one-half times wider than long.* Gray, brown, light green, or purplish above, with individual dots or wavy lines; white below, with grayish outer edges; shading changes with surroundings; several dark bars on tail. *Tail very short, no spine.*

Habitat: Shallow nearshore waters over sand.

Range: MA to Brazil, including Gulf of Mexico and Caribbean; rare occurrences north of Chesapeake Bay based on summer waifs.

Similar Species: Spiny Butterfly Ray (*G. altavela*) has disk reaching width of 7′ (2.1 m), tail spine, and tentacle-like structure on posterior edge of spiracle. California Butterfly Ray (*G. marmorata*) has disk reaching width of 7′ (2.1 m) and short tail with spine; occurs to depths of about 180′ (55 m) in Pacific.

Comments: Smooth Butterfly Ray lacks a tail spine and is harmless to people. Individuals reported to be 5–6′ (1.5–1.8 m) wide are probably misidentified specimens of Spiny Butterfly Ray.

EAGLE RAYS
Family Myliobatidae

4 genera and about 24 species worldwide; 2 genera and 4 species in North America (2 Atlantic, 1 Pacific, 1 shared), plus 2 species confined to Mexican Pacific waters. These rays, found in tropical and temperate seas, have robust bodies with roughly falcate pectoral fins; the entire disk is wider than it is long. The anterior parts of the pectoral fins form one or two subrostral lobes under the snout; the pectoral fins themselves are narrow and pointed near the tips. The eyes and spiracles are located on the sides of the head, which is separate from the rest of the disk. Eagle

rays have long tails, distinct from their bodies; there is a small fleshy dorsal fin on the tail base, behind which is a venomous spine. The pectoral fins function in a flapping motion, which serves to propel the fish through the water; this motion is different from the undulating movement of skates (family Rajidae), whiptail and round stingrays (Dasyatidae and Urolophidae), and butterfly rays (Gymnuridae).

319 Spotted Eagle Ray
Aetobatus narinari

Description: To 9′ (2.7 m) wide. Disk wider than long. *Gray, olive gray, or chestnut brown above; with whitish, yellowish, or bluish spots, variable in size and shape;* white below. Head distinct from body; eye and spiracle both on side of upper body; 1 row of large flat tooth plates in each jaw. Pectoral fin more or less falcate, tapering to acute point. Tail very long, whip-like, with dorsal fin and usually 2 spines at base. Skin smooth.

Habitat: Surface of coastal waters.

Range: In w Atlantic from Chesapeake Bay to Brazil, including Bermuda, Bahamas, Gulf of Mexico, and Caribbean; abundant in e FL and Antilles. In e Pacific from s Gulf of California to Panama.

Comments: The usually solitary Spotted Eagle Ray sometimes travels in small groups of two or more; it is found in large schools only when spawning and migrating. It is capable of sustaining long-distance travel, and occurs worldwide in tropical seas. This ray is a graceful swimmer and looks as if it were flying through the water. When pursued, it makes spectacular leaps into the air. Spotted Eagle Ray feeds chiefly on bivalve mollusks, such as clams and oysters, which it cracks with its tooth plates, but its diet may sometimes also include fishes and other types of invertebrates. When large numbers of this species are present, clam and oyster beds can become decimated in a very short time.

320 Bat Ray
Myliobatis californica

Description: To 6' (1.8 m) wide. Disk diamond-shaped, wider than long, with long blunt-pointed wings. Brown, olive, or black above; white below. *Head and eyes extend beyond front of disk.* Tail whip-like, with dorsal fin and at least 1 spine at base. Skin smooth.

Habitat: Shallow sandy areas in bays, on coast to depths of 150' (46 m), and in kelp beds.

Range: OR to Gulf of California.

Comments: Bat Ray is an excellent fighter and is popular with anglers, but few fish are kept for eating. The young develop within the female and are released in late summer and fall. The venomous tail spines can cause a painful injury.

COWNOSE RAYS
Family Rhinopteridae

1 genus with about 5 species worldwide; 1 species in North America, plus 1 species confined to Mexican Pacific waters. Members of this family, found in tropical to warm-temperate seas, resemble the closely related eagle rays (family Myliobatidae) and mantas (Mobulidae); similar to the mantas, the pectoral fins of these rays are deeply divided into subrostral lobes. All species have a small dorsal fin. Cownose rays are unique among myliobatiform fishes in having heads with a concave anterior depression.

---

318 Cownose Ray
Rhinoptera bonasus

Description: To 3' (91 cm) wide. Disk slightly more than one and one-half times wider than long, anterior edges nearly straight, posterior edges concave, outer corners falcate. Brownish above; whitish or yellowish white below. Front of head moderately concave; usually 7 rows of tooth plates in each jaw. *Pectoral fin deeply notched in middle, forming 2 subrostral lobes joined at base;* head and subrostral lobes form shape resembling cow's nose. Tail with spine immediately behind dorsal fin. Skin smooth.

Habitat: Primarily bottoms of shallow bays and over continental shelf.

Range: New England to Brazil, including n Cuba, Gulf of Mexico, and s Caribbean.

Comments: Cownose Ray occasionally jumps out of the water, landing on the surface with a loud smack, probably as a territorial display. Its stinging spines make it potentially dangerous. This ray feeds primarily on hard-shelled mollusks, which it crushes with its powerful tooth plates. During the summer, Cownose Ray sometimes occurs in bays in schools that disappear in the winter. The species migrates south in large schools; fish tagged in northern Florida have been recovered off northern South America. The population in the Gulf of Mexico migrates clockwise; in the fall, schools of up to 10,000 fish leave the western coast of Florida for the Yucatán Peninsula.

MANTAS
Family Mobulidae

2 genera and 13 species worldwide; 2 genera and 3 species in North America (1 Atlantic, 1 Pacific, 1 shared), plus 3 species confined to Mexican Pacific waters. In contrast to cownose rays (family Rhinopteridae) and eagle rays (Myliobatidae), mantas lack large tooth plates. The pectoral fins are subdivided anteriorly and modified into two separate cephalic fins (on the head). The posterior edges of the pectoral fins are falcate. The small dorsal fin is located on the tail; all North American mantas have spineless tails. These fishes occur worldwide in tropical and warm to temperate seas, and feed on large planktonic crustaceans or schools of small fishes that they strain with the branchial sieve.

317 Atlantic Manta
Manta birostris

Description: To 22' (6.5 m) wide. Disk about twice as wide as long. Coloration varies:

reddish to olive brown to black above, paler on edges; shoulders uniformly colored, or with white patches or series of dark spots; blotched slate gray or black below. *Mouth terminal; teeth only in lower jaw. Cephalic fins large, widely set, forward-directed, horn-like;* posterior edge of pectoral fin falcate. Tail relatively short; no spine at base.

Habitat: Shallow nearshore to deep offshore waters.

Range: NC to Brazil, including Bermuda, Bahamas, and Gulf of Mexico; occasionally north to New England; common in Bermuda and Gulf of Mexico.

Comments: This pelagic species is often seen leaping out of the water or basking on the surface. The cephalic fins are used for steering and to direct food into the mouth. Regardless of size, Atlantic Manta is harmless to people.

RAY-FINNED FISHES
Class Actinopterygii

Living bony fishes are separated into two classes, Sarcopterygii and Actinopterygii, but only the latter, the ray-finned fishes, occurs in North America. Actinopterygii contains most of the known marine and freshwater fishes. This class is the most valuable to people because of the large number of species that support commercial and sport fisheries. Worldwide, there are 45 orders with nearly 24,000 species in the class (about 40 percent in fresh water); 38 orders with roughly 2,500 species occur in North America (about 800 species native to fresh water) north of Mexico.

Ray-finned fishes are characterized by the presence, in most species, of fins with soft rays or spines, one of several types of scales, a single pair of gill openings, branchiostegal rays, a swim bladder or functional lung, and a skeleton that is at least partially composed of bone.

The eggs and embryos are never enclosed in cases, and fertilization is usually external. Some members of this class live for less than a year, whereas others live for more than 100 years.

Usually considered to be the most recent in evolutionary terms, this class first appeared in the Silurian period, about 440 million years ago. Many species have become so specialized that they face extinction when some aspect of their habitat is threatened.

Order Acipenseriformes

This order, confined to the Northern Hemisphere, contains two families, the sturgeons (Acipenseridae) and the paddlefishes (Polyodontidae), both of which occur in North America. These fishes are found in fresh water; however, some are anadromous. They are among the largest freshwater fishes, and are the remnants of an ancient and primitive group. Members of this order have largely cartilaginous skeletons, upper jaws that are not united with the skull, and heterocercal caudal fins.

STURGEONS
Family Acipenseridae

4 genera and 24 species worldwide; 2 genera and 8 species in North America. This family includes anadromous and freshwater fishes. Sturgeons are large fishes with comparatively elongate snouts. They have a total of five rows of bony plates on the body (one dorsal row, two mid-lateral rows, and two ventrolateral rows), scale-like plates on the skin between the bony plates, and bony plates covering the head. There are four barbels anterior to the ventral mouth, which lacks teeth. Species in the genus *Acipenser* have two smooth lobes on the lower lip, whereas species in *Scaphirhynchus* have four papillose lobes. The dorsal and anal fins are located on the rear one-third of the body. Females are usually larger and mature later than males.

VENTRAL VIEW OF HEADS

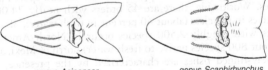

genus *Acipenser*   genus *Scaphirhynchus*

31 Lake Sturgeon
Acipenser fulvescens

Description: To 8′ (2.4 m); 309 lb (141 kg). Elongate. Dark olive to gray above; sides lighter, often reddish; off-white to yellowish below. Body with 5 rows of bony plates: 8–17 in dorsal row, 29–43 in each mid-lateral row, 6–12 in each ventrolateral row; young have sharp spine on each bony plate, with adjacent plates usually touching; adults have small, more rounded, separated plates. Snout rounded above, flat below; *4 smooth barbels anterior to mouth; lower lip with 2 smooth lobes; spiracles above and behind eyes.* Caudal fin heterocercal. Caudal peduncle short, roundish, incompletely armored.

Habitat: Rivers and lakes over clean sand, gravel, or rocks.

Range: Lower Hudson Bay west to s AB and south through s Canada; St. Lawrence River, Great Lakes, and Mississippi River system to AR, ne LA, and nw MS; Coosa River, AL and GA.

Comments: Lake Sturgeon is probably the largest freshwater fish in North America; the record catch, taken in Lake Superior in 1922, measured 7′11″ (2.4 m). It can live to be very old; one fish, 154 years old and weighing 208 lb (95 kg), was caught in Lake of the Woods, on the Minnesota–Canada border, in 1953. The Lake Sturgeon population has been greatly reduced by exploitation, dams, and pollution.

32, 635 White Sturgeon
Acipenser transmontanus

Description: To 12′6″ (3.8 m); 1,386 lb (630 kg). Elongate, rounded in cross section. Gray above, lighter below. Body with 5 rows of bony plates: 11–14 in dorsal row, *38–48 in each mid-lateral row,* 9–12 in each ventrolateral row. Head slightly flat; snout short, broad, pointed; *4 smooth barbels anterior to mouth, nearer tip of snout than mouth;* mouth ventral, below eye; *lower lip with 2 smooth lobes.* Caudal fin heterocercal.

Habitat: Oceans over soft bottoms; deep pools of large rivers.

Range: In Pacific from Gulf of Alaska to n Baja California; in fresh water south only to Sacramento River, n CA.

Similar Species: Green Sturgeon *(A. medirostris)* has long snout, concave in profile, 4 smooth barbels closer to mouth than to snout tip, and 23–30 bony plates in mid-lateral row.

Comments: White Sturgeon spawns in rivers in the spring. Males do not mature until they are 11 to 22 years old; females mature when they are 11 to 34 years old. This large sport fish feeds on small fishes, crustaceans, and mollusks. Sturgeons are highly regarded commercially for their caviar and meat and for sport.

33, 636   Atlantic Sturgeon
Acipenser oxyrinchus

Description: To 14′ (4.3 m). Elongate, heavy-bodied, pentagonal in cross section. Bluish black to brownish olive above; lighter below. Body with 5 rows of bony plates: 7–13 in dorsal row, 24–35 in each mid-lateral row, 8–11 in each ventrolateral row. Snout elongate; *4 smooth barbels anterior to mouth; mouth width one-third to one-half distance from mouth to snout tip, flat below; lower lip with 2 smooth lobes; spiracles above and behind eyes.* Caudal fin heterocercal.

Habitat: Large rivers, tidal fresh waters near shore, and coastal marine waters.

Range: Atlantic coast from George River and Ungava Bay, n QC, to central FL; Gulf coast from FL to LA, possibly TX.

Similar Species: Shortnose Sturgeon *(A. brevirostrum)* has short snout not upturned at tip and mouth width about equal to distance from mouth to snout tip.

Comments: Atlantic Sturgeon has been the subject of a commercial fishery since the early 1600s, when it was pickled and shipped to England. The fishery in the 1800s and 1900s was for both meat and roe for caviar. For many years in New York, sturgeon meat was referred to as "Albany beef." Currently, the Atlantic Sturgeon fishery is limited, and in some states take is prohibited.

34 Shovelnose Sturgeon
Scaphirhynchus platorynchus

Description: To 3′ (91 cm); 7 lb (3.2 kg). Elongate. Olive to yellowish brown above; sides lighter; white below. Body with 5 rows of *sharply keeled bony plates:* 14–19 in dorsal row, 38–47 in each mid-lateral row, 10–14 in each ventrolateral row. *Bony plates on head, without short spines* at snout tip or anterior to eye; snout shovel-shaped; *4 barbels with lateral projections anterior to mouth, bases in straight line; lower lip with 4 papillose lobes; no spiracles.* Caudal fin heterocercal; upper lobe with long, thread-like filament. Caudal peduncle long, depressed, fully armored.

Habitat: Channels of large turbid rivers with moderate current over firm sand or gravel.

Range: Ohio, Mississippi, and Missouri Rivers; Rio Grande, TX and NM.

Similar Species: Pallid Sturgeon (*S. albus*) has shorter inner barbels with bases anterior to outer barbels, and belly lacks small, scale-like plates. Alabama Sturgeon (*S. suttkusi*) has patch of sharp spines on snout tip and large eye.

Comments: Shovelnose Sturgeon is the most common sturgeon in North America. It is becoming less common in some areas, but remains a part of the commercial fishery industry along some reaches of the Mississippi and Missouri Rivers.

PADDLEFISHES
Family Polyodontidae

2 genera and 2 species worldwide; 1 species in North America. This freshwater family is represented by one species in the Mississippi River system and one species in the Yangtze River of China. Paddlefish (*Polyodon spathula*) is probably the most distinctive of all North American fishes, due to its elongate snout that expands into a thin flat paddle; its body is covered with smooth skin similar in appearance to that of the freshwater catfishes (family Ictaluridae).

30 Paddlefish
Polyodon spathula

Description: To 7'1" (2.2 m); 200 lb (91 kg).
Slightly compressed. Back dark bluish
gray, often mottled; sides lighter; belly
white. *Snout paddle-shaped;* eye small,
above front edge of mouth; *mouth very
large;* gill rakers slender, numerous;
*opercular flap large, tapering, extending to
pelvic fins. Caudal fin deeply forked,* lobes
about equal. Unscaled except caudal
peduncle.

Habitat: Backwaters, bayous, impoundments,
lakes, and pools of large rivers.

Range: Mississippi River system; Mobile Bay
drainage, AL west to e TX; 19th- and
early-20th-century records from a few
localities in Lakes Superior, Michigan,
and Huron and w Lake Erie.

Comments: This large fish lives up to 30 years.
Considered good eating, it is caught by
snag-fishing during spawning in April
and June, when the species congregates
below obstructions, such as dams, and
on gravel shoals. Paddlefish populations
have declined recently due to pollution,
channelization, dams, and overfishing.

GARS
Order Lepisosteiformes
Family Lepisosteidae

This order consists of a single family: 2
genera and 7 species worldwide; 2 genera and 5 species in
North America, plus 1 species confined to Mexico. These
fishes are found in eastern North America and Central
America south to Costa Rica and Cuba. Gars are predominantly freshwater (some species enter brackish and marine
waters). They are long, slender, predatory fishes covered
with interlocking ganoid scales that protect them from
most predators. Extremely hardy, gars typically inhabit
quiet, weedy, often stagnant backwater areas. They have
elongate jaws with needle-like teeth, and are equipped with
a vascularized swim bladder to permit aerial respiration.
The single dorsal fin is located posteriorly on the body
above the anal fin; the abbreviated heterocercal caudal fin is
rounded.

29, 639 Alligator Gar
Atractosteus spatula

Description: To 10′ (3 m); 301 lb (137 kg).
Cylindrical. Dark brown above,
occasionally spotted; yellowish below;
median fins with few dark spots. Young
have light mid-dorsal stripe from snout
tip to upper base of caudal fin, bordered
by dark lateral stripes. *Snout short, broad;
length of jaw shorter than rest of head; teeth
large, in 2 rows on each side of upper jaw.*
Caudal fin short, rounded. Scales thick,
diamond-shaped. *Lateral line with 58–62
scales.*

dorsal view
of head

Habitat: Large rivers, sluggish lakes, bayous, and
reservoirs; frequently enters brackish
and marine waters in coastal areas.
Young in or near aquatic vegetation.

Range: Ohio River from sw OH westward;
Mississippi River from IL southward;
Gulf coastal plain from w FL to
Veracruz, Mexico.

Comments: Alligator Gar is one of the largest
freshwater fishes. In some areas it is
fished commercially and by anglers, and
it has become very rare in certain parts
of its range. There have been unconfirmed
reports of attacks on people.

28 Spotted Gar
Lepisosteus oculatus

Description: To 3′ (91 cm); 8 lb (3.6 kg). Cylindrical.
Brown to olive above; sides lighter;
whitish below; *body, head, and all fins
with olive brown to black spots.* Young have
dark mid-dorsal and mid-lateral stripe.
*Snout short, less than twice as long as rest of
head;* teeth in 1 row on upper jaw; bony
plates on isthmus. Caudal fin short,
rounded. Scales thick, diamond-shaped.
Lateral line with 53–59 scales.

dorsal view
of head

Habitat: Clear pools with aquatic vegetation in
streams, swamps, and lakes; sometimes
enters brackish water along Gulf coast.
Young in or near aquatic vegetation.

Range: Lake Erie and s Lake Michigan

drainages; Mississippi River drainage
from IL to e OK and e TN; Gulf coast
streams from FL to central TX.

Similar Species: Shortnose Gar *(L. platostomus)* has jaw
longer than rest of head and dark spots
on head and pectoral and pelvic fins;
occurs in backwaters and pools of
streams. Florida Gar *(L. platyrhincus)*
lacks bony plates on isthmus; occurs in
sluggish streams, canals, and lakes with
vegetation.

Comments: Spotted Gar spawns in shallow waters
over vegetation during the spring. The
hatched larvae of gars have an adhesive
pad on the upper jaw, by which they
attach themselves to aquatic plants.

27 Longnose Gar
Lepisosteus osseus

Description: To 6′ (1.8 m); 50 lb (23 kg). Cylindrical.
Dark olive to brownish above; sides
lighter, with dark spots usually
posteriorly; whitish below; median fins
yellowish brown, with many dark spots.

dorsal view
of head

Young have dark mid-dorsal and mid-
lateral stripes. *Snout very long, more than
twice as long as rest of head;* teeth large, in
1 row on upper jaw. Caudal fin short,
rounded. Scales thick, diamond-shaped.
Lateral line with 60–64 scales.

Habitat: Backwaters, large creeks, lakes, and
reservoirs; sometimes enters brackish
water. Young in or near aquatic
vegetation.

Range: St. Lawrence River drainage; along
Atlantic coast from NJ to s FL; s Great
Lakes and Mississippi River system to
Rio Grande drainage in TX.

Comments: Longnose Gar is occasionally sought for
sport, but it is rarely eaten, and the roe
is poisonous. It is considered a nuisance
by anglers because it feeds on sport
fishes. It can also damage commercial
gill nets. In summer, this fish can often
be observed floating motionless near the
surface of quiet waters.

BOWFINS
Order Amiiformes
Family Amiidae

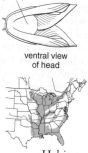

This order of ancient and highly predatory fishes consists of a single family: 1 species native to fresh waters of eastern North America. Fossil records are known from freshwater and marine deposits dating from the Jurassic period, 213 million years ago. Bowfins are a transitional group, related to the gars (family Lepisosteidae), but possessing some characteristics of bony fishes. For example, the primitive skeleton consists of bone and cartilage, but its vertebrae are concave at each end, a characteristic of bony fishes. These fishes have bony plates covering the head and a bony gular plate. There is a single dorsal fin, and the abbreviated heterocercal caudal fin is rounded.

46 Bowfin
Amia calva

gular plate

ventral view
of head

Description: To 34″ (86 cm); 22 lb (9.8 kg). Elongate, moderately robust. Dark olive green above; sides lighter, often with net-like pattern; cream to greenish yellow below; fins dark olive to greenish. Males have dark spot and yellow to orange halo on upper base of caudal fin. Head massive; *nostrils tubular;* jaws with numerous teeth; maxilla extends beyond eye. Pelvic and pectoral fins small, rounded; *dorsal fin long, with 42–53 rays; 9–12 anal fin rays; caudal fin rounded.* Lateral line complete.

Habitat: Low-gradient, sluggish streams, swamps, and oxbow lakes in quiet, usually clear waters with vegetation.

Range: Lake Champlain and St. Lawrence River west through Great Lakes; Mississippi River system from MN to TX; Long Island, NY; along coastal plain from s PA south to FL and west to TX.

Similar Species: The introduced Bullseye Snakehead (*Channa marlius*) is native to India, lacks gular plate, and has scaled head and long anal fin with 28–36 rays.

Comments: Bowfin, also known as Mudfish, Dogfish, and Grinnel, is often thought of as a pest, since it consumes the same food items as sport fishes. It spawns in early spring in shallow waters, where the male clears vegetation and excavates a shallow nest. After spawning, the male protects the eggs until they hatch and guards the young for several weeks. This species is one of the hardiest of North American freshwater fishes. It has a swim bladder that can function as a lung, allowing the fish to gulp air in waters with little or no dissolved oxygen.

MOONEYES
Order Hiodontiformes
Family Hiodontidae

This order consists of a single family: 1 genus with 2 species confined to fresh waters of North America. Mooneye fossils are known from the Cretaceous period, approximately 145 million years ago, in China. Representatives of this group probably entered North America from China via rivers and streams that traversed the Bering land bridge. Mooneyes may be confused with the herrings (family Clupeidae), but can be distinguished by the presence of teeth on the tongue and jaws, the absence of scutes on the belly, and the position of the dorsal fin, which is over the anal fin. All family members have a lateral line. This group was formerly included in the order Osteoglossiformes.

171 Goldeye
Hiodon alosoides

Description: To 20″ (51 cm); 3 lb (1.4 kg). Moderately deep, compressed; *keel on midline of belly extends from pectoral fins to anus.* Bluish above; silvery below; eye bright golden yellow. Eye very large; *mouth large, with small sharp teeth. Dorsal fin with 9–10 rays, origin just behind anal fin origin;* 29–35 anal fin rays; caudal fin deeply forked. Lateral line complete, with 55–62 scales.

Habitat: Clear to turbid rivers, lakes, reservoirs, and quiet backwaters.

Range: James Bay drainage, ON and QC, west to Mackenzie River, Northwest Territories, and south to AB; Mississippi

River system from se OH and w MT south to n AL and LA.

Similar Species: Mooneye *(H. tergisus)* has keel on belly from pelvic fins to anus and dorsal fin with 11–12 rays, its origin anterior to anal fin origin.

Comments: Caught with live bait and artificial lures, Goldeye is commercially important in Canada as a smoked fish. It appears to be more tolerant of turbid waters than Mooneye.

Order Elopiformes

This order consists of two families, both of which occur in North America. Members of this order are silvery elongate fishes with spineless fins. The pelvic fins are abdominal, and the pectoral fins are inserted below the mid-side of the body. The single dorsal fin is located at mid-body, and the caudal fin is forked. These fishes lack adipose fins. Scales are cycloid; each pectoral and pelvic fin has a large axillary scale. An adipose eyelid is present. The gular plate is well developed on the underside of the head. Members of this order share a ribbon-like leptocephalus larval stage with the closely related orders Albuliformes and Anguilliformes, a characteristic that is presumed to be indicative of a natural phylogenetic relationship among these groups.

leptocephalus

TENPOUNDERS
Family Elopidae

1 genus with at least 6 species worldwide; 3 species in North America (2 Atlantic, 1 Pacific), including a presumably unnamed Caribbean species that ranges north into the Gulf of Mexico and along the southern U.S. Atlantic coast. Found throughout the world in tropical to warm-temperate seas, tenpounders (also known as lady-fishes) are silvery, herring-like fishes with elongate stream-lined bodies. The Elopidae at one time also included the tarpons (now in the family Megalopidae); tenpounders differ from tarpons in having a more slender body, much finer (thus more numerous) scales, more branchiostegal rays, more pelvic and dorsal fin rays, no posterior extension to the

dorsal fin, fewer anal fin rays, unbranched tubes in the lateral line, and the swim bladder not lying against the skull. The taxonomy of the genus *Elops* is poorly understood; the different species closely resemble one another and differ primarily in the number of myomere segments in the larvae, and in the numbers of vertebrae, gill rakers, and lateral line scales in adults.

641 Machete
Elops affinis

Description: To 3' (91 cm); 10 lb (4.5 kg). Very elongate, slender, compressed. Silvery above and below. Snout pointed; 22–32 gill rakers. Pelvic and pectoral fins each with large axillary scale; *dorsal fin soft-rayed;* caudal fin deeply forked.

Habitat: Shallow waters over sand.

Range: Mandalay Beach, s CA, to Peru.

Similar Species: Ladyfish *(E. saurus)* has 16–23 gill rakers.

Comments: This smaller relative of Tarpon *(Megalops atlanticus)* is an excellent fighter, and thus a desirable sport fish. It has no value as a food fish, however, because of its oily flesh.

640 Ladyfish
Elops saurus

Description: To 3'3" (99 cm). Fusiform, elongate. Bluish gray above; sides silvery; yellowish below; fins dusky, yellow-tinged. Adipose eyelid present; mouth terminal, oblique; upper jaw reaches well beyond eye; gular plate in lower jaw; 23–25 branchiostegal rays. Pelvic fin slightly in front of dorsal fin origin; pelvic and pectoral fins each with large axillary scale; dorsal fin short, *last ray not thread-like;* anal fin short, origin well behind dorsal fin; caudal fin deeply forked. *Scales very small.* Lateral line with 100–120 scales.

branchiostegal rays

gular plate

ventral view of head

Habitat: Primarily shallow marine and brackish waters; occasionally enters fresh waters.

Range: Cape Cod, MA, to Brazil, including
Bermuda, Bahamas, Gulf of Mexico, and
Caribbean; sporadically north of
Chesapeake Bay.

Comments: Ladyfish spawns offshore, and the larvae
transform into adults in coastal waters.

This species is also known as
Tenpounder, a common name also
collectively given to the family Elopidae;
although small, when hooked this
species fights like a "tenpounder," hence
this common name. It is a good light-
tackle fish and jumps frequently, but has
no value as a food fish. Most or all South
American and Caribbean Ladyfish
populations apparently represent an
unnamed species, which is distinguished
by lower total myomere counts in the
leptocephali and, presumably, by lower
vertebral counts in the adults; small
numbers of leptocephali identifiable as
the southern form have been recorded
from the northern Gulf of Mexico and
Atlantic coastal waters as far north as
North Carolina.

TARPONS
Family Megalopidae

1 genus with 2 species worldwide; 1
species in North America. Tarpons, found in tropical seas
worldwide, differ from the closely related tenpounders, also
known as ladyfishes (family Elopidae, in which they were
formerly included), in having a deeper and more robust
body, much coarser (thus fewer) scales, fewer branchiostegal
rays, fewer pelvic and dorsal fin rays, a posterior extension
to the dorsal fin, more anal fin rays, branched tubes in the
lateral line, and the swim bladder lying against the skull.

643 Tarpon
Megalops atlanticus

Description: To 8′ (2.4 m); 282 lb (128 kg). Large,
elongate, moderately deep and
compressed. Back bluish gray; sides and
belly silvery; fins dusky or pale. Mouth

huge, oblique, superior; upper jaw reaches well beyond eye; lower jaw projects well beyond upper; gular plate in lower jaw. Pelvic fins abdominal, in front of dorsal fin origin; pelvic and pectoral fins each with large axillary scale; dorsal fin short, *last ray elongate and thread-like;* anal fin origin behind dorsal fin base; caudal fin deeply forked. *Scales extremely large, cycloid.* Lateral line with 40–48 scales.

Habitat: Primarily shallow coastal waters and estuaries. Young, and sometimes adults, enter fresh waters.

Range: NS to Brazil, including Bermuda, Bahamas, Gulf of Mexico, and Caribbean; infrequent north of NC. Also in e Atlantic.

Comments: Tarpon is also given the name Silverking, and it is indeed the king of sport fishes. It takes an experienced angler to land a large Tarpon, for this extremely strong fish is a fast swimmer and makes spectacular leaps out of the water in an effort to throw the hook. It is not regarded as a good food fish. This species spawns offshore, and the larvae develop inshore.

Order Albuliformes

This order contains three families, all of which are found in North America; the family Albulidae (bonefishes) occurs in shallow inshore waters, and the Halosauridae (halosaurs) and Notacanthidae (spiny eels) in deep offshore waters. Members of this order share a leptocephalus larval stage, absence of an adipose fin, and other basic characteristics with the closely related orders Elopiformes (in which they were once placed) and Anguilliformes. They differ from elopiform fishes in having a weakly developed gular plate, the insertion of the pectoral fins sometimes high on the body (family Halosauridae), fin spines sometimes present (family Notacanthidae), and the caudal fin not always forked (the caudal skeleton is greatly reduced in both Halosauridae and Notacanthidae). Adults of the family Albulidae are conventionally shaped fishes, whereas adult halosaurs and notacanthids are elongate fishes whose body shapes partially reflect their close relationship to anguilliform fishes.

BONEFISHES
Family Albulidae

1 genus with probably 7–8 species worldwide; 2 species (1 unnamed) in North America. One-third of all North American bonefishes are found in tropical waters of the western Atlantic and eastern Pacific. These fishes have an elongate fusiform body with an undivided dorsal fin and a large caudal fin. Their eggs hatch into leptocephalus larvae, which move offshore to the open ocean where they spend their early lives before returning inshore as juveniles.

642 Bonefish
Albula vulpes

Description: To 3′ (91 cm); 19 lb (8.6 kg). Fusiform, elongate. Silvery bluish or greenish; sides occasionally with dusky stripes and bars (fading upon death); fin bases often yellow. *Upper jaw projects beyond lower;* maxilla lacks teeth. Pelvic fins abdominal; 16–21 dorsal fin rays; *caudal fin large, deeply forked.* Scales cycloid.

Habitat: Shallow waters over soft bottoms.

Range: In Atlantic from Bay of Fundy to Rio de Janeiro, Brazil; most common in s FL, Bermuda, and Bahamas. In Pacific from San Francisco, CA, to Peru.

Comments: Bonefish feeds on clams, snails, shrimps, and small fishes. Although it has been virtually ignored on the U.S. Pacific coast, it is a prized sport fish on the U.S. Atlantic coast because it is easy to catch on shallow sand flats. Although Bonefish has been considered to comprise a single worldwide species, recent research has demonstrated that there are actually at least seven species, of which two (one unnamed) occur in North American Atlantic waters; these species are virtually indistinguishable morphologically, but are genetically quite distinct. In areas of Florida where both *A. vulpes* and the unnamed species

are found, the populations apparently
are ecologically separated, the unnamed
form consistently occurring in slightly
deeper waters.

Order Anguilliformes

This order includes three suborders and 15 families worldwide. Within the three suborders and nine families found in
North America, virtually all species occur in inshore marine
waters; one species occurs in fresh water. Many species are
found in deeper waters offshore and are rarely seen. These
long, snake-like fishes lack pelvic fins or girdles, premaxillary bones, and spines in the fins. Most eels are unscaled;
freshwater eels (family Anguillidae) have very small, deeply
embedded cycloid scales. The pectoral fins are often rudimentary or absent. The caudal fin is sometimes absent;
when present, it is continuous with the dorsal and anal fins.
Gill rakers are absent, and the gill openings are usually
very small. Many of the bones usually found in the heads
of fishes are absent or fused. Members of this order share a
ribbon-like leptocephalus larval stage with the closely related orders Elopiformes and Albuliformes, although in
some families the leptocephalus stage is of relatively short
duration. The leptocephalus stage is highly pelagic; this
mobility is probably a major factor in the unusually wide
distributions of certain eel species.

PARTS OF AN EEL

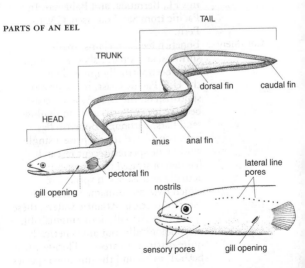

FRESHWATER EELS
Family Anguillidae

1 genus with 15 species worldwide; 1 species in North America. Unlike other eels, members of this family have small scales embedded in the skin. In addition, they have pectoral fins, and the dorsal and anal fins are continuous with the caudal fin. After reaching sexual maturity, the two Atlantic freshwater eel species migrate to the Sargasso Sea to spawn. The eggs hatch into leptocephalus larvae that pass through several stages as they transform into adults. Apparently only the females ascend rivers, where they remain for a number of years.

44, 500 **American Eel**
Anguilla rostrata

Description:	To 4′11″ (1.5 m). Elongate, snake-like, circular in cross section anteriorly, compressed posteriorly. Coloration variable, depending on habitat and age: usually dark brown or greenish above, fading to yellowish white on belly. Head large, about one-eighth of length; mouth terminal, nearly horizontal; lower jaw projects slightly. Pectoral fin well developed; dorsal fin origin far behind pectoral fin; anal fin origin behind dorsal fin origin; dorsal and anal fins continuous with caudal fin. *Scales small, elliptical, deeply embedded in skin.*
Habitat:	Brackish or fresh waters; migrates to sea to spawn.
Range:	Along Atlantic coast and to headwaters of associated rivers from Labrador to Guyana, including Gulf of Mexico and Antilles.
Similar Species:	The introduced Asian Swamp Eel *(Monopterus albus)*, in family Synbranchidae, lacks pectoral fins; occurs in streams, canals, lakes, wetlands, and swamps. Lampreys (class Cephalaspidomorphi) have eel-like bodies, but lack jaws and paired fins.
Comments:	Freshwater eels are eaten fresh and smoked. The exportation of young eels (called elvers) to Europe and Japan for

use in aquaculture is now prohibited in
most areas due to overfishing.

MORAYS
Family Muraenidae

15 genera and roughly 200 species world-
wide; 6 genera and 19 species in North America (5 Atlantic,
1 Pacific), plus 4 genera and 21 species confined to Mexican
Atlantic and Pacific waters. These fishes are found throughout the world, mostly in reefs and rocky areas of inshore tropical oceans. The body is heavy and compressed in some
species, more so than in most other eels; in such heavy-
bodied species, the forehead is elevated in adults. Most have
long, fang-like teeth in the jaws and on the roof of the
mouth; adults of some species have low, molar-like teeth.
Morays are also distinguished by having an unscaled body; a
small round gill opening on each side of the head; lateral line
pores on the head but not the body; a posterior nostril high
on the head, usually above the front portion of the eye; and
reduced gill arches. They lack pectoral fins, and the reduced
tail is continuous around the tip of the body. The leptocephalus larval stage is relatively short-lived, and very small
transformed morays are encountered more frequently than
in other eels. Morays are most readily confused with those
species of the family Chlopsidae, appropriately called false
morays, which lack pectoral fins. Many chlopsids have pectoral fins, but for those that do not, the only obvious external difference between the two families is the position of the
posterior nostril, which is ventrally placed in the chlopsids
(dorsally situated in the morays).

495, 496   Chain Moray
Echidna catenata

Description: To 28" (71 cm). Relatively small, laterally
compressed. *Chocolate brown to blackish,
with yellow or cream chain-like pattern*
(yellow more extensive in young). Head
short, blunt; posterior nostril above front
of eye, with low, scalloped, fleshy rim;
jaw teeth of adults thick, relatively blunt;
vomer teeth molar-like. Dorsal fin origin
above a point in front of gill opening.

Habitat: Common in shallow reefs and rocky
inshore areas in clear waters to depths of
65' (20 m).

Range: Southern FL, Bermuda, and Bahamas south throughout Caribbean to Brazil. Also around several offshore islands in South Atlantic east to Ascension Island.

Comments: Chain Moray feeds primarily on small crustaceans, especially crabs, and is often seen by snorkelers and divers. Due to the distinct combination of a strongly reticulated pigmentation pattern, blunt head, and blunt teeth, this moray should not be confused with any other species of eel. Time and place of spawning is a mystery. Although common, very few individuals in sexual condition have been examined, and no identifiable larvae have been seen.

493 Green Moray
Gymnothorax funebris

Description: To 6' (1.8 m). *Very large, relatively compressed. Uniformly dark green to brown.* Young blackish, with white chin. Snout long, pointed; eye well forward, with center slightly before mid-jaw; 4 sensory pores below eye; posterior nostril not tubular; *inner edge of jaw not curved; not exposed when mouth closed,* teeth not serrate, *not exposed when mouth closed,* most developed near front of upper jaw and on roof of mouth.

Habitat: Common in shallow reefs and tide pools; usually to depths of 102' (31 m).

Range: Southern FL, Bermuda, and Bahamas south throughout Caribbean to n Brazil. Also disjunctly in s Brazil and nearby offshore islands.

Similar Species: Chestnut Moray (*Enchelycore carychroa*) and Viper Moray (*E. nigricans*) adults also have uniform coloration, but have curved inner edge of jaw and teeth exposed when mouth closed. Chestnut Moray reaches length of 18" (46 cm); Viper Moray reaches length of 3' (91 cm).

Comments: Green Moray is diurnal and feeds mostly on small fishes and crustaceans. Most moray eels in the tropical western Atlantic have some degree of mottling or spotting on the body. Because it is large, common, and occurs in shallow reefs, this species is one of the western Atlantic morays most likely to be encountered by snorklers and divers. It is usually seen with its head protruding from a hole and the rest of the body concealed. It may become aggressive if provoked. No identifiable larvae of this species have been seen.

491 California Moray
Gymnothorax mordax

Description: To 5′ (1.5 m). Elongate. *Brown to greenish brown. Forehead elevated;* mouth large; inner edges of jaws not curved; teeth strong, not exposed when mouth closed; gill openings small, round. Body unscaled. Skin thick.

Habitat: Shallow rocky reefs with crevices and caves to depths of 192′ (59 m); usually to 66′ (20 m).

Range: Point Conception, CA, to Bahía Magdalena, Baja California.

Similar Species: Pacific Snake Eel *(Ophichthus triserialis)* has pectoral fins and dark-spotted body; occurs over soft bottoms.

Comments: This is the only moray found north of Baja California. It feeds on crabs, shrimps, lobsters, and various fishes. Females deposit eggs that develop into leptocephalus larvae. Although not usually aggressive, if disturbed, this moray may bite divers.

492 Spotted Moray
Gymnothorax moringa

Description: To 3′3″ (99 cm). Robust, moderately compressed. *Yellow above; white or yellow elsewhere, with dense, irregular, brownish to purplish-black spots and small blotches;* spotting continues out to near edge of fins; number of spots varies, some individuals pale with relatively few spots; anterior edge of dorsal fin black; posterior edges of dorsal, anal, and caudal fins white. Young to 4″ (10 cm) long uniformly brown, with pale sides and white lower jaws. Forehead elevated; posterior nostril not tubular; rear jaw teeth not serrate.

Habitat: Shallow coral reefs and rocky coasts; rarely to depths of 656′ (200 m).

Range: SC (possibly NC) to Rio de Janeiro, Brazil, including Bermuda, Bahamas, Gulf of Mexico, and Caribbean. Also in e Atlantic.

Similar Species: Purplemouth Moray (*G. vicinus*) also has freckled or mottled pattern, but has white edges on anal and caudal fins and rear one-third of dorsal fin.

Comments: Spotted Moray is one of the most common morays in shallow waters in the Bahamas, but it is not often seen by divers due to its secretive nature.

---

494 Honeycomb Moray
Gymnothorax saxicola

Description: To 24″ (61 cm). Stout. Brownish or purplish brown, *with numerous pale spots varying in size; dorsal fin with large, ocellated, disconnected black spots along edge;* anal fin with connected spots forming uninterrupted dark edge. Forehead somewhat elevated; posterior nostril not tubular; teeth serrate, shark-like. Dorsal fin origin at head.

Habitat: Sea-grass beds and over sand or mud on continental shelf at depths of 30–300′ (9–91 m).

Range: Bermuda, NC south to s FL and e Gulf of Mexico, and west to Mississippi Delta; absent from Bahamas; disjunctly off Yucatán.

Similar Species: Blackedge Moray (*G. nigromarginatus*) has usually smaller white spots on body, and connected elongate black blotches along edge of dorsal fin; occurs in more turbid waters over muddier bottoms.

Comments: Honeycomb and Blackedge Morays are probably most active at night, when they feed primarily on fishes and squids.

SNAKE EELS AND WORM EELS
Family Ophichthidae

52 genera and about 250 species worldwide; 17 genera and 36 species in North America (32 Atlantic, 4 Pacific), plus 10 genera and 37 species confined to Mexican waters. Found in tropical to warm-temperate inshore waters, these fishes comprise a morphologically diverse family of unscaled eels, some of which have reduced or absent fins and resemble snakes. Some are very colorful, and a number of species are active in the daytime. Within the restricted framework of eel morphology, there are broad differences among species. The snout varies from rounded to pointed, although the latter condition is probably more prevalent. Pectoral, dorsal, and anal fins are usually present, but some species may lack one or more of these fins; in extreme cases, some lack fins altogether. The position of the gill openings may vary from the underside to the side of the body or some position in between. The posterior nostril is located on or near the upper lip and, like the anterior nostril, may be either a simple opening or situated at the end of a tube. The teeth are fang-like in some species and blunt in others. The family is divided into two subfamilies: the Ophichthinae (snake eels), which have hard-tipped tails usually without visible caudal fin rays; and the Myrophinae (worm eels), which have tails with flexible tips and short but visible caudal fin rays. Those species that burrow into hard bottoms in relatively deep water are usually difficult to collect and may be known from very few specimens. For similar reasons, new species continue to be discovered, probably more so than for any other family of eels.

498 Goldspotted Eel
Myrichthys ocellatus

Description: To 3'7" (1.1 m). Slender. Pale tan or greenish brown, shading to pale green ventrally; distinctive pattern of *diffuse dark spots with bright yellow centers (fading upon death)*. Pectoral fin well developed, broad-based; dorsal fin origin at head.

Habitat: Sea-grass beds, areas with sand and coral rubble, and coral reefs to depths of 24' (7.5 m).

Range: Bermuda, Bahamas, and Florida Keys south throughout Antilles to South America.

Similar Species: The slightly larger Sharptail Eel
(M. breviceps) has more numerous
light spots on body not outlined with
dark pigment.

Comments: Goldspotted Eel has been known
as *M. oculatus* in past literature
references.

499 Speckled Worm Eel
Myrophis punctatus

Description: To 17" (43 cm). Slender, worm-like.
Brownish or yellowish brown above
and on entire posterior half of body;
belly lighter; *tiny dark speckles everywhere
except belly.* Snout rounded; eye oval;
anterior nostril tubular, posterior nostril
on edge of lip; mouth extends beyond
eye; upper jaw projects beyond lower.
No pelvic fins; pectoral fins short,
broad-based; *dorsal fin origin on anterior
one-third of body, about midway between
head and anus; dorsal and anal fins
continuous around tip of tail.*

Habitat: Coastal waters, bays, and tidal creeks;
usually over soft mud, sometimes over
sand.

Range: NC to n South America, including
Bermuda, Bahamas, ne and e Gulf of
Mexico, and Caribbean.

Similar Species: Key Worm Eel *(Ahlia egmontis)* has
blunter head and dorsal fin origin much
farther back (above anus); occurs usually
around reefs.

Comments: This is one of the most common eels in
the northern Gulf of Mexico. It appears
in shrimp trawls and seine collections
made in shallow waters over mud, but
because of its burrowing habits is
unlikely to be seen by divers.

497 Spotted Snake Eel
Ophichthus ophis

Description: To 4'7" (1.4 m). Elongate, snake-like.
Pale, tan to yellowish, *with 2 rows of large
blackish spots;* 20 large spots at mid-

body; 25–35 pairs of smaller spots along dorsal fin base; spots on head much smaller, often dash-like; *broad blackish collar across nape and cheek.* Eye above middle of upper jaw; anterior nostril tubular; 1 row of teeth on vomer, front teeth not enlarged. Pectoral fin well developed; dorsal fin origin well behind gill opening, above tip of pectoral fin; *no caudal fin. End of tail stiff.*

Habitat: Over open sand bottoms from inshore to depths of 165′ (50 m).

Range: Bermuda to s FL, n Cuba, and Lesser Antilles, and e Caribbean from Colombia to Brazil; apparently absent from Bahamas. Also around offshore islands in e Atlantic.

Similar Species: Giant Snake Eel *(O. rex)* reaches length of 7′ (2.1 m), and has 12–13 large, vertically rectangular blotches on sides. Shrimp Eel *(O. gomesii)* reaches length of 28″ (71 cm), is dark brown to dark gray above and paler below, and lacks spots and other conspicuous markings.

Comments: Spotted Snake Eel is nocturnal, as are probably most other snake eel species. It lies buried in the sand, with only its head exposed.

Order Clupeiformes

This order consists of five families: the herrings and the anchovies, both of which are found in North American waters, and three smaller families. The majority of these usually small, delicate, silvery fishes are marine. Anchovies and herrings usually have laterally compressed bodies (a few herring species have rounded bodies), normally without dark pigment. Members of this order are rather primitive, with such features as abdominal pelvic fins, pectoral fins low on the sides of the body, no adipose fin, fins lacking spiny rays, and cycloid scales that in many species are highly deciduous. They are unique in having a peculiar connection between the swim bladder and the inner ear, together with special characteristics of the portion of the skeleton that supports the caudal fin. The pectoral and pelvic fins may each have a large axillary scale in the posterior angle between the fin and the body. The dorsal fin is never divided into segments, but in some cases the last ray may have a long extension. A lateral line is absent, but in some species sensory canals on the head extend onto the shoulder region. All have a single pair of nostrils. Most species have numerous long, fine, closely set gill rakers attached to the inner sides of the gill arches; these are used to strain small planktonic organisms from the water. In some species the number of gill rakers increases with size and age; in other species the number remains stable throughout adult life. The number of gill rakers, as well as the number of branchiostegal rays, are often of considerable taxonomic importance. Many species swim in large compact schools, usually numbering in the thousands. Many anchovies and herrings are important as forage for larger carnivorous fishes, and some species are of commercial importance.

ANCHOVIES
Family Engraulidae

16 genera and 139 species worldwide; 4 genera and 13 species in North America (9 Atlantic, 4 Pacific), plus 1 genus and 17 species confined to Mexican waters. There is an unusually high percentage of species concentrated in the tropical eastern Pacific region. Some occur in fresh water, although rarely in North America. Anchovies are small, usually not exceeding 4″ (10 cm) in length, delicate, and moderately laterally compressed. These fishes are unmistakable, due to the combination of a silvery translucent body, often with a bright silvery stripe along the side, large eyes, and a very large inferior mouth coupled with an overhanging conical snout. The gill arches extend well forward on the floor of the mouth, nearly to the tip of the lower jaw, and contain numerous closely spaced gill rakers. The pelvic fins are abdominal, and the pectoral fins are low on the body. The caudal fin is deeply forked. The large cycloid scales are deciduous; unlike in herrings, the scales do not form a keel on the midline of the belly.

Many anchovies are similar in appearance but differ in the number of fin rays, position of the dorsal fin relative to the anal fin, shape and length of the maxilla, and number of gill rakers. They play an invaluable role in the food web, and are eaten extensively by predators such as mackerels and bluefishes. Widely used for bait and food, these fishes also are important commercially.

645 Striped Anchovy
Anchoa hepsetus

Description: To 6" (15 cm). Relatively large, slender. *Well-defined silvery lateral stripe contrasts sharply with areas immediately above and below.* Snout moderately long, length slightly less than width of eye; *maxilla long, sharply pointed, extends to edge of opercle;* 33–44 (usually 37–39) gill rakers. 15–18 (usually 16–17) pectoral fin rays; dorsal fin with 14–17 (usually 16) rays, *origin above a point well in front of anal fin,* ends above front rays of anal fin; *18–23 (usually 20–21) anal fin rays.* Melanophores outline all dorsal scales, especially those behind dorsal fin.

Habitat: Shallow coastal waters to depths of 210' (64 m).

Range: Chesapeake Bay south throughout Gulf of Mexico and Caribbean to Uruguay; rarely north to NS, but sometimes seasonally common off NJ and NY.

Similar Species: The smaller Bay Anchovy *(A. mitchilli)* has deeper, more compressed body, less sharply delineated silvery stripe along side, and usually at least 25 anal fin rays.

Comments: Striped Anchovy is an important forage fish throughout its range.

184, 644 Bay Anchovy
Anchoa mitchilli

Description: To 4" (10 cm). *Small. Silvery lateral stripe not contrasting sharply with areas immediately above and below. Snout relatively blunt, projecting slightly beyond tip of jaw;* eye large, width greater than length of snout; maxilla long, slender, pointed, not quite reaching edge of opercle; 35–45 (usually 38–42) gill rakers. 11–14 (usually 12–13) pectoral fin rays; dorsal fin with 14–16 rays, *origin almost directly above anal fin origin; 23–31 (usually 25–28) anal fin rays.*

Habitat: Abundant in inshore waters, particularly in shallow bays and estuaries; frequently enters brackish water, occasionally fresh water.

Range: Continental waters from Gulf of Maine to FL and throughout Gulf of Mexico to Yucatán.

Similar Species: The larger Striped Anchovy *(A. hepsetus)* has slightly more slender and less compressed body, more sharply delineated silvery stripe along side, dorsal fin well in front of anal fin, and 18–23 anal fin rays.

Comments: This species is unique among North American anchovies in having the dorsal fin origin almost directly above the anal fin origin. Bay Anchovy is one of the most abundant of all fishes in bays and estuaries along the Atlantic and Gulf coasts of North America. As such, it is an extremely important forage species.

---

646 Northern Anchovy
Engraulis mordax

Description: To 9″ (23 cm), rarely more than 7″ (18 cm). Fusiform, elongate, *round.* Metallic blue to green above; silvery below. Maxilla reaches almost to rear edge of opercle. *Each pectoral fin with axillary scale more than half of fin length;* anal fin origin under or posterior to last few dorsal fin rays; 19–26 anal fin rays.

Habitat: Surface of coastal waters, usually near shore; occasionally to depths of 720′ (220 m).

Range: Northern BC to Cabo San Lucas, Baja California.

Similar Species: Deepbody Anchovy *(Anchoa compressa)* has pectoral fin with axillary scale less than half of fin length, anal fin origin anterior to middle of dorsal fin base, and 29–33 anal fin rays. Slough Anchovy *(A. delicatissima)* has anal fin origin anterior to middle of dorsal fin base and 23–26 anal fin rays. Both occur in bays and estuaries.

Comments: The pelagic Northern Anchovy is usually found in tightly packed schools. Tagging studies indicate that the schools move fairly large distances up and down the coast. Northern Anchovy spawns during the winter and early spring, and the pelagic eggs take between two and four days to hatch. This anchovy rarely lives longer than four years. An extremely important commercial fish, it is also a major food source for other fishes, birds, and mammals. Northern Anchovy supports a bait fishery; most fish sold as "anchovies" are this species. It is also caught commercially for processing into fish meal and oil.

HERRINGS
Family Clupeidae

56 genera and about 180 species worldwide; 11 genera and 33 species in North America, plus 1 genus and 5 species confined to Mexican waters. Members of this large, primarily saltwater family have variable body shapes. The clupeid mouth is typically large and terminal, with the lower jaw projecting beyond the upper; however, the lower jaw is deep and the maxilla is broad posteriorly. The anal fin is larger than the dorsal fin, which is at about mid-body. There is no lateral line. Most herring species have scutes, modified cycloid scales with keel-like ridges, on the belly.

ventral scutes

161, 652 **Skipjack Herring**
Alosa chrysochloris

Description: To 21″ (53 cm). Elongate, strongly compressed; *dorsal and ventral profiles evenly rounded.* Back dark blue-green to gray; sides silvery; no dark humeral spot. *Lower jaw projects beyond upper;*

20–24 gill rakers on lower limb of first arch. Dorsal fin origin just before pelvic fin insertion; last dorsal fin ray not elongate.

Habitat: Open areas of medium to large rivers and reservoirs with clear to slightly turbid waters; occasionally enters marine waters.

Range: Large tributaries of Mississippi River from MN and PA southward; Gulf coast rivers from Suwannee River, FL, to central TX.

Comments: Skipjack is a popular sport fish, taken with light tackle using small spoons and spinners. Populations near the Gulf coast may enter marine environments but spawn in fresh water. Inland landlocked populations complete their entire life cycle in fresh water.

159, 651 Alewife
Alosa pseudoharengus

Description: To 15″ (38 cm). Elongate, strongly compressed, depth less than one-quarter length; *ventral profile more convex than dorsal profile.* Back iridescent grayish green or violet; sides paler; belly silvery; humeral spot dusky. Head less than one-fifth length; *eye large, width greater than length of snout;* mouth oblique, with deeply notched upper jaw; maxilla wide, reaches middle of eye. Dorsal fin origin just before pelvic fin insertion; last dorsal fin ray not elongate.

Habitat: Bays, estuaries, and fresh water.

Range: Inland along coast from NF to SC; Great Lakes.

Similar Species: Blueback Herring *(A. aestivalis)* has blue-green back and smaller eyes.

Comments: This schooling species feeds on plankton and small crustaceans while at sea. Populations established in lakes remain there to spawn; all others enter freshwater streams to spawn, and then return to the sea.

162, 680 American Shad
Alosa sapidissima

Description: To 30″ (76 cm); 9 lb (4.2 kg). Elongate, strongly compressed, depth about one-fourth length; *dorsal and ventral profiles evenly rounded.* Back dark bluish or greenish; sides much paler; belly silvery; *humeral spot dusky, usually followed by several small, less distinct dusky spots.* Head one-fifth or less of length; *eye width much less than length of snout;* mouth oblique; maxilla reaches posterior edge of eye; *adults lack jaw teeth; 59–73 gill rakers on lower limb of first arch.* Dorsal fin origin slightly anterior to pelvic fin insertion; last dorsal fin ray not elongate.

Habitat: Bays, estuaries, and fresh water.

Range: Southern Labrador to St. Johns River, FL. Introduced in Pacific from AK to Mexico.

Similar Species: Hickory Shad *(A. mediocris)* has almost straight, ventrally well-rounded dorsal profile, teeth on lower jaw that projects well beyond upper jaw, and 18–23 gill rakers on lower limb of first arch. Alabama Shad *(A. alabamae)* has 42–48 gill rakers on lower limb of first arch; occurs in coastal waters and large rivers.

Comments: American Shad is taken as a sport fish, and during spawning runs is caught commercially. It is marketed fresh; in some areas the roe is sold as a delicacy. All fishes in the genus *Alosa* are schooling species that enter freshwater streams to spawn. Adults of most species do not remain long in fresh water, nor do they travel far out at sea.

653 Atlantic Menhaden
Brevoortia tyrannus

Description: To 18″ (46 cm). Oval, deep, compressed. Blue or green, sometimes bluish brown above; sides and belly silvery; distinct humeral spot often followed by several rows of smaller spots; fins yellowish.

Head very large; mouth oblique; maxilla reaches posterior edge of eye. Pectoral fin slightly falcate, insertion near ventral profile of body; dorsal fin origin slightly behind pelvic fin insertion. *Exposed edges of scales almost vertical, fringed.*

Habitat: At or near surface over continental shelf and near large estuaries.

Range: NB to s FL.

Similar Species: Gulf Menhaden (*B. patronus*) has larger head, and dorsal fin is farther forward.

Comments: Both Atlantic and Gulf Menhadens are also known as Pogy. Each species occurs in huge schools, often weighing hundreds of tons, and together support a large industry on the Atlantic and Gulf coasts. Although all parts of these fishes have value, the oil is the principal product.

160 Pacific Herring
Clupea pallasii

Description: To 18″ (46 cm). Fusiform, laterally compressed. Dark bluish green above; silvery white below; no humeral spot. Vomer teeth present; *no striations on opercle.* Dorsal fin with 15–21 rays, origin slightly anterior to pelvic fin. *Ventral scutes lack bony keel.*

Habitat: Inshore waters.

Range: Gulf of Alaska to n Baja California.

Similar Species: Pacific Sardine (*Sardinops sagax*) lacks vomer teeth, is black-spotted, and has elongate last anal fin ray and ventral scutes with bony keel.

Comments: Pacific Herring spawns during the winter and early spring. The eggs are deposited on objects, such as kelp, rocks, and eelgrass, in very shallow water and hatch in 10 days. Large quantities of eggs are harvested commercially, often to be exported to Japan. Pacific Herring adults feed on a variety of crustaceans and small fishes, and are themselves prey for many important commercial and sport fishes, such as salmons.

164, 678 Gizzard Shad
Dorosoma cepedianum

Description: To 16″ (41 cm). Deep, moderately
compressed. Back dark blue or gray;
sides silvery, with 6–8 horizontal
dusky stripes on upper sides; belly
white; humeral spot dusky. Head small;
adipose eyelid present; *mouth small,
inferior; upper jaw with notch on ventral
edge.* Pelvic fin almost directly under
dorsal fin origin; *last dorsal fin ray
elongate, filamentous; anal fin long, with
25–37 rays.* Ventral scutes form distinct
keel.

Habitat: Large rivers, reservoirs, lakes, and
estuaries; may enter nearshore marine
waters.

Range: Atlantic coast and associated rivers from
NY to central FL; Gulf of Mexico from
central FL to central Mexico; St.
Lawrence River; Great Lakes;
Mississippi River system.

Similar Species: Threadfin Shad *(D. petenense)* has deep
and moderately compressed body and
elongate last dorsal fin ray, but lacks
scales on ridge of back anterior to dorsal
fin. Atlantic Thread Herring
(Opisthonema oglinum) has elongate last
dorsal fin ray, and scales on ridge of back
anterior to dorsal fin.

Comments: Gizzard Shad is a very common
herbivorous fish associated primarily
with freshwater habitats. It has no
commercial value, but is a forage fish
for larger carnivorous fishes.

163, 679 Threadfin Shad
Dorosoma petenense

Description: To 9″ (23 cm). Deep, moderately
compressed. Back gray to green; sides
silvery; belly white; *humeral spot large,
black;* all fins except dorsal fin yellowish.
Head small; mouth small, terminal; *no
notch on ventral edge of upper jaw.* Dorsal
fin small, origin slightly posterior to

pelvic fin; last dorsal fin ray greatly
elongate, reaching near caudal fin base;
anal fin short, with 17–27 rays.

Habitat: Large, low- to moderate-gradient rivers,
reservoirs, lakes, and estuaries;
occasionally enters brackish water.

Range: Mississippi River basin from IN and IL
south to Gulf of Mexico and ne Mexico.
Widely introduced outside native range,
including Atlantic coast drainages from
Chesapeake Bay to FL; also widely
introduced in reservoirs and large rivers
in sw U.S.

Comments: Threadfin Shad is an important forage
species for sport fishes in large rivers
and reservoirs. It is not as tolerant
of cold water as Gizzard Shad
(*D. cepedianum*).

165 Atlantic Thread Herring
Opisthonema oglinum

Description: To 12″ (30 cm). Deep, moderately
elongate, strongly compressed. Bluish
black to green above, shading to silvery
on sides; *5–7 dark stripes on back; dark
humeral spot at upper end of gill opening.*
Head small; mouth terminal; *no median
notch on upper jaw. Dorsal fin with 19–20
rays, origin anterior to pelvic fin; last dorsal
fin ray greatly elongate, reaching near
caudal fin base*; 17–22 anal fin rays.
*32–36 sharply edged scutes on midline of
breast and belly.*

Habitat: Shallow nearshore marine waters to
depths of 164′ (50 m); enters brackish
and rarely fresh waters in lower reaches
of rivers.

Range: ME to Brazil, including Bermuda,
Bahamas, Gulf of Mexico, and
Caribbean.

Comments: Atlantic Thread Herring is a schooling
pelagic species. It is caught for bait
with seines or cast nets, but is of no
sporting or commercial interest. This
species is known to enter Florida's St.
Johns River.

Order Cypriniformes

This is the second-largest order of fishes; there are five families worldwide, two of which occur in North America. This is usually the dominant group of freshwater fishes, very rarely entering brackish water, and adapted to the most extreme freshwater environments. Members of this order have a single rayed dorsal fin, and most species lack fin spines. The scales are cycloid. These fishes have a series of modified vertebrae connecting the swim bladder with the inner ear, which facilitates an acute sense of hearing.

CARPS AND MINNOWS
Family Cyprinidae

210 genera and about 2,000 species worldwide; 45 genera and 254 species native to North America north of Mexico, plus 5 genera and 41 species confined to Mexico. The largest family of fishes in the world, Cyprinidae has the most extensive continuous distribution of any family of freshwater fishes; carps and minnows occur throughout North America, Europe, Asia, and Africa, but are absent from South America. The widespread distribution and abundance of these fishes make them very important in the ecology of freshwater ecosystems. They have jaws without teeth and cycloid scales, and lack an adipose fin. Some species are as small as ½″ (12 mm) long, and some are as big as 9′10″ (3 m). The largest North American species, Colorado Pikeminnow *(Ptychocheilus lucius)*, reaches a length of 5′ (1.5 m).

131 Chiselmouth
Acrocheilus alutaceus

Description: To 12″ (30 cm). Elongate. Back grayish brown; sides lighter, with small black dots; dorsal and caudal fins grayish brown; anal fin reddish orange. Snout bluntly rounded, slightly overhanging wide mouth; *upper jaw with fleshy lip and straight cartilaginous plate; lower jaw with straight-edged, hard sheath;* no barbels. Anal fin origin posterior to dorsal fin origin; *caudal fin deeply forked.* Caudal peduncle slender. Scales embedded. Lateral line complete, with 85–93 scales.

ventral view of mouth

Habitat: Creeks and rivers with slow to swift

current and lakes over firm bottoms; enters streams to spawn.

Range: BC to OR, ID, and ne NV.

Comments: Chiselmouth feeds by scraping its chisel-like lower jaw over algae-covered surfaces. Other adaptations for feeding on algae include stout pharyngeal teeth with well-developed grinding surfaces and a long intestine.

174 Longfin Dace
Agosia chrysogaster

Description: To 3½" (9 cm). Robust. Dark olive gray above, *with dark mid-lateral stripe ending in darker spot;* whitish below. Head blunt; mouth terminal, reaching front of eye; *small barbel at corner of jaw.* Fins rounded except forked caudal fin; anterior half of anal fin elongate in females. Scales small. Lateral line complete, with 75–90 scales.

Habitat: Warm desert streams to cooler mountain brooks.

Range: Bill Williams and Gila Rivers, sw NM and s AZ; Colorado River, n Sonora, Mexico.

Comments: Longfin Dace is less common in large rivers and at high elevations. It is omnivorous, feeding on debris, aquatic invertebrates, and algae.

141 Central Stoneroller
Campostoma anomalum

Description: To 9" (23 cm). Elongate, stout. Dark olive to gray above; sides with dark flecks; whitish below. Breeding males have black band through central part of pelvic, dorsal, and anal fins; tubercles on head, body, and median fins. *Head blunt; snout overhangs mouth;* upper lip fleshy; *lower jaw with cartilaginous ridge; no barbels; 21–33 gill rakers on first arch. 36–46 scales around body at dorsal fin origin.* Lateral line complete, with 47–56 scales.

ventral view of mouth

Habitat: Riffles and shallow pools of clear creeks to small rivers with moderate to steep gradient over gravel or bedrock.

Range: Thames River, s ON, south through most of e and central U.S. to San Juan River, ne Mexico.

Similar Species: Largescale Stoneroller *(C. oligolepis)* has larger scales; breeding males lack tubercles around nostrils and dark band through anal fin. Bluefin Stoneroller *(C. pauciradii)* has 11–17 gill rakers on first arch and 33–38 scales around body at dorsal fin origin. Dace (genus *Rhinichthys*) have barbel at corner of jaw and smaller scales.

Comments: Stonerollers are common in small streams, where they feed on algae and other microorganisms, which they scrape from rocks and other hard surfaces using the blade-like lower jaw. They move small stones as they feed, hence the common name stoneroller.

---

167 Goldfish
Carassius auratus

Description: To 16″ (41 cm); 3½ lb (1.6 kg). Robust. Coloration varies: usually olive, sometimes gold, orange, or creamy white; fins match color of body. Young may have dark blotches. *No barbels. Dorsal and anal fins each with 1 heavy serrate spine; dorsal fin with 15–18 branched rays; 5–6 anal fin rays.* Caudal peduncle deep, short. Lateral line complete, with 27–31 scales.

Habitat: Warm lakes, ponds, and sloughs with aquatic vegetation over soft bottoms.

Range: Introduced in s Canada, United States, and Mexico.

Similar Species: Common Carp *(Cyprinus carpio)* has 2 pairs of barbels on upper lip and 32–39 smaller scales in lateral line.

Comments: Goldfish is native to China. It can tolerate extreme temperatures of 32–106° F (0–4° C) and low levels of dissolved oxygen, but is usually found in warmer waters of regions where winters are not severe. Goldfish and Common Carp hybridize, making identification difficult. Since large Goldfish populations can suppress native fishes, this species should not be released into the wild.

176 Rosyside Dace
Clinostomus funduloides

Description: To 4″ (10 cm). Oblong, moderately deep and compressed. Back olive; *sides rosy, with dusky mid-lateral stripe and scattered dark scales;* belly whitish. Breeding males bright red, covered with tubercles. Mouth large, extending to eye; lower jaw protrudes; no barbels. Dorsal fin origin posterior to pelvic fin insertion. Lateral line decurved, complete, *with 48–57 scales.*

Habitat: Clear creeks with moderate current over gravel or rocks.

Range: Western NJ and s PA to Savannah River, GA, and west to w TN, ne MS, and sw KY; s OH and e KY.

Similar Species: Redside Dace *(C. elongatus)* has slender elongate body and 59–70 lateral line scales.

Comments: Rosyside Dace is generally common within its range. It reaches sexual maturity after one year, and lives for three to four years.

211 Lake Chub
Couesius plumbeus

Description: To 9″ (23 cm). Elongate, moderately compressed. Bluish gray to dark greenish above; mid-lateral stripe lead-colored (faded in older fish); silvery white below. *Breeding males bright reddish orange at bases of paired fins.* Snout moderately pointed, same length eye; *mouth extends to front of eye; barbel near corner of jaw.* Dorsal fin with 8 rays, origin just posterior to pelvic fin insertion; caudal fin moderately forked. Lateral line complete, *with 56–69 scales.*

Habitat: Rivers, creeks, and lakes in clear to turbid waters over sand or gravel.

Range: Eastern AK, Canada, and n U.S. south to n CO, s WI, and s NY.

Similar Species: Pearl Dace (*Margariscus margarita*) has more rounded body; breeding males have bright red along lower sides.

Comments: Lake Chub is used for bait in some areas. The abundance of this species suggests it may be an important forage fish. It is the only minnow that occurs in Alaska, representing the most northerly distribution of a cyprinid in North America.

158 Grass Carp
Ctenopharyngodon idella

Description: To 3'3" (99 cm); 100 lb (45 kg). Robust. *Back olive brown; sides silvery;* whitish below; fins olive to dusky; *scales outlined with dusky pigment, creating crosshatched pattern.* Head blunt, broad; snout short; *pharyngeal teeth serrate, not molar-like.* Dorsal fin with 8–9 rays, origin over pelvic fin insertion; *anal fin with 8–9 rays, origin closer to caudal fin base than dorsal fin origin. Caudal peduncle short, deep.* Lateral line complete, with 40–42 scales.

Habitat: Rivers and large creeks; adaptable to ponds and reservoirs.

Range: Widely introduced in U.S.

Similar Species: Black Carp (*Mylopharyngodon piceus*) has bluish-gray sides, whitish belly, grayish-black fins, small terminal mouth without barbels, and serrate, molar-like, pharyngeal teeth; introduced in fish culture ponds and may have escaped into open waters.

Comments: This carp, native to eastern Asia, was introduced in experimental ponds in Alabama and Arkansas in 1963 for aquatic weed control and as a food fish. It feeds primarily on vegetation, grows rapidly, and may eat more than its body weight daily; all are traits that could destroy fish and waterfowl habitats.

Because of widespread stocking, Grass Carp could be encountered in any water body in the continental United States except Alaska.

225 Satinfin Shiner
Cyprinella analostana

Description: To 3½″ (9 cm). Deep, moderately compressed. Dark olive above; sides silvery to bluish gray; no caudal spot; *posterior membranes of dorsal fin pigmented,* other fins plain; *scales dark-edged.* Breeding males have white-edged fins and white-tipped caudal fin. Snout pointed; eye small; mouth slightly subterminal, oblique. *13–14 pectoral fin rays; 9 anal fin rays. Scales diamond-shaped.* Lateral line complete, with 34–37 scales.

Habitat: Small to large streams with clear to turbid waters and slow to moderate current over sand or gravel.

Range: Lake Ontario drainage, NY, and Atlantic coast streams from NY to s NC.

Similar Species: Ocmulgee Shiner *(C. callisema)* has blue mid-lateral stripe and small black blotch on bottom of first few dorsal fin rays. Bannerfin Shiner *(C. leedsi)* has enlarged dorsal fin with small black blotch on first 2 rays near outer edge.

Comments: Satinfin Shiner breeds from May to August. Spawning males defend their territory against other males by swimming toward them with their fins erect and making knocking sounds. Males produce a purring noise as they circle the females during courtship.

223 Whitetail Shiner
Cyprinella galactura

Description: To 5″ (12.5 cm). Cylindrical, terete, slightly compressed. Back olive to dusky; *sides silvery to bluish gray;* dark diffuse lateral stripe on upper side;

dorsal fin reddish, *posterior ray membranes black;* anal fin reddish; *caudal fin dusky, upper and lower bases creamy white; scales black-edged.* Mouth terminal; eye small. 9 anal fin rays. *Scales diamond-shaped.* Lateral line complete, with 39–41 scales.

Habitat: Large creeks to small rivers with cool clear waters and moderate current over gravel or rocks.

Range: Tennessee and Cumberland River drainages, sw VA and s KY, south to nw SC and west to ne MS; s MO and n AR.

Similar Species: Bluntface Shiner *(C. camurus)* has blunt snout and deeper body.

Comments: Whitetail Shiner feeds on aquatic and terrestrial insects. It is an active swimmer and is constantly moving.

---

226 Red Shiner
Cyprinella lutrensis

Description: To 3½" (9 cm). *Very deep, compressed.* Back dark olive to bluish; *sides steel blue to silvery blue, with dark wedge-shaped bar behind opercle; border of gill opening reddish;* dorsal fin dusky, no black blotch on posterior membranes; other fins dusky to reddish orange. Head short, deep; eye small; mouth terminal, oblique. 9 anal fin rays. Caudal peduncle short. Lateral line complete, with 32–37 scales.

Habitat: Small to large, turbid streams with slow to moderate current over sand or gravel.

Range: Northern IL west to s SD and se WY, southeast to LA, and west to Rio Grande in TX, NM, and Mexico. Widely introduced.

Similar Species: Proserpine Shiner *(C. proserpina)* has yellowish-orange dorsal fin.

Comments: The most common shiner in the turbid silty streams of the midwestern plains, Red Shiner is an important forage and bait fish. Its bright colors and hardiness make it a popular aquarium fish.

221 Spotfin Shiner
Cyprinella spiloptera

Description: To 4½" (11.5 cm). Deep, moderately compressed. Back olive; *sides silvery blue, with dark-edged scales;* posterior dusky stripe below lateral line; *fins plain, bases yellowish; posterior membranes of dorsal fin dusky.* Breeding males have fins with milky white edges. Snout pointed; eye small; mouth slightly ventral, oblique. *14 pectoral fin rays;* posterior dorsal fin straight-edged; 8 anal fin rays. *Scales diamond-shaped.* Lateral line complete, with 35–40 scales.

Habitat: Clear to slightly turbid pools and channels of large creeks and rivers with moderate current over firm sand or gravel.

Range: St. Lawrence River and Great Lakes drainage in sw QC and se ON, south through NY to w NC and n AL, and west to e OK, MN, and se ND.

Similar Species: Steelcolor Shiner *(C. whipplii)* has 15 pectoral fin rays and 9 anal fin rays.

Comments: This fish spawns in the summer. The eggs are deposited under loose bark and in crevices of submerged logs and roots. Several males may engage in combat until one remains over the spawning site.

224 Blacktail Shiner
Cyprinella venusta

Description: To 7" (18 cm). Deep, compressed. Olive above; *sides silvery to steel blue, with dark-edged scales; large black caudal spot* extends onto base of dorsal fin; posterior 3 membranes of dorsal fin black. Breeding males have small tubercles on head and body. Head pointed; eye small; mouth slightly inferior, oblique. *Scales diamond-shaped.* Lateral line complete, with 36–41 scales.

Habitat: Medium to large streams with clear to turbid waters over sand, gravel, or rocks.

Range: Southern IL, w KY, and se MO south to w GA and n FL, and west in Gulf coast drainages to Rio Grande drainage, TX.

Similar Species: Alabama Shiner *(C. callistia)* has
blunt snout overhanging upper lip;
occurs in streams with moderate
current over gravel or rocks. Tricolor
Shiner *(C. trichroistia)* has orange
to yellowish orange on leading
edge of fins.

Comments: Blacktail Shiner, a common and
important forage species, is considered
good bait, especially for basses and
sunfishes. When it occurs in the same
area as Red Shiner *(C. lutrensis)*, the two
species occasionally hybridize.

---

156 Common Carp
Cyprinus carpio

Description: To 30″ (76 cm); 60 lb (27 kg). Robust,
moderately compressed. Dark olive
above; sides lighter; yellowish below;
fins dusky olive. *2 pairs of barbels on upper
lip. Dorsal and anal fins each with 1 stout
serrate spine; dorsal fin long, with 17–21
rays;* 5–6 anal fin rays. Lateral line
complete, with 32–39 scales.

Habitat: Streams, lakes, ponds, sloughs, and
reservoirs with clear to turbid waters
and aquatic vegetation over mud or silt;
more common in warm waters.

Range: Introduced in s Canada, throughout
U.S., and Mexico.

Similar Species: Goldfish *(Carassius auratus)* lacks
barbels and has larger scales. Tench
(Tinca tinca), native to Eurasia, has short
dorsal fin with 8 rays, and 95–105
lateral line scales; widely introduced and
perhaps established in U.S. lakes, ponds,
and reservoirs with mud bottoms and
vegetation.

Comments: This species was introduced in the
United States during the late 1880s by
the U.S. Fish Commission as a food fish.
It proved detrimental to native fish
populations, and has never become as
popular as a sport and food fish in North
America as it is in Europe. It is a good
fighter and will take a variety of bait,
such as dough balls, corn, and worms.

203 Roundnose Minnow
Dionda episcopa

Description: To 2½″ (6.5 cm). Stout, rounded. Back dark olive; *sides brassy to silvery; mid-lateral stripe dusky,* less prominent on head, terminates as caudal spot; middle of dorsal fin base dark. Head rounded; snout blunt, slightly longer than eye; *mouth small, extends to nostril.* Dorsal and anal fins each with 8 rays. Lateral line complete, *with 35–43 scales.*

Habitat: Clear shallow pools of low-gradient rivers and creeks with vegetation.

Range: Colorado River, south-central TX, southwest to Rio Grande, e NM and ne Mexico.

Similar Species: Devils River Minnow *(D. diaboli)* has wedge-shaped caudal spot separated from mid-lateral stripe, dark-edged scales above stripe creating crosshatched pattern, and fewer lateral line scales.

Comments: This species, formerly abundant in eastern New Mexico, has disappeared from much of its range because of habitat alteration.

172 Spotfin Chub
Erimonax monachus

Description: To 3½″ (9 cm). Elongate, compressed. Back olive; *sides silvery to steel blue,* no blotches or speckles; *caudal spot large, dark;* dark spot on posterior dorsal fin rays. Snout extends beyond upper lip; eye small, laterally placed; *barbels small,* sometimes absent. Lateral line complete, *with 52–62 scales.*

Habitat: Large clear streams in or near moderate to swift current over gravel or rocks.

Range: Tennessee River drainage from sw VA to nw GA and n AL.

Similar Species: The robust Thicklip Chub *(Cyprinella labrosa)* has dark pigment on pelvic and median fins and 34–40 lateral line scales. The slender elongate Santee Chub *(C. zanema)* lacks dark markings on pelvic, anal, and caudal fins; occurs in warm, clear to turbid streams over sand or rocks.

Comments: Spotfin Chub has disappeared from much of its former range and is on the United States list of threatened species. This chub feeds mainly on larval aquatic insects. It spawns in the late spring and early autumn.

190 Slender Chub
Erimystax cahni

Description: To 3¾" (9.5 cm). Slender. Back yellowish tan to brown, with predorsal stripe of alternating gold and dusky areas; *sides with iridescent pale green mid-lateral band;* caudal spot dark; upper and lower 3 rays of caudal fin pigmented near base. Snout extends beyond upper lip; eye large; *barbels present.* Lateral line with 39–45 scales.

Habitat: Medium to large rivers in moderate to swift current over small gravel.

Range: Upper Tennessee River system, TN and VA.

Comments: Slender Chub was probably more widespread prior to impoundment of much of the main channel of the Tennessee River. This threatened species is one of the most geographically restricted minnows in the United States.

213 Streamline Chub
Erimystax dissimilis

Description: To 4½" (11.5 cm). Slender. Back olive yellow, with narrow predorsal stripe of alternating gold and dusky areas; *sides silvery, with 6–9 large, dark, horizontal, mid-lateral blotches underlaid by dusky stripe;* belly silvery to white. Snout extends beyond upper lip; eye large; *barbels present.* Dorsal fin origin anterior to pelvic fin insertion. Lateral line complete, with 44–49 scales.

Habitat: Medium to large, clear streams with moderate to swift current over clean gravel.

Range: Ohio River drainage from w NY and n IN south to n AL.

Similar Species: Blotched Chub *(E. insignis)* has rows of spots above and below dusky mid-lateral stripe and vertical mid-lateral blotches. Gravel Chub *(E. x-punctatus)* has scattered X-shaped markings on sides. Ozark Chub *(E. harryi)* has row of mid-lateral blotches, but lacks scattered X-shaped markings on sides.

Comments: Streamline, Blotched, Gravel, and Ozark Chubs are intolerant of habitat alterations such as impoundments, channelization, and pollution; consequently, their numbers have been reduced over much of their range. They spawn during May and June, and feed on aquatic insects and snails.

198 Cutlip Minnow
Exoglossum maxillingua

Description: To 5″ (12.5 cm). Stout, thick. Back dark olive; sides grayish silver; fins plain, dusky. Head broad, flat above; snout blunt; *mouth ventral; lower jaw 3-lobed, outer lobes fleshy,* formed by lower lip; *no barbels.* Pectoral fin short; caudal fin shallowly forked. Caudal peduncle deep. *Scales crowded anteriorly.* Lateral line complete, with 50–53 scales.

ventral view of mouth

Habitat: Clear pools and riffles of creeks and rivers over gravel or rocks.

Range: St. Lawrence River south to n NC.

Similar Species: Tonguetied Minnow *(E. laurae)* has barbel near corner of upper jaw and lips are not lobed.

Comments: During the late spring and early summer, Cutlip Minnow spawns in streams, building a mound-shaped nest of gravel 12–18″ (30–46 cm) wide and 3–6″ (7.5–15 cm) high.

132 Tui Chub
Gila bicolor

Description: To 16″ (41 cm). Plump, robust. Back
dark olive to brassy; sides lighter; lower
body and fins pinkish in adults. Young
have dark mid-lateral stripe. Head
short, somewhat pointed; eye large;
*mouth small, oblique, not reaching front of
eye; no barbels. Dorsal fin with 8–9 rays,
origin usually over or anterior to pelvic fin
insertion;* anal fin small, with 7–9 rays.
Caudal peduncle deep, thick. Lateral line
complete, *with 44–60 scales.*

Habitat: Ponds, lakes, and large slow streams
with quiet shallow waters and
vegetation.

Range: Southern WA south through OR, sw
ID, NV, and e and s CA.

Similar Species: Arroyo Chub *(G. orcuttii)* has dorsal fin
origin slightly behind pelvic fin origin.
Oregon Chub *(Oregonichthys crameri)*
reaches length of 2¾″ (7 cm), and has
clusters of dark brown to black spots on
back and sides and 35–49 lateral line
scales.

Comments: Tui Chub is omnivorous, but feeds
primarily on invertebrates. It is a
good forage fish, but has overpopulated
some reservoirs, adversely affecting
some sport fishes. Several subspecies are
endangered, and most are restricted to
streams and springs in isolated desert
basins.

170 Bonytail
Gila elegans

Description: To 24″ (61 cm). Moderately elongate;
hump on nape in adults. Greenish gray
above; sides lighter; whitish below.
Breeding males reddish orange below
and on paired fins. Head short; *snout
depressed, broadly rounded, usually not
overhanging upper lip.* Fins large, slightly
falcate; usually 10 dorsal fin rays; 10–11
anal fin rays; caudal fin deeply forked.

Caudal peduncle very narrow. Scales embedded or absent on predorsal area, belly, and caudal peduncle. *Lateral line with 75–88 scales.*

Habitat: Swift channels of large turbid rivers.

Range: Upper Colorado River system, CO and UT; lower Colorado River system, AZ and NV.

Similar Species: Humpback Chub *(G. cypha)* has snout slightly overhanging mouth, 9 dorsal fin rays, and at least 10 anal fin rays.

Comments: Bonytail and Humpback Chub are both endangered species threatened by predation, competition from exotic fishes, and man-made habitat changes. Bonytail presently occurs only in isolated populations in the Colorado River system.

---

130 Roundtail Chub
Gila robusta

Description: To 17″ (43 cm). Moderately thick, streamlined. Dusky to olive or silvery above; dorsal fin olive. Breeding males reddish on sides. Head flat above; eye small; *mouth terminal, reaching front of eye; no barbels.* Fins large; dorsal fin with 9–10 rays, origin behind pelvic fin insertion; 9–10 anal fin rays; caudal fin deeply forked. *Caudal peduncle moderate to slender. Lateral line complete, with 75–95 scales.*

Habitat: Lakes and pools of rivers and creeks with warm, often turbid waters.

Range: Colorado River system from sw WY to w NM.

Similar Species: Chihuahua Chub *(G. nigrescens)* has reddish snout and pelvic and anal fin bases. Rio Grande Chub *(G. pandora)* has silvery sides with 2 dusky stripes. Both occur in areas with cover.

Comments: This is the most common chub in the Colorado River system. There are four subspecies of Roundtail Chub, which exhibit different body forms and proportions.

212 Flame Chub
Hemitremia flammea

Description: To 3″ (7.5 cm). Moderately stout. Back
dark olive to brown; sides light olive to
buff, with dusky mid-lateral stripe
extending from snout to caudal spot;
belly whitish. Breeding males reddish
on belly and bases of dorsal, anal, and
caudal fins. Head short; *snout bluntly
rounded; mouth small, oblique, extending to
front of eye;* no barbels. Fins rounded.
34–42 scales in lateral series. *Lateral line
incomplete, with 7–24 pored scales.*

Habitat: Clear cool springs, creeks, and pools of
small rivers with slow current.

Range: Tennessee River, n AL and nw GA; one
tributary of Coosa River in Talladega
County, AL.

Comments: Habitat alteration has reduced or
eliminated some Flame Chub
populations. It is generally rare
throughout its range, but can be found
in large numbers in some springs.

231 California Roach
Hesperoleucus symmetricus

Description: To 4″ (10 cm). Elongate. Back dusky
gray to steel blue; sides dull silvery, with
small dusky dots. Breeding males
reddish orange on chin, opercle, bases of
paired fins, and base of anal fin. Snout
slightly longer than eye; mouth slightly
oblique, not reaching eye; *no barbels.
Dorsal fin origin far behind pelvic fin
insertion; anal fin short, with 6–9 rays;*
caudal fin forked. Lateral line decurved,
complete, with 47–63 scales.

Habitat: Small intermittent tributaries of large
streams with moderate gradient.

Range: Pit River drainage, s OR; Sacramento and
San Joaquin River drainages, central CA;
coastal streams from Humboldt County
south to Santa Barbara County, CA.

Comments: California Roach is one of the most
common fishes in many U.S. Pacific coast

streams, partly because it can survive in isolated pools of intermittent streams, where conditions are too harsh for most other fishes. It feeds on filamentous algae, crustaceans, and aquatic insects.

199 Brassy Minnow
Hybognathus hankinsoni

Description: To 4″ (10 cm). Moderately elongate, compressed. Back dark olive to blackish; *sides yellowish, with brassy reflections;* fins clear, plain. Head blunt, rounded; snout slightly overhangs small mouth; no barbels. *Dorsal and anal fins with rounded tips; dorsal fin origin just in front of pelvic fin insertion;* 8 anal fin rays. Lateral line complete, with 36–41 scales.

Habitat: Cool sluggish streams and dark-stained waters of bogs and ponds with vegetation over silt or mud.

Range: Central BC and MT east to sw QC and NY, and south to n MO and n KS.

Similar Species: Cypress Minnow *(H. hayi)* has black-edged scales on back and upper sides, appearing diamond-shaped.

Comments: Brassy Minnow is common in the central and eastern part of its range, where it is often used for bait. In May it spawns over plants in quiet pools.

200 Mississippi Silvery Minnow
Hybognathus nuchalis

Description: To 7″ (18 cm). Thick, stout. Back olive to silvery, with dark mid-dorsal stripe; *silvery below, no dark stripe;* fins clear. Snout blunt, rounded, overhanging mouth; eye width greater than width of mouth; no barbels. *Dorsal fin pointed, origin anterior to pelvic fin insertion;* 8 anal fin rays. Caudal peduncle moderately deep. Lateral line complete, with 33–41 scales.

Habitat: Clear pools and backwaters of large creeks and rivers with slow current over mud to sandy mud bottoms.

Range: Mississippi River system from WI and MN to e TN, AL, and e TX.

Similar Species: Western Silvery Minnow (*H. argyritis*) has eye width less than width of mouth; occurs in pools of large silty streams. Eastern Silvery Minnow (*H. regius*) has deeper body and more scales in lateral line.

Comments: Mississippi Silvery Minnow usually stays on or near the bottom, where it forms large schools. It feeds on algae and organic ooze found on the mud to sandy mud bottom.

---

187 Bigeye Chub
Hybopsis amblops

Description: To 3″ (7.5 cm). Moderately slender. Back olive yellow, with dark-edged scales; sides silvery; *prominent dusky mid-lateral stripe extends from snout to caudal fin base.* Head large, flat above; snout blunt, rounded, projecting beyond upper lip; *eye slightly longer than snout;* mouth small, ventral; *barbels present.* Dorsal fin origin over or just posterior to pelvic fin insertion; 8 anal fin rays. Lateral line complete, with 33–38 scales.

Habitat: Pools of medium to large, clear streams with slow current over sand, gravel, or rocks.

Range: Western NY, se MI, and central IL south to n AL and central AR; w NC and n GA west to ne OK.

Similar Species: Lined Chub (*H. lineapunctata*) has dusky lateral band narrowing posteriorly, terminating in caudal spot. Rosyface Chub (*H. rubrifrons*) has reddish snout and fins.

Comments: Bigeye Chub's large eyes and clear-water habitat suggest that it locates its food by sight. It is intolerant of silt, and has disappeared from some streams.

192 Pallid Shiner
Hybopsis amnis

Description: To 3¼" (8.5 cm). Moderately
elongate; *back arched at origin of
dorsal fin.* Yellowish above; sides
silvery; *lateral stripe continues around
snout.* Snout projects beyond upper lip;
eye large, about equal to snout length;
mouth small; no barbels. 8 anal fin
rays. 13–15 predorsal scales. Lateral
line with 35–36 scales.

Habitat: Rivers with quiet waters over sand to
silt bottoms.

Range: Central Mississippi River valley from
MN and WI south to LA and west on
Gulf coast to central TX.

Similar Species: Clear Chub *(H. winchelli)* has slender,
more compressed body.

Comments: Although widespread geographically,
Pallid Shiner is uncommon in most
areas.

233 Silver Carp
Hypophthalmichthys molitrix

Description: To 3'3" (99 cm). Heavy-bodied; *keel
on belly extends from head to anus.* Back
olive to silvery; sides silvery. Head
large; eye large; mouth small. First ray
of pectoral, dorsal, and anal fins thick,
spine-like in adults; 15–18 pectoral fin
rays; 12–13 anal fin rays. Lateral line
complete, with 95–105 scales.

Habitat: Pools of large to medium rivers,
backwater sloughs, oxbow lakes, and
reservoirs.

Range: Mississippi River system from IL and
IN south to LA. Widely introduced
in s U.S.

Similar Species: Bighead Carp *(H. nobilis)* has ventral
keel extending forward to pelvic fin
base.

Comments: Silver Carp is native to the Amur
River of eastern Russia south to the
Pearl River, China, and possibly to
northern Vietnam.

232 Least Chub
Iotichthys phlegethontis

Description: To 2½″ (6.5 cm). Moderately deep, compressed. Back olive green; *upper sides steel blue; golden stripe extends from upper end of gill opening to caudal fin base;* lower sides and belly golden; fins yellowish. Breeding males reddish on belly and lower sides. Mouth very oblique, extending to front of eye; eye large; *no barbels.* Dorsal fin with 8–9 rays, origin just posterior to pelvic fin insertion; caudal fin slightly forked. *34–38 scales in lateral series. Lateral line absent or with 1–3 pored scales.*

Habitat: Clear shallow streams, springs, ponds, and swamps with abundant vegetation over clay, mud, or organic debris.

Range: Bonneville Basin, north-central UT.

Similar Species: Desert Dace *(Eremichthys acros)* has 68–78 scales in lateral series and complete or incomplete lateral line; occurs in hot springs. Relict Dace *(Relictus solitarius)* has very robust body, 50–70 scales in lateral series, and incomplete lateral line; occurs in isolated spring pools. Moapa Dace *(Moapa coriacea)* has black caudal spot, small embedded scales, and complete lateral line with 70–80 pored scales; occurs in clear pools of thermal springs at 66–90° F (19–32° C) and their outflow with moderate current.

Comments: In some areas Least Chub survives in harsh habitats with highly alkaline waters, low dissolved oxygen, and temperatures varying by 59° F (15° C) in a day. It is sexually mature after one year, when just more than 1″ (2.5 cm) long, and spawns from April to August, peaking in May. Its maximum life span is about three years.

135 Hitch
Lavinia exilicauda

Description: To 13″ (33 cm). Deep, compressed. Back dark brownish yellow; sides lighter,

silvery; scales with dusky edges; median fins clear to dusky. Head small; mouth terminal, oblique, not reaching eye; *no barbels.* Dorsal fin origin just posterior to pelvic fin insertion; *anal fin long, with 10–14 rays;* caudal fin deeply forked. Caudal peduncle slender. *Lateral line decurved, complete, with 54–62 scales.*

Habitat: Ponds, lakes, reservoirs, and warm sluggish streams and sloughs; usually with vegetation.

Range: Sacramento, San Joaquin, Pajaro, and Salinas Rivers and Clear Lake, CA.

Comments: Although less common than it once was, Hitch has survived habitat alterations and the introduction of exotic predators and competitors. In some California reservoirs, large populations may inhibit the growth of sport fishes.

---

182 Little Colorado Spinedace
Lepidomeda vittata

Description: To 4″ (10 cm). Robust anteriorly, moderately compressed. Back olive to bluish gray; *sides silvery, with fine black spots and blotches* and thin dark vertical lines extending to dorsal fin; fins clear. Head broad; eye large; mouth moderately oblique; *no barbels. Dorsal fin with 2 spines,* 6 rays; 8 anal fin rays. Lateral line complete, *with 90–103 scales.*

Habitat: Clear streams with large pools 12–36″ (30–91 cm) deep over rocks or gravel.

Range: Upper Little Colorado River system, east-central AZ.

Similar Species: White River Spinedace (*L. albivallis*) has 9 anal fin rays and 79–92 lateral line scales; occurs in springs. Virgin Spinedace (*L. mollispinis*) has 9 anal fin rays and 77–90 lateral line scales.

Comments: In recent decades, this species has declined in numbers due to habitat changes, such as dams and water diversion, and the introduction of exotic minnows and sport fishes.

222 Striped Shiner
Luxilus chrysocephalus

ventral view
of head

Description: To 7″ (18 cm). Deep, compressed. Back
olive, with broad dusky predorsal stripe;
*dusky to dark stripes above, converging behind
dorsal fin;* sides silvery to bluish gray;
chin tip dusky; fins pinkish. Breeding
males rosy on sides. Eye large; mouth
terminal, oblique. Fins rounded; dorsal
fin origin in front of pelvic fin insertion;
9 anal fin rays. *21 or fewer predorsal scales;
scales on sides of body high, narrow.* Lateral
line complete, with 37–40 scales.

Habitat: Riffles and pools of clear creeks and
small rivers with moderate current over
sand, gravel, or rocks.

Range: Southeastern ON and w NY west to se
WI, south to s AL, and east to sw MO, e
OK, and e TX.

Similar Species: Crescent Shiner *(L. cerasinus)* has black
crescent-shaped markings on sides.

Comments: This fish was formerly considered a
subspecies of Common Shiner *(L.
cornutus),* to which it is closely related.
Striped Shiner is common throughout
most of its range, and is often found in
large schools.

214 Warpaint Shiner
Luxilus coccogenis

Description: To 5″ (12.5 cm). Moderately elongate
and compressed. Back olive yellow; sides
and belly silver; *vertical red line behind
eye; edge of gill opening black;* upper lip
reddish; base of pectoral fin red; *base of
dorsal fin reddish anteriorly, blue to black
posteriorly;* other fins plain. Head
moderately large; eye large; mouth
terminal, oblique. Dorsal fin origin
behind pelvic fin insertion. Lateral line
complete, with 39–43 scales.

Habitat: Medium to large, clear streams with
swift current over gravel or rocks.

Range: Southwestern VA and e TN south to nw
SC and n GA, and west to south-central
TN and nw AL.

Similar Species: Bandfin Shiner *(L. zonistius)* has black band through center of dorsal fin and bright red caudal fin.

Comments: The specific name, *coccogenis,* means "berry-red cheeks"; the common name also refers to the red line on the cheek of this colorful shiner.

---

217 Common Shiner
Luxilus cornutus

ventral view of head

Description: To 6" (15 cm). Deep, compressed. Back dusky olive, with wide dark predorsal stripe; *no dusky pigment on chin; fins clear to rosy.* Breeding males silvery to bluish purple on sides. Head moderately large, blunt; eye large; mouth large, terminal, oblique. *Fins rounded;* dorsal fin origin over or in front of pelvic fin insertion; 8–9 anal fin rays. *22–32 predorsal scales; scales on sides of body high, narrow.* Lateral line complete, with 36–44 scales.

Habitat: Riffles and pools of clear cool creeks and small rivers with moderate current over firm bottoms.

Range: NS west to se SK, south to se WY and e CO, and east to central VA.

Similar Species: White Shiner *(L. albeolus)* has sharp snout, and scales on sides of body are not high or narrow.

Comments: Common Shiner, as its name implies, is found frequently in much of its range. It is often replaced by Striped Shiner *(L. chrysocephalus)* in streams that have become warm, turbid, and silty. It is often used as bait for basses and other sport fishes.

---

206 Bleeding Shiner
Luxilus zonatus

Description: To 4½" (11.5 cm). Elongate, slender. Back olive brown, with broad dark mid-dorsal stripe; *upper sides with dark golden yellow and black mid-lateral stripes* extending from head to tail; *edge of gill opening black; fins plain.* Breeding males with red head; fins red, with clear edges. Eye moderately large; mouth terminal, oblique. 9 anal fin rays. Lateral line complete, with 38–43 scales.

Habitat: Small to medium, clear streams with moderate to swift current over gravel or rocks.

Range: Southern MO and ne AR.

Similar Species: Duskystripe Shiner *(L. pilsbryi)* has white to creamy lower half of body and lacks dark edge along gill opening. Cardinal Shiner *(L. cardinalis)* has red lower half of body.

Comments: Bleeding Shiner is often found in large schools with other shiners. Most spawning takes place in May and early June in gravel riffles, frequently over the nests of other minnows.

220 Redfin Shiner
Lythrurus umbratilis

Description: To 3½″ (9 cm). *Deep, very compressed.* Light olive above, with overlying dusky pigment; sides silvery; fins black or black and red; *black spot on base of anterior dorsal fin rays.* Breeding males bluish gray on top of head, reddish on sides; numerous small tubercles on head. Mouth terminal, oblique; eye moderately large. Dorsal fin origin posterior to pelvic fin insertion; 10–12 anal fin rays. *Scales crowded anteriorly;* 25 predorsal scales. Lateral line decurved, complete, with 38–50 scales.

Habitat: Pools of small to moderately large streams with slow to moderate current over sand, gravel, or rocks; often with aquatic vegetation.

Range: Southeastern ON, w NY, and w PA west to se WI and se MN, and south to s LA, e TX, and e OK.

Similar Species: Rosefin Shiner *(L. ardens)* has slender body and reddish fins.

Comments: Redfin Shiner spawns over the nests of sunfishes (family Centrarchidae), to which it is attracted by the scent of fluids released by sunfishes during spawning. As many as 30 to 100 male Redfin Shiners have been observed over a single large Green Sunfish nest.

191 Speckled Chub
Macrhybopsis aestivalis

Description: To 3" (7.5 cm). Slender. Olive to brownish yellow above; *sides yellow to silvery, with small, dark, rounded speckles;* faint dusky mid-lateral stripe often present; belly silvery. *Snout rounded, projecting well beyond upper lip;* eye high on head, width much less than length of snout; mouth ventral; *barbels long.* 7–8 anal fin rays. Lateral line complete, with 34–41 scales.

Habitat: Channels of large, clear to turbid streams with moderate current over sand or gravel.

Range: OH, s MN, and NE south to Rio Grande drainage in ne Mexico; w FL, nw GA, and AL west to TX.

Comments: Speckled Chub lives on or near the bottom, using taste buds on the head, body, and fins to find the aquatic insects on which it feeds. It spawns in deep swift water around midday from May through August. It seldom lives longer than one and a half years.

188 Sicklefin Chub
Macrhybopsis meeki

Description: To 4" (10 cm). Cylindrical, terete. Yellowish to tan, with silvery reflections above; silvery white below; lower lobe of caudal fin dark, white-edged. Head bluntly rounded; snout extends just beyond upper lip, not depressed; mouth small; barbels present. *Pectoral fin long,* extending beyond pelvic fin base; *dorsal fin strongly falcate.* Caudal peduncle slender. Breast unscaled. Lateral line complete, with 43–50 scales.

Habitat: Large rivers with warm turbid waters and swift current over sand or gravel.

Range: Mississippi and Missouri Rivers from
MT to LA.

Similar Species: Sturgeon Chub *(M. gelida)* has depressed
head and scales with keels above lateral
line.

Comments: Both Sicklefin and Sturgeon Chubs, with
their reduced eyes and external taste
buds, are well adapted to turbid water.

---

189 Silver Chub
Macrhybopsis storeriana

Description: To 9″ (23 cm). Moderately stout. Back
olive; *silvery white below, no dark
markings;* lower lobe of caudal fin dusky,
white-edged. Snout blunt, rounded,
extending beyond upper lip; mouth
small; *barbels present.* Dorsal fin with 7–8
rays, origin before pelvic fin insertion.
Lateral line complete, with 35–41 scales.

Habitat: Pools or slow current of large streams
over sand or gravel; occasionally lakes
and reservoirs.

Range: Southeastern ON and w NY west to se
MB and ND, and south to AL and e TX;
absent from Great Lakes except Lake
Erie.

Comments: Silver Chub, the second-largest species
in the genus, is widespread and fairly
common in the rivers of the Mississippi
River valley. It feeds primarily on
aquatic insects and crustaceans. Its life
span is about three years.

---

178 Spikedace
Meda fulgida

Description: To 3″ (7.5 cm). Elongate, slender,
slightly compressed. Back olive brown,
with dark mottling; *sides silvery, with
scattered black speckles;* all fins except
caudal have reddish bases. Snout short;
eye large; mouth extends to below eye;
no barbels. *Dorsal fin with 2 spines,* 7
branched rays, origin posterior to pelvic
fin insertion; 9 anal fin rays. *Scales
embedded or absent.* No lateral line.

Habitat: Pools of large streams with moderate to swift current over sand or gravel.

Range: Gila River system in sw NM and central and se AZ.

Comments: Spikedace was once widespread in the drainages of the Gila River, but it has been displaced in many areas by the introduced Red Shiner (*Cyprinella lutrensis*).

128 Hardhead
Mylopharodon conocephalus

Description: To 18″ (46 cm). Elongate, moderately compressed. *Brown to dusky bronze above;* lighter below. Head broad, cone-shaped; mouth horizontal; lips thick; upper jaw extends to eye; *no barbels; frenum present.* Dorsal fin with 8 rays, origin posterior to pelvic fin insertion; anal fin short, with 8–9 rays; caudal fin moderately forked. Caudal peduncle moderately slender. Lateral line complete, *with 69–81 scales.*

Habitat: Quiet deep pools of large, warm, clear streams over rocks or sand.

Range: Pit, Sacramento, Russian, and San Joaquin River systems, CA.

Comments: Once abundant, Hardhead populations have been much reduced by habitat changes and the introduction of exotic fishes. It feeds on plant and animal matter taken on or near the bottom. Hardhead reaches sexual maturity after two years, and has a life span of five to six years.

138 Hornyhead Chub
Nocomis biguttatus

Description: To 10″ (25 cm). Stout, heavy-bodied. Olive brown above; sides light olive; caudal spot dusky; dorsal fin olive; caudal fin reddish. Young have dusky to black lateral stripe. *Breeding males have bright red spot behind eye; head with 60–130 tubercles, but no swollen crest.* Head blunt, wide; mouth almost terminal; small barbel at corner of jaw.

Dorsal and anal fins each with 8 rays; caudal fin with rounded tips. Lateral line complete, with 38–46 scales.

Habitat: Clear pools of creeks and small rivers with moderate current over gravel.

Range: Southeastern ON and NY southwest to n AR and west to s MB, se WY, and e CO.

Similar Species: Redspot Chub *(N. asper)* breeding males have tubercles on front of body. Redtail Chub *(N. effusus)* has reddish-orange pelvic, anal, and caudal fins; breeding males have tubercles on head and body.

Comments: Hornyhead Chub feeds on algae, other plants, aquatic insects, snails, and crustaceans. Although hardy and used as bait in some areas, it has become less abundant in silty streams.

139 Bluehead Chub
Nocomis leptocephalus

Description: To 8″ (20 cm). Stout, robust, not compressed. Back olive brown; sides bluish to brassy reddish orange in adults. Young have dark lateral stripe and caudal spot. *Breeding males have 5–15 tubercles on swollen crest between eyes; no tubercles on snout tip.* Head large; small barbel at corner of jaw. Fins rounded; *8 anal fin rays.* Breast almost completely scaled. Lateral line complete, with 36–43 scales.

Habitat: Pools of small streams 10–50′ (3–15 m) wide with clear to slightly turbid waters over sand, gravel, or rocks.

Range: Atlantic coast streams from n VA to GA; Gulf coast streams from w GA to s MS and e LA; Tennessee River system in nw AL and ne MS.

Comments: Bluehead Chub, like others in the genus *Nocomis,* constructs a large, dome-shaped nest of pebbles during the spawning period from late April to July. The nest, up to 3′ (91 cm) wide and 15″ (38 cm) high, is built by the male, which picks up and carries pebbles in its mouth to the nest site.

140 River Chub
Nocomis micropogon

Description: To 10″ (25 cm). Cylindrical, stout
anteriorly. Olive brown above; sides
silvery; *no red spot behind eye;* dorsal and
caudal fins olive yellow to reddish
orange. Young have dusky lateral stripe. *Breeding
males rosy; 30–65 tubercles on snout tip and
between nostrils,* none between eyes. Head
broad; snout blunt; mouth large; small
barbel at corner of jaw. Breast unscaled
or slightly scaled posteriorly. Lateral line
complete, with 37–43 scales.

Habitat: Pools of medium to large creeks and
rivers with clear waters and moderate to
swift current over gravel or rocks.

Range: Southeastern ON and s NY west to MI
and IN, and south to s VA, nw SC, and
nw AL.

Similar Species: Bigmouth Chub (*N. platyrhynchus*) has
mostly scaled breast; breeding males
have fewer than 100 small tubercles from
tip of snout to top of head. Bull
Chub (*N. raneyi*) breeding males have
more than 100 tubercles from tip of
snout to top of head.

Comments: As in other *Nocomis* species, spawning
occurs intermittently over a pebble
nest, which is guarded by the male.
Other small minnows often spawn on
the nest while the male chub is gathering
pebbles. River Chub feeds on algae,
aquatic insects, crustaceans, and
mollusks. This species lives for about
five years and reaches sexual maturity
when three years old. It is used for bait
in some areas.

166 Golden Shiner
Notemigonus crysoleucas

Description: To 12″ (30 cm). Deep, compressed;
*pronounced unscaled keel on belly between
pelvic and anal fins.* Back golden to olive;
sides light olive, with silvery reflections;
belly silvery yellow; some individuals
entirely silvery; fins orange to yellowish

orange. Mouth upturned; maxilla extends to nostril; snout blunt. Dorsal fin slightly falcate. Lateral line decurved, complete, *with 44–55 scales.*

Habitat: Clear quiet streams, lakes, ponds, and swamps over mud, sand, or rocks; usually near aquatic vegetation.

Range: Eastern North America from s Canada to TX. Widely introduced.

Similar Species: Rudd *(Scardinius erythrophthalmus),* native to Europe, has bright red fins, scaled keel on belly, 10–13 gill rakers on first arch, 10–11 dorsal fin rays, and 36–45 lateral line scales.

Comments: Golden Shiner is the most common bait fish sold in the United States and is an important forage fish for several species of sport fishes. It is a schooling species that stays mainly near shore but may venture into open water.

204 Emerald Shiner
Notropis atherinoides

Description: To 4″ (10 cm). Elongate, streamlined, *strongly compressed.* Back yellowish olive to blue-green; *sides silvery, with iridescent emerald band most visible posteriorly;* belly silvery; *fins plain.* Snout pointed; eye large; mouth oblique, terminal, moderately large. Dorsal fin origin posterior to pelvic fin insertion; *10–13 anal fin rays;* caudal fin moderately forked. Lateral line complete, with 35–43 scales.

Habitat: Large streams, lakes, and reservoirs in open, clear to slightly turbid waters.

Range: Mackenzie River drainage, s Northwest Territories, south and east through s Canada, MT, Great Lakes, St. Lawrence River drainage, and NY to Gulf coast of AL and e TX.

Similar Species: Silver Shiner *(N. photogenis)* reaches length of 5″ (12.5 cm) and has dark crescent-shaped markings between nostrils; occurs in large clear streams with moderate current. Silverstripe Shiner *(N. stilbius)* has large eye and black oval caudal spot.

Comments: Emerald Shiner, often found in large
streams and sometimes in lakes, lives in
sizable schools at mid-depths, where it
feeds on small crustaceans and aquatic
insects. It is an important forage species
for a variety of sport fishes and is used
for bait.

219 Bigeye Shiner
Notropis boops

Description: To 3″ (7.5 cm). Cylindrical, terete,
slightly compressed. Greenish to olive
yellow above, with dark-edged scales;
sides silvery; dark lateral stripe about
width of pupil extends from snout tip;
unpigmented area above lateral stripe;
lateral line pores outlined in black; fins
clear. Breeding males have tubercles on
head. *Eye large, width more than one-third
head length;* mouth terminal, oblique.
Dorsal and anal fins slightly falcate; *8
anal fin rays. 17 or fewer predorsal scales.*
Lateral line complete, with 34–38 scales.

Habitat: Clear pools of medium to large streams
with moderate current over sand, gravel,
or rocks.

Range: Northwestern OH and n IL south to n
AL; ne MO and se KS south to ne LA
and west to se OK.

Comments: Bigeye Shiner cannot withstand long
periods in turbid water. It feeds
primarily on insects, which it locates by
sight. On occasion, it will leap a few
inches out of the water to capture insects
hovering just above the surface.

197 Silverjaw Minnow
Notropis buccatus

Description: To 3½″ (9 cm). Cylindrical, terete; *bones
of underside and lower part of head have
cavernous channels.* Pale olive yellow above,
with dark-edged scales; mid-dorsal stripe
narrow, most prominent anterior to dorsal
fin; silvery below; no caudal spot; fins
clear. Breeding males lack bright colors

ventral view of head

and tubercles. Snout broad, flat, longer than eye; *no barbels.* Lateral line almost straight, complete, with 31–36 scales.

Habitat: Small creeks to rivers with moderate current over sand or fine gravel.

Range: Southern PA, se MI, and n IL south to n and sw VA, n TN, and se MO; Gulf coast drainages from n GA and ne MS south to w FL and e LA.

Comments: Silverjaw Minnow runs in schools near the bottom, where it feeds on larval insects. Its life span is about three years.

209 Spottail Shiner
Notropis hudsonius

Description: To 6″ (15 cm). Deep, moderately robust. Back yellowish; *silvery below, with faint lateral stripe; caudal spot black; lower rays of caudal fin whitish;* other fins plain. Snout blunt, rounded; eye large; mouth extends to eye. Dorsal and anal fins often slightly falcate; 8 anal fin rays. Lateral line complete, with 36–42 scales.

Habitat: Creeks and rivers with slow to moderately swift current over sand, gravel, or rocks; lakes.

Range: Mackenzie River system, Northwest Territories, south and east through s Canada and the Dakotas to St. Lawrence River system; along Atlantic coast from MA to central GA; Mississippi River valley south to s MO.

Comments: Spottail Shiner is one of the most widespread minnows. It is an important forage fish and is often used for bait, especially for Walleye. This species seems to be most common in large bodies of water.

210 Longnose Shiner
Notropis longirostris

Description: To 2½″ (6.5 cm). Elongate, slender; belly flat. Yellowish above; sides silvery; *fins yellowish.* Snout long, rounded; *eye*

small, directed upward; mouth
subterminal. Dorsal fin origin anterior
to pelvic fin origin; 7 anal fin rays.
Lateral line with 34–37 scales.

Habitat: Pools and runs of creeks and small to
medium rivers over sand.

Range: Upper Altamaha River system, GA;
Apalachicola River drainage, FL and
GA, west along Gulf coast to LA, except
Mobile Bay basin in AL.

Similar Species: Orangefin Shiner *(N. ammophilus)* has
orange fins and snout, and dorsal fin
origin is over pelvic fin origin. Bigmouth
Shiner *(N. dorsalis)* has silvery back and
sides, clear fins, and 8 anal fin rays. Sabine
Shiner *(N. sabinae)* has olive yellow back,
silvery sides, dorsal fin origin anterior
to pelvic fin origin, and 7 anal fin rays.

Comments: This species is one of the most successful
fishes in exploiting the shifting sand
bottoms of coastal plain streams. It is
often seen in large schools moving along
the bottom in search of food.

205 Taillight Shiner
Notropis maculatus

Description: To 3″ (7.5 cm). Elongate, slender. Olive
to yellowish brown above; *dusky lateral
stripe extends from snout to caudal fin,
ending in large black caudal spot;* scales
dark-edged, creating crosshatched
pattern; pelvic, dorsal, and anal fins
with dusky edges; leading edge of dorsal
fin black. Breeding males reddish. Snout
rounded; mouth subterminal. Dorsal
and anal fins falcate; 8 anal fin rays.
Lateral line incomplete, with 34–39 scales.

Habitat: Clear to dark-stained backwaters and
quiet areas of lowland rivers, streams,
and lakes with some aquatic vegetation.

Range: Coastal plain from s NC south to s FL
and west to e TX; Mississippi River
valley from s IL to e TX.

Comments: The life span of Taillight Shiner is 13 to
15 months. It grows rapidly, sometimes
reaching sexual maturity and spawning
at six to nine months.

201 Ozark Minnow
Notropis nubilus

Description: To 3″ (7.5 cm). Slender, slightly compressed. Dusky yellow to olive above, with dark-edged scales; *dark lateral stripe extends from snout to caudal fin, ending in small caudal spot;* yellow to orange below; *outer half of fins clear, bases orange.* Eye large; mouth slightly oblique. *Fins rounded;* dorsal fin origin over pelvic fin insertion; 8 anal fin rays. *13–14 predorsal scales.* Lateral line complete, with 33–38 scales.

Habitat: Clear pools of small to medium streams with steep gradient over sand, gravel, or rocks.

Range: Southern WI and se MN south to n AR and ne OK.

Comments: One of the most common minnows in the Ozark uplands, this species spawns from late April to early July over the gravel nests of chubs. Breeding males maintain a small territory during spawning.

215 Rosyface Shiner
Notropis rubellus

Description: To 3½″ (9 cm). elongate, slender, compressed. Olive to bluish above, with dusky to orange lateral stripe; darker posteriorly; *fins plain; lateral line pores dark-edged.* Breeding males reddish on head and fin bases. Snout sharp; mouth terminal, slightly oblique. *Dorsal fin origin behind pelvic fin insertion; 10–13 anal fin rays.* 17–21 predorsal scales. Lateral line complete, with 36–40 scales.

Habitat: Clear pools and riffles of large creeks to small rivers with moderate current over gravel or rocks.

Range: Southwestern QC west through Great Lakes drainage to s MB and south to n AL, s AR, and e OK.

Similar Species: Tennessee Shiner *(N. leuciodus)* has reddish body, rectangular black caudal spot, and 8–9 anal fin rays.

Comments: This shiner is less abundant in some
streams that have become silty and
turbid. The specific name, *rubellus,*
which means "reddish," describes the
color of breeding males.

207 Weed Shiner
Notropis texanus

Description: To 3" (7.5 cm). Elongate, moderately
compressed. Straw-colored above, with
dusky predorsal stripe; *prominent dark
lateral stripe ends as dark caudal spot;*
area around stripe pale; scales dark-edged;
*fins plain; fourth to seventh rays of anal fin
with dusky edges. Breeding males have rosy
fins.* Head short; snout blunt; mouth
terminal, oblique; eye large, high on
head. *7 anal fin rays.* Lateral line
complete, with 31–37 scales.

Habitat: Slow lowland streams with clear open
waters over sand or gravel; often with
some vegetation.

Range: Winnipeg River, se MB; MN, WI, and s
MI south to n FL and along Gulf coastal
plain from s GA to s TX.

Similar Species: Ironcolor Shiner *(N. chalybaeus)* has 8
anal fin rays with dusky edges. Dusky
Shiner *(N. cummingsae)* has wide black
mid-lateral stripe extending posteriorly
onto caudal fin and 10–11 anal fin rays.
Coastal Shiner *(N. petersoni)* has 7 anal
fin rays with dusky edges.

Comments: Weed Shiner is common in the southern
part of its range, but rare in northern
areas. It was first collected in Texas, thus
the specific name, *texanus.*

208 Mimic Shiner
Notropis volucellus

Description: To 3" (7.5 cm). Slender, slightly
compressed. Back yellowish olive, with
dark-edged scales; *sides silvery, with faint
dusky lateral stripe; dark around anus;* fins
plain. Breeding males lack bright colors;
have small tubercles on head and

pectoral fins. Snout rounded; eye large; mouth small, slightly oblique. Pelvic fin tip not reaching front of anal fin; 8 anal fin rays. Lateral line complete, with 32–39 scales; anterior scales high, narrow.

Habitat: Medium to large streams with clear to turbid waters and moderate current over sand, gravel, or rocks; clear lakes.

Range: Southern QC west to s MB and south to AL and s TX; Atlantic coast streams in se VA and ne NC.

Similar Species: Ghost Shiner *(N. buchanani)* lacks dark-edged scales on back, and pelvic fin tip reaches front of anal fin; occurs in large turbid streams.

Comments: Mimic Shiner is common over much of its range. It is an important forage species for some fishes, especially basses, and is also preyed upon by terns and other birds.

202 Pugnose Minnow
Opsopoeodus emiliae

Description: To 2½" (6.5 cm). Moderately deep, compressed. Back yellowish olive; *sides silvery,* with dark-edged scales; *dusky mid-lateral stripe* extends from snout; fins plain. Breeding males have dusky front and rear dorsal fin rays. *Snout blunt; mouth small, upturned, almost vertical;* barbels occasionally present. *9 dorsal fin rays.* Lateral line complete or incomplete, with 36–40 scales.

Habitat: Clear lakes and streams with slow current and abundant vegetation over organic debris.

Range: Lake St. Clair drainage in ON and MI; along coastal plain from s SC to FL and west to TX; e OH west to se MN and south to s TX.

Comments: The upturned mouth of Pugnose Minnow suggests that it feeds at mid-depths or near the surface. The specific name, *emiliae,* honors Mrs. Emily Hay, whose husband, Oliver P. Hay, discovered and described the species.

133 Sacramento Blackfish
Orthodon microlepidotus

Description: To 18″ (46 cm). Elongate, round, slightly compressed. Back dark olive to dark gray; sides lighter. Young silvery. Head flat above; eye small; *mouth terminal; maxilla not reaching eye.* Fins rather large; *dorsal fin with 9–11 rays,* origin just anterior to pelvic fin insertion; caudal fin deeply forked. Caudal peduncle moderately slender. *Lateral line decurved anteriorly, complete, with 105 or fewer scales.*

Habitat: Lakes, reservoirs, sloughs, and sluggish streams with shallow, warm, usually turbid waters.

Range: Clear Lake, Sacramento and San Joaquin River systems, and Pajaro, Salinas, Russian, and Carmel Rivers, CA; Truckee River, NV.

Comments:  Sacramento Blackfish is unusual among North American cyprinids in being predominantly a filter feeder, with adaptations such as long, slender, fringed gill rakers and long, straight, slender pharyngeal teeth to break up ingested clumps. It grows rapidly to about 14″ (36 cm) by the end of its third year.

195 Suckermouth Minnow
Phenacobius mirabilis

Description: To 4″ (10 cm). Elongate, slightly compressed. Olive above, *with dark-edged scales;* silvery below, with dusky mid-lateral stripe ending in small caudal spot; fins plain. *Snout long, rounded; mouth sucker-like, ventral; no barbels.* Fins rounded; dorsal fin with 8 rays, origin in front of pelvic fin insertion; 7 anal fin rays. 18–22 rows of predorsal scales; *breast unscaled.* Lateral line complete, with 40–50 scales.

Habitat: Riffles of medium to large streams with clear to turbid waters over sand or gravel.

Range: Southern and w OH west to se ND and
se WY, south to nw AL, and southwest
to n TX and e NM; se TX.

Similar Species: Kanawha Minnow (*P. teretulus*) has scales
on breast and lacks caudal spot; occurs
in swift rocky streams.

Comments: This fish has increased its range in areas
where streams have become more turbid.
It feeds primarily on aquatic insects
obtained by rooting in gravel riffles.

193 Stargazing Minnow
Phenacobius uranops

Description: To 4½" (11.5 cm). *Elongate, slender,
almost cylindrical.* Olive above; dusky
mid-lateral stripe ends in small dusky
caudal spot; silvery below; fins plain.
*Snout long, rounded; eye high on head; mouth
sucker-like, ventral; small barbels above
upper lip.* Dorsal fin with 8 rays, origin
over or in front of pelvic fin insertion; 7
anal fin rays. *Breast and midline of belly
unscaled.* Lateral line complete, with
52–61 scales.

Habitat: Riffles of medium to large streams with
swift clear waters over gravel or rocks.

Range: Southwestern VA and s KY south to nw
GA and n AL.

Similar Species: Riffle Minnow (*P. catostomus*) has scales
on belly and 59–69 lateral line scales.
Fatlips Minnow (*P. crassilabrum*) has
long pelvic fin extending to anus.

Comments: Stargazing Minnow is intolerant of
prolonged exposure to silty turbid
waters. Its presence generally indicates a
high-quality stream habitat.

175 Southern Redbelly Dace
Phoxinus erythrogaster

Description: To 3" (7.5 cm). Elongate. Olive above,
with dark spots; *sides with 2 black stripes
separated by cream stripe, lower black stripe
wider, ending in caudal spot*; fins plain,
yellowish. Breeding males yellowish to
bright red on lower sides and belly.

Mouth small, terminal; no barbels. Dorsal fin origin behind pelvic fin insertion; 7–8 anal fin rays. 65–85 scales in lateral series. *Lateral line incomplete or absent.*

Habitat: Springs and small, cool, clear streams with moderate to swift current over gravel or rocks.

Range: Western PA, s MI, and s MN south to n AL and n AR; sporadically in sw MS, ne NM, and e CO.

Similar Species: Northern Redbelly Dace (*P. eos*) reaches length of 2″ (5 cm) and has more upturned mouth; occurs in small streams, lakes, and boggy ponds.

Comments: Southern Redbelly Dace spawns during the spring and early summer in swift riffles over the gravel nests of other minnows. It reaches sexual maturity at one year of age and lives for two to three years.

---

179 Finescale Dace
Phoxinus neogaeus

Description: To 4¼″ (11 cm). Moderately robust. Dark olive above, with black speckles; sides silvery, with dark lateral stripe; caudal spot black. Breeding males reddish on sides. Head short; *mouth terminal, large; no barbels.* Dorsal and anal fins each with 8 rays. Lateral line incomplete, with 63–90 scales.

Habitat: Cool boggy ponds, lakes, creeks, and small rivers with aquatic vegetation.

Range: Northwest Territories south to WY and east through upper Mississippi River, Great Lakes, and Hudson Bay drainages to Atlantic drainages in ME.

Comments: This hardy minnow is used as a bait fish in southeastern Canada.

---

177 Mountain Redbelly Dace
Phoxinus oreas

Description: To 2½″ (6.5 cm). Moderately deep, robust, slightly compressed. Olive above, with large dark spots; light creamy lateral stripe on side; *black stripe extends from upper edge of opercle to anal fin base; narrow black stripe on rear half of body;* silvery below; fins plain, yellowish. Breeding males bright red below. Head small; mouth terminal, oblique. 8 anal fin rays. 65–70 scales in lateral series. *Lateral line incomplete or absent.*

Habitat: Small clear streams with moderate to swift current over sand, gravel, or rocks.

Range: Atlantic coast drainages from n VA to n NC; upper Tennessee River drainage, sw VA.

Similar Species: Blackside Dace *(P. cumberlandensis)* has 1 broad black lateral stripe. Tennessee Dace *(P. tennesseensis)* has smaller dark spots, thin black stripe along sides, and red extending onto caudal fin base.

Comments: Breeding males of this species are among the most colorful fishes found in North America. The specific name, *oreas,* means "mountain nymph."

---

194 Bluntnose Minnow
Pimephales notatus

Description: To 4″ (10 cm). Slender; back broad. Yellowish olive above; sides silvery to bluish; scales dark-edged, creating crosshatched pattern; narrow dark mid-lateral stripe ends in caudal spot; *lining of body cavity black;* dusky blotch on first and second dorsal fin rays and membranes. Snout blunt, rounded; mouth small, slightly oblique. *First dorsal fin ray short, stout, separated by membrane; 7 anal fin rays. Scales crowded on back behind head. Lateral line complete,* with 39–45 scales.

Habitat: Clear to turbid pools of creeks, small rivers, and lakes over sand, gravel, or rocks.

Range: Southwestern QC and NY west to s MB and e Dakotas, and south through s Great Lakes and Mississippi River system to AL and LA.

Similar Species: Bullhead Minnow *(P. vigilax)* has terminal, slightly oblique mouth, black spot at front of dorsal fin and caudal fin base, and silvery body cavity lining.

Comments: Bluntnose Minnow spawns from early spring throughout the summer. The male prepares a nest by clearing a small depression beneath a flat rock. The female then deposits the eggs on the underside of the rock, and the male guards the nest until the young leave.

227 Fathead Minnow
Pimephales promelas

Description: To 4″ (10 cm). Stout, chubby. Back tan to olive; sides silvery to brassy; caudal spot dark. Breeding males grayish black, with pale fleshy pad behind head; pale below dorsal fin. *Snout blunt; mouth nearly terminal, oblique.* Fins low, rounded; *first dorsal fin ray short, stout, separated by membrane;* 7 anal fin rays. *Scales behind head crowded;* 42–48 scales in lateral series. *Lateral line incomplete.*

Habitat: Clear pools of creeks and shallow ponds and lakes over sand, gravel, or mud.

Range: Great Slave Lake, Northwest Territories, southeast to sw QC and south through central and ne U.S. to ne Mexico. Widely introduced.

Similar Species: Slim Minnow (*P. tenellus*) has more elongate body and prominent caudal spot.

Comments: Fathead Minnow, often sold as bait, is easily propagated in small ponds, which may yield 400,000 fish per acre.

229 Woundfin
Plagopterus argentissimus

Description: To 3″ (7.5 cm). Moderately slender. *Back olive to silvery, with minute black dots; silvery below.* Head broad, flat above; *snout slightly overhangs upper lip;* mouth extends to eye; *barbels present.* Pectoral fins long, reaching pelvic fin base; *dorsal fin with 2 spines,* 7 rays, origin posterior to pelvic fin insertion. *Scales deeply embedded.* Lateral line complete, with thickened scales.

Habitat: Warm, turbid, seasonally swift streams over shifting sand.

Range: Virgin River in sw UT, w AZ, and se NV; Moapa River in se NV.

Comments: Woundfin is an endangered species. Water storage and diversion projects eliminated the population in the Gila River drainage in New Mexico and Arizona, and, along with the introduction of exotic fishes, have reduced populations in some regions of the Virgin River. In undisturbed habitat in the Virgin River, Woundfin is often the most common fish.

---

137 Flathead Chub
Platygobio gracilis

Description: To 12½" (32 cm). Slender. Brownish to silvery above; silvery white below, no dark spots or blotches; lower lobe of caudal fin dusky. Head wedge-shaped; snout flat, extending beyond upper lip; eye small; mouth somewhat oblique, extending to eye; *barbels present. Breast scaled. Pectoral and dorsal fins falcate.* Lateral line complete, with 42–59 scales.

Habitat: Large turbid rivers and lower parts of large tributaries with moderate to swift current over sand, gravel, or rocks; rarely lakes.

Range: Great Slave Lake and Mackenzie River drainage, Northwest Territories, south through s AB to s MB and east to Mississippi River in LA; common in Missouri River.

Comments: This is the largest species of its genus. It feeds on terrestrial and aquatic insects, vegetation, and small fishes.

---

230 Splittail
Pogonichthys macrolepidotus

Description: To 14" (36 cm). Elongate, somewhat compressed. Dusky olive gray above; *sides silvery;* paired and caudal fins light reddish

orange. Mouth extends to eye; barbel at
corner of jaw; 14–18 gill rakers. *Anal fin
with 7–9 rays, entirely posterior to dorsal fin
base; caudal fin large, deeply forked,* upper
lobe longer than lower. *Lateral line
decurved,* complete, with 57–66 scales.

Habitat: Lakes and large sluggish rivers; tolerant
of brackish water.

Range: Sacramento and San Joaquin Rivers, CA,
and their delta.

Similar Species: Clear Lake Splittail *(P. ciscoides)* has
terminal mouth with underdeveloped
barbels (sometimes absent), usually
21–23 gill rakers, and more symmetrical
caudal fin; occurs in open lakes.

Comments: Splittail spawns from March to May in
sloughs over submerged vegetation. It
was formerly widespread throughout its
range, but its numbers have declined
because of man-made habitat changes.
There is a limited sport fishery for this
species.

---

228 Bluehead Shiner
Pteronotropis hubbsi

Description: To 2½" (6.5 cm). Elongate, moderately
deep. Back and upper sides dusky; lower
portion of head and body creamy; *broad
dark lateral stripe extends from chin to
caudal fin base, absent from upper lip and
snout.* Breeding males have blue head
and greatly enlarged dorsal and anal fins.
Snout short; mouth terminal. *9–10
dorsal fin rays; 9–11 anal fin rays.* 34–36
scales in lateral series. Lateral line absent
or with 2–9 pored scales.

Habitat: Small to medium, sluggish streams and
oxbow lakes with dark-stained waters
and dense vegetation.

Range: Mississippi River valley from s IL south
to AR, LA, and extreme ne TX.

Similar Species: Bluenose Shiner *(P. welaka)* has 8 dorsal
fin rays and 8 anal fin rays; breeding
males have bright blue nose.

Comments: Bluehead and Bluenose Shiner breeding
males are among the most spectacular
members of the family.

26 Sailfin Shiner
Pteronotropis hypselopterus

Description: To 2½" (6.5 cm). Deep, compressed. Back dark olive, with dark predorsal stripe; upper sides with golden pink stripe; *broad steel blue lateral band;* dorsal fin black, with clear tip; anal fin olive yellow; *caudal fin base dusky olive, with 2 small bright red spots;* outer half of caudal fin olive yellow. Dorsal fin large, slightly rounded, origin far behind pelvic fin insertion; 10–11 anal fin rays. *22–24 predorsal scales.* Lateral line decurved, complete, with 33–38 scales.

Habitat: Creeks with clear to dark-stained waters, slow to moderate current, and abundant vegetation.

Range: SC south to peninsular FL and west to sw AL.

Similar Species: Flagfin Shiner *(P. signipinnis)* has large yellow spots at caudal fin base. Broadstripe Shiner *(P. euryzonus)* has clear "window" at caudal fin base.

Comments: Sailfin and Flagfin Shiners are attractive fishes that are easily kept in aquariums. The genus name *Pteronotropis* is derived from *ptero,* meaning "winged," and *notropis,* meaning "keeled back," describing the deep body and very large dorsal fin of these fishes.

169 Sacramento Pikeminnow
Ptychocheilus grandis

Description: To 3' (91 cm). Elongate, slightly compressed. Back dark olive brown; *sides silvery grayish;* fins plain. Young have dark caudal spot. Breeding males have reddish fins. Head long, flat above; eye small; mouth terminal, large, extending to eye; *no barbels.* Dorsal fin with 8 rays, origin behind pelvic fin insertion; 8 anal fin rays; caudal fin moderately forked. *13–15 rows of scales above lateral line. Lateral line complete, with 73–86 scales.*

Habitat: Clear deep pools of creeks, rivers, and lakes over sand or rocks.

Range: Sacramento, Russian, San Joaquin,
Pajara, and Salinas Rivers and Clear
Lake system, CA.

Similar Species: Northern Pikeminnow *(P. oregonensis)*
has 9 anal fin rays and 67–75 lateral
line scales. Umpqua Pikeminnow
(P. umpquae) has 9 dorsal fin rays,
8 anal fin rays, and 19–24 rows of
scales above lateral line.

Comments: This fish was once considered a
major predator of young salmons;
however, while both fishes may
compete for food and space, most
waters inhabited by Sacramento
Pikeminnow are too warm for young
salmons and trouts.

136 Colorado Pikeminnow
Ptychocheilus lucius

Description: To 5′ (1.5 m). Elongate, somewhat
compressed. Back olive to dusky; *sides
silvery;* fins plain. *Young have wedge-shaped
caudal spot.* Head long, flat; eye small;
mouth slightly oblique, terminal, large,
extending to eye. *Dorsal fin with 9 rays,*
origin behind pelvic fin insertion; 9 anal
fin rays; caudal fin moderately forked.
*Lateral line decurved, complete, with 80–95
scales.*

Habitat: Large streams with turbid to nearly clear
water and moderate current over sand,
gravel, or rocks. Young in backwater
pools along stream edges.

Range: Colorado River basin of sw WY, w CO,
and e UT south to s AZ, se CA, and nw
Mexico.

Comments: Colorado Pikeminnow is the largest
minnow in North America. During the
late 1800s, individuals 5′ (1.5 m) long
and weighing 80 lb (36 kg) were not
unusual. Today, this species has
disappeared from the southern half of its
range and is on the United States
endangered species list. Its decline has
resulted from impoundments, water
diversions, and the introduction of
exotic fishes.

180 Blacknose Dace
Rhinichthys atratulus

ventral view
of head

Description: To 3½″ (9 cm). Elongate, moderately robust. *Yellowish olive to dark brown above, with black blotches;* dusky to dark mid-lateral stripe extends from snout to caudal fin base. *Snout long; mouth small, subterminal, horizontal; barbels present.* Fins small, rounded; dorsal fin with 8 rays, origin behind pelvic fin insertion; 7 anal fin rays; caudal fin shallowly forked. Lateral line complete, with 56–71 scales.

Habitat: Springs and cool clear creeks with moderate to swift current over gravel or rocks.

Range: NS and New England west to MB, e ND, and e NE, and south to nw SC, n GA, and n AL.

Comments: Blacknose Dace spawns during the spring and early summer in riffles over shallow gravel. This dace spawns at two years of age and lives for three or four years. It feeds primarily on aquatic insect larvae.

181 Longnose Dace
Rhinichthys cataractae

ventral view
of head

Description: To 7″ (18 cm). Elongate, moderately stout. Dark olive to dusky above; *wide black mid-lateral band extends from head;* fins plain. Breeding males have rosy fins. Head flat above; *snout long, overhanging mouth;* eye small; *mouth small, ventral; barbels present.* Pelvic fin with axillary scale; dorsal fin with 8 rays, origin behind pelvic fin insertion; 7 anal fin rays. *Caudal peduncle long, deep.* Scales small. Lateral line complete, with 50–76 scales.

Habitat: Clear to turbid streams, usually in swift riffles over gravel or rocks; lakes.

Range: Much of Canada and n U.S. south in Appalachian Mountains to ne GA, and south in Rocky Mountains to Rio Grande, TX and NM.

Similar Species: Umpqua Dace *(R. evermanni)* has narrow caudal peduncle with keel above and below, deeply forked caudal fin, and 57–61 lateral line scales.

Comments: Longnose Dace feeds almost exclusively on aquatic insects that it gleans from its riffle habitat. It is sexually mature at three years of age and lives for up to five years. It may be an important forage fish for Smallmouth Bass, which is found in similar habitat.

196 Loach Minnow
Rhinichthys cobitis

Description: To 2½" (6.5 cm). Elongate; belly flat. Olive above, with dark blotches; *2 large light spots at base of caudal peduncle separated by black caudal spot.* Breeding males reddish on lower part of head and around fin bases. Head small, somewhat depressed; eye high on head; mouth small, terminal; lips fleshy; no barbels. 8 dorsal fin rays; 7 anal fin rays. Lateral line complete, with about 65 scales.

Habitat: Large streams with swift current and algae over gravel riffles.

Range: Restricted to Gila River, sw NM and s AZ, and Colorado River, n Sonora, Mexico.

Similar Species: Leopard Dace *(R. falcatus)* has falcate dorsal fin, deeply forked caudal fin, slender caudal peduncle, and 52–57 lateral line scales; occurs in large streams with slower current.

Comments: Loach Minnow feeds primarily on aquatic insect larvae. It has become less abundant, probably due to deteriorating habitats and the introduction of exotic fishes.

183 Speckled Dace
Rhinichthys osculus

Description: To 4" (10 cm). Elongate, rounded; belly flat. Back dusky to dark olive; *sides grayish green, with dark lateral stripe,* often obscured by dark speckles or blotches;

fins plain. Breeding males reddish on lips and fin bases. *Snout moderately pointed; eye small; mouth small, ventral; barbels present.* 8 dorsal fin rays; 7 anal fin rays; caudal fin moderately forked. *Lateral line complete, with 60–90 scales.*

Habitat: Cool to warm creeks, rivers, and lakes over gravel or rocks; desert springs and their outflow.

Range: West of Continental Divide from s BC to s AZ.

Comments: Speckled Dace is one of the most widespread minnows in western waters. It is highly variable, and there are several subspecies. This dace is an important forage fish in some trout streams and is used for bait.

218 Redside Shiner
Richardsonius balteatus

Description: To 7″ (18 cm). *Deep, compressed.* Back dark olive; upper sides dusky, with narrow unpigmented stripe; mid-lateral stripe dark; fins yellowish. Breeding males reddish below. Mouth oblique, almost reaching front of eye; eye width equal to snout length; no barbels. *Dorsal fin with 9 rays, origin just in front of anal fin origin; 10–22 anal fin rays.* Lateral line complete, with 55–67 scales.

Habitat: Sluggish creeks, rivers, and ditches; ponds and lakes in deep water or shallow weedy areas.

Range: Northern BC and w AB south to OR, ne NV, and w UT. Introduced in Colorado River drainage from w WY to nw AZ.

Similar Species: Lahontan Redside (*R. egregius*) has slender body and 8–9 anal fin rays; occurs in streams and lakes. Peamouth (*Mylocheilus caurinus*) has small mouth with barbel at corner of jaw, deeply forked caudal fin, well-developed axillary scales on pelvic fin, and complete lateral line with 68–79 scales; occurs in lakes, deep sluggish rivers, and brackish waters at mouths of rivers.

Comments: Increasing Redside Shiner populations
have overcrowded some lakes, reducing
trout populations. Costly efforts to
eradicate them have failed.

150 Creek Chub
Semotilus atromaculatus

Description: To 12″ (30 cm); ¾ lb (300 g). Chubby.
Back olive; sides silvery, with greenish-
purple sheen; dusky lateral stripe ends
in caudal spot; edge of gill opening
dusky; *dark spot at anterior base of dorsal
fin.* Head large; *mouth large; small barbel
on upper lip near corner of jaw.* Fins
rounded; *dorsal fin with 8 rays,* origin
behind pelvic fin insertion. Scales on
anterior portion of body crowded.
Lateral line complete, with 52–69 scales.

Habitat: Small, clear to turbid streams and lakes
over sand, gravel, or rocks.

Range: Eastern North America, except
peninsular FL, west to MB, e MT, WY,
and ne NM.

Similar Species: Sandhills Chub *(S. lumbee)* has 9
dorsal fin rays and lacks dark spot at
anterior base of dorsal fin. Dixie Chub
(S. thoreauianus) has fewer than 52
lateral line scales; breeding males have
yellow fins.

Comments: This fish is often used for bait, and is
frequently caught by fly-fishing anglers.

Creek Chub spawns in the spring over a
nest excavated by the male. The female
lays the eggs in the depression, and then
the eggs are covered with gravel from
the downstream side of the nest, which
is abandoned after spawning.

134 Fallfish
Semotilus corporalis

Description: To 20″ (51 cm). Elongate, moderately
compressed. Back olive brown; *sides
silvery;* black bar behind opercle. Dorsal
fin with 8 rays, origin over pelvic fin
insertion. Lateral line with 43–50 scales.

Habitat: Clear streams with slow to moderate
           current over gravel; lakes.

Range: NB, s QC, and e ON south along
           Atlantic coast to VA.

Comments: Fallfish spawns in the spring over
           a mound of rocks constructed by
           the male, which carries the stones
           in its mouth. This species is the
           largest native minnow in eastern
           North America.

129 Leatherside Chub
Snyderichthys copei

Description: To 6″ (15 cm). Elongate, slender,
              slightly compressed. *Back and sides
              silvery blue, with black speckles.* Breeding
              males red on upper edge of gill opening
              and fin bases. Head short; eye large;
              mouth small; no barbels. Dorsal and
              anal fins each with 8 rays. *Scales small,
              leather-like. Lateral line with 68–84 scales.*

Habitat: Pools of cool to cold creeks and rivers
              with turbid to muddy waters and
              vegetation over sand, rubble, or
              boulders.

Range: Snake River system in se ID, w WY, ne
              NV, ne UT; Bonneville Basin, UT.
              Introduced in Colorado River system.

Similar Species: Utah Chub *(Gila atraria)* has 9 dorsal
                  fin rays, 8 anal fin rays, and 45–65
                  lateral line scales; breeding males have
                  yellowish sides of head and fin bases.

Comments: Many of the clear, cool to cold creeks
              preferred by Leatherside Chub have been
              drastically altered by water diversions
              and development. This species has been
              greatly reduced in abundance and is
              threatened in much of its native habitat.

SUCKERS
Family Catostomidae

14 genera and 73 species worldwide; 13
genera and 63 species in North America, plus 6 species in
Mexico. Suckers are small to moderately large, bottom-
dwelling freshwater fishes that inhabit rivers, creeks, and

lakes. They usually have ventral mouths with thick lips and jaws without teeth. In most species the mouth can be extended ventrally during feeding. They lack adipose fins and barbels. There are at least 10 rays in the dorsal fin, and the short anal fin is placed well back on the body. Members of the genus *Catostomus,* which occur mainly in the western United States in somewhat restricted ranges, can be distinguished by a cylindrical body with a flat or rounded head and an inferior horizontal mouth with thick fleshy lips that are either plicate or have papillae. *Catostomus* suckers have fewer than 20 dorsal fin rays, and more than 55 scales in the lateral line.

157 Quillback
Carpiodes cyprinus

Description: To 24″ (61 cm); 12 lb (5.4 kg). Deep, compressed; *back highly arched.* Olive to brownish; *sides silvery; fins plain; median fins dusky, paired fins clear.* Head small; snout blunt; mouth ventral, narrow, horizontal; lips plicate; tip of lower lip anterior to nostril. *Dorsal fin with 27–30 rays, anterior rays long,* longest ray almost as long as fin base; usually 7 anal fin rays; caudal fin forked, with pointed tips. Lateral line straight, complete, with 37–41 scales.

Habitat: Large creeks, rivers, and lakes with clear to turbid waters over soft or firm bottoms.

Range: Southwestern QC and s ON west to s AB; Atlantic coast drainages from ne PA to SC; Mississippi River system; Gulf coast drainages from w FL to LA.

Similar Species: River Carpsucker *(C. carpio)* has nipple-like structure at middle of lower lip and dorsal fin with anterior rays about half as long as fin base. Highfin Carpsucker *(C. velifer)* has nipple-like structure on lower lip, blunter snout, and dorsal fin with anterior rays as long as fin base.

Comments: Quillback and other carpsuckers are rarely sought by anglers, but are occasionally taken by snag-fishing. They are caught in gill nets and sold commercially; as a group, however, they are not generally considered to be important as food fishes.

143 White Sucker
Catostomus commersonnii

Description: To 24″ (61 cm). Elongate, cylindrical.
Back dusky olive; sides greenish yellow,
with brassy luster; fins plain. Young
mottled on sides. Head flat above; snout
blunt; mouth large, ventral; *lips thick,
with many papillae.* Pelvic fin with
axillary scale; *10–13 dorsal fin rays; 6–8
anal fin rays.* Caudal peduncle moderately
slender. *Anterior scales crowded;* 8–10
rows of scales above lateral line. *Lateral
line complete, with 55–74 scales.*

Habitat: Cool clear streams and lakes over sand,
gravel, or rocks.

Range: Canada and n U.S. east of Continental
Divide to nw SC, n AL, n AR, and n
NM.

Similar Species: Longnose Sucker *(C. catostomus)* has long
fleshy snout extending beyond mouth
and 91–120 lateral line scales.

Comments: White Sucker is the most common
Catostomus sucker in North America. It
is not sought by anglers, but some are
taken during spawning runs in large lift
nets and in commercial fisheries.

149 Flannelmouth Sucker
Catostomus latipinnis

Description: To 30″ (76 cm). Elongate, slender. Back
dusky olive green; sides lighter; belly
yellowish; *fins yellowish orange to red.*
Head short; *lips thick; upper lip with 5–8
rows of papillae.* 11–13 dorsal fin rays; 7
anal fin rays. Caudal peduncle narrow.
Scales small. Lateral line with 95–110 scales.

lips

Habitat: Pools and swift runs of large creeks
to rivers over sand, cobble, or boulders.

Range: Colorado River system in sw WY,
w CO, e UT, se NV, se CA, and AZ.

Similar Species: Mountain Sucker *(C. platyrhynchus)*
reaches length of 9¾″ (25 cm), and has
dark greenish-black lateral band, 10
dorsal fin rays, and 75–92 lateral line
scales; occurs in cool clear creeks and
small rivers.

Comments: Flannelmouth Sucker is the most common and widespread sucker in the Colorado River system.

---

147 Blue Sucker
Cycleptus elongatus

Description: To 3'4" (1 m); 16 lb (7.3 kg). Elongate, slightly compressed. Back and fins bluish black; sides light bluish gray; belly white. Breeding males dark, with tubercles on head, body, and fins. *Snout blunt, extends beyond mouth;* lips with low blunt papillae. *Dorsal fin long, falcate anteriorly, with 28–37 rays; 7–8 anal fin rays;* caudal fin deeply forked. Caudal peduncle long, *with 19–20 rows of scales. Lateral line with 53–58 scales.*

Habitat: Deep, moderately swift channels in rivers over firm bottoms; some populations survive in reservoirs.

Range: Mississippi River system from PA, MN, and MT south to LA; AL to NM; ne Mexico.

Similar Species: Southeastern Blue Sucker (*C. meridionalis*) has 16–17 caudal peduncle scales and 49–53 lateral line scales.

Comments: Blue Sucker and Southeastern Blue Sucker are most closely related to Chinese Sucker (*Myxocyprinus asiaticus*), which is known only from the Yangtze and Huang Ho River basins in eastern China.

---

151 Creek Chubsucker
Erimyzon oblongus

Description: To 11" (28 cm). Robust, chubby. Olive bronze above, with dark-edged scales creating crosshatched pattern; 5–8 saddles across back, ending in dark mid-lateral blotches; creamy below; dorsal and caudal fins dusky olive. Mouth small, subterminal; lower lip plicate, with halves meeting to form acute V-shaped angle. *Dorsal fin with 9–12 rays, edge rounded; anal fin of breeding males*

2-lobed. Caudal peduncle narrow. *No lateral line; 39–41 scales in lateral series.*

Habitat: Streams and small rivers with slow current and vegetation over soft bottoms.

Range: Southern ME to NY and south along Atlantic coastal plain to central GA; w OH west to s WI and south to w FL and e TX.

Similar Species: Lake Chubsucker *(E. sucetta)* has rounded dorsal fin and 34–38 scales in lateral series. Sharpfin Chubsucker *(E. tenuis)* has straight-edged, sharply pointed dorsal fin; anal fin not 2-lobed in breeding males.

Comments: Although Creek Chubsucker is widely distributed, it is not common in most areas. It appears to be intolerant of silty streams.

148 Northern Hog Sucker
Hypentelium nigricans

snout

Description: To 24″ (61 cm). Moderately elongate, heavy anteriorly, tapering posteriorly. Back dark olive to reddish brown, mottled with darker brown; *3–4 dark saddles across back, extending obliquely forward onto sides;* sides greenish yellow; belly white; fins olive. *Head large, concave between eyes;* snout long, blunt; mouth ventral; lips large, thick, fleshy, with coarse papillae. *11 dorsal fin rays. Lateral line complete, with 44–54 scales.*

Habitat: Riffles and pools below riffles of shallow clear streams with moderate to swift current over gravel or rocks.

Range: Southeastern ON and NY west to MN and south to e LA and s MS; north-central NC and ne GA west to ne OK.

Similar Species: Alabama Hog Sucker *(H. etowanum)* has 10 dorsal fin rays, and area between eyes is not concave. Roanoke Hog Sucker *(H. roanokense)* has light streaks along upper sides and usually 40–45 lateral line scales.

Comments: Northern, Alabama, and Roanoke Hog Suckers are common but intolerant of turbid silty streams. They feed on aquatic invertebrates and minute plants that they scrape off small rocks or find under gravel.

168 Smallmouth Buffalo
Ictiobus bubalus

Description: To 3' (91 cm); 51 lb (23 kg). Deep, moderately compressed; *back arched, often with anterior ridge.* Dark olive to gray; *sides grayish to bronze; pelvic fins grayish black,* other fins dusky. Head small; snout bluntly rounded; *mouth small, horizontal, ventral, below level of eye;* lips thick, plicate. 24–31 dorsal fin rays, anterior rays nearly half as long as fin base; 8–9 anal fin rays. Lateral line straight, with 35–39 scales.

Habitat: Rivers with clear to slightly turbid water and moderate current; lakes and reservoirs.

Range: Mississippi River system and Gulf coast drainages from AL west to Rio Grande in TX, NM, and ne Mexico.

Similar Species: Bigmouth Buffalo *(I. cyprinellus)* has terminal mouth and tip of upper lip above lower edge of eye; occurs in sluggish rivers, backwaters, and lakes. Black Buffalo *(I. niger)* has subterminal, slightly oblique mouth, and lacks ridge on arched back.

Comments: Buffalo fishes are not popular for sport, but are fished commercially in the Mississippi River and some large lakes. The collective common name refers to their large size and humped back.

144 Spotted Sucker
Minytrema melanops

Description: To 20" (51 cm). Elongate, slightly compressed. Back olive, usually with dark blotch near dorsal fin base; sides and belly silvery; *black-spotted scales on sides form horizontal stripes;* median fins light olive. Lips ridged, thin; posterior edge of lower lip V-shaped. Dorsal fin short, posterior edge concave, usually with 11–12 rays; caudal fin deeply forked. *No lateral line; 42–47 scales in lateral series.*

Habitat: Deep clear pools of lowland streams over firm bottoms; overflow ponds, sloughs, lakes, and reservoirs.

Range: Atlantic coast drainages from NC south to Gulf coast drainages of n and w FL, and west to central TX; s Great Lakes drainage; Mississippi River system from MN to LA.

Similar Species: Redhorses (genus *Moxostoma*) have lateral line and scales on sides usually without spots.

Comments: Spotted Sucker makes spawning runs up rivers and small streams in early spring, and spawns from March to May in swift shallow riffles. It is intolerant of silty turbid water.

---

154 Silver Redhorse
Moxostoma anisurum

Description: To 25″ (64 cm). Moderately stout, compressed. Back greenish brown; sides brassy yellowish to silvery; paired and anal fins orange to red; *dorsal and caudal fins gray.* Head large; *lips plicate, broken into low papillae; lobes of lower lip meet at acute angle.* 14–17 (usually 14–15) dorsal fin rays. 12 rows of scales on caudal peduncle. Lateral line with 39–43 scales.

Habitat: Pools or slow current of large creeks to rivers over soft mud to rock bottoms.

Range: Hudson Bay drainage, s Canada; Great Lakes and St. Lawrence River drainages; upper Mississippi River system; Atlantic coast drainages from s VA to central GA.

Similar Species: Shorthead Redhorse *(M. macrolepidotum)* has short head (about 20 percent of length from tip of snout to base of caudal fin), posterior edge of lower lips forming straight line, 12–13 dorsal fin rays, and red caudal fin; occurs in large creeks and rivers with moderate to swift current over gravel or rocks.

Comments: In some areas in the spring, just prior to spawning runs, Silver Redhorse is taken by anglers using worms as bait.

155 River Redhorse
Moxostoma carinatum

Description: To 30″ (76 cm); 14 lb (6.4 kg). Moderately robust, slightly compressed. Back olive to dusky; *sides silvery;* fins plain; *median fins reddish olive; paired fins pale red.* Head large; snout moderately long, blunt, slightly overhanging mouth; eye small; mouth ventral; *lips fleshy, plicate; rear edge of lower lip almost straight.* 12–13 dorsal fin rays; anal fin long, pointed, with 7–9 rays. Lateral line complete, with 41–47 scales.

Habitat: Clear waters of large creeks and rivers with moderate to swift current over gravel or rocks.

Range: St. Lawrence River and Great Lakes drainages in s QC, se ON, OH, and MI; Mississippi River system; Gulf coast drainages in w FL, AL, and MS.

Similar Species: Robust Redhorse *(M. robustum)* is darker and deeper bodied.

Comments: River Redhorse feeds on aquatic insects, crustaceans, and small mollusks. It is occasionally caught by snag-fishing in shallow gravel shoals during spring spawning runs. Its numbers have declined in some areas due to siltation and pollution.

153 Golden Redhorse
Moxostoma erythrurum

Description: To 24″ (61 cm); 4½ lb (2 kg). Moderately stout, slightly compressed. Back olive; *sides golden to bronze;* fins plain; *dorsal and caudal fins grayish olive, other fins pale orange.* Breeding males have tubercles on head. Head moderately large; snout blunt; mouth large, ventral; lips thick, fleshy, plicate;

rear edge of lower lip broadly V-*shaped.* 9 pelvic fin rays; 12–14 dorsal fin rays. *Lateral line complete, with 39–42 scales.*

Habitat: Pools of creeks and rivers with slow to moderate current and clear to slightly turbid waters over sand or gravel.

Range: Southeastern ON and w NY west to MN and e ND, and south to ne TX; Atlantic coast drainages from MD to NC; s MS; Mobile Bay drainage of nw GA and AL.

Similar Species: Black Redhorse *(M. duquesnii)* has slender body, 10 pelvic fin rays, and 44–47 lateral line scales; breeding males lack tubercles on head.

Comments: Golden Redhorse is the most common of the 18 species of *Moxostoma* restricted to eastern North America. It is of little importance as either a sport or food fish.

---

152 Blacktail Redhorse
Moxostoma poecilurum

Description: To 18″ (46 cm). Elongate, moderately compressed. Back yellowish olive to dusky; sides silvery to golden; *scales dark-edged, forming vague alternating dark and light stripes;* fins plain, faint orange; *lower lobe of caudal fin dusky to black, with white lower edge.* Head short; snout blunt; mouth ventral; lips plicate; rear edge of lower lip forms broad angle. *13 dorsal fin rays.* Caudal peduncle slender. Lateral line complete, with 39–45 scales.

Habitat: Creeks and rivers with moderate current over sand or gravel; occasionally reservoirs.

Range: Western TN, w GA, AL, and Gulf coast drainages from w FL to e TX.

Similar Species: Silver Redhorse *(M. anisurum)* has grooves in lower lip with transverse creases forming low papillae, 14–17 (usually 14–15) dorsal fin rays, and 12 rows of scales on caudal peduncle.

Comments: Blacktail Redhorse ascends small streams during April and May and spawns over shallow gravel shoals with swift current.

142 Striped Jumprock
Scartomyzon rupiscartes

snout

Description: To 10″ (25 cm). Elongate. Back olive to yellowish brown; *sides yellowish to silvery, with faint striped pattern; caudal fin yellowish.* Young have dark blotches. *Head long, wider than deep,* flat to slightly convex between eyes; snout blunt; mouth wide; lips plicate, with transverse creases. Pelvic, pectoral, and anal fins rounded; 9 pelvic fin rays; 7 anal fin rays; *caudal fin lobes rounded. Lateral line complete, with 45–50 scales.*

Habitat: Creeks with moderate to swift riffles over sand, gravel, or rocks.

Range: Santee River drainage, sw NC, southwest to Chattahoochee River drainage, ne GA.

Similar Species: Black Jumprock *(S. cervinum)* has narrow mouth, black-tipped dorsal and caudal fins, and 39–44 lateral line scales. Greater Jumprock *(S. lachneri)* has 12 dorsal fin rays and caudal fin with pointed lobes and white lower edge.

Comments: The specific name, *rupiscartes,* means "rock jumper" and refers to Striped Jumprock's habit of darting around rocks in the swift riffles where it lives.

145 Torrent Sucker
Thoburnia rhothoeca

Description: To 7½″ (19 cm). Elongate, torpedo-shaped. Top of head and back yellowish tan to olive; *mid-lateral stripe orange to reddish orange, 2 scales wide; 2 large pale areas at base of caudal fin. Lobes of lower lip triangular.* Pectoral fin large; 10 dorsal fin rays; 7 anal fin rays. Caudal peduncle deep. Lateral line complete, with 43–51 scales.

Habitat: Cold to warm waters of creeks and small rivers with moderate to very swift riffles and runs.

Range: Central VA and e WV.

Similar Species: Rustyside Sucker *(T. hamiltoni)* has lower lip with larger, broadly rounded lobes. Blackfin Sucker *(T. atripinnis)* has large blotch on outer half of first through fifth dorsal fin rays; occurs in slow or gently flowing pools of medium to large creeks.

Comments: Torrent Sucker is the smallest species in the family. Its small size, torpedo-shaped body, poorly developed swim bladder, and large expansive pectoral fins are all adaptations allowing it to thrive in swift shallow riffles of high-gradient streams.

146 Razorback Sucker
Xyrauchen texanus

Description: To 3' (91 cm). Deep; *back with high sharp ridge extending from head to dorsal fin.* Dark olive to brownish black above; sides lighter; belly yellowish orange. Breeding males grayish black, with bright orange belly. Head long, rounded; snout long, fleshy; mouth ventral, wide; lobes of lower lip meet at V-shaped angle. *Dorsal fin low, with 12–15 rays, origin in front of pelvic fin insertion.* Lateral line almost straight, complete, with 68–87 scales.

Habitat: Large rivers with deep, clear to turbid water over mud, sand, or gravel; occasionally reservoirs.

Range: Colorado River system from sw WY to s AZ and se CA.

Comments: Razorback Sucker, once common, is now an endangered species. Its numbers have declined throughout its range, and it has disappeared in some areas due to impoundments, water diversions, and the introduction of exotic fishes.

Order Characiformes

This order contains 10 families, only one of which occurs in North America. These fishes are found from the southwestern United States south to South America and in Africa. Most are small and colorful, and many are utilized in the aquarium fish trade. Other species are important food fishes.

CHARACINS
Family Characidae

About 170 genera and 900 species worldwide; 1 species in North America north of Mexico. Members of this large family, one of the two families of freshwater fishes that occur in South America and Africa, are found from Texas and New Mexico south through Central and South America and in Africa. The family includes herbivorous fishes as well as the carnivorous piranhas (genus *Serrasalmus*). Most characins have jaws with teeth and an adipose fin, and all lack barbels.

173 Mexican Tetra
Astyanax mexicanus

Description: To 5″ (12.5 cm). Moderately deep, compressed. Back olive; sides silvery to brassy; lateral stripe dusky, larger and more intense near caudal fin base, narrowing on caudal fin; fins yellowish to pale reddish; front tip of anal fin white, middle rays dusky to black. Head narrow, short; mouth terminal, with *multicuspid teeth. Anal fin long, with 21–25 rays; adipose fin present.* Caudal peduncle short, deep. Lateral line almost straight, complete, with 35–40 scales.

Habitat: Rivers, creeks, and springs with slow to moderate current.

Range: Rio Grande and Pecos and Nueces Rivers from TX and NM south to Mexico and Panama. Introduced outside native range in TX and NM, and in OH, LA, OK, AZ, and CA.

Comments: Mexican Tetra is the northernmost representative of the family. It has been kept by aquarists and used for bait; it should not be released outside its natural range, because it may cause damage to native fishes if it becomes established. It is sensitive to temperature and is not likely to survive in the cooler areas of the United States north of central New Mexico and Texas.

Order Siluriformes

This large order contains 34 families. In North America there are two native families, plus one in Mexico; there are three introduced families of freshwater catfishes in the United States. These marine and freshwater catfishes are distributed in temperate and tropical waters worldwide. They are closely related to the Cypriniformes; members of both groups have an apparatus that connects the swim bladder with the inner ear, providing an acute sense of hearing. Many species are commercially important as food, sport, and aquarium fishes.

NORTH AMERICAN CATFISHES
Family Ictaluridae

6 genera and 39 species confined to fresh waters of North America, plus 1 genus with 7 species in Mexico. These catfishes are found east of the Rocky Mountains, from southern Canada south to Guatemala. They range in length from 2" (5 cm) to more than 5' (1.5 m). They have four pairs of barbels, an adipose fin, and each dorsal and pectoral fin has a single spine. In some species the pectoral fin spines have serrations. The madtoms (genus *Noturus*) are equipped with a venom gland at the base of the pectoral fin spine, which is often grooved, enabling them to inflict a painful sting. Species in the genera *Ameiurus, Ictalurus,* and *Pylodictus* are important sport and food fishes.

55, 56 Snail Bullhead
Ameiurus brunneus

Description: To 12½" (32 cm). Robust, heavy anteriorly. Back and sides pale olive brown to grayish brown, not mottled; *fins dark-edged; dark blotch at dorsal fin base.* Head flat; *14–17 gill rakers on first arch.* Pectoral fin spine without strong serrations; *anal fin short, with 17–20 rays; caudal fin emarginate.*

dorsal fin

Habitat: Flowing pools and riffles of medium to large creeks and rivers.

Range: Roanoke River drainage, VA, south to St. Johns River, FL; Apalachicola River basin in AL, FL, and GA.

Similar Species: Flat Bullhead *(A. platycephalus)* has 11–13 gill rakers on first arch and

21–24 anal fin rays. Spotted Bullhead (*A. serracanthus*) has dark body with numerous light round spots and strong serrations on pectoral fin spine.

Comments: Snail Bullhead is a good food fish.

---

60 White Catfish
Ameiurus catus

Description: To 24″ (62 cm); 19 lb (8.6 kg). Moderately robust. Back dark bluish gray; sides lighter, *no scattered dark spots;* chin barbels yellowish to white; *no dark blotch at dorsal fin base; adipose fin dusky to black.* Posterior edge of pectoral fin spine without strong serrations; *anal fin rounded, with 22–25 rays; caudal fin moderately forked.*

Habitat: Pools or slow current of medium to large creeks and rivers, ponds, and reservoirs; may enter brackish water.

Range: Atlantic coast drainages from NY to FL and west into Gulf coast drainages of se AL and w FL. Widely introduced in Mississippi River basin and states on U.S. Pacific coast.

Comments: White Catfish is an important sport fish throughout its native range and where introduced.

---

57 Black Bullhead
Ameiurus melas

Description: To 24″ (62 cm); 8 lb (3.6 kg). Heavy anteriorly. Back olive to black; sides yellowish olive to black, *not mottled;* belly yellowish; *chin barbels grayish black or spotted; fins dusky to black, membranes darker than rays;* pale bar at caudal fin base. Head large, rounded above; eye small; mouth terminal, short, wide; 16–18 gill rakers on first arch. *Pectoral fin spine rough, without strong serrations; anal fin edge rounded, with 20–24 rays;* adipose fin present; *caudal fin slightly notched, not deeply forked.* Caudal peduncle short, moderately deep.

Habitat: Low-gradient sections of streams, backwaters, lakes, and reservoirs; frequently over silty soft mud.

Range: Southeastern ON west to s SK and south throughout central U.S. Widely introduced outside native range.

Comments: Black Bullhead appears to be more tolerant of turbid, silty, polluted waters than other bullheads. It feeds on a variety of plant and animal material taken off the bottom.

59 Yellow Bullhead
Ameiurus natalis

Description: To 18″ (46 cm); 4 lb (1.9 kg). Robust, heavy. Back dark olive brown; sides yellowish brown, *not mottled;* belly yellowish; *chin barbels yellow to white; fins dusky to olive; anal and caudal fins black-edged.* Head thick, long, rounded above; eye small; mouth terminal. Posterior edge of pectoral fin spine with serrations; *24–28 anal fin rays;* adipose fin present; caudal fin truncate to rounded.

Habitat: Pools, backwaters, and sometimes slow riffles of sluggish streams, ponds, and lakes; usually with heavy vegetation.

Range: Southeastern ON west to s ND and south throughout central and e U.S. Widely introduced outside native range.

Comments: Yellow Bullhead is a good sport and food fish. It is active at night, relying on its barbels and sense of smell to search out food along the bottom.

58 Brown Bullhead
Ameiurus nebulosus

Description: To 19″ (48 cm); 6 lb (2.7 kg). Robust, heavy, rounded anteriorly. Back olive to black; sides lighter, *strongly mottled with brownish blotches;* belly whitish; *chin barbels dusky or black;* fins dusky to black. Young are drab gray to black on sides, without blotches. Mouth terminal; upper jaw slightly overhangs lower; *barbels on upper jaw long, extending beyond pectoral fin base;* 12–15 gill rakers. *Pectoral fin spine with strong serrations on rear edge;* 20–24 anal fin rays; adipose fin present; caudal fin emarginate.

Habitat: Clear deep pools with submerged vegetation.

Range: NS west to se SK, south to n LA, and east to Atlantic coast. Widely introduced in w U.S.

Comments: Brown Bullhead appears to be intolerant of silty polluted waters. It has been raised commercially and widely stocked in ponds and lakes.

63 Blue Catfish
Ictalurus furcatus

Description: To 5'5" (1.7 m); 111 lb (50 kg). Moderately stout, compressed posteriorly. *Head and body blue to slate gray above;* sides lighter; belly white. Head small, wedge-shaped; eye small, below midline of head; mouth small, upper jaw overhangs lower. *Anal fin with 30–36 rays, outer edge straight;* posterior edge of adipose fin free; *caudal fin deeply forked.*

Habitat: Large creeks and rivers with moderate to swift current over rock, gravel, or clean sand bottoms.

Range: Mississippi River system from WV west to SD and south to Gulf coast; AL and GA west to TX and Mexico. Introduced in 14 states outside native range.

Similar Species: White Catfish (*Ameiurus catus*) has rounded anal fins with 22–25 rays and shallowly forked caudal fin.

Comments: Its large size and firm, well-flavored flesh make this species a highly valued sport and commercial food fish. It is one of the largest North American freshwater fishes. The decline in abundance of Blue Catfish has been attributed to overfishing and dams, which destroy its habitat and limit its migration.

61 Channel Catfish
Ictalurus punctatus

Description:	To 3′11″ (1.2 m); 58 lb (26 kg). Slender. Back bluish gray; *sides light blue to silvery, with scattered dark olive to black spots;* belly white; fins olive to dusky. Head wide, flat to slightly rounded above; eye large, above midline of head; upper jaw overhangs lower. *Anal fin with 24–31 rays, outer edge rounded;* adipose fin present; *caudal fin deeply forked.*
Habitat:	Large creeks and rivers with slow to moderate current over sand, gravel, or rocks; ponds, lakes, and reservoirs.
Range:	Southern QC west to s AB and south throughout central and east-central U.S. Widely introduced.
Similar Species:	Headwater Catfish *(I. lupus)* has deeper caudal peduncle, 20–26 anal fin rays, and less deeply forked caudal fin; occurs in pools and runs of springs, creeks, and small rivers over sand or rocks. Yaqui Catfish *(I. pricei)* has shorter pectoral and dorsal fin spines; occurs in pools of small rivers over sand or rocks.
Comments:	Channel Catfish is a very popular sport and food fish. It is a principal catfish raised in aquaculture.

52 Mountain Madtom
Noturus eleutherus

Description:	To 5″ (12.5 cm). Moderately robust. Brown to yellowish brown, mottled; *dark blotch near middle of adipose fin, confined to basal half; dark brown bar at caudal fin base.* Head flat. *Pectoral fin spine with 6–9 large barbs,* 1 venom gland at base; 12–16 anal fin rays; caudal fin straight-edged.
Habitat:	Sediment-free riffles, runs, and shoals of large creeks and rivers; often associated with rooted vegetation.
Range:	Ohio River basin from w PA west to IL and south to n AL; se MO, s AR, and se OK.

Similar Species: Frecklebelly Madtom *(N. munitus)* has dark blotch near middle of adipose fin extending to edge and usually dark speckles on belly. Northern Madtom *(N. stigmosus)* has dark blotch near middle of adipose fin extending into upper half and almost to edge.

Comments: This species spawns in early to mid-summer. The female deposits about 90 eggs in a nest, where they are fertilized by the male. The eggs are guarded by the male until they hatch. The nest is usually under a flat rock in moderate current. This behavior is typical of most madtom species.

53 Slender Madtom
Noturus exilis

Description: To 6" (15 cm). Slender. Back grayish to

toothband

mouth

dark olive, *with light yellow blotch under last 3 rays of dorsal fin;* sides light gray to yellow; belly grayish white; *median fins olive to gray, black-edged. Head very depressed; mouth usually terminal; toothband on upper jaw without backward projections.* Pectoral fin with distinct serrations on posterior edge of spine, venom gland at base, 8–10 rays; *adipose fin long, with low keel-like ridge;* caudal fin truncate, slightly rounded.

Habitat: Riffles of clear creeks and small rivers with moderate to swift current.

Range: Central Mississippi River system from w IN, s WI, and s MN south to n AL, central AR, and e OK.

Similar Species: Margined Madtom *(N. insignis)* has dusky-edged median fins and upper jaw overhangs lower.

Comments: Slender Madtom is generally intolerant of silty turbid streams. Like the other madtom species, this fish is active at night, hiding under rocks or debris during the day.

49 Stonecat
Noturus flavus

toothband

mouth

Description: To 12″ (30 cm). Moderately elongate. *Coloration uniform;* back slate gray to olive green; sides yellowish olive; *belly, lower lip, and chin whitish;* yellowish blotch at end of dorsal fin base; caudal fin with clear edge. Head depressed; eye small; upper jaw overhangs lower; *toothband on upper jaw with backward projections.* Pectoral fin with a few barbs on anterior edge of spine near tip, venom gland at base, 9–11 rays; adipose fin continuous with caudal fin; *caudal fin truncate.*

Habitat: Riffles of medium to large streams over gravel or rocks; on shoals of lakes.

Range: St. Lawrence River drainage and n NY west to s AB and south to n AL, w TN, and e AR.

Similar Species: Orangefin Madtom *(N. gilberti)* has median fins with broad light borders; occurs in clear streams over rocks.

Comments: Stonecat is secretive, emerging from its cover at night to feed on aquatic insects and crustaceans. This is the largest species of madtom.

54 Tadpole Madtom
Noturus gyrinus

Description: To 5″ (12.5 cm). *Tadpole-shaped,* robust anteriorly, strongly compressed posteriorly. Back golden brown to olive gray; sides gray, with narrow dark mid-lateral stripe branching out to outline muscle segments; belly yellowish; median fins olive. Head deep, rounded above; eye small; *mouth terminal. Pectoral fin spine without serrations,* venom gland at base; *adipose fin continuous with caudal fin; caudal fin broad, rounded.*

Habitat: Low-gradient, quiet, slow streams, sloughs, ponds, and lakes with vegetation over mud.

Range: Southwestern QC west to se MB and south to s FL and s TX; absent from

Appalachian highlands. Introduced in parts of ID, OR, WA, and several New England states.

Comments: Tadpole Madtom is the most widespread species in the genus. Like most madtoms, it is secretive and frequently hides in empty cans and bottles.

---

50 Speckled Madtom
Noturus leptacanthus

Description: To 3½" (9 cm). Slender. Back dark brown to russet; sides brownish yellow; belly whitish; *back, sides, and median fins with scattered grayish-black blotches.* Head narrow; eye small; upper jaw overhangs lower. *Pectoral fin spine without serrations,* venom gland at base; adipose fin continuous with caudal fin; caudal fin truncate.

Habitat: Creeks with moderate current over sand or gravel; often with vegetation or debris.

Range: Northwestern SC, se TN, and ne MS south to n FL and west to e LA.

Similar Species: Black Madtom *(N. funebris)* is dark gray to black without dark blotches. Brown Madtom *(N. phaeus)* is dark brown and has strong serrations on rear edge of pectoral fin spine. Ouachita Madtom *(N. lachneri)* lacks scattered grayish-black blotches on back, sides, and median fins; occurs in pools and runs of creeks and small rivers over rocks.

Comments: Speckled Madtom frequently nests in old cans and bottles, in which females often lay 15 to 30 large eggs during July and August. The nest is guarded by the male until the eggs hatch and the young leave.

---

51 Brindled Madtom
Noturus miurus

Description: To 5" (12.5 cm). Heaviest just anterior to dorsal fin spine. *Back dark yellowish brown, with 3 saddles;* sides mottled; belly yellowish; *dusky band at end of caudal peduncle and near caudal fin edge; black* blotch on edge of first 4 dorsal fin rays; blotch near edge of posterior anal fin rays. Eye large; upper jaw overhangs lower. *Pectoral fin spine strongly serrate,* venom gland at base; adipose fin low, with shallow notch posteriorly, continuous with caudal fin; caudal fin rounded.

Habitat: Pools or riffles of clear, low-gradient streams; often with debris.

Range: Southern Lake Ontario drainage southwest to e LA; e WV and e KY west to se KS and ne OK.

Similar Species: Checkered Madtom (*N. flavater*) has black blotch on edge of dorsal fin rays, adipose fin separated from caudal fin by deep notch, and caudal fin with black bands at base and near edge; occurs in high-gradient streams. Yellowfin Madtom (*N. flavipinnis*) has brown band near middle of dorsal fin, with outer one-third of fin clear.

Comments: Brindled Madtom is known to utilize discarded beer and soda cans for a nest site. This madtom usually selects a can with a large opening that is oriented downstream.

48 Freckled Madtom
Noturus nocturnus

Description: To 6″ (15 cm). *Moderately robust. Coloration uniform;* back brown; sides lighter; *back and sides with many dark freckles;* belly yellowish; median fins dusky at bases, each with lighter area toward edge followed by dark submarginal band and clear outer edge. Head depressed, rounded above; upper jaw overhangs lower. Pectoral fin spine with smooth anterior edge, posterior edge roughened or with 3–5 serrations, venom gland at base; anal fin short, with 15–20 rays; *adipose fin broadly continuous with caudal fin; caudal fin rounded.*

Habitat: Pools or deep riffles of large streams with moderate current over gravel, sand, or rocks.

Range: IL south to s AL and central TX; e KY west to se KS and e OK.

Comments: Although Freckled Madtom is widely distributed, it is not very common.

---

62 Flathead Catfish
Pylodictis olivaris

Description: To 5'1" (1.5 m); 123 lb (56 kg). Elongate, slender. Back and sides olive yellow to light brown, with dark mottling; belly yellowish; *caudal fin dark brown to black, upper lobe clear;* other fins yellowish to light brown. *Head large, wide, very flat;* eye small; mouth wide, lower jaw projects beyond upper; barbels short. *Pectoral fin spine serrate on anterior and posterior edges; dorsal fin spine weak; 14–17 anal fin rays; adipose fin large; caudal fin truncate, weakly notched.*

Habitat: Large creeks, rivers, and reservoirs; usually near cover of rocks, logs, or other debris.

Range: Southeastern ON, w PA, sw WI, and ND south to TX and ne Mexico; east in Gulf coast drainages to Mobile Bay drainage of AL and GA. Introduced along Atlantic coast from VA to GA and in w U.S.

Comments: Flathead Catfish, a good sport and food fish, is commercially important in some areas. The young feed on aquatic insects, but gradually shift their diet to fishes and crayfishes as they mature.

---

66 Widemouth Blindcat
Satan eurystomus

Description: To 5½" (13.5 cm). Moderately robust. *White or pinkish.* Head broad, flat, with well-developed sensory canal pores; no eyes; *well-developed teeth in jaws.* Adipose fin long, relatively high; posterior edge of caudal fin slightly notched.

Habitat: Subterranean pools to depths of 2,000' (610 m).

Range: San Antonio pool of Edwards Aquifer, Bexar County, TX.

Similar Species: Toothless Blindcat *(Trogloglanis pattersoni)* lacks teeth.

Comments: The subterranean Widemouth and Toothless Blindcats evolved from stream-dwelling catfishes. Widemouth Blindcat appears to be most closely related to Flathead Catfish *(Pylodictis olivaris)*, and Toothless Blindcat appears to be related to catfishes of the genus *Ictalurus.*

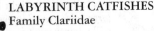

LABYRINTH CATFISHES
Family Clariidae

13 genera and about 100 species worldwide; 1 species introduced in North America. These freshwater catfishes are native to Africa, Syria, India, and the area encompassed by Java, Borneo, and the Philippines. Many are important food fishes, some attaining lengths of 3′4″ (1 m). Members of this family have a unique accessory respiratory organ, which rises from the gill arches, that enables them to breathe air by increasing the surface area for absorption of oxygen. This adaptation allows some species to leave the water and move about on land. The dorsal fin is long, with usually more than 30 rays, and lacks a spine at the anterior end. The adipose fin is often absent.

---

47 Walking Catfish
Clarias batrachus

Description: To 14″ (36 cm). Elongate, broad anteriorly, compressed posteriorly. Dark brown to olive above; lighter below; frequent albino populations white to pinkish. *4 pairs of barbels.* Pectoral fin with 1 spine, 8–11 rays; *dorsal fin long, with 60–75 rays; anal fin long, with 47–58 rays; no adipose fin; caudal fin with rounded posterior edge, not continuous with dorsal and anal fins.*

Habitat: Lakes, swamps, and sluggish canals with debris and aquatic vegetation over mud.

Range: Established in s FL. Introduced but not established in MA, CT, GA, NV, and CA

rivers, ponds, lakes, and swamps with vegetation.

Range: St. Lawrence River west through s Great Lakes and south to Gulf coast from FL to TX; absent from Appalachian Mountains.

Similar Species: Chain Pickerel *(E. niger)* has dark chain-like pattern on sides, vertical bar under eye, and 14–17 (usually 15) branchiostegal rays.

Comments: This is the smallest member of the family and the only one not considered an important sport fish.

---

38 Northern Pike
Esox lucius

Description: To 4'4" (1.3 m); 46 lb (21 kg). Elongate. Back dark olive green to greenish brown; sides lighter, *with irregular rows of small oval yellow spots and small gold spot on exposed edge of each scale;* belly creamy white; *median fins green to white, occasionally reddish orange, with dark markings.* Head one-fourth total length; lower jaw protrudes, *with 5 large sensory pores on each side;* 14–15 branchiostegal rays. Cheek and upper half of opercle scaled. Lateral line complete, with 105–148 scales.

ventral view of jaw

Habitat: Large slow-moving streams, lakes, and reservoirs with abundant aquatic vegetation.

Range: AK south and east throughout Canada to MT, NE, MO, PA, and NY. Widely introduced.

Comments: The large Northern Pike was formerly harvested commercially. It is now primarily considered a desirable and important sport fish. This pike is the most widely distributed freshwater fish.

---

35 Muskellunge
Esox masquinongy

Description: To 6' (1.8 m); 67 lb (31 kg). Elongate. Back greenish to light brown; *sides greenish gray to silvery, usually with dark*

ventral view
of jaw

spots or diagonal bars; belly creamy white;
median fins greenish to reddish brown,
with dark markings. Head broad, flat to
concave above; 6–9 large sensory pores on
each side of lower jaw; 16–19
branchiostegal rays. Cheek and opercle
usually scaled only on upper half. Lateral
line complete, with 132–167 scales.

Habitat: Lakes and reservoirs with thick
vegetation; slow-moving streams and
rivers with abundant plant cover.

Range: St. Lawrence River west through Great
Lakes to sw ON and se MB, and south to
PA, WV, VA, n GA, OH, and KY; upper
Mississippi River from MN to MO.
Widely introduced.

Comments: The largest species in the family, the
"Musky" is eagerly sought by anglers.
It feeds primarily on fishes, but will eat
any animal it can swallow, including
small ducks and amphibians. This
species and Northern Pike (E. lucius)
have been crossed to produce a more
robust fish called Tiger Muskellunge,
which is stocked in some areas.

36 Chain Pickerel
Esox niger

Description: To 31″ (79 cm); 9½ lb (4.3 kg).
Elongate, moderately compressed. Olive
to yellowish brown above; sides with dark
chain-like markings; belly whitish; bold
vertical dark bar under eye; fins greenish
yellow to dusky, without dark spots.
Head long; snout long, with concave profile;
4 large sensory pores on each side of lower
jaw; 14–17 (usually 15) branchiostegal
rays. Caudal fin deeply forked. Cheek and
opercle fully scaled. Lateral line complete,
with 110–138 scales.

Habitat: Clean clear lakes, ponds, swamps,
reservoirs, and pools of streams with
vegetation.

Range: NS, NB, sw QC, and from ME to NY
south in Atlantic coast streams to s FL;
Mississippi River system from s IN and
se MO south to LA and GA. Introduced

outside native range in Ohio and upper
Mississippi River drainages, and in CO.

Similar Species: Redfin Pickerel *(E. americanus)* has
smaller body, short snout, and 11–13
(usually 12) branchiostegal rays.

Comments: In the northeastern United States, Chain
Pickerel is an especially popular sport
fish in the winter; large numbers are
caught through the ice.

MUDMINNOWS
Family Umbridae

3 genera and 7 species worldwide; 3 gen-
era and 4 species in North America. These freshwater fishes
are small, reaching a maximum length of about 8″ (20 cm).
They are very hardy, capable of withstanding extreme cold,
and are able to utilize atmospheric oxygen. Under adverse
conditions they are reputed to become dormant in mud.
Members of this family have short snouts, non-protractile
jaws with small teeth, cycloid scales on the head and body,
and faint or absent lateral lines. The pelvic fins are small,
and the caudal fin is rounded. The North American mudminnows are found in western Alaska and Washington, in
the Great Lakes, and on the Atlantic coastal plain.

258 Alaska Blackfish
Dallia pectoralis

Description: To 13″ (33 cm). Elongate, cylindrical
anteriorly, compressed posteriorly. Dark
olive brown; sides with 4–6 bars or
blotches; belly whitish; fins have
reddish-brown speckles. Head flat; snout
short; maxilla extends beyond middle of
eye. *Pelvic fin small, with 3 rays;* pectoral
fin large, rounded; dorsal fin with 10–14
rays, above anal fin. Scales small, cycloid,
embedded; *76–100 scales in lateral series.*

Habitat: Lowland swamps, ponds, lakes, and
streams with vegetation; more abundant
in tundra than forest.

Range: Arctic and subarctic fresh waters of AK
and Bering Sea islands.

Comments: In the past, Alaska Blackfish was an
important staple in the diet of Alaskan
natives and their dogs. Large quantities

caught in the fall were packed in woven grass bags in batches of 50–100 lb (23–45 kg) each and frozen for use during the winter.

246 Central Mudminnow
Umbra limi

Description: To 5½″ (14 cm). Broad anteriorly, compressed posteriorly. Back brownish olive, mottled with black; *sides mottled with olive,* sometimes barred; belly yellowish; fins dusky. Mouth terminal, extends to middle of eye. Pectoral fin rounded; *dorsal fin above anal fin; anal fin about half length of dorsal fin;* caudal fin rounded, *with dark bar at base.* No lateral line; 34–37 scales in lateral series.

Habitat: Cool ponds, bogs, swamps, and pools of slow-moving streams with abundant vegetation.

Range: St. Lawrence River drainage, Great Lakes, and s MB south to w TN and ne AR; w PA west to e SD.

Similar Species: Eastern Mudminnow (*U. pygmaea*) has 10–14 light stripes. Olympic Mudminnow (*Novumbra hubbsi*) lacks dark bar at caudal fin base and has more than 47 scales in lateral series.

Comments: Central Mudminnow is used as bait in some areas.

Order Salmoniformes

This order contains two families, both of which are found in North America. They include freshwater, marine, anadromous, and deep-sea species. All have soft-rayed fins, adipose fins, and abdominal pelvic fins. Most of these fishes are commercially valuable.

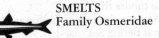

SMELTS
Family Osmeridae

7 genera and 13 species worldwide; 6 genera and 10 species in North America, including 1 species introduced from Asia. Smelts are found in marine

and freshwater environments in cold-temperate to arctic waters throughout the Northern Hemisphere. They resemble the closely related trouts and salmons (family Salmonidae) in many ways, including having a streamlined body, pelvic fins midway on the underside of the abdomen, low pectoral fins, an adipose fin, firmly attached small scales covering the body, and an incomplete lateral line. Smelts lack the axillary scale above the pelvic fin that is characteristic of trouts and salmons. During spawning, these fishes exhibit sexual differences, such as breeding tubercles and a modified anal fin in the male. They are popular sport fishes and are captured in nets from the shore. Smelts are important commercially, used for both food and bait.

127, 648 Rainbow Smelt
Osmerus mordax

Description: To 13″ (33 cm). Elongate, slender, moderately compressed. Translucent; purple above; sides with purplish iridescence; silvery below. Maxilla reaches to middle of eye; *strong canine teeth on vomer and tongue.* Dorsal fin with 8–11 rays, origin over or in front of pelvic fin insertion; 12–16 anal fin rays; *adipose fin above end of anal fin;* caudal fin deeply forked. 62–72 scales in lateral series. *Lateral line incomplete, with 14–30 pored scales.*

Habitat: Nearshore marine and estuarine waters, inland streams, and lakes; anadromous and freshwater populations.

Range: Labrador south to n VA; coastal AK. Widely introduced in Great Lakes and ND; North Dakota introduction is most likely source of population in Mississippi River drainage, which ranges south seasonally to LA.

Comments: Rainbow Smelt is one of the most valuable sport and commercial fishes on the Atlantic coast and in the Great Lakes. Anglers take it on hook and line through the ice in the winter, and with dip nets in small streams during the spring spawning runs. When first removed from the water, this fish smells similar to freshly cut cucumber. Lake populations of *Osmerus* from southern Quebec, New

Brunswick, and Maine have sometimes been considered a separate species, Pygmy Smelt (*O. spectrum*).

126 Eulachon
Thaleichthys pacificus

Description: To 10" (25 cm). Fusiform, elongate, compressed. Bluish brown above, with fine black speckling on back; shading to bright silvery below; *caudal fin often speckled.* Maxilla reaches to posterior edge of eye; usually no enlarged teeth; 4–6 gill rakers on upper limb of outer arch; *parallel, vertical, slightly curved grooves on opercle.* Pelvic fin insertion below and slightly anterior to dorsal fin origin; 10–13 dorsal fin rays; 18–23 anal fin rays. Thickened ridge along sides in adult males.

Habitat: Fresh water, coastal inlets, and near shore to depths of 600' (183 m).

Range: Pribilof Islands, AK, to Bodega Bay, CA.

Similar Species: All other smelt species lack grooves on opercle. Whitebait Smelt (*Allosmerus elongatus*) has eye width equal to depth of caudal peduncle, maxilla reaching beyond eye, pelvic fin insertion slightly anterior to dorsal fin origin, and 12–18 anal fin rays; occurs over soft bottoms and does not enter fresh water. Night Smelt (*Spirinchus starksi*) has eye width less than depth of caudal peduncle, maxilla reaching middle of eye, pelvic fin insertion slightly anterior to dorsal fin origin, and pectoral fin extending almost to pelvic fin insertion; occurs over soft bottoms and does not enter fresh water. Surf Smelt (*Hypomesus pretiosus*) has maxilla not reaching beyond middle of eye, pelvic fin insertion directly beneath dorsal fin origin, and 12–18 anal fin rays; occurs in nearshore waters off sandy beaches and enters fresh water. Capelin (*Mallotus villosus*) has pelvic fin insertion slightly anterior to dorsal fin origin; occurs in nearshore waters off sandy beaches, sometimes to depths of 250′ (76 m), in arctic and cold-temperate seas and probably enters fresh water.

Comments: The body of Eulachon is rich in oil; a wick is sometimes inserted into dried specimens to be used as a torch. As a result, this species is sometimes called Candlefish.

TROUTS AND SALMONS
Family Salmonidae

11 genera and about 66 species world-wide; 7 genera and 39 species in North America north of Mexico (38 native, 1 introduced), plus 1 species in Mexico. These fishes occur in temperate fresh and salt waters of the Northern Hemisphere and have been widely introduced throughout North America. All salmonids have an adipose fin and an axillary scale above each pelvic fin, and most species have well-developed teeth in both jaws. The gill membranes extend far forward and are free of the isthmus. The swim bladder is connected to the alimentary canal, allowing these fishes to change depth rapidly. Many species exhibit significant sexual differences in color and morphology during the spawning season. Many trouts and salmons are important sport fishes.

67 Cisco
Coregonus artedi

nostrils

Description: To 22″ (57 cm); 5½ lb (2.5 kg). Elongate, compressed. Back bluish black to grayish green; sides silvery; fins clear to opaque; *edges of pelvic, dorsal, and caudal fins dusky. Profile of head flat behind eye; 2 flaps of skin between nostrils; mouth terminal; lower jaw with small knob at tip, projecting slightly beyond upper jaw;* 46–50 *gill rakers.* 10–15 dorsal fin rays; adipose fin present. Lateral line complete, with 63–94 scales.

Habitat: Primarily lakes; may enter large rivers in n part of range.

Range: Northwest Territories southeast to QC, Great Lakes, and St. Lawrence River drainage. Introduced in MT.

Similar Species: Bloater *(C. hoyi)* reaches length of 13¾″ (35 cm), lacks knob at tip of lower jaw, and has 40–47 gill rakers and shorter pelvic fin not reaching anal fin. Kiyi *(C. kiyi)* reaches length of 14½″ (37 cm), and has black upper lip, small knob at tip of lower jaw, and long pelvic fin usually reaching anal fin.

Comments: Similar morphology and coloration of the 14 species of *Coregonus* make identification extremely difficult. Cisco is important ecologically as a prey species for other salmonids and as a sport fish. In some areas, it is marketed as Lake Herring. Millions of pounds are harvested annually for food; it is excellent prepared fresh or smoked.

71 Lake Whitefish
Coregonus clupeaformis

Description: To 31″ (80 cm); 42 lb (19 kg). Elongate, compressed. Back olive to bluish black; sides and belly silvery; fins clear to dusky. *Profile of head concave behind eye; snout overhangs mouth; 2 flaps of skin between nostrils; maxilla extends beyond front of eye;* teeth on tongue, absent from jaws; 26–33 gill rakers. 11–13 dorsal fin rays; adipose fin present; caudal fin forked. Lateral line complete, with 70–97 scales.

Habitat: Large rivers and lakes.

Range: AK, Canada, n New England, Great Lakes, and n MN. Stocked in lakes of central and w U.S., but is not reproducing in most cases.

Comments: Lake Whitefish, the most widely distributed species in the genus *Coregonus,* is one of the most valuable commercial freshwater fishes of North America. However, commercial landings have declined, especially in the Great Lakes, due to the deterioration of habitat and depletion of stocks. Lake Whitefish is also sought for sport in some areas. It is a superlative table delicacy.

76 Apache Trout
Oncorhynchus apache

Description: To 19¼" (49 cm); 5 lb (2.3 kg). Moderately stout, compressed. Dark olive to brown above; *sides and belly yellow to golden yellow;* lower part of head orange to yellowish orange; *large prominent dark spot behind eye;* many dark spots about half width of pupil on head, back, sides, and fins; pelvic, dorsal, and anal fins white-tipped. Dorsal fin large; adipose fin present. Lateral line complete, with 112–124 scales.

Habitat: Riffles and pools of clear mountain streams at elevations of 7,545′ (2,300 m) or more.

Range: Headwaters of Salt and Little Colorado Rivers, east-central AZ.

Similar Species: Gila Trout *(O. gilae),* now an endangered species, has smaller, closely set dark spots extending onto belly and small dark spots on dorsal and caudal fins.

Comments: Apache Trout, also known as Arizona Trout, was almost totally exterminated by exotic trouts, which hybridize with it and compete for food and habitat. It is classified as a threatened species.

75, 545 Cutthroat Trout
Oncorhynchus clarkii

Description: To 3′3″ (99 cm); 41 lb (18.5 kg). Elongate, cylindrical or terete, moderately compressed. Back dark olive; coloration on sides variable: silvery, olive, or reddish to yellowish orange; belly lighter; *dark spots on back, sides, and median fins; bright red to reddish-orange slash mark on each side of throat* (particularly visible in breeding males). Mouth extends beyond eye; basibranchial teeth present. 8–11 dorsal fin rays; 9–12 anal fin rays; adipose fin present; caudal fin slightly forked. Caudal peduncle narrow. Lateral line complete, with 120–230 (usually at least 150) scales.

Habitat: Inshore and estuarine waters; lakes; coastal, inland, and alpine streams.

Range: Along coast from s AK south to n CA; inland from s BC and AB south to NM and e CA east to central CO. Introduced in parts of w U.S.

Comments: Cutthroat Trout is a highly variable species, and many populations have in the past been classified as distinct species or subspecies. Currently there are about 14 recognized subspecies.

83, 556 Pink Salmon
Oncorhynchus gorbuscha

Description: To 30″ (76 cm); 14 lb (6.3 kg). Elongate, moderately compressed. *Back steel blue to blue-green, with large black spots; black spots on adipose and caudal fins.* Breeding males pale red, with olive to brown blotches; head and back darker; *hump on back; upper jaw hooked.* Lateral line straight, complete, with 147–205 scales.

Habitat: Coastal waters; enters streams to spawn.

Range: Pacific Ocean from ne Asia, Siberia, and AK south to La Jolla, CA; coastal streams south to Sacramento River, CA. Introduced in NS, Labrador, Gulf of St. Lawrence, and upper Great Lakes.

Comments: Pink Salmon is the most abundant salmonid in the Pacific Ocean. The common name is derived from its pink flesh, compared to the deeper red of Sockeye (*O. nerka*) and other salmons. It is a less desirable food fish than other members of the family.

85, 554 Chum Salmon
Oncorhynchus keta

Description: To 3′4″ (1 m); 35 lb (16 kg). Elongate, compressed, streamlined. Back steel blue; sides silvery; *back, upper sides, and dorsal, adipose, and caudal fins finely speckled with black; anal and pelvic fins white-tipped.* Spawning adults brownish red on sides, with greenish bars or mottling. 18–26 gill rakers on first arch. Lateral line with 124–153 scales.

Habitat: Coastal waters; enters streams to spawn.

Range: Pacific and Arctic Oceans from Japan to AK and south to CA; coastal streams south to Sacramento River, CA.

Comments: This is an important commercial species, especially to native peoples, who use it dried or smoked as winter food for themselves and dogs. It is sometimes referred to as Dog Salmon. The markings on the sides of spawning adults often resemble paint that has run.

79, 80, 81, 550, 551, 552   **Coho Salmon**
Oncorhynchus kisutch

Description: To 3'3" (99 cm); 33 lb (15 kg). Fusiform, elongate, moderately compressed. Blue-green above; silvery white below; irregular dark spots on back and sometimes on upper lobe of caudal fin. *Gums at base of teeth white or gray.* Adipose fin present; *caudal fin with rough striations on rays.*

Habitat: Coastal waters at mid-depths or near surface; enters coastal streams to spawn, sometimes far inland.

Range: Bering Strait to Baja California; coastal streams south to Monterey Bay, CA. Introduced elsewhere, especially in Great Lakes.

Similar Species: Chinook Salmon (*O. tshawytscha*) has oblong black spots on back and entire caudal fin, black gums at base of teeth, and smooth striations on caudal fin rays.

Comments: Like all Pacific salmons, Coho Salmon is anadromous. The adult spawns in small streams, where the female deposits 2,500 to 5,000 eggs in the gravel during the fall. Both the male and the female die after spawning. The young stay in the stream for about a year before migrating to the ocean, where they remain for two or three years. Coho Salmon is a sport fish prized both as a fighter and for eating. It supports a large commercial fishery.

78, 547   Rainbow Trout
Oncorhynchus mykiss

Description: To 3′9″ (1.1 m); 42 lb (19 kg).
Fusiform, elongate. Marine coloration:
metallic blue above; silvery white below;
small black spots on back, sides, and
dorsal and caudal fins. Freshwater
coloration: spots more prominent;
distinctive red band on sides. *Gums at
base of teeth white; no teeth on back of tongue.
8–12 anal fin rays;* adipose fin present,
usually black-edged.

Habitat: Lakes and freshwater streams and rivers;
sea-run populations in inshore waters at
mid-depths and near surface.

Range: Native freshwater range confined to
streams and lakes along Pacific coast
from AK to Baja California; sea-run
populations in Bering Sea to s CA.
Introduced throughout Canada and U.S.

Comments: A sea-run Rainbow Trout, often called
Steelhead by anglers, usually spends two
to four years in its home stream before
venturing to sea, where it remains for
about three years; it returns to the home
stream in the winter to spawn, and will
continue this pattern as long as it
survives natural predators. Fish that
exist solely in fresh water spawn in the
spring. Most males spawn at one year of
age, while females may take six years to
mature. Rainbow Trout is a popular
sport fish; it is rarely taken at sea by
anglers using bait, but does succumb
readily to trolled shrimp-like flies. It
provides good eating and is raised for
market through aquaculture.

86, 557   Sockeye Salmon
Oncorhynchus nerka

Description: To 33″ (84 cm); 15 lb (6.8 kg).
Fusiform, elongate, moderately
compressed. Marine coloration: blue-
green above; silvery below; *fine speckling,
no spots.* Freshwater coloration: bright
red; head pale green. Females often with

green and yellow blotches. Snout
bluntly pointed; mouth terminal; gill
rakers long, slender, closely spaced,
28–40 on first arch. Adipose fin present.

Habitat: Surface of open seas; enters streams,
rivers, and lakes with tributary streams
to spawn; some landlocked populations.

Range: Bering Strait to Sacramento River, CA.
Introduced in lakes and reservoirs in
Canada and n U.S.

Comments: Sockeye Salmon spawns during the
summer in small tributaries of lakes,
where the young spend one to three years
before migrating to the ocean. After
living at sea for two to four years,
maturing adults return to their home
stream. This species has the greatest
commercial value of all the Pacific
salmons; few are caught by anglers in the
ocean, however, because it rarely strikes
lures or trolled bait. The landlocked
populations are known as Kokanee.

84, 555 Chinook Salmon
Oncorhynchus tshawytscha

Description: To 4′10″ (1.5 m); 126 lb (57 kg).
Fusiform, elongate. Marine coloration:
greenish-blue to black above; silvery
white below; oblong black spots on back
and entire caudal fin. Freshwater
coloration: very dark overall. *Gums at
base of teeth black.* Adipose fin present;
caudal fin with smooth striations on rays.

Habitat: Oceans near surface and at mid-depths,
may feed near bottom; enters large rivers
to spawn.

Range: Bering Strait to s CA; in freshwater
streams south to Sacramento River, CA.
Widely introduced.

Similar Species: Coho Salmon *(O. kisutch)* lacks spots on
lower lobe of caudal fin, has white or
gray gums at base of teeth, and strong
rough striations on caudal fin rays.

Comments: Chinook Salmon enters fresh water most
months of the year, but the major
spawning runs occur in the spring and
fall. Similar to Coho Salmon, it feeds on

a variety of crustaceans and fishes, such as anchovies, herrings, young rockfishes, and sand lances. This species is the most highly prized ocean sport fish from Alaska to northern California. It also supports a large valuable commercial troll fishery.

70 Round Whitefish
Prosopium cylindraceum

Description: To 22" (56 cm); 6 lb (2.7 kg). Elongate, cylindrical. Back greenish to bluish gray, with dark-edged scales; sides silvery; dorsal and caudal fins slightly dusky, other fins amber. Young silvery, with 2–3 rows of black spots along lateral line. Snout narrow, pointed; *1 flap of skin between nostrils;* mouth small, ventral, extends to eye; teeth on tongue, absent from jaws; 13–20 gill rakers. Adipose fin present; caudal fin forked. *Lateral line complete, with 74–108 scales.*

nostrils

Habitat: Lakes to depths of 50′ (15 m) and streams.
Range: AK, nw Canada, and se Canada to Great Lakes and New England.
Similar Species: Pygmy Whitefish *(P. coulterii)* has 55–70 lateral line scales. Mountain Whitefish *(P. williamsoni)* has 20–25 gill rakers. Bonneville Cisco *(P. gemmifer)* has long pointed snout and 37–45 gill rakers on first arch.
Comments: Round Whitefish is fished commercially in the Great Lakes, but is not very valuable because of its small size and restricted population. It is an important forage fish for Lake Trout in some areas.

82, 553 Atlantic Salmon
Salmo salar

Description: To 4′5″ (1.3 m); 79 lb (36 kg). Elongate, moderately compressed. *Brownish above; sides silvery; numerous small black spots, sometimes X-shaped, without halos,* on head, body, and dorsal fin. Breeding males bronzish-purple on sides, with red spots; lower jaw upward-hooked. Young have

8–11 dusky bars on sides. Head large, depth about one-fifth length; maxilla extends beyond eye. Pectoral fin insertion well below axis of body; dorsal fin short-based, midway between snout and caudal fin base; adipose fin present; caudal fin slightly forked or emarginate.

Habitat: Coastal waters; freshwater streams and lakes.

Range: Native in North Atlantic and ne Canada from Arctic Circle and n QC south to Delaware River; Lake Ontario. Landlocked populations in several New England states.

Comments: This anadromous species spawns in the fall in high-gradient streams over gravel. After spawning, it is weak and emaciated but does not necessarily die like some other salmonid species. Atlantic Salmon is a well-known and highly valued food and sport fish. Individuals as large as 40–50 lb (18–23 kg) are unusual in the Atlantic; most weigh much less.

73, 548 Brown Trout
Salmo trutta

Description: To 3′4″ (1 m); 40 lb (18 kg). Fusiform, elongate, moderately compressed. Back and sides olive, becoming lighter; belly silvery; *numerous red or orange spots, often with halos,* scattered on head, body, and dorsal and adipose fins. Maxilla extends well beyond eye. Pectoral fin insertion well below axis of body; dorsal fin short-based, about midway between snout and caudal fin base; adipose fin present; caudal fin truncate.

Habitat: Primarily high-gradient freshwater streams and in lakes; sea-run populations in nearshore waters.

Range: Southern Canada, ne U.S., and Great Lakes south in Appalachian Mountains and Mississippi River valley; w U.S. at higher elevations; sea-run populations in NB and NF.

Comments: Brown Trout, native to Europe and western Asia, was introduced in the

United States in 1883 and is presently one of the most widespread salmonids. It can tolerate higher temperatures than other members of the family. The young feed on aquatic insects; adults feed primarily on other fishes. Brown Trout is difficult to catch, and as a food fish is not as highly regarded as Brook Trout (*Salvelinus fontinalis*) or Rainbow Trout (*Oncorhynchus mykiss*).

77, 546 Brook Trout
Salvelinus fontinalis

Description: To 28″ (70 cm); 14½ lb (6.6 kg). Fusiform, elongate, depth about one-fifth length. Marine coloration: back bluish green, becoming silvery on sides; belly white. Freshwater coloration: red or yellowish tint on back and sides, *with lighter wavy lines;* red spots within blue halos on sides; belly ordinarily white (reddish in adult males); *pelvic, pectoral, and anal fins light orange, with white leading edges followed by dark area; dorsal fin with dark undulating lines.* Maxilla extends well beyond eye. Fins relatively large; adipose fin present; caudal fin slightly forked.

Habitat: Clear cool freshwater streams and tidal streams; rarely in salt water.

Range: Eastern Canada, ne U.S., and Great Lakes south to n GA. Introduced in w U.S. at higher elevations.

Similar Species: Arctic Char *(S. alpinus)* has upper sides with reddish spots about equal to width of pupil, 7–13 gill rakers on upper limb of first arch, and 12–19 on lower limb; occurs in rivers, lakes, and inshore Arctic, Atlantic, and Pacific waters. Dolly Varden *(S. malma)* has upper sides with orangish-red spots smaller than width of pupil, 3–9 gill rakers on upper limb of first arch, and 8–14 on lower limb; occurs in rivers, lakes, and nearshore Pacific waters.

Comments: Brook Trout, also known as Squaretail or Speck, is one of the most colorful freshwater fishes. It feeds on a variety of organisms, including other fishes, but primarily on aquatic insects. Spawning occurs in small headwater streams. It is highly esteemed as a food and sport fish. The largest Brook Trout on record, weighing 14½ lb (6.6 kg), was caught in 1916 in the Nipigon River, Ontario.

74, 549 Lake Trout
Salvelinus namaycush

Description: To 4′2″ (1.3 m); 102 lb (46 kg). Elongate, slightly compressed. Dark olive to grayish green above; bluish gray to greenish bronze below; *creamy spots on head, body, and median and adipose fins;* leading edges of pelvic, pectoral, and anal fins reddish orange, with narrow whitish border. Mouth terminal, extends beyond eye; teeth on vomer. Adipose fin present; *caudal fin deeply forked.* Caudal peduncle slender. Scales small; 175–200 in lateral series.

Habitat: Deep cold lakes and far northern rivers.

Range: AK, Canada, Great Lakes, and ME south to NY and west to e MN. Introduced outside native range.

Comments: Lake Trout is the largest trout native to North America. It is highly esteemed as a food fish and is sought by anglers. A large commercial fishery in the Great Lakes was decimated by pollution and by Sea Lampreys after the rapid expansion of their population in the 1940s. Lake Trout feeds on a wide range of aquatic organisms.

72 Arctic Grayling
Thymallus arcticus

Description: To 30″ (76 cm); 6 lb (2.7 kg). Elongate, compressed. Back bluish black to purple; *sides silvery bluish gray, often with pinkish cast and anterior dark spots;* dark stripe along lower side extends from pectoral fin to pelvic fin; belly grayish;

fins dusky to dark; dorsal fin light-edged.
Head short; mouth extends to middle of
eye; teeth small. *Dorsal fin long, with
17–25 rays;* adipose fin present; caudal
fin deeply forked. Lateral line straight,
complete, with 77–103 scales.

Habitat: Clear cold rivers, creeks, and lakes.

Range: Hudson Bay west to AK and south to
MT; n Great Lakes. Widely introduced
outside native range.

Comments: The attractive Arctic Grayling is one of
the most highly prized sport fishes in
northern Canada and Alaska. It has been
an important food source for native
people in remote areas.

Order Aulopiformes

This order contains 13 families, seven of which are found in
shallow to deep marine waters of North America. Only the
lizardfish family (Synodontidae) contains species that predominantly occur in inshore waters. Members of this order
are soft-rayed fishes with abdominal pelvic fins; some families have an adipose fin. The scales are cycloid; certain
species have luminescent photophores on the body. These
features are also characteristic of the order Myctophiformes,
in which the aulopiform fishes were formerly included. The
separation of the Aulopiformes from the Myctophiformes is
based on several specializations of the gill arches that are
unique among bony fishes.

LIZARDFISHES
Family Synodontidae

5 genera and 55 species worldwide; 3
genera and 11 species in North America. Found in tropical
to temperate waters, members of this group are oblong or
elongate, almost round in cross section, and reach lengths of
6–18″ (15–46 cm). The mouth is large, wide, and slightly
oblique, with the upper jaw bordered entirely by the premaxilla and a rudimentary maxilla extending well behind
the eyes. The jaws bear numerous cardiform teeth, and teeth
are also present on the tongue and roof of the mouth. These
teeth, together with a pointed scaly head, give these fishes
a distinctive lizard-like appearance, hence the collective
common name lizardfishes. The abdominal pelvic fins have
the inner rays either distinctly longer than the outer, or vice

versa (depending upon genus). The dorsal fin is short and undivided. An adipose fin is present, and the caudal fin is forked. Lizardfishes are typically seen resting motionless on sand or mud bottoms. Post-larvae are transparent and have a series of black spots in the body cavity lining, the number and distribution of which are of taxonomic importance.

422 Inshore Lizardfish
Synodus foetens

Description: To 18″ (46 cm). Elongate, cylindrical. Brownish or olive, with greenish cast above; about 8 diamond-shaped marks on upper sides; whitish or yellowish below; light wavy lines on head; pectoral fin dusky, yellowish, or light green; dark spot on adipose fin. Head depressed; snout pointed; eye large, above midpoint of maxilla. Pelvic fin with inner rays much longer than outer rays; *anal fin with 10–14 (usually 11–13) rays,* base same length or longer than dorsal fin base. *4–6 rows of scales between lateral line and dorsal fin base. Lateral line complete, with 56–65 (usually 60–62) scales.*

Habitat: On bottom to depths of about 90′ (27 m); usually near shore.

Range: MA to Brazil, including Bermuda, Bahamas, Gulf of Mexico, and Caribbean; uncommon north of NC.

Similar Species: Offshore Lizardfish *(S. poeyi)* has obscure blotches along lateral line, knob at tip of lower jaw, 3 rows of scales between lateral line and dorsal fin base, and 43–48 lateral line scales; occurs in deeper waters. Snakefish *(Trachinocephalus myops)* has alternating yellow and blue stripes on sides, very short snout with eye far forward, and much longer anal fin base than dorsal fin base. The 3 North American species in genus *Saurida* differ from genera *Synodus* and *Trachinocephalus* in having 2 (vs. 1) pairs of toothbands on roof of mouth and inner and outer pelvic fin rays of equal length; occur in deeper waters.

Comments: This very common lizardfish is often caught in shrimp trawls and discarded as a trash fish.

423 Sand Diver
Synodus intermedius

Description: Usually to 11″ (28 cm), reportedly to 18″ (46 cm). Elongate, cylindrical, cigar-shaped. Light brown or greenish; *brown bars extend along mid-side from pectoral fin to caudal fin base; thin horizontal yellow lines extend from head to tail; black humeral spot partly covered by opercle;* belly pale; fins orange. Snout relatively blunt; eye slightly anterior to midpoint of maxilla. Anal fin rays 10–12 (usually 11); adipose fin present. 3 rows of scales between lateral line and dorsal fin base. Lateral line complete, with 45–52 (usually 47–49) scales.

Habitat: Offshore over sand to depths of 1,050′ (320 m); occasionally in shallow waters or around rocks.

Range: NC to Brazil, including Bermuda, Bahamas, Gulf of Mexico, and Caribbean.

Similar Species: California Lizardfish (*S. lucioceps*) is brown above and has tan belly and yellow gill membranes and pelvic fin; occurs over sand or mud to depths of 50′ (15 m) in Pacific.

Comments: Sand Diver, whose common name is derived from its habit of burying itself in the sand when disturbed, has no value as a food or sport fish.

Order Lampridiformes

This morphologically diverse order of pelagic fishes contains seven families, five of which are found in North America. Some species have a unique protractile upper jaw. All have fins without true spines, and the pelvic fins are sometimes absent. One group (composed of two families) has a deep body, a symmetrical caudal fin, and a well-developed skeleton; this group includes the large, widely distributed, and commercially important Opah (*Lampris guttatus*). The other group (composed of five families) are among the most morphologically bizarre of all fishes, with a laterally compressed, ribbon-like body, a sometimes asymmetrical caudal fin, and a weak skeleton.

OARFISHES
Family Regalecidae

2 genera and probably 2 species worldwide; 1 species in North America. Oarfishes have extremely elongate bodies and relatively blunt heads without extended snouts. The eyes are small, and teeth are absent. The pelvic fins are extremely slender and elongate, each with a single ray and a paddle-like membrane near the tip. The bright red dorsal fin is extremely long, extending the entire length of the fish from just behind the tip of the snout to the base of the tail; the first few rays are elongate, highly elevated as a flag-like crest on the head, and the remainder of the fin is extremely low in relation to the body. The anal fin is absent, and the caudal fin is tiny. These fishes are unscaled, but have tubercles on the skin. They lack a swim bladder. The number of gill rakers differs in the two species, suggesting different feeding habits.

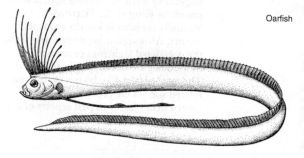

Oarfish

Oarfish
Regalecus glesne

Description: To 26′ (8 m), unconfirmed reports to 56′ (17 m). *Extremely elongate; dorsal fin elevated on head as flag-like crest.* Grayish, variously marked; *dorsal fin red.* Head blunt; eye small; no teeth; 40–58 gill rakers. Pelvic fin extremely slender, elongate, with 1 ray and paddle-like membrane near tip; dorsal fin with 260–412 rays, extending from head to base of tail; no anal fin; caudal fin tiny. Body unscaled.

Habitat: Open seas; usually at mid-depths, sometimes at surface.

Range: Bermuda and both coasts of FL.

Similar Species:

Three other families in the order contain equally bizarre, elongate fishes: tube-eyes (Stylephoridae), with extremely long anterior dorsal fin rays, greatly extended lowermost caudal fin ray, and mouth and gill cavities adapted for large and rapid changes in volume; ribbonfishes (Trachipteridae), with rough skin, bluntish snout, very long pelvic and dorsal fin rays, and upper caudal fin lobe sometimes angled sharply upward; and crestfishes (Lophotidae), with smooth skin, tiny or absent pelvic fin, sometimes extremely elongate dorsal fin crest, and internal ink sac. All families occur in Atlantic and Pacific.

Comments: Oarfish, which occurs worldwide in tropical to warm-temperate seas, is also known as King of the Herrings. Virtually nothing is known about its life history. Although it is infrequently seen, the occasional sightings of stranded individuals are usually well publicized. The long ribbon-like bodies of this and related species are probably the main contributing factor to past reports of sea serpents.

Order Percopsiformes

This order contains two families, both of which are confined to the fresh waters of North America north of Mexico. These fishes are small and usually robust, with relatively large heads. The dorsal fin is preceded by up to four weak spines, and the anal fin by up to three weak spines. When present, the pelvic fins are situated behind the pectoral fins and are composed of eight to nine rays.

TROUT PERCHES
Family Percopsidae

    1 genus with 2 species confined to fresh waters of North America north of Mexico. The common name for this family was assigned to it by early naturalists, who thought it to be an intermediate form in the evolution from trouts to perches. These fishes have pelvic fins with eight to nine rays. The pectoral fin extends beyond the pelvic fin insertion. One to three spines precede each dorsal and anal fin. Trout perches have an adipose fin and small ctenoid scales.

264 Trout Perch
Percopsis omiscomaycus

Description: To 8″ (20 cm). Moderately elongate, stout. *Pale olive to straw yellow above; somewhat translucent, with rows of dark spots on upper half of body;* fins clear. Snout long; mouth small, ventral. *Dorsal fin with 2–3 weak spines, 8–11 rays,* origin behind pelvic fin insertion; *adipose fin present;* caudal fin forked. Caudal peduncle long. Head, cheek, and opercle unscaled. *Lateral line complete, with 41–60 scales.*

Habitat: Lakes and streams over sand or gravel.

Range: Much of AK and Canada, including drainages of s Hudson and James Bays; nw CT south to Potomac River; Great Lakes and upper Mississippi River system. Introduced and possibly established in UT.

Similar Species: Sand Roller (*P. transmontana*) has highly arched back, lacks rows of spots on upper half of body, and lateral line is incomplete; occurs in large streams over sand or rocks.

Comments: Trout Perch seeks food at night along the bottom of shallow open waters, retiring to deeper water or undercut banks during the day. In northern lakes, where it is abundant, it is an important forage fish for several species of sport fishes.

PIRATE PERCHES
Family Aphredoderidae

1 species confined to fresh waters of eastern North America. Pirate perches are unusual in that, as they mature, the anus moves forward from just in front of the anal fin in juveniles to a point anterior to the pelvic girdle in the throat region in adults.

263 Pirate Perch
Aphredoderus sayanus

anus —
ventral view
of adult head

Description: To 5½″ (14 cm). Oblong, stout anteriorly, compressed posteriorly. *Dark olive gray to purplish, with dark spots;* yellowish to brownish below; fins dusky to black; 1–2 dark bars at caudal fin base. Maxilla extends to front of eye; opercular spine sharp; preopercle strongly serrate. *Dorsal fin with 2–4 weak spines, 10–11 rays; no adipose fin.* Caudal peduncle deep. *Ctenoid scales on head and body.* Lateral line incomplete.

Habitat: Backwaters of low-gradient streams, ponds, swamps, and bayous with clear to murky waters and abundant aquatic plant cover.

Range: Atlantic coastal plain from Long Island, NY, south to s FL and west to e TX; s Great Lakes drainage from w NY west to se MN, and south in Mississippi River valley.

Comments: Pirate Perch hides in aquatic vegetation and debris by day and emerges in darkness to feed on aquatic insects, crustaceans, and small fishes. It lives for four years. It is more abundant in the southern part of its range.

CAVEFISHES
Order Amblyopsiformes
Family Amblyopsidae

This order consists of a single family: 5 genera and 6 species confined to fresh waters of North America. These fishes are found in caves, springs, and swamps of the east-central and eastern United States. Their evolution exhibits the transition from surface water to springs to subterranean habitats; they share morphological adaptations, including blindness or small rudimentary eyes and exposed sensory papillae in rows on the head and body. The species found in the surface water of swamps and those adapted to springs have rudimentary eyes and sensory papillae on the head and are pigmented (see below, left); those adapted to habitats in, or around the entrance to, caves are blind, have numerous sensory papillae on the head, body, and tail, and lack pigmentation (see below, right). Other interesting cave adaptations include a decrease in metabolic rate and a reproductive strategy in which the few large eggs are held in the gill chamber of the female after being fertilized and during the early stages of development. All family members have a single dorsal fin either lacking spines or with one or two spines, and seven to 12 rays. The anal fin is either spineless or has one or two spines, and has seven to 11 rays. Small embedded cycloid scales are present on the body, but absent on the head. In adults, the anus is situated anteriorly near the junction of the gill membranes.

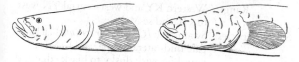

236 Northern Cavefish
Amblyopsis spelaea

Description: To 4¼" (11 cm). Robust, very wide anteriorly. *Pinkish white;* head and body covered with short vertical rows of sensory papillae; fins plain, clear. Head large, somewhat depressed; eye beneath skin, nonfunctional; mouth moderately large; lower jaw projects beyond upper. *Pelvic fin small, often absent; 9 dorsal fin rays;* anal fin under dorsal fin; *caudal fin rounded, with 4–6 rows of sensory papillae.* Scales small, embedded.

Habitat: Clear pools in caves over mud, sand, or rocks.

Range: South-central IN and n KY south to Mammoth Cave, KY.

Similar Species: Ozark Cavefish (*A. rosae*) has 7 dorsal fin rays.

Comments: Northern Cavefish feeds on small crustaceans it locates with external sensory organs that are sensitive to the slightest vibrations. It swims very slowly just a few inches off the bottom.

234 Spring Cavefish
Forbesichthys agassizii

Description: To 3½" (8.5 cm). Elongate, somewhat rounded. Dark brown above; *light olive brown on sides, with pale mid-lateral stripe;* belly yellowish; head and body covered with short rows of sensory papillae; *median fins olive; dusky bar at caudal fin base.* Head flat above; *eye very small, functional;* mouth moderately large; lower jaw projects beyond upper. *No pelvic fins; caudal fin broad, rounded.* Caudal peduncle long, deep. Scales small, embedded.

Habitat: Cool clear waters in springs and caves.

Range: Western KY and west-central TN west to s IL and se MO.

Similar Species: Swampfish *(Chologaster cornuta)* lacks pale mid-lateral stripe, and has clear dorsal fin with dusky to black edge and black caudal fin with 2 white blotches near base; occurs in sluggish streams and swamps.

Comments: While Spring Cavefish is sometimes seen in caves, it is most often found in springs or streams flowing from caves. It is active at night and retreats to overhanging banks or other cover during the day.

235 Southern Cavefish
Typhlichthys subterraneus

Description: To 3½" (8.5 cm). Slender, elongate. *Unpigmented except for pinkish cast where blood vessels show through skin;* individuals exposed to light become dusky; body appears naked. Head blunt, broad; *eye absent;* mouth small. *No pelvic fins;* anal fin well behind anus; *caudal fin rounded, with 2 rows of sensory papillae.* Scales small, somewhat embedded.

Habitat:	Underground pools and caves at or near water table; occasionally near cave openings.
Range:	Southern IN south to nw GA and n AL; s MO, ne AR, and ne OK.
Similar Species:	Alabama Cavefish (*Speoplatyrhinus poulsoni*) has very long, flat snout.
Comments:	Southern Cavefish is the most widespread of the cavefishes, occurring east and west of the Mississippi River.

Order Ophidiiformes

This order contains five families; in North America, three families are known to occur in inshore waters, and two are found in deeper waters. There are also a number of unnamed species in North America and throughout the world. Previously considered part of the broad order Gadiformes, these benthic fishes are slender and elongate, with bodies tapering to pointed tips. The bases of the dorsal and anal fins are long, extending to the end of the body, where they either meet with each other or with the caudal fin. When present, the pelvic fins are inserted at the level of the preopercle, sometimes even forward to beneath the eye; each pelvic fin has one or two elongate rays, and occasionally a spine. There are paired nostrils on each side. Some species are unscaled. The families Carapidae (pearlfishes) and Ophidiidae (cuskeels) are oviparous and lack external copulatory organs. The family Bythitidae (viviparous brotulas), with at least six species in North America (plus many still unnamed), is viviparous, and includes several freshwater species in the Bahamas, Cuba, and Mexico. A pelagic vexillifer larval stage is present in the Carapidae, but is absent in the other families.

PEARLFISHES
Family Carapidae

7 genera and 32 species worldwide; 2 genera and 2 species in North America. Found in tropical seas, these small, very slender, unscaled fishes have long bodies tapering to pointed tips. Pectoral fins are sometimes absent. The long dorsal and anal fins meet at the tip of the body; the tail usually disappears as the fish develops. The rays of the anal fin are longer than those of the dorsal fin. The anus and anal fin origin are far forward in adults, located behind the head and usually beneath the pectoral fins. The gill openings are wide and extend far forward, and

there are six to seven branchiostegal rays. There are teeth in the jaws and on the bones in the roof of the mouth, with prominent fangs sometimes present on the premaxilla. The opercle is spineless. Some species are inquiline (living within the bodies of various marine invertebrates without doing any harm to the host). Pearlfishes pass through two distinct larval stages: a pelagic vexillifer stage, which looks like a plant stem with small leaves, and then a demersal tenuis stage, which is extremely elongate and ribbon-like.

530 Pearlfish
Carapus bermudensis

Description: To about 8″ (20 cm). *Slender, elongate, tapering. Pallid, semi-transparent; series of silvery blotches along anterior side.* No enlarged fangs on premaxilla. *Anal fin long, origin under throat,* with rays longer than those of dorsal fin; caudal fin usually absent. Tail pointed.

Habitat: Inquiline; in bodies of sea cucumbers to depths of 720′ (220 m).

Range: NC to Brazil, including Bermuda, Bahamas, Gulf of Mexico, and Caribbean.

Similar Species: Chain Pearlfish (*Echiodon dawsoni*) is free-living (non-inquiline) and has fang-like, canine teeth; occurs at depths of 78–900′ (24–275 m).

Comments: This fish lives in the body cavity of a sea cucumber. It enters tail-first through the anus of its host and backs into the body cavity; it leaves the host to feed, probably during the night. Although reported from several species of sea cucumbers, its most common host in shallow water is *Actinopyga agassizii*. Pearlfish lays free-floating eggs in gelatinous masses.

CUSK-EELS
Family Ophidiidae

 46 genera and about 209 species worldwide; 7 genera and 18 species in North America, plus at least 9 species in Mexican waters. Cusk-eels are found in tropical to temperate waters. These bottom-dwelling fishes

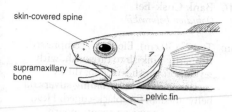

skin-covered spine

supramaxillary bone

pelvic fin

live in burrows or rocks and occur over an extraordinarily wide depth range, from the shoreline to the greatest depth at which any fish species has been collected, almost 27,560′ (8,400 m). Some species are spotted, but most lack distinctive markings; all are scaled. Most cusk-eels have two elongate rays in each pelvic fin, located below the opercle or under the eye. Some species have one or more spines on the opercle, and some have a spine underneath the skin near the snout tip. The dorsal fin rays are usually equal to or longer than the anal fin rays. The anus and anal fin origin are usually behind the pectoral fin tip. A supramaxillary bone is present. Males lack an external copulatory organ. Cusk-eel larvae do not go through a vexillifer larval stage, in contrast to the related pearlfishes (family Carapidae).

501 Spotted Cusk-Eel
Chilara taylori

Description: To 14″ (36 cm). Elongate, eel-like. Light brown to creamy, *with small dark spots.* Fins spineless; *pelvic fin filamentous, located on throat;* dorsal fin long-based; anal fin similar in shape to dorsal fin; dorsal, anal, and caudal fins continuous around body.

Habitat: Soft bottoms to depths of 798′ (243 m).

Range: OR to s Baja California.

Similar Species: Basketweave Cusk-Eel *(Ophidion scrippsae)* lacks spots and has strong crosshatched scale pattern on sides.

Comments: Spotted Cusk-Eel burrows tail-first into the sand or mud during the day, coming out at night to feed. It is occasionally captured by divers and makes an interesting aquarium fish. This fish is sometimes accidentally caught by commercial anglers in trawls and round haul nets.

516 Bank Cusk-Eel
Ophidion holbrookii

Description: To 12″ (30 cm). Elongate, compressed. Primarily pinkish to brownish, with several brownish stripes or dusky mottling on back; becoming silvery on belly; median fins black-edged. Head conical; no spine on snout; mouth inferior; 4 gill rakers. *Pelvic fin rays rather long, with 2 filamentous rays of unequal length,* insertion behind chin; dorsal and anal fins long, continuous with caudal fin around tip of tail. *Scales not overlapping, in oblique rows creating herringbone pattern.*

Habitat: Continental shelf from shoreline to depths of 240′ (73 m).

Range: NC to TX.

Similar Species: Longnose Cusk-Eel *(O. beani)* has 5–6 gill rakers and short pelvic fin rays; occurs at depths of 48–240′ (14.5–73 m). Blotched Cusk-Eel *(O. grayi)* has robust body with prominent brown spots or blotches; occurs at depths of 30–210′ (10–70 m). Crested Cusk-Eel *(O. welshi)* and Striped Cusk-Eel *(O. marginatum)* have 3 rows of dark spots on body, those in upper 2 rows partly fused into solid stripe; both occur to depths of 180′ (55 m). Mottled Cusk-Eel *(Lepophidium jeannae)* has overhanging snout with sharp spine at tip, pelvic fin with 2 filamentous rays of equal length, black blotches on edges of dorsal fin, and overlapping scales in regular rows; occurs to depths of 300′ (91 m).

Comments: Bank Cusk-Eel is often accidentally caught by shrimp trawlers. The taxonomy of the genus *Ophidion* and of related genera is still not completely resolved, and some species remain unnamed.

Order Gadiformes

This order contains 12 families, seven of which are found in North American waters. Members of this order occur in cold-temperate to arctic waters of the Northern Hemisphere.

Most are marine; one species is primarily marine but also occurs in isolated inland waters, and another species is confined to fresh water. These fishes have elongate tapering bodies and spineless fins. When present, the pelvic fins are located below or in front of the pectoral fins; each pelvic fin has up to 11 rays. The dorsal and anal fins are long, and the dorsal fin is often deeply divided into segments. The maxilla is not united with the edge of the upper jaw, and in some species the mouth is protractile. There are six to eight branchiostegal rays. Most species have cycloid scales. A swim bladder is usually present, without a pneumatic duct. Classification of this order has recently undergone many changes. One major group was placed in its own order, the Ophidiiformes; several groups formerly included in the family Gadidae have been recognized as separate families, including the phycid hakes (Phycidae) and the merlucciid hakes (Merlucciidae).

PHYCID HAKES
Family Phycidae

5 genera and 27 species worldwide; 3 genera and 9 species in North America (all Atlantic). Phycid hakes have pelvic fins with moderately to greatly elongate rays. The dorsal fin is separated into two or three segments; when divided into two segments, the first has eight to 13 rays and the second has 43 to 68 rays. All phycid hakes have chin barbels; some also have barbels on the snout (absent in North American species).

511 Red Hake
Urophycis chuss

Description: 20–51″ (52–130 cm), best estimate 30″ (76 cm); 7 lb (3.2 kg). Elongate, cylindrical anteriorly, compressed posteriorly. Coloration variable: usually reddish, often dark or mottled; belly whitish; dorsal and anal fins without dark edges. *Maxilla reaches rear edge of eye;* chin barbel minute. *Pelvic fin extends beyond anus to anal fin origin, with long filamentous third ray; first dorsal fin with elongate third ray;* second dorsal and anal fins long, straight; caudal fin rounded. Caudal peduncle narrow. Lateral line with about 140 scales.

Habitat: On bottom near shore to depths of 3,000' (915 m) or more. Larger individuals in deeper waters.

Range: Labrador to Cape Hatteras, NC.

Similar Species: Longfin Hake *(U. chesteri)* has unpatterned body, dark-edged dorsal and anal fins, first dorsal fin with long, thread-like ray, and longest pelvic fin ray reaching almost to end of anal fin. Gulf Hake *(U. cirrata)* is pale brown, has dark-edged dorsal and anal fins, and lacks elongate dorsal fin ray. Carolina Hake *(U. earllii)* has dark brown body with pale blotches and spots on sides, dark-edged dorsal and anal fins, and lacks elongate dorsal fin ray. Southern Hake *(U. floridana)* is reddish brown above, with series of distinct black spots above and behind eye and on opercle, and has dark-edged dorsal and anal fins, pale lateral line, and lacks elongate dorsal fin ray. Spotted Hake *(U. regia)* is brownish, with 2 dusky streaks from eye to pectoral fin and white streak along mid-side, has first dorsal fin with conspicuous white-black-white pattern, and lacks elongate dorsal fin ray.

Comments: Red and White Hake *(U. tenuis)* are both important commercially, but are not highly esteemed as food or sport fishes. Their flesh is soft and their fighting qualities are too poor to make them attractive to anglers. The young of hake species may occur inshore in shallow water during the winter; in Florida, for example, Southern Hake is common in the winter in shallow bays in the eastern Gulf of Mexico, but disappears as the water warms up.

510 White Hake
Urophycis tenuis

Description: To 4'5" (1.4 m); 48 lb (22 kg). Elongate, cylindrical anteriorly, compressed posteriorly. Back and dorsal fin brown or purplish brown; belly and anal fin dirty white or yellowish; dorsal and anal fins

black-edged; *lateral line pale.* Head pointed, depressed; *maxilla reaches rear edge of eye;* chin barbel small. *Pelvic fin filamentous, not extending beyond anus;* first dorsal fin short, high, triangular, with extended third ray; second dorsal and anal fins long, straight; caudal fin rounded. Caudal peduncle narrow. Lateral line with about 110 scales.

Habitat: Over mud or silt at depths of 36–360′ (11–110 m).

Range: Southern Labrador to Cape Hatteras, NC.

Similar Species: Red Hake *(U. chuss)* has about 140 smaller scales in lateral line.

Comments: White Hake is not popular as a sport fish, but is important commercially.

MERLUCCIID HAKES
Family Merlucciidae

1 genus with 13 species worldwide; 3 species in North America (2 Atlantic, 1 Pacific). These fishes are found at mid-depths in northern and southern temperate regions of the world. Each pelvic fin has seven rays. The dorsal fin is divided into two segments; the first segment has eight to 13 rays, and the second deeply notched segment has 34 to 46 rays. The anal fin is notched, with 35 to 46 rays. The caudal fin is separate from the dorsal and anal fins; it is either squared at the tip or is slightly notched. Members of this family have tiny cycloid scales. The anus and urogenital opening are close together. The long terminal mouth has a black interior and long teeth; vomer teeth are present, but palatine teeth are absent. There are seven branchiostegal rays. Unlike phycid hakes (family Phycidae), merlucciid hakes do not have chin barbels.

---

568 Silver Hake
Merluccius bilinearis

Description: To 30″ (76 cm); 5 lb (2.3 kg). Elongate, rounded to anus, compressed posteriorly. Brownish, with silvery iridescence; silvery below; fins with light greenish borders; axil and edges of pectoral fin black. Maxilla reaches middle of eye; lower jaw projects beyond upper; *no chin barbels;* 15–22 gill rakers. Pelvic fin not filamentous; *first dorsal fin short, high; second dorsal fin long, with deep notch,* similar to anal fin; caudal fin slightly truncate. *Lateral line prominent, appears double.*

Habitat: On or near bottom in deep continental shelf waters; occasionally in shallow waters in pursuit of food.

Range: Grand Banks, NF, to offshore waters of the Carolinas; most abundant in sw Gulf of Maine.

Similar Species: Offshore Hake *(M. albidus)* has 9–11 gill rakers; occurs in deeper waters. Hakes in genus *Urophycis* have chin barbels and long filamentous pelvic fin with 2 rays.

Comments: Commonly marketed as Whiting, this species has a good flavor and is an important commercial fish. Because of its soft flesh, Silver Hake must be processed promptly in order to prevent deterioration. It occurs too deep to be a sport fish.

567 Pacific Hake
Merluccius productus

Description: To 3′ (91 cm). Elongate, slightly compressed. Back metallic silvery gray, with black speckles; silvery below; opercle black. Maxilla extends to middle of eye; *lower jaw projects beyond upper; no chin barbels. Second dorsal and anal fins deeply notched;* caudal fin truncate.

Habitat: Near bottom, at mid-depths, or higher in water column; to depths of 3,000′ (915 m), usually to 750′ (229 m); occasionally in inshore waters.

Range: Gulf of Alaska to Gulf of California.

Similar Species: Walleye Pollock *(Theragra chalcogramma)* has weak or absent chin barbel, jaws of about equal length, dorsal fin divided into 3 segments, and divided anal fin; occurs over soft bottoms.

Comments: The schooling Pacific Hake spawns from January to June. It feeds mostly at night, chiefly on other fishes, shrimps,

and plankton. Anglers trolling for
salmons commonly catch this fish,
but they rarely eat it. Russians eat
large amounts of Pacific Hake; in
the United States this species is
used chiefly for animal food. It is
an important prey for sea lions and
small marine mammals.

CODS
Family Gadidae

15 genera and about 30 species world-
wide; 12 genera and 16 species in North America (7 Atlantic, 4 Pacific, 4 shared, 1 fresh water). These fishes are
confined to cold-temperate or arctic waters of the Northern
Hemisphere; one species is restricted to fresh water, and at
least one has occasional freshwater, or even landlocked, populations. Cods have spineless fins. The long dorsal and anal
fins are both sometimes deeply divided, the dorsal fin into as
many as three segments and the anal fin sometimes into two
segments. Some species have a barbel on the chin. The scales
are small and cycloid. Valuable as food, most cods are harvested commercially and sold fresh, dried, or salted. Histor-
ically, they were important as a major trading item. Some
species are sought by anglers. The eggs of cods are usually
free-floating. Because of recent changes in classification, the
family is now much reduced in size.

515 Cusk
Brosme brosme

Description: To 3'6" (1.1 m); 27 lb (12 kg).
Moderately elongate, cylindrical
anteriorly, compressed posteriorly. Dark
slate to reddish brown above; sides
yellowish, sometimes mottled brown;
belly whitish; *dorsal, anal, and caudal
fins white-edged, each with black
submarginal stripe.* Head flat; mouth
oblique; maxilla reaches beyond eye;
chin barbel present. *Dorsal and anal fins
not divided, not elevated, both partly joined
to caudal fin;* dorsal fin origin above
anterior half of pectoral fin; caudal fin
rounded.

Habitat: Over hard bottoms at depths of
60–3,000′ (18.5–915 m); usually to
600′ (183 m).

Range: Greenland and Grand Banks, NF, to s
New England; occasionally south to NJ.
Also in e North Atlantic.

Comments: Cusk is an important commercial fish.
The annual catch has totaled hundreds
of tons in the United States alone. It is
marketed both fresh and salted.

---

544 Atlantic Cod
Gadus morhua

Description: To 4′ (1.2 m), usually to 24″ (61 cm); 60
lb (27 kg), usually to 10 lb (4.5 kg).
Moderately elongate, slightly
compressed, tapering to slender caudal
peduncle. Coloration varies: greenish,
brownish, yellowish, whitish, or
reddish; *numerous brownish spots on back
and sides; no black blotch on shoulder; lateral
line pale;* fins dark. Eye large; maxilla

reaches anterior edge of eye; upper jaw
projects beyond lower; *chin barbel large.*
Pelvic fin not filamentous; dorsal fin in 3
segments; anal fin in 2 segments; caudal
fin emarginate.

Habitat: On or near hard irregular bottoms
of continental shelf; usually at depths
of 36–120′ (11–37 m), sometimes
deeper.

Range: Western Greenland and Baffin Island,
Canada; south in winter to Cape
Hatteras, NC; most common from
Labrador to New York. Also in e
Atlantic.

Similar Species: Greenland Cod (*G. ogac*) lacks dark
spots on body.

Comments: Atlantic Cod feeds on a variety of
animals, mostly mollusks, sea squirts,
and other fishes. The annual catch of
this commercially important fish
amounts to tens of thousands of tons. It
is often caught on a hand line by anglers
in New England. The largest individual
on record was 6′ (1.8 m) long and
weighed 209 lb (95 kg).

45 Burbot
Lota lota

Description: To 3′2″ (97 cm); 18½ lb (8.5 kg).
Elongate, robust, compressed posteriorly.
Yellowish brown to dark olive above;
sides mottled light and dark; *pelvic fin
pale;* other fins dark, mottled. Head
broad, flat; nostril tubular; maxilla
reaches eye; *chin barbel slender. Pelvic fin
far forward; first dorsal fin short, with 8–16
rays;* second dorsal fin long, with 60–80
rays; anal fin long, with 60–76 rays;
caudal fin rounded.

Habitat: Deep cold rivers and lakes.

Range: AK, most of Canada, and Great Lakes
south to Ohio and Missouri River
drainages; strays downstream to w TN.

Comments: Burbot is unusual among freshwater
fishes in that it spawns in the winter
under ice. From December to March it
spawns at night in shallow water over
clean sand, gravel, or rocks, where the
eggs lie unattended. Adults feed mainly
on other fishes. This the only exclusively
freshwater species in the cod family. It is
occasionally caught by anglers.

562 Haddock
Melanogrammus aeglefinus

Description: To 3′8″ (1.1 m), usually to 30″ (76 cm);
37 lb (17 kg), usually to 10 lb (4.5 kg).
Moderately elongate, slightly
compressed, tapering to slender caudal
peduncle. Dark gray above; whitish
below; *large dark blotch on shoulder; lateral
line black;* dorsal and caudal fins dusky.
Maxilla not reaching eye; *chin barbel very
small. Pelvic fin not filamentous;* dorsal fin
in 3 segments, anterior rays of first long
and ending in sharp point; anal fin in 2
segments.

Habitat: Usually at depths of 150–450′
(46–137 m); rarely in shoal waters.

Range: Grand Banks, NF, to Cape Cod, MA;
south in winter to deep waters off Cape
Hatteras, NC. Also in e North Atlantic.

Comments: Haddock lives in deeper waters than Atlantic Cod *(Gadus morhua)* and prefers smooth bottoms of sand, gravel, or clay. It feeds indiscriminately on available fauna. This species is somewhat more important commercially than Atlantic Cod; it has been greatly depleted by overfishing.

564 Pacific Tomcod
Microgadus proximus

Description: To 12″ (30 cm). Elongate, moderately compressed. Olive green above; creamy white below; fin tips dusky. *Chin barbel small, equal in length to width of pupil. Dorsal fin in 3 segments, first above anus; anal fin in 2 segments.*

Habitat: Over soft bottoms; usually at depths of 90–720′ (27–220 m). Young in shallower waters, often around piers and jetties in bays.

Range: Bering Sea to Point Sal, CA.

Similar Species: The larger Pacific Cod *(Gadus macrocephalus)* has longer chin barbel, equal in length to width of entire eye, and anus is below second dorsal fin; occurs in deeper waters.

Comments: Pacific Tomcod grows fast but lives only about five years. During occasional runs of abundance, it is popular with pier and skiff anglers. This species is considered a fine food fish, but is not large enough to support a commercial fishery.

565 Atlantic Tomcod
Microgadus tomcod

Description: To 15″ (38 cm); 1¼ lb (600 g). Moderately elongate, tapering, slightly compressed. Olive to dark green above, with yellowish tinge; becoming pale on sides; *body and fins mottled with indefinite dark spots or blotches;* lateral line pale. Snout conical, overhanging lower jaw; eye small; chin barbel relatively large.

Second pelvic fin ray filamentous, twice as long as rest of fin; dorsal fin in 3 segments; anal fin in 2 segments; caudal fin rounded.

Habitat: Shallow waters to depths of about 18′ (5.5 m); brackish and fresh waters in estuaries and rivers.

Range: Labrador to VA; enters rivers, with landlocked populations in some lakes in NS and QC.

Comments: This small cod is known to ascend the Hudson River nearly to Albany, New York. It is tolerant of cold, and spawns in water temperatures as low as 34° F (1° C). During the winter when other fishes may be scarce, this excellent food fish is often sought by anglers.

---

560 Pollock
Pollachius virens

Description: To 3′6″ (1.1 m), usually to 3′ (91 cm); 46 lb (21 kg), usually 4–15 lb (1.8–6.8 kg). Rather elongate, somewhat compressed. Olive green, brownish green, or grayish above; sides paler; belly silvery; *lateral line white;* paired fins tinged with pink; median fins olive gray or greenish. Maxilla reaches anterior edge of eye; *lower jaw projects beyond upper; chin barbel minute, absent in large individuals.* Pelvic fin short; dorsal fin in 3 segments, first segment roughly triangular; anal fin deeply incised, in 2 nearly separate segments; caudal fin deeply emarginate or lunate.

Habitat: Over rocks to depths of 600′ (183 m); sometimes at mid-depths or surface.

Range: Southwestern Greenland and Labrador to NJ, apparently reaching greatest abundance in Gulf of Maine; south in winter to NC. Also in e North Atlantic.

Comments: Pollock usually runs in schools and is an important part of the New England and North Atlantic fishery, but less so than Atlantic Cod *(Gadus morhua)* and Haddock *(Melanogrammus aeglefinus).*

TOADFISHES
Order Batrachoidiformes
Family Batrachoididae

This order consists of a single family: 19 genera and more than 69 species worldwide; 2 genera and 6 species in North America (4 Atlantic, 2 Pacific), plus 2 genera and 12 species confined to Mexican waters (including 1 restricted to fresh water). These fishes occur mostly in tropical to temperate seas; several species live permanently in fresh water. Toadfishes live on the bottom, mostly in bays, lagoons, and coastal waters along continental shelves. A few species are found around coral reefs, and one occurs to depths of 1,200′ (366 m). Toadfishes are small to medium, slow-moving, carnivorous fishes. Most are drab brown and variously blotched and mottled, but a few are strikingly marked and colorful. Members of the genus *Porichthys* have rows of photophores on the underside of the head and body. All have a moderately broad and flat head, with eyes near the top of the head and directed upward. The dorsal fin is separated into two segments, and the first segment has two or three low stout spines. In two tropical genera, the opercular spine and two dorsal fin spines are hollow and serve to conduct poison from underlying venom glands. The anal and second dorsal fins are low and long, with at least 15 and 18 fin rays, respectively. The pelvic fins are small and situated under the throat. The small caudal fin is usually rounded. When present, the scales are small and cycloid. Toadfishes have at least one lateral line. There is no larval stage; the young are miniature replicas of the adults.

514 Oyster Toadfish
Opsanus tau

Description: To 15″ (38 cm). Robust, compressed. Olive brown above; belly paler, with pale bars or irregular blotches; paired fins pale; median fins dusky; *complete pale bars across pectoral and caudal fins.* Head large, depressed; *mouth very large, wide; fleshy flaps on upper and lower lips;* teeth strong, blunt. Pectoral fin broad at base, fan-like, *with 19–20 rays,* insertion posterior to pelvic fin; *usually 25–26 dorsal fin rays;* anal fin spineless, similar to dorsal fin but shorter; caudal fin rounded. Body unscaled.

Habitat: Shallow waters with vegetation or among debris and man-made objects over sand or mud.

Range: Cape Cod, MA, to n FL; stragglers south to Miami area in cold years.

Similar Species: Gulf Toadfish *(O. beta)* has lighter blotches on body and pectoral fin, 18–19 pectoral fin rays, and usually 24–25 dorsal fin rays. Leopard Toadfish *(O. pardus)* has yellowish, buff, or straw-colored head and body with darker brown markings, irregular blotching on fins not forming complete bars, and 20–22 pectoral fin rays.

Comments: Oyster, Gulf, and Leopard Toadfishes have powerful jaws and should be handled with caution. They remain in hiding, awaiting their prey, which includes a variety of crustaceans, annelids, mollusks, and fishes.

---

518 Plainfin Midshipman
Porichthys notatus

Description: To 15″ (38 cm). Elongate, tapering. Purplish bronze above; yellowish white below; rows of photophores on underside, *second row under head V-shaped and with apex toward front;* pectoral, dorsal, and anal fins plain. Head large, broad; *eyes widely separated, protruding.* 33–38 dorsal fin rays; 28–34 anal fin rays.

Habitat: Over sand or mud from shoreline to depths of 1,200′ (366 m).

Range: Sitka, AK, to Gulf of California.

Similar Species: Specklefin Midshipman *(P. myriaster)* has U-shaped second row of photophores under head, spots on pectoral, dorsal, and anal fins, and 33–39 anal fin rays.

Comments: Plainfin Midshipman enters shallow water during the late spring to spawn. The male becomes emaciated while guarding the eggs and young, causing a high mortality rate among egg-tending males. This species feeds at night on other fishes and crustaceans. It often appears in the catches of sport and commercial anglers.

519 Atlantic Midshipman
Porichthys plectrodon

Description: To 12½″ (31.5 cm). Elongate, tapering.
Light to very dark brown; usually with
numerous small to medium brown to
black spots above and on dorsal fin; 10
blotches on sides; *rows of golden
photophores on underside, those under head
with forward-directed, U-shaped extension.*
Usually 12–14 gill rakers. Usually
17–18 pectoral fin rays; usually 35–37
dorsal fin rays; usually 32–34 anal fin
rays; caudal fin not connected to dorsal
or anal fin. 4 lateral lines.

Habitat: Offshore banks over soft bottoms;
usually in relatively shallow waters,
recorded to depths of 840′ (256 m).

Range: Cape Henry, VA, to n Brazil, including
Gulf of Mexico and Caribbean except
West Indies.

Comments: Atlantic Midshipman is often found in
commercial shrimp grounds.
Midshipman species are bottom-dwelling
fishes; they burrow a short distance into
the substrate and most likely are active
at night. The common name
midshipman relates to the arrangement
of the photophores on the underside of
the body, which may be likened to gold
buttons on the front of a midshipman's
uniform. The genus *Porichthys* is one of
only a very few groups of shallow-water
fishes with bioluminescent properties.
The function of the photophores is
something of a mystery, perhaps related
to mate recognition during breeding,
which probably occurs at night.

Order Lophiiformes

This order contains 16 families, six of which are found in
North America. A number of additional species occur in
deeper waters offshore. All species are marine; a high percentage are restricted to deep water, some living at mid-
depths and most on the bottom. The bodies of these fishes
are usually strongly compressed, either laterally or dorso-
ventrally. The small gill opening on each side is situated

partly in front of the pectoral fin base. The pelvic fins are well in front of the pectoral fins, which sometimes function as "legs" for locomotion. The first ray of the spiny dorsal fin is often greatly elongate and modified into a "fishing pole" (the illicium) of varying length; the spine tip contains a fleshy appendage (the esca) that functions as a "lure." In some deep-sea families the male is tiny and permanently attached to the body of the female. The highly modified morphology and unusual life history of some families make the lophiiform fishes among the most bizarre of all fish groups.

GOOSEFISHES
Family Lophiidae

4 genera and 25 species worldwide; 2 genera and 5 species in North America (3 Atlantic, 2 Pacific). Found in tropical to cold-temperate seas throughout the world, members of this family have broad, rounded, flat heads and tapering bodies, squarish pectoral fins, and wide superior mouths that are equipped with many thin sharp teeth. The dorsal fin is divided into two segments; the soft-rayed segment is long and squarish, and the spiny segment is separated into several free spines that extend forward to the front of the head. The foremost dorsal fin spine, located just behind the upper lip, is modified to form a "fishing pole," complete with a fleshy "lure" at the tip; this structure attracts the smaller fishes that are part of a goosefish's diet. Goosefish flesh has an excellent flavor and is sold as a delicacy in Japan, Europe, and North America.

341 Goosefish
Lophius americanus

Description: To 4′ (1.2 m); 48 lb (22 kg). Tapering. Tan to chocolate brown above, finely mottled; whitish below; membranes of dorsal fin behind head black; other fins darker than body; *inner edge of pectoral fin not black;* fringe of fleshy flaps on lower jaw, head, and sides. Head flat, rounded; mouth wide, opens upward; teeth numerous, thin, sharp; gill opening round, behind pectoral fin axis. *Pectoral fin broad, squarish;* first dorsal fin spine modified as "fishing pole," *third spine on top of head shorter than width of ridge between eyes.*

Habitat:	On bottom to depths of about 1,200′ (366 m); frequents shallow waters north of NC.
Range:	Bay of Fundy to n FL.
Similar Species:	Blackfin Goosefish *(L. gastrophysus)* has pectoral fin with black inner edge and long third dorsal fin spine on top of head, and lacks membranes between dorsal fin spines behind head; occurs in deep waters.
Comments:	Goosefish species have an enormous capacity for food and eat almost any kind of fish, turtles, and invertebrates; some species have been reported to eat birds, including geese. They apparently can swallow fishes that are equal to their own weight. This species is widely marketed as Monkfish.

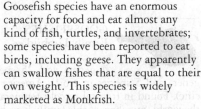

FROGFISHES
Family Antennariidae

14 genera and 43 species worldwide; 2 genera and 7 species in North America (6 Atlantic, 1 Pacific). Found in tropical and warm-temperate seas, these small fishes have globular, slightly to moderately compressed bodies. They are poor swimmers; their coloration changes to match their environment, and they depend on this camouflage for concealment from predators. The skin is either prickly or smooth and often has fleshy flaps. The mouth is strongly superior and oblique. The pectoral fins are limb-like. The first dorsal fin spine, located near the snout tip, is separated from the rest of the long dorsal fin and modified into a "fishing pole" with a "lure" at its tip. Frogfishes feed by waiting in ambush, or by enticing other fishes. The "lure" is wiggled to mimic a live animal, attracting potential prey. Faster than the eye can follow, the frogfish gulps the unsuspecting victim.

---

346 Longlure Frogfish
Antennarius multiocellatus

Description:	To 6″ (15 cm). Globular, compressed. Light phase: usually pale yellow; small spot beneath and above pectoral fin; small spot at base of third dorsal fin spine;

342 Pancake Batfish
Halieutichthys aculeatus

Description: To 4″ (10 cm). Disk-shaped, fringed
with fleshy papillae; eyes included well
within borders of disk when viewed
from above. Light brown above, *with
irregular dark lines and small blotches
creating net-like pattern;* very small white
speckles over entire dorsal surface;
unpigmented and unscaled below; eye
blue; fins dusky; dark diffuse crossbars
on pectoral and caudal fins. *Snout not
protruding, without prominent horn-like
projection on each side;* "fishing pole"
retracts into groove beneath snout;
mouth small. Paired fins limb-like;
pectoral fin connected to tail by
membrane. Tail section short, broad,
greatly depressed, with dorsal fin at base.

Habitat: Shoreline to edge of continental shelf
over sand; most abundant at depths of
252–390′ (77–119 m).

Range: NC to n South America, including
Bahamas, Gulf of Mexico, and
Caribbean.

Similar Species: Tricorn Batfish (*Zalieutes megintyi*) has
prominent horn-like projection on each
side of snout; occurs usually at depths of
300–600′ (91–183 m).

Comments: This fish, sometimes called Spiny
Batfish, remains partially covered by
sand during the day and becomes active
at night. It swims by moving its
pectoral fins in an oar-like fashion,
seeming to "walk" along the bottom.

344 Roughback Batfish
Ogcocephalus parvus

Description: To 4″ (10 cm). Triangular, very wide;
tail round in cross section. Dark brown
above, with light net-like pattern;
uneven lavender spots on sides; cheek
white with orange spots; small black
dots on tail section; *pectoral fin bicolored,
buff to red at base, blackish at tip;*

caudal fin usually pale, with dark reddish or blackish tip. *Snout protrudes, short, upturned;* "fishing pole" 3-lobed, retracts to groove beneath snout; mouth small. Pectoral fin with 10–11 rays, tip rounded. Body and tail covered with large rough bucklers.

Habitat: Offshore over sand or mud; usually at depths of 180–450′ (55–137 m).

Range: Cape Hatteras, NC, to n Brazil, including e Gulf of Mexico and Caribbean.

Similar Species: Polka-dot Batfish (*O. radiatus*) reaches length of 15″ (38 cm), and has pectoral fin with many large spots and usually 13 rays. Palefin Batfish (*O. rostellum*) is similar to Polka-dot Batfish, but has mostly plain pectoral fin; occurs at depths of 92–750′ (28–229 m). Longnose Batfish (*O. corniger*) also has bicolored pectoral fin, but snout is much longer; occurs at depths of 60–760′ (18.5–232 m). Shortnose Batfish (*O. nasutus*) has uniformly brown to dark brown pectoral fin; occurs to depths of 1,000′ (305 m). Spotted Batfish (*O. pantostictus*) reaches length of 12″ (30 cm), and has many large spots on entire upper body; occurs at depths of 30–100′ (9–30 m). Slantbrow Batfish (*O. declivirostris*) has short snout with downward-pointed tip and pectoral fin with pointed tip; occurs at depths of 12–1,280′ (3.7–390 m).

Comments: The snout length varies among different batfish species; although the length is of diagnostic importance, it is sometimes difficult to evaluate taxonomically. In some species the snout remains long throughout life, whereas in others it becomes much reduced with increasing age and size of the individual.

343 **Polka-dot Batfish**
Ogcocephalus radiatus

Description: To 15″ (38 cm). Triangular, very wide. Dark brown, with reddish- to yellowish-orange patches above; diffuse stripe of

dark spots extends along side from eye
to caudal fin; coppery red below; cheek
spotted; *pectoral fin tan to yellowish to
whitish above, with many large dark brown
spots sometimes dense and creating net-like
pattern;* caudal fin with blackish
posterior edge. Snout always very short,
sometimes with stout upturned
projection, never longer than eye.
Pectoral fin with 12–14 (usually 13) rays,
tip rounded.

Habitat: Inshore waters to depths of 230′ (70 m);
usually over hard-packed sand or mud.

Range: Western Bahamas, se FL, and n Gulf of
Mexico to Bay of Campeche.

Similar Species: Palefin Batfish *(O. rostellum)* has mostly
plain pectoral fin; occurs at depths of
92–750′ (28–229 m). Roughback
Batfish *(O. parvus)* reaches length of 4″
(10 cm), and has bicolored, black-tipped
pectoral fin with 10–11 rays.

Comments: This is the most common batfish in
North American inshore waters; it is
sometimes found in water so shallow
that the fish can be observed from shore.
It is sometimes referred to as *O. cubifrons.*

MULLETS
Order Mugiliformes
Family Mugilidae

This order consists of a single family:
about 17 genera and at least 66 species worldwide; 2 genera
and 7 species in North America, plus 2 genera and 5 species
confined to Mexican waters. Mullets live primarily in
coastal waters and in estuaries in warm-temperate and tropical regions throughout the world. Early development is in
the ocean; adults of some species enter fresh water and may
ascend rivers for considerable distances, and others spend
their entire adult life in fresh water. These fast-swimming
fishes often jump clear of the surface. They range in size
from small to fairly large, reaching lengths of 3′ (91 cm).
They have elongate bodies that are almost cylindrical near
the head, but become compressed posteriorly. The snout is
blunt, the mouth is small and wide, and the premaxilla is
protractile. The adipose eyelid is sometimes well developed.
The pelvic fins are located about midway between the middle of the abdomen and the pectoral fin base. The pectoral

fins are inserted above the axis of the body. The dorsal fins are well separated, the first consisting of four spines. The scales are usually described as cycloid; however, they actually change from a cycloid to a ctenoid condition in adults of many species. The lateral line is very faint or absent. This group was previously placed in the order Perciformes, and shares a number of characteristics generally associated with that order, such as spiny pelvic, dorsal, and anal fins, abdominal pelvic fins, and scales either cycloid or ctenoid.

68, 559 Striped Mullet
Mugil cephalus

Description: To 18″ (46 cm). Elongate, cylindrical anteriorly, compressed posteriorly. Silvery; back olive green or blue-green; *6–7 dark stripes on side.* Head flat between eyes; adipose eyelid well developed; mouth small, wide, terminal; *fleshy knob at tip of lower jaw.* Pelvic fin abdominal; pectoral fin inserted high on shoulder; first dorsal fin with 4 spines, well separated from second dorsal fin; anal fin with 3 spines, *8 rays* (2 spines and 9 rays in small young); caudal fin forked. *Scales cycloid, covering body, top of head, and bases of second dorsal and anal fins.* No lateral line; *38–42 scales in lateral series.*

Habitat: Coastal waters and estuaries; often ascends far up into fresh water.

Range: In Atlantic from Cape Cod, MA, to Bay of Campeche, Mexico; occasionally north to NS. In Pacific from s CA to n Chile; occasionally north to San Francisco Bay.

Similar Species: Liza (*M. liza*) reaches length of 3′ (91 cm), and has 31–36 scales in lateral series; occurs in Atlantic and enters fresh water. Fantail Mullet (*M. trichodon*) has blackish blotch at pectoral fin base, tiny scales on second dorsal and anal fins, and 33–37 scales in lateral series; occurs in Atlantic and does not enter fresh water. Mountain Mullet (*Agonostomus monticola*) has brownish body with yellowish fins and ctenoid scales, lacks adipose eyelid, and lower jaw is not angular at tip; adults restricted to fresh water. White

Mullet *(M. curema)* lacks stripes, and has 9–10 anal fin rays, densely scaled second dorsal and anal fins, and usually 38–39 scales in lateral series.

Comments: This important food fish forms small to medium schools in tropical to warm-temperate seas. It is known to travel several hundred miles up rivers, but spawning always takes place in the sea. Striped Mullet feeds on small algae and debris gleaned from the mud. Past records of this species from the West Indies and adjacent areas to the south are believed to be based on the similar and closely related Liza. Striped Mullet is one of the small number of inshore marine species that have a worldwide distribution.

69, 563 White Mullet
Mugil curema

Description: To 15" (38 cm), reputedly to 3' (91 cm). Elongate, cylindrical anteriorly, compressed posteriorly. Silvery; back olive green or blue-green; *no noticeable stripes;* 2 bronze blotches on each side of head; bluish-black axillary blotch at pectoral fin base. Head flat between eyes; adipose eyelid well developed; mouth small, wide, terminal; *fleshy knob at tip of lower jaw.* Pelvic fin abdominal; pectoral fin inserted high on shoulder; first dorsal fin with 4 spines, well separated from second dorsal fin; anal fin with 3 spines, 9–10 (usually 9) rays (2 spines and 10 rays in small young); caudal fin forked. Scales cycloid, covering body, top of head; *second dorsal and anal fins densely covered with tiny scales.* No lateral line; 37–40 (usually 38–39) scales in lateral series.

Habitat: Coastal waters and estuaries; occasionally enters fresh water.

Range: New England (seasonally) to s Brazil, including Bermuda, Bahamas, Gulf of Mexico, and Caribbean. Also in e Atlantic and e Pacific.

Similar Species: Fantail Mullet *(M. trichodon)* also has
small dense scales covering second dorsal
and anal fins, but has 33–37 scales in
lateral series; does not enter fresh water.
Liza *(M. liza)* has distinct stripes on
body, 8 anal fin rays, scales restricted to
bases of second dorsal and anal fins, and
31–36 scales in lateral series; enters
fresh water. Striped Mullet *(M. cephalus)*
resembles Liza, but has 38–42 scales in
lateral series.

Comments: White Mullet enters fresh water, though
much less frequently and not nearly as
far inland as Striped Mullet.

Order Atheriniformes

This order contains eight families, two of which occur in
North America north of Mexico. Members of this order are
morphologically diverse and are distributed worldwide in
virtually all tropical and temperate marine, brackish, and
freshwater environments. The pelvic fins are abdominal,
subabdominal, or thoracic. There are usually two dorsal
fins; when present, the first consists of weak flexible spines.
The anal fin usually has a single spine preceding the rays.
The lateral line is absent or very faint, and the pores are not
joined by tubes. The nostril openings are paired. Classification of the order has undergone radical changes, with many
families now included in the orders Beloniformes and
Cyprinodontiformes. One indication of the close relationship among these orders is the evolution of live-bearing
species and the ability of the eggs in certain genera to completely develop in a dry environment.

NEW WORLD SILVERSIDES
Family Atherinopsidae

13 genera and about 74 species world-
wide; 6 genera and 13 species in North America, plus 6 genera and 44 species confined to Mexico, mostly in fresh water.
These fishes, found in temperate and tropical marine, brackish, or fresh waters, are mostly small, delicate, elongate, and
slightly compressed. All have a silvery lateral stripe on each
side extending from the pectoral fin to the caudal fin. The
mouth is terminal and oblique. The two dorsal fins are well
separated; the first consists of a few weak spines. The pelvic,
second dorsal, and anal fins each have a single spine preced-

ing the rays. The scales are large and cycloid, and the lateral
line, when present, is placed low on the side. This family was
formerly included in the family Atherinidae (now known as
the Old World silversides); external characteristics are virtually
ally identical in both families.

---

647 Topsmelt
Atherinops affinis

Description: To 14½" (37 cm). Elongate, compressed.
Green-blue above, with silvery mid-lateral
stripe; silvery below. *Teeth forked, in 1 row
on each jaw.* Dorsal fins well separated; first
dorsal fin small, with 5–9 delicate spines;
anal fin origin posterior to first dorsal
fin. 5–8 scales between dorsal fins.
Habitat: Surface waters near shore, in bays, and
around kelp beds.
Range: Vancouver Island, BC, to Gulf of
California.
Similar Species: Jacksmelt *(Atherinopsis californiensis)* also
has anal fin origin behind first dorsal fin,
but has unforked teeth in bands on jaws
and 10–12 scales between dorsal fins.
Comments: This schooling species matures in two to
three years and spawns during the late
winter and spring. The large eggs are
attached to kelp and other algae.
Topsmelt and the larger Jacksmelt are
caught by anglers from piers. The
annual commercial haul of both species
in California totals about 250 tons.

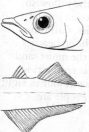

---

185 Brook Silverside
Labidesthes sicculus

Description: To 4" (10 cm). Elongate, slender,
compressed, depth one-seventh length.
Pale greenish yellow, translucent; silvery
lateral stripe bordered above by dark
line; fins clear; tips of dorsal fin spines
black in males. Head long, flat above,
narrow below; snout longer than eye;
jaws pointed, beak-like; maxilla not
reaching eye. Dorsal fins separate; *origin
of first dorsal fin slightly posterior to anal
fin origin; anal fin long, with 1 spine,*

21–25 rays; caudal fin forked. Lateral line incomplete.

Habitat: Quiet clear lakes, ponds, rivers, creeks, and reservoirs.

Range: Great Lakes and St. Lawrence River; Atlantic coastal plain from SC to FL; PA southwest to w OK; Mississippi River system. Introduced in NE.

Similar Species: Inland Silverside *(Menidia beryllina)* has first dorsal fin origin anterior to anal fin origin.

Comments: Brook Silverside is adapted for living near the surface, where it forms large schools during the day and feeds on zooplankton and small insects. It is an important forage and bait fish.

60 California Grunion
Leuresthes tenuis

Description: To 7½″ (19 cm). Fusiform, elongate. Greenish above; silvery below, with mid-lateral stripe; bluish blotch on cheek. Snout bluntly rounded; *teeth minute or absent.* Dorsal fins separate; origin of first dorsal fin slightly anterior to anal fin origin. 7–9 scales between dorsal fins.

Habitat: Off sandy beaches to depths of about 60′ (18.5 m).

Range: San Francisco, CA, to Bahía San Juanico, Baja California.

Similar Species: Surf Smelt *(Hypomesus pretiosus),* in smelt family (Osmeridae), has adipose fin and 1 dorsal fin.

Comments: This fish is smaller and more slender than other Pacific coast silversides; it also differs in having a bluish blotch on the cheek, rather than the yellowish blotch of other Pacific coast species. During spring high tides, California Grunion spawns at night on beaches. The eggs are buried in the moist sand and hatch when the next spring tide occurs. Each female spawns four to eight times during a season. People are allowed to use only their hands to

capture these fishes during spawning.
Gulf Grunion *(L. sardina),* which spawns
during the day, replaces California
Grunion in the Gulf of California.

186, 649 Inland Silverside
Menidia beryllina

Description: To 4″ (10 cm). Elongate, slender,
moderately compressed. Pale greenish
above; paler below; *silvery lateral stripe,*
with dark line above; posterior edges of
scales dusky; fins pale; *peritoneum silvery.*
Snout shorter than eye; mouth terminal,
oblique; maxilla not reaching eye.
Dorsal fins well separated; origin of first
dorsal fin anterior to anal fin origin; anal
fin long, with 16–18 rays; caudal fin
forked. *Scales with smooth edges, not rough
to touch;* usually 37–39 scales in lateral
series.

Habitat: Coastal waters and freshwater streams
and rivers; usually over sand.

Range: Along coast and in associated freshwater
streams from MA to Veracruz, Mexico;
inland in lower Mississippi River
drainage and Rio Grande.

Similar Species: Atlantic Silverside *(M. menidia)* has
black peritoneum and longer anal fin;
occurs in salt water. Tidewater Silverside
(M. peninsulae) has deeper body; occurs
in salt and brackish waters. Key
Silverside *(M. conchorum)* has 12–15 anal
fin rays; occurs in salt water. Rough
Silverside *(Membras martinica)* has
scalloped scales, rough to touch; occurs
in salt and fresh waters.

Comments: The taxonomy of the genus *Menidia* is
complex. Texas Silverside *(M.
clarkhubbsi)* is an all-female species.
Until recently, Inland Silverside and
Tidewater Silverside were considered to
be the same species; however, the two
are now known to be distinct species,
based largely on genetic differences.
They occasionally occur together in
some brackish situations.

Order Beloniformes

This order contains five families, four of which are found in North America. Many species are confined to fresh water or weak brackish water. These fishes have elongate bodies; the back is not elevated. The jaws are very elongate in some groups; the upper jaw is not protractile. The pelvic fins are usually abdominal, sometimes subabdominal; the pectoral fins are usually high on the body. The dorsal and anal fins are far back on the body. The lower lobe of the caudal fin has more rays than the upper lobe. Reproduction in these fishes is usually oviparous, occasionally viviparous.

NEEDLEFISHES
Family Belonidae

10 genera and 32 species worldwide; 4 genera and 8 species in North America. Needlefishes are found in tropical to temperate waters; most species are marine, but some occasionally occur in fresh water. They have very elongate bodies that are either cylindrical or compressed. The jaws are usually very long, beak-like, and armed with numerous sharp teeth. The spineless fins are similar to those of flyingfishes (family Exocoetidae) and halfbeaks (family Hemiramphidae). The pelvic fins are abdominal; the dorsal and anal fins are far back on the body and similar in size and shape; and the lower lobe of the caudal fin is longer than the upper. Needlefishes are found near the surface and skitter over the water. They are predators that feed primarily on small fishes. These fishes are often called gars or saltwater gars because of their physical and behavioral similarities to freshwater gars (family Lepisosteidae), but the two families are not closely related.

25, 477 Atlantic Needlefish
Strongylura marina

Description: To 25″ (64 cm). Very elongate, round in cross section. Greenish to blue-green above; silvery below; often with dark stripe on each side extending from above pectoral fin to caudal fin base; side of head pale, at least below mid-eye level. *Upper and lower jaws very elongate, with numerous sharp teeth.* Fins spineless; pelvic fin small, abdominal; pectoral fins inserted high on side; dorsal and anal fins far back on body; 14–17 dorsal fin rays; 16–20 anal fin rays; caudal fin not deeply forked, lower lobe slightly longer than upper. Caudal peduncle without keels, not strongly depressed; only right gonad developed. Scales small, cycloid. Lateral line follows ventral profile.

Habitat: Coastal waters; enters freshwater coastal streams.

Range: ME to FL and along coasts of Gulf of Mexico and Central and South America to Rio de Janeiro, Brazil; absent from Bahamas and Antilles.

Similar Species: Timucu *(S. timucu)* has broad dusky stripe behind eye with darker area in front of eye, and both gonads are developed; does not enter fresh water. Redfin Needlefish *(S. notata)* has black bar along front edge of opercle, reddish or orangish (in life) dorsal, anal, and caudal fins, and dorsal and anal fins each with 13–15 rays; does not enter fresh water, sometimes enters brackish water.

Comments: Needlefishes often occur in small schools, readily visible near the surface, and are most active at night. They feed primarily on small fishes. It is believed that Atlantic Needlefish spawns in both fresh and salt water. Atlantic Needlefish and Timucu were once thought to be the same species.

FLYINGFISHES
Family Exocoetidae

7–8 genera and about 53 species worldwide; 6 genera and 14 species in North America (10 Atlantic, 3 Pacific, 1 shared), plus 1 genus and 13 species confined to Mexican waters. Flyingfishes are found in tropical to temperate seas. They have nearly cylindrical bodies that are bluish above, shading to silvery on the sides, and white on the belly. All fins are spineless. The pelvic fins are abdominal, sometimes very elongate and extending beyond the anus. The pectoral fins are located high on the sides and are usually greatly enlarged (only slightly enlarged in the genus *Oxyporhamphus*). The dorsal and anal fins are placed far back on the body. The lower lobe of the caudal fin is longer than the upper. The elongate caudal fin lobe propels the fish out of the water, and the enlarged pectoral fins function as "wings" as the fish glides through the air (although actual flapping of the fins does not occur). The scales are cycloid, and the lateral line pores follow the ventral contour of the body. Young flyingfishes have a very elongate lower jaw, which regresses during development and is equal in length to the upper jaw in adults. In the closely related halfbeaks (family Hemiramphidae), the elongate lower jaw in most species is retained throughout life. Flyingfishes live near the surface of open oceans, where they are often abundant, but the young may enter bays, and adults approach shores of oceanic islands to spawn. They are commercially important food fishes in some areas in the Greater Antilles.

695 Fourwing Flyingfish
Hirundichthys affinis

Description: To 12″ (30 cm). Nearly cylindrical. Bluish above; lighter below; *pectoral fin dusky, with pale triangle at base and narrow clear border;* dorsal fin clear, with dark area at edge in young. Pelvic fin elongate; pectoral fin greatly enlarged, with unbranched first ray; dorsal fin low; *anal fin origin slightly in front of dorsal fin origin;* dorsal and anal fins with approximately same number of rays (rarely as many as 2 rays' difference).

Habitat: Surface of open seas.

Range: Gulf Stream off VA and n Gulf of Mexico to Brazil, including Bermuda, Bahamas, and Caribbean. Widespread in tropical Atlantic; absent from e Atlantic.

Similar Species: Blackwing Flyingfish *(H. rondeletii)* lacks pale triangle at pectoral fin base. Oceanic Two-winged Flyingfish *(Exocoetus obtusirostris),* Tropical Two-Winged Flyingfish *(E. volitans),* and Smallfin Flyingfish *(Parexocoetus brachypterus)* have short pelvic fin. Smallwing Flyingfish *(Oxyporhamphus micropterus)* has only slightly enlarged pectoral fin. Bluntnose Flyingfish *(Prognichthys occidentalis)* has dorsal fin with 2–5 more rays than anal fin. Clearwing Flyingfish *(Cheilopogon comatus),* Margined Flyingfish *(C.*

cyanopterus), Bandwing Flyingfish *(C. exsiliens),* Spotfin Flyingfish *(C. furcatus),* and Atlantic Flyingfish *(C. melanurus)* have dorsal fin with 2–5 more rays than anal fin, and anal fin origin is beneath or behind dorsal fin origin.

Comments: Because of their great mobility, flyingfishes generally have wide distributions, with several species occurring worldwide.

HALFBEAKS
Family Hemiramphidae

12 genera and about 85 species worldwide; 4 genera and 9 species in North America (5 Atlantic, 3 Pacific, 1 shared). These fishes are found in tropical to temperate waters; four genera occur in fresh water. Until recently, they were included in the closely related flyingfish family (Exocoetidae). They have similar cylindrical bodies that are bluish above, shading to silvery on the sides, and white on the belly. The upper jaw is usually much shorter than the lower jaw throughout life (in flyingfishes, this is true only in young). All fins are spineless. The pelvic fins are abdominal, and the pectoral fins are located high on the sides; in contrast to the flyingfishes, the paired fins are not enlarged. The dorsal and anal fins are placed far back on the body. The lower lobe of the caudal fin is elongate in some species. Some halfbeaks have internal fertilization and viviparous reproduction (none in North America).

479 Atlantic Silverstripe Halfbeak
Hyporhamphus unifasciatus

Description: To 10½" (27 cm). Very elongate, slightly compressed. Greenish above; 3 black lines on mid-dorsal area between head and dorsal fin; silvery below; scales dark-edged; *tip of lower jaw bright orangish red;* upper caudal fin lobe yellowish red. *Bony ridge in front of eye; lower jaw very long, extending well beyond short upper jaw.* Pelvic fin small, abdominal, with tip falling well short of a point below dorsal fin origin; pectoral fin short, insertion above axis of body; dorsal and anal fins similar in size and

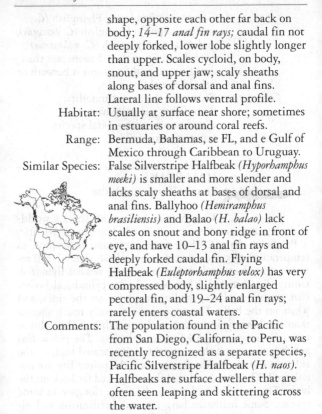

shape, opposite each other far back on body; *14–17 anal fin rays;* caudal fin not deeply forked, lower lobe slightly longer than upper. Scales cycloid, on body, snout, and upper jaw; scaly sheaths along bases of dorsal and anal fins. Lateral line follows ventral profile.

Habitat: Usually at surface near shore; sometimes in estuaries or around coral reefs.

Range: Bermuda, Bahamas, se FL, and e Gulf of Mexico through Caribbean to Uruguay.

Similar Species: False Silverstripe Halfbeak *(Hyporhamphus meeki)* is smaller and more slender and lacks scaly sheaths at bases of dorsal and anal fins. Ballyhoo *(Hemiramphus brasiliensis)* and Balao *(H. balao)* lack scales on snout and bony ridge in front of eye, and have 10–13 anal fin rays and deeply forked caudal fin. Flying Halfbeak *(Euleptorhamphus velox)* has very compressed body, slightly enlarged pectoral fin, and 19–24 anal fin rays; rarely enters coastal waters.

Comments: The population found in the Pacific from San Diego, California, to Peru, was recently recognized as a separate species, Pacific Silverstripe Halfbeak *(H. naos)*. Halfbeaks are surface dwellers that are often seen leaping and skittering across the water.

Order Cyprinodontiformes

This order contains eight families, seven of which are found in North America. Members of this order inhabit marine, estuarine, and fresh waters. They are characterized by a symmetrical caudal fin, well-developed sensory canal pores on the head, pitted scales, and the absence of a lateral line. They exhibit marked sexual dimorphism, with brightly colored males.

TOPMINNOWS
Family Fundulidae

4 genera and about 48 species worldwide; 4 genera and 36 species in North America, plus 3 species in Mexico. These small fishes occur in fresh, brackish, and coastal marine waters; they spend most of their

time near the surface of the water, where they are easily observed. Topminnows have teeth, and the single dorsal fin is far back on the body. The males lack external reproductive organs, and the females lay eggs; both characteristics are important in distinguishing topminnows from the closely related livebearers (family Poeciliidae).

397 Diamond Killifish
Adinia xenica

Description:
To 2″ (5 cm). Very deep and compressed, depth about half of length. *Dark green, with 10–14 narrow pearly bands and wider interspaces;* belly yellowish; lower jaw orange; pelvic fin dusky, with yellowish tip; caudal fin barred, with some pale spots. Males have dusky dorsal and anal fins, with pale blue or orange spots. Head flat above, anterior profile concave; snout pointed; mouth terminal; teeth conical. Dorsal fin origin anterior to anal fin origin. Caudal peduncle deep.

Habitat:
Shallow lagoons, tide pools, ditches, and salt marshes.

Range:
Gulf of Mexico from s FL to s TX.

Similar Species:
Sheepshead Minnow *(Cyprinodon variegatus)* has humeral scale and blunter snout.

Comments:
This beautiful killifish is often locally abundant in shallow tidal waters of marshes and barrier islands.

247, 248 Northern Studfish
Fundulus catenatus

Description:
To 7″ (18 cm). Elongate, moderately stout, somewhat compressed posteriorly. Yellowish brown to olive above; median fins with small brown speckles; edges of dorsal and anal fins not dusky or black. *Males bluish on sides, with 7–11 rows of spots forming stripes; females lighter on sides, somewhat silvery, with short brown horizontal dashes often forming interrupted stripes.* Head broad, flat above; mouth upturned. *13–16 dorsal fin rays; 14–18 anal fin rays.* 39–52 scales in lateral series.

Habitat: Clear streams with moderate gradient over clean sand, gravel, or rocks.

Range: Southwestern VA, south-central IN, central KY, TN, nw GA, n AL, sw MS, s MO, n AR, and e OK.

Similar Species: Barrens Topminnow *(F. julisia)* has irregular spots on head and body; occurs in small spring-fed brooks. Speckled Killifish *(F. rathbuni)* has dark spots on head and unmarked body. Southern Studfish *(F. stellifer)* has scattered reddish-brown spots on sides and black-edged dorsal and caudal fins. Stippled Studfish *(F. bifax)* has short interrupted rows of reddish-brown spots on sides and black-edged dorsal and caudal fins.

Comments: From May to August during spawning, the colorful male Northern Studfish establishes and defends small territories in quiet shallow waters near shore, but does not prepare a nest.

---

249 Golden Topminnow
Fundulus chrysotus

Description: To 3" (7.5 cm). Robust, short. Back dark olive; sides greenish yellow. *Males have reddish spots; 7–10 dusky bars on rear two-thirds of body;* median fins yellowish orange, with red spots. *Females have cream or golden spots.* Head short, wide, flat above; snout short, blunt; mouth upturned. Fins small, rounded; dorsal fin with 7–9 rays, origin behind anal fin origin; 9–11 anal fin rays; caudal fin rounded. Head scaled. 31–35 scales in lateral series.

Habitat: Clear backwaters, sloughs, and pools of sluggish streams, lakes, and marshes with abundant vegetation.

Range: SC south to FL and west along coast to e TX; sw KY and se MO south to Gulf coast.

Comments: Golden Topminnow feeds on a variety of aquatic invertebrates and some plant material. It spawns from March through August. The large eggs, 1/16" (2 mm)

wide, are usually deposited in thick
masses of aquatic vegetation.

250 Banded Topminnow
Fundulus cingulatus

Description: To 3″ (8 cm). Elongate. Olive green
above; *4–5 irregular rows of reddish spots
and 12–15 dark green bars on sides;* white
to reddish orange below; jaws and side
of head without red pigment; fins clear
to reddish orange. 6 sensory pores on
lower jaw. Dorsal fin with 6–8 rays,
origin anterior to anal fin origin; 9–11
anal fin rays.

Habitat: Sluggish creeks and rivers, oxbow lakes,
and floodplain ponds; usually associated
with vegetation.

Range: Lower portions of Gulf coast drainages
from Waccasassa River, FL, to eastern
tributaries of Mobile Bay, AL.

Similar Species: Redface Topminnow *(F. rubrifrons)* has
red pigment on jaws and sides of head.

Comments: The attractive Banded Topminnow is a
popular aquarium fish, due in part to its
nonaggressive behavior. It is also easy to
breed in an aquarium.

242 Banded Killifish
Fundulus diaphanus

Description: To 5″ (12.5 cm). *Elongate.* Olive brown
above; sides silvery, with *12–20 greenish-
brown bars;* throat and fins yellowish.
Snout flat. Dorsal fin with 13–15 rays,
origin anterior to anal fin origin; 10–12
anal fin rays. 39–49 rows of scales in
lateral series.

Habitat: Quiet rivers, creeks, ponds, and lakes
with some vegetation over sand or gravel.

Range: Southern NF southwest in St. Lawrence
River system to Great Lakes; south in
upper Mississippi River system to
north-central IL, and south along
Atlantic coast to SC. Introduced on
Pacific coast in OR and WA.

Similar Species: Waccamaw Killifish *(F. waccamensis)* has
slender body and 54–64 rows of scales in
lateral series; occurs in open lakes near
vegetation.

Comments: Banded Killifish is used as live bait in
some areas; it is a hardy fish and will
survive for hours in a bait bucket.

254, 396 Gulf Killifish
Fundulus grandis

Description: To 6″ (15 cm). Elongate, *moderately
robust.* Males dark greenish blue or olive
above; sides lighter, with small pearly
spots; belly yellowish; pelvic and anal
fins yellowish; small light spots on
median fins. Females olive above; silvery
below; 12–15 narrow bars on sides; anal
fin yellow. Head rather large; snout
bluntly rounded; *10 sensory pores on lower
jaw.* Dorsal fin origin above or anterior
to anal fin origin; dorsal and anal fins
each with 11–12 rays. 39 or fewer scales
in lateral series.

Habitat: Bays, tidal marshes, pools, and ditches
over sand or mud.

Range: Along Gulf coast from ne FL to Veracruz,
Mexico. Introduced in NM and TX.

Similar Species: Mummichog *(F. heteroclitus)* has 8
sensory pores on lower jaw; occurs in
shallow coastal waters over sand.

Comments: Gulf Killifish can tolerate adverse
conditions, such as low oxygen, and
great variation in salinity, ranging from
fresh water to a salt concentration several
times that of seawater. It feeds primarily
on crustaceans and small fishes. This
killifish is valued as a bait fish.

251 Bayou Topminnow
Fundulus nottii

Description: To 3″ (7.5 cm). Short, moderately deep.
Back dark; sides olive to silvery; silvery
spot on top of head; *large square black
blotch under eye. Males have 10–15 faint
dusky bars extending forward to near*

pectoral fin base. Females have dark spots
forming stripes on sides. *Mouth upturned.
Fins small; dorsal fin with 7–8 rays,
origin posterior to anal fin origin.
18–20 scales on caudal peduncle; 30–35
scales in lateral series.*

Habitat: Lowland marshes, ponds, swamps, and
sluggish streams with vegetation.

Range: Gulf coastal plain streams from Mobile
Bay basin drainage, AL, to Lake
Pontchartrain, se LA.

Similar Species: Lined Topminnow *(F. lineolatus)* has
sides with few or no dark dashes or
speckles and 16 caudal peduncle scales;
males have 11–15 dark green bars;
females have 5–8 black stripes; occurs in
clear lowland streams and lakes with
vegetation. Starhead Topminnow *(F.
dispar)* has sides with few or no dark
dashes or speckles and 18–20 caudal
peduncle scales; males have 5–13 dark
green bars; females have 5–8 fine stripes.
Russetfin Topminnow *(F. escambiae)*
males have 11 or fewer (sometimes
absent) dark bars on sides extending
forward only to pelvic fin; females lack
dark speckles between stripes. Western
Starhead Topminnow *(F. blairae)* has
17–18 caudal peduncle scales; males
usually lack dark bars; females have dark
speckles and 6–8 dark thin stripes.

Comments: Bayou Topminnow swims at the surface,
where it feeds on aquatic as well as
terrestrial insects. Spawning occurs
during May and June over dense
growths of aquatic plants.

253 Blackspotted Topminnow
Fundulus olivaceus

Description: To 4″ (10 cm). Elongate. *Back olive to
tan; sides yellowish brown, with broad black
mid-lateral stripe extending from snout;
many distinct black spots on upper sides;
median fins olive, with distinct black
spots.* Head flat above; snout moderately
long. Dorsal fin with 9–10 rays, origin
posterior to anal fin origin; caudal fin

rounded. Head scaled; 33–36 scales in
lateral series.

Habitat: Clear streams with slow to moderate
current over sand, gravel, or rocks.

Range: Western KY, s IL, s MO, e TN, AL, and
w FL west to e TX.

Similar Species: Blackstripe Topminnow *(F. notatus)* has
generally smaller body, and spots are
absent, diffuse, or irregular in shape and
lighter than lateral stripe; occurs in low-
gradient streams, sloughs, and quiet
edges of larger streams, often with
vegetation. Broadstripe Topminnow *(F.
euryzonus)* has very wide purplish-brown
lateral stripe extending almost to lower
edge of caudal peduncle and anteriorly
through upper pectoral fin base.

Comments: Blackpotted Topminnow feeds at the
surface on small crustaceans and insects.
It is common throughout its range.

241, 395 Bayou Killifish
Fundulus pulvereus

Description: To 3″ (7.5 cm). Elongate, rather robust
anteriorly, tapering to slender caudal
peduncle. Olive, with fine brownish
spots (except on breast); *sides with 12 or
more spots, each as large as pupil, sometimes
joining to form oblong blotches.* Head broad,
depressed; eye width greater than length
of snout; mouth superior, slightly
oblique; teeth pointed, in several series,
outer teeth larger. Dorsal fin origin
slightly anterior to anal fin origin.

Habitat: Brackish and saltwater marshes, bayous,
coastal ditches, and ponds; sometimes
freshwater coastal streams.

Range: York River, VA, to ne FL; disjunctly
from Mobile Bay, AL, to s TX.

Similar Species: Marsh Killifish *(F. confluentus)* has
14–18 distinct irregular bars.

Comments: Bayou and Marsh Killifishes may
represent a single species. They
hybridize in northeastern Florida and on
the Gulf coast from the Apalachicola
River in Florida to the Mobile Bay in
Alabama.

252 Plains Topminnow
Fundulus sciadicus

Description: To 2¾" (7 cm). Stout, short, slightly
compressed. Back dusky olive; *sides
greenish to silvery, unmarked;* belly
yellowish; *fins plain, reddish orange in
males, yellowish in females.* Head flat
above; mouth upturned. Dorsal fin with
10–11 rays, origin behind anal fin
origin; 12–15 anal fin rays. Caudal
peduncle deep. Head scaled; 31–39
scales in lateral series.

Habitat: Clear pools and backwaters of springs
and small streams with aquatic
vegetation over sand or gravel.

Range: Western IA, s SD, NE, se WY, and ne
CO; central and sw MO, se KS, and ne
OK.

Comments: Plains Topminnow is usually found near
the surface. It feeds on small crustaceans,
aquatic insects, and some filamentous
algae. Spawning occurs from May
through July in shallow water over
aquatic vegetation.

244 Seminole Killifish
Fundulus seminolis

Description: To 6½" (16.5 cm). Elongate, stout. Back
olive; *sides greenish yellow to silver; scales
dark-edged.* Males have irregular rows of
numerous small black spots on sides;
dorsal and caudal fins with rows of dark
spots, dusky edges. Females have 10–15
faint dusky bars on sides. Mouth
upturned, with 2 rows of teeth. Fins
large, rounded; *dorsal fin with 13–20
rays, origin anterior to anal fin origin.*
50–55 scales in lateral series.

Habitat: Open shallow lakes and streams with
vegetation over sand.

Range: Northern FL to near tip of peninsula.

Comments: Seminole Killifish feeds on bottom-
dwelling invertebrates in shallow open
waters over sand. Spawning takes place
throughout the year, but most breeding
occurs during April and May around

clumps of aquatic vegetation. This is an important forage fish in the lakes of peninsular Florida.

240, 394 Longnose Killifish
Fundulus similis

Description: To 6″ (15 cm). Elongate, relatively slender. Olive or bluish gray above, becoming bronze or silvery below; sides have up to 16 dark bars with wider interspaces, *last bar on caudal peduncle below distinct black spot;* large dark humeral blotch. *Head long; snout pointed,* length greater than width of eye; maxilla not reaching eye. Dorsal fin origin slightly anterior to anal fin origin; dorsal and anal fins relatively high. About 33 scales in lateral series.

Habitat: Tide pools, salt marshes, ditches, and lagoons over sand or mud.

Range: Southern FL, including Florida Keys.

Similar Species: Striped Killifish *(F. majalis)* females have dark stripes on sides.

Comments: Although it does not enter fresh water, Longnose Killifish is very tolerant of low oxygen and fluctuating salinity. Recent evidence suggests that it may be a subspecies of Striped Killifish.

238 Plains Killifish
Fundulus zebrinus

Description: To 5″ (12.5 cm). Elongate, stout anteriorly. Back dark olive; *sides silvery yellow to white, with 12–28 dark bars;* bars wider, fewer, and darker in males; belly yellowish; fins yellowish to reddish. Head flat above; mouth upturned, with band of teeth on jaws. *Fins large, rounded;* dorsal fin with 14–15 rays, origin anterior to anal fin origin; *caudal fin straight-edged.* Caudal peduncle deep. Scales small, present on head; 38–67 scales in lateral series.

Habitat: Shallow pools, backwaters, and edges of streams with slow to moderate current over sand.

Range: Great Plains east of Rocky Mountains from n WY, sw SD, and NE south through nw MO to TX. Introduced in AZ, NV, MT, and UT.

Comments: Plains Killifish tolerates saline and alkaline waters in which few, if any, other fishes are found. It is occasionally used for bait.

---

243 Pygmy Killifish
Leptolucania ommata

Description: To 1¼" (3 cm). Slender, compressed. *Back greenish yellow; belly yellowish.* Males have pale yellow stripe above *black lateral stripe, ending in caudal spot with creamy yellow halo;* 5–7 dusky bars on posterior half of body; dark stripe above anal fin. Females have black lateral stripe ending in caudal spot. Mouth small, upturned; *eye longer than snout.* Dorsal fin with 6–7 rays, origin posterior to anal fin origin. 27–32 scales in lateral series.

Habitat: Dark-stained waters of swamps, slow lowland streams, overflow ponds, and ditches with abundant vegetation.

Range: Southern GA south to s FL and west to se MS.

Comments: Pygmy Killifish is the second-smallest fish in North America. It is attractive, hardy, peaceful, and easily kept in aquariums.

---

245 Bluefin Killifish
Lucania goodei

Description: To 2" (5 cm). Small, relatively elongate, moderately compressed. Back yellowish olive to brown; *black-edged scales on back and sides create crosshatched pattern; well-developed bluish-black to black mid-lateral stripe extends forward to tip of snout;* pelvic fin orangish red; dorsal fin with black base and dusky edge, bright blue in center. Eye large, width greater than length of snout; mouth small; lower jaw projects beyond upper. 9–12 dorsal fin rays. *29–32 scales in lateral series.*

Habitat: Edges of streams, lakes, and ponds with vegetation; especially common along edges of spring runs.

Range: Lower portions of Atlantic coast drainages from GA south throughout peninsular FL and west along Gulf coast to Chipola River in w FL and se AL. Introduced in the Carolinas.

Comments: This species is one of the most attractive killifishes. It is easy to maintain in home aquariums.

239, 391 **Rainwater Killifish**
Lucania parva

Description: To 2″ (5 cm). Small, *relatively elongate, moderately compressed.* Light brown or olive above; lighter below; *scales diamond-shaped to hexagonal, with dusky edges creating crosshatched pattern;* lateral stripe faint, more intense on caudal peduncle in some populations; pelvic and pectoral fins orange to yellow; dorsal and caudal fins with thin black border; *dorsal fin dusky orange in males, with black membranes between first 3 rays.* Eye width greater than length of snout; mouth small, superior; lower jaw projects beyond upper; teeth conical, 1 series in each jaw. No large humeral scale; *23–29 scales in lateral series.*

Habitat: Bays, marshes, estuaries, saltwater ponds, and bayous with vegetation; enters fresh water.

Range: Along coast from MA to Mexico; inland populations in FL and TX. Introduced in OR, CA, NV, UT, and NM.

Comments: Rainwater Killifish tolerates a wide range of salinity. It makes a good aquarium fish.

LIVEBEARERS
Family Poeciliidae

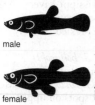

male

female

30 genera and about 300 species worldwide; 4 genera and 13 species native to
North America north of Mexico, plus 8
genera and 77 species in Mexico. Members of this family are found in North
America, Central America, South Amer-
ica, and Africa; they occur in a variety of habitats in fresh,
brackish, and salt waters. Livebearers are elongate, small-
bodied fishes, usually reaching lengths of less than 8″ (20
cm), with a small upturned mouth. They have a single dorsal fin placed near the mid-body. There are 35 or fewer rows
of scales in the lateral series. Unlike the closely related topminnows (family Fundulidae), these fishes give birth to live
young after internal fertilization. The male transmits packets of sperm into the female by a complex copulatory organ
(the gonipodium) formed from the first few rays of the anal
fin. The sperm packets may be held by the female for up to
10 months and used to fertilize several broods.

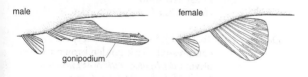

male

female

gonipodium

259, 392 Western Mosquitofish
Gambusia affinis

Description: To 2½″ (6.5 cm). Rather robust,
compressed. Tan to olive gray above;
pale yellowish below; *dark blotch below
eye; small dusky spots near edges of scales;*
many spots on dorsal and caudal fins.
Females particularly robust, with
conspicuous black spot on belly during
reproductive period. Head depressed;
mouth small, oblique; lower jaw
projects beyond upper; teeth small, in 1
villiform band on each jaw. *6 dorsal fin
rays; 9 anal fin rays;* anal fin in males
modified to form reproductive organ.

Habitat: Near surface of ponds, lakes, ditches,
backwaters, and sluggish streams with
fresh or brackish waters.

Range: Central and lower Mississippi River
system and Gulf coast drainages from
MS west to TX and ne Mexico. Widely
introduced.

Similar Species: Eastern Mosquitofish *(G. holbrooki)*
has 8 dorsal fin rays and 10 anal fin rays.
Mangrove Gambusia *(G. rhizophorae)* has
2–3 rows of small dark spots on upper
sides and lacks dark blotch below eye;
occurs in tidal creeks in stands of
mangroves.

Comments: Mosquitofishes eat aquatic mosquito
larvae, hence their common name.
They have been introduced into many
areas in a misguided attempt to control
mosquitoes; although these fishes
consume large numbers of larvae, they
are incapable of actually controlling
mosquito populations.

237 Least Killifish
Heterandria formosa

Description: To 1½" (3.5 cm). Moderately
compressed. Back golden brown to
olive; *sides lighter, with 6–9 indistinct
bars and dusky mid-lateral stripe ending
in darker spot; dark spot on dorsal fin
base;* dark spot on anal fin base in
females. Snout short; eye large;
mouth terminal. Dorsal fin origin
posterior to anal fin origin; anal
fin in males modified to form
reproductive organ. 24–30 scales
in lateral series.

Habitat: Swamps, ditches, ponds, and bayous
with fresh or brackish waters and
abundant aquatic vegetation.

Range: Coastal drainages from s NC south
throughout peninsular FL and west
to TX.

Comments: Least Killifish is very hardy and makes
an interesting aquarium fish. It is the
smallest live-bearing vertebrate found
in the United States.

262, 398 Sailfin Molly
Poecilia latipinna

Description: To 5″ (12.5 cm). Oblong, compressed; *males with about equal depth from dorsal fin posteriorly;* females with rounded belly and narrower caudal peduncle. *Olive on sides; blackish or reddish-orange to yellowish dots on scales form stripes;* caudal fin with dark spots forming bars, less pronounced in females. Head small, depressed; mouth small; teeth in several series, outer teeth largest. *12–16 dorsal fin rays;* dorsal fin in males very tall, sail-like, with blackish spots on membranes between rays forming interrupted narrow bands; anal fin in males located forward, modified as reproductive organ. 23–28 scales in lateral series.

Habitat: Saltwater marshes, ponds, and ditches; freshwater pools, ponds, and ditches.

Range: Along coast from NC to Yucatán; inland streams in FL, LA, and TX. Introduced in lower Colorado River system.

Similar Species: Amazon Molly *(P. formosa)* has 10–12 dorsal fin rays.

Comments: This beautiful fish feeds primarily on plants and organic debris. A variety with black coloring is bred as a popular aquarium fish. Like many members of the family, Sailfin Molly is extremely tolerant of wide ranges in salinity.

255 Gila Topminnow
Poeciliopsis occidentalis

Description: To 2½″ (6 cm). Moderately elongate, greatest depth anterior to dorsal fin. Back dark olive; sides olive to tan, with dark lateral stripe extending from upper edge of opercle to caudal fin base; dark-edged scales on back and sides; *fin rays dark-edged.* Head small; *mouth small, upturned; teeth pointed.* Pelvic fin small; dorsal fin origin posterior to anal fin origin; anal fin in males modified to form reproductive organ; *caudal fin*

rounded to almost square. Scales large; 29
in lateral series.

Habitat: Springs, pools, backwaters, and edges of
streams; usually with debris and aquatic
vegetation.

Range: Gila River drainage from s AZ and sw
NM to Sonora, Mexico.

Comments: Once one of the most common fishes in
the southern Colorado River drainage,
Gila Topminnow was added to the list of
endangered species in 1967. Efforts are
underway to recover it by removing
competitors from isolated springs and
reintroducing it to its native waters.

GOODEIDS
Family Goodeidae

19 genera and 40 species confined to
fresh waters of Nevada and Mexico. Goodeids from the two
regions differ in morphology and reproductive biology and
are placed in different subfamilies. The subfamily Empetrichthyinae (2 genera and 4 species) is found only in desert
springs in southern Nevada. They lack pelvic fins; the dorsal fin, which has 10 to 12 rays, and the anal fin are both located on the posterior part of the body. There are 25 to 33
scales in the lateral series. Members of this subfamily are
small, reaching a maximum length of 3½″ (9 cm), and the
eggs are deposited in vegetation and fertilized externally.
The subfamily Goodeinae (17 genera and 36 species) is
found only in west-central Mexico. They are morphologically similar to the Empetrichthyinae, except males have
short crowded anterior anal rays that are separated from
the remainder of the fin by a deep notch; this structure is
used by the males to accomplish internal fertilization. The
young are born live; embryos and newborns typically have
ribbon-like extensions on the anal region, which are associated with nutrition and respiration during development.
Members of this subfamily often reach a length of 8″ (20
cm). The differences between the subfamilies reflect the
long period of geographic isolation between the two groups.

---

256 White River Springfish
Crenichthys baileyi

Description: To 3½″ (9 cm). Deep, stout, slightly
compressed. Back dark olive to dusky;

sides silvery, with 2 rows of dark spots; belly
yellowish to whitish; fins black-edged.
Head large, flat above; snout blunt;
mouth wide, small; *teeth bicuspid.* Fins
small; *no pelvic fins;* pectoral fin rounded,
insertion low on body; dorsal and anal
fins placed posteriorly; caudal fin
straight-edged. 27 scales in lateral
series.

Habitat: Warm desert spring pools and runs.
Range: White River drainage of se NV.
Similar Species: Railroad Valley Springfish *(C. nevadae)*
has 1 row of dark mid-lateral spot.
Pahrump Killifish *(Empetrichthys latos)*
has conical teeth.
Comments: White River Springfish feeds on
microscopic and filamentous algae and
aquatic invertebrates. Like many other
fishes in desert springs, it is threatened
by the alteration of its limited habitat
and the introduction of exotic fishes.

PUPFISHES
Family Cyprinodontidae

9 genera and about 100 species world-
wide; 3 genera and 14 species in North America, plus 2 genera and 23 species in Mexico. Pupfishes are found in fresh and
brackish waters and coastal marine habitats in North America, parts of northern South America, northern Africa, and
the Mediterranean region. They have relatively short deep
bodies with upturned mouths. Some lack pelvic fins (present in most North American species), and all have a single
dorsal fin. These fishes tolerate extreme environmental conditions, with some species inhabiting waters ranging from
near freezing to 113° F (45° C), saline waters more than
four times saltier than seawater, or waters with the lowest
levels of dissolved oxygen known for any gill-breathing fish.

260 Desert Pupfish
Cyprinodon macularius

Description: To 2¾" (7 cm). Stout, deep; females
deeper-bodied than males. Back silvery
to olive; *sides silvery, with 6–9 dusky bars
often forming irregular lateral band;* dorsal
fin often with posterior dusky blotch.

Breeding males iridescent blue. Head short; mouth terminal, upturned; *1 series of tricuspid teeth.* Dorsal and anal fins rounded, *each with 9–12 rays;* caudal fin edge slightly convex. Head scaled; 24–28 scales in lateral series.

Habitat: Marshy backwaters of desert streams and springs.

Range: Southern CA, s AZ, and nw Mexico.

Similar Species: Devils Hole Pupfish *(C. diabolis)* reaches length of ¾″ (2 cm), lacks pelvic fins, and has rounded caudal fin.

Comments: Desert Pupfish grows very rapidly, sometimes reaching a length of 2″ (5 cm) in one year. Most of the 13 species of *Cyprinodon* in the United States are restricted to springs or streams in the deserts of Texas, New Mexico, Arizona, Nevada, and California. Several species are endangered by desert development and the introduction of exotic fishes. The best known is Devils Hole Pupfish, which was the focal point of a Supreme Court water rights case in the 1970s.

257, 393   Sheepshead Minnow
Cyprinodon variegatus

Description: To 3″ (7.5 cm). Robust, moderately compressed. Breeding males olive, iridescent blue, or greenish blue above; poorly defined bars on sides; belly yellowish; 1–2 spots on posterior dorsal fin rays; black bar on caudal fin edge and base. Females olive or brassy, sometimes light orange above; black bars on sides. Snout blunt; mouth small, terminal; *teeth incisor-like, tricuspid.* Dorsal fin origin midway between snout and caudal fin, anterior to anal fin base; caudal fin truncate. Caudal peduncle deep. *Humeral scale present.*

Habitat: Shallow coastal marshes and tide pools, usually over sand; enters fresh water.

Range: Along Atlantic and Gulf coasts from MA to n Mexico. Introduced in inland waters of TX.

Similar Species: Diamond Killifish *(Adinia xenica)* has more pointed snout and lacks humeral scale. Goldspotted Killifish *(Floridichthys carpio)* has irregular bands confined to lower sides; breeding males have gold spots on cheek and body and lack dark spots on dorsal fin; may enter low-salinity waters.

Comments: Sheepshead Minnow is usually found in brackish water, but can survive in water up to four times saltier than seawater. It is also tolerant of extreme temperatures.

---

261 **Flagfish**
Jordanella floridae

Description: To 2½″ (6.5 cm). Short, deep, compressed. Back olive; *sides greenish gold to brassy;* belly yellowish. Males have 7–9 reddish-orange stripes between scale rows; dark blotch below dorsal fin origin. Head short, flat above; mouth small, upturned; 1 row of incisor-like, tricuspid teeth on each jaw. *16–18 dorsal fin rays; first dorsal fin ray short, thick, spine-like.* 25–27 scales in lateral series.

Habitat: Quiet shallow ditches, lakes, and ponds with vegetation; commonly enters brackish water.

Range: North-central FL south throughout peninsula.

Comments: Flagfish is primarily herbivorous. It spawns from April to August over dense mats of vegetation or in small depressions. The male fans the eggs and remains with them until they hatch.

Order Beryciformes

This order contains seven families, three of which occur in North American Atlantic inshore waters. Other families are found in deeper waters offshore. Many of these fishes are bottom dwellers. Most have large eyes, and one family, the Anomalopidae (flashlight fishes), is bioluminescent. Members of this order have a relatively deep body. The pelvic, dorsal, and anal fins each have a single strong spine preceding the rays. Each pelvic fin has more than five rays, and is either thoracic or placed beneath the middle of the pectoral fin. The caudal fin has 18 to 19 rays. Several families formerly included in this group have been placed in different orders.

SQUIRRELFISHES
Family Holocentridae

8 genera and about 65 species worldwide; 7 genera and 11 species in North America, plus 5 species confined to Mexican waters. These relatively deep-backed, compressed fishes are usually colored various shades of red. They have large eyes, a large terminal mouth, and hard spiny scales. The bones around the eye and opercle are serrate. Most species have a large spine at the angle of the preopercle and another on the upper edge of the opercle; these spines can inflict wounds. Each pelvic fin has a single spine preceding seven rays. The dorsal fin is long-based; the well-developed spiny segment has 10 to 12 spines and is nearly separated from the much shorter soft segment. The anal fin has four spines, the third one greatly enlarged. Most squirrelfishes live in shallow tropical coral reefs; some occur over sand or mud to depths of 900′ (275 m) or more. They are most active at night.

470 Squirrelfish
Holocentrus adscensionis

Description: To 14″ (36 cm). Relatively slender. *Bright silvery red, with faint stripes on body; snout and top of head dark red;* whitish below; *upper maxilla white; membranes of dorsal fin orange just behind spines, the orange running length of spines;* other fins pinkish. Eye large; mouth terminal; maxilla reaches beyond middle of eye; preopercular spine long, slender; *14–17 gill rakers.* Anterior rays of soft dorsal fin falcate; 4 anal fin spines; *upper lobe of caudal fin slightly longer than lower lobe.* Caudal peduncle narrow.

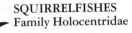

Habitat: Coral and rocky reefs from near shore to depths of at least 600′ (183 m).

Range: NC to Brazil, including Bermuda, Bahamas, parts of Gulf of Mexico, and Caribbean. Also around Ascension Island in South Atlantic.

Similar Species: Longspine Squirrelfish *(H. rufus)* has dorsal fin with white spots on edges of membranes just behind spines.

Comments: All squirrelfishes hide by day in crevices or under coral ledges, and feed by night away from the reef over sand and seagrass beds. The large eyes afford good night vision, and the red colors make them almost invisible in dim light.

471 Longspine Squirrelfish
Holocentrus rufus

Description: To 12" (30 cm). Oblong, relatively slender. *Bright silvery red;* diffuse red lines above, becoming indistinct and pink on sides and belly; top of head and area below eye brick-red; *white spots near upper edge of dorsal fin spine membranes.* Maxilla reaches just beyond anterior edge of eye; preopercular spine long, slender; *14–17 gill rakers.* Anterior rays of soft dorsal fin elongate; 4 anal fin spines; *upper lobe of caudal fin elongate. Caudal peduncle very narrow.*

Habitat: Coral reefs to depths of 90' (27 m).
Range: Bermuda, Bahamas, se FL, w Gulf of Mexico, and West Indies to South America.

Similar Species: Squirrelfish *(H. adscensionis)* has dorsal fin with orange edges on membranes bordering spines.

Comments: Longspine Squirrelfish is active at night, feeding away from the coral reefs where it hides during the day. This species feeds on a variety of crustaceans, gastropods, and brittle stars.

468 Blackbar Soldierfish
Myripristis jacobus

Description: To 8½" (22 cm). Oblong, relatively deep, moderately compressed. Reddish orange above; silvery and pinkish on sides; *broad bar extends from upper end of gill opening to pectoral fin base;* median fins blue and red; leading edges of pelvic, soft dorsal, anal, and caudal fins white. Snout blunt; eye very large; mouth terminal; maxilla reaches well beyond middle of eye; *no opercular or preopercular spines.* Last dorsal fin spine joined to soft dorsal fin; 4 anal fin spines. Scales cover basal half of soft dorsal and anal fins.

Habitat: Shallow coral reefs and offshore to depths of 270' (82 m).

Range: Bermuda; GA to Brazil, including Bahamas, n Gulf of Mexico, and Caribbean. Also around Cape Verde Islands in e Atlantic and Ascension Island in South Atlantic.

Comments: This nocturnal species feeds mostly on planktonic organisms. It is rather common on offshore reefs.

472 Dusky Squirrelfish
Sargocentron vexillarium

Description: To 6" (15 cm). Relatively deep. *Alternating stripes of red and silvery white:* red more prominent on upper sides where thick black lines separate red and white stripes; *axil of pectoral fin deep red or dusky;* dorsal fin red, with white next to spines; other fins reddish. Maxilla not reaching middle of eye; lower jaw not projecting beyond upper; opercular and preopercular spines well developed. Last dorsal fin spine well separated from first dorsal fin ray; lobes of caudal fin nearly equal. Lateral line with 40–44 pored scales.

Habitat: Tide pools, coral reefs, and rocky areas.

Range: Bermuda; FL to n South America, including Bahamas, s Gulf of Mexico, and West Indies.

Similar Species: Reef Squirrelfish *(S. coruscum)* has longer maxilla and large black spot between third and fourth dorsal fin spines. Deepwater Squirrelfish *(S. bullisi)* has alternating red and white stripes on sides and black spot on dorsal fin between first and second spines; occurs in deeper waters. Saddle Squirrelfish *(S. poco)* has red body and fins, with black blotch on membranes between first 4 dorsal fin spines. Longjaw Squirrelfish *(Neoniphon marianus)* has red, yellow, and silver stripes, yellow spiny dorsal fin with white spots, prominent lower jaw projecting beyond upper, and elongate third anal fin spine; occurs in slightly deeper waters.

Comments: The red on the body of this species is much less prominent overall than in most other North American squirrelfishes. Dusky and Reef Squirrelfishes are reportedly the most common inshore squirrelfishes in Bermuda, Florida, and the West Indies.

Order Gasterosteiformes

This order contains 11 families, six of which occur in North America. Members of this order are found in tropical to cold-temperate marine and fresh waters throughout the world. Most species are marine, but nearly one-fourth occur in either fresh or brackish waters. Many families are highly modified morphologically. These fishes usually have a very elongate, tube-like snout with a tiny mouth at the end. The body is usually pencil-like, often partially or completely covered with bony plates, and sometimes has long fleshy appendages and a prehensile tail. A brood pouch may be present on the belly in males. Classification of the order is unsettled, with some families proposed for addition.

TUBESNOUTS
Family Aulorhynchidae

2 genera and 2 species worldwide; 1 species in North America. These fishes are confined to the cold-temperate waters of the North Pacific Ocean from Japan and Korea to California. The body is elongate, with a series of 24 to 26 very short and isolated dorsal fin spines followed by a soft dorsal fin with about 20 rays; the soft dorsal fin is situated directly above the anal fin on the posterior one-third of the body. The small pelvic fins are located beneath the pectoral fins. The sides of the body are covered with thin bony plates. The snout is tube-like (hence the family's common name), with a terminal, moderately prominent mouth. Tubesnouts were previously included in the stickleback family (Gasterosteidae).

483 Tubesnout
Aulorhynchus flavidus

Description: To 7″ (18 cm). Fusiform, very elongate.
Olive green to tan, sometimes with
silvery patch between opercle and pectoral
fin. Breeding males have bright red pelvic
fin. Snout very long, tubular. *23–26
isolated dorsal fin spines in front of soft
dorsal fin.* Caudal peduncle long, slender.

Habitat: Giant kelp and eelgrass beds in shallow
bays and to depths of 102′ (31 m).

Range: Sitka, AK, south to Punta Rompiente,
Baja California; possibly north to Prince
William Sound, AK.

Similar Species: Bay Pipefish *(Syngnathus leptorhynchus)*
lacks isolated spines in front of soft
dorsal fin.

Comments: The male Tubesnout builds a nest in
giant kelp fronds. The eggs, deposited
in the nest by the female, adhere to these
fronds. This fish feeds on small
planktonic crustaceans and fish larvae,
including its own young. Tubesnout is
rarely caught by anglers, but it is
familiar to most divers.

STICKLEBACKS
Family Gasterosteidae

5 genera and about 7 species worldwide;
4 genera and 5 species in North America. Sticklebacks are
widely distributed in the Northern Hemisphere in fresh,
brackish, and salt waters. These small fishes are characterized by the presence of three to 16 isolated dorsal fin spines
followed by a soft dorsal fin with 14 to 16 rays. They have
a fusiform body with a very long slender caudal peduncle.
They are unscaled, but the sides are often covered with bony
plates. Sticklebacks are widely known for their complex
mating behavior and nest-building activity.

265 Brook Stickleback
Culaea inconstans

Description: To 3½″ (9 cm). Compressed. Back green
to olive; sides lighter, with yellowish
spots or wavy lines. Breeding males

dusky green to black. *4–7 dorsal fin spines, length less than width of eye,* curved slightly backward, followed by soft dorsal fin. *Caudal fin rounded.* Caudal peduncle slender, without keel. Minute bony plates along lateral line.

Habitat: Small streams, ponds, and lakes with clear cold waters and abundant aquatic vegetation; rarely enters brackish water.

Range: Northwest Territories and e BC south and east to s Hudson Bay drainage, Great Lakes, upper Mississippi River system, St. Lawrence River, New England, and NS. Introduced in CT, AL, and NM.

Similar Species: Ninespine Stickleback (*Pungitius pungitius*) has 9 dorsal fin spines inclined alternately to left and right and lacks distinct bony plates on sides.

Comments: Brook Stickleback spawns in shallow water, where the male uses vegetation to construct a small, ball-shaped nest with a cavity through the center.

266, 399 **Threespine Stickleback**
Gasterosteus aculeatus

Description: To 4″ (10 cm). Fusiform. Gray to olive brown; sides paler; belly silvery. Breeding adults reddish on head and belly. Head one-fourth length; lower jaw projects beyond upper. Pelvic fin with 1 spine, 1 ray; *usually 3 stout dorsal fin spines, widely separated,* followed by soft dorsal fin; caudal fin triangular. Caudal peduncle narrow. *Series of bony plates on sides,* number of plates varies geographically.

Habitat: Marine, estuarine, and fresh waters; usually in vegetation.

Range: In Atlantic from Hudson Bay to Chesapeake Bay. In Pacific from Bering Sea to n Baja California. Also associated freshwater streams on both coasts.

Similar Species: Blackspotted Stickleback (*G. wheatlandi*) has black spots, pelvic fin with 1 spine and 2 rays, 3 weaker dorsal fin spines, and 6–11 bony plates anteriorly on each side of body, none posteriorly. Fourspine

Stickleback *(Apeltes quadracus)* has 4 dorsal fin spines and lacks bony plates.

Comments: This is the only stickleback found in Mexico. This shore fish enters brackish water or ascends freshwater streams to spawn from April to July. The female deposits 75 to 100 eggs in a nest built by the male; the male then guards the eggs and remains with the fry until they can fend for themselves.

PIPEFISHES AND SEAHORSES
Family Syngnathidae

pipefish

seahorse

52 genera and about 215 species (190 pipefishes, 25 seahorses) worldwide; 9 genera and 28 species (24 pipefishes, 4 seahorses) in North America (21 Atlantic, 7 Pacific), plus 1 genus and 5 species in Mexican waters. Members of this family are found in tropical to cold-temperate waters. All North American species are marine, with two pipefish species also occurring in fresh water; one of these may have some permanent freshwater populations. They are small atypical fishes, with bodies encased in bony rings perpendicular to several discontinuous longitudinal ridges running along the sides of the body. Pipefishes have a straight body, and seahorses have a curved prehensile tail; a few genera are morphologically intermediate and appear to bridge the gap between the two groups. Characteristics important in identification include the number of bony rings on the body, particularly the total number and relative numbers before and behind the anal fin; length and position of longitudinal ridges along the sides of the body; snout length; position of the dorsal fin relative to the body rings; number of dorsal fin rays; presence or absence of an anal fin; and length, position, and morphology of the brood pouch on the belly of the male.

484 Lined Seahorse
Hippocampus erectus

Description: To 6″ (15 cm). Deep, compressed; *head perpendicular to vertical body.* Coloration varies with background: light brown, dusky, gray, blackish, or brick-red;

unmarked or variously mottled; sometimes speckled with fine white or golden dots. Dorsal fin fan-shaped, with 16–20 rays; *no caudal fin. Tail prehensile.*

Habitat: Usually associated with vegetation such as eelgrass and sargassum weed.

Range: NS to Argentina, including Bermuda, n Bahamas, Gulf of Mexico, and Greater Antilles.

Similar Species: Dwarf Seahorse *(H. zosterae)* reaches length of 3″ (7.5 cm), and has green to blackish body and 10–13 dorsal fin rays. Longsnout Seahorse *(H. reidi)* has many dark spots on body, slightly longer snout, and 16–19 dorsal fin rays.

Comments: Seahorses are poor swimmers. Their camouflage hides them from both enemies and prey. They blend so well into the background that they are rarely seen by the casual observer. Seahorses feed by rapid intake of water. The incubation period in the brood pouch is thought to be about two weeks.

---

480 Bay Pipefish
Syngnathus leptorhynchus

Description: To 14″ (36 cm). Very elongate, hexagonal in cross section anteriorly. Green to brown; mottled, depending on habitat. Snout very long; mouth small, terminal. *No pelvic fins; 28–44 dorsal fin rays;* caudal fin very small. *Covered with bony plates; 53–63 body rings.*

Habitat: Eelgrass beds in bays.

Range: Sitka, AK, to s Baja California.

Similar Species: Barred Pipefish *(S. auliscus)* has long snout and 48–55 body rings. Kelp Pipefish *(S. californiensis)* has 46–52 body rings. Chocolate Pipefish *(S. euchrous)* has usually 61–68 body rings. Barcheek Pipefish *(S. exilis)* has usually 63–68 body rings. Snubnose Pipefish *(Bryx arctus)* is only Pacific pipefish with short snout. Tubesnout *(Aulorhynchus flavidus)* has 23–26 isolated dorsal fin spines in front of soft dorsal fin.

Comments: No other Pacific pipefish species occurs north of California. Bay Pipefish feeds on small crustaceans. All pipefishes mate in early summer, and the female deposits the eggs in the brood pouch of the male. Observers rarely notice these relatives of the seahorses unless they are seen swimming away from vegetation.

26, 481 Gulf Pipefish
Syngnathus scovelli

Description: To 7″ (18 cm). Slender, very elongate. Females with deeper body, V-shaped belly; usually olive brown with white or silvery bars; pectoral fin plain; dorsal and caudal fins dusky. Males similar, but usually lighter. Snout moderately short. No pelvic fins; *dorsal fin with 27–35 rays, usually located over 3 bony rings on body and 5 on tail;* caudal fin present. 46–51 body rings.

Habitat: Shallow grassy flats in salt and fresh waters.

Range: Coastal FL, Gulf of Mexico, and through Caribbean (except West Indies) to Brazil; enters fresh water in FL and LA.

Similar Species: Dusky Pipefish *(S. floridae),* Northern Pipefish *(S. fuscus),* Chain Pipefish *(S. louisianae),* and Bull Pipefish *(S. springeri)* have longer snout. Fringed Pipefish *(Anarchopterus criniger),* Insular Pipefish *(A. tectus),* Pugnose Pipefish *(Bryx dunckeri),* Crested Pipefish *(Cosmocampus brachycephalus),* Whitenose Pipefish *(C. albirostris),* and Banded Pipefish *(Micrognathus crinitus)* have shorter snout (lacking pigment in Whitenose Pipefish). Opossum Pipefish *(Microphis brachyurus)* has longer snout and serrations on ridges along sides of body; enters fresh water.

Comments: Of the Atlantic species of North American pipefishes, only Gulf and Opossum Pipefishes enter fresh water. Gulf Pipefish sometimes occurs well inland, where there are some permanent freshwater populations.

TRUMPETFISHES
Family Aulostomidae

1 genus with 3 species worldwide; 1 species in North America. These unmistakable fishes are found in tropical seas. They are similar to the pipefishes and seahorses (family Syngnathidae) and the cornetfishes (Fistulariidae) in that they have a very long body with the mouth at the end of a tubular snout. They differ by having a chin barbel; a series of seven to 12 isolated dorsal fin spines, together resembling a small sail, followed by a short soft dorsal fin; the anal fin placed below, and about equal in size and shape to, the soft dorsal fin; and the pelvic fins located below the middle dorsal fin spines.

482 Trumpetfish
Aulostomus maculatus

Description: To 3' (91 cm), usually to 20" (51 cm). Very elongate, compressed. Brown or reddish brown, with lengthwise pale lines and irregular rows of dark spots; black bar or spot near bases of soft dorsal and anal fin anterior rays; 1–2 black spots on caudal fin. Head and snout very long, about one-third total length; mouth oblique, at end of tubular snout; 1 chin barbel. *Dorsal fin with usually 10 isolated spines;* soft dorsal and anal fins similar in size and shape; caudal fin without long filament.

Habitat: Reefs in shallow waters. Early stages in oceans at mid-depths.

Range: Bermuda, Bahamas, s FL, and along Gulf coast south through Caribbean to Brazil. Also in e Atlantic.

Comments: This fish often aligns itself vertically with its head down among sea feathers (gorgonian corals), where it cannot readily be seen in order to take unwary prey by surprise. Trumpetfish feeds on shrimps and small fishes, which it pounces on then sucks into its mouth.

CORNETFISHES
Family Fistulariidae

1 genus with 4 species worldwide; 3 species in North America (2 Atlantic, 1 Pacific), plus 1 species confined to Mexican waters. These fishes are found in subtropical coastal waters. They are more slender than trumpetfishes (family Aulostomidae) and have depressed, mostly unscaled bodies (some species are completely unscaled). The head is long, and the mouth is at the end of a tubular snout. They do not have chin barbels. The dorsal and anal fins are spineless, short-based, posteriorly placed, and similar in size and shape. The small caudal fin is forked, with the middle two rays forming a long filament.

478 Red Cornetfish
Fistularia petimba

Description: To 6′ (1.8 m), not including caudal filament. Elongate, slender, depressed. Red to reddish brown above; sides iridescent; belly silvery; pectoral and median fins pink or red; pelvic fins orange. Head more than one-third length excluding caudal filament; snout very long, tubular; mouth oblique; lower jaw projects beyond upper. Dorsal and anal fins small, falcate, posteriorly placed opposite each other; caudal fin forked, with middle 2 rays forming long filament. *Series of embedded, elongate, bony plates on dorsal midline;* forward-projecting spines on posterior lateral line.

Habitat: Near shore over soft bottoms to depths of about 30′ (9 m).

Range: MA to Venezuela, including e Gulf of Mexico and Jamaica; apparently absent from Bermuda, Bahamas, and perhaps other West Indian islands.

Similar Species: Bluespotted Cornetfish *(F. tabacaria)* has blue spots on back and lacks bony plates on dorsal midline; occurs usually in shallower waters.

Comments: Cornetfishes tend to live among sea grasses, and apparently feed on shrimps and small fishes. Unlike the related trumpetfishes (family Aulostomidae), they are active.

Order Scorpaeniformes

This order contains 24 families, 12 of which occur in North America. Nearly all species are marine, the exception being about 52 species in the sculpin family (Cottidae), which are confined to fresh water in cool-temperate regions of North America, Asia, and Europe. Members of this order are collectively called "mail-cheeked" fishes because of the characteristic bony ridge running along the side of the head from the snout to the preopercle. The head and body usually have spines and sometimes bony plates. The pelvic, pectoral, dorsal, and anal fins often have well-developed spines. The pectoral fins are usually rounded; the caudal fin is also usually rounded, rarely forked. This group was previously included in the order Perciformes, and the relationships among these fishes are not completely resolved.

SCORPIONFISHES
Family Scorpaenidae

At least 56 genera and about 388 species worldwide; 8 genera and 92 species in North America (24 Atlantic, 68 Pacific). These fishes, found in tropical to cold-temperate waters throughout the world, have fusiform compressed bodies. They have ridges and spines on the head, including coronal spines (those located where the top of the head and the nape come together); in addition, there are usually five spines on the preopercle and two on the opercle. All members of the family have a bone beneath the eye that extends across the cheek. They have a single dorsal fin, often notched, with 11 to 17 spines and eight to 18 rays. The anal fin has one to three spines and three to nine rays. The pelvic, dorsal, and anal fin spines often contain venom glands that may cause very painful wounds. When present, the scales are ctenoid or cycloid. Fertilization is internal, and some species lay eggs. Many of the species in the genus *Sebastes* are difficult to distinguish from one another; they all have palatine teeth and a dorsal fin with 12 to 15 (usually 13) spines and nine to 16 rays, and all are ovoviviparous. Those family members found in the North Pacific are often known as rockfishes.

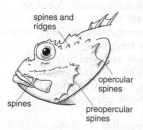

spines and ridges

opercular spines

spines

preopercular spines

433 Barbfish
Scorpaena brasiliensis

Description: To 9″ (23 cm). Robust, depth about one-
third length. Pinkish or reddish, with
lighter mottling; *2–3 large brown spots on
sides between pectoral and anal fins; axil of
pectoral fin pale, with small brown spots;*
caudal peduncle pale. Head large, with
numerous spines; pit between eyes;
mouth terminal; maxilla reaches beyond
eye; usually large tentacle over eye.
Pectoral fin broad, fan-like, with 18–19
(usually 19) rays; dorsal fin deeply
notched, with 2 spines, 9 rays; caudal fin
truncate or slightly rounded. Scales
cycloid. Lateral line complete.

Habitat: Inshore over mud, silt, sand, rocks, or
coral reefs to depths of 300′ (92 m).

Range: VA to Brazil, including Gulf of
Mexico, Greater Antilles, and coastal
Caribbean.

Comments: This is a common scorpionfish in Florida
waters. It has the most toxic fin spines of
all western Atlantic scorpionfishes.

431 California Scorpionfish
Scorpaena guttata

Description: To 17″ (43 cm). Elongate, rounded in
cross section, slightly depressed. Red to
brown, with spots overall. Head robust,
ridged; snout rounded; maxilla reaches
middle of eye; *teeth palatine;* opercular
and preopercular spines present. Pectoral
fin large, broad, rounded; dorsal fin
notched, *with 12 spines,* 8–10 rays;
caudal fin truncate. Scales large, ctenoid.
Lateral line straight.

Habitat: Shallow rocky reefs and kelp beds to
depths of 600′ (183 m).

Range: Santa Cruz, CA, to Uncle Sam Bank,
Baja California; upper Gulf of
California.

Similar Species: Stone Scorpionfish (*Scorpaena mystes*) is
only other Pacific scorpionfish with
fewer than 13 dorsal fin spines. Rainbow
Scorpionfish (*Scorpaenodes xyris*) lacks

palatine teeth and has 13 dorsal fin spines; occurs in caves and crevices to depths of about 84′ (26 m). Sculpins (family Cottidae) lack anal fin spines.

Comments: Unlike most other members of the family, California Scorpionfish deposits eggs embedded in transparent, pear-shaped cases. It is considered an excellent food fish and makes up a minor portion of the southern California commercial and sport catch.

432 Spotted Scorpionfish
Scorpaena plumieri

Description: To 17″ (43 cm), rarely more than 12″ (30 cm). Robust, depth about one-third length. Pale, with dark brown or black blotches above; reddish below; colors in variegated pattern; *axil of pectoral fin black, with white spots or blotches; 3 dark bands on caudal fin.* Head large, with numerous spines; *deep pit under eye,* another between eyes; 3–4 free spiny points on preorbital bone; mouth terminal; maxilla reaches beyond eye. Pectoral fin broad-based, fan-like; dorsal fin deeply notched, with 12 spines, 9 rays; caudal fin truncate. Scales cycloid. Lateral line complete.

Habitat: Reefs in shallow waters, rocky areas, and around oil platforms to depths of about 180′ (55 m).

Range: MA to Rio de Janeiro, Brazil, including Bermuda, Bahamas, Gulf of Mexico, and Caribbean. Also around St. Helena and Ascension Islands in South Atlantic.

Similar Species: Hunchback Scorpionfish *(S. dispar)* is only other Atlantic *Scorpaena* species with more than 2 free spiny points on preorbital bone; occurs in rocky areas or over rubble at depths of 120–390′ (37–119 m). Plumed Scorpionfish *(S. grandicornis)* has tan pectoral fin axil with small white dots; occurs in grassy areas and bays. Spotfin Scorpionfish *(Scorpaenodes tredecimspinosus)* has 13 dorsal fin spines; occurs at depths of

25–270′ (7.5–82 m). Reef Scorpionfish
(Scorpaenodes caribbaeus) has 13 dorsal fin
spines; occurs around coral reefs to
depths of 60′ (18.5 m).

Comments: Spotted Scorpionfish feeds on small fishes
and crustaceans. When disturbed, this
fish spreads its pectoral fins as a
warning, apparently to display the
characteristic black and white coloration
underneath. Populations in the eastern
Pacific are now recognized as a separate
species, Stone Scorpionfish *(S. mystes)*.

---

613 Pacific Ocean Perch
Sebastes alutus

Description: To 20″ (51 cm). Fusiform, elongate,
compressed. Light red, with dark areas
under soft dorsal fin and on caudal
peduncle. Head with 1 pair of spines
above eyes and usually 5 additional pairs
of small weak spines; *lower jaw projects,
with prominent knob at tip.* Dorsal fin
deeply notched, spiny segment longer-
based, membranes between spines
incised; 8–9 (rarely 6–7) anal fin rays.

Habitat: Over soft bottoms and around rocky
reefs at depths of 180–300′ (55–92 m).

Range: Bering Sea to La Jolla, CA. Also in
Japan.

Similar Species: Darkblotched Rockfish *(S. crameri)*
has depth at pelvic fin insertion greater
than head length and 5 dark bars or
blotches on back; occurs at depths of

96–1,800′ (30–549 m). Stripetail
Rockfish *(S. saxicola)* has green stripes
on caudal fin membranes; occurs at
depths of 150–1,380′ (46–421 m).
Halfbanded Rockfish *(S. semicinctus)*
has blackish-red bar below dorsal
fin and dark reddish-brown
spots on dorsal and caudal fins;
occurs at depths of 192–1,320′
(59–403 m). Sharpchin Rockfish
(S. zacentrus) has dark forked bar
extending from eye to edge of opercle
and 7 anal fin rays; occurs at depths of
300–1,050′ (92–320 m).

Comments: This species is the most commercially
important rockfish on the Pacific coast,
with annual foreign and domestic
landings of more than 50,000 tons.

467 Kelp Rockfish
Sebastes atrovirens

Description: To 17" (43 cm). Fusiform, deep,
compressed. Body and fin membranes
*light gray or brown to golden brown, with
mottling.* 5 or more pairs of head spines;
no coronal spines; snout moderately
sharp; *gill rakers on first arch long, slender.*
Dorsal fin deeply notched, spiny segment
longer-based, membranes between spines
incised, spines and rays same length;
caudal fin rounded. Lower jaw scaled.
Habitat: Rocky reefs and kelp beds to depths of
150' (46 m).
Range: Timber Cove, CA, to Punta San Pablo,
Baja California.
Similar Species: Brown Rockfish *(S. auriculatus)* has
coronal spines, dark blotch on rear edge
of opercle, and pinkish membranes of
pelvic, pectoral, and caudal fins. Grass
Rockfish *(S. rastrelliger)* has short blunt
gill rakers on first arch and unscaled
lower jaw.
Comments: Kelp Rockfish occurs singly or in large
aggregations. It feeds on small crabs,
shrimps, squids, and some fishes. This
species forms a small portion of the
catches of sport anglers and scuba divers.

450 Brown Rockfish
Sebastes auriculatus

Description: To 22" (55 cm). Fusiform, deep,
compressed. Olive brown above, with
light orangish-brown mottling; lighter
below; *dark brown spot on rear of opercle;*
pelvic, pectoral, and caudal fins pinkish.
Head flat between eyes, with 6 pairs of
spines *(including coronal spines);* snout
moderately sharp. Dorsal fin deeply
notched, spiny segment longer-based,

membranes between spines incised,
spines and rays about same length;
caudal fin truncate.

Habitat: Shallow, low-profile, rocky reefs and
occasionally over soft bottoms; to depths
of 420′ (128 m), usually to 180′ (55 m).

Range: Prince William Sound, AK, to Bahía
San Hipólito, Baja California.

Similar Species: Kelp Rockfish *(S. atrovirens)* lacks
coronal spines and spot on rear edge of
opercle, and membranes of pelvic,
pectoral, and caudal fins are not pinkish.
Grass Rockfish *(S. rastrelliger)* lacks spot
on rear edge of opercle and has short
blunt gill rakers on first arch.

Comments: This fish is born in the late spring; after
a short period during which it floats
with the plankton community, it settles
to the bottom, usually in calm areas.
Brown Rockfish makes up a minor
portion of the sport and commercial
rockfish catch.

---

445 Gopher Rockfish
Sebastes carnatus

Description: To 15″ (38 cm). Fusiform, deep,
elongate. *Dark olive brown or brown, with
pinkish or white blotches and spots; lower lip
yellow to orange.* Head concave between
eyes, with 5 pairs of spines; snout
moderately sharp; no knob at tip of
lower jaw. Dorsal fin deeply notched,
spiny segment longer-based, membranes
between spines incised; usually 5–7 anal
fin rays; caudal fin slightly rounded.

Habitat: Shallow rocky waters to depths of 180′
(55 m).

Range: Eureka, CA, to Punta San Roque, Baja
California.

Similar Species: Black-and-yellow Rockfish *(S. chrysomelas)*
has black body with orangish-yellow to
light yellow blotches and dark gray
lower lip.

Comments: Gopher Rockfish feeds on crabs,
squids, and small fishes. It is considered
fine eating, particularly when freshly
caught.

460 Copper Rockfish
Sebastes caurinus

Description: To 22″ (56 cm). Fusiform, deep, compressed. Orangish brown, olive, dull yellow, or copper above; white below and on head; *posterior two-thirds of lateral line whitish or pinkish, with white blotches.* 5 pairs of head spines; snout moderately sharp. Dorsal fin deeply notched, spiny segment longer-based, membranes between spines incised, spines at least as long as rays; caudal fin truncate. Lower jaw smooth, unscaled.

Habitat: Low-profile rocky and shale reefs to depths of 600′ (183 m).

Range: Kenai Peninsula, AK, to Islas San Beníto, Baja California.

Similar Species: Calico Rockfish (*S. dallii*) has orangish-brown bars extending down sides from dorsal fin and orangish-brown spots on and below dorsal fin; occurs over rocky reefs or soft bottoms.

Comments: The coloration of this species varies greatly. Most individuals from southern California are more reddish, and may be a separate species, Whitebelly Rockfish (*S. vexillaris*). Copper Rockfish feeds on fishes and crustaceans. It is common, and is a popular sport fish.

444 Black-and-yellow Rockfish
Sebastes chrysomelas

Description: To 15″ (38 cm). Fusiform, deep, elongate, compressed. *Black, with yellow or yellowish-orange blotches and spots; lower lip dark gray.* Head concave between eyes, with 5 pairs of spines; snout moderately sharp; no knob at tip of lower jaw. Dorsal fin deeply notched, spiny segment longer-based, membranes between spines incised; 6–7 anal fin rays.

Habitat: Shallow rocky intertidal waters to depths of 120′ (37 m); usually to 60′ (18.5 m).

Range: Eureka, CA, to Isla Natividad, Baja California.

Similar Species: Gopher Rockfish *(S. carnatus)* has brown or olive brown body with pinkish or whitish blotches. China Rockfish *(S. nebulosus)* has continuous yellow stripe extending from membranes of third and fourth dorsal fin spines along lateral line to caudal fin.

Comments: Black-and-yellow Rockfish is valued as a food fish, but is not caught in large numbers. As are the other species in the genus, it is ovoviviparous; fertilization is internal and the embryos develop within the female.

454 Widow Rockfish
Sebastes entomelas

Description: To 21″ (53 cm). Fusiform, elongate, compressed. Brassy brown above; often whitish below; *membranes of pelvic, pectoral, and anal fins black.* Head convex between eyes, spines not prominent; snout fairly sharp; maxilla reaches middle of eye. Dorsal fin deeply notched, spiny segment longer-based, membranes between spines incised, spines and rays about same length; *rear edge of anal fin straight;* caudal fin emarginate.

Habitat: Over deep rocky reefs and soft bottoms from surface to depths of 1,200′ (366 m). Young in shallow waters.

Range: Kodiak Island, AK, to Bahía de Todos Santos, Baja California.

Similar Species: Squarespot Rockfish *(S. hopkinsi)* has dark squarish blotches on back and sides, and second anal fin spine extends beyond tip of third; occurs at depths of 60–600′ (18.5–183 m). Speckled Rockfish *(S. ovalis)* is orangish brown above, yellowish tan below, and covered with small black spots; occurs at depths of 102–1,200′ (31–366 m).

Comments: This species occurs in large aggregations at mid-depths, where it feeds on plankton. Widow Rockfish contributes to the catches of anglers, and is now one of the most important commercial rockfishes on the Pacific coast. A single trawler has been known to catch more than 50 tons in one day.

463 Yellowtail Rockfish
Sebastes flavidus

Description: To 26" (66 cm). Fusiform, deep, compressed. Brown to dark gray; *reddish-brown speckles on scales;* pelvic, pectoral, anal, and caudal fins yellowish. Head convex between eyes, *spines not prominent; 33–39 gill rakers on first arch.* Dorsal fin deeply notched, spiny segment longer-based, membranes between spines incised, spines and rays about same length; *anal fin with 8 (rarely 7 or 9) rays,* rear edge straight and vertical; caudal fin slightly emarginate or forked.

Habitat: Over deep rocky reefs and soft bottoms from surface to depths of 900' (275 m); usually at 78–150' (24–46 m).

Range: Kodiak Island, AK, to San Diego, CA.

Similar Species: The very similar Olive Rockfish (*S. serranoides*) lacks reddish-brown speckles on scales and has light blotches on back, 29–36 gill rakers on first arch, and 9 (rarely 8 or 10) anal fin rays. Puget Sound Rockfish (*S. emphaeus*) has copper red body with greenish-brown bars and blotches and rounded rear lobe of anal fin; occurs at depths of 36–1,200' (11–366 m). Bank Rockfish (*S. rufus*) has dusky back, black spots on red body and dorsal fin, and anal fin with black membranes; occurs at depths of 102–810' (11–247 m).

Comments: This species is born in January, February, and March. Large aggregations occur at mid-depths, usually over deep rocky reefs. It feeds on crustaceans, squids, and small fishes. Yellowtail Rockfish is one of the three most important rockfishes caught for sport in central and northern California.

447 Quillback Rockfish
Sebastes maliger

Description: To 24″ (61 cm). Fusiform, deep, compressed. Back brown, with orange spots and blotches; *rear of head to pectoral fin insertion yellow, with brown spots; orange spots below;* paired fins blackish; dorsal fin brown, with creamy spines. Head flat between eyes, with 5 pairs of spines. Dorsal fin deeply notched, membranes between spines deeply incised, spines very long.

Habitat: Rocky reefs with caves and crevices to depths of 900′ (275 m); in shallower waters in n part of range.

Range: Gulf of Alaska to Point Conception, CA.

Similar Species: China Rockfish *(S. nebulosus)* has black body and yellow stripe extending from dorsal fin spines to and along lateral line with bluish-white spots below.

Comments: This inshore rockfish is common in British Columbia and northward. It is caught in small numbers by sport and commercial anglers.

451 Black Rockfish
Sebastes melanops

Description: To 24″ (61 cm); 10½ lb (4.8 kg). Fusiform, deep, compressed. Black, with gray mottling; *usually gray to white stripe along lateral line;* black spots on dorsal fin. Head convex between eyes, *spines not prominent;* maxilla reaches to rear of eye; no knob at tip of lower jaw. Dorsal fin deeply notched, spiny segment longer-based, membranes between spines incised; rear edge of anal fin rounded; caudal fin truncate to emarginate.

Habitat: Over rocks and soft bottoms to depths of 1,200′ (366 m).

Range: Amchitka Island, AK, to Huntington Beach, CA.

Similar Species: Dusky Rockfish *(S. ciliatus)* has blackish-brown body with brown

speckles, medium knob at tip of lower
jaw, and straight rear edge of anal fin.
Blue Rockfish *(S. mystinus)* has dark
blue body with light blue mottling,
lacks gray stripe on lateral line, maxilla
does not reach rear of eye, and rear
edge of anal fin is straight or slightly
indented.

Comments: Black Rockfish occurs both singly and
in large aggregations near the bottom or
at mid-depths. It feeds on crabs and
other crustaceans as well as on fishes.
This species is an important sport and
commercial fish.

---

457 Vermilion Rockfish
Sebastes miniatus

Description: To 30″ (76 cm); 15 lb (6.8 kg).
Fusiform, deep, compressed. Red to
orange, with gray mottling; *mouth and
fins reddish* (shallow-living individuals
more brown); posterior two-thirds of
lateral line gray to white; *fins usually
black-edged.* Head convex between eyes,
with 6 pairs of spines. Dorsal fin deeply
notched, spiny segment longer-based,
membranes between spines incised;
caudal fin truncate. *Rough scales on
underside of jaw.*

Habitat: Over rocky reefs and soft bottoms to
depths of 900′ (275 m).

Range: Queen Charlotte Islands, BC, to Islas
San Benito, Baja California.

Similar Species: Rougheye Rockfish *(S. aleutianus)*
lacks gray mottling and has 2–10
sharp spines on ridge below eye.
Canary Rockfish *(S. pinniger)* has
gray band along lateral line and
underside of jaw is smooth and
unscaled; young have black blotch
on spiny dorsal fin.

Comments: Vermilion Rockfish is popular with
anglers because it is large and makes
good eating. It is also an important
commercial species caught with hook
and line off southern California.

452   Blue Rockfish
Sebastes mystinus

Description: To 21″ (53 cm). Fusiform, deep, elongate, compressed. Dark blue, with light blue mottling; *no spots on dorsal fin membranes.* 4 or fewer pairs of weak head spines; snout moderately sharp; *maxilla not reaching rear edge of eye.* Dorsal fin deeply notched, spiny segment longer-based, membranes between spines incised; rear edge of anal fin straight or slightly indented; caudal fin emarginate.

Habitat: Shallow to deep rocky reefs and kelp beds to depths of 1,800′ (549 m); usually at mid-depths.

Range: Vancouver Island, BC, to Punta Santo Tomás, Baja California; possibly north to Bering Sea.

Similar Species: Dusky Rockfish *(S. ciliatus)* has blackish-brown body with brown speckles. Black Rockfish *(S. melanops)* has black spots on dorsal fin, maxilla reaching rear edge of eye, and rounded rear edge of anal fin.

Comments: In late winter, Blue Rockfish bears its young, which spend several weeks as part of the plankton community. Large aggregations of adults occur at mid-depths, where they feed on small crustaceans, jellyfishes, pelagic tunicates, algae, and small fishes. This species is often the most abundant rockfish in the catches of charter boat and skiff anglers off the U.S. Pacific coast. The annual sport catch in California is close to half a million fish.

443   China Rockfish
Sebastes nebulosus

Description: To 17″ (43 cm). Fusiform, deep, compressed. Black, with yellow mottling; *yellow stripe extends from spiny dorsal fin down to and along lateral line; bluish-white spots below.* Head deeply concave between eyes, with 5 pairs of prominent spines; snout moderately sharp. Dorsal fin deeply notched, membranes between spines incised, some spines longer than rays; usually 7 anal fin rays; caudal fin slightly rounded.

Habitat: Rocky reefs with caves and crevices at depths of 12–420′ (3.7–128 m).

Range: Prince William Sound, AK, to San Miguel Island, CA.

Similar Species: Black-and-yellow Rockfish *(S. chrysomelas)* lacks yellow stripe and bluish-white spots, and head is convex between eyes. Quillback Rockfish *(S. maliger)* lacks yellow stripe and has orange spots below.

Comments: This solitary fish uses its large pectoral fins to support itself on the cave floor and maneuver in crevices. It feeds on brittle stars, crabs, and shrimps. China Rockfish makes up a minor portion of sport and commercial hook-and-line catches off the U.S. Pacific coast.

459 Tiger Rockfish
Sebastes nigrocinctus

Description: To 24″ (61 cm). Fusiform, deep, compressed. Pink, rose, or gray, *with 5 dark red or black bars; 2 red or black stripes radiate posteriorly from eyes to rear edge of opercle.* Young have black-tipped pelvic and anal fins. Head concave between eyes, with 6 pairs of prominent spines; snout moderately sharp; lower jaw projects beyond upper. Dorsal fin deeply notched, spiny segment longer-based, membranes between spines incised; rear edge of caudal fin rounded.

Habitat: Deep rocky reefs with caves and crevices at depths of 78–900′ (24–275 m).

Range: Prince William Sound, AK, to Point Buchon, CA.

Similar Species: Redbanded Rockfish *(S. babcocki)* has 4 dark bars, first mostly behind opercle. Flag Rockfish *(S. rubrivinctus)* has white or light pink body with 4 dark red to reddish-brown bars, first mostly on opercle.

Comments: This solitary rockfish prefers caves and other hiding places, and is seldom part of either sport or commercial catches. However, it is commonly observed by divers at depths of 78–102′ (24–31 m) off British Columbia and Alaska, and taken by anglers in waters to depths of 180′ (55 m) to the south.

453 Bocaccio
Sebastes paucispinis

Description: To 3′ (91 cm); 15 lb (6.8 kg). Fusiform, elongate, compressed. Brown to dusky red or bronze above; lighter below. *Young have dark brown spots.* Head convex between eyes, with 3 pairs of weak spines; snout sharp; *maxilla reaches beyond eye;* lower jaw projects beyond upper; 28–31 gill rakers. Dorsal fin deeply notched, spiny segment longer-based, with 12–14 (usually 13) spines, membranes between spines incised; usually 9 anal fin rays; caudal fin slightly forked.

Habitat: Over rocky reefs and soft bottoms to depths of 1,050′ (320 m). Young around shallow rocky reefs and in bays.

Range: Kodiak Island, AK, to Punta Blanca, Baja California.

Similar Species: Silvergray Rockfish *(S. brevispinis)* is dark gray above, silvery below, and has 4 pairs of weak head spines; occurs at depths of 102–1,200′ (31–366 m). Bronzespotted Rockfish *(S. gilli)* has brown spots on back and usually 8 anal fin rays; occurs at depths of 246–1,230′ (75–375 m). Chilipepper *(S. goodei)* has bright red stripe along lateral line, maxilla not reaching rear edge of eye, and usually 8 anal fin rays.

Comments: A single Bocaccio female releases 20,000 to two million larvae in the winter. This species feeds on a variety of fishes, crabs, and squids. Small numbers are taken by ocean anglers, and it is an important commercial fish in California.

455 Canary Rockfish
Sebastes pinniger

Description: To 30″ (76 cm). Fusiform, deep, compressed. Orange, with gray blotches and bands along lateral line; pelvic, pectoral, and anal fins yellowish orange; fins not black-edged. *Young have dark blotch on spiny dorsal fin.* Head convex between eyes, with 6 pairs of spines; snout moderately sharp; *lower jaw projects slightly,* no knob at tip. Dorsal fin deeply notched, spiny segment longer-based, membranes between spines incised; rear edge of anal fin straight; caudal fin moderately forked. *Underside of jaw smooth, unscaled.*

Habitat: Around deep rocky reefs and over soft bottoms at depths of 300–900′ (92–275 m). Adults in shallower waters in n part of range; young in shallower waters throughout range.

Range: Cape San Bartolome, AK, to Cabo Colnett, Baja California.

Similar Species: Vermilion Rockfish *(S. miniatus)* has deep red pelvic, pectoral, dorsal, and anal fins with usually black edges and rough scales on underside of lower jaw.

Comments: During winter months, Canary Rockfish releases its young, which become part of the plankton community.

465 Rosy Rockfish
Sebastes rosaceus

Description: To 14″ (36 cm), rarely more than 11″ (28 cm). Fusiform, deep, compressed. Back bright red or orangish red, with lavender blotches and *3–6 white blotches ringed by pale purplish red;* purple bar across nape. Head concave between eyes, with 6 pairs of prominent spines; snout moderately sharp. *Usually 17 pectoral fin rays;* dorsal fin deeply notched, spiny segment longer-based, membranes between spines incised; caudal fin truncate. Lower jaw smooth, unscaled.

Habitat: Around rocky reefs with crevices and caves at depths of 48–420' (14.5–128 m); usually 102–150' (31–46 m).

Range: Northern CA to Bahía Tortugas, Baja California; possibly north to Puget Sound, WA.

Similar Species: Greenspotted Rockfish (*S. chlorostictus*) has bright green vermiculations and spots; occurs at depths of 162–656' (49–200 m). Starry Rockfish (*S. constellatus*) has white spots overall; occurs at depths of 78–900' (24–275 m). Rosethorn Rockfish (*S. helvomaculatus*) has white blotches on back not ringed by purplish red and usually 16 pectoral fin rays; occurs at depths of 390–1,800' (119–549 m).

Comments: This small, distinctive fish makes excellent eating, but it is discarded by many anglers because of its small size.

---

456 Yelloweye Rockfish
Sebastes ruberrimus

Description: To 3' (91 cm). Fusiform, deep, compressed. Orangish yellow above; paler below; *eye bright yellow; fins black-edged. Young have 2 silvery white stripes on sides;* coloration changes with growth: individuals more than 12" (30 cm) long lose pale stripes, lower stripes disappearing first. Head concave between eyes, *with serrate ridges in older individuals,* 6 or more pairs of spines; mouth terminal, large; knob at tip of lower jaw broad, low, rounded. Dorsal fin deeply notched, spiny segment longer-based, membranes between spines incised; caudal fin rounded. Lower jaw smooth, unscaled.

Habitat: Around rocky reefs with caves and crevices at depths of 150–1,800' (46–549 m).

Range: Gulf of Alaska to Ensenada, Baja California.

Similar Species: Cowcod (*S. levis*) has head ridges not serrate, eyes are not yellow, and spiny dorsal fin membrane is deeply incised.

Redstripe Rockfish (*S. proriger*) lacks
serrate ridges on head, and has light red
or yellow pelvic and pectoral fin
membranes, gray lateral line bordered
by red stripes, and 5 pairs of head
spines; occurs at depths of 42–900'
(13–275 m).

Comments: This species is also known as Turkey-red
Rockfish. A single female may release
up to three million young in late spring.
Yelloweye Rockfish feeds on fishes and
crustaceans. Because it is large and
makes fine eating, this rockfish is highly
prized by both sport and commercial
bottom-anglers. However, since it
remains in a single location and is
solitary, not many catches are sizable.

448 Flag Rockfish
Sebastes rubrivinctus

Description: To 20″ (51 cm). Fusiform, deep,
compressed. White or light pink, with 4
dark red to reddish-brown bars, *first
extending over rear of opercle anterior to
pectoral fin,* second and third extending
to dorsal fin, bars sometimes faint in
individuals more than 14″ (36 cm) long.
5 pairs of head spines; snout moderately
sharp. Dorsal fin deeply notched, spiny
segment longer-based, membranes
between spines incised; caudal fin
truncate to slightly rounded. *Lower jaw
smooth, unscaled.*

Habitat: Over soft bottoms and around rocky
reefs at depths of 102–600' (31–183 m).
Range: San Francisco, CA, to Cabo Colnett,
Baja California.
Similar Species: Redbanded Rockfish (*S. babcocki*) has
first red bar extending across body
behind pectoral fin insertion and scaled
lower jaw; occurs at depths of
300–1,560' (92–476 m). Tiger Rockfish
(*S. nigrocinctus*) has pink, rose, or gray
body, with 5 dark red or black bars.
Comments: Flag Rockfish is occasionally caught
by commercial trawlers and hook-and-
line anglers. Reports of large individuals

to 25" (64 cm) long may have been based on misidentified Redbanded Rockfish.

464 Olive Rockfish
Sebastes serranoides

Description: To 24" (61 cm). Fusiform, elongate, compressed. Olive brown, with *light blotches beneath dorsal fin;* ivory below; pelvic, pectoral, and anal fins yellowish. Head usually lacks spines; snout moderately sharp; 29–36 gill rakers on first arch. Dorsal fin deeply notched, spiny segment longer-based, with 12–13 (usually 13) spines, membranes between spines incised; *usually 9 anal fin rays;* caudal fin emarginate.

Habitat: Shallow rocky reefs and kelp beds to depths of 480' (146 m); usually to 102' (31 m).

Range: Redding Rock, n CA, to Islas San Beníto, Baja California.

Similar Species: Yellowtail Rockfish *(S. flavidus)* has reddish-brown speckles on scales, 33–39 gill rakers on first arch, and usually 8 anal fin rays. Kelp Bass *(Paralabrax clathratus)* has dorsal fin with 10–11 spines and 12–14 rays, with longest spine longer than longest ray.

Comments: The young of this species are born during winter and late spring. Often confused with Kelp Bass, the adult occurs singly as well as in small aggregations. It is an excellent sport fish, readily taking surface lures. It feeds on crustaceans and small fishes.

461 Treefish
Sebastes serriceps

Description: To 16" (41 cm). Fusiform, deep, compressed. *Bright yellow to olive yellow, with 6 black bars; lips pinkish or red.* Young more yellowish, without pink on chin or lips; fins white-edged. 6 pairs of sharp prominent head spines; snout moderately sharp; *lips thick.* Dorsal fin deeply notched, spiny segment longer-based, membranes between spines incised; caudal fin rounded.

Habitat: Around shallow rocky reefs with crevices and caves to depths of 150' (46 m).

Range: San Francisco, CA, to Isla de Cedros, Baja California; rare north of Santa Barbara, CA.

Comments: Treefish is often observed by divers off southern California. This solitary species is territorial, defining its area by its constant presence.

---

466 Honeycomb Rockfish
Sebastes umbrosus

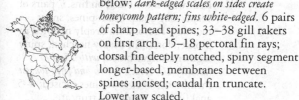

Description: To 10½" (27 cm). Fusiform, elongate, compressed. Back orangish brown, with 5 or fewer white blotches; light orange below; *dark-edged scales on sides create honeycomb pattern; fins white-edged.* 6 pairs of sharp head spines; 33–38 gill rakers on first arch. 15–18 pectoral fin rays; dorsal fin deeply notched, spiny segment longer-based, membranes between spines incised; caudal fin truncate. Lower jaw scaled.

Habitat: Around moderately deep rocky reefs and sometimes over soft bottoms at depths of 90–1,590' (27–485 m); usually to 228' (70 m).

Range: Monterey Bay, CA, to Punta San Juanico, Baja California; rare north of Point Conception, CA; common in s CA.

Similar Species: Swordspine Rockfish *(S. ensifer)* has slightly projecting lower jaw, second anal fin spine equal to or longer than anal fin rays, and scales without dark edges. Pink Rockfish *(S. eos)* has 26–31 gill rakers on first arch, 4–7 of these rudimentary and spiny, usually 18 pectoral fin rays, and scales without dark edges; occurs at depths of 252–1,206' (77–368 m). Freckled

Rockfish *(S. lentiginosus)* has green freckles, front of upper jaw extending forward, forming 2 toothed knobs, and scales without dark edges; occurs at depths of 132–552' (40–168 m). Greenblotched Rockfish *(S. rosenblatti)* has green spots, 29–34 gill rakers on first arch, usually 17 pectoral fin rays, and scales without dark edges; occurs at depths of 204–1,308' (62–399 m).

Comments: A very small number of this species are caught by sport or commercial anglers. Divers occasionally encounter a solitary individual around low-profile rocky reefs at depths of 90–102' (27–31 m).

469 Shortspine Thornyhead
Sebastolobus alascanus

Description: To 30" (76 cm). Fusiform, elongate. Red, with some black on fins. 7 pairs of very strong sharp head spines; snout rounded. Pectoral fin deeply notched in profile; dorsal fin deeply notched, spiny segment longer-based, *with 15–17 (usually 16) spines, fourth and fifth longest,* membranes between spines incised; 4–5 anal fin rays; caudal fin truncate. *Branchiostegal rays unscaled.*

Habitat: Over soft bottoms and sometimes around rocky reefs to depths of 5,028' (1,534 m); usually to 360' (110 m); in shallower waters in n part of range.

Range: Bering Sea to n Baja California.

Similar Species: Longspine Thornyhead *(S. altivelis)* has usually 15 (rarely 16) dorsal fin spines, third spine longest, and scales on branchiostegal rays.

Comments: Both Shortspine and Longspine Thornyheads lay eggs that float in masses near the surface. Shortspine Thornyhead feeds on crustaceans and other invertebrates. Although it is rarely caught by anglers, it makes up a major share of the catches of commercial trawlers working at depths of 1,020' (311 m) or more.

SEAROBINS
Family Triglidae

10 genera and about 70 species world-wide; 2 genera and 17 species in North America (15 Atlantic, 2 Pacific), plus 5 species confined to Mexican Pacific waters. Searobins are small to medium, variably colored fishes that live on the bottom. They are easily recognized by their large heads with many ridges and spines; broad flat snouts and equally broad, terminal or slightly inferior mouths; and usually large, wing-like, often brightly colored pectoral fins with the first three rays free and detached from the rest of the fin. The free pectoral fin rays are used in "walking" along the bottom and as sense organs for probing the bottom in search of food. The spiny dorsal fin is triangular, with 10 spines in the genus *Prionotus* and 11 in *Bellator*. The soft dorsal fin and the anal fins are long and continuous. The body is covered with small, firmly set ctenoid scales. These fishes inhabit continental and insular shelves of tropical and temperate seas to depths of about 570' (174 m). Until recently, the armored gurnards (now classified as the family Peristediidae), which occur in deeper water than searobins, were considered a subfamily of the Triglidae; they have two free pectoral fin rays, two forward-projecting spines on the snout, long fleshy barbels on the lower jaw, and scales modified into four rows of bony scutes.

---

428 Northern Searobin
Prionotus carolinus

Description: To 17" (43 cm), rarely more than 12" (30 cm). Elongate, robust anteriorly, tapering posteriorly. Grayish or reddish above; pale below; pelvic fin white; pectoral fin reddish brown to black above, grayish or whitish below; *black spot between fourth and sixth dorsal fin spines, surrounded by light halo extending through membrane between third and fourth, sixth and seventh spines.* Head large, with many ridges and spines, some disappearing with growth; 11–13 gill rakers on lower limb of outer arch; branchiostegal ray membranes black. Pectoral fin wing-like, extending to middle of soft dorsal fin, with 14 attached rays and 3 free rays anteriorly; usually 12 anal fin rays. Breast fully scaled.

Habitat: Coastal waters over open sand or mud from near shore to depths of 558' (170 m); migrates offshore in winter.

Range: Bay of Fundy to Palm Beach, FL; most common between Cape Hatteras, NC, and Cape Cod, MA; migrates south in winter; absent from Bermuda and Bahamas.

Similar Species: Leopard Searobin *(P. scitulus)* has spot between first and second and fourth and fifth dorsal fin spines, 9–11 gill rakers on lower limb of outer arch, 13 attached pectoral fin rays, and incompletely scaled breast. Barred Searobin *(P. martis)* has spot between first and second and fourth and fifth dorsal fin spines, and 9–11 gill rakers on lower limb of outer arch.

Comments: This is perhaps the most common searobin in Chesapeake Bay. It feeds on various crustaceans, bivalves, squids, and fishes. Searobins are good food fishes, but are not often sold commercially.

---

429 Bandtail Searobin
Prionotus ophryas

Description: To 8" (20 cm). Elongate, slightly compressed. Usually brownish or coppery, with several dark oblique bands; lateral area of snout with light areas between dark blotches; pectoral fin brown, sometimes with spots and bands; alternating light and dark bands on free pectoral fin rays; *3 dark bars on caudal fin*. Head broad, ridged, profile very steep; preopercular spine well developed, other spines on head and snout relatively small or absent; *tentacle above eye; long filament on nostril*. Pectoral fin relatively long, wing-like, extending well beyond middle of soft dorsal fin, with 14 attached rays.

Habitat: Shallow grassy areas over sand; usually to depths of 180' (55 m).

Range: GA to Bahamas and Gulf of Mexico; in coastal waters south to Venezuela.

Similar Species: Bluespotted Searobin *(P. roseus)* has
pectoral fin with usually prominent
blue spots and 13 attached rays; occurs
at depths of 132–288′ (40–88 m).

Comments: Bandtail Searobin is the only searobin
known from the Bahamas. Rarely
seen elsewhere, it also is the only
searobin in North America with a
nasal filament and a tentacle above the
eye. It has been recorded to depths of as
much as 570′ (174 m) in the Gulf of
Mexico. Like other searobins, it has free
pectoral fin rays used for support on the
bottom.

426 Leopard Searobin
Prionotus scitulus

Description: To 10″ (25 cm). Elongate, relatively
slender, slightly compressed; *dorsal
profile rounded.* Brown or olive brown
above; abruptly lighter and unmarked
below lateral line; *darker spots on back,
upper sides, and pectoral, dorsal, and caudal
fins;* black spot on membrane between
first and second dorsal fin spines, larger
spot between fourth and fifth. Head
relatively small; *snout relatively narrow,*
no prominent spines. Pectoral fin wing-
like, not greatly expanded, usually
extending to third anal fin ray.

Habitat: Bays and nearshore waters to depths of
150′ (46 m); often over sand.

Range: VA to Venezuela, including n Gulf of
Mexico.

Similar Species: Northern Searobin *(P. carolinus)* lacks
spot on spiny dorsal fin between first
and second rays.

Comments: The Atlantic population of this species
has a higher gill raker count (averaging
one higher) and usually more scales on
the sides of the body than those fishes
found in the Gulf of Mexico; these
populations are sometimes recognized as
subspecies. This and other searobins live
on the bottom and feed primarily on
invertebrates.

430 Bighead Searobin
Prionotus tribulus

Description: To 14″ (36 cm). *Robust,* slightly compressed, depth one-fourth length. Light to olive brown above, with darker spots, especially on head; often with irregular oblique bands, especially under soft dorsal fin and on caudal peduncle; whitish below; pelvic fin pale; pectoral fin crossed with dark lines, no bright spots; no membranes between fourth and sixth dorsal fin spines; caudal fin blackish, with pale band near base. *Head large, two-fifths length; very large, well-developed spines on snout, head, and shoulders;* snout broad, flat; maxilla reaches front of eye. Pectoral fin large, wing-like, extending well beyond anal fin origin.

Habitat: Nearshore waters, bays, and sounds over sand or mud.

Range: Chesapeake Bay to n FL, and Gulf of Mexico from s FL to TX; occasionally north to NY.

Comments: The young of this species are less than 3″ (7.5 cm) long; with their oversize head armed with large spines, they make interesting aquarium fish. The adults are too large to be kept in most aquariums.

SABLEFISHES
Family Anoplopomatidae

2 genera and 2 species worldwide; both species in North America. Members of this family are confined to temperate waters of the North Pacific. Sablefishes have elongate, fusiform, slightly compressed bodies. They lack spines, ridges, and cirri on the head. The dorsal fin is divided; the spiny first segment is rounded, and the soft second segment is smaller and triangular. The small triangular anal fin has three or fewer weak spines (sometimes absent) and 11 to 23 rays. The caudal fin is truncate or indented. The scales are ctenoid, and a lateral line is present.

421 Sablefish
Anoplopoma fimbria

Description: To 3'4" (1 m), usually to 30" (76 cm);
126 lb (57 kg), usually to 24 lb (11 kg).
Fusiform, elongate, almost round in
cross section. *Blackish gray above; gray to
white below.* Snout moderately sharp;
upper jaw projects slightly beyond
lower, not reaching posterior part of eye.
Dorsal fin widely separated; first dorsal
fin rounded, *with 17–30 spines;* second
dorsal fin triangular; anal fin spineless,
with 16–23 rays; caudal fin indented.

Habitat: Over soft bottoms to depths of 6,000'
(1,830 m). Young in shallow waters.

Range: Bering Sea to Isla de Cedros, Baja
California. Also in Japan.

Similar Species: Skilfish *(Erilepis zonifer)* has light
blotches on head and anterior part of
body, 12–14 dorsal fin spines, and anal
fin with 2–3 spines and 11–14 rays.

Comments: Sablefish spawns during the winter, and
the eggs drift near the surface. This
species feeds on fishes, worms, and
crustaceans. It is wide-ranging and often
migratory. Smoked and sold for food, it
is very important commercially, but it
lives too deep to be pursued by anglers.

GREENLINGS
Family Hexagrammidae

5 genera and 11 species worldwide; 5
genera and 9 species in North America. Restricted to the
North Pacific, the colorful greenlings have elongate, slender, slightly compressed bodies with cirri but no ridges or
spines on the head. The snout is sharp, blunt, or rounded.
The long dorsal fin usually has a notch separating the 15 to
27 spines from the 11 to 26 rays. The long anal fin has four
or fewer spines, which are sometimes longer than one-third
of the body length. The caudal fin is truncate or forked.
These fishes have one to five lateral lines, and the scales are
either ctenoid or cycloid. Combfishes (genus *Zaniolepis*),
which have the unique ability of contorting their bodies
into a U-shape, are sometimes considered a separate family.

449 Kelp Greenling
Hexagrammos decagrammus

Description: To 21″ (53 cm). Fusiform, elongate, slightly compressed. Males dark gray, with bright blue (occasionally black-edged) spots. Females grayish brown, with gold or brown spots. Snout moderately sharp; *pair of cirri above eyes, length less than three-fourths width of eye; pair of cirri on nape very small, occasionally absent;* mouth yellowish inside; lips fleshy; palatine teeth present. Dorsal fin long, deeply notched; caudal fin slightly indented. Ctenoid scales cover opercle. 5 lateral lines; *fourth extends well beyond anal fin origin.*

Habitat: Rocky inshore waters and over sand to depths of 150′ (46 m); common in kelp beds.

Range: Aleutian Islands, AK, to La Jolla, CA; rare in s CA, common northward.

Similar Species: Rock Greenling *(H. lagocephalus)* has pair of cirri above eyes with length more than three-fourths width of eye, and mouth is bluish inside. Whitespotted Greenling *(H. stelleri)* has white spots on back, lacks palatine teeth, and fourth lateral line does not extend beyond anal fin origin. Masked Greenling *(H. octogrammus)* reaches length of 11″ (28 cm), lacks white spots on back, and has very short fourth lateral line.

Comments: Kelp Greenling spawns in the fall. The mass of blue eggs is attached to rocks and guarded by the male. This very colorful fish is popular with anglers. It feeds on polychaete worms, shrimps, small crabs, small fishes, and the siphons of clams.

424 Lingcod
Ophiodon elongatus

Description: To 5′ (1.5 m), usually to 4′ (1.2 m); 105 lb (48 kg), usually to 40 lb (18 kg); females larger than males. Fusiform, elongate, almost round in cross section.

Grayish brown to green, with darker
spots and mottling. *Snout sharp;* pair of
cirri above eyes; *mouth large; lower jaw
projects beyond upper;* jaws with very sharp
large canine and smaller conical teeth.
Dorsal fin long, deeply notched, with
25–28 spines, 19–24 rays; anal fin
sometimes with 1–2 visible spines, 21
or more rays; caudal fin truncate. *1
lateral line.*

Habitat: Near rocks from shallow waters to
depths of 1,398′ (426 m). Young in bays
and inshore areas over sand or mud.

Range: Kodiak Island, AK, to Punta San Carlos,
Baja California; possibly in Bering Sea.

Similar Species: Painted Greenling *(Oxylebius pictus)* has
very small mouth, 15–17 dorsal fin
spines, and anal fin with 3–4 spines and
12–13 rays. Shortspine Combfish
(Zaniolepis frenata) has 21 dorsal fin
spines, second slightly longer than
third, and 15–16 anal fin rays; occurs
over soft bottoms. Longspine Combfish
(Z. latipinnis) has long first 3 dorsal fin
spines, second spine notably longer than
first and third.

Comments: Lingcod feeds on various large fishes,
crustaceans, and mollusks. This
voracious predator is one of the most
highly esteemed sport fishes, primarily
because it makes excellent eating. It is
also a valuable commercial species.

---

458 Painted Greenling
Oxylebius pictus

Description: To 10″ (25 cm), usually to 6″ (15 cm).
Elongate, moderately deep, compressed.
Usually grayish to brown, occasionally
quite dark; sometimes with white spots;
*5–7 red or reddish-brown bars extend onto
fins;* throat usually dark-spotted; 3 dark
bands radiate from eye (1 forward, 2
backward); dark spots on pelvic,
pectoral, and dorsal fins. *Snout pointed;*
pair of cirri above eyes; 1 cirrus midway
between eye and dorsal fin; *mouth small.*
Dorsal fin with 15–17 spines, 14–16 rays;

anal fin with 3–4 spines (often embedded
and not visible), 12–13 rays. *1 lateral
line.*

Habitat: Rocky intertidal waters to depths of
162′ (49 m).

Range: Kodiak Island, AK, to north-central
Baja California; rare north of WA.

Similar Species: Lingcod *(Ophiodon elongatus)* has larger
mouth, 25–28 dorsal fin spines, 19–24
anal fin rays, and 1 lateral line.

Comments: Painted Greenling is commonly seen
hovering motionless by divers, but it is
rarely caught on baited hook. It is also
known as Convict Fish.

GRUNT SCULPINS
Family Rhamphocottidae

1 species worldwide. Grunt sculpins are
found in the North Pacific from Japan to Alaska and south
to southern California. These distinctive fishes have a very
long head, about half as long as the length of the body from
the tip of the snout to the base of the tail, and an elongate
snout. There are six branchiostegal rays, and all fin rays are
unbranched. This family was formerly included in the
sculpin family (Cottidae).

---

440 Grunt Sculpin
Rhamphocottus richardsonii

Description: To 3¼″ (8.5 cm). Deep, compressed.
Creamy yellow, with brown bars and
streaks; caudal peduncle and all fins
except pelvic fins bright red. *Snout long,
sharp;* mouth small, terminal; upper lip
with small, flap-like cirrus. *Lowest
pectoral fin rays free;* dorsal fin separated

by notch, first dorsal with 7–9 spines,
second dorsal with 12–14 rays; 6–8
anal fin rays; caudal fin rounded.
Scales reduced to plates bearing
minute spines.

Habitat: Rocky areas over soft bottoms in
intertidal zone and below low-tide level
to depths of 540′ (165 m).

Range: Bering Sea to Santa Monica Bay, CA.
Also in Japan.

Comments: This fish is thought to spawn in the winter. Aquarium observations show that during the spawning season the female chases the male until he is trapped among rocks; she keeps him trapped until her eggs are laid. Grunt Sculpin makes an amusing aquarium fish; it uses its pectoral fins to virtually jump over rocks on the bottom, and the eyes operate independently. It produces grunt-like sounds when removed from the water, hence its common name. This distinctive sculpin feeds on the larvae of small crustaceans and of fishes.

SCULPINS
Family Cottidae

About 70 genera and about 300 species worldwide; 34 genera and 108 species in North America (5 Atlantic, 69 Pacific, 8 shared, 26 freshwater), plus a few species in deeper offshore waters. These fishes are mostly marine, but some (nearly all in the genus *Cottus*) are strictly freshwater. The family is restricted to cold-temperate and arctic waters, with the majority of marine species concentrated in the North Pacific; they frequently occur in rocky intertidal zones. Most sculpins have a large head and mouth, and an elongate tapering body partly covered with scales or prickles; a few are completely unscaled. The large eyes are placed high on the head, and there are usually one to five well-developed preopercular spines. These fishes have a lateral line. Each pelvic fin has a single spine and two to five rays. The pectoral fins are broad and fan-like. Most species have a deeply notched or divided dorsal fin. The soft-rayed anal fin is usually about as long as the second dorsal fin. Fourteen North American marine species recently included in this family are now placed in the closely related families Rhamphocottidae (grunt sculpins), Psychrolutidae (fathead sculpins), and Hemitripteridae (searavens).

434 Scalyhead Sculpin
Artedius harringtoni

Description: To 4″ (10 cm). Moderately elongate and deep, tapering. Brownish to olive above, *with 5–7 dark saddles on back;* prominent rounded pale areas on lower sides merge

onto white belly; underside of head
orange in adults; red bars radiate from
eye; red spot near tip of first 2 dorsal fin
spines; pectoral, dorsal, and caudal fins
with brown spots forming bands. Head
cirri present (better developed in males);
snout rounded; cirri above front of eyes;
upper preopercular spine short. 15–18
(usually 17) dorsal fin rays; 10–14
(usually 13–14) anal fin rays; caudal fin
slightly rounded. *Anus directly in front of
anal fin; genital papillae of mature males
markedly elongate, forming penis* with
tapering tip. *Scales on head,* sometimes
on cheek, absent on snout; *broad band of
scales on back,* in 38–51 oblique rows,
9–16 scales in longest row.

Habitat:
Common in intertidal and subtidal
rocky waters and around pilings to
depths of 70′ (21 m).

Range:
Kodiak Island, AK, to s CA.

Similar Species:
Coralline Sculpin *(A. corallinus)* has
unscaled head. Padded Sculpin *(A.
fenestralis)* has scales on head, cheek, and
usually below front of eye, and is nearly
fully scaled between dorsal fin base and
lateral line; occurs to depths of 180′
(55 m). Smoothhead Sculpin *(A. lateralis)*
has unscaled head with steep profile and
narrow band of scales on back; occurs to
depths of 43′ (13 m).

Comments:
Species of the genus *Artedius* are among
the most common tide-pool inhabitants
along the North American Pacific coast.

---

427 Mottled Sculpin
Cottus bairdii

Description:
To 6″ (15 cm). Robust, thick anteriorly.
Back olive to tan; sides lighter, with
dark mottling; belly whitish; traces of 2
dark saddles sometimes beneath second
dorsal fin; other fins dusky or with faint,
narrow, dusky to brown bands. Males
have dusky back; *black first dorsal fin,
with bright orange edge in breeding males.*
Head broad, depressed; mouth extends
to below eye; palatine teeth present; *gill*

membranes broadly joined, attached to isthmus. *Pelvic fin with 1 slender spine, 3–4 rays; dorsal fin deeply notched. Caudal peduncle deep, compressed.* Lateral line incomplete, with 18–25 pored scales.

Habitat: Clear, cool or cold creeks, rivers, and lakes over gravel or rocks.

Range: QC, ON, and central MB south to n GA and n AR; s BC and s AB south to OR, UT, w CO, and nw NM.

Similar Species: Banded Sculpin *(C. carolinae)* has pelvic fin with 1 spine and 4 rays, slender caudal peduncle, and complete lateral line. Slimy Sculpin *(C. cognatus)* has pelvic fin with 1 spine and usually 3 rays, slightly joined dorsal fins, slender caudal peduncle, and incomplete lateral line. Black Sculpin *(C. baileyi)* reaches length of 2½″ (6.5 cm), and lacks palatine teeth; occurs in headwater spring creeks.

Comments: Mottled Sculpin feeds on aquatic insects. It is frequently cited as a major predator of trout eggs, but this does not appear to be true. Trouts, however, may prey on sculpins.

435 Buffalo Sculpin
Enophrys bison

Description: To 14½″ (37 cm). Elongate, tapering, almost round in cross section, greatest depth at pectoral fin insertion. Dark gray, green, or brown above, often with light blotches. Head large; snout rounded; *upper preopercular spine extremely long, sharp,* extending to rear edge of opercle; lower preopercular spine points downward. Pelvic fin with 1 spine, 3 rays; second dorsal fin with 9–13 rays; 8–10 anal fin rays; caudal fin truncate. *Heavy bony plates on lateral line.*

Habitat: Common in rocky or sandy inshore waters to depths of 66′ (20 m); often around piers and wrecks.

Range: Kodiak Island, AK, to Monterey Bay, CA.

Similar Species: Bull Sculpin *(E. taurina)* has upper
preopercular spine extending beyond
opercle, and 6–7 anal fin rays. Pacific
Staghorn Sculpin *(Leptocottus armatus)*
has antler-like upper preopercular spine
not reaching rear edge of opercle and
lacks bony plates.

Comments: Buffalo Sculpin feeds heavily on algae. It
spawns in late winter and early spring in
low intertidal areas. The male guards
the egg cluster and fans the eggs with
its pectoral fins. Although this is one of
the larger sculpins, the few that are
caught by anglers are seldom retained
because they lack sufficient flesh.

446   Red Irish Lord
Hemilepidotus hemilepidotus

Description: To 20″ (51 cm), usually to 12″ (30 cm).
Robust, tapering. Reddish, with brown
and black mottling above; *usually 4 dark
saddles on back;* whitish below. Head
depressed, large, with cirri; snout
moderately sharp; *4 short unbranched
preopercular spines; gill membranes
united, narrowly joined to isthmus.* Dorsal
fin with 10–13 spines, notched between
third and fourth spines (sometimes
between fourth and fifth), 17–20 rays;
13–16 anal fin rays; caudal fin slightly
rounded. *Scales on body in 2 main rows, on
back and below lateral line; upper row 4–5
scales wide, lower row about 10 scales wide.*

Habitat: Shallow rocky areas from intertidal zone
to depths of 156′ (48 m).

Range: Kamchatka Peninsula, Russia, and
Bering Sea to Monterey Bay, CA;
common in AK, rare in CA.

Similar Species: Brown Irish Lord *(H. spinosus)* has light
to dark brown body, band of 6–8 rows
of scales below dorsal fin, and band of
4–5 rows of scales below lateral line.
Coralline Sculpin *(Artedius corallinus)*
has unscaled head, first dorsal fin
with 9 spines, second dorsal fin with
15–16 rays, and 39–49 oblique rows of
scales in dorsal band. Smoothhead

Sculpin *(A. lateralis)* has unscaled head and 18–29 oblique rows of scales in dorsal band.

Comments: In the spring, the colorful Red Irish Lord lays its egg masses in intertidal areas. Adults feed on crabs, barnacles, and mussels. Anglers only occasionally catch this edible sculpin.

---

437 Lavender Sculpin
Leiocottus hirundo

Description: To 10″ (25 cm). Elongate, slightly compressed. Brownish or olive green, with blue blotches; 3–4 brownish or reddish bars on sides; orangish brown below, often with pale spots; iridescent blue stripes on dorsal fin. Snout moderately sharp; *no cirrus above eye;* upper preopercular spine 2-pointed. 3 pelvic fin rays; *first 2 dorsal fin spines elongate;* caudal fin truncate. Anus midway between pelvic fin base and anal fin origin. *Body unscaled;* cirri on preopercle, rear of upper jaw, base of nasal spine, and anterior part of lateral line.

Habitat: Shallow waters over rocks or soft bottoms; around kelp beds to depths of 120′ (37 m).

Range: Point Conception, CA, to Punta Banda, Baja California.

Similar Species: Roughback Sculpin *(Chitonotus pugetensis)* has deeply notched spiny dorsal fin, with first spine twice as long as second. Threadfin Sculpin *(Icelinus filamentosus)* has very elongate first 2 dorsal fin spines, about two-thirds free of membrane. Sailfin Sculpin *(Nautichthys oculofasciatus)* has very high spiny dorsal fin, with first 4 spines almost 3 times height of rays. Species in genera *Clinocottus* and *Oligocottus* are also unscaled, but first 2 dorsal fin spines are not elongate.

Comments: Although anglers rarely catch the distinctive Lavender Sculpin, it is commonly encountered by divers.

441 Longhorn Sculpin
Myoxocephalus octodecimspinosus

Description: To 18″ (46 cm), rarely more than 14″
(36 cm). Elongate, rather slender.
Usually dark olive to pale greenish
yellow above; fading to white on belly;
usually 4 obscure irregular crossbars,
sometimes broken into blotches. Head
blunt, heavy, flat; *preopercular spine very
long;* 2 sharp opercular spines. Dorsal fin
with 8–9 spines, first 3 spines long,
third longest (half length of head),
15–16 rays. *Body unscaled. Lateral line
marked by series of bony plates.*

Habitat: Common in harbors and shallow coastal
waters; deeper waters in winter.

Range: Eastern NF and Gulf of St. Lawrence
to VA.

Similar Species: Grubby *(M. aeneus)* rarely reaches
length of 6″ (15 cm), has deeper body,
lower spiny dorsal fin, and shorter
preopercular spine, and lacks bony
plates on lateral line; occurs in open
coastal waters and estuaries to depths
of 420′ (128 m).

Comments: Longhorn Sculpin spawns in the winter.
It feeds heavily on offal discarded
around wharves, as well as on a wide
range of living food, including crabs,
shrimps, mollusks, squids, and small
fishes.

439 Fluffy Sculpin
Oligocottus snyderi

Description: To 3½″ (9 cm). Elongate, slightly
compressed. Coloration extremely
variable: green to reddish brown to pink;
belly often bluish; usually 4–6 dark
saddles on back; sides spotted and
mottled; white spots usually on
underside of head; pelvic fin clear; other
fins banded. *1 cirri at nasal spine;* tufts of
cirri on head, dorsal fin base, and lateral
line; *no cirri on upper jaw or below eye; upper
preopercular spine with usually 2 points.* 3
pelvic fin rays; 13–15 pectoral fin rays;

dorsal fin with 7–9 spines, 17–20 rays; anal fin directly behind anus, with 12–15 rays, first ray enlarged and (with next 2 rays) separate from rest of fin in adult males. *No prickles or scales on body.*

Habitat: Common in tide pools; prefers sheltered waters.

Range: Sitka, AK, to n Baja California.

Similar Species: Rosy Sculpin *(O. rubellio)* has upper preopercular spine with usually 3 points and 1–4 cirri at rear of upper jaw. Tidepool Sculpin *(O. maculosus)* lacks cirri at nasal spine and has a few cirri on head or body. Saddleback Sculpin *(O. rimensis)* has prickles on skin.

Comments: Species of the genus *Oligocottus* are among the most common tide-pool inhabitants along the Pacific coast of North America.

436 Snubnose Sculpin
Orthonopias triacis

Description: To 4″ (10 cm). Elongate, slightly compressed. Brown, with light and dark mottling and bright red patches; about 5 saddles on back; black spot at front of first dorsal fin. Head large; *snout very blunt;* upper preopercular spine small, sharp, usually with 2 or more points. Pelvic fin with 1 spine, 3 rays; caudal fin rounded. *Anus much closer to pelvic fin base than to anal fin in adults; about midway between pelvic and anal fins in young.* Dense scales on top of head and over most of back. Cirri along lateral line.

Habitat: Rocks between high- and low-tide levels and rocky reefs below intertidal zone to depths of 102′ (31 m).

Range: Monterey Bay, CA, to Isla de San Jeronimo, Baja California.

Similar Species: The 7 species of genus *Artedius* all have anus directly in front of anal fin. Woolly Sculpin *(Clinocottus analis)* has anus midway between pelvic and anal fins and numerous cirri and minute prickles between dorsal fin and lateral line. Mosshead Sculpin *(C. globiceps)* has bluntly rounded head and cirri in front of and between eyes, and lacks scales between dorsal fin and lateral line. Bald Sculpin *(C. recalvus)* has bluntly rounded head and lacks scales between dorsal fin and lateral line. Fluffy Sculpin *(Oligocottus snyderi)* has anus close to anal fin and unscaled skin; first anal fin rays longest in males.

Comments: This small sculpin is rarely caught by anglers, but is familiar to divers.

---

442 Cabezon
Scorpaenichthys marmoratus

Description: To 3'3" (99 cm); 24 lb (11 kg). Elongate, slightly compressed. Red to olive green to brown, with dark and light mottling. Snout moderately blunt; *large fleshy cirri on midline of snout and over each eye; upper preopercular spine stout, slightly curved.* Pelvic fin with 1 spine, 5 rays; 11–14 anal fin rays; caudal fin truncate. *Body unscaled.*

Habitat: Rocky areas in intertidal zone and below low-tide level to depths of 252' (77 m).

Range: Sitka, AK, to Punta Abreojos, Baja California.

Similar Species: Rosylip Sculpin *(Ascelichthys rhodorus)* reaches length of 6" (15 cm), has bluntly rounded head, and lacks pelvic fins. Lingcod *(Ophiodon elongatus),* of greenling family (Hexagrammidae), lacks mottling on body, and has more pointed head and much longer spiny dorsal fin. Blackfin Sculpin *(Malacocottus kincaidi),* in closely related fathead sculpin family (Psychrolutidae), reaches length of 8" (20 cm), lacks large cirri on head, and has 3 pelvic fin rays and thin loose skin.

Comments: Cabezon spawns in the winter, and the male guards the mass of greenish to purplish eggs until they hatch. The eggs are poisonous if eaten. This large tasty sculpin is highly desired by anglers, who catch it from the shore.

SEARAVENS
Family Hemitripteridae

3 genera and 8 species worldwide; 3 genera and 7 species in North America (1 Atlantic, 6 Pacific). The characteristics distinguishing this family from other closely related families in the order Scorpaeniformes mostly involve details of the internal anatomy. The one prominent external feature that sets apart the searavens is the presence of minute spines covering the body.

---

438 Sailfin Sculpin
Nautichthys oculofasciatus

Description: To 8″ (20 cm). Relatively slender. Brown to gray above; pale brown to cream below, usually with black blotches; black diagonal bar across cheek, through eye, and onto cirrus above eye; dark bars on all fins except pelvic fin; dorsal fin sometimes flecked with red. 13–14 pectoral fin rays; *first dorsal fin spiny, highly elevated;* second dorsal fin long, with 27–30 rays; 16–21 (usually 19) anal fin rays. *Prickles cover body.*

Habitat: Over rocks from inshore to depths of 360′ (110 m); often with algae.

Range: Kodiak Island, AK, to San Miguel Island, s CA; common from Puget Sound, WA, northward. Possibly in Bering Sea and Japan.

Similar Species: Smallsail Sculpin *(N. robustus)* and Eyeshade Sculpin *(N. pribilovius)* have much lower first spiny dorsal fin and fewer rays in soft dorsal fin.

Comments: This species does well in captivity and is a popular display fish in public aquariums.

POACHERS
Family Agonidae

20 genera and 44 species worldwide; 15 genera and 27 species in North America (24 Pacific, 3 Atlantic and Pacific). These fishes are restricted to cold-temperate to arctic marine waters. One species is confined to the eastern North Atlantic, and another four species are

restricted to the area around the southern tip of South America. Most poachers have elongate slender bodies tapering to small caudal fins and dorsal fins divided into two distinct segments. When separated, the first dorsal fin is spiny and the second is soft-rayed. The pelvic fins have one spine and two rays and are situated below the pectoral fins. There are no spines in the anal fin. A few species have cirri, usually on the lower jaw. Poachers are sometimes confused with juvenile sturgeons (order Acipenseriformes), since both groups have scales modified as bony plates.

425 Sturgeon Poacher
Podothecus accipenserinus

Description: To 12″ (30 cm). Elongate, tapering. Grayish brown above, with dark saddles across back; light yellow to orange below; orange spot beneath each eye. Snout long, sharp; 2 projecting rostral spines, widely separated; *mouth ventral, with patch of long yellow to cream cirri in front and at corners.* Pelvic fin with 1 spine, 2 rays; 16–18 pectoral fin rays; 2 dorsal fins; 6–9 anal fin rays; caudal fin rounded. Caudal peduncle long, slender. 4 rows of bony plates on each side.

Habitat: Shallow rocky reefs and over soft bottoms to depths of 180′ (55 m).

Range: Bering Sea to Eureka, CA.

Similar Species: Northern Spearnose Poacher *(Agonopsis vulsa)* lacks large yellow cirri on snout and has terminal mouth and 2 closely set, projecting rostral spines. Rockhead *(Bothragonus swanii)* has deep robust body and deep pit on head behind eyes. Warty Poacher *(Chesnonia verrucosa)* has terminal mouth, 15 pectoral fin rays, and knobby, plate-like scales on breast in front of pelvic fins; males have pelvic and pectoral fins of equal length. Pygmy Poacher *(Odontopyxis trispinosa)* has shallow pit on top of head behind eyes and upright rostral spines. Pricklebreast Poacher *(Stellerina xyosterna)* has terminal mouth, 17–19 pectoral fin rays, and smooth breast with minute spines.

Comments: Sturgeon Poacher, rarely caught by anglers, is often netted by trawlers but not kept. The physical appearance of this fish is similar in certain respects to that of a small armored gurnard (family Peristediidae).

LUMPFISHES
Family Cyclopteridae

7 genera and 28 species worldwide; 5 genera and 11 species in North America (7 Pacific, 2 Atlantic, 2 shared). Lumpfishes are found in cold-temperate to arctic waters of the Northern Hemisphere. They have a globose body usually covered with tubercles (one genus has a naked body). When present, the pelvic fins are modified into a sucking disk. The dorsal fin is usually divided into two short segments, the first with four to eight spines (concealed beneath the skin in some species), the second with eight to 13 rays; it is never joined to the caudal fin. The anal fin is short, with seven to 13 rays. This family formerly included the snailfishes (family Liparidae).

365 Lumpfish
Cyclopterus lumpus

Description: To 24" (61 cm); 21 lb (9.5 kg). *Very robust, somewhat triangular in cross section.* Bluish, olive, brownish, reddish, or greenish; paler below, often with darker blotches and black dots; tips of largest tubercles sometimes black. Eye small, on anterior one-third of head; mouth small, terminal, oblique. *Pelvic fins inserted just behind throat, modified to form ventral sucking disk; pectoral fins broad-based, almost meeting at throat;* first dorsal fin segment beneath surface of skin; second dorsal fin segment and anal fin similar, posteriorly placed opposite each other; caudal fin truncate. Skin rough, with 7 lengthwise ridges formed by large tubercles.

Habitat: Primarily over rocks in shallow waters; sometimes semipelagic, hiding under floating seaweed.
Range: Hudson Bay to NF and along coast to Chesapeake Bay. Also in e Atlantic.

Similar Species: Leatherfin Lumpsucker (*Eumicrotremus derjugini*) and Atlantic Spiny Lumpsucker (*E. spinosus*) have much larger eye and divided dorsal fin with prominent spiny segment.

Comments: This ungainly fish clings to rocks or debris. It is noted for its tasty roe. Males make good eating, but females are inedible during the breeding season.

SNAILFISHES
Family Liparidae

About 19 genera and at least 195 species worldwide; 6 genera and 36 species in North America (7 Atlantic, 26 Pacific, 3 shared). Most species occur in cold-temperate to arctic waters of the Northern Hemisphere, but at least 45 species are found in the Antarctic region and perhaps some in deep waters in intervening tropical latitudes. These fishes occur over a wide depth range, from the shoreline to depths of more than 23,100′ (7,046 m). The body is elongate and unscaled (some species have small prickles), and sometimes tadpole-like in appearance. Snailfishes have either single or paired nostrils, and the skin is very soft and flabby. When present, the pelvic fins are joined together as an adhesive disk; this disk is absent in at least 45 species (including three in North America). The dorsal and anal fins are long and continuous (or nearly so) with the caudal fin. Members of this family reach a maximum length of about 20″ (51 cm). They were formerly included in the lumpfish family (Cyclopteridae).

517 Tidepool Snailfish
Liparis florae

Description: To about 7″ (18 cm). Elongate, moderately deep, laterally compressed. Brown, olive, or purplish, sometimes yellowish or various shades of greenish brown to reddish brown; fins about same color as body. Teeth tricuspid; gill slit extends down in front of pectoral fin. Pectoral fin with 3–5 rays, *lower rays elongate; front rays of dorsal fin form bluntly pointed, nearly separate lobe; dorsal and anal fins extend only slightly onto caudal fin;* 25–27 anal fin rays.

Habitat: Inshore waters and tide pools on exposed coasts.

Range: Kodiak Island, AK, to Point Conception, CA.

Similar Species: Spotted Snailfish (*L. callyodon*) also has lobe in front of dorsal fin, but has spots on sides. Lobefin Snailfish (*L. greeni*) has teeth with 1 cusp and at least 30 anal fin rays.

Comments: Tidepool Snailfish is perhaps the most common snailfish found in tide pools over much of its range.

FLYING GURNARDS
Order Dactylopteriformes
Family Dactylopteridae

This order contains a single family: 2 genera and 7 species worldwide; 1 species in North America. This group, which at various times has been allied with either the orders Syngnathiformes or Scorpaeniformes, is now regarded as a separate order, closely related to the Scorpaeniformes. These bottom-dwelling fishes are found in tropical to temperate seas, absent only from the eastern Pacific; the sole North American representative of the order is widespread in the tropical and warm-temperate areas of the Atlantic. The elongate body is squarish in cross section, tapers posteriorly, and is covered with scute-like scales. Thick bones on the top of the large blunt head are fused into a bony shield, and there is a large, spine-like apparatus on each side of the nape. The mouth is small and low. The eyes are relatively large, and there is a pointed, extremely long preopercular spine on each side of the head. The pelvic fins are thoracic, each with one spine and four rays. Each pectoral fin is separated into two segments, the upper part relatively short and the lower part greatly expanded and reaching almost to the caudal fin base. The dorsal fin is also separated into two segments; the first one or two spines of the first part are free, not connected to the rest of the fin. The caudal fin is emarginate, and there are two sharp keels on each side of the caudal peduncle.

542, 543 Flying Gurnard
Dactylopterus volitans

Description: To 18″ (46 cm); 4 lb (1.8 kg). Elongate, squarish in cross section, tapering. Usually brilliant shades of brownish to greenish olive above; paler below; irregularly blotched with reddish or pinkish-yellow tints; pectoral fin membranes brightly colored, usually with rows of large blue to lavender spots and several blue lines (1 line along edge of fin). *Head encased in bony shield, with long preopercular spine extending back from top of skull to below middle of first dorsal fin.* First 2 dorsal fin spines not widely separated from rest of fin, not immediately adjacent to skull, *closely joined at bases,* first spine usually offset to right and second spine offset to left.

Habitat: Over open bottoms from shallow waters to mid-depths; often around coral reefs. Young at surface.

Range: NC to Argentina, including Bermuda, Bahamas, Gulf of Mexico, and Caribbean; seasonally north to ME and possibly e Canada. Also in e Atlantic and around Ascension Island in South Atlantic.

Similar Species: Searobins (family Triglidae, in order Scorpaeniformes) also have expanded pectoral fins, but lack extremely long preopercular spine on each side of head and lower pectoral fin rays are free.

Comments: This species is sufficiently distinct that it should not be confused with any other fish. Flying Gurnard apparently employs the pelvic fins to move along the bottom, unlike searobins, which use the free pectoral "fingers" for this purpose. Adults feed primarily on bottom crustaceans, especially crabs, as well as clams and small fishes.

Order Perciformes

This is the largest order of bony fishes, which as presently constituted includes 18 suborders and 148 families; 13 suborders and 81 families are found in North America, plus at least 200 species in Mexican waters. Classification of the order is unsettled; there have been many recent changes, and others are expected in the future. These typical spiny-rayed fishes occur in marine and fresh waters. The pelvic fins usually consist of a single spine and five rays, and there are spines on the anterior parts of the dorsal and anal fins. The scales are typically ctenoid, and a lateral line is almost always present.

SNOOKS
Family Centropomidae

3 genera and 22 species worldwide; 1 genus with 4 species in marine and fresh waters of eastern North America, plus 8 species confined to Mexican Atlantic and Pacific waters. These rather large fishes have elongate compressed bodies with well-separated dorsal fins. The short-based anal fin has three spines, with the second spine enlarged. The lateral line extends to the caudal fin tip. The snout is pointed, the mouth is large, and the lower jaw projects well beyond the upper. Snooks inhabit tropical coastal waters, estuaries, and lagoons, and often enter fresh water.

561 Snook
Centropomus undecimalis

Description: To 4' (1.2 m); 53 lb (24 kg). Slender, elongate. Yellowish brown or greenish brown above; silvery below; *lateral line dark; fins dusky.* Snout pointed; mouth large; teeth in jaw and on roof of mouth; lower jaw protrudes; usually 7–9 gill rakers; preopercle serrate. Dorsal fins well separated, with very strong second spine; anal fin with 3 spines, usually 6 rays; caudal fin deeply forked. Scales small, ctenoid; 67–77 *(usually 69–74) scales in lateral series. Lateral line extends to tip of caudal fin,* with 70–77 scales.

Habitat: Shallow coastal and fresh waters, estuaries, lagoons, and canals.

Range: Cape Fear River, NC, to s FL; along Gulf coast to Destin, FL, disjunctly to TX; Caribbean to Brazil; probably only summer migrants north of s FL.

Similar Species: Fat Snook *(C. parallelus)* also has anal fin with 3 spines and 6 rays, but has 10–13 gill rakers and 79–92 (usually 81–89) scales in lateral series. Tarpon Snook *(C. pectinatus)* has usually 21–22 gill rakers in outer arch, anal fin with somewhat longer second spine and usually 7 rays, and 61–72 (usually 64–67) scales in lateral series. Swordspine Snook *(C. ensiferus)* has usually 15–19 gill rakers, anal fin with much longer second spine and 6 rays, and 49–59 (usually 51–56) scales in lateral series.

Comments:　Snook is a highly esteemed food and sport fish. It feeds on other fishes and various crustaceans. It is sensitive to low temperatures, and avoids water cooler than about 61° F (16° C). This fish should be handled carefully, as the sharp gill cover can cause deep cuts. The other North American species in the genus are much smaller, with none exceeding 24″ (61 cm) in length.

TEMPERATE BASSES
Family Moronidae

　　1 genus with 4 species confined to North America. These fishes are found in fresh, brackish, and salt waters. They are characterized by the presence of one or two preopercular spines; two dorsal fins, deeply divided or separate, the first with eight to 10 spines and the second with one spine and 10 to 13 rays; an anal fin with three spines and nine to 12 rays; and a complete lateral line extending onto a forked caudal fin. Many temperate basses are important food and sport fishes. During the past few decades, fishery biologists have cultured hybrids of several species. The cross between a female White Bass *(Morone chrysops)* and a male Striped Bass *(M. saxatilis)* is known as Sunshine Bass; the reciprocal cross is called Palmetto Bass. Other names for hybrids between White Bass and Striped Bass are Wiper (or Wiper Bass) and White Rock Bass. The cross between a male Yellow Bass *(M. mississippiensis)* and a female Striped Bass is known as Paradise Bass. Crosses between White Perch *(M. americana)* and Striped Bass are called Virginia Bass and Maryland Bass. Of all these crosses, the most frequently stocked were Sunshine Bass and Palmetto Bass. However, with increased success in stocking Striped Bass in inland waters, the interest in releasing hybrids has declined in many states. Some of the hybrids are known to backcross with the parental species, which genetically contaminates the stock of the native species.

108, 588 White Perch
Morone americana

Description: To 23″ (58 cm); 4¾ lb (2.2 kg). Oblong,
moderately compressed; back elevated.
*Back greenish gray or nearly black; sides
paler, sometimes with indistinct stripes;* belly

whitish. Head depressed between eyes;
maxilla reaches eye; lower jaw slightly
protrudes; teeth small, in bands on jaw,
vomer, and palatine bones; *lateral tooth
patch on edge of tongue, absent on base of
tongue;* 2 preopercular spines. Dorsal

tongue

fins slightly connected, first with 8–10
strong spines; *anal fin with 3 spines, second
and third about equal in length, 8–9 rays.*
Scales extend onto base of median fins
and head.

Habitat: Brackish waters of bays and estuaries;
freshwater populations in rivers and
lakes, especially in north of range.

Range: Cape Breton Island, NS, St. Lawrence
River, and Lake Ontario south to SC;
most abundant in Hudson River and
Chesapeake Bay. Introduced in Great
Lakes and central U.S.

Comments: White Perch is an important sport fish.

It averages 8–10″ (20–25 cm) in length,
and usually weighs up to 1 lb (500 g).
In 1949, a record catch of 4¾ lb (2.2 kg)
was taken in Messalonskee Lake, Maine.
White Perch probably entered Lake
Ontario through the Erie Barge Canal
and the Oswego River. It is a recent
immigrant to Lake Erie.

105 White Bass
Morone chrysops

Description: To 18″ (46 cm); 7 lb (3.1 kg). Deep,
compressed. Back olive to silvery gray;
*sides silvery to white, with 6–9 dark narrow
stripes,* sometimes interrupted below
lateral line; belly yellowish. Mouth
reaches middle of eye; lower jaw
protrudes; *lateral tooth patch on edge and
base of tongue. Dorsal fins separate; anal fin*

tongue

with second spine about half length of third,
11–13 rays. Scales extend onto head.
Lateral line with 50–60 scales.

Habitat: Moderately clear waters of large
streams, lakes, and reservoirs over
firm sand, gravel, or rocks.

Range: Lake Winnipeg, MB; St. Lawrence
River; s Great Lakes; Mississippi
River system; Gulf coast from
LA to TX and NM. Widely
introduced in U.S.

Comments: White Bass is found in schools in
open waters. It feeds primarily
on fishes, but also on aquatic insects
and crustaceans, which it locates
by sight rather than scent. It is an
important sport fish, especially in
reservoirs, and minnows and lures
are excellent bait.

107 Yellow Bass
Morone mississippiensis

Description: To 18″ (46 cm); 2½ lb (1.1 kg). Deep,
compressed. Back greenish yellow; *sides
silvery to brassy yellow, with 7–9 bold dark
greenish to black stripes, those below lateral
line just anterior to anal fin interrupted and
offset;* belly yellowish. Mouth reaches
eye; lower jaw not protruding; *no teeth on
tongue. Dorsal fins slightly joined at bases;
anal fin with second spine about same length
as third,* 9–10 rays. Lateral line with
49–55 scales.

tongue

Habitat: Backwaters and quiet pools of lowland
rivers, lakes, and reservoirs.

Range: Central Mississippi River system; Gulf
coast from AL to e TX. Introduced in
AZ and possibly KS.

Comments: Although Yellow Bass is smaller and
has a more restricted range than
White Bass *(M. chrysops),* it also is a
popular sport fish. It lives in schools
and feeds on fishes, crustaceans, and
insects from mid-depths to the surface.
During the spring it makes spawning
runs up streams.

106, 610 Striped Bass
Morone saxatilis

Description: To 6′ (1.8 m); 125 lb (57 kg). Elongate,
moderately compressed, depth usually
more than one-fourth length. Back olive
green to dark blue; sides silvery, *upper
sides with 6–9 dark uninterrupted stripes;*
belly white; median fins dusky. Mouth
large; lower jaw protrudes slightly; teeth
small, in bands on jaws, vomer, and
palatine bones; *lateral tooth patch on edge
of tongue, 2 parallel patches on middle of
tongue posteriorly;* 2 flat spines near
posterior edge of opercle. Dorsal fins
separate, first with 8–10 strong spines,
second usually with 12 rays; anal fin
with 3 spines, second distinctly shorter
than third, 11–13 rays. Scales extend
onto all fin bases except first dorsal fin.

tongue

Habitat: Inshore over various bottoms; some
populations permanently in fresh water.

Range: Atlantic Ocean and associated rivers
from St. Lawrence River to St. Johns
River, FL; Apalachicola River, w FL, to
Lake Pontchartrain, se LA; most
abundant from Hudson River to
Chesapeake Bay. Widely introduced in
rivers and lakes in much of Mississippi
River system, Colorado River, and
coastal streams in WA, OR, and CA.

Comments: Striped Bass is a very important sport and
commercial fish throughout its range;
large individuals are caught by surf
fishing, especially on the Atlantic coast. It
is a delicious food fish. This anadromous
species spawns prolifically in fresh water.

WRECKFISHES
Family Polyprionidae

2 genera and 2 species worldwide; both
species in North America (1 Atlantic, 1 Pacific). These very
large fishes are widespread in the Atlantic and in the eastern and western North Pacific (but absent from intervening
boreal waters) and occur disjunctly in temperate regions of
the South Pacific and Indian Oceans. They are very similar

externally to members of other generalized perciform families; this has led to past uncertainty in classification, and the species at various times have been included in the sea bass family (Serranidae) or the temperate perch family (Percichthyidae). One of the most distinctive external features is the dorsal fin ray count (nine to 12), which is lower than for other perciform fishes of similar appearance and size.

632 Giant Sea Bass
Stereolepis gigas

Description: To 7'5" (2.3 m); 556 lb (253 kg). Heavy, robust, slightly compressed, greatest depth near head. Dark gray; *usually large black spots on sides.* Young red, with black spots. Eye relatively small; lower jaw protrudes slightly; *2 opercular spines.* Dorsal fin with 11 spines, 10–11 (possibly 9) rays; caudal fin square to slightly indented.

Habitat: Rocky waters and kelp beds from inshore to depths of 150' (46 m).

Range: Humboldt Bay, CA, to Gulf of California. Also disjunctly in w North Pacific.

Similar Species: Wreckfish *(Polyprion americanus)*, also in family Polyprionidae, reaches length of 7' (2.1 m), has rough head with numerous protuberances, strong bony ridge on opercle, and 11–12 dorsal fin rays; occurs around rocky ledges, outcroppings, and wrecks, usually at depths of 300–2,000' (91–610 m). Gulf Grouper *(Mycteroperca jordani)* has 3 opercular spines and caudal fin with smooth posterior edge. Broomtail Grouper *(M. xenarcha)* has 3 opercular spines and caudal fin with jagged tip.

Comments: Giant Sea Bass was formerly placed in the sea bass family (Serranidae); it has a lower dorsal fin ray count than any grouper or true sea bass in the eastern Pacific. It spawns in the summer and does not mature until about 11 to 13 years of age, when it weighs 51–60 lb (23–27 kg). This huge fish is highly prized by anglers and divers. Its numbers have declined drastically, and in 1981 the capture of this species by commercial and sport anglers was prohibited in California.

SEA BASSES
Family Serranidae

About 62 genera and 449 species worldwide; 21 genera and 80 species in North America (66 Atlantic, 14 Pacific), plus 28 species confined to Mexican waters. As the common name implies, all sea basses are marine. Since these are generalized perciform fishes, our understanding of interrelationships within the family is still not completely resolved. Some groups formerly placed in other families, including the soapfishes (formerly the Grammistidae), are now included in the Serranidae; others have been removed and placed in other families, such as the cardinalfishes (Apogonidae). Some, including the temperate basses and the wreckfishes, have been accorded family status (Moronidae and Polyprionidae, respectively). As now constituted, the sea basses can be characterized as perch-like fishes with a usually slightly notched dorsal fin and an anal fin with usually three to five spines. The mouth is generally large, with a broad exposed maxilla and teeth on the jaws and the roof of the mouth. The upper edge of the opercle is free and usually has three flat spines. The lateral line is complete and extends to the caudal fin base. Sizes of species within this family vary tremendously; some are less than an inch long and weigh only a few ounces, while others reach a length of 8′ (2.4 m) and a weight of at least 700 lb (318 kg). Many sea basses change color patterns during the transformation from juvenile to adult. Coloration may also alter as the fish moves around and as the light intensity changes, so that red colors become more prominent as the light dims. Sex reversal has been documented in a number of species; typically, younger individuals are females, changing into males with increasing age. The common name grouper is often applied to large species in the closely related genera *Mycteroperca* and *Epinephelus* and in other related genera, including *Cephalopholis*.

633 Black Sea Bass
Centropristis striata

Description: To 24″ (61 cm); 8 lb (3.6 kg). Elongate, moderately compressed, depth one-third length. Dark brown or bluish black;

light-centered scales form stripes above;
dorsal fin striped. Head large; maxilla
reaches middle of eye; lower jaw projects
beyond upper; *preopercle weakly serrate,
without large spines.* Dorsal fin high,
spiny and soft segments separated by
notch, interspinal membrane deeply
notched, fleshy flaps on spines; 3 anal
fin spines; caudal fin round or ends in 3
lobes, upper lobe often with elongate ray
in adults. Bases of soft dorsal and anal
fins lack scales and thick skin. Lateral
line extends to caudal fin base.

Habitat: Shallow continental shelf waters;
common around jetties, pilings, and
wrecks over rocks.

Range: ME to FL and e Gulf of Mexico; reaches
extreme s FL in cold winters.

Comments: Populations in the eastern Gulf of
Mexico represent a subspecies *(C. striata
melana)* that attains a length of only
about half that of the Atlantic
populations. Black Sea Bass is an
important food fish, especially in the
mid-Atlantic states. It is often caught
by anglers fishing with rods from boats
for other kinds of fishes.

620 Coney
Cephalopholis fulva

Description: To 16″ (41 cm), usually to 12″ (30 cm).
Small, rather elongate, robust. *Coloration
variable:* body and head most often
dark brown or sharply bicolored (dark
above, pale tan below), sometimes
reddish, occasionally golden yellow;
*numerous small, prominent, electric blue spots,
each surrounded by black ring;* individuals
from deeper waters with fewer spots,
often without blue centers; *2 black spots
always present on chin, 2 black spots on top
of caudal peduncle.* Head pointed; mouth
large, reaching just beyond eye; lower
jaw projects beyond upper. Dorsal fin
with 9 spines, 15–16 rays; anal fin with 3
spines, 9 rays; caudal fin slightly
rounded.

Habitat: Common in coral reefs and rocky areas from inshore to depths of 500' (152 m).

Range: NC to Brazil, including Bermuda, Bahamas, Gulf of Mexico, and Caribbean.

Similar Species: Graysby *(C. cruentata)* lacks small blue spots on body, is never golden yellow (generally with much less variable pigmentation), and has 4 relatively large dark spots evenly spaced along upper side below length of entire dorsal fin, 14 dorsal fin rays, 8 anal fin rays, and more rounded caudal fin.

Comments: Coney and Graysby have frequently been included in the genus *Epinephelus.* They are probably the most commonly seen groupers in the coral reefs of the western Atlantic.

---

587 Sand Perch
Diplectrum formosum

Description: To 12" (30 cm). Small, slender, elongate. *Indistinct dark bars and alternating blue and orange stripes;* narrow blue lines on cheek. Head and mouth large; *preopercle with 2 bony lobes,* 1 at angle, 1 above, each with radiating spines; 3 flat preopercular spines. Dorsal fin not notched; 3 anal fin spines; caudal fin slightly forked, upper rays sometimes thread-like. Lateral line extends to caudal fin base.

Habitat: Coastal waters over sand or mud and near reefs or upper edges of depressions in ocean floor from inshore to depths of 240' (73 m).

Range: VA to FL, Cuba, e Gulf of Mexico, and Bay of Campeche, Mexico; absent from coast of Central America, but occurs along coast of n South America to Brazil and possibly Uruguay; apparently absent from West Indies; scarcity of insular records (one each from Bahamas and Virgin Islands) raises possibility of erroneous locality data.

Similar Species: Dwarf Sand Perch *(D. bivittatum)* reaches length of 5" (12.5 cm) and has 1 bony lobe on preopercle.

Comments: Rather common in certain areas, this little sea bass is often caught by anglers who are pursuing something larger. Disjunctly distributed populations in North and South America differ in certain respects, most notably gill raker counts, which average lower in North American populations.

618 Rock Hind
Epinephelus adscensionis

Description: To 24″ (61 cm). Robust, not strongly compressed. Light olive; *body and fins covered with reddish-brown spots, larger below than on sides; 2–3 dark saddles on back under dorsal fin, 1 on caudal peduncle;* soft dorsal, anal, and caudal fins greenish, without black edges. Head long; mouth oblique; maxilla reaches eye. Dorsal fin with 11 spines, 16–17 rays, some spines longer than anterior rays, interspinal membrane notched; anal fin with 3 spines, 8 rays; caudal fin rounded. Bases of soft dorsal and anal fins covered with scales and thick skin. Lateral line extends to caudal fin base.

Habitat: Over coral reefs and rocks in shallow waters to depths of 250′ (76 m).

Range: Bermuda, s FL, Gulf coast, and along Caribbean coast and throughout West Indies to Brazil; occasional stragglers north to MA.

Similar Species: Graysby *(Cephalopholis cruentata)* is similarly spotted, but has 3–4 small distinct spots under dorsal fin base. Red Hind *(E. guttatus)* lacks spots on fins and dark saddles on back, and spots below and on sides are same size.

Comments: This common shallow-water species is frequently seen by divers and snorkelers. It is reported to be a better food fish than Red Hind *(E. guttatus),* but is more wary of taking bait.

617 Speckled Hind
Epinephelus drummondhayi

Description: To 3'7" (1.1 m), usually to 22" (56 cm);
52 lb (24 kg). Robust, not strongly
compressed. Reddish brown above;
bluish purple below; *covered with small
creamy white spots,* sometimes merging in
large individuals; pelvic fin blackish
toward tip. Young occasionally yellow,
with white spots, sometimes with 2–3
pale areas below dorsal fin. Head long;
mouth oblique; maxilla reaches middle
of eye. Dorsal fin with 11 spines, 16
rays, some spines longer than anterior
rays, interspinal membrane notched;
anal fin with 3 spines, 9 rays; caudal fin
truncate or slightly emarginate. Bases of
soft dorsal and caudal fins covered with
scales and thick skin. Lateral line
extends to caudal fin base.

Habitat: Rocky ledges and seamounts with
strong current; usually at depths of
about 600' (183 m).

Range: Bermuda, e FL, and ne Gulf of Mexico;
rarely to w Gulf of Mexico.

Comments: This beautiful grouper is unique in
having a dark background color
profusely scattered with white spots. It
is apparently uncommon throughout
most of its range, although this may be
largely an artifact of sampling
difficulties caused by a combination of
the depth and rugged habitat in which
this species lives.

619 Red Hind
Epinephelus guttatus

Description: To 24" (61 cm), usually to 18" (46 cm).
Robust, not strongly compressed; *light
pinkish, with numerous uniform small red
spots; no saddle-shaped blotch on caudal
peduncle or along base of dorsal fin;* no spots
on fins; soft dorsal, anal, and caudal fins
with broad black border. Head long, not
depressed; mouth oblique; maxilla
reaches beyond middle of eye. Dorsal fin

with 11 spines, 15–16 rays, some spines longer than anterior rays, interspinal membrane notched; anal fin with 3 spines, 8 rays; caudal fin truncate. Bases of soft dorsal and anal fins covered with scales and thick skin. Lateral line extends to caudal fin base.

Habitat: Over coral reefs and rocks in shallow waters to depths of 330′ (101 m).

Range: Bermuda, Bahamas, and NC south throughout s Gulf of Mexico, along Caribbean Coast, and West Indies.

Comments: Red Hind is commonly caught off the bottom on hook and line. Like other *Epinephelus* species, it probably feeds primarily on crustaceans.

631 Goliath Grouper
Epinephelus itajara

Description: To 7′10″ (2.4 m); 678 lb (308 kg), usually to 88 lb (40 kg). *Very robust, broad.* Greenish or gray, *with small black spots;* smaller individuals have relatively larger dark spots and 4–5 irregular, oblique dark bars along sides. *Head large, somewhat flat;* eye small; mouth oblique; maxilla reaches well beyond eye. Pelvic fin smaller than pectoral fin; dorsal fin not notched, with 11 spines, 15–16 rays, spines much shorter than anterior rays; soft dorsal and anal fins rounded; anal fin with 3 spines, 8 rays; caudal fin rounded. Scales small, strongly ctenoid; bases of soft dorsal and anal fins covered with scales and thick skin. Lateral line extends to caudal fin base.

Habitat: Shallow inshore waters to mid-depths; sometimes close to shore around mangroves and often around wrecks and other sheltered areas to depths of 165′ (50 m) or more. Young enter estuaries, sometimes canals.

Range: Bahamas, both coasts of FL, Gulf of Mexico, West Indies, and Caribbean coasts of Central and South America from Yucatán to Brazil. Also in e Pacific from Gulf of California to Peru.

Similar Species:	Warsaw Grouper *(E. nigritus)* reaches length of 6' (1.8 m) and weight of 580 lb (264 kg), has more compressed body, dark reddish brown to almost black above, and 10 dorsal fin spines, with greatly extended second spine.
Comments:	Until recently, this species was known by the common name Jewfish. The world's angling record is 680 lb (309 kg). Goliath Grouper is sought by spearfishers around oil rigs in Louisiana and Texas. It is a popular sport fish and often occurs in accessible places; consequently it has declined in numbers and is now protected in many areas. Goliath Grouper feeds mostly on crustaceans, but it is known to feed on fishes and even on turtles.

---

629 Red Grouper
Epinephelus morio

Description:	To 3' (91 cm), usually to 28" (71 cm). Robust, not strongly compressed. *Reddish brown, with scattered pale blotches;* some dark spots on cheeks and opercle; soft dorsal, anal, and caudal fins with narrow black border. Head long; eye green; mouth large; maxilla reaches posterior edge of eye. Dorsal fin with 11 spines, 16–17 rays, second spine longest and longer than anterior rays, *interspinal membrane not notched;* anal fin with 3 spines, 9 rays; caudal fin truncate or slightly lunate. Bases of soft dorsal, anal, and caudal fins covered with scales and thick skin. Lateral line extends to caudal fin base.

Habitat:	Usually over rocks to depths of about 450' (137 m); over flat limestone with pitted surfaces in e Gulf of Mexico.
Range:	Bermuda, Bahamas, FL, Gulf of Mexico, and Caribbean south to Brazil; seasonally north to MA; most abundant in FL and Gulf of Mexico.
Comments:	Red Grouper is one of the most common and commercially important groupers, especially in Florida, Cuba, and Mexico,

where thousands of tons are caught each year. It is also an important sport fish. This species feeds on a variety of small fishes, squids, and crustaceans.

627 **Warsaw Grouper**
Epinephelus nigritus

Description: To 6' (1.8 m); 580 lb (264 kg). Robust, not strongly compressed. *Dark reddish brown to almost black above; dull reddish gray below;* no intense spots or saddles on dorsal area or caudal peduncle. Young to 12" (30 cm) long have few irregularly arranged pearly spots on sides. Head long; maxilla reaches to or beyond posterior edge of eye. Dorsal fin with 10 spines, 14–15 rays, second spine longer than rays, *interspinal membrane deeply notched;* soft dorsal and anal fins well rounded; anal fin with 3 spines, 9 rays; caudal fin truncate or slightly rounded. Bases of soft dorsal and anal fins covered with scales and thick skin. Lateral line extends to caudal fin base.

Habitat: Deep rocky ledges, seamounts, and sometimes around oil platforms at depths of 120–1,500' (37–458 m). Young sometimes in inshore waters.

Range: MA to FL and Gulf of Mexico; sporadically in Greater Antilles; most abundant in FL and Gulf of Mexico; absent from Bermuda and Bahamas. Scattered records from n South America south to Brazil.

Similar Species: Misty Grouper *(E. mystacinus)* is gray to dark brown and has 8–9 forward-sloping dark bands on body and dorsal fin and 3 oblique bars on head.

Comments: Warsaw Grouper was once thought to occur in the tropical eastern Pacific, but that population is now recognized as a distinct species, Tenspine Grouper *(E. exsul)*. Like other *Epinephelus* species, the young are females and change into males as they grow older.

630 Nassau Grouper
Epinephelus striatus

Description: To 3′3″ (1 m); 60 lb (27 kg). Robust,
not strongly compressed. Brownish or
brownish orange above, often pinkish or
red in deep water; *5 dusky bars on sides;
dark blotch on top of caudal peduncle;* intense
dark dots around eye; *dark stripe between
eye and dorsal fin origin.* Head long;
maxilla reaches posterior edge of eye.
Dorsal fin with 11 spines, 16–17 rays,
spiny and soft segments separated by
shallow notch, interspinal membrane
notched; anal fin with 3 spines, 8 rays;
caudal fin rounded in young, becoming
truncate in adults. Bases of soft dorsal and
anal fins covered with small dense scales.

Habitat: Over coral reefs from close inshore to
depths of at least 300′ (92 m).

Range: NC to Brazil, including Bermuda,
Bahamas, s Gulf of Mexico, and
Caribbean.

Similar Species: Spotted Cabrilla *(E. analogus)* has reddish-
brown body, dark brown spots, and
16–18 dorsal fin rays; occurs in Pacific.

Comments: Nassau Grouper changes color phases
rapidly, except for the black blotch on
the top of the caudal peduncle, which
remains constant at all times. It feeds
primarily on crustaceans. This grouper is
considered excellent eating and is an
important sport fish; it is a good fighter,
and will take various kinds of bait. It is
not very wary, and readily takes food
from the hands of divers.

628 Black Grouper
Mycteroperca bonaci

Description: To 4′ (1.2 m); 180 lb (82 kg) or more.
Elongate, rather robust. Usually light
brown, with irregular rows of dark
rectangular blotches; cheek and belly
gray, with hexagonal spots. Head large;
mouth oblique; maxilla completely
exposed, reaching beyond eye; lower jaw
projects beyond upper; preopercle evenly

rounded, smooth; *pectoral fin with narrow orange border;* median fins with black border. Dorsal fin not notched, with 11 spines, 17 rays, spiny and soft segments separated by shallow notch; anal fin with 3 spines, 12 rays; caudal fin truncate. Bases of soft dorsal and anal fins covered with scales and thick skin.

Habitat: Over rocks and coral reefs from shallow waters to depths of about 70′ (21 m).

Range: Bermuda, Bahamas, s FL, e Gulf of Mexico, and Caribbean south to s Brazil; reported from New England.

Similar Species: The 13 New World species of the genus *Mycteroperca* differ from all other New World grouper genera in having 11–14 anal fin rays, rather than 7–9. Scamp (*M. phenax*) has tan body and small brown spots on fins; occurs at depths of 78–150′ (24–46 m).

Comments: Black Grouper inhabits shallow water when small. As it grows larger, it moves into deeper waters.

608 Kelp Bass
Paralabrax clathratus

Description: To 28″ (71 cm). Elongate, moderately compressed. Greenish brown above; white below; white blotches between dorsal fin and lateral line. Head bluntly pointed; mouth reaches middle of eye. *Dorsal fin with 10–11 spines, third spine about same length as fourth and fifth, 12–14 rays;* 3 anal fin spines. Lateral line extends to caudal fin base.

Habitat: Around reefs, wrecks, and kelp beds to depths of 150′ (46 m).

Range: Columbia River, nw U.S., to Bahía Magdalena, Baja California; rare north of s CA.

Similar Species: Spotted Sand Bass (*P. maculatofasciatus*) has small black spots on body and fins, and third dorsal fin spine is much longer than fourth and fifth. Barred Sand Bass (*P. nebulifer*) lacks spots and has dorsal fin with very long third spine. Goldspotted Sand Bass (*P. auroguttatus*) is olive with bright golden oblong spot. Olive Rockfish *(Sebastes serranoides)* has dorsal fin with 12–13 spines and 15–17 rays.

Comments: Kelp Bass spawns from late spring to early fall. It is one of the sport fishes most sought after in southern California; the annual catch is estimated to be more than one million fishes. It feeds on crustaceans, squids, octopuses, polychaete worms, and fishes. It is a slow-growing fish, taking four to six years to reach a length of 12″ (30 cm); an individual 24″ (61 cm) long might be 20 years old.

596 Atlantic Creolefish
Paranthias furcifer

Description: To 15″ (38 cm). Small, robust, moderately compressed; dorsal and ventral profiles equally rounded. Reddish brown above, becoming pinkish below; *3 small, well-separated, intense white spots above lateral line; bright orange spot at pectoral fin base.* Head small; mouth moderately large, oblique. Dorsal fin not notched, with 9 spines, 18–19 rays; anal fin with 3 spines, 9–10 rays; caudal fin deeply forked. Bases of soft dorsal and anal fins covered with scales and thick skin. Lateral line extends to caudal fin base.

Habitat: Near deep reefs and rocky ledges at depths of 36–198′ (11–60 m).

Range: SC to s Brazil, including Bermuda, Bahamas, Gulf of Mexico, and Caribbean. Also around Ascension Island in South Atlantic.

Comments: This small sea bass usually lives in schools near the bottom, where it feeds on zooplankton. The eastern Pacific population, which does not range north into U.S. waters, was previously considered to be a disjunct population of *P. furcifer;* it is now regarded as a separate species, Pacific Creolefish *(P. colonus).* Recognition of the populations as distinct species necessitated a change in common name for the Atlantic species, from Creolefish to Atlantic Creolefish.

625   Greater Soapfish
Rypticus saponaceus

Description: To 13″ (33 cm). Elongate, compressed; *anterior profile pointed.* Brown, gray, or almost black, with irregular lighter blotches on sides; smaller light spots on dorsal fin; edges of median fins pale. *Lower jaw projects well beyond upper;* 2 flat spines on preopercle, 3 on opercle. Pectoral fin rounded; dorsal fin long, not notched, with 3 spines, posterior rays longest and similar to anal fin; anal fin lacks spines; caudal fin rounded. Scales small, embedded.

Habitat: Over sand, rocks, or reefs in relatively shallow waters.

Range: Bermuda, s FL, and West Indies and Caribbean coast of Central America to Brazil. Also in South Atlantic to w Africa and around Ascension and St. Helena Islands.

Similar Species: Whitespotted Soapfish *(R. maculatus)* has 2 dorsal fin spines. Spotted Soapfish *(R. subbifrenatus)* has pale body with dark spots.

Comments: The species of soapfish were formerly classified as a separate family, the Grammistidae. Recent studies have reunited them with the Serranidae, the family in which they originally resided. Greater Soapfish is the largest, most common, and most widespread soapfish. It is seldomly used as a food fish, however, because its slimy mucus contains a toxic substance.

598   Tattler
Serranus phoebe

Description: To 6″ (15 cm). Oblong, robust anteriorly; dorsal profile nearly straight.

Light brown, with lighter blotches and dusky bars; *dark belt extends from front of dorsal fin to belly; conspicuous white bar on sides;* 1–2 dark saddles below soft dorsal fin. Head large, about one-fourth length; eye width equal to snout length; maxilla reaches middle of eye; lower jaw not projecting; teeth canine, small. Pectoral fin long; dorsal fin not notched, with strong spines, fourth spine longest; 3 anal fin spines; caudal fin emarginate or moderately forked. Top of head unscaled; about 8 rows of scales on cheek; soft dorsal fin partly scaled. Lateral line with about 53 scales.

Habitat: Over sand or rocks to depths of 1,320' (403 m); usually 180–600' (55–183 m). Young sometimes in water as shallow as 78' (24 m).

Range: SC to Brazil, including Bermuda and Gulf of Mexico; apparently absent from Bahamas and West Indies.

Comments: This small bass has been collected in large numbers in the northeastern Gulf of Mexico at depths of 252–402' (77–123 m).

626 Belted Sandfish
Serranus subligarius

Description: To 4½" (11.5 cm). Oblong, robust, deep. Brownish olive; broad dark bars on sides; dark stripe extends from snout through eye to upper edge of opercle; *large white blotch on belly between pelvic and anal fins; large blackish spot at anterior end of soft dorsal fin;* all fins except pelvic fin have dark spots forming bands with light interspaces; *pelvic fin blackish, with white leading edge;* scales light-centered. *Head small, pointed, with straight dorsal profile;* maxilla reaches posterior edge of eye; lower jaw projects slightly beyond upper. 15–16 (usually 16) pectoral fin rays; dorsal fin slightly notched, with 12 spines, 12–13 rays; anal fin with 3 spines, 7 rays. Front of head, area in front of eyes, jaws, and fins unscaled.

Habitat: Around rocky jetties and over sand from shore to depths of at least 60′ (18.5 m); often in silty waters.

Range: NC to FL and throughout Gulf of Mexico.

Comments: This little bass has no commercial value. It differs from other members of the family by having six branchiostegal rays, rather than seven. Belted Sandfish has both functional gonads and ovaries; individuals will occasionally lay and fertilize their own eggs.

JAWFISHES
Family Opistognathidae

3 genera and about 90 species (some unnamed) worldwide; 2 genera and 8 species in North America, plus 8 species confined to Mexican waters. Jawfishes are found in tropical seas; the North American species all occur in the Atlantic. These fishes dwell in burrows, usually with only their heads exposed, and they use their large mouths for excavation. Males often have an extremely well-developed maxilla. The body is covered with cycloid scales, but the head is unscaled. The pectoral fins are located on the midside of the body, and the pelvic fins are slightly in front of the pectoral fins. Each pelvic fin has a single spine and five rays. The dorsal fin is of even height throughout, without an obvious notch between the spiny and soft segments; there are nine to 12 dorsal fin spines. The low anal fin is also even throughout; it has three spines and is about half the length of the dorsal fin. Both the dorsal and anal fins terminate at the same level, and are not connected to the rounded or lanceolate caudal fin. Jawfishes have a high lateral line, ending near the middle of the dorsal fin. These fishes reach lengths of about 4–16″ (10–41 cm), depending upon the species. Males practice oral incubation.

634 Mottled Jawfish
Opistognathus maxillosus

Description: To 5″ (12.5 cm). Elongate, slightly compressed, tapering posteriorly. Light tan; brownish bands and mid-lateral stripe with evenly spaced light interspaces; *4–5 evenly spaced non-ocellated oblong blotches on lower part of dorsal fin*

adjacent to back, beginning at fourth spine, second blotch (between sixth and ninth spines) noticeably darker and slightly larger; no large ocellated spot on anterior part of spiny dorsal fin. Head rounded, relatively blunt; maxilla projects slightly in males. 20–21 pectoral fin rays; dorsal fin with usually 11 spines, 15 rays; anal fin with 3 spines, 15 rays; caudal fin rounded. Scales small; more than 85 in lateral series.

Habitat: Shallow coral reefs at depths of 6–42′ (1.8–13 m); usually in clear water with sand and rubble.

Range: Bahamas, Florida Keys, and throughout most of Caribbean to Panama and Tobago; apparently absent from Gulf of Mexico and n South America.

Similar Species: Banded Jawfish *(O. macrognathus)* has smaller eye, prominent blotch on dorsal fin more oblong and located in upper one-third of fin, 14 dorsal fin rays, and 14 anal fin rays; occurs to depths of 145′ (44 m). Yellowhead Jawfish *(O. aurifrons)* has yellow head and delicate blue to blue-green wash on rear two-thirds of body and fins; occurs over mud at depths of 8–135′ (2.4–41 m). Swordtail Jawfish *(Lonchopisthus micrognathus)* has long pointed caudal fin; occurs over mud at depths of 30–325′ (9–99 m).

Comments: Mottled Jawfish is perhaps the most common shallow-water jawfish species in the western Atlantic. Most jawfishes live in burrows with only their heads exposed; Yellowhead Jawfish is unusual in that it swims above the bottom, descending into its burrow at the sign of danger.

SUNFISHES
Family Centrarchidae

7 genera and 31 species confined to North America. Sunfishes are one of the most widespread and popular groups of freshwater sport fishes in North America. The dorsal fin usually has a notch

between the spiny and soft segments, and the anal fin has at least three spines. The caudal fin is usually forked. The gill membranes are usually separate. Most members of the genus *Lepomis* are characterized by a fleshy extension of the posterior edge of the opercle, which is referred to as the "ear flap"; this structure is important in the identification of many species. Most sunfishes are nest builders; the nest is usually a depression 12–24" (30–61 cm) wide in shallow waters. The male excavates the nest using his anal and caudal fins, then guards the eggs after spawning. Except for a single species native to California, Sacramento Perch *(Archoplites interruptus),* sunfishes are indigenous to warm waters of North America east of the Rocky Mountains. However, as a result of their popularity with anglers, they have been introduced in other areas.

---

97 Mud Sunfish
Acantharchus pomotis

Description: To 10" (25 cm). Oblong, robust. Back dusky green; sides greenish olive, with *3–5 irregular dull greenish-yellow stripes;* head greenish, with 2–3 dark stripes; large dark blotch on upper part of opercle; fins greenish, with darker edges. Snout short; mouth wide; *maxilla reaches beyond middle of eye. Anal fin with 4–6 spines, 9–12 rays; caudal fin rounded.* Caudal peduncle short, deep. Scales cycloid. Lateral line complete, with 35–43 scales.

Habitat: Usually dark-stained waters of sluggish coastal plain streams, swamps, and backwaters with abundant vegetation over mud.

Range: NY south to n FL and west to St. Marks River, w FL.

Comments: Mud Sunfish spends much of the day hiding under overhanging banks, submerged debris, or vegetation. It is active at night, coming out to forage.

---

103 Rock Bass
Ambloplites rupestris

Description: To 17" (43 cm); 3½ lb (1.6 kg). Oblong, robust. Olive above, mottled with dark saddles and bronze blotches; *lighter below, with rows of dusky to dark spots. Head large; mouth reaches to or beyond middle of eye; eye red, large;* gill rakers long, slender, 7–10 on first arch. 13–15 pectoral fin rays; *dorsal fin with 10–13 spines,* 10–11 rays; *anal fin with 5–7 spines,* 9–10 rays. *Usually 7–8 rows of scales on cheek.* Lateral line complete, with 36–46 scales.

Habitat: Cool, clear, rocky streams and shallow lakes with vegetation and other cover.

Range: Southern QC west to s MB and south through Great Lakes drainage to n AL and n GA. Widely introduced in central and w U.S.

Similar Species: Shadow Bass *(A. ariommus)* has deeper body, dark brown blotches on sides, and 4–5 rows of scales on cheek; occurs in creeks and rivers. Roanoke Bass *(A. cavifrons)* has gold spots on upper body and unscaled cheek; occurs in upland streams. Ozark Bass *(A. constellatus)* is uniformly colored, with scattered dark spots; occurs in upland streams.

Comments: Although small, Rock Bass is a popular sport fish.

104 Sacramento Perch
Archoplites interruptus

Description: To 24″ (61 cm); 9 lb (4.1 kg). Moderately elongate, compressed. Back olive to black; *sides olive brown; upper sides mottled, with 6–8 irregular olive brown bars;* belly whitish. Mouth large, reaches middle of eye; *preopercle and subopercle serrate. 12–13 dorsal fin spines; 6–7 anal fin spines;* caudal fin slightly forked. Lateral line complete, with 38–48 scales.

Habitat: Sloughs, sluggish streams, and lakes with vegetation.

Range: Sacramento, San Joaquin, Pajaro, and Salinas Rivers and Clear Lake, CA. Introduced in other areas of CA and in OR and UT; stocked but not established in other parts of w U.S.

Comments: Sacramento Perch is the only sunfish native to the western United States. It has declined in its native range due to habitat destruction and the introduction of exotic fishes. Although it has been introduced in the midwestern and western United States, most populations have not survived. In some Oregon lakes where this fish has flourished, it is causing a decline of the native fishes' fauna.

101 Flier
Centrarchus macropterus

Description: To 7½″ (19 cm), usually to 6″ (15 cm); 1¼ lb (600 g). Oval, strongly compressed. Dusky above; *greenish yellow below, with 8–12 rows of small dark brown spots; dark wedge-shaped spot through eye;* soft dorsal and anal fins with narrow dark markings. Young have black blotch with orange halo on soft dorsal fin. Snout short; mouth small, reaches middle of eye. Dorsal and anal fins large, about equal in size; *dorsal fin with 11–13 spines, 12–15 rays; anal fin with 7–8 spines, 13–15 rays.* Caudal peduncle length and depth about equal. Cheek and opercle scaled. Lateral line with 38–45 scales.

Habitat: Clear quiet lowland streams, swamps, and ditches with heavy vegetation.

Range: Southern MD south to FL and west to e TX; Mississippi River valley from s IL and sw IN south to Gulf coast.

Comments: The very attractive Flier is locally abundant. Its small size makes it relatively unimportant as a sport fish.

98 Bluespotted Sunfish
Enneacanthus gloriosus

Description: To 4″ (10 cm). Short, moderately deep, compressed. Back olive brown; *sides greenish brown, with irregular rows of bright blue spots,* faint in females; belly light yellowish olive; dark spot with pearly

edge on upper end of opercle. Snout short; mouth terminal, slightly oblique. Dorsal fin with 8–9 spines, 10–11 rays; caudal fin rounded. *16–18 rows of scales on caudal peduncle.* Lateral line complete or incomplete, with 30–32 scales.

Habitat: Clear to dark-stained waters of sluggish coastal streams, swamps, and lakes with abundant vegetation.

Range: Southern NY south to s FL and west to s AL and s MS.

Similar Species: Blackbanded Sunfish *(E. chaetodon)* lacks blue spots and has 6–8 broad dark bars. Banded Sunfish *(E. obesus)* has blue spots, 4–8 dark bars, and 19–22 rows of caudal peduncle scales.

Comments: Bluespotted Sunfish is small, hardy, and colorful. Its mild disposition makes it a good aquarium fish.

92 Redbreast Sunfish
Lepomis auritus

Description: To 11″ (28 cm); 1¾ lb (800 g). Oblong, compressed. Back dark olive to dusky; sides greenish to yellowish brown, with reddish spots; belly reddish orange; bluish lines below eye; *ear flap black, without light edge;* fins plain; median fins yellowish orange, occasionally dusky. Mouth extends to eye; *ear flap elongate, no wider than eye;* 11 short gill rakers. *Pectoral fin short, rounded, with 13–15 rays;* 3 anal fins spines. Lateral line complete, with 43–50 scales.

Habitat: Streams with slow to moderate current over sand, gravel, or rocks; ponds and lakes.

Range: Atlantic coast streams from NB south to central FL and west in Gulf coast drainages to Apalachicola River system in FL and AL. Introduced outside native range.

Comments: Redbreast Sunfish inhabits streams more frequently than most other sunfishes. It is usually found alone, but forms compact hibernating schools at low temperatures. Unlike most other sunfishes in the genus *Lepomis,* this species does not produce sounds during courtship. Where Redbreast Sunfish has been introduced, Longear Sunfish (*L. megalotis*) appears to be declining, even disappearing in some streams.

93 Green Sunfish
Lepomis cyanellus

Description: To 12″ (30 cm); 2¼ lb (1 kg). Robust, moderately elongate; depth less than distance from snout tip to dorsal fin origin. Back yellowish olive; sometimes dusky bars on sides; belly pale olive; median fins olive to dusky, with whitish to light orange edges; *black blotch often on posterior base of soft dorsal and anal fins.* Head broad; mouth reaches middle of eye; ear flap not elongate. Pectoral fin short, rounded. Lateral line complete, with 40–52 scales.

Habitat: Clear to turbid swamps, ponds, and smaller streams with little or no current.
Range: Southern Great Lakes and Mississippi River basin south to TX; AL west to NM. Widely introduced outside native range in U.S. and n Mexico.
Comments: Green Sunfish, one of the most common sunfishes, is tolerant of a wide range of environmental conditions.

90 Pumpkinseed
Lepomis gibbosus

Description: To 16″ (41 cm); 1½ lb (600 g). Deep, short, compressed. Back dark greenish gold, mottled with reddish orange; sides greenish yellow, mottled with orange and blue-green; belly yellowish orange; wavy bluish lines on cheek; *spot on ear flap, black anteriorly, bordered by white above and below, red posteriorly; soft dorsal fin spotted,* with yellowish to white edge. Head small; mouth reaches eye; *ear flap stiff. Pectoral fin long, pointed;* 3 anal fin spines. Lateral line complete, with 36–47 scales.

Habitat: Cool, quiet, shallow waters of slow
streams, ponds, marshes, and lakes with
dense vegetation.

Range: NB west to s MB; south along Atlantic
coast to ne GA; Great Lakes and upper
Mississippi River system south to s IL.
Widely introduced.

Comments: Pumpkinseed is not sought by most
experienced anglers, but is often caught
by beginners. It is aggressive and will
take a variety of bait.

---

102 Warmouth
Lepomis gulosus

Description: To 12″ (30 cm); 2½ lb (1.1 kg). Oblong,
robust. Back and median fins dark olive
brown, with dusky mottling; sides
lighter, with scattered dusky spots; belly
yellowish; *eye reddish,* with 4–5 radiating
dusky lines extending to edge of opercle;
dark spot on upper part of opercle. Head
large, wide; *mouth reaches beyond middle of
eye; teeth on tongue; ear flap not elongate.*
Pectoral fin short, rounded; 9–11 dorsal
fin spines; 3 anal fin spines. Lateral line
complete, with 36–44 scales.

Habitat: Ponds, swamps, lakes, and sluggish
streams with vegetation or debris.

Range: MD, s MI, and s WI south to FL and
west to TX. Introduced in w and sw
U.S.

Comments: Warmouth spends much of its time in
the cover of dense vegetation. It feeds on
small fishes, crayfishes, and aquatic
insects. During the late spring and
summer, it nests in shallow water. Due
to its small size, this species is generally
not very important as a sport fish.

---

95 Bluegill
Lepomis macrochirus

Description: To 16″ (41 cm); 4¾ lb (2.2 kg). Deep,
compressed; profile rounded under
dorsal fin. Back and median fins dark
olive green; sides lighter olive, with

brassy reflections, often with dusky bars; belly whitish; ear flap dusky to black; *black blotch near middle of soft dorsal fin posterior rays.* Mouth terminal, reaching front edge of eye; *ear flap broad, moderately long. Pectoral fin long, pointed;* anal fin base about half length of dorsal fin base. Lateral line complete, with 39–45 scales.

Habitat: Clear warm pools of streams, lakes, ponds, sloughs, and reservoirs; usually in shallow waters with vegetation.

Range: Southern QC, s ON, and Great Lakes drainage south to FL and west to s TX. Widely introduced in U.S. and n Mexico.

Comments: Bluegill is the most common sunfish and probably the most popular freshwater sport fish in the United States. It is commonly stocked in ponds as forage for larger fishes.

---

91 Longear Sunfish
Lepomis megalotis

Description: To 9″ (23 cm); 1¾ lb (800 g). Deep, compressed. Back dark olive to blue-green; sides light olive, with yellow and blue-green speckles; belly yellow to reddish; *cheek reddish, with wavy blue-green stripes; ear flap often with white or red edge;* soft dorsal, anal, and caudal fins reddish orange. Mouth reaches eye; *ear flap long, wider than eye. Pectoral fin short, rounded, with 13–14 rays;* 3 anal fin spines. *5–6 rows of scales on cheek.* Lateral line complete, with 33–41 scales.

Habitat: Pools of streams with moderate current over sand, gravel, or rocks; reservoirs and lakes.

Range: Southwestern QC west to se MB; Mississippi River valley; Gulf coast drainages from w FL west to Rio Grande in TX and NM. Introduced outside native range.

Similar Species: Orangespotted Sunfish *(L. humilis)* has light olive to silvery sides with scattered bright orange spots, blue-green side of head with orange spots often merging to form lines, and long dark ear flap with wide white border; occurs in pools of rivers and creeks near vegetation or brush. Dollar Sunfish *(L. marginatus)* has deeper body, 12 pectoral fin rays, and 4 rows of scales on cheek; occurs in slow streams and swamps with vegetation.

Comments: Longear Sunfish is a popular sport fish throughout most of its range. It feeds on aquatic insects, snails, crustaceans, and small fishes. It appears to decline or disappear in streams where Redbreast Sunfish *(L. auritus)* has been introduced.

94 Redear Sunfish
Lepomis microlophus

Description: To 14″ (36 cm); 5½ lb (2.5 kg). Moderately elongate, compressed. Back olive, with brown speckles; sides greenish yellow, with brassy reflections and dark speckles; belly yellowish orange; dark olive spots on sides of head, no wavy lines; *black spot on ear flap, with broad bright reddish-orange border posteriorly.* Young have 5–8 dusky bars on sides. Mouth reaches eye. *Pectoral fin long, pointed, extending to near middle of anal fin base;* 3 anal fin spines. Lateral line complete, with 35–44 scales.

Habitat: Clear quiet pools of warm streams, ponds, lakes, and reservoirs with vegetation or other cover.

Range: NC and FL west to s IL and s MO, and south to Rio Grande drainage, TX. Widely introduced.

Comments: Because this fish has specialized molar-like teeth for crushing snails, it is often given the common name Shellcracker.

99 Spotted Sunfish
Lepomis punctatus

Description: To 6½″ (16.5 cm). Small, deep, moderately compressed. Back dark olive to black; *rows of dark-spotted scales on sides;*

black speckles on sides of head; ear flap dark olive to black; *pelvic fin dusky to black; dorsal, anal, and caudal fins dusky reddish brown, with narrow silvery to white border. Ear flap short.* 20–23 scales on caudal peduncle. Lateral line with 38–44 scales; usually 7–8 rows of scales above lateral line, 13–15 rows below.

Habitat: Pools and sluggish waters of creeks and small rivers, ponds, and lakes; usually with vegetation.

Range: Atlantic coast drainages from se NC south through peninsular FL and west to Ochlockonee River, w FL and w GA.

Similar Species: Redspotted Sunfish *(L. miniatus)* has rows of reddish-orange spots on sides and reddish-orange pigment on breast.

Comments: Populations found in the Apalachicola River basin in Florida and Georgia west to the Mobile Bay basin in Alabama are Spotted Sunfish and Redspotted Sunfish hybrids.

96 Bantam Sunfish
Lepomis symmetricus

Description: To 3¾" (9.5 cm). Small, robust, chubby. *Back and sides dark olive to brownish, with rows of dark brown spots often forming longitudinal rows of irregular vertical bands;* belly pale yellow to creamy; *ear flap dark, with light edge;* all fins except pectoral fins dusky; *dark spot near posterior base of soft dorsal fin.* Mouth moderately large; upper jaw reaches near middle of eye; *ear flap short;* gill rakers long, slender. Pectoral fin short, rounded, not extending beyond eye when bent forward. *Lateral line incomplete,* with 30–37 scales.

Habitat: Clear to turbid lowland creeks, swamps, bayous, and oxbow lakes with vegetation, logs, and sticks over mud and debris.

Range: Mississippi River valley from s IL south to sw MS and west to e TX.

Comments: Bantam Sunfish is the smallest species in the genus *Lepomis;* its small size renders it insignificant as a food fish.

110 Shoal Bass
Micropterus cataractae

Description: To 25″ (64 cm); 9 lb (4 kg). Elongate, compressed. Back olive green to almost black; *10–15 dark vertically elongate mid-lateral blotches, with interspaces about equal to width of blotches;* 6–8 dark vertically elongate blotches on lower back to upper sides; 5–7 weakly developed rows of spots on lower sides. *No teeth on tongue.* Usually 16 pectoral fin rays; dorsal fin with 9–11 spines, 10–13 rays; anal fin with 3 spines, 9–12 rays. 27–35 scales on caudal peduncle. Lateral line with 68–71 scales.

Habitat: Medium to large creeks and rivers with rocky or gravel shoals; rarely reservoirs.

Range: Apalachicola River basin in GA, FL, and AL. Introduced outside native range in upper Altamaha River, GA.

Similar Species: Suwannee Bass *(M. notius)* reaches length of 12″ (30 cm), and has blue-green belly.

Comments: This recently named species is a member of the spotted bass group. However, unlike Spotted Bass *(M. punctulatus),* it does not tolerate reservoir habitats. It has declined in many areas due to dams and channel-alteration projects.

111 Smallmouth Bass
Micropterus dolomieu

Description: To 27″ (69 cm); 12 lb (5.4 kg). Elongate, compressed. Back dark olive to brown; *sides greenish yellow, with bronze reflections;* diffuse mid-lateral bars form dark mottling; median fins olive. Mouth reaches eye; *small round tooth patch usually on tongue.* 16–18 pectoral fin rays; dorsal fin with 10 spines, 13–14 rays; anal fin with 3 spines, 11 rays. *Bases of soft dorsal and anal fins scaled;* 29–31 rows of scales on caudal peduncle. Lateral line complete, with 68–81 scales; 11–13 rows of scales above lateral line, 20–23 rows below.

Habitat: Cool clear streams with moderate to
swift current over gravel or rocks; lakes
and reservoirs.

Range: Southwestern QC, se ON, and NY west
to MN and south in Mississippi River
system to n AL, n AR, and e OK.
Widely introduced.

Similar Species: Redeye Bass *(M. coosae)* rarely exceeds
length of 16″ (41 cm), has rows of dark
spots forming lines on lower sides, teeth
on tongue, 12 dorsal fin rays, and 7–10
rows of scales above lateral line, 16–17
rows below.

Comments: Smallmouth Bass is one of the most
popular sport fishes in eastern North
America. It takes a variety of live bait,
minnows, and crayfishes, as well as
artificial lures. This species spawns earlier
than other sunfishes in the same range.

109 Spotted Bass
Micropterus punctulatus

Description: To 24″ (61 cm); 9½ lb (4.3 kg).
Elongate, compressed. Back dark olive;
sides olive to yellowish, with dark
diamond-shaped mid-lateral blotches;
*rows of dusky spots form stripes on lower
sides;* median fins olive. Mouth reaches
middle of eye; *oval to rectangular tooth
patch on tongue.* 15–16 pectoral fin rays;
dorsal fin with 10 spines, 12–13 rays;
anal fin with 3 spines, 10 rays. *Bases of
soft dorsal and anal fins scaled;* 23–28
rows of scales on caudal peduncle.
Lateral line complete, with 60–75
scales; 8–9 rows of scales above lateral
line, 15–18 rows below.

dorsal fin

Habitat: Warm, clear to slightly turbid pools of
creeks and rivers; ponds, lakes, and
reservoirs.

Range: Western WV, sw VA, nw GA, and w FL
west to e TX; s OH west to se KS.
Introduced outside native range.

Similar Species: Guadalupe Bass *(M. treculii)* reaches
length of 15½″ (40 cm), has 10–14
greenish to dusky bands extending from

lower sides to above midline, and 26–27
rows of caudal peduncle scales.

Comments: There are two subspecies of Spotted
Bass, which are often confused with
Largemouth Bass *(M. salmoides).* Spotted
Bass readily takes live or artificial bait
and is a prized sport fish.

112 Largemouth Bass
Micropterus salmoides

dorsal fin

Description: To 3'2" (97 cm); 22 lb (10 kg).
Moderately deep, robust. Back dark
olive to green, mottled; *sides olive to
greenish yellow, with dark mid-lateral
stripe;* head greenish gold, with 2–3 dark
lines across cheek and opercle; median
fins dusky olive. *Mouth large, reaches
beyond posterior edge of eye in adults; usually
no teeth on tongue.* 14–15 pectoral fin rays;
*dorsal fin deeply divided, almost separate,
middle spines longest,* with 10 spines,
12–14 rays; anal fin with 3 spines,
10–12 rays. *Bases of soft dorsal and anal
fins unscaled; 24–28 rows of scales on
caudal peduncle.* Lateral line complete,
with 59–77 scales; 7–9 rows of scales
above lateral line, 14–17 rows below.

Habitat: Quiet, clear to slightly turbid streams,
ponds, lakes, and reservoirs; often with
vegetation or other cover.

Range: Southern ON south through Great
Lakes and Mississippi River system;
coastal plain from n NC to TX and nw
Mexico. Widely introduced in s Canada
and U.S.

Comments: Largemouth Bass, one of the most
highly sought-after sport fishes in the
United States, is caught with live and
artificial bait. There are generally two
recognized subspecies: One is wide-
ranging and occurs throughout most of
the Mississippi River basin and the Gulf
coast; the second, known as Florida
Largemouth Bass, was originally
confined to peninsular Florida, but has
been widely introduced. Largemouth

Bass is more tolerant of warm water than Smallmouth Bass *(M. dolomieu),* but at higher temperatures it becomes less active. It is also more likely to enter low-salinity waters than other basses. Adults feed primarily on other fishes and crayfishes. The average life span is about 16 years.

100 Black Crappie
Pomoxis nigromaculatus

Description: To 19½″ (49 cm); 5 lb (2.3 kg). Deep, strongly compressed; dorsal profile rounded. Back greenish; sides silvery green, with scattered dark green to black mottling not forming bars; belly silvery; median fins green, with dusky wavy lines and white spots. Head long, concave near eye; mouth oblique, reaches beyond middle of eye; 27–32 long slender gill rakers. *Length of dorsal fin base about equal to distance from dorsal fin origin to middle of eye; dorsal fin with 7–8 spines, no notch between spiny and soft segments; anal fin large, with 6–7 spines.* Lateral line complete, with 35–44 scales.

Habitat: Quiet, warm, clear streams, ponds, lakes, and reservoirs.

Range: Southern QC, s ON, and s MB; e and central U.S. except Atlantic coast streams from ME to VA. Stocked throughout U.S. and established in most areas.

Similar Species: White Crappie *(P. annularis)* has more elongate body, 6 dorsal fin spines, and length of dorsal fin base less than distance from dorsal fin origin to middle of eye.

Comments: This is a very popular sport and food fish, especially in the southern part of its range. It is generally less abundant than White Crappie and less tolerant of silty and turbid waters. It feeds throughout the day and night, and is most active in the evening.

PERCHES
Family Percidae

10 genera and more than 190 species worldwide; 6 genera and more than 180 species in North America, plus Ruffe *(Gymnocephalus cernuus)*, an introduced European native now firmly established in the Great Lakes. Perches occur in the fresh waters of Eurasia and North America. The dorsal fin of these fishes is usually separated into two segments. The anal fin has one to two spines, and the second spine is not enlarged. The larger species, which reach lengths of 3' (91 cm), are important sport fishes and have been widely introduced. The smaller species are among the most colorful fishes in the world. The four genera of darters, *Percina*, *Ammocrypta*, *Crystallaria*, and *Etheostoma*, together total more than 175 species and form one of the most diverse and colorful groups of North American freshwater fishes. With few exceptions, darters are found in North America east of the Continental Divide. Many have very restricted ranges and habitats. The collective common name describes their habit of "darting" about, using the tail and pectoral fins for locomotion. These movements are largely confined to the bottom, since most species lack a swim bladder. *Percina* (40 species) darters tend to be tan or brown with darker markings (any bright coloration is usually yellow or orange) and have two anal fin spines and a complete lateral line; males have specialized scales on the midline of the belly that are used during spawning to maintain their position and stimulate the female. *Ammocrypta* (six species) and *Crystallaria* (one species) darters are translucent with a faint yellow to orange wash, have a single anal fin spine and a complete lateral line, and males lack specialized scales on the midline of the belly. *Etheostoma* (130 species) darters have one to two anal fin spines and either a complete or incomplete lateral line, and males lack specialized scales on the belly. Males in the genus *Etheostoma* are usually brightly colored, as are some *Percina* males.

VENTRAL VIEW OF MALE DARTERS

genus *Percina*

genera *Ammocrypta, Crystallaria,* and *Etheostoma*

specialized scales

273 Naked Sand Darter
Ammocrypta beanii

Description: To 2½" (6.5 cm). *Elongate, cylindrical.*
Translucent; yellowish orange; pelvic fin
whitish; first dorsal fin with black
blotch anteriorly, dusky band
posteriorly; second dorsal, anal, and
caudal fins with central gray black band.
Snout pointed; mouth reaches eye; *no
opercular spine. Distance between dorsal fins
about equal to or greater than snout length.
Unscaled, except 1–5 mid-lateral rows.*
Lateral line complete, with 55–77 scales.

Habitat: Creeks and rivers with moderate current
over clean sand.

Range: Hatchie River, w TN; Big Black River,
w MS, south to Lake Pontchartrain, se
LA, and east to Mobile Bay drainage, AL.

Similar Species: Florida Sand Darter *(A. bifascia)* males
have 2 black bands on dorsal and anal
fins.

Comments: Naked Sand Darter, like other sand
darters, dives head-first into the sand,
emerges with only the snout and eyes
protruding, and darts from this position
to capture food. It feeds on drifting
aquatic insects and crustaceans.

268 Western Sand Darter
Ammocrypta clara

Description: To 2¾" (7 cm). Elongate, cylindrical.
Translucent; yellowish; 9–13 dark
elongate blotches centered along dusky
narrow mid-lateral stripe; fins clear,
yellowish; pelvic fin not dusky. *Opercular
spine present. Distance between dorsal fins
about equal to or greater than snout length.*
Body, cheek, and opercle partially
scaled. Lateral line complete, with
63–81 scales; *1–3 rows of scales below
lateral line, 1 row above.*

Habitat: Medium to large rivers with moderate to
slow current over sand.

Range: Ohio River drainage in IN, KY, and
TN; Mississippi River system from s
MN south to MS and e TX.

Comments: Western Sand Darter spawns from July to August. It has been found buried more than an inch below the surface of the sand.

267 Eastern Sand Darter
Ammocrypta pellucida

Description: To 3¼″ (8.5 cm). Slender, very elongate, length 8–11 times depth. Yellowish; lighter below, with *9–15 dark oval blotches just below lateral line;* pectoral, dorsal, and anal fin membranes clear. Maxilla reaches eye; no opercular spine. *Distance between dorsal fins about equal to or greater than snout length;* anal fin origin under or just anterior to first ray of second dorsal fin. Lateral line complete, with 65–84 scales; *1–4 rows of scales above lateral line, 4–7 rows below.*

Habitat: Creeks and rivers with moderate current over sand; protected beaches of Lake Erie islands.

Range: St. Lawrence River; s Lake Huron, Lake St. Clair, and Lake Erie islands; Ohio River drainage from PA to w KY.

Similar Species: Southern Sand Darter *(A. meridiana)* has more rows of scales above and below lateral line.

Comments: Eastern Sand Darter was once fairly common, but habitat changes have reduced population levels. It feeds primarily on midge larvae, which are captured as they drift over sandy shoals. The female probably buries itself in the sand to deposit eggs.

274 Scaly Sand Darter
Ammocrypta vivax

Description: To 3″ (7.5 cm). Elongate. Translucent; yellowish orange; sides lighter, with *9–16 dark, oval, vertically oriented mid-lateral blotches; 2 dark bands on median fins.* Maxilla reaches front of eye; no opercular spine. *Distance between dorsal fins about equal to or greater than snout*

length. Cheek and opercle scaled; body partially scaled. Lateral line complete, with 58–79 scales.

Habitat: Creeks and rivers with moderate current over clean sand.

Range: Mississippi River system from w KY and se MO south to extreme se AL, MS, LA, and e TX.

Comments: The burying behavior of all sand darters reduces the time needed to maintain themselves swimming, thus conserving energy, and also offers protection from predators.

269 Crystal Darter
Crystallaria asprella

Description: To 6¼" (16 cm). Very slender, length 8–10 times depth. Opaque; back olive to tan, with *4 dark saddles extending downward and forward to lateral line, first saddle anterior to first dorsal fin;* sides usually with brownish mid-lateral stripe; belly whitish; *fin membranes clear.* Head broad; snout long, rounded; frenum present; eye large; maxilla not reaching eye. *Dorsal and anal fins high;* caudal fin slightly forked. *Completely scaled.* Lateral line complete, with 77–97 scales.

Habitat: Moderate to swift rivers over sand, gravel, or rocks; occasionally pools.

Range: Mississippi River system from WV, OH, and MN south to se OK and LA; Gulf coast drainages from w FL to LA.

Comments: Crystal Darter has been eliminated from much of its range because many of its habitats have been destroyed by canalization and dams.

293 Greenside Darter
Etheostoma blennioides

Description: To 6" (15 cm). Elongate, robust. Olive above, *mottled with 6–7 dark saddles and reddish-orange spots; yellowish below, with dark green V- or W-shaped markings;* dorsal

ventral view of mouth

fins red, with greenish-blue edges; anal fin green; pelvic and anal fins barred. *Snout blunt, overhangs mouth;* frenum present; *mouth small, horizontal; nipple-like projection on middle of upper lip;* gill membranes broadly joined. Pectoral fin large; first dorsal fin with 12–15 spines, second dorsal fin with 12–14 rays. Lateral line complete, with 53–83 scales.

Habitat: Riffles of large clear creeks and rivers with moderate to swift current over gravel or rocks.

Range: Southeastern ON and NY south to w NC, n GA, and n AL; s MI, e IL, s MO, and se KS to s AR.

Similar Species: Rock Darter *(E. rupestre)* has clear to dusky pelvic and anal fins and lacks frenum. Harlequin Darter *(E. histrio)* has 2 dark brown to dark green spots on caudal fin base and brown to black speckles on underside of head and belly.

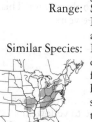

Comments: Greenside Darter is the largest species in the genus *Etheostoma*. It lives three to four years.

---

291 Slackwater Darter
Etheostoma boschungi

Description: To 2½" (6.5 cm). Moderately stout, compressed. Back olive to brown, with 3 dark saddles, 3–5 lighter blotches; sides with greenish-black blotches, often forming band posteriorly; yellowish olive below, orange in breeding males; *dark bluish-black bar under eye;* first dorsal fin orange, base blue-green; other fins spotted. *Frenum broad; eye longer than snout;* gill membranes narrowly joined. 2 anal fin spines. 43–58 scales in lateral series. *Lateral line incomplete, with 30–40 pored scales.*

Habitat: Edges of clear, small to medium streams with moderate current around leaf litter and debris.

Range: Tennessee River drainage, south-central TN and n AL.

Similar Species: Stippled Darter *(E. punctulatum)* has compressed body with wide blue-green mid-lateral stripe posteriorly, beginning behind anal fin origin, 2 anal fin spines, and 58–80 scales in lateral series. Trispot Darter *(E. trisella)* has thin bar under eye, 1 anal fin spine, and complete lateral line with 44–52 scales.

Comments: Slackwater Darter leaves its stream habitat in January and February and moves into the marshy seepage areas of wetlands to spawn. Eventually both the larvae, which are about ⅜" (1 cm) long, and the adults return to the stream. This darter lives two to three years.

---

298 Rainbow Darter
Etheostoma caeruleum

Description: To 3" (7.5 cm). Robust, greatest depth at first dorsal fin. Olive to yellowish green above; bluish green below; *encircled by 8–11 dark blue-green bands,* areas between posterior bands reddish; gill membranes reddish orange; first dorsal fin reddish, with wide blue border; second dorsal and caudal fins reddish, with narrow blue border; *anal fin blue-green, with reddish base.* Snout pointed; frenum present; gill membranes narrowly joined. *Lateral line incomplete, with 12–30 pored scales.*

Habitat: Riffles of clear swift creeks and small rivers over gravel or rocks.

Range: Southeastern ON and w NY west to s MN and south to n AL and n AR; sw MS and e LA.

Comments: Rainbow Darter is sensitive to pollution and silt. It spawns in clean gravel riffles from March to June. Its lives for about four years.

---

288 Iowa Darter
Etheostoma exile

Description: To 3" (7.5 cm). Slender. Olive above, with 7–9 dark blotches; *sides with 10–12 dark squarish mid-lateral blotches,* dark red between blotches; belly yellowish orange; base and edge of first dorsal fin blue, center red; brown spots forming bars on second dorsal and caudal fins. Frenum present; uninterrupted sensory canal below eye, with 8 pores; gill membranes narrowly joined. *Caudal peduncle long, slender.* 45–63 scales in lateral series. *Lateral line incomplete,* with 18–35 pored scales; *5–6 rows of scales above lateral line.*

Habitat: Quiet, clear, cool streams and lakes with vegetation over sand, mud, clay, or organic debris.

Range: Southern QC, w NY, and n OH west to AB, e MT, se WY, and ne CO.

Similar Species: Slough Darter *(E. gracile)* has 10–12 greenish bars on sides, uninterrupted sensory canal below eye with 8 pores, and 3–4 rows of scales above anteriorly arched lateral line; occurs in sluggish streams over mud, silt, or debris. Backwater Darter *(E. zonifer)* has 8–10 greenish bars on sides and interrupted sensory canal below eye with 6 pores; occurs in sluggish streams.

Comments: Iowa Darter spawns from April to June in quiet shallow water, depositing eggs on the roots and stems of plants.

---

284 Fantail Darter
Etheostoma flabellare

Description: To 3″ (7.5 cm). Deep, compressed. Back olive brown; *sides lighter, with narrow dark stripes* and dusky bars; belly yellowish orange; first dorsal fin with orange edge; second dorsal and caudal fins orange, with dark bars. Frenum present; gill membranes broadly joined. *First dorsal fin has fleshy knobs at tips of 6–9 low spines,* knobs smaller in females; *caudal fin rounded.* 45–60 scales in lateral series. Lateral line incomplete, with 15–36 pored scales.

Habitat: Clear cool streams with moderate to swift current over gravel or rocks.

Range: Southwestern QC, se ON, and NY
west to s MN and south to NC, n AL,
and n AR.

Similar Species: Stripetail Darter *(E. kennicotti)* lacks
stripes on sides and has fewer than 45
scales in lateral series. Spottail Darter
(E. squamiceps) lacks stripes on sides and
has 45–56 scales in lateral series.

Comments: Fantail Darter spawns upside-down
under flat rocks, which the male scrapes
clean with the fleshy tips of its dorsal
fin. After spawning, the male remains
with the eggs until they hatch.

271 Swamp Darter
Etheostoma fusiforme

Description: To 2″ (5 cm). Elongate. Back dark olive,
with 8–12 dark mid-dorsal blotches;
*sides tan to greenish, mottled, often with mid-
lateral blotches;* belly whitish, with dark
speckles; first dorsal fin with dusky base,
darker anteriorly; *caudal fin barred, with
3 dark spots at base. Snout shorter than eye,
decurved; frenum present; opercular spine
strong;* gill membranes narrowly joined.
First dorsal fin with 9–11 spines, second
dorsal fin with 10–12 rays. Caudal
peduncle long, slender. Lateral line
arched upward, incomplete, with 5–30
pored scales.

Habitat: Sluggish, clear to dark-stained coastal
streams, ponds, and swamps with
vegetation over mud, sand, or debris.

Range: Southern ME south to FL and west
to se OK and e TX; w TN and e AR
south to LA.

Similar Species: Sawcheek Darter *(E. serriferum)* has
serrate preopercle, second dorsal fin
with 13–15 rays, and 4 black spots at
caudal fin base. Carolina Darter *(E.
collis)* has tan to light greenish-brown
sides with numerous small dark spots
and mid-lateral row of dark brown
dashes.

Comments: Swamp Darter is common over most of
its range, but little is known of its life
history or habits.

303 Spotted Darter
Etheostoma maculatum

Description: To 3″ (7.5 cm). Deep, compressed. Dark
olive brown above; *sides lighter, with
dusky spots, many bright red spots in males;*
median fins olive to reddish in males,
dark spotted with light edge in females;
paired fins lighter. Snout pointed,
longer than eye; frenum present; *gill
membranes narrowly joined.* Caudal
peduncle deep. Cheek unscaled; opercle
scaled. *Lateral line usually complete, with
52–67 scales;* when incomplete, last 1–5
scales unpored.

Habitat: Clear large creeks and rivers with swift
current over rocks or rubble.

Range: Southwestern NY and w PA west to n
IN and south to sw NC and e TN.

Similar Species: Bluebreast Darter *(E. camurum)* has blue-
green breast, reddish-orange fins, and
black-edged second dorsal, anal, and
caudal fins. Wounded Darter *(E.
vulneratum)* has dusky teardrop under
eye, dark olive to dusky first dorsal fin
with reddish pigment on first two and
last membranes, and black-edged second
dorsal, anal, and caudal fins.

Comments: Spotted Darter spawns during May and
June in riffles 6–24″ (15–61 cm) deep.
The female deposits the eggs in a
wedge-shaped mass on the underside of
a rock. The nests are at least 4′ (1.2 m)
apart, and are guarded by the male.

282 Least Darter
Etheostoma microperca

Description: To 1¾″ (4.5 cm). Small, elongate,
moderately compressed. Olive to green;
*8–10 dark mid-lateral blotches; pelvic and
anal fins red or orange.* Mouth small, not
reaching beyond anterior edge of eye;
sensory canal below eye, with 2–3 pores; gill
membranes moderately joined. *1–2
(usually 2) anal fin spines.* Cheek unscaled;
opercle scaled; 30–36 scales in lateral
series. *Lateral line with 1–3 pored scales.*

Habitat: Quiet streams, lakes, and swamps with
            vegetation over mud or sandy mud.

Range: Great Lakes drainage from WI and MN
            south to n KY, south-central MO, nw
            AR, and e OK.

Similar Species: Cypress Darter *(E. proeliare)* has mid-

            lateral row of round to oval dark
            blotches, scaled cheek, sensory canal
            below eye with 4 pores, and usually 2
            anal fin spines. Fountain Darter *(E.
            fonticola)* has dark brown crosshatching
            on upper and lower sides, mid-lateral
            row of dark dashes, unscaled cheek,
            sensory canal below eye with 4 pores,
            and 1 anal fin spine; occurs in spring
            pools and runs with aquatic vegetation.

Comments: Least Darter is one of the smallest
            species in the family. It reaches sexual
            maturity at one year of age, and its life
            span is less than two years.

277 Johnny Darter
Etheostoma nigrum

Description: To 2½″ (6.5 cm). Slender. *Yellowish to
                straw-colored;* usually with 5–7 dark
                saddles; *sides usually with small dark* X-,
                V-, *and* W-*shaped markings,* often
                merging to form zigzag lines; dark lines
                extend from snout to eye, not joined at
                midline; rows of dark spots form bands
                on fins; pectoral fin varies from clear to
                barred. Breeding males blackish; spots

                on fins dusky. Snout blunt, decurved; no
                frenum; gill membranes narrowly
                joined. Anal fin with 1 spine, 7–9 rays.
                Cheek usually unscaled. *Lateral line
                nearly complete, with 40–55 scales.*

Habitat: Pools near riffles of clear to slightly
            turbid creeks and rivers over sand,
            gravel, or rocks; lake shores.

Range: Southern QC and s Hudson Bay
            drainage east to e SK; Atlantic coast
            drainages in s VA and n NC; Great
            Lakes and upper Mississippi River
            drainages west to se WY and ne CO and
            south to sw AR; Mobile Bay drainage in
            AL and MS.

Similar Species: Bluntnose Darter *(E. chlorosomum)* has dark bridle around snout, scaled cheek, and incomplete lateral line with fewer than 25 pored scales; occurs in sluggish streams over mud, sand, or clay.

Comments: This is the most widespread species in the genus *Etheostoma*. It provides food for sport fishes, but its populations are too small for it to be considered an important forage fish. One of the easiest darters to maintain in captivity, Johnny Darter is often used in behavioral studies. The common name was first used by Dr. David Starr Jordan and Dr. Barton Warren Evermann in 1896 in reference to a specimen in their aquarium that they referred to as "little Johnny, our earliest aquarium friend."

278 Tessellated Darter
Etheostoma olmstedi

Description: To 3½" (9 cm). Elongate. Olive brown above, with 6 dark saddles; upper sides mottled with zigzags and *9–11 dark mid-lateral* X- *and* W-*shaped markings;* yellowish below; thin alternating dark and light bands on dorsal and caudal fins; pelvic and anal fins black in males. Gill membranes narrowly joined. Fins large; anal fin with 1–2 spines, 6–9 rays. Cheek and opercle sometimes scaled. *Lateral line complete, with 37–58 scales.*

Habitat: Clear pools of streams with slow current over sand, mud, or gravel; lake shores.

Range: St. Lawrence River and Lake Ontario drainages in s QC and se ON, and south in Atlantic coast drainages to ne FL.

Similar Species: Waccamaw Darter *(E. perlongum)* has more elongate body and 58–66 lateral line scales; occurs along lake shores over sand. Glassy Darter *(E. vitreum)* has translucent body with yellowish wash, 6–9 dark mid-lateral dashes, and numerous dark speckles on upper sides.

Comments: Tessellated Darter spawns in a nest cavity, usually under rocks, logs, or other debris. The eggs are deposited in a single layer over an area 1–3″ (2.5–7.5 cm) wide. Occasionally three or four males may maintain territories under the same rock. The common name refers to the checkered pattern of the lateral markings.

292 Stippled Darter
Etheostoma punctulatum

Description: To 3½″ (9 cm). Moderately deep, compressed. Brownish above, with 4 prominent dark saddles; sides with broad blue-green mid-lateral band posteriorly; *broad black bar below eye;* first dorsal fin with orange edge and black base in males, lighter in females; other fins spotted. Males bright reddish orange below, with reddish-orange gill membranes. Snout longer than eye; frenum present; gill membranes narrowly joined. *58–80 scales in lateral series. Lateral line incomplete, with 35–50 pored scales.*

Habitat: Quiet pools of cool clear creeks with moderate current over clean gravel or rocks.

Range: Southern MO, n AR, se KS, and ne OK.

Similar Species: Arkansas Darter *(E. cragini)* has 40–55 scales in lateral series and incomplete lateral line with 8–20 pored scales; occurs in small clear springs and seepage areas with vegetation. Paleback Darter *(E. pallididorsum)* has wide light olive stripe along midline of back, 44–52 scales in lateral series, and incomplete lateral line with 8–19 pored scales; occurs in small creeks and springs and shallow pools with vegetation over gravel.

Comments: Stippled Darter spawns during the spring and early summer. Other details of its life history are unknown.

302 Redline Darter
Etheostoma rufilineatum

Description: To 3½″ (9 cm). Deep, compressed. *Males with olive brown back; sides marked with* cream, red, orange, green, and dusky dashes; breast blue; second dorsal, anal, and caudal fins with dark greenish base, red bands, and narrow black border. Females with olive brown back; sides greenish, with dark bars; breast dusky blue; fins yellowish, with black spots and black edge. Caudal fin of males and females with dark spot in center, cream spot at upper and lower base. Snout short, pointed; frenum present. Lateral line complete, with 41–57 scales.

Habitat: Swift riffles of clear cool creeks and rivers over gravel or rocks.

Range: Cumberland and Tennessee River drainages, sw VA and s KY, south to n GA and n AL.

Similar Species: Etowah Darter (*E. etowahae*) lacks red spots on sides, has blue-green anal fin without red band, and opercle is scaled. Greenbreast Darter (*E. jordani*) has red spots on sides and blue-green anal fin without red band.

Comments: Redline Darter is generally common throughout its range. The colors of the male and female are so different that they are often thought to be different species.

296 Tennessee Snubnose Darter
Etheostoma simoterum

Description: To 3″ (7.5 cm). Robust anteriorly. Back olive, with 8–10 dark saddles; *upper sides tan, with reddish scales often forming zigzag lines;* dark mid-lateral blotches merge to form irregular band; white below, bright orange in males; dorsal fins dusky to black at base, with dark spots or bands near middle, outer portion reddish. *Snout very blunt, strongly decurved; frenum narrow;* mouth small, subterminal; gill membranes broadly joined. *14 pectoral fin rays. 18–22 rows of scales on caudal peduncle.*

Habitat: Shallow riffles of clear creeks and small rivers with moderate current over sand, gravel, or rocks.

Range: Southwestern VA and w NC south to n
AL.

Similar Species: Blackside Snubnose Darter *(E. duryi)*
lacks frenum and has 13 pectoral fin rays
and 15–18 rows of caudal peduncle
scales.

Comments: There are more than a dozen species of
snubnose darters; they are very closely
related, and most have restricted
distributions. These fishes are very
difficult to identify when adult males
are not in full breeding color.

---

299 Orangethroat Darter
Etheostoma spectabile

Description: To 2½" (6.5 cm). Compressed, *greatest
depth at dorsal fin origin.* Olive above,
with 7–10 dark square blotches; *sides
mottled, with 7–10 blue-green bands and
reddish-orange interspaces;* belly pale blue-
green; cheek ivory; gill membranes
orange; first dorsal fin with reddish base,
cream to orange center, blue-green edge;
pelvic and anal fins blue-green; caudal fin
dusky to olive, with 2 orange spots at
base. Gill membranes narrowly joined.
Lateral line incomplete, with 15–25 pored
scales.

Habitat: Riffles of clear creeks with moderate to
swift current over gravel or rocks.

Range: Western OH, se MI, s IA, and w NE
south to TN, s AR, and south-central TX.

Comments: Orangethroat Darter spawns in shallow
gravel riffles during the early spring.
After hatching, the fry move into pools
near the nest of a Smallmouth Bass
(Micropterus dolomieu), which defends the
nest and protects them along with its
own young.

---

297 Speckled Darter
Etheostoma stigmaeum

Description: To 2½" (6.5 cm). Slender. Yellowish
brown above, with 5–7 dark saddles;
8–10 dark mid-lateral blotches, becoming

bright blue bars in breeding males; lower sides of head pale blue in males, bright blue in breeding males; belly yellowish; first dorsal fin with blue base, orange band near center, black-edged; *pelvic, second dorsal, anal, and caudal fins dusky.* Snout decurved; no frenum; gill membranes narrowly joined. First dorsal fin with 10–12 spines. *Lateral line incomplete, with 21–50 pored scales.*

Habitat: Pools and riffles of clear creeks and small rivers with moderate current over sand, gravel, or rocks.

Range: Southern KY, s MO, and se KS south to w FL and e TX.

Similar Species: Blueside Darter *(E. jessiae)* has frenum.

Comments: Speckled Darter is common over most of its range. It spawns from late March to May. The eggs are deposited in gravel and fertilized, then abandoned.

---

295 Gulf Darter
Etheostoma swaini

Description: To 2½″ (6.5 cm). Moderately elongate, compressed. Olive above, with 7–9 dark saddles; sides brownish, *males with 5–7 reddish-orange bars posteriorly;* belly of males yellowish orange to red; fins spotted in females; *dorsal fins with red and blue bands, edges dusky blue;* bases of pelvic, anal, and caudal fins bluish. Snout short, pointed; frenum present; gill membranes narrowly joined. 35–48 scales in lateral series. *Lateral line complete or almost so, with 7 or fewer unpored scales.*

Habitat: Clear creeks and small rivers with vegetation or debris over sand or gravel.

Range: Western KY and w TN south to sw GA, w FL, and e LA.

Similar Species: Mud Darter *(E. asprigene)* has 44–54 scales in lateral series and incomplete lateral line with 8 or more unpored scales; males have spots forming bars on second dorsal fin; occurs in sluggish lowland streams and ponds with debris over mud or sand.

Comments: Almost nothing is known about the life history of this darter, except that it spawns during the spring.

289 Striped Darter
Etheostoma virgatum

Description: To 3″ (7.5 cm). Slender, elongate. Olive brown above, with 6–7 small dark saddles; *sides with 10 narrow stripes, 9–11 dusky mid-lateral blotches; cheek dusky, with bicolored bar,* red above, silvery below; fins with spots forming bars in females; first dorsal fin black at base in males, with reddish edge; second dorsal, anal, and caudal fins reddish orange; anal fin blue-edged. Snout pointed; frenum present; gill membranes narrowly joined. Caudal peduncle long. *Lateral line incomplete, with 6–20 pored scales.*

Habitat: Pools of creeks and small rivers with slow to moderate current over flat bedrock, sand, or gravel.

Range: Cumberland River drainage, se KY and central TN.

Similar Species: Teardrop Darter (*E. barbouri*) lacks narrow stripes and has well-defined dark bar below eye. Barcheek Darter (*E. obeyense*) lacks stripes on sides.

Comments: Striped Darter spawns during the spring. The female deposits the eggs on the underside of a flat rock, and the male guards them until they hatch.

275 Glassy Darter
Etheostoma vitreum

Description: To 2½″ (6.5 cm). Elongate. *Translucent, washed with yellow;* breeding males dusky to black; 7–9 dark mid-dorsal blotches; upper sides with numerous small black speckles, 6–9 *dark mid-lateral dashes; fins plain.* Head pointed. Pectoral fin very large; first dorsal fin with 7–9 spines, second dorsal fin with 6–9 rays. Scales strongly ctenoid, rough; cheek and opercle scaled; breast and back anterior to dorsal fin unscaled. *Lateral line complete, with 47–62 scales.*

Habitat: Creeks and small rivers with moderate current over sand or gravel.

Range: Atlantic coast streams from n MD to central NC.

Comments: During spawning season, in March and April, males and females gather over rocks or logs in fast currents, where the eggs are deposited and fertilized. This communal spawning is unique among darters. Glassy Darter is also the only species of *Etheostoma* that spends most of its time partially buried in the sand.

294 Redfin Darter
Etheostoma whipplii

Description: To 3½" (9 cm). Compressed. Olive above, with 8–10 dark saddles; sides with 6–9 dark blotches, *males with red spots;* yellowish orange below; *median fins with reddish base and blue edge in males, spotted in females;* 2 red spots at base of caudal fin. Snout long, pointed; frenum present; gill membranes narrowly joined. *59–73 scales in lateral series; usually 27–32 rows of scales on caudal peduncle.* Lateral line incomplete, with more than 40 pored scales.

Habitat: Creeks and rivers with moderate to swift current over gravel or sand.

Range: Eastern AL west to s AR, se OK, and e TX.

Similar Species: Redspot Darter *(E. artesiae)* has usually 47–57 scales in lateral series and usually 19–26 rows of scales on caudal peduncle. Orangebelly Darter *(E. radiosum)* lacks red spots and has 49–62 larger scales in lateral series.

Comments: Redfin Darter spawns in gravel riffles during March and April. It feeds on aquatic insects and other invertebrates.

286 Banded Darter
Etheostoma zonale

Description: To 3″ (7.5 cm). Elongate. Back olive, with 6–7 dark saddles; *sides greenish yellow; dusky mid-lateral band with 9–12 green bars, interspaces narrower than bars;* belly greenish; *no dark spot on cheek or opercle;* gill membranes greenish; pectoral fin plain; dorsal fins with reddish base, green bands, clear to dusky edge; pelvic and anal fins greenish. Snout short, blunt, decurved; frenum present; gill membranes broadly joined. Pectoral fin rounded, with 14–15 rays; anal fin with 2 spines, first spine enlarged, 6–9 rays. *Lateral line complete, with 38–58 scales.*

Habitat: Riffles and shoals of large creeks and rivers with moderate to swift current over gravel, sand, or rubble.

Range: Mississippi River system from w NY west to WI and MN and south to s AR.

Similar Species: Brighteye Darter *(E. lynceum)* has 8–10 dark bars with interspaces about equal to width of bars.

Comments: This darter spawns in riffles between April and June, depositing the eggs in the algae and moss growing on the surface of stones and boulders. It reaches maturity in one to two years and lives no longer than four years.

304 Ruffe
Gymnocephalus cernuus

Description: To 10″ (25 cm). Elongate, moderately robust. Back greenish brown; sides brown to yellowish; *numerous irregular dark spots on back and sides; rows of dark spots on dorsal fin membranes;* rows of dark spots on caudal fin. Head relatively small; snout rounded, overhanging mouth. *Dorsal fins broadly joined, first dorsal fin with 12–16 spines, second dorsal fin with 11–15 rays; anal fin with 2–3 spines of equal length, 5–6 rays;* caudal fin slightly forked. *Lateral line complete, with 35–40 scales.*

Habitat: Streams with slow current and lakes; enters low-salinity marine waters.

Range: Introduced in Great Lakes. Native to w and central Europe.

Similar Species: Yellow Perch *(Perca flavescens)* has 5–8 dusky bars across back and sides and separate dorsal fins.

Comments: This European native avoids swift water. It usually forms small schools and can be very common within limited areas. It was first discovered in tributaries of Lake Superior in 1986. Ruffe feeds on crustaceans, aquatic insects, and other benthic organisms. Its diet overlaps that of Yellow Perch, and it appears to be a direct competitor. This species lives a maximum of six years.

119 Yellow Perch
Perca flavescens

Description: To 15″ (38 cm); 4¼ lb (1.9 kg). Oblong, moderately compressed. Brassy green to golden yellow above; *5–8 dusky bars across back almost to belly;* dorsal and caudal fins dusky to olive; pelvic and anal fins light grayish green to reddish orange. Mouth reaches middle of eye; *no canine teeth; preopercle serrate. Anal fin with 2 spines,* 6–8 rays. Cheek and opercle scaled. Lateral line complete, with 53–59 scales.

Habitat: Open areas in clear streams, lakes, ponds, and reservoirs with aquatic vegetation.

Range: Great Slave Lake, Northwest Territories, south to MT and east to NS; Atlantic coast from St. Lawrence River drainage south to SC; Great Lakes drainage and south in Mississippi River drainage to MO; Gulf coast drainages, w FL and extreme s AL. Introduced outside native range.

Similar Species: Ruffe *(Gymnocephalus cernuus)* has joined dorsal fins with 12–16 spines and 11–15 rays, and 35–40 lateral line scales.

Comments: Yellow Perch lives in schools in deep water, moving into shallower areas to

feed at dawn and dusk. It is a sport and
food fish, and is harvested commercially
in parts of Canada and the Great Lakes.
Anglers use worms and minnows and
other fishes as live bait.

300 Tangerine Darter
Percina aurantiaca

Description: To 7″ (18 cm). Elongate. Back olive
yellow, with row of small black spots
above wide black mid-lateral stripe;
*underside of head, lower sides, and belly
bright orange in breeding males, yellowish in
females; second dorsal fin orangish; pelvic
and anal fins dusky to black. First dorsal
fin with 13–16 spines, second dorsal fin
with 12–15 rays. Scales small. Lateral line
with 82–99 scales.*

Habitat: Deep riffles, runs, and pools of medium
to large creeks and rivers with steep
gradient over bedrock, cobble, rubble, or
boulders.

Range: Upper Tennessee River system in sw VA,
e TN, w NC, and ne GA.

Comments: Tangerine Darter feeds primarily on
aquatic insects, which are picked off
plants growing along the stream bottom
attached to rocks. One of North
America's largest and most colorful
darters, this fish is occasionally caught
on small baited hooks or artificial flies.
It is known as River Slick in some
regions. It lives up to four years.

279 Logperch
Percina caprodes

Description: To 7″ (18 cm). Elongate, almost
cylindrical. Olive to yellowish, with
15–22 dark saddles; yellowish below;
first dorsal fin with black base, narrow
black border; second dorsal and caudal
fins with rows of dark spots; other fins
plain; *caudal spot usually present. Head
cone-shaped; snout pointed, overhanging
mouth;* frenum present; gill membranes

narrowly joined. First dorsal fin with 14–16 spines. Nape completely scaled. Lateral line complete, with 71–91 scales.

Habitat: Riffles and pools of medium to large streams over sand, gravel, or rocks; lakes and reservoirs.

Range: QC west to SK; Hudson River drainage, VT and NY; St. Lawrence River system, Great Lakes, and Mississippi River system south to LA.

Similar Species: Blotchside Logperch *(P. burtoni)* has 8–10 oval to round mid-lateral blotches, orange band on first dorsal fin, black spot at middle of caudal fin base, and usually unscaled nape; occurs in clear large creeks and rivers with moderate current over gravel or rocks. Bigscale Logperch *(P. macrolepida)* lacks band on first dorsal fin.

Comments: Logperch is the most widespread *Percina* species, but it has disappeared from streams contaminated by silt and pollution. It feeds on aquatic insects, frequently using its long snout to flip stones in search of prey.

272 Channel Darter
Percina copelandi

Description: To 2½″ (6 cm). Elongate, slender. Back olive to olive brown; *sides with 8–10 oval to squarish mid-lateral blotches;* dusky bar under eye; first dorsal fin with dusky to black band along base and edge; second dorsal, anal, and caudal fins clear to dusky; *small black spot at middle of caudal fin base. Snout short, somewhat blunt; frenum very narrow or absent.* First dorsal fin with 10–12 spines, second dorsal fin with 10–13 rays; anal fin with 2 spines, 7–9 rays. *More than half of nape, cheek, and opercle scaled.* Lateral line with 45–64 scales.

Habitat: Riffles, channels, and pools of large creeks and rivers over sand or gravel; lake shores.

Range: St. Lawrence River system, sw QC, se ON, and NY west to Lakes Ontario and

Erie; OH south to e TN and w KY; sw
MO and se KS south to n LA.

Similar Species: Pearl Darter *(P. aurora)* has unscaled
nape and scaled cheek and opercle;
occurs in large creeks and small rivers
with moderate to swift current over
gravel or rocks. Coal Darter *(P.
brevicauda)* lacks frenum and has
unscaled or partially scaled nape,
unscaled cheek, and scaled opercle.

Comments: Channel and Coal Darters are the
smallest species in the genus *Percina*.

290 Bluestripe Darter
Percina cymatotaenia

Description: To 4″ (10 cm). Elongate, moderately
compressed. Dark olive brown above;
*sides have irregular, usually brownish-black
mid-lateral band, with blue-green stripe and
cream to yellowish wavy stripe above;* cream
to yellow below; fins with faint rows of
dark spots forming bars; first dorsal fin
with dusky edge; *caudal fin base
yellowish, with black spot.* Head short; eye
large; gill membranes narrowly joined.
Lateral line complete, with 64–73
scales.

Habitat: Pools and backwaters of large creeks and
small rivers over sand, gravel, debris, or
vegetation.

Range: Gasconade and Osage River drainages,
south-central MO.

Comments: Bluestripe Darter feeds on aquatic
insects and other invertebrates. It
spawns during May in gravel riffles.

287 Gilt Darter
Percina evides

Description: To 3″ (7.5 cm). Moderately stout,
compressed. Dark olive, *with 6–8 dark
saddles ending in large dark mid-lateral
blotches;* yellowish orange below; dark
bar under eye; cheek orange; gill
membranes yellowish orange; pelvic and
anal fins bluish black; first dorsal fin

dusky to orange, with clear edge; second dorsal and caudal fins dusky. Head and snout short, decurved; frenum present; gill membranes narrowly joined. Lateral line complete, with 52–67 scales.

Habitat: Clear, deep, swift riffles of large creeks and rivers over gravel, rubble, or boulders.

Range: Western NY west to Mississippi River system in n WI and e MN, and south to n GA, n AL, and n AR.

Similar Species: Bronze Darter *(P. palmaris)* has 10–11 dark saddles.

Comments: During the spring and summer, adult male Gilt Darters are found in deep swift shoals, while females and young males stay in the adjacent shallows. In the winter, all move into deeper pools. The maximum life span of this species is about four years.

270 Blackside Darter
Percina maculata

Description: To 4″ (10 cm). Elongate, moderately robust. Back greenish brown, with 7–10 dark saddles (sometimes uniformly brown); upper sides dusky to yellow; *7–9 oval bluish-black mid-lateral blotches connected by dusky band;* yellowish below; median fins dusky or with rows of dark spots forming bars; *black spot at caudal fin base.* Snout pointed; frenum present; gill membranes narrowly joined. Lateral line complete, with 57–70 scales.

Habitat: Riffles and pools of large creeks and rivers over sand, gravel, or rocks; often around vegetation or debris; uncommon in lakes.

Range: Southeastern ON west to s MB and se SK; Great Lakes and Mississippi River systems; Gulf coast drainages from AL west to ne and e OK and extreme ne TX.

Similar Species: Longhead Darter *(P. macrocephala)* has dark broad mid-lateral band with light stripe above. Leopard Darter *(P. pantherina)* has 10–14 black oval to round mid-lateral blotches and dark brown to black spots on back and upper sides.

Comments: Unlike most darters, Blackside Darter swims in mid-depths during the day and rests on the bottom at night. The young feed on very small crustaceans; when they reach a length of 1½–2½" (4–6.5 cm), the diet changes to aquatic insects. This species lives up to four years.

283 Blackbanded Darter
Percina nigrofasciata

Description: To 4" (10 cm). Elongate, stout. Yellowish tan to dark brown above, with darker saddles; *dark mid-lateral band with 10–15 blotches, diamond-shaped anteriorly, oval posteriorly;* whitish below; dusky bar under eye; fins somewhat dusky; *3 small dark blotches at caudal fin base.* Snout pointed; frenum present; gill membranes narrowly joined. Fins large; first dorsal fin with 11–13 spines, second dorsal fin with 11–12 rays; anal fin with 2 spines, 8–10 rays. Lateral line complete, with 50–64 scales.

Habitat: Riffles of creeks and small rivers with moderate current and vegetation or debris over rocks, sand, or gravel.

Range: Coastal plain drainages from SC to e LA; peninsular FL south to Lake Okeechobee.

Similar Species: Freckled Darter *(P. lenticula)*, the longest darter, reaching length of 8" (20 cm), has black spot on anterior base of second dorsal fin and small scales, 80–93 in lateral line; occurs in large creeks to medium rivers in deep swift water over gravel or rocks. Dusky Darter *(P. sciera)* has 8–12 oval mid-lateral blotches and 2 merged blotches on lower caudal fin base.

Comments: This species can change its color pattern rapidly to match its environment. It feeds primarily on aquatic insects. Spawning occurs during May and June.

280 Shield Darter
Percina peltata

Description: To 3″ (7.5 cm). Elongate, stout. Yellowish to tan above; *dark blotch on nape with light oval inner spot;* upper sides with 6–7 blackish saddles connected by dark, narrow, wavy line; *mid-lateral band formed by large dark blotches and small, lighter, squarish blotches;* yellowish to white below; dark bar under eye and on midline of chin; first dorsal fin with black base, clear band, dusky band at edge; second dorsal and caudal fins spotted. Snout moderately blunt. Lateral line complete, with 52–64 scales.

Habitat: Riffles of creeks and rivers with moderate to swift current over vegetation, gravel, or rubble.

Range: Atlantic coast drainages from se NY to s NC.

Similar Species: Stripeback Darter *(P. notogramma)* lacks black bar on midline of chin and has oval mid-lateral blotches.

Comments: The spawning period of Shield Darter lasts from mid-April to May.

285 Slenderhead Darter
Percina phoxocephala

Description: To 4″ (10 cm). Elongate, slender. Yellowish brown, with 14–20 dark saddles; *dusky mid-lateral band with 10–15 dark blotches;* first dorsal fin with dusky to black base, orange band through middle, and clear edge; second dorsal and caudal fins with dark spots; other fins plain; *black spot at caudal fin base.* Head long, slender; *snout long, pointed, length about equal to width of eye;* frenum present; gill membranes broadly joined; 6 branchiostegal rays. *Lateral line complete, with 62–72 scales.*

Habitat: Riffles over gravel or rocks and pools over sand in rivers and large creeks with moderate to swift current.

Range: OH to WI, s MN, and ne SD, and south to n AL, se KS, and e OK.

Similar Species: Longnose Darter *(P. nasuta)* has 12–15
dark mid-lateral blotches and bars,
irregular dark blotches on back and
upper sides, long snout, and 65–83
lateral line scales. Olive Darter
(P. squamata) has snout longer than
width of eye, dorsal fin with dusky
to black edge, and complete lateral
line with 72–88 scales; occurs
in rivers with swift current around
boulders.

Comments: The male Slenderhead Darter moves
to spawning grounds in May and
establishes a territory in swift shallow
riffles over gravel. After spawning in
May and June, it returns to deeper
water. Populations have declined in
some silty streams.

301   Roanoke Darter
Percina roanoka

Description: To 3″ (7.5 cm). Elongate, moderately
robust. Back dark olive to brown, with
6–9 dark square saddles; upper sides
dusky, with dark flecks; *sides bluish, with
9–12 black mid-lateral bars or blotches;
first dorsal fin with pale edge, followed by
narrow black band, wide orange band, and
black band at base;* light orange spots at
upper and lower caudal fin base. Snout
short, rounded, moderately blunt.
15–17 rows of scales on caudal
peduncle. Lateral line complete, with
38–54 scales; 4–5 rows of scales above
lateral line.

Habitat: Large creeks and rivers with moderate
to swift current over sand, gravel, or
rubble.

Range: James, Neuse, and upper New Rivers
from central VA and e WV south to
north-central NC.

Similar Species: Piedmont Darter *(P. crassa)* has 7–9 dark
mid-lateral blotches, black bar on
middle of chin, and yellow band on first
dorsal fin.

Comments: Roanoke Darter is one of the most
colorful *Percina* darters.

276 River Darter
Percina shumardi

Description: To 3¼" (8.5 cm). Elongate, moderately robust. Back olive brown, with 5–8 dark irregular saddles, less distinct anteriorly; *sides olive gray, with 8–15 dark blue-green vertically elongate mid-lateral blotches; dark bar under eye; dorsal fin membranes with small dark spot anteriorly, large dark blotch posteriorly;* small caudal spot present. Snout short, pointed. *Anal fin in breeding males enlarged, elongate.* Lateral line complete, with 46–63 scales.

Habitat: Deep large creeks and rivers with moderate to swift current over gravel or rubble; reservoirs.

Range: Hudson Bay drainage, south-central Canada; w Lake Huron and Lake Erie; Mississippi and Ohio Rivers south to Gulf coast from AL to TX.

Comments: As the common name implies, River Darter almost always occurs in large bodies of water. Unlike most other darters, it is also found in some reservoirs with slow-moving current.

281 Snail Darter
Percina tanasi

Description: To 3" (7.5 cm). Robust, thick anteriorly. Back olive brown, *with 4 broad dark saddles extending to lateral line, first saddle under anterior dorsal fin spines;* mid-lateral blotches on sides; pale green to yellowish below; pelvic and anal fins clear; other fins with dark spots forming bars on rays. Head small; *snout decurved; mouth almost horizontal.* Fins large; pectoral fin rounded, extends in breeding males to 17th through 19th lateral line scales; 11–12 anal fin rays. Lateral line complete, with 49–56 scales.

Habitat: Clean gravel riffles and shoals of clear, medium to large streams.

Range: Tennessee River drainage in se TN, nw GA, and ne AL.

Similar Species: Amber Darter *(P. antesella)* has 4 dark
narrow saddles, first saddle anterior to
first dorsal fin. Stargazing Darter *(P.
uranidea)* has 4 dark saddles, first saddle
under first dorsal fin, saddles extending
ventrally to merge with lateral blotches,
and large black bar under eye.
Saddleback Darter *(P. vigil)* has 5 dark
brown saddles extending across back and
onto sides, not merging with lateral
blotches, and faint dusky bar under eye.

Comments: Snail Darter became the focus of a legal
controversy in 1977 when its status as
an endangered species delayed the
construction of a dam on the Little
Tennessee River in southeastern
Tennessee that threatened its habitat.
Congress eventually passed legislation
exempting that dam project from the
Endangered Species Act, and
construction went forward. In recent
years, conservation actions have resulted
in a partial recovery, and this species is
currently considered to be threatened,
no longer in danger of extinction.

---

120 Sauger
Sander canadense

Description: To 28″ (71 cm); 12½ lb (5.6 kg).
Elongate, almost cylindrical. Gray to
dull brown, *often with 3–4 dark saddles
extending to mid-sides;* sides brassy to
orange, with dark markings; belly
whitish; *first dorsal fin with 2–3 rows of
small black spots, narrow dusky border;*
second dorsal fin with 2 light narrow
bands. *Mouth reaches beyond middle of eye;*
teeth canine; preopercle partially serrate.
Caudal fin moderately forked. Lateral
line complete, with 85–95 scales.

Habitat: Large creeks and rivers with moderate to
swift current, lakes, and reservoirs; often
in somewhat turbid waters.

Range: QC to AB; St. Lawrence River and Great
Lakes; Mississippi River drainage south
to TN, n AL, and AR. Introduced
outside native range.

Comments: Sauger is an important sport and food
fish, and is harvested commercially in
parts of Canada. It feeds on a variety of
small fishes and aquatic invertebrates,
which it locates with its large eyes.

121 Walleye
Sander vitreum

Description: To 3'5" (1 m); 25 lb (11.5 kg). Elongate,
slightly compressed. Olive brown to
brassy greenish yellow above, *with dusky
to black mottling;* belly whitish, with
yellowish-green tinge; first dorsal fin
dusky, black-edged, *with black blotch on
membranes of last 2–3 spines;* tip of lower
caudal fin lobe white. *Mouth reaches eye;*
teeth canine; preopercle serrate. Caudal
fin moderately forked. Lateral line
complete, with 82–92 scales.

Habitat: Deep large streams, lakes, and reservoirs
over firm sand, gravel, or rocks.

Range: Mackenzie River, Northwest Territories,
southeast to s Hudson Bay drainage and
south through Great Lakes and
Mississippi River system to AR; e Gulf
coast drainages in AL and MS. Widely
introduced.

Comments: Walleye is the largest North American
species in the perch family and one of
the most sought-after sport and food
fishes. The largest catch on record was
taken in Old Hickory Lake, Tennessee,
in 1960. This species feeds on aquatic
insects, crustaceans, amphibians, and
almost any available species of fish.

BIGEYES
Family Priacanthidae

4 genera and 18 species worldwide; 3
genera and 5 species in North America (4 Atlantic, 1 Pacific), plus 1 species confined to Mexican Pacific waters.
Bigeyes are found in tropical and temperate seas, and occur
primarily in rock or coral reef habitats at depths of 6–420'
(1.8–128 m) or more. These small to medium fishes are easily distinguished by their deep bodies and very large eyes.

The mouth is large and quite oblique, and the lower jaw projects beyond the upper. The large pelvic fins are anteriorly placed and broadly joined to the body by a membrane. The dorsal fin has 10 spines and 11 to 15 rays. The anal fin has three spines and 10 to 16 rays. The caudal fin is emarginate to rounded. Bigeyes have ctenoid scales; the lateral line does not extend onto the caudal fin.

475   Bigeye
Priacanthus arenatus

Description: To 14½" (37 cm). Compressed, *depth one-third length. Bright red; pelvic fins black.* Profile of head less curved above than below, nearly straight from snout to dorsal fin origin; eye large, width greater than length of snout; mouth large, oblique; lower jaw projects well beyond upper; *preopercular spine very small.* Pelvic fin connected to body by membrane; dorsal fin not notched, with usually 10 spines, 14 rays; anal fin evenly rounded, with 3 spines, 15 rays; caudal fin emarginate.

Habitat: Around coral reefs and rocks at depths of 66–656′ (20–200 m); sometimes over open sand bottoms.

Range: NC to Argentina, including Bermuda, Bahamas, Gulf of Mexico, and Caribbean; seasonally north to MA. Also in e Atlantic.

Similar Species: The nocturnal Glasseye Snapper (*Heteropriacanthus cruentatus*) reaches length of 12″ (30 cm), with depth about two-fifths length, is not uniformly bright red, and has strong prominent preopercular spine, 13 dorsal fin rays, and 14 anal fin rays; occurs to depths of 66′ (20 m).

Comments: Bigeye and Glasseye Snapper are carnivores and feed on small fishes, crustaceans, and polychaete worms.

474   Short Bigeye
Pristigenys alta

Description: To 10″ (25 cm). Compressed, *depth more than half of length*; profile about equally rounded above and below. *Bright red, including fins; median fins black-edged.* Eye very large, width much greater than length of snout; mouth very oblique; maxilla reaches middle of eye; lower jaw projects well beyond upper; *2 small spines at lower angle of preopercle.* Pelvic fin reaches beyond anal fin origin, attached by membrane to body; length of pectoral fin rays about equal to width of eye; dorsal fin notched, with 10 strong spines, 11 rays; anal fin with 3 spines, 10 rays; soft dorsal and anal fins pointed posteriorly, both reaching beyond caudal fin base; caudal fin truncate or slightly rounded. Scales strongly ctenoid.

Habitat: Over rocks at depths of about 18–420′ (5.5–128 m); usually deeper than 30′ (9.2 m).

Range: Gulf of Maine to FL, including Bermuda, Bahamas, Cuba, n and s Gulf of Mexico, and w Caribbean; apparently uncommon in West Indies.

Comments: The rocky habitat of this secretive, bottom-dwelling fish provides ample hiding places.

CARDINALFISHES
Family Apogonidae

22 genera and at least 207 species world-wide; 3 genera and 20 species in North America, plus 5 species confined to Mexican waters. Cardinalfishes are found mostly in tropical seas, but a few Indo-Pacific species occur in fresh or brackish waters. These small fishes have large eyes and a large, terminal, oblique mouth. The dorsal fin is well separated into two segments, the first with six to eight spines and the second with a single spine and eight to 14 rays. The anal fin has two spines and eight to 18 rays. The lateral line does not extend onto the caudal fin. Members of this family are found primarily around tropical coral reefs, usually to depths of 150′ (46 m) or more. Because cardinal-fishes are generalized perciform fishes, an accurate defini-tion of the family has been difficult. Several groups once included in this family have been removed and placed in other families, most notably the Epigonidae (deepwater car-dinalfishes) and Acropomatidae (temperate ocean basses).

476 **Flamefish**
Apogon maculatus

Description: To 4" (10 cm). Elongate. *Bright red, with dusky stripe on head between eye and opercle; round diffuse black spot beneath soft dorsal fin; dark dusky saddle on caudal peduncle.* Eye large; mouth large, terminal, oblique; small villiform teeth on jaws and roof of mouth; posterior edge of preopercle finely serrate, *without protruding lobe on fleshy flap at lower corner.* 12 pectoral fin rays. Scales ctenoid; *20 rows of scales in series around caudal peduncle.*

Habitat: Around coral and rocky reefs and oil platforms; usually to depths of 30' (9 m).

Range: NC to n South America, including Bermuda, Bahamas, Gulf of Mexico, and Caribbean.

Similar Species: Whitestar Cardinalfish *(Apogon lachneri)* has small but distinct black blotch beneath soft dorsal fin, immediately followed by distinct white spot; occurs in slightly deeper waters. Twospot Cardinalfish *(Apogon pseudomaculatus)* has well-defined black blotch beneath soft dorsal fin and on upper part of caudal peduncle in front of tail; occurs at depths of 5–1,200' (1.5–366 m). Barred Cardinalfish *(Apogon binotatus),* Pale Cardinalfish *(A. planifrons),* Broadsaddle Cardinalfish *(A. pillionatus),* Belted Cardinalfish *(A. townsendi),* and Mimic Cardinalfish *(A. phenax)* have narrow but distinct band between soft dorsal and anal fins, broader band of varying width and intensity on caudal peduncle, and 16 or fewer rows of scales around caudal peduncle; all occur in somewhat deeper waters. Bronze Cardinalfish *(Astrapogon alutus),* Blackfin Cardinalfish *(A. puncticulatus),* and Conchfish *(A. stellatus)* have smooth preopercular edge without protruding lobe, 14–16 pectoral fin rays, and cycloid scales; all occur in cavities of conchs and other shells.

Comments: Flamefish occurs frequently in shallow
Caribbean waters, where it is the most
common cardinalfish. It hides during
the day and is active at night. Like all
other cardinalfishes, this species
practices oral incubation, holding the
eggs in the mouth while they develop.

473 Dusky Cardinalfish
Phaeoptyx pigmentaria

Description: To 3″ (7.5 cm). Rather short-bodied.
Head and body brownish, never reddish;
large melanophores form star-shaped
spots all over body, usually 1 per scale
below lateral line; *no bar or spot beneath
soft dorsal fin;* no dark streaks along bases
of soft dorsal and anal fins; dark oblong
blotch extends along entire depth of
caudal peduncle, immediately in front of
caudal fin. Posterior edge of preopercle
serrate, *with protruding lobe on fleshy flap
at lower corner;* usually 11–12 gill rakers
on lower limb of outer arch. Usually
11–13 pectoral fin rays.

Habitat: Around coral reefs from shoreline to
depths of 78′ (24 m); occasionally to
144′ (44 m).

Range: NC to Brazil, including Bermuda,
Bahamas, parts of Gulf of Mexico, and
Caribbean. Also in e Atlantic.

Similar Species: Freckled Cardinalfish *(P. conklini)* is also
brownish with no trace of red, but more
boldly marked, with dark streaks placed
slightly away from bases of soft dorsal
and anal fins, and usually 15 gill rakers
on lower limb of outer arch. Sponge
Cardinalfish *(P. xenus)* has pigmentation
more or less intermediate between other
two species of *Phaeoptyx,* with dusky
streaks along bases of soft dorsal and anal
fins, and usually 14 gill rakers on lower
limb of outer arch; occurs around coral
reefs and in tubular sponges.

Comments: Dusky Cardinalfish seems to be less
common than Freckled Cardinalfish,
although the two species are often found
together.

TILEFISHES
Family Malacanthidae

5 genera and 39 species worldwide; 3 genera and 9 species in North America (6 Atlantic, 3 Pacific). These fishes reach lengths of 3′6″ (1.1 m) and are found to depths of 300′ (92 m). The pelvic fins are thoracic in position, each with one spine and five rays. The very long dorsal and anal fins are continuous and composed mostly of rays. The caudal fin is emarginate to lunate. Tilefishes are elongate, varying from relatively robust to slender. Some species have a ridge or fleshy keel on the nape, and all have an opercular spine that varies from flat to sharp and strong. Some tilefishes are quite colorful. The larger species are important sport and commercial fishes.

---

676   Ocean Whitefish
Caulolatilus princeps

Description: To 3′4″ (1 m). Fusiform, compressed. Yellowish brown above; whitish below; pelvic fin with yellow or yellowish-green edge; yellow streak at center of pectoral fin; dorsal and anal fins with blue stripe near edges. Head blunt. *Dorsal fin with 8–9 spines,* 23–26 rays; *anal fin long,* with 1–2 spines, 23–25 rays.

Habitat: Mostly around islands over soft bottoms and rocky reefs to depths of 300′ (92 m).

Range: Vancouver Island, BC, to Peru, including Galápagos Islands, Ecuador; rare north of central CA.

Similar Species: Yellowtail Jack *(Seriola lalandi)* has short dorsal fin with usually 6 visible low spines separated from 31–39 rays. Dolphinfish *(Coryphaena hippurus)* has dorsal fin extending farther forward onto head.

Comments: Ocean Whitefish is a popular sport fish; it is a good fighter, and its flesh is very tasty. It feeds on other fishes, squids, shrimps, and crabs.

---

520   Tilefish
Lopholatilus chamaeleonticeps

Description: To 3′6″ (1.1 m); 35 lb (16 kg). Stout, compressed. *Blue-green, with many yellow*

*spots on upper body; large yellow spots on
dorsal and anal fins. Prominent fleshy
triangular yellow crest on top of head,* equal
to height of dorsal fin; eye near top of
head; mouth large, terminal. Dorsal fin
with 7 spines, 14–15 rays; anal fin with
1 spine, 13–14 rays; caudal fin deeply
emarginate. Scales fine; about 93 in
lateral series.

Habitat: In burrows over open bottoms along
edge of continental shelf and beyond at
depths of 270–1,020′ (82–311 m).

Range: Labrador south throughout Gulf of
Mexico.

Comments: This colorful species is the only tilefish
with a prominent triangular crest on the
top of the head. It is the best-known and
most commercially utilized species in
the family. There are unconfirmed
reports of individuals weighing up to 50
lb (23 kg). Tilefish apparently occupies
an unusually narrow temperature range,
probably 47–53° F (8.25–11.65° C). A
mass die-off occurred in 1892, after
which the fish was rare for decades; this
is believed to have been the result of
freak conditions that temporarily
eliminated water in the required
temperature range.

---

521 Sand Tilefish
Malacanthus plumieri

Description: To 24″ (61 cm). Elongate, slender.
Generally pale gray to tan, with bluish
cast; pelvic fin white; pectoral fin clear;
dorsal and anal fins mostly yellow, with
clear bands; *caudal fin with sharply
defined dusky area above center, lobes
yellowish orange. Head pointed, not abruptly
elevated, without fleshy triangular crest;* eye
small, near top of head; opercular spine
strong, pointed. Dorsal fin long, low,
with 4–5 spines, 53–57 rays; anal fin
long, with 1 spine, 50–52 rays; caudal
fin lunate, with long lobes.

Habitat: Over sand and rubble from near shore to
depths of about 150′ (46 m).

Range: Cape Lookout, NC, to Santos,
Brazil, including Bermuda, Bahamas,
Gulf of Mexico, and Caribbean. Also
around Ascension Island in South
Atlantic.

Similar Species: Tilefish *(Lopholatilus chamaeleonticeps)*
has more robust blue-green body with
yellow spots and prominent fleshy
triangular crest on head.

Comments: Young Sand Tilefish are pelagic, but
adults are bottom dwellers. This species
builds a refuge of sand and rubble into
which it retreats when disturbed.

BLUEFISHES
Family Pomatomidae

2 genera and 3 species worldwide; 1
species in North America, plus 1 genus with 1 species in
offshore waters to depths of 656–1,980′ (200–604 m) off
southern Florida. Bluefishes are found in tropical and temperate seas. Moderately large, robust, and relatively elongate, they superficially resemble certain species in the jack
family (Carangidae). The dorsal fin is separated into two
segments, the first with seven to eight low spines and the
second with one spine and 13 to 28 rays. The anal fin has
two to three spines and 12 to 27 rays. The second dorsal fin
and the anal fin are covered with scales, and there is a black
blotch at the base of each pectoral fin. Members of this family have a membranous flap over the subopercle.

675 Bluefish
Pomatomus saltatrix

Description: To 3′7″ (1.1 m); 32 lb (14.5 kg).
Elongate, compressed. *Greenish or grayish
blue above; silvery below;* median fins
yellowish. Head large; mouth large,
terminal; *teeth prominent, sharp, flat,
triangular, in 1 series.* First dorsal fin with
7–8 spines, second dorsal fin with
23–28 rays; anal fin similar to second
dorsal fin, with 2 spines, 25–27 rays;
caudal fin forked. Scales small, cycloid;
head, body, and bases of fins scaled.
Lateral line straight, complete, follows
dorsal profile.

Habitat: Surface of nearshore to offshore waters. Young enter bays and estuaries.

Range: NS to Argentina, including Bermuda and Gulf of Mexico; apparently absent from Bahamas; rare or absent between s FL and n South America. Also irregularly distributed in e Atlantic and Indian Oceans.

Comments: Bluefish occurs in large schools. It is voracious, often foraging on squids or schools of small fishes; it is reported to feed until its belly is full, regurgitate, and feed again as long as food is present. Bluefish is an exciting sport fish and good food if consumed when fresh. It has been known to attack people.

ROOSTERFISHES
Family Nematistiidae

1 species confined to eastern Pacific from California to Peru. Roosterfishes were previously placed in the jack family (Carangidae). Evidence suggests that these two families, together with the remoras (Echeneidae), cobias (Rachycentridae), and dolphinfishes (Coryphaenidae), form a natural lineage.

621 Roosterfish
Nematistius pectoralis

Description: To 4' (1.2 m), usually to 3' (91 cm); 99 lb (45 kg). Large, compressed, jack-like. Back slightly dusky, iridescent; 2 dark curved stripes on sides; silvery below; elongate dorsal fin spines dark at tips, yellow in middle, dusky at base. Head deep, moderately long, with gently rounded forehead; snout short; mouth reaches posterior edge of eye. Pectoral fin pointed, long, extending nearly to anal fin origin; *first dorsal fin with 7 elongate, thread-like spines anteriorly;* second dorsal fin with 1 spine, 25–28 rays; anal fin with 3 spines, 15–17 rays. Scales small, cycloid; 120–130 scales in irregular series along lateral line. No scutes along lateral line.

Habitat: Shallow inshore areas, including sandy
           shores along beaches. Young sometimes
           in tide pools.
Range: San Clemente Island, CA, to Peru,
           including Galápagos Islands, Ecuador;
           rare north of Baja California.
Comments: This jack-like fish is easily recognized
           by its "comb" of elongate dorsal fin
           spines, a feature that is the source of its
           common name. A scrappy fighter on
           light tackle, Roosterfish is a popular
           sport and food fish.

REMORAS
Family Echeneidae

4 genera and 8 species worldwide; all
found in North America (1 Atlantic, 7 Atlantic and Pacific).
Seven of the eight species have worldwide distributions in
tropical to warm-temperate seas. Remoras are instantly recognizable by the unique sucking disk on the top of the head;
this oval disk is actually a modified spiny dorsal fin. Other
than the disk, these fishes bear a close resemblance to cobias
(family Rachycentridae) and are believed to have evolved
from that family. Remoras are elongate fishes with superior
mouths that open just anterior to the disk. They attach
themselves to a variety of large marine fishes, mammals, and
turtles, and sometimes to ships or other floating objects.
They not only save energy and get a free ride, but feed on
scraps of food left by their hosts. Species in the genus *Echeneis*
are not host-specific, in contrast to the other genera.

637 Sharksucker
Echeneis naucrates

Description: To 32" (81 cm). *Very elongate, depth about
              one-tenth length; head about one-fifth length.*
              Dark gray, brown, or blackish; belly
              whitish; *dark stripe extends from snout
              through eye to caudal fin, with whitish area on
              each side;* dorsal and anal fins with whitish
              edges. Mouth superior; sucking disk oval,
              with usually 23 lamellae. Dorsal and anal
              fins similarly shaped, long-based; usually
              39 dorsal fin rays; usually 36 anal fin rays.
Habitat: Usually near surface of inshore and
              offshore waters in open seas.

Range: In w Atlantic from NS and Bermuda to Uruguay. In e Pacific from s CA to n South America.

Similar Species: Whitefin Sharksucker *(E. neucratoides)* has sucking disk with 21 lamellae, more white in fins, 36 dorsal fin rays, and 32 anal fin rays. Cobia *(Rachycentron canadum)* lacks sucking disk, and has short isolated dorsal fin spines. White Suckerfish *(Remorina albescens)* has relatively deep, short body and sucking disk with 12–13 lamellae; attaches to sharks, mantas, and Black Marlins. Slender Suckerfish *(Phtheirichthys lineatus)* has sucking disk with 10 lamellae; attaches most often to Great Barracudas (also reported to be free-swimming). Whalesucker *(Remora australis)* has very large disk with 25–27 lamellae; attaches to whales and porpoises. Spearfish Remora *(R. brachyptera)* has smaller disk with 15–17 lamellae; attaches to Swordfishes, Ocean Sunfishes, and marlins. Marlinsucker *(R. osteochir)* has disk with 17–20 lamellae and stiff pectoral fin with 20–23 rays; attaches to marlins, sailfishes, spearfishes, and Wahoos. Remora *(R. remora)* is very similar to Marlinsucker, but has flexible pectoral fin with 26–29 rays; attaches to sharks.

Comments: Sharksucker is found worldwide in tropical seas. Unlike some remoras, it is indiscriminate in choosing a host. It has been observed to remain with Bull Shark *(Carcharhinus leucas)* even in fresh water.

COBIAS
Family Rachycentridae

1 species worldwide. These fishes are found nearly worldwide, absent only from the eastern Pacific. The depressed head, protruding lower jaw, and short isolated dorsal fin spines distinguish cobias from other fishes. Like their apparent relatives, the remoras (family Echeneidae), they linger around larger fishes for food scraps and protection.

638 Cobia
Rachycentron canadum

Description: To 6'7" (2 m); 110 lb (50 kg). Elongate, almost cylindrical. Dark brown above, with 2 narrow silvery bands; belly gray or yellowish. *Head large, broad, flat;* mouth terminal, lower jaw protrudes; teeth in villiform bands on jaws, roof of mouth, and tongue. *First dorsal fin with 7–9 (usually 8) short disconnected spines;* second dorsal fin long, elevated anteriorly; anal fin similar to second dorsal fin, smaller; caudal fin rounded to slightly lunate. Scales small, embedded.

Habitat: Open seas, usually in association with buoys and floating shelter; sometimes near shore around barrier islands and coral reefs.

Range: Mid-Atlantic states to Argentina, including Bermuda, Bahamas, Gulf of Mexico, and Caribbean; sometimes seasonally north to MA.

Similar Species: Bluefish *(Pomatomus saltatrix)* is greenish or grayish blue, lacks silvery bands, and head is not flat. Sharksucker *(Echeneis naucrates)* has sucking disk.

Comments: Cobia is often seen basking on the surface around boats or flotsam, where it will take a hook baited with almost any fish, squid, or crustacean. This species may be confused with remoras when viewed from the side.

DOLPHINFISHES
Family Coryphaenidae

1 genus with 2 species worldwide; both species in North America. Dolphinfishes occur in tropical seas worldwide; they exhibit beautiful iridescent colors that fade soon after death. The body is elongate and moderately laterally compressed. The extremely long dorsal fin contains 48–65 rays; it begins just behind the eyes and extends the length of the back. The origin of the anal fin is at about mid-body, and the fin continues almost to the caudal fin. These fishes have a narrow caudal peduncle, a long forked tail, and small cycloid scales. Adult males develop a heavy

bony crest on the forehead, resulting in an almost vertical anterior profile. Until recently these fishes were known as dolphins; the name of the family has been modified in order to avoid confusion with the marine mammals of the same name. Dolphinfishes are usually marketed as Mahi-mahi.

696 Dolphinfish
Coryphaena hippurus

Description: To 6′6″ (2 m); 87 lb (40 kg). Elongate, moderately laterally compressed, greatest depth at nape. Iridescent blue and green, tinged with yellow; scattered small dark or golden blotches and spots; dorsal fin black; anal fin black, white-edged. Head blunt; mouth large, terminal; lower jaw projects. Pectoral fin length more than half of head length; pelvic fin about same length as pectoral fin; each pelvic and pectoral fin fits into depression on side of body; *dorsal fin undivided,* with more than 56 (usually 59–65) rays, *begins at nape, extends almost to caudal fin; anal fin long, low,* similar to posterior half of dorsal fin, *outer edge concave;* caudal fin deeply forked.

Habitat: Surface of open seas; usually over deep water, sometimes near shore.

Range: In w Atlantic from NS to Brazil, including Bermuda, Bahamas, Gulf of Mexico, and Caribbean. In e Pacific from Grays Harbor, WA, to Chile, including Galápagos Islands, Ecuador; rare north of s CA.

Similar Species: Pompano Dolphinfish *(C. equiselis)* reaches length of 30″ (76 cm), has deeper body, pectoral fin usually less than half of head length, dorsal fin with fewer than 56 rays, and anal fin with convex outer edge; occurs farther offshore and perhaps to greater depths.

Comments: Dolphinfish and Pompano Dolphinfish are important sport and commercial fishes. They are found near rafts of sargassum weed, where they apparently feed. The young, to lengths of about 3″ (7.5 cm), are part of the sargassum fauna.

JACKS
Family Carangidae

About 32 genera and 140 species worldwide; 14 genera and 40 species in North America (25 Atlantic, 12 Pacific, 3 shared), plus 15 species confined to Mexican waters. Jacks are found in tropical to temperate seas. This is an extremely diverse family morphologically, ranging from streamlined, fast-swimming, torpedo-like fishes to slow-moving fishes with extraordinarily laterally compressed bodies. They have two dorsal fins. In some species, the dorsal and anal fin spines are persistent throughout the life of the fish; in others, the spines are evident only in the young, becoming extremely short and covered by skin as the fish increases in size. Some jacks have finlets behind the dorsal and anal fins. All have a forked caudal fin. Several genera have scutes, usually on the posterior one-third of the lateral line. These fishes usually form schools; their habitats range from inshore brackish waters to open seas. Some species are highly esteemed food and sport fishes, although a few have been linked to ciguatera poisoning.

389 African Pompano
Alectis ciliaris

Description: To 3′6″ (1.1 m), possibly to 4′7″ (1.4 m); 51 lb (23 kg). Deep, compressed; rear half of body triangular in outline, becoming relatively longer with age. Metallic blue-green above; silvery below. Front of head steep, rounded; snout blunt; eye moderately large, adipose eyelid present. Pectoral fin falcate, longer than head; *pelvic fin longer than maxilla;* first dorsal fin not persistent, greatly reduced, usually not visible in adults; *second dorsal and anal fins falcate, anteriormost 6 rays in both long and thread-like (exceeding body length in young);* caudal fin forked, with paired keels at base. Scales minute, embedded; scutes inconspicuous. Arched part of lateral line follows dorsal profile of body.

Habitat: Usually near rocky reefs to depths of about 180′ (55 m). Young in open seas.

Range: In w Atlantic from MA south to Brazil, including Bermuda, Bahamas, Gulf of Mexico, and Caribbean. Also in e Pacific from s Mexico to Peru.

Comments: This solitary fish is valued by sport
anglers as a good fighter. Young up to 3″
(7.5 cm) long have four bars on the sides.
Those up to 6″ (15 cm) long have thread-
like extensions on the first dorsal and
anal fins; when the fish grows beyond
this length, the seven dorsal and two anal
fin spines disappear. This is the only
species in the family that does not retain
obvious dorsal fin spines throughout life.
The young drift in the open ocean, their
long fins trailing, thus accounting for
the common name Threadfish, which is
often applied to this species.

685 Crevalle Jack
Caranx hippos

Description: To 3′4″ (1 m), possibly to 5′ (1.5 m); 54
lb (25 kg), possibly to 70 lb (32 kg).
Robust, somewhat compressed; anterior
profile steep. Green-blue or bluish black
above; sides silvery; *belly yellowish; black
spot on upper edge of opercle and near lower
base of pectoral fin; first dorsal fin dusky,
other fins yellow.* Head large; snout blunt;
adipose eyelid present; mouth terminal;
lower jaw projects beyond upper;
maxilla reaches posterior edge of eye; 16–19
gill rakers on lower limb of outer arch.
First dorsal fin persistent; second dorsal
fin with 18–21 rays; anal fin similar in
size and shape to second dorsal fin, with
2 spines well separated from rays. Breast
largely unscaled; well-developed scutes
on caudal peduncle.

Habitat: Inshore, shallow bays, and estuaries to
deep waters of continental shelf; enters
waters of very low salinity (nearly fresh)
in FL.

Range: NS to Uruguay, including Gulf of
Mexico and Caribbean; possibly in
Bahamas; absent from Lesser Antilles.
Also in e Atlantic.

Similar Species: Horse-eye Jack *(C. latus)* has less steep
front of head, fully scaled breast in
individuals longer than 3″ (7.5 cm), and
poorly defined (sometimes absent) small

black blotch at edge of opercle, and
lacks dark blotch on pectoral fin.

Comments: Crevalle Jack is a large, fast, strong
swimmer that provides plenty of
excitement for anglers. It is primarily
a bottom scavenger, but is sometimes
found at the surface. Reports of this
species in the eastern Pacific,
including California, are based on
the closely related Pacific Crevalle
Jack *(C. caninus)*.

684 Horse-eye Jack
Caranx latus

Description: To 31″ (79 cm); 30 lb (13.5 kg).
Elongate, moderately deep, depth
about one-third length. Dark blue to
bluish gray above; silvery white or
sometimes golden below; usually small
diffuse black spot on opercle; *no dark
blotch on pectoral fin;* dorsal fins black-
tipped; first dorsal fin dusky; caudal fin
yellow. Young have 5–6 dark bars on
body, 1 on nape. Head large; snout
bluntish, not steep; eye width equal to
snout length, adipose eyelid present;
maxilla reaches beyond eye; 14–18 gill
rakers on lower limb of outer arch.
Pectoral fin falcate, longer than head;
first dorsal fin persistent; second dorsal
fin with 20–22 rays; anal fin similar to
second dorsal fin, with 2 spines well
separated from rays. Scales small,
cycloid; *breast fully scaled* in individuals
longer than 3″ (7.5 cm); well-developed
scutes on caudal peduncle.

Habitat: Around islands, over sand, or offshore;
enters brackish waters in lower reaches
of estuaries.

Range: NJ to Rio de Janeiro, Brazil, including
Bermuda, Bahamas, Gulf of Mexico,
and Caribbean. Also in e Atlantic,
including Ascension Island in South
Atlantic.

Similar Species: Crevalle Jack *(C. hippos)* has blunter
head, incompletely scaled breast,
prominent blotch on edge of opercle,

and distinct dark blotch on lower part of pectoral fin near base.

Comments: This jack is usually found in small schools. It feeds primarily on shrimps and other invertebrates.

---

682 Bar Jack
Caranx ruber

Description: To 22″ (56 cm); 15 lb (6.8 kg). Elongate, moderately compressed; *dorsal and ventral profiles about equal.* Bluish gray above; silvery below; *dark stripe extends from base of second dorsal fin through caudal peduncle and onto lower lobe of caudal fin; pale blue stripe immediately below dark stripe,* sometimes extending forward onto snout. Mouth terminal, slightly oblique; maxilla not reaching eye; 31–35 gill rakers on lower limb of outer arch. Pectoral fin falcate, reaching well beyond anal fin origin; second dorsal fin with 26–35 rays. Scutes on posterior part of lateral line and on caudal peduncle. 2 keels on caudal peduncle.

Habitat: Shallow clear waters; common around coral reefs.

Range: NJ to s Brazil, including Bermuda, Bahamas, nw and s Gulf of Mexico, and Caribbean.

Similar Species: Yellow Jack (*C. bartholomaei*) has yellowish cast and lacks dark and pale stripes on back; young are brassy, with many pale spots (only w Atlantic *Caranx* species with spots). Blue Runner (*C. crysos*) is usually dark olive to bluish above with conspicuous black spot at tip of opercle, and lacks dark and blue stripes on back.

Comments: Bar Jack, Yellow Jack, and Blue Runner are sometimes included in the genus *Carangoides.* Bar Jack is often found in schools, commonly seen in the Bahamas. It rarely occurs in the northern Gulf of Mexico, perhaps because of its preference for very clear water.

655 Round Scad
Decapterus punctatus

Description: To 8¼" (21 cm). Fusiform, elongate. Green-blue, fading to silver on sides; belly white; narrow yellowish stripe extends from head to caudal peduncle; *black spot on upper edge of opercle; conspicuous row of widely spaced black spots on front half of lateral line;* caudal fin lacks red pigment. Eye width almost equal to length of snout; adipose eyelid present. *2 well-separated, well-developed dorsal fins,* second long and low; anal fin similar to second dorsal fin, shorter; *finlet behind second dorsal and anal fins.* Lateral line strongly arched, with 37–56 scales in arched part; scutes on anterior arched part not expanded, *scutes on posterior straight part prominent and greatly enlarged vertically.*

Habitat: Mid-depths or on bottom to depths of about 300' (92 m); sometimes at surface, especially young.

Range: Georges Bank, MA, to Rio de Janeiro, Brazil, including Bermuda, Bahamas, Gulf of Mexico, and Caribbean. Also in e Atlantic and around Ascension and St. Helena Islands in mid–South Atlantic.

Similar Species: Mackerel Scad *(D. macarellus)* lacks spots on lateral line, and has slightly arched lateral line with 61–79 scales on arched part and scales slightly enlarged vertically on posterior part. Redtail Scad *(D. tabl)* has bright red caudal fin, lacks spots on lateral line, and lateral line has about 61–79 scales on arched part. Bigeye Scad *(Selar crumenophthalmus)* has much larger eye and lacks finlets behind second dorsal and anal fins.

Comments: Although used as food in some areas, Round Scad is primarily a bait fish.

656 Rainbow Runner
Elagatis bipinnulata

Description: To 4' (1.2 m); 37 lb (17 kg). Fusiform, very elongate, slender. Coloration gaudy; blue-green above; silvery below; series of

stripes on sides: broad dark blue stripe
extends from snout to caudal fin base,
narrow pale blue stripe immediately
below, broad yellow stripe along mid-
side, followed by another narrow blue
stripe; fins dusky, with yellowish tint.
Head long, pointed; maxilla not reaching
eye. Pectoral fin short; 2 dorsal fins, 6
anterior spines of first fin separated from
second by deep notch; *detached finlet with
2 rays behind second dorsal and anal fin;*
caudal fin large, deeply forked. *Grooves
on upper and lower sides of caudal peduncle.*
No scutes on lateral line.

Habitat: At or near surface over deep waters.
Range: In w Atlantic from MA to n Brazil,
including Bermuda, Bahamas, Gulf
of Mexico, and Caribbean. In e Pacific
from Cabo San Lucas, Baja California,
to n South America.
Similar Species: Cobia *(Rachycentron canadum)* lacks
bright colors and finlets.
Comments: This is the only gaudily colored jack in
North American waters. Found
worldwide in tropical seas, Rainbow
Runner is often seen in the company of
sharks and pilotfishes. It is highly
esteemed as a food and sport fish.

654 Bigeye Scad
Selar crumenophthalmus

Description: To 12″ (30 cm). Fusiform, elongate,
moderately compressed. Blue-green or
metallic blue above; silvery below; snout
and median fins dusky; pelvic and
pectoral fins clear. *Eye width greater than
length of snout;* adipose eyelid well
developed; mouth relatively large,
oblique; lower jaw projects beyond
upper; 2 widely separated fleshy papillae
on shoulder girdle, lower papilla larger
than upper. Pectoral fin falcate, about

shoulder girdle

same length as head; first dorsal fin
triangular; anal fin with 2 spines,
persistent; *no detached dorsal or anal finlets.
Enlarged scutes on posterior straight part of
lateral line,* smaller scutes on arched part.

Habitat: Shallow inshore waters.

Range: In w Atlantic from NS to Brazil, including Bermuda, Bahamas, Gulf of Mexico, and Caribbean. In e Pacific from Gulf of California to Ecuador.

Similar Species: Rough Scad *(Trachurus lathami)* has well-developed scutes on curved part of lateral line. Scads in genus *Decapterus* have similar body shape with much smaller eyes and detached finlets behind second dorsal and anal fins.

Comments: The finlets and the two small papillae on the shoulder girdle distinguish scads from other members of the jack family. Bigeye Scad is found in schools. It is not highly esteemed as a food fish, but is commonly used as bait, especially for sailfishes. There are unconfirmed reports of individuals reaching lengths of up to 24″ (61 cm).

---

692 Atlantic Moonfish
Selene setapinnis

Description: To 15″ (38 cm). *Very deep, extremely compressed;* ventral profile more convex than dorsal profile. Silvery; sometimes metallic blue above; fins clear; dusky or olive-yellow tints on second dorsal fin and caudal fin lobes. Young have black spot over straight part of lateral line. *Profile of head bluntly rounded above, steep and concave in front of eye;* mouth terminal; lower jaw projects beyond upper. First dorsal fin with 8 spines, persistent; second dorsal and anal fins slightly elongate anteriorly, not falcate. Scales small, cycloid; scutes inconspicuous.

Habitat: Inshore on bottom.

Range: NS to Argentina, including Gulf of Mexico and most of Caribbean; absent from Bahamas and possibly Bermuda.

Similar Species: Lookdown *(S. vomer)* has more convex head profile and elongate dorsal and anal fin rays.

Comments: Atlantic Moonfish is found in schools; it is often abundant within limited areas during the summer. It is rarely used as food in North America because of the lack of flesh on the body. This species was previously placed in the genus *Vomer*. Reports from the eastern Atlantic are based on a closely related species, African Lookdown *(S. dorsalis).*

689 Lookdown
Selene vomer

Description: To 16″ (41 cm); 4½ lb (2.1 kg). *Very deep, extremely compressed; dorsal and ventral profiles anteriorly straight, almost parallel.* Mostly metallic overall; bluish on back; silvery or golden elsewhere; second dorsal and anal fins blackish. *Profile of head very steep; mouth ventral, terminal;* lower jaw projects beyond upper. Pelvic fin very short, much shorter than maxilla; first dorsal fin with 8 spines, persistent; *second dorsal and anal fins long, falcate;* anal fin with 2 spines, not persistent. Scales small, cycloid; scutes inconspicuous.

Habitat: Shallow coastal waters over sand or mud.
Range: ME to Uruguay, including Bermuda, Bahamas, Gulf of Mexico, and most of Caribbean; possibly north to NS; absent from Lesser Antilles.
Similar Species: Atlantic Moonfish *(S. setapinnis)* has more concave and less steeply sloping head profile and much shorter dorsal and anal fin rays.
Comments: Unlike adults, the young of this species have long pelvic fins and long filaments extending from the first dorsal fin spines. In adults, the second dorsal fin and anal fin are greatly extended. This change is complete by the time the fish reaches a length of 4–5″ (10–12.5 cm).

681 Greater Amberjack
Seriola dumerili

Description: To 6′2″ (1.9 m); 177 lb (81 kg). Fusiform, elongate, slightly compressed.

Bluish or olive; brownish or pinkish tinge on sides, sometimes with amber stripe from eye to tail; belly silvery or whitish; olive stripe from eye to origin of first dorsal fin. Head bluntly pointed; mouth large, terminal; *maxilla very broad posteriorly, reaches middle of eye. Pectoral fin shorter than head,* equal in length to pelvic fin; first dorsal fin low, usually with 7 spines, persistent; *second dorsal fin much longer than anal fin;* front lobe of second dorsal and anal fins low, outer edges curved, not sickle-shaped; anal fin origin well behind origin of second dorsal fin; *no dorsal or anal finlets.* Caudal peduncle relatively deep, *with grooves on upper and lower sides. No scutes.*

Habitat: Open seas to depths of 1,200′ (366 m); small individuals in shallow waters.

Range: Cape Cod, MA, to Brazil, including Bermuda, Bahamas, Gulf of Mexico, and Caribbean. Also in e Atlantic and much of tropical Indo-Pacific region; absent from e Pacific.

Comments: This is the largest species of amberjack. It is sought by both sport and commercial anglers. Some species of amberjacks are believed to be responsible for ciguatera poisoning.

683 Yellowtail Jack
Seriola lalandi

Description: To 5′ (1.5 m); 79 lb (36 kg), usually 10–20 lb (4.5–9.1 kg). Fusiform, elongate, compressed. Olive brown to brown above; *yellow stripe on sides;* slightly oblique dark stripe extends from snout through eye; fins yellowish. *Head longer than body depth at origin of first dorsal fin.* First dorsal fin low, with usually 6 visible spines; anal fin origin well behind origin of second dorsal fin. No scutes on lateral line.

Habitat: Near surface around reefs, islands, and kelp beds in summer and fall; to depths of 222′ (68 m) in colder months.

Range: BC to Chile.

Similar Species: Green Jack *(Caranx caballus)* has pectoral fin reaching beyond origin of second dorsal fin and scutes on lateral line. Almaco Jack *(S. rivoliana)* has silvery body, lacks yellow stripes, and dark bar extends from eye to rear of head. Ocean Whitefish *(Caulolatilus princeps),* of tilefish family (Malacanthidae), has dorsal fin spines and rays of about equal height.

Comments: Yellowtail Jack feeds on anchovies, sardines, mackerels, squids, and pelagic red crabs. Second only to the elusive Albacore *(Thunnus alalunga),* it is one of the most popular sport fishes in southern California. Its migration north into this area depends upon water temperature, and the annual catch fluctuates between 5,000 and 400,000 fish. It is illegal to use purse seines for Yellowtail Jack in California waters; most are caught by hook and line.

---

686 Florida Pompano
Trachinotus carolinus

Description: To 25″ (64 cm); 7½ lb (3.4 kg). Short, deep, moderately compressed; dorsal and ventral profiles similar. Back bluish gray or blue-green; sides silvery; belly silvery yellowish; fins dusky or yellowish. Snout blunt; *mouth slightly inferior. Pectoral fin shorter than head;* pelvic fin shorter than pectoral fin; first dorsal fin with 6 short spines, *second dorsal fin with 22–27 (usually 23–25) rays; base of second dorsal fin only slightly longer than anal fin base;* anal fin with 3 spines, first 2 spines detached, *20–24 (usually 21–22) rays;* no dorsal or anal finlets. *Caudal peduncle relatively deep;* no scutes or grooves.

Habitat: Shallow waters along sandy beaches; breeding males known to occur at depths of 177–197′ (54–60 m).

Range: MA to Brazil, including Gulf of Mexico and Caribbean coasts of Central and South America; occasionally in Greater Antilles; rare north of NC; absent from

Bermuda and Bahamas; migrates north in summer, south in winter.

Similar Species: Permit *(T. falcatus)* reaches length of 3′9″ (1.1 m) and weight of 50 lb (23 kg), and has 17–21 dorsal fin rays and 16–19 anal fin rays. Palometa *(T. goodei)* has 4–5 distinct narrow dark bars on sides, 19–20 dorsal fin rays, 16–18 anal fin rays, and notably elongate anterior dorsal and anal fin rays in subadults and adults.

Comments: Florida Pompano is a favorite food fish and commands a high price. It is caught using light tackle over shallow sand flats. This species often makes long horizontal "flights" out of the water. Supposed record-size reports of Pompano are usually based on misidentified Permit individuals.

687 Palometa
Trachinotus goodei

Description: To 20″ (51 cm). Deep, compressed; dorsal and ventral profiles about equally rounded. Silvery; *4–5 distinct narrow dark bars on sides; leading edges of second dorsal and anal fins and caudal fin lobes black.* Snout blunt; mouth slightly inferior; maxilla reaches middle of eye. Pectoral fin relatively small, not falcate; *dorsal and anal fins very long, falcate, reaching beyond fork of caudal fin;* first dorsal fin with 6 short spines, second dorsal fin with 19–20 rays; anal fin with 3 spines, first 2 spines detached, 16–18 rays; no dorsal or anal finlets. No grooves on caudal peduncle. Scales small, cycloid, partially embedded; no scutes.

Habitat: Surf zone and sandy beaches; around reefs and rocky areas.

Range: MA to Argentina, including Bermuda, Bahamas, Gulf of Mexico, and Caribbean.

Similar Species: Permit *(T. falcatus)* reaches length of 3′9″ (1.1 m) and weight of 50 lb (23 kg), lacks bars on sides, and has shorter dorsal and anal fin lobes. Florida

Pompano *(T. carolinus)* lacks bars on sides and has more dorsal and anal fin rays. Gafftopsail Pompano *(T. rhodopus)* has faint yellow bars and reddish-yellow fins; occurs in Pacific.

Comments: Palometa occurs in large schools, mostly in clear tropical waters. It feeds on small fishes and invertebrates. This fish was formerly known as *T. glaucus*.

659 Jack Mackerel
Trachurus symmetricus

Description: To 32″ (81 cm). Fusiform, compressed. Metallic blue to olive green above; silvery below, darkening with age; *dark spot on upper rear part of opercle; caudal fin yellowish to reddish, other fins mostly clear.* Pectoral fin extends to base of first anal fin ray; dorsal fins barely separated; anal fin with 2 detached spines often buried or absent in individuals longer than about 6″ (15 cm); *no dorsal or anal finlets,* but some large individuals have last few dorsal and anal fin rays almost entirely separated from rest of fin. *Lateral line dips strongly at end of pectoral fin,* covered throughout length with 40–55 scutes.

Habitat: Offshore from surface to depths of at least 600′ (183 m). Young around reefs and kelp beds.

Range: Southeastern AK to Galápagos Islands, Ecuador.

Similar Species: Mexican Scad *(Decapterus scombrinus)* always has dorsal and anal finlets, and lateral line lacks dorsal branch and has scutes only posteriorly. Atlantic Chub Mackerel *(Scomber colias)* has dark green to bluish-black back with dark wavy streaks and 5 dorsal and anal finlets.

Comments: Large Jack Mackerel individuals are important commercially in southern California. This species feeds on krill, squids, anchovies, and lanternfishes. It often occurs in schools, and is a major food source for seals, sea lions, porpoises, swordfishes, sea basses, and pelicans.

SNAPPERS
Family Lutjanidae

21 genera and about 125 species worldwide; 5 genera and 21 species in North America (17 Atlantic, 4 Pacific), plus 7 species confined to Mexican waters. Snappers occur in tropical to warm-temperate seas throughout the world, living around reefs and on the outer continental shelf. They are oblong, moderately compressed fishes. Due to their generalized perciform characteristics, it is often difficult to identify them as members of the family Lutjanidae; in particular, snappers can be difficult to distinguish from species of the family Serranidae (sea basses).

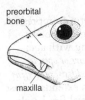

When the large terminal mouth is closed, the maxilla is nearly covered by the preorbital bone. The teeth are conical and sharp, never molar-like, and there are teeth on the roof of the mouth. The chin has no barbels or pores, and there are no spines on the opercle. Small ctenoid scales cover the body, except between the mouth and eyes. A prominent, narrowly triangular scale is present in the axil of the pelvic fin. The dorsal fin is continuous, and the caudal fin varies from deeply forked to truncate. The lateral line extends to the base of the caudal fin. Most snappers are carnivorous. They are very important economically as commercial and sport fishes.

606 Schoolmaster
Lutjanus apodus

Description: To 24″ (61 cm); 8 lb (3.6 kg). Moderately deep. Olive gray, with yellow tinge above; lighter below; *8 narrow pale bars on back and upper sides under dorsal fin base; solid or broken blue line under eye;* fins yellow or yellowish green. Profile of upper head nearly straight; snout long, pointed; *canine teeth in upper jaw visible when mouth closed;* vomer tooth patch anchor-shaped, with posterior extension. Dorsal fin slightly notched, with 10 spines, *14 rays; anal fin rounded,* with 3 spines, 8 rays; caudal fin emarginate. 5–6 scales, counted diagonally, between dorsal fin origin and lateral line.

Habitat: Coastal waters around coral reefs and over rocks; mangrove swamps, tide pools, and estuaries.

Range: NC to Brazil, including Bermuda, Bahamas, Gulf of Mexico, and Caribbean; seasonally north to ME.

Similar Species: Dog Snapper *(L. jocu)* lacks yellow and blue pigment on body, and has pale, narrow, triangular patch and blue stripe below eye (particularly well developed in young) tending to be broken into series of dots at a smaller body size. Amarillo Snapper *(L. argentiventris)* has rosy red body anteriorly, light yellow posteriorly, with blue spots or streaks under eye; occurs in shallow inshore Pacific waters, usually around reefs or mangrove swamps. Lane Snapper *(L. synagris)* and Mahogany Snapper *(L. mahogoni)* have 12 dorsal fin rays (all other w Atlantic *Lutjanus* species have 14). Blackfin Snapper *(L. buccanella)* has conspicuous black blotch at base and axil of pectoral fin; occurs at depths of 200–300' (61–91 m). Red Snapper *(L. campechanus),* Mutton Snapper *(L. analis),* and Silk Snapper *(L. vivanus)* have angular anal fin. Gray Snapper *(L. griseus)* and Cubera Snapper *(L. cyanopterus)* lack yellow and blue pigment on upper body; Cubera Snapper occurs in deep offshore waters.

Comments: Schoolmaster is very common around coral reefs, where it associates with Gray Snapper during the day. At night Schoolmaster goes its separate way to feed, like other snappers, mainly on fishes and crabs.

614 Red Snapper
Lutjanus campechanus

Description: To 3'3" (99 cm); 35 lb (16 kg). Rather deep, depth one-fourth length. *Scarlet above, fading to rosy red below,* sometimes with silvery sheen; fins red or reddish orange, sometimes with dusky edges;

individuals to 12″ (30 cm) long have dark spot on upper side just above lateral line and below anterior soft dorsal fin. Head large, anterior profile steep, rounded behind eye; snout long; eye small; maxilla not reaching below front edge of eye; canine teeth prominent; vomer tooth patch anchor-shaped, with posterior extension. Dorsal fin long, slightly notched, with 10 spines, 14 rays; anal fin angular in outline, with 3 spines, usually 9 rays; caudal fin emarginate. Usually 8–9 scales, counted diagonally, between dorsal fin origin and lateral line.

Habitat: Over rocks or natural and artificial reefs at depths of 30–330′ (9.2–101 m).

Range: NC to Yucatán; absent from Caribbean.

Similar Species: Caribbean Red Snapper (L. purpureus) has 8 anal fin rays and 10–11 scales between dorsal fin origin and lateral line; replaces Red Snapper in Caribbean.

Comments: This species was formerly known as Lutjanus aya. It accounts for a substantial part of the food fishery on the Gulf coast of the United States and Mexico. In the northeastern Gulf of Mexico, artificial reefs have been constructed to attract this and other fishes for sport fishing.

615 Gray Snapper
Lutjanus griseus

Description: To 3′ (91 cm), usually to 18″ (46 cm). Relatively slender. Gray or olive above, with reddish tinge or blotches; grayish or yellowish pink below; broad dark stripe usually extends from snout tip through eye toward dorsal fin; scales sometimes with orange centers, white-edged; no black spot on side below soft dorsal fin; edge of spiny dorsal fin red. Profile of head slightly concave; snout long, pointed; lower jaw projects slightly beyond upper; large pair of canine teeth in upper jaw; vomer tooth patch anchor-shaped, with posterior extension. Pectoral fin relatively short, not reaching anus; dorsal fin long, slightly notched, with 10 spines, *14 rays; anal fin rounded,* with 3 spines, 8 rays; caudal fin emarginate.

Habitat: Estuaries, mangrove swamps, around coral reefs, and over rocks from inshore to depths of about 540′ (165 m). Young and subadults inshore; occasionally in fresh water.

Range: MA to Rio de Janeiro, Brazil, including Bermuda, Bahamas, Gulf of Mexico, and Caribbean.

Similar Species: Cubera Snapper *(L. cyanopterus)* reaches length of 5′ (1.5 m) and weight of 125 lb (57 kg), is steely gray to dark brown, sometimes with purplish metallic reflections, and lacks posterior extension of vomer tooth patch; occurs in deeper offshore waters. Mutton Snapper *(L. analis)* has small but conspicuous black spot on side below soft dorsal fin and lacks posterior extension of vomer tooth patch. Mahogany Snapper *(L. mahogoni)* reaches length of 15″ (38 cm), and has larger spot on side, part of which is below lateral line, and 12 dorsal fin rays.

Comments: Gray Snapper is an excellent food fish.

616 Dog Snapper
Lutjanus jocu

Description: To 3′ (91 cm); 31 lb (14 kg). Deep; depth and head length each about one-third length. *Olive brown, with bronzy tinge above; pinkish below, with coppery cast;* no spots or bars on sides; *pale, narrow, triangular patch and row of blue dots beneath eye;* fins orange. Profile of head more or less straight from snout to nape; snout pointed; eye large; mouth terminal, slightly oblique; *large canine teeth in upper jaw visible when mouth closed;* vomer tooth patch anchor-shaped, with posterior extension. Dorsal fin long, slightly notched, with 10 spines, *14 rays; anal fin rounded,* with 3 spines, usually 8 rays; caudal fin emarginate or slightly forked. 8–11 scales, counted diagonally, between dorsal fin origin and lateral line.

Habitat: Around coral reefs in continental and
island shelf waters. Young inshore and
around estuaries; sometimes in low-
salinity waters.

Range: NC to Brazil, including n Gulf of
Mexico, Bahamas, Caribbean, and
Yucatán; seasonally north to MA;
supposedly introduced in Bermuda.

Similar Species: Schoolmaster *(L. apodus)* has yellow and
blue pigment on body, blue stripe below
eye (particularly well developed in
young) tending to be broken into series
of dots at larger body size, finer scales,
and lacks pale triangle beneath eye.

Comments: Dog Snapper is a voracious predator that
feeds mainly on fishes and bottom-
dwelling invertebrates. It has been
implicated in ciguatera poisoning.

---

602 Lane Snapper
Lutjanus synagris

Description: To 14″ (36 cm). Moderately deep.
Pinkish above, with green tinge, diffuse
dusky bars visible when resting; silvery
below, with yellow tinge; *8–10 yellow
or golden stripes on body, 3–4 on head;
prominent black spot between lateral line
and anterior soft dorsal fin,* lateral line
runs through bottom of spot; outer
edges of dorsal, anal, and pelvic fins
yellow; caudal fin light red. Snout
pointed; mouth rather large, canine
teeth not visible when mouth closed.
Dorsal fin slightly notched, with 10
spines, *12 rays;* anal fin rounded, with
3 spines, 8 rays.

Habitat: Continental and shallow island shelf
waters.

Range: NC to Brazil, including Bermuda,
Bahamas, Gulf of Mexico, and
Caribbean.

Similar Species: Mahogany Snapper *(L. mahogoni)*
reaches similar size, lacks yellow lines
on body, and lateral line runs through
middle of dark spot on upper posterior
part of back.

Comments: Lane Snapper is often found in large
schools. It is used as a food fish,
although it is less important than
most snappers because of its smaller
size.

603 Yellowtail Snapper
Ocyurus chrysurus

Description: To 30″ (76 cm); 5 lb (2.3 kg). *Fusiform;*
dorsal and ventral profiles evenly
rounded. Back and sides olive, blue, or
bluish gray, *with yellow spots; prominent
yellow mid-lateral stripe* begins on snout,
becoming progressively broader and
covering entire caudal peduncle; narrow
alternating reddish and pale yellow
stripes on lower sides and belly; *caudal
fin yellow.* Head and mouth relatively
small; *no canine teeth.* Dorsal fin long,
low, no discernible notch, with 10
spines, 12–13 rays; anal fin relatively
short, with 3 spines, 9 rays; *caudal fin
deeply forked.*

Habitat: Most common in coastal waters to
depths of about 60′ (18.5 m); usually
around coral reefs and over rocks.
Range: NC to s Brazil, including Bermuda,
Bahamas, Gulf of Mexico, and
Caribbean; seasonally north to MA,
possibly to Gulf of Maine. Also around
Cape Verde Islands in e Atlantic.
Comments: The schooling Yellowtail Snapper is an
excellent food fish. Evidence suggests
that the genera *Ocyurus* and *Lutjanus* are
very closely related, despite differences
in their appearance and habits.

TRIPLETAILS
Family Lobotidae

2 genera and about 7 species worldwide;
1 genus with 2 species in North America (1 Atlantic, 1 Pacific). Species in the genus *Lobotes* are marine, whereas those
in the genus *Datnoides* occur in Indo-Pacific fresh and brackish waters. The collective common name is derived from

the long rounded posterior dorsal and anal fin lobes that extend well beyond the base of the caudal fin, giving the appearance of three tails. The body is deep and compressed. The dorsal fin is very slightly notched, and has 12 stiff spines and 15 to 16 rays. There are two spines on the opercle, and the top of the head is scaled. The vomer and palatine bones are toothless. Adults float on their sides in the shade of flotsam; the young do the same, mimicking drifting leaves.

---

624   Atlantic Tripletail
Lobotes surinamensis

Description: To 3′4″ (1 m). Deep, compressed; *rounded caudal fin and long soft dorsal and anal fins give appearance of 3 tails.* Dark brown to bronzy to yellowish brown; often blotched or mottled, especially in young; pectoral fin pale, other fins dark. Teeth in jaws pointed; preopercle strongly serrate. Dorsal fin slightly notched; 3 anal fin spines. Scales embedded, adherent, strongly ctenoid.

Habitat: Inshore to offshore; bays and estuaries near buoys and channel markers.

Range: Cape Cod, MA, to Argentina, including Bermuda, Bahamas, Gulf of Mexico, and Caribbean; most abundant south of Cape Hatteras, NC. Records from FL northward mainly of young that drift north with Gulf Stream during summer.

Comments: Atlantic Tripletail is an excellent food fish; it can be taken around piers, pilings, wrecks, or flotsam using live shrimps for bait. It feeds primarily on crustaceans. Until recently, *Lobotes surinamensis* was thought to comprise a single worldwide species; now, however, records from the eastern Pacific are known to be based on a different species, Pacific Tripletail *(L. pacificus)*. In addition to the eastern Pacific species, populations elsewhere may be divisible into one or two additional species.

MOJARRAS
Family Gerreidae

8 genera and about 40 species world-wide; 4 genera and 12 species in North America (9 Atlantic, 2 Pacific, 1 shared), plus 10 species confined to Mexican waters. Members of this family occur in tropical and warm-temperate waters; they are mostly marine, but some species enter fresh water and a few are found there permanently. These usually small fishes are never brightly colored, but may have pigment patterns of tan and brown. They are covered with silvery scales; the scales are usually embedded and adherent, but are sometimes deciduous. The top of the head, cheek, and opercle are scaled. The body is moderately to deeply compressed, and the snout is pointed. The ventral

profile of the head is concave. The jaws are extremely protractile; this is made possible by long extensions of the premaxillary bone, which slip into a sheath that extends along the upper snout. When extended, the jaws point downward. A prominent axillary scale is present at the insertion of each pelvic fin. The dorsal fin, which has nine to 10 spines and nine to 17 rays, is interrupted by a shallow notch; it and the anal fin each fold into a deep sheath of scales. The anal fin has two to three (usually three) spines; the second spine is longest and often very stout. The caudal fin is deeply forked. Mojarras are bottom-dwelling fishes, usually less than 12″ (30 cm) long, and are found mostly in relatively shallow water over grass, sand, or other open bottoms, but seldom around reefs. Some species, particularly those in the genus *Eucinostomus,* are very similar in appearance and are difficult to identify.

protractile jaws

113, 611 Spotfin Mojarra
Eucinostomus argenteus

Description: To 8″ (20 cm). Oblong, compressed. Silvery; grayish green when viewed from above; dusky oblique bars or stripes; tips of dorsal fin spines dusky (especially noticeable in young). Jaws extremely protractile; *premaxillary groove constricted but not completely interrupted by transverse row of scales, groove acutely triangular in*

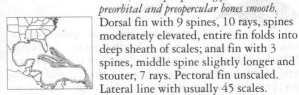

outline, with apex pointing forward;
preorbital and preopercular bones smooth.
Dorsal fin with 9 spines, 10 rays, spines
moderately elevated, entire fin folds into
deep sheath of scales; anal fin with 3
spines, middle spine slightly longer and
stouter, 7 rays. Pectoral fin unscaled.
Lateral line with usually 45 scales.

Habitat: Coastal waters over shallow sand flats;
absent from reefs; does not enter fresh
water.

Range: NJ to se Brazil, including Bermuda,
Bahamas, Gulf of Mexico, and
Caribbean.

Similar Species: Mottled Mojarra *(E. lefroyi)* has 2 anal
fin spines. Bigeye Mojarra *(E. havana)*
has scaled pectoral fin. Flagfin Mojarra
(E. melanopterus) has tricolored spiny
dorsal fin, with jet black tip and pale
center. Silver Jenny *(E. gula)* has deeper
body, rectangular premaxillary groove
interrupted anteriorly by transverse row
of scales, and usually 43–44 lateral line
scales. Slender Mojarra *(E. jonesii)* has
more slender body, narrow, straight,
open premaxillary groove not
interrupted by transverse row of scales,
and usually 47 lateral line scales.
Tidewater Mojarra *(E. harengulus)* has
less intensely pigmented top of snout
and broad open premaxillary groove not
interrupted anteriorly by row of
transverse scales; enters fresh water.

Comments: The downward-directed, extremely
protractile jaws enable this and other
mojarras to feed on bottom-dwelling
invertebrates. Western Atlantic species
of the genus *Eucinostomus* are generally
very similar in appearance. Those closely
related to Spotfin Mojarra have posed
special difficulties (particularly Slender
and Tidewater Mojarras), and only
recently have characteristics been
identified that allow separation of these
species. Spotfin Mojarra was also once
considered to occur in the eastern Pacific
Ocean, but that population is now
recognized as a separate species, Pacific
Spotfin Mojarra *(E. dowii)*.

612 Striped Mojarra
Eugerres plumieri

Description: To 12″ (30 cm). Deep, compressed. Dark
olive above; tan to silvery on sides, often
with metallic sheen; *about 12 conspicuous
stripes along centers of scale rows on sides,*
except toward belly; all fins except
pectoral fin dusky in large adults; pelvic
and anal fins sometimes dark orange;
pelvic fin spine and first 2 anal fin
spines pale. Ventral profile of head
concave; snout pointed; jaws extremely
protractile; preorbital bone serrate.
*Dorsal fin highly elevated, not obviously
notched,* with 9 spines, 10 rays, *posterior
edge deeply and evenly rounded;* anal fin
with 3 spines, *second spine long and
extremely stout,* 8 rays. Lateral line with
usually 34–36 pored scales.

Habitat: Usually grassy brackish coastal waters;
enters fresh water in areas with
underlying limestone substrate.

Range: SC to Brazil, including Gulf of Mexico
and much of Caribbean; absent from
Bermuda, Bahamas, and smaller islands
in West Indies.

Similar Species: Yellowfin Mojarra *(Gerres cinereus)* has
7–8 dark bluish or pinkish bars on sides,
yellow pelvic fin, and shorter and
weaker dorsal and anal fin spines. Irish
Pompano *(Diapterus auratus)* lacks
lateral stripes and has smooth preorbital
bone. Species of genus *Eucinostomus* have
less deep and less compressed body
without lateral stripes, less elevated
dorsal fin, and weaker second anal fin
spine.

Comments: This species has often been included in
the genus *Diapterus* in past literature
references.

607 Yellowfin Mojarra
Gerres cinereus

Description: To 16″ (41 cm). Deep, compressed.
*Silvery, with 7–8 dark bluish or pinkish
straight bars on sides; fins yellow;* dorsal

and caudal fins dusky. Jaws extremely protractile; maxilla barely reaches eye; posterior part of premaxillary groove broad. *Pectoral fin reaches anal fin origin;* dorsal fin slightly notched; dorsal and anal fin each with sheath of scales at base; anal fin with 3 spines, second spine moderately enlarged.

Habitat: Shallow coastal waters; usually over open sand in surf zone, mangrove channels, and sea-grass beds near coral reefs.

Range: Bermuda, Bahamas, ne FL to TX, and Caribbean to Rio de Janeiro, Brazil. Also in e Pacific from Mexico to Peru.

Comments: Yellowfin Mojarra is the only western Atlantic mojarra that has yellow fins and straight dark bars on the sides. No other western Atlantic species in the family is likely to be seen around coral reefs. Reef-dwelling individuals have pinkish bars on the sides. This species feeds primarily on crustaceans and worms that it grubs from bottom sediments.

GRUNTS
Family Haemulidae

17 genera and about 150 species world-wide; 7 genera and 21 species in North America (16 Atlantic, 5 Pacific), plus 24 species confined to Mexican waters. These perch-like fishes occur in a variety of habitats in tropical and subtropical coastal marine waters around the world; a few species regularly enter fresh water, and a small number occur in temperate waters. They have oblong bodies with relatively large heads. The continuous dorsal fin is shallowly notched, and the caudal fin is moderately forked. Two small pores are located under the chin. Ctenoid scales cover the body, opercle, cheeks, and the area between the mouth and eyes. These fishes have teeth in the jaws and on the pharyngeal bones, but none on the roof of the mouth. The maxilla slips under the preorbital bone when the mouth is closed, giving grunts a characteristic smiling appearance. The inside of the mouth is orangish red in most Atlantic species. The young of most species have a dark stripe along the mid-side of the body that ends in a caudal spot. Members of this family produce a grunting sound by rubbing the pharyngeal teeth together, hence their common

name. Some species pair in a peculiar "kissing" display, the reason for which is unknown. Past literature references classified this family as the Pomadasyidae.

601 Porkfish
Anisotremus virginicus

Description: To 15″ (38 cm). Deep, compressed. Alternating silvery blue and yellow stripes on sides; *black stripe extends diagonally from chin through eye to nape, another from below first dorsal fin spine to pectoral fin base;* pelvic and spiny dorsal fins dusky to black, other fins yellow. Young have large dark spot near caudal fin base; lack black stripes. Head short; snout blunt; mouth small, with thick lips; preopercle finely serrate. Dorsal fin with 12–13 spines, 17 rays; anal fin with 3 spines, middle spine longer and stouter, 10 rays. *Bases of soft dorsal and anal fins scaled. Lateral line with 56–60 scales.*

Habitat: Shallow waters over reefs or rocks.

Range: FL to Brazil, including Bermuda, Bahamas, e and s Gulf of Mexico, and Caribbean.

Similar Species: Black Margate (*A. surinamensis*) has silvery gray body without bright coloration or dark bands on head.

Comments: The adult Porkfish feeds on a variety of invertebrates. The young are popular aquarium fish and are known to pick parasites from the skin of larger fish.

605 Tomate
Haemulon aurolineatum

Description: To 10″ (25 cm). Oblong, compressed. Silvery white; head dusky; *broad bronze to yellow stripe extends from eye to dusky spot at caudal fin base,* spot particularly obvious in young; narrow yellow stripe just above lateral line; mouth red inside; fins chalky to light gray. Snout pointed; maxilla reaches beyond middle of eye;

upper jaw extends beyond lower; 24–28 (usually 26–27) gill rakers on outer arch. *Dorsal fin with 13 spines,* 14–15 rays; anal fin with 3 spines, 9 rays. Usually 22 rows of scales around caudal peduncle; scales above and below lateral line of about equal size.

Habitat: Sea-grass beds and sand flats at night, near coral reefs during day; to depths of about 100′ (30 m).

Range: Chesapeake Bay to Brazil, including Bermuda, Bahamas, Gulf of Mexico, and Caribbean; seasonally north to MA.

Similar Species: Striped Grunt *(H. striatum)* also has 13 dorsal fin spines (all other w Atlantic species in genus have 12), and has 27–36 gill rakers and at least 24 scales around caudal peduncle; occurs over reefs to depths of about 324′ (99 m). French Grunt *(H. flavolineatum)* has bright yellow to orange stripes below lateral line, and scales below lateral line are larger than those above.

Comments: Tomtate seems to be the dominant species of *Haemulon* along the eastern coast of Florida, and it is common over shrimp grounds in the Tortugas and around reefs and oil platforms in the Gulf of Mexico. The specific name, *aurolineatum,* refers to the golden lateral stripe. Adults of the various species of *Haemulon* congregate around coral reefs during the day, and feed at night over grassy areas or other open bottoms; the young occur primarily in sea-grass beds in bays and other coastal waters.

594 French Grunt
Haemulon flavolineatum

Description: To 12″ (30 cm). Oblong, compressed. Yellow above; *many bright yellow to orange stripes below lateral line, top 3 stripes straight, others oblique;* creamy to white below; yellow spots on lower head; fins yellow. Young have oblong dark spot at caudal fin base not connected to dusky lateral stripe. Usually 23 gill rakers on

outer arch. *Dorsal fin with 12 spines,*
14–15 rays; anal fin with 3 spines, 8
rays. Pectoral fin scaled; usually 22 rows
of scales around caudal peduncle; *scales
below lateral line larger than those above, in
oblique rows.*

Habitat: Sea-grass beds and sand flats at night,
near coral reefs during day; to depths of
about 100′ (30 m).

Range: FL to Brazil, including Bermuda,
Bahamas, Gulf of Mexico, and
Caribbean.

Similar Species: Other North American *Haemulon* species
lack oblique yellow to orange stripes on
body. Tomtate *(H. aurolineatum)* and
Striped Grunt *(H. striatum)* have 13
dorsal fin spines; Striped Grunt occurs
over reefs to depths of about 324′ (99
m). Margate *(H. album)* has 12 dorsal fin
spines and 23–26 rows of scales around
caudal peduncle. Cottonwick *(H.
melanurum)* has 12 dorsal fin spines and
23–26 rows of scales around caudal
peduncle, and back, upper half of caudal
peduncle, and caudal fin are black.
Smallmouth Grunt *(H. chrysargyreum)*
has smaller mouth, usually 13 dorsal fin
rays, and 29–43 gill rakers on outer
arch. Sailors Choice *(H. parra)* has
17–18 dorsal fin rays and scales on more
than one-third of pectoral fin.
Bluestriped Grunt *(H. sciurus)* has pale
blue stripes on head and body. White
Grunt *(H. plumierii)* has alternating blue
and bronze stripes on head.

Comments: This is one of the most common and
obvious species of *Haemulon* in reef
habitats in the tropical western Atlantic.

595 White Grunt
Haemulon plumierii

Description: To 16″ (41 cm). Oblong, compressed.
Light yellowish or bronze; *alternating
blue and bronze stripes on head;* black
blotch often beneath edge of preopercle;
mouth red inside; paired fins pale; dorsal
fin chalky or yellowish white; anal and

caudal fins grayish brown; *each scale has white or blue spot and bronze edge.* Snout long, pointed; mouth terminal; maxilla reaches eye; 25 gill rakers. Dorsal fin with 12 spines, 15–17 rays; anal fin with 3 spines, 9 rays. Soft dorsal and anal fins scaled; usually 22 rows of scales around caudal peduncle; *scales above lateral line larger than those below.*

Habitat: Sea-grass beds and sand flats at night; near coral reefs during day.

Range: Chesapeake Bay to Brazil, including Bahamas, Gulf of Mexico, and Caribbean; absent from Bermuda.

Similar Species: Bluestriped Grunt *(H. sciurus)* has pale blue stripes on head and body and scales of equal size above and below lateral line; occurs over reefs to depths of about 96′ (29 m). Striped Grunt *(H. striatum)* has slender yellow body with 4 dark brown stripes; occurs over reefs to depths of about 324′ (99 m).

Comments: White Grunt, like other grunts, displays "kissing" behavior; that is, two individuals will face each other and push with open mouths.

PORGIES
Family Sparidae

29 genera and about 100 species worldwide; 6 genera and 16 species in North America (15 Atlantic, 1 Pacific), plus 2 species confined to Mexican waters and 2 species sometimes entering coastal fresh waters in Florida. Porgies have oblong compressed bodies and large steep heads. The mouth is small and terminal; the maxilla is covered by a sheath when the mouth is closed, and never reaches beyond the middle of the eye. The opercle is scaled, but has no spines or serrations. The teeth are well developed, and include incisors or canines in the front of the jaws and molars in the sides. Most North American porgies have a slit-like posterior nostril. The pectoral fins are long. The continuous dorsal fin usually has 10 to 13 spines and 10 to 15 rays. The anal fin has three spines and eight to 14 rays. Some porgies live over hard bottoms, others over mud; a few species are sometimes found around coral reefs, but this is not the usual habitat. Practically all porgies occur inshore, but some are found in brackish or fresh waters.

462 Sheepshead
Archosargus probatocephalus

Description: To 3' (91 cm); 20 lb (9 kg). Deep, compressed. Gray; 5–6 *slightly diagonal dark bars on body, 1 on nape,* with slightly wider pale interspaces; bars darker in young than adults. Profile of head very steep; snout pointed; mouth terminal; *broad incisor teeth in front jaws;* 3 rows of lateral molar-like teeth on sides of upper jaw, 2 rows in lower jaw. Pectoral fin long; dorsal fin continuous, with 12 spines, 10–12 rays, preceded by small, forward-directed spine embedded in skin; anal fin with 3 spines, 10–11 rays.

Habitat: Shallow waters over mud or oyster beds; frequently around piers and piles of bridges; occasionally enters fresh water.

Range: Cape Cod, MA, to Brazil, including Gulf of Mexico and Caribbean coast; occasionally north to NS; absent from Bermuda, Bahamas, and West Indies.

Similar Species: Sea Bream *(A. rhomboidalis),* the only other North American *Archosargus* species, has numerous narrow bronze stripes on body and dark blotch on shoulder; occurs around mangrove shorelines and in brackish water.

Comments: This excellent food fish is a bottom dweller; it forms feeding groups but does not school. The stout dorsal and anal fin spines can cause punctures. It should not be confused with a North American freshwater species in the drum and croaker family (Sciaenidae), Freshwater Drum *(Aplodinotus grunniens),* which is called Sheepshead in the Great Lakes region.

---

690 Jolthead Porgy
Calamus bajonado

Description: To 27" (69 cm); 8 lb (3.6 kg). Deep, compressed, oblong. *Brassy or silvery; blue stripe below eye; 2 white stripes on each cheek;* lower jaw and corner of mouth orange; *centers of scales shiny blue.* Profile of head moderately steep; snout bluntly pointed; eye midway between snout and dorsal fin origin; posterior nostril slit-like; mouth terminal; maxilla not reaching eye; *teeth slender, canine-like in front of jaw,* molar-like on sides. *Pectoral fin long, with 15 rays;* dorsal fin continuous, with 12 spines, usually 12 rays; anal fin with 3 short spines, 10 rays. *Lateral line with 51–57 scales.*

Habitat: Along coast around coral reefs, over coralline sand, or in tidal creeks; usually at depths of 20–150′ (6–46 m), sometimes to 600′ (183 m) or more.

Range: NC to Brazil, including Bermuda, Bahamas, most of Gulf of Mexico, and Caribbean; seasonally north to RI.

Similar Species: Sheepshead Porgy *(C. penna)* has fewer than 49 lateral line scales; occurs over reefs or sea-grass beds to depths of 250′ (76 m). Grass Porgy *(C. arctifrons)* and Whitebone Porgy *(C. leucosteus)* have 16 pectoral fin rays and fewer than 49 lateral line scales; Grass Porgy occurs in shallow sea-grass beds; Whitebone Porgy occurs along coast, sometimes near reefs. Saucereye Porgy *(C. calamus),* Knobbed Porgy *(C. nodosus),* and Littlehead Porgy *(C. proridens)* have 14 pectoral fin rays; Knobbed Porgy occurs over hard bottoms at depths of 23–300′ (7–91 m). Red Porgy *(Pagrus pagrus)* has reddish body and oval posterior nostril; occurs over open bottoms in continental shelf waters to depths of 656′ (200 m).

Comments: Jolthead Porgy is one of the largest porgies. It feeds on hard-bodied invertebrates such as sea urchins and crabs. The sharp front teeth are used to dislodge mollusks and crustaceans that are then crushed with the strong molar-like teeth.

691 **Saucereye Porgy**
Calamus calamus

Description: To 16″ (41 cm). Deep, oval, depth about half of length. *Silver, with bluish reflections;*

bony
tubercle

alternating brassy and pearly or bluish stripes; *deep blue streak below eye;* cheek blue, with yellowish spots creating net-like pattern. Anterior profile of head steep; snout rather long; bony tubercle opposite eye; posterior nostril slit-like; maxilla not reaching eye; teeth slender, canine-like in front of jaw, molar-like on sides. Pectoral fin large, with 14 rays; dorsal fin continuous, third and fourth spines longest; anal fin with 3 spines, 11 rays. Lateral line with 51–55 scales.

Habitat: Over hard bottoms or near reefs to depths of 240′ (73 m). Young in sea-grass beds.

Range: NC to Brazil, including Bermuda, Bahamas, ne and se Gulf of Mexico, and Caribbean.

Similar Species: Knobbed Porgy *(C. nodosus)* has deeper body and head with steeper profile.

Comments: This and other species in the genus *Calamus* contribute significantly to the commercial fishing industry in southern Florida and in the West Indies. Like most other porgies, Saucereye Porgy produces free-floating eggs and gives no parental care.

---

599 Pinfish
Lagodon rhomboides

Description: To 15″ (38 cm). Oval, compressed. *Silvery sheen overall; back olive; sides bluish, with straight to wavy yellow stripes and 5–6 faint dusky bars; dark spot on shoulder, centered on lateral line; fins yellow; no dark blotch on caudal peduncle.* Profile of head slightly concave at eye; snout relatively short, rather pointed; posterior nostril oval; mouth terminal; maxilla just reaches eye; front teeth strongly flat, incisor-like, deeply notched; side teeth molar-like, 2½ rows in each jaw. Pectoral fin long; dorsal fin continuous, with 12 spines, 11 rays, preceded by tiny, forward-directed spine; anal fin with 3 spines, 11 rays.

Habitat: Primarily shallow waters, often around vegetation; enters fresh water in a few coastal areas of w FL.

Range: Cape Cod, MA, south along coast to Yucatán; possibly including n Cuba and Andros Island, Bahamas; generally absent from insular areas.

Similar Species: Spottail Pinfish *(Diplodus holbrookii)* and Silver Porgy *(D. argenteus)* both have large prominent dark blotch on caudal peduncle. Longspine Porgy *(Stenotomus caprinus)* has much deeper body and very long dorsal fin spines. Scup *(S. chrysops)* lacks bars and spot on shoulder, and anterior dorsal fin spines are much shorter. Sea Bream *(Archosargus rhomboidalis)* has dark blotch on shoulder centered below (rather than on) lateral line; occurs around mangrove shorelines and enters brackish water.

Comments: This is a very common porgy, but because of its small size it is seldom used as food. Its greatest value is as forage for larger fishes.

THREADFINS
Family Polynemidae

7 genera and 33 species worldwide; 1 genus with 5 species in North America (3 Atlantic, 2 Pacific). Members of this family occur in shallow tropical to warm-temperate marine and brackish waters; four species, none in North America, are found in fresh water. The young are pelagic. Most threadfins are small to medium fishes less than 18″ (46 cm) long; one Indo-Pacific species reaches a length of 6′ (1.8 m). Each subabdominal pelvic fin has a single spine and five rays. Each pectoral fin is divided into two segments, the upper with attached rays and the lower with three to 15 long unattached rays. The dorsal fin is widely separated into spiny and soft-rayed segments, and the caudal fin is deeply forked. The mouth is on the underside of the head. Threadfins are important food fishes in some parts of world, but not in North America.

Atlantic Threadfin
Polydactylus octonemus

Description: To 12″ (30 cm). Moderately deep, compressed, tapering; caudal peduncle relatively deep. Generally silvery;

Atlantic Threadfin

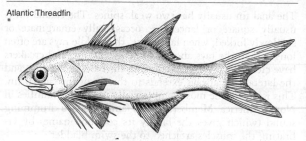

somewhat dusky above; upper pectoral fin sometimes dark, especially in adults. *Pectoral fin with 8 free rays;* dorsal fin with 8 spines, 12–13 rays; anal fin with 3 spines, 13–15 rays. Lateral line with about 70 scales.

Habitat: Shallow nearshore waters over sand or mud; often in surf zone.

Range: Continental shorelines from NY to Yucatán.

Similar Species: Barbu *(P. virginicus)* has 7 free rays in lower pectoral fin, 15 rays in upper pectoral fin, and 53–63 lateral line scales. Littlescale Threadfin *(P. oligodon)* has 7 free rays in lower pectoral fin, 16 rays in upper pectoral fin, and 68–74 lateral line scales.

Comments: Atlantic Threadfin and its relatives feed mostly on bottom invertebrates.

DRUMS AND CROAKERS
Family Sciaenidae

70 genera and about 270 species worldwide; 18 genera and 32 species in North America (23 Atlantic, 8 Pacific, 1 restricted to fresh water), plus 5 genera and 43 species confined to Mexican waters (2 Atlantic, 41 Pacific). Family members occur in tropical and temperate waters; one North American species, the only species in the genus *Aplodinotus,* is restricted to fresh water. These elongate and moderately compressed fishes occur in a variety of habitats, but most are bottom dwellers that live close to shore over open sand or mud. They often have chin and rostral pores, and some have chin barbels. The top of the head in some species is very cavernous. Teeth are present in the jaws, but absent on the roof of the mouth; some species have molar-like teeth on the pharyngeal bones. The dorsal fin is divided into two segments, separated by a distinct notch.

The anal fin usually has two weak spines. The caudal fin is usually square or lanceolate, occasionally emarginate or shallowly forked; when lanceolate, the middle rays are often longer than the rays above and below. Drums and croakers have ctenoid scales, often covering the bases of the fins, and the lateral line always extends to the tip of the caudal fin. This is one of the most commercially important families in North America. Members of this family make a drumming sound (which gives the family its common name) by vibrating the muscles attached to the swim bladder.

114 Freshwater Drum
Aplodinotus grunniens

caudal fin of adult

Description: To 35" (89 cm); 55 lb (25 kg). Oblong, robust; greatest depth at dorsal fin origin. *Silvery bluish above; sides silvery;* whitish below; pectoral fin whitish, median fins dusky. Mouth ventral. *Outer ray of pelvic fin an elongate filament;* dorsal fin deeply notched, with 10 spines, *26–32 rays; anal fin with 2 spines, second spine enlarged,* 7 rays; caudal fin pointed in young, moderately pointed to rounded in adults. Scaly sheath at dorsal fin base. Lateral line extends to tip of caudal fin.

Habitat: Small to large rivers with slow to moderate current; deeper waters of lakes and reservoirs.

Range: Hudson Bay drainage in e MB and s SK; St. Lawrence River and s Great Lakes; Mississippi River drainage; Gulf coast drainages from AL west to TX and south to Guatemala.

Comments: Freshwater Drum, the only North American member of the family restricted to fresh water, has the widest distribution in latitude of any freshwater fish in the United States and Canada. It is fished commercially and for sport throughout much of its range. This species is known as Sheepshead in the Great Lakes region, but it should not be confused with the primarily saltwater species Sheepshead *(Archosargus probatocephalus),* in the porgy family (Sparidae).

558 White Seabass
Atractoscion nobilis

Description: To 5′ (1.5 m); 90 lb (41 kg). Fusiform, elongate, slightly compressed. Bluish gray above; silvery below; black spot at pectoral fin base. Young to 2′ (61 cm) long have 3–6 dusky bars on side and dusky yellow fins. *No large canine teeth in middle of upper jaw;* pores on snout and chin; no chin barbels. Dorsal fin with 9–10 spines, 19–23 rays, segments slightly joined by membrane; anal fin with 2 spines, 8–10 rays, base less than half length of soft dorsal fin base. Lateral line extends to tip of caudal fin.

Habitat: Usually over rocks and in kelp beds from shore to depths of 400′ (122 m). Young in bays and along sandy beaches.

Range: Juneau, AK, to Bahía Magdalena, Baja California, and upper Gulf of California; rare north of s CA.

Comments: White Seabass spawns from April to August, congregating inshore. This large species is an important sport and commercial fish. It feeds on squids, sardines, and anchovies. White Seabass migrates north along the coast in the spring, returns south in the fall, and generally spends the winter off Baja California. It is sometimes placed in the closely related genus *Cynoscion.*

575 Silver Perch
Bairdiella chrysoura

Description: To 12″ (30 cm). Oblong, compressed. Silvery; darker above; *obscure dark stripes along scale rows on sides, especially on upper body; parallel stripes on posterior body;* pelvic, dorsal, anal, and caudal fins pale yellowish. Top of head not cavernous; mouth large, usually terminal or nearly so; no enlarged teeth; no chin barbels; *edge of preopercle with distinct strong spines at angle.* Dorsal fin with 10–11 spines, *19–23 (usually 20–22) rays;* anal fin with 2 spines, second spine moderately long and strong, 8–10 (usually 9) rays. Lateral line extends to tip of caudal fin.

Habitat: Open shorelines in shallow waters over sand or mud.

Range: NY to s FL, and e and n Gulf of Mexico to n Mexico.

Similar Species: Striped Croaker *(B. sanctaeluciae)* has darker, more prominent stripes slanting sharply upward below notch in dorsal fin, usually 22–24 dorsal fin rays, and shorter and weaker second anal fin spine. Blue Croaker *(B. batabana)* has distinctive bluish-gray cast overall, dark stripes confined to below lateral line, and 25–29 dorsal fin rays. Reef Croaker *(Odontoscion dentex)* has generally darker body, black spot at pectoral fin base, and slightly enlarged teeth in upper and lower jaws. White Perch *(Morone americana),* in temperate bass family (Moronidae), has shallowly forked tail and lateral line not extending to tip of caudal fin.

Comments: Silver Perch is one of the species most frequently caught by anglers from piers and wharfs. It is too small to be of much value as a food fish.

---

571 Spotted Seatrout
Cynoscion nebulosus

Description: To 28″ (71 cm); 16 lb (7.3 kg). Fusiform, elongate, moderately compressed. Dark gray above, with bluish iridescence; silvery below; *black spots extend onto dorsal and caudal fins;* spiny dorsal fin dusky, other fins pale yellowish. Mouth oblique; upper jaw reaches beyond eye; lower jaw projects beyond upper; *2 large canine teeth in front of upper jaw; no barbels or pores on chin;* edge of preopercle smooth. Dorsal fin deeply notched into separate segments, with 10 spines, 24–26 rays, base much longer than anal fin base; anal fin with 2 spines, 10–11 rays; caudal fin truncate or emarginate. Scales large; *soft dorsal fin unscaled.* Lateral line extends to tip of caudal fin.

Habitat: Mostly in shallow coastal waters over sand. Young in estuaries, tidal mud flats, sea-grass beds, and salt marshes.

Range: Cape Cod, MA, to FL; Gulf of Mexico from w FL to Laguna Madre, Mexico; absent from Caribbean.

Comments: Spotted Seatrout is also known as Speck. It is a valued food and sport fish, especially around the barrier islands off Florida and the Gulf coast.

572 Silver Seatrout
Cynoscion nothus

Description: To 14″ (36 cm). Fusiform, elongate, moderately compressed. Grayish above; silvery below; *no conspicuous markings; dorsal fin dusky, other fins pale. Maxilla reaches middle of eye;* 2 large canine teeth in upper jaw; no barbels or pores on chin. Dorsal fin deeply notched, with 10 spines, 27–29 rays; anal fin with 2 spines, 8–10 (usually 9) rays; caudal fin truncate or *with rounded lower lobe, longer than upper lobe. Scales extend beyond basal half of soft dorsal fin.* Lateral line extends to tip of caudal fin.

Habitat: Offshore over sand to depths of more than 36′ (11 m); enters inshore waters and bays during winter.

Range: Chesapeake Bay to FL and sw TX; occasionally north to NY.

Similar Species: Sand Seatrout *(C. arenarius)* has 25–27 (usually 26) dorsal fin rays and 10–12 (usually 11) anal fin rays.

Comments: Silver Seatrout is used for pet food. It is not of much interest to anglers due to its relatively small size and because it occupies deep waters well outside the reach of the cane-pole angler.

570 Weakfish
Cynoscion regalis

Description: To 35″ (89 cm); 17½ lb (8 kg). Fusiform, elongate, moderately compressed. Greenish olive above; *small irregular*

dark dots on back form oblique streaks on
scale rows; sides iridescent; silvery below;
pelvic and anal fins usually yellow; other
fins dusky, yellow-tinged. Mouth
oblique; lower jaw protrudes; maxilla
reaches posterior edge of eye; 2 large
canine teeth in upper jaw; no barbels or
pores on chin or lower jaw; 14–17 gill
rakers on outer arch; edge of preopercle
smooth. Dorsal fin with 10 spines,
24–29 (usually 26–27) rays; anal fin
with 2 spines, 10–13 (usually 12) rays;
caudal fin truncate or emarginate. Basal
half of soft dorsal fin scaled. Lateral line
extends to tip of caudal fin.

Habitat: Shallow coastal waters over sand or mud;
summer feeding and nursery grounds in
estuaries.

Range: NS to FL; most abundant from NJ to
Chesapeake Bay.

Similar Species: The closely related Sand Seatrout (C.
arenarius) has fainter spots on body and
fins, 12–14 gill rakers on outer arch,
and usually 11 anal fin rays. Spotted
Seatrout (C. nebulosus) has fewer and
more distinct dark spots on body and
fins and 24–26 dorsal fin rays. Silver
Seatrout (C. nothus) lacks conspicuous
spots on body and fins.

Comments: Weakfish is an important sport and
commercial fish. The majority caught by
anglers are up to 18″ (46 cm) long.

390 Jackknife-fish
Equetus lanceolatus

Description: To 10″ (25 cm). Compressed, deep
anteriorly; tapering to narrow caudal
peduncle. Light-colored, with 3 broad dark
stripes or bands, each bordered by thin silvery
stripes: first band through eye, second
obliquely from forehead to pelvic fin
base; third (longest and most obvious)
from spiny dorsal fin lengthwise to end
of caudal fin; broad dark band on
leading edges of pelvic and spiny dorsal
fins. Profile of head very steep; mouth
small, inferior; no enlarged teeth in

jaws. *Spiny dorsal fin very tall;* caudal fin pointed. Lateral line extends to tip of caudal fin.

Habitat: Relatively shallow waters around coral reefs and over mud or rocks.

Range: SC to Brazil, including Bahamas, e and sw Gulf of Mexico, and Caribbean; absent from Bermuda.

Similar Species: Spotted Drum (*E. punctatus*) has principal dark stripe on body and spiny dorsal fin extending only to caudal fin base, and numerous white spots on soft dorsal, anal, and caudal fins.

Comments: Small individuals have an especially tall spiny dorsal fin; that of a 3″ (7.5 cm) specimen is as high as the fish is long. Jackknife-fish is valued as an aquarium fish.

---

580 White Croaker
Genyonemus lineatus

Description: To 16″ (41 cm), usually to 12″ (30 cm). Relatively deep and compressed, tapering. Silvery above, sometimes brassy, with dark speckles; lighter below; *indistinct wavy lines along scale rows;* fins white to yellowish; *usually small black spot at top of pectoral fin base;* caudal fin usually dark-edged. Snout projects slightly beyond mouth; upper jaw projects beyond lower; chin barbels minute or absent. *Dorsal fin with 12–16 spines,* 18–25 rays; anal fin with 1–2 spines, 10–12 rays. Lateral line extends to tip of caudal fin.

Habitat: Inshore waters and bays, usually to depths of 100′ (30 m); occasionally to 600′ (183 m).

Range: Barkley Sound, BC, to s Baja California; rare north of CA.

Similar Species: California Corbina (*Menticirrhus undulatus*) has 1 chin barbel. Yellowfin Croaker (*Umbrina roncador*) has dark wavy lines on body and 1 chin barbel. Spotfin Croaker (*Roncador stearnsii*) has large black spot at pectoral fin base. Black Croaker (*Cheilotrema saturnum*) has black on upper rear gill cover.

Comments: No other Pacific croaker has more than 11 dorsal fin spines. This species and White Seabass *(Atractoscion nobilis)* are the only croakers found north of central California. White Croaker often occurs in schools. It is an important sport and commercial fish, and is commonly caught from piers and boats.

576 **Spot**
Leiostomus xanthurus

Description: To 14″ (36 cm). Short, deep; back elevated. Bluish to brownish above, with *12–15 diagonal, straight, narrow dark bars on back; distinct brownish spot on shoulder* just behind edge of upper gill slit; sides brassy; silvery to white below. Mouth low; teeth not prominent; *no chin barbels;* 30–36 gill rakers on outer arch. Dorsal fin with 9–11 spines, 29–35 rays; anal fin with 2 spines, 12–13 rays; *caudal fin shallowly forked.* Lateral line extends to tip of caudal fin.

Habitat: Open shorelines in shallow waters over sand or mud.

Range: MA to n Mexico; absent from s FL.

Similar Species: Atlantic Croaker *(Micropogonias undulatus)* lacks distinct spot on shoulder, and has 20–22 irregular bars on back, numerous chin barbels, 26–30 dorsal fin rays, 7–9 anal fin rays, and weakly lanceolate caudal fin.

Comments: This is the only drum in North America with a shallowly forked caudal fin. It is a popular food fish.

569 **Northern Kingfish**
Menticirrhus saxatilis

Description: To 20″ (51 cm); 2¼ lb (1 kg). Fusiform, elongate, moderately compressed. Dusky; darker above; belly almost white; *7–8 intensely dark oblique bands on sides; V-shaped mark on shoulder;* gill cavity lining dusky; pectoral fin dusky, black-edged; pelvic, anal, and caudal fins dusky, sometimes yellow-tinged; spiny dorsal fin dusky, apex black; soft dorsal fin plain. Snout conical; mouth small, horizontal, inferior; no enlarged teeth in jaws; *1 short stout chin barbel.* Dorsal fin with 9–10 spines, usually 22–27 rays, spiny dorsal fin extends beyond base of soft dorsal fin when depressed; anal fin with 1 spine, *usually 8 rays.* Scales small, adherent; scales on breast about as large as lateral line scales. Lateral line extends to tip of caudal fin.

Habitat: Over sand, mud, or silt to depths of 60′ (18.5 m). Young typically in surf zone in water no more than a few inches deep.

Range: MA to Yucatán.

Similar Species: Southern Kingfish *(M. americanus)* has faint bars on body, lacks obvious V-shaped mark on shoulder, and has usually 7 anal fin rays. Gulf Kingfish *(M. littoralis)* has silvery body, smaller breast scales, and 19–26 dorsal fin rays.

Comments: Northern Kingfish is one of several kingfishes known as Ground Mullet. This tasty fish is caught by bait-casting in the surf.

578 Atlantic Croaker
Micropogonias undulatus

Description: To 24″ (61 cm); 4 lb (1.8 kg). Moderately elongate, compressed. Dusky bluish or grayish above; silvery bronze below; small brownish dots form about 20 irregular oblique bars on sides and 1–2 horizontal rows on soft dorsal fin; other fins clear or pale yellowish. Top of head not cavernous; snout conical; *mouth small,* slightly oblique, inferior; no enlarged teeth in jaws; *3–5 pairs of minute barbels and 5 pores on chin;* preopercle serrate, with strong spines at angle. Dorsal fin with 2 spines, 26–30 (usually 28–29) rays; anal fin with 2 spines, 7–9 (usually 8) rays; caudal fin weakly lanceolate in adults. 8–9 scales in vertical series between dorsal fin origin and lateral line. Lateral line extends to tip of caudal fin.

Habitat: Coastal waters and estuaries over mud
            or sand; enters fresh water.

Range: Cape Cod, MA, to Yucatán; not common
            north of NJ or in s FL.

Similar Species: Spot *(Leiostomus xanthurus)* lacks chin
            barbels, and has 12–15 straight bars on
            back, 29–35 dorsal fin rays, 12–13 anal
            fin rays, shallowly forked caudal fin, and
            distinct spot on shoulder.

Comments: In the southern part of its range,
            Atlantic Croaker matures in one year
            and lives another one or two years; in the
            north, it matures later and lives longer.
            Important commercially, it is taken by
            the thousands of tons. This species is
            known to ascend well into Florida's St.
            Johns River.

581 Reef Croaker
Odontoscion dentex

Description: To 10″ (25 cm). Oblong, compressed.
            *Brownish silver; dark dots on scales; large
            black blotch at pectoral fin base.* Top of
            head not cavernous; *mouth terminal,
            oblique;* maxilla reaches posterior edge
            of eye; teeth large, conical, 1 row in
            each jaw; no chin barbels; 19–26 long
            gill rakers on outer arch. Dorsal fin
            with 11–12 spines, 23–26 rays; anal
            fin with 2 spines, 8–9 rays; caudal
            fin truncate. Lateral line extends to
            tip of caudal fin.

Habitat: Shallow waters around rocks or coral
            reefs.

Range: Southern FL, s Gulf of Mexico, and from
            Caribbean to Brazil; apparently absent
            from Bermuda and Bahamas.

Similar Species: Species in genus *Bairdiella* often have
            more silvery body without black blotch
            at pectoral fin base and lack row of
            enlarged teeth in jaws.

Comments: Reef Croaker is active at night, feeding
            on shrimps and small fishes. During the
            day it retreats to crevices in coral reefs
            and caves. The preferred coral reef
            habitat of this fish is unusual among the
            family Sciaenidae.

574 Black Drum
Pogonias cromis

Description: To 5'7" (1.7 m); 145 lb (66 kg). Deep, moderately compressed; back elevated, ventral profile nearly straight. Silvery to dark gray; *4–5 broad black bars on sides,* less vivid in large individuals; fins dusky or black. Mouth nearly horizontal, inferior; maxilla reaches middle of eye; no large canine teeth in upper jaw; pharyngeal teeth large; *numerous small chin barbels,* longer posteriorly on chin; gill rakers short, 16–21 in outer arch; *preopercle smooth.* Dorsal fin with 10 spines, 19–23 rays; anal fin with 2 spines, *second spine much larger, 5–7 rays;* caudal fin truncate to slightly emarginate. Scales large. Lateral line extends to tip of caudal fin.

Habitat: Bays and estuaries over sand or sandy mud.

Range: NS to Laguna Madre, Mexico. Also from s Brazil to Argentina.

Similar Species: Sheepshead *(Archosargus probatocephalus),* in porgy family (Sparidae), lacks chin barbels, and has 5–6 distinct but narrower black bars on body, broad incisor teeth in front and molar-like teeth on sides of jaws, and deeply emarginate or forked caudal fin.

Comments: Black Drum feeds on fishes, crustaceans, and oysters, which it crushes with its huge pharyngeal teeth. Although it is a popular sport fish, and the flesh is quite palatable (especially when marinated), this drum is often discarded by anglers because of parasites in its muscles.

579 Spotfin Croaker
Roncador stearnsii

Description: To 27" (69 cm); 10½ lb (4.8 kg). Deep, compressed. Bluish gray to metallic gray above; sides brassy; silver to white below, occasionally golden; *large black spot at pectoral fin base.* Breeding males have golden paired fins. Females have black streaks on belly. Snout blunt, projects beyond mouth; teeth not prominent; *no chin barbels.* Dorsal fin with 9–10 spines, 21–25 rays; anal fin with 2 strong spines, 7–9 rays. Lateral line extends to tip of caudal fin.

Habitat: Sandy shores and bays, common in shallow surf zone, sometimes to depths of 50′ (15 m); often near rocks and entrances to bays.

Range: Point Conception, CA, to Mazatlán, Mexico, including Gulf of California; rare north of Los Angeles.

Similar Species: White Croaker *(Genyonemus lineatus)* has small dark spot at upper pectoral fin base and 12–16 dorsal fin spines. White Seabass *(Atractoscion nobilis)* is more elongate and snout does not project beyond mouth.

Comments: This species is typically found in small groups, but it aggregates for spawning. An excellent sport fish, Spotfin Croaker is caught in the surf and off piers. Adults feed on invertebrates, such as marine worms, clams, crabs, and small crustaceans.

---

573   Red Drum
Sciaenops ocellatus

Description: To 5′ (1.5 m); 90 lb (41 kg). Elongate, moderately compressed; ventral profile nearly straight. *Iridescent silvery gray, copper, bronze, or reddish; at least 1 large ocellated black spot on caudal peduncle;* pelvic and anal fins pale; dorsal and caudal fins dusky. Snout conical; mouth horizontal, inferior; maxilla reaches posterior edge of eye; *no chin barbels;* 12–14 gill rakers on outer arch; edge of preopercle smooth. Dorsal fin with 10 spines, third and fourth spines longest, 23–25 rays; anal fin with 2 spines, 7–9 rays; caudal fin rounded in young, squared off in adults. Scales large. Lateral line extends to tip of caudal fin.

Habitat: Surf zone to offshore waters, depending
            on season and age of individuals;
            occasionally enters fresh water. Young in
            estuaries and salt marshes.

Range: NY to Laguna Madre, Mexico; most
            abundant from FL to TX.

Comments: Red Drum has a variety of common
            names. It is known as Redfish in
            Florida, and as Channel Bass in other
            eastern states; large individuals are
            called Bullred and small ones Ratred.
            This drum runs in schools during the
            spring and fall migrations, which makes
            it popular with anglers. It migrates in
            response to temperature, salinity, and
            food availability. It is an important sport
            and commercial fish, and has achieved
            great culinary popularity as "blackened
            redfish." For this reason, regulations
            have been passed to prevent overfishing.

---

566 Queenfish
Seriphus politus

Description: To 12″ (30 cm). Moderately elongate,
              moderately compressed. Bluish above;
              silvery below; fins yellowish. Snout not
              projecting beyond mouth; mouth large,
              slightly oblique; no chin barbels. Dorsal
              fin with 7–9 spines, 19–21 rays, *spiny
              and soft segments separated by wide gap;* soft
              dorsal and anal fins of about equal length;
              anal fin with 2 spines, 21–23 rays.
              Lateral line extends to tip of caudal fin.

Habitat: Usually over sand to depths of 27′ (8 m)
              or more; common around pilings in bays
              and tidal sloughs.

Range: Yaquina Bay, OR, to south-central Baja
              California; common in CA.

Similar Species: White Seabass *(Atractoscion nobilis)* has
                 8–10 anal fin rays.

Comments: Queenfish is the only North American
              croaker with a wide gap between the
              spiny and soft dorsal fin segments. It is
              frequently caught on a baited hook and
              occasionally fished commercially. It has
              limited value as a food fish partly

because of its small size, but is often
used as a bait fish. It feeds mostly on
small fishes and crustaceans. Queenfish
moves into deeper waters at night; it has
been reported to depths of 70′ (21 m).

---

577   **Yellowfin Croaker**
Umbrina roncador

Description: To 20″ (51 cm); 4 lb (1.8 kg). Elongate,
compressed; greatest depth at origin
of spiny dorsal fin. Iridescent blue to
gray above; sides silvery; dark, oblique,
wavy stripes on back and sides; *fins
mostly yellowish,* dorsal fin darker.
Snout bluntly rounded; upper jaw
projects beyond lower; *chin with 1
short tubular barbel; preopercle serrate.*

Dorsal fin deeply notched, with
10–11 spines, 25–30 rays; anal fin
with 2 strong spines, 6–7 rays;
caudal fin emarginate. Lateral line
extends to tip of caudal fin.

Habitat: Over sand in surf zone, often near rocks
or kelp; in bays to depths of 26′ (8 m).

Range: Point Conception, CA, to Gulf of
California; old records from as far north
as San Francisco.

Similar Species: California Corbina *(Menticirrhus
undulatus)* also has 1 chin barbel, but
body is more elongate, stripes on back
(when present) are not oblique, and
anal fin has only 1 weak spine; occurs
along sandy shores and in bays. White
Croaker *(Genyonemus lineatus)* has faint
wavy lines on sides, minute or absent
chin barbels, and dorsal fin with 12–16
spines and 10–12 rays. Queenfish
(Seriphus politus) has terminal mouth,
snout not projecting beyond lower jaw,
and widely separated spiny and soft
dorsal fin segments.

Comments: This croaker spawns in the summer.
It is caught by surf anglers and speared
by skin divers. In California it is a sport
fish and is protected by law. It feeds on
invertebrates and small fishes.

GOATFISHES
Family Mullidae

6 genera and about 55 species world-wide; 4 genera and 5 species in North America (4 Atlantic, 1 Pacific), plus 1 species confined to Mexican Pacific waters. These rather elongate bottom dwellers, usually bright red or yellow, are found in tropical and warm-temperate seas. The dorsal fin is divided into two well-separated segments; the first segment has six to eight spines and the second has eight to nine rays. The anal fin has two small spines and five to eight rays. Goatfishes locate food with two large barbels that trail from the chin and fit into a groove on the throat; these movable tactile structures are used to stir up the bottom and dislodge the small organisms that occur there.

Red Goatfish

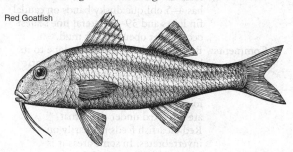

Red Goatfish
Mullus auratus

Description: To 10″ (25 cm). Elongate, depth greatest at nape, tapering posteriorly. *Bright scarlet or crimson, somewhat blotched; 2 yellow to reddish stripes on sides;* pelvic fin plain; pectoral fin reddish; first dorsal fin with 1 orange stripe near base sometimes covering basal one-third of fin, 1 red to brownish-red stripe near tip; second dorsal fin with red or yellow spots forming stripes across fin; caudal fin scarlet, sometimes with white markings. Profile of head steep; mouth terminal, horizontal; maxilla reaches eye; small teeth on roof of mouth and in lower jaw; *2 large chin barbels;* no opercular spines. Dorsal fin with 8 spines, first spine very short, 6 rays; anal fin with 2 spines, 6 rays. Lateral line with 34–37 scales.

Habitat: Continental coastal waters over mud to
depths of about 240' (73 m).

Range: NS to n South America, including Gulf
of Mexico and most of Caribbean; absent
from Bermuda, Bahamas, and West
Indies; records north of NC probably
based on summer waifs.

Similar Species: Yellow Goatfish *(Mulloidichthys
martinicus)* has bright yellow stripe on
sides and 39–42 lateral line scales;
occurs around coral reefs. Spotted
Goatfish *(Pseudupeneus maculatus)* has
2–3 blackish spots on sides and 31–33
lateral line scales; occurs around coral
reefs. Dwarf Goatfish *(Upeneus parvus)*
has 4–5 oblique dusky bands on caudal
fin lobes and 39–40 lateral line scales;
occurs over open sand or mud.

Comments: Red Goatfish has a steeper slope to its
head than any other western Atlantic
goatfish. All goatfishes use their long
chin barbels to probe the bottom for
food. When not in use, the barbels
are retracted under the throat.
Red Goatfish feeds primarily on
invertebrates. In some areas it is
highly prized as a food fish.

SWEEPERS
Family Pempheridae

2 genera and about 25 species world-
wide; 1 genus with 2 species in North America. Sweepers
are found in tropical seas, but are absent from the eastern
Pacific; both North American sweepers occur in the tropical western Atlantic. These usually coppery red, nocturnal
fishes form large schools at mid-depths around coral reefs or
rock ledges, where they feed on small planktonic organisms.
Most species inhabit shallow water, but some may occur to
depths of 300' (91 m). They have a deep compressed body
that usually tapers strongly to a slender caudal peduncle.
The maxilla does not reach beyond the middle of the eye.
The preorbital area is smooth, and the eyes are large, without adipose lids. The dorsal fin is continuous, located midway along the back, with four to seven spines and seven to
12 rays. The anal fin has two (rarely three) spines and 17 to
45 rays. The pelvic fins are thoracic in position, each with a

single spine and five rays. There are usually 40 to 82 scales in the lateral line, which extends onto the caudal fin. Most sweepers are less than 6″ (15 cm) long; one Indo-Pacific species reaches a length of 12″ (30 cm).

---

694 **Glassy Sweeper**
Pempheris schomburgkii

Description: To 5¼″ (13.5 cm). *Ventral profile deep, angular; straight in front of anal fin, sharply upturned behind that point. Copper,* with dark streak along anal fin base. Young pale red. 31–38 (usually 32–34) anal fin rays.

Habitat: Mid-depths around shallow coral reefs at night; in recesses of reefs during day.

Range: Bermuda, Bahamas, se FL, and Caribbean to Brazil.

Similar Species: Curved Sweeper *(P. poeyi)* has more rounded ventral profile, lacks dark streak along anal fin base, and has usually 23–24 anal fin rays.

Comments: Glassy Sweeper bears a superficial resemblance to alfonsinos of the family Berycidae, a small unrelated group of deep-sea fishes; these similarities include a deep compressed body, large eyes, a short dorsal fin with no break or obvious notch between the spiny and soft-rayed segments, and a long anal fin.

 BUTTERFLYFISHES
Family Chaetodontidae

10 genera and 114 species worldwide; 2 genera and 8 species in North America (6 Atlantic, 2 Pacific), plus 2 genera and 3 species confned to Mexican Pacific waters. Butterflyfishes are found in tropical coral reefs throughout the world; they are among the most characteristic and obvious fishes in this type of habitat. These small to medium fishes have deep, compressed, disk-shaped bodies. Yellow coloration dominates in many species, and most have a dark band through the eye. The snout is pointed, and the small mouth has protractile jaws. The long continuous dorsal fin has only a slight notch (sometimes no notch) between the spiny and soft-rayed segments; there are

six to 16 dorsal fin spines and 15 to 30 rays. The anal fin has three to five (usually three) spines and 14 to 23 rays. The lateral line extends onto the caudal peduncle. Some butterflyfish species are solitary; others pair off early and for life.

369 Foureye Butterflyfish
Chaetodon capistratus

Description: To 6″ (15 cm), usually to 4″ (10 cm). Deep, compressed, disk-shaped. Silvery gray to pale yellow or whitish; *dark oblique lines above and horizontal lines below, meeting at about a 45-degree angle to form chevrons;* black bar on head through eye; pelvic fin mostly yellow; *large ocellated black spot below end of dorsal fin.* Snout pointed; mouth small; jaws protractile. Dorsal fin with usually 13 spines, 20 rays; anal fin with 3 spines, 18 rays. Lateral line extends onto caudal peduncle.

Habitat: Shallow coral and rocky reefs.

Range: NC to n South America, including Bermuda, Bahamas, Gulf of Mexico, and Caribbean; occasionally north to MA in summer.

Similar Species: Longsnout Butterflyfish *(C. aculeatus)* has golden or bronze yellow body, paler below, with dark stripe from nape to eye, where it turns forward onto side of snout (only w Atlantic species without continuation of dark bar below eye), and has noticeably longer snout than any other w Atlantic butterflyfish; occurs around coral reefs to depths of 200′ (61 m). Bank Butterflyfish *(C. aya)* has pale body with 2 broad blackish diagonal bands and dark brown bar along midline of snout; occurs around coral reefs at depths of 66–550′ (20–168 m). Scythe Butterflyfish *(Prognathodes falcifer)* has yellow body with black scythe-shaped stripe; occurs around deep rocky reefs in Pacific.

Comments: This species is one of the most common butterflyfishes. Foureye Butterflyfish feeds primarily on coral polyps, sea anemones, tubeworms, and algae.

368 Spotfin Butterflyfish
Chaetodon ocellatus

Description: To 8″ (20 cm). Deep, strongly
compressed, disk-shaped. *Whitish; dark
bar extends from cheek through eye and onto
front of dorsal fin;* pelvic fin yellow;
pectoral fin pale, with yellow stripe
running from base to edge of opercle;
median fins yellow, with thin blue line
near edges; *dark blotch at base of soft dorsal
fin, smaller spot at tip.* Young have dark
bar between soft dorsal and anal fins.
Profile of head steep, concave in front of
eye; snout pointed. Dorsal fin with
12–13 spines, 20–21 rays; anal fin with
3 spines, 17 rays; soft dorsal and anal
fins similar in size and shape.

Habitat: Shallow coral and rocky reefs; around
rock jetties in areas without reefs.

Range: NC to Brazil, including Bermuda,
Bahamas, Gulf of Mexico, and Greater
Antilles; most common in FL and
Central and South America.

Comments: The scarcity of Spotfin Butterflyfish
in the West Indies is difficult to
explain.

367 Reef Butterflyfish
Chaetodon sedentarius

Description: To 6″ (15 cm). Deep, compressed,
disk-shaped. Yellow above, shading to
white below; dark bar on head through
eye; *dorsal fin darker, chocolate brown
posteriorly, with color extending downward
as well-defined dark band across caudal
peduncle and along rear edge of anal fin.*
Snout pointed; mouth small; jaws
protractile. Dorsal fin with 13 spines,
22–23 rays; anal fin with 3 spines, 18
rays; *soft dorsal and anal fins rounded
posteriorly.* Lateral line extends onto
caudal peduncle.

Habitat: Coral and rocky reefs from inshore to
depths of 280′ (85 m) or more; most
common below 50′ (15 m).

Range: NC to n South America, including
Bermuda, Bahamas, Gulf of Mexico, and
Caribbean.

Comments: Young Reef Butterflyfishes are often
seen in shallow water. Adults are found
in deeper water on average, and are
observed less frequently than some other
butterflyfishes. This fish generally
occurs in deeper water than other North
American species of *Chaetodon,* except for
Bank Butterflyfish *(C. aya).*

370 Banded Butterflyfish
Chaetodon striatus

Description: To 6″ (15 cm). Deep, compressed, disk-
shaped. Whitish, with lines forming
chevrons; black band on head through
eye; *2 broad black bars on sides; black or
dusky bar extends from base of soft dorsal fin
to caudal peduncle;* pelvic fin spine white,
rays black; *median fins with black
submarginal bands* and white edges.
Snout pointed; mouth small; jaws
protractile. Dorsal fin with 12 spines, 21
rays; anal fin with 3 spines, 17 rays; soft
dorsal and anal fins not noticeably
rounded.

Habitat: Shallow coral and rocky reefs.

Range: NC to Brazil, including Bermuda,
Bahamas, Gulf of Mexico, and
Caribbean; seasonally north to NJ.

Comments: Reports of Banded Butterflyfish in the
eastern Atlantic are probably erroneous.

ANGELFISHES
Family Pomacanthidae

9 genera and 74 species worldwide; 3
genera and 7 species in North America (6
Atlantic, 1 Pacific), plus 2 species con-
fined to Mexican Pacific waters. Found in tropical seas, these
brightly colored fishes have deep compressed bodies. They
are so close anatomically to butterflyfishes (family
Chaetodontidae) that they once were included in that
group. Angelfishes differ in having a blunter snout and a
large spine on the angle of the preopercle; in addition, the

rays of the dorsal and anal fins are often long and filamentous. Some angelfishes are small, but others reach lengths of 24" (61 cm), larger than any species in the family. Most species inhabit shallow reefs, and are active during the day and lethargic at night. The young of some species feed on ectoparasites of other fishes, and adults sometimes feed on sponges. The color pattern of the young is sometimes different from that of adults. Two species found in the western Atlantic, Queen Angelfish (*Holacanthus ciliaris*) and Blue Angelfish (*H. bermudensis*), commonly hybridize, an extremely rare phenomenon in reef-dwelling marine fishes.

380 Cherubfish
Centropyge argi

Description: To 2¾" (7 cm). Oval. *Deep blue; head and breast yellow; narrow blue ring around eye; pectoral fin pale yellowish; other fins deep blue, with pale blue edges.* Head blunt, not concave over eyes; eye width greater than length of snout; bone anterior to eye with 2 large decurved spines; preopercle strongly serrate, with large spine. Dorsal fin with 14–15 spines, 15–16 rays; dorsal and anal fins not filamentous; caudal fin rounded.

Habitat: Coral and rocky reefs from near shore to depths of 250' (76 m); most common below 100' (30 m).

Range: Bermuda, Bahamas, s FL, Gulf of Mexico, West Indies, and Caribbean coast to n South America.

Similar Species: Flameback Angelfish (*C. aurantonotus*) is darker, with entire head yellow or orange.

Comments: This beautiful little fish seems to prefer deep water, and is apparently not often encountered.

373 Queen Angelfish
Holacanthus ciliaris

Description: To 18" (46 cm). Deep, compressed. *Bluish; head yellowish, with blue markings on snout, opercle, and breast; large black spot encircled by blue ring on nape; scales with yellowish-orange edges; pelvic, pectoral, and caudal fins yellowish; black blotch at pectoral fin base;* dorsal and anal fins with narrow light blue borders; last few rays of soft dorsal and anal fins adjacent to tail dark. Young yellowish green, with narrow bluish-white bars; bluish-black band through eye. Profile of upper head nearly straight to slightly concave above eye; no spine on bone anterior to eye; preopercular spine present. Dorsal fin with 14 spines, 17–20 rays; dorsal and anal fins long, filamentous, extending beyond end of caudal fin; caudal fin rounded, without upper filament.

Habitat: Shallow coral reefs.

Range: Bahamas, FL, Gulf of Mexico, and Caribbean to Brazil.

Similar Species: Blue Angelfish *(H. bermudensis)* lacks ocellus on nape, intensely darkened blotch at base of pectoral fin, and noticeably darkened posteriormost rays of anal and dorsal fins, and has mostly dark caudal fin with relatively narrow yellowish border; young very similar to young Queen Angelfishes, with bluish-white bars on body (next to last bar not always curved) and yellow rear edges of soft dorsal and anal fins.

Comments: Despite its bright colors, Queen Angelfish blends well with its natural habitat. The young may exhibit cleaning behavior typical of some wrasses (family Labridae). In most areas of the Gulf of Mexico, this species is replaced by the closely related Blue Angelfish. Although hybridization among species of reef-dwelling fishes is extremely rare, Queen and Blue Angelfishes commonly hybridize, and their offspring are intermediate in appearance; individuals from Bermuda are apparently such hybrids.

376 Rock Beauty
Holacanthus tricolor

Description: To 14″ (36 cm). Deep, compressed. *Head, breast, and belly yellow; remainder of body black; first few dorsal fin spines, posterior edges of dorsal and anal fins, and pectoral, pelvic, and caudal fins yellow;* lips black or blue. Young have large ocellus surrounded by large black area on upper back and lower part of soft dorsal fin; black area expands to cover most of posterior two-thirds of body with increasing size and age. Profile of head concave in front of eye; preopercular spine very long. Dorsal fin with 13–15 (usually 14) spines, 17–19 (usually 17–18) rays; anal fin with 3 spines, 17–20 (usually 18) rays; dorsal and anal fins not filamentous, with straight posterior edges; caudal fin rounded, with short filament at upper corner.

Habitat: Shallow coral and rocky reefs; sometimes offshore.

Range: NC to Brazil, including Bermuda, Bahamas, and Caribbean; offshore reefs in nw Gulf of Mexico.

Comments: This attractive species is conspicuous and not likely to be confused with any other fish. It is very common on West Indian reefs. Like certain other small angelfishes, Rock Beauty feeds on sponges, tunicates, and algae.

375 Gray Angelfish
Pomacanthus arcuatus

Description: To 24″ (61 cm). Compressed, depth about three-fourths length. *Gray or brown; chin and mouth area white; most large scales dark, with pale edges; median fins with light blue or white edges.* Young black, with 5 yellow bars across head and body; prominent yellow semicircle on inner part of tail. Profile of head very steep; mouth small; lower jaw projects beyond upper; preopercular spine well developed. Dorsal fin with 8–10 (usually 9) spines, 29–32 (usually 30–32) rays; anal fin with 3 spines, 17–20 (usually 18–19) rays; soft dorsal and anal fins filamentous; caudal fin truncate.

Habitat: Shallow reefs; occasionally to depths of
           200′ (61 m).

Range: New England to se Brazil, including
           Bahamas and Caribbean; rare on offshore
           reefs in Gulf of Mexico; absent from
           Bermuda; n records based on summer
           waifs.

Similar Species: French Angelfish *(P. paru)* has 10 dorsal

fin spines; young also have dark bodies
with bright yellow bars, but narrow
yellowish border completely encircles
more rounded caudal fin, with large
dark area in center.

Comments: References to Gray Angelfish in
            literature prior to 1968 appear as *P.
            aureus.* Perhaps the largest of the
            angelfishes, this species is reported to be
            among the least wary of the reef fishes.
            It is believed to have formerly occurred
            in Bermuda, presumably as an
            introduction.

---

374   French Angelfish
Pomacanthus paru

Description: To 14″ (36 cm). Deep, compressed.
              *Blackish; yellow ring around eye; most scales
              with crescent-shaped yellow marks; yellow
              bar at pectoral fin base; dorsal fin filament
              yellow.* Young black; 5 yellow bars on
              head, body, and caudal fin base. Profile
              of head very steep; mouth small; lower
              jaw projects beyond upper; preopercular
              spine well developed. Dorsal fin with 10

spines, 27–31 (usually 29–30) rays; anal
fin with 3 spines, 21–24 (usually
22–23) rays; dorsal and anal fins
filamentous; caudal fin rounded.

Habitat: Shallow reefs; occasionally to depths of
           228′ (69 m).

Range: Bermuda, n FL, Bahamas, and
           Caribbean to n South America; reported
           in w Gulf of Mexico around West
           Flower Garden Bank. Also around
           Ascension Island in South Atlantic.

Similar Species: Gray Angelfish *(P. arcuatus)* has usually
                   9 dorsal fin spines; young also have dark
                   bodies with bright yellow bars, but

broad yellow border does not entirely
encircle more truncate caudal fin, with
less extensive black center.

Comments: References to French Angelfish in
literature prior to 1968 appear as *P.
arcuatus,* which is now the accepted
scientific name for Gray Angelfish. This
may partly account for confusion
regarding geographical distribution and
the relative abundance of the two
species. Another factor possibly
contributing to this confusion is the
similarity of young French and Gray
Angelfishes.

SEA CHUBS
Family Kyphosidae

15 genera and about 42 species world-
wide; 5 genera and 7 species in North America (2 Atlantic,
5 Pacific), plus 2 species confined to Mexican Pacific waters.
This family is found in tropical to temperate marine waters
throughout the world; it has recently been expanded to include several groups once considered distinct families,
among them the nibblers (formerly family Girellidae) and
the halfmoons (formerly family Scorpidae), each with a single species in North American eastern Pacific waters. Sea
chubs are perch-like fishes, with oval compressed bodies
and small mouths. The dorsal fin has nine to 17 spines and
11 to 28 rays. The anal fin has three spines and 10 to 21
rays. The caudal fin is lunate to almost truncate. Most
species feed on algae. Some are referred to as rudderfishes
because of their penchant for following ships.

383 Opaleye
Girella nigricans

Description: To 26″ (66 cm), usually to 9″ (23 cm).
Deep, compressed. Dark olive green,
with blue eyes; *usually 2 yellowish-white
spots below dorsal fin.* Snout rounded.
Dorsal fin with 12–14 spines, 12–15
rays; anal fin with 3 spines, 17–21 rays,
rear profile rounded; caudal fin almost
square in profile. Scales prominent.

Habitat: Shallow rocky areas and kelp beds to
depths of 100′ (30 m). Early life stages

pelagic; young are prominent members of tide-pool communities.

Range: San Francisco, CA, to Cabo San Lucas, Baja California.

Similar Species: Zebra Perch *(Hermosilla azurea)* has about 10 dark bars on sides, bright blue spot on opercle, and dorsal fin with 11 spines and 11 rays.

Comments: This species was formerly included in the nibbler family (Girellidae). Opaleye reaches maturity at two to three years of age and spawns during April, May, and June. It feeds on algae and eelgrass, apparently taking most of its nourishment from small animals living on the plants. Anglers take about 74,000 Opaleyes annually from the shore and from skiffs. Commercial anglers using round haul nets or purse seines catch only small amounts.

---

600 Bermuda Chub
Kyphosus sectatrix

Description: To 20″ (51 cm). Oval, compressed. *Bluish gray to dark gray, with pale yellow stripes;* horizontal yellow bands on head; upper opercular membrane blackish. Young have pale spots same size as eye on head, body, and fins. Head short; snout blunt; mouth small, horizontal; maxilla partly hidden; *teeth incisor-like, roots horizontal, visible in mouth.* Pectoral fin short; dorsal fin continuous, slightly notched, with 10 spines, spiny segment retractable into sheath of scales, usually 12 rays; anal fin with 3 spines, usually 11 rays; caudal fin forked. Scales ctenoid, covering most of head, body, and all fins except spiny dorsal fin.

Habitat: Near shore around coral reefs or rocks.

Range: MA to Brazil, including Bermuda, Bahamas, Gulf of Mexico, and Caribbean; n records probably based on seasonal waifs. Probably also around Ascension Island in mid–South Atlantic; reported from e Atlantic.

Similar Species: Yellow Chub *(K. incisor)* has brighter yellow stripes and 1–2 more rays in dorsal and anal fins. Blue-bronze Chub *(K. analogus)* has brassy stripes on sides and prominent stripe under eye; occurs around rocks and kelp beds to depths of about 100′ (30 m) in Pacific.

Comments: Bermuda and Yellow Chubs are both schooling fishes that feed primarily on bottom-dwelling algae. Neither species is highly regarded as a food fish. Young Bermuda Chubs are occasionally found in rafts of sargassum weed.

604 Halfmoon
Medialuna californiensis

Description: To 19″ (48 cm), usually to 8″ (20 cm). Compressed, deep. Dark blue above; light blue to whitish below; *bright blue spot above gill opening;* fins dark. Mouth small. Dorsal fin with 9–10 spines, 22–27 longer rays; anal fin with 3 spines, 17–21 rays; *caudal fin lunate. Scales extend onto dorsal fin rays.*

Habitat: Rocky areas and kelp beds from near surface to depths of 130′ (40 m). Young pelagic.

Range: Vancouver Island, BC, to Gulf of California; rare north of Point Conception, CA.

Comments: Halfmoon probably spawns during the summer and fall. It reaches sexual maturity at two years of age, and the maximum known age is eight years. Halfmoon feeds on small invertebrates, particularly those living among algae. The annual sport catch in California amounts to about 67,000, with fish averaging about ½ lb (200 g) each.

HAWKFISHES
Family Cirrhitidae

9 genera and about 32 species worldwide; 1 species in North America, plus 3 genera and 3 species confined to Mexican Pacific waters. Hawkfishes are

small to medium, brightly colored fishes. The lower five to seven pectoral fin rays are thickened and unbranched, with the rays projecting well beyond the fin membrane. The dorsal fin has 10 spines with cirri at the tips and 11 to 17 rays. The anal fin has three spines and five to seven rays. Hawkfishes have cycloid or ctenoid scales. Found in tropical marine shore waters, these bottom-dwelling fishes live in rock and coral habitats, where they may be observed resting on the bottom propped up by their pectoral fins.

597 Redspotted Hawkfish
Amblycirrhitus pinos

Description: To 4″ (10 cm). Moderately compressed. Olive, with series of narrow and broad alternating dark bands in various shades of green to greenish brown; *last band black, encircling caudal peduncle; small red spots sprinkled over head, dorsal fin, and upper anterior part of body;* large black spot on lower part of soft dorsal fin, with orange band below. Snout pointed. *Pectoral fin with anterior 5 rays thickened and unbranched;* dorsal fin with 10 spines, 10 rays; anal fin with 3 spines, 6 rays.

Habitat: Shallow coral reefs; occasionally to depths of 150′ (46 m).

Range: Bermuda; nw Gulf of Mexico; s FL south throughout Caribbean to n South America. Also around St. Helena Island in South Pacific.

Comments: Solitary individuals are often observed resting in crevices or on the top of coral heads, supported by their thickened pectoral fin rays.

PYGMY SUNFISHES
Family Elassomatidae

1 genus with 6 species confined to North America. In the recent past, these fishes were considered to be part of the sunfish family (Centrarchidae). As currently recognized, the family's single genus, *Elassoma,* is confined to fresh water in the central and southeastern United States. Pygmy sunfishes are small fishes, all less than 2″ (5 cm) long, with cycloid scales. The dorsal fin has three to five

spines, and the anal fin has three spines. The caudal fin is rounded. These fishes lack a lateral line.

124, 125 Carolina Pygmy Sunfish
Elassoma boehlkei

Description: To 1¼" (3 cm). Oblong, moderately compressed. Back dark olive to brown; alternating dark and light bars on sides; no dark spots anteriorly on upper body. *Breeding males black, except pectoral fin; 12–16 narrow brilliant blue-green bars with irregular edges. Dorsal fin with 4 spines, 8–12 rays. Top of head unscaled;* 24–30 scales in lateral series.

Habitat: Creeks, sloughs, swamps, and roadside ditches with dense aquatic vegetation.

Range: Along coastal plain from Waccamaw River drainage, se NC, south to Santee River drainage, central SC.

Similar Species: Bluebarred Pygmy Sunfish *(E. okatie)* has 10–11 wide bars on sides, usually 5 dorsal fin spines, and unscaled top of head.

Comments: This colorful pygmy sunfish is short lived; few individuals live longer than one and a half years.

---

123 Everglades Pygmy Sunfish
Elassoma evergladei

Description: To 1¼" (3 cm). Oblong, compressed. Back grayish green to dark olive brown; sides lighter; no large black spots anteriorly on upper sides; *front of lower jaw darkly pigmented. Breeding males grayish black, with iridescent blue bars.* Mouth small, upturned, reaching front edge of eye. *Dorsal fin with 4 spines, 8–10 rays. Top of head scaled;* 23–31 scales in lateral series.

Habitat: Coastal lowlands in sluggish streams, swamps, oxbow lakes, and wetlands with dense vegetation.

Range: Atlantic and Gulf coast drainages from se NC to Mobile Bay basin, AL.

Similar Species: Okefenokee Pygmy Sunfish *(E. okefenokee)* has dorsal fin with 4 spines and 10–13 rays, unscaled top of head, and 31–34 scales in lateral series.

Comments: Everglades Pygmy Sunfish, like related species, is secretive and rarely ventures into open waters. It completes its life cycle in dense vegetation. Females deposit 50 to 75 eggs on submerged aquatic plants where the eggs hatch. This species grows rapidly and reaches sexual maturity in about one year.

122 Banded Pygmy Sunfish
Elassoma zonatum

Description: To 2" (5 cm). Oblong, compressed. Dark olive green above; *sides lighter, with 9–12 irregular dark bars; black spot below dorsal fin origin;* dark bands on median fins. Snout short; mouth terminal, reaches eye. 4–5 dorsal fin spines; 3 anal fin spines; *caudal fin rounded. Top of head and cheek scaled;* 33–36 scales in lateral series.

Habitat: Quiet, sluggish, clear to dark-stained streams, sloughs, and swamps with abundant vegetation.

Range: Atlantic coast from NC south to FL and west along Gulf coast to TX; Mississippi River valley from sw IN and s IL south to LA.

Similar Species: Spring Pygmy Sunfish *(E. alabamae)* has 6–7 wide dark bars on sides with iridescent blue-green to creamy interspaces, unscaled head, and clear area at posterior end of soft dorsal fin near base; occurs in springs and spring runs.

Comments: Banded Pygmy Sunfish feeds on crustaceans and aquatic insects. It rarely lives more than three years. This diminutive fish makes an interesting aquarium fish.

CICHLIDS
Family Cichlidae

About 105 genera and 1,300 species worldwide; 9 genera and 58 species in North America (including 15 species in 8 introduced genera). Noted for their elaborate breeding behavior and bright colors, cichlids are important aquarium fishes. This is a widespread, abundant, and diverse group of primarily freshwater fishes, but many species tolerate brackish to salt waters. Cichlids superficially resemble the sunfishes (family Centrarchidae), but are easily distinguished by the single nostril on each side of the snout and by the usually posteriorly interrupted lateral line. Several species have been introduced for the purpose of weed control, pond culture, and sport fishing, often adversely affecting native fishes.

609 Peacock Bass
Cichla ocellaris

Description: To 18″ (46 cm); 11½ lb (5.2 kg). Elongate, moderately compressed. Back dark olive to black; *3 wide dark bars on sides, widest on upper sides, narrowing ventrally; large black spot encircled by bright yellow on upper caudal fin base.* Head large; snout pointed; mouth large; jaw reaches near middle of eye. Dorsal fin with longest spines anteriorly. *Scales on bases of soft dorsal, anal, and caudal fins;* 68–79 scales in lateral series, *continuing onto caudal fin base.* Lateral line incomplete.

Habitat: Canals and man-made lakes over mud, sand, or rocks.

Range: Introduced in s FL. Native to tropical fresh waters of South America.

Comments: The northerly distribution of Peacock Bass in southern Florida is limited by cold winter temperatures. This is a popular sport fish in southern Florida as well as in its native waters.

115 Rio Grande Cichlid
Cichlasoma cyanoguttatum

Description: To 12″ (30 cm). Deep, compressed; dorsal profile gently curved. Dusky to olive above; *sides greenish gray, with numerous small blue or blue-green to whitish spots* and 4–6 dusky bars; dusky below; dark spots below middle of dorsal fin and near caudal fin base. Breeding males have hump at nape. Maxilla not reaching eye. Dorsal fins joined, spines longer than rays; *anal fin with 5–6 spines, 8–9 rays.* 27–30 scales in lateral series. Lateral line incomplete.

Habitat: Pools and sluggish waters of warm streams; usually with aquatic vegetation.

Range: Gulf coast drainages from Rio Grande, TX, to n Mexico. Introduced in central FL, s TX, and s U.S.

Similar Species: Black Acara *(C. bimaculatum),* an

aquarium fish introduced from South America, has dark blotch under eye, 4–5 anal fin spines, and banded caudal fin. Mayan Cichlid *(C. urophthalmus),* an aquarium fish introduced from Central America, has dark bands on body, often with narrow grayish-white borders, and black blotch at end of caudal peduncle; occurs in sloughs, canals, and brackish water.

Comments: This very attractive fish is easy to keep in an aquarium, but like other cichlids it digs up the bottom, uproots plants, and is somewhat aggressive if kept with other fishes.

116, 622 Mozambique Tilapia
Oreochromis mossambica

Description: To 15″ (38 cm). Deep, compressed. Dark olive to gray above; sides grayish green to yellowish; yellowish below; *dorsal and caudal fins with reddish edges. Breeding males bluish to black,* with large blue lips. Young silvery, with 6–8 dusky bars on sides. *Profile of snout concave;* mouth moderately large; *18–26 gill rakers. Dorsal fins joined, with 15–17 spines, 10–12 rays;* anal fin with 3–4 spines, 9–10 rays; dorsal and anal fins pointed posteriorly; caudal fin rounded. Caudal peduncle short, deep. 29–33 scales in lateral series. Lateral line incomplete posteriorly.

Habitat: Warm sluggish streams, ponds, and canals with abundant aquatic vegetation; enters brackish water.

Range: Widely introduced in s U.S. south of
VA, MO, and central CA. Native to
tropical fresh waters of e Africa.

Similar Species: Blue Tilapia *(O. aureus)* has 26–32 gill
rakers, 12–15 dorsal fin rays, and 3 anal
fin spines.

Comments: Mozambique Tilapia, introduced for the
purpose of weed control, has escaped
from ponds where it was cultured for the
tropical fish trade. It feeds on aquatic
insects and small fishes as well as on
aquatic weeds, and competes with native
sport fishes for food and space.

---

623 Spotted Tilapia
Tilapia mariae

Description: To 12″ (30 cm). Deep, moderately
compressed, heavy. Back dark olive
brown to black; *sides olive brown, with
4–5 dark mid-lateral blotches on posterior
two-thirds of body;* lower sides deep red
behind pectoral fin and above pelvic
fin; *fins dusky; upper edge of dorsal fins
reddish; red marginal band on caudal fin.
Posterior dorsal fin spines of about equal
length;* anal fin with 3 spines, 9–11 rays;
caudal fin truncate. 3 rows of scales on cheek;
14–16 scales on caudal peduncle; 26–28
scales in lateral series. Lateral line
incomplete.

Habitat: Creeks, lakes, ponds, canals, and
roadside ditches; usually with aquatic
vegetation.

Range: Introduced in s FL, s AZ, and s NV;
established in AZ and FL. Native to
tropical w Africa.

Similar Species: Blackchin Tilapia *(Sarotherodon
melanotheron),* an introduced aquarium
fish, has conspicuous irregular black
markings on lower jaw, occasionally
extending onto cheek, and 2 rows of
scales on cheek; occurs in fresh and
brackish waters.

Comments: Since its introduction in the early
1970s, Spotted Tilapia has become one
of the most common fishes in the canal
systems of southern Florida.

SURFPERCHES
Family Embiotocidae

13 genera and about 22 species world-wide; 11 genera and 19 species in North America. Members of this family are found in cold-temperate waters along the Pacific coasts of North America and northeastern Asia, including Japan; one North American species is confined to fresh water. Surfperches have a deep compressed body with a fully exposed maxilla. The continuous dorsal fin is usually slightly notched but never deeply divided, with usually six to 11 spines (15 to 19 in one species) and nine to 28 rays. The anal fin has three spines and 15 to 35 rays. The caudal fin is notched or deeply forked. These fishes have cycloid scales, and there is usually a sheath of scales extending onto the dorsal fin. All species are viviparous; internal fertilization is facilitated by the thickened forward end of the anal fin, which aids in the transfer of sperm from the male to the female. The developing embryos receive nourishment from the female through a series of capillaries in their enlarged dorsal and anal fins.

---

590   Redtail Surfperch
Amphistichus rhodoterus

Description: To 16″ (41 cm). Deep, very compressed. Silvery; *light reddish to brownish bars on sides; all fins reddish, especially caudal fin.* Lower edge of eye below tip of upper lip; maxilla fully exposed; 10–14 gill rakers on lower limb of first arch. Dorsal fin with usually 10 spines, 25–29 (usually 27) rays, *longest spine longer than rays;* anal fin with 3 spines, 28–31 rays.

Habitat: Surf zone over steeply sloping sandy beaches and other sandy areas to depths of about 25′ (7.5 m).

Range: Vancouver Island, BC, to Monterey Bay, CA.

Similar Species: Barred Surfperch *(A. argenteus)* lacks red on fins, has lower edge of eye above upper lip, and dorsal fin spines are shorter than rays. Calico Surfperch *(A. koelzi)* also has lower edge of eye below upper lip, but dorsal fin spines and rays are about equal in length.

Comments: This fish feeds on sand-dwelling crustaceans and mollusks. Highly sought after by surf anglers in northern

California, Redtail Surfperch also supports a small commercial hook-and-line fishery.

---

585 Kelp Perch
Brachyistius frenatus

Description: To 8½″ (22 cm). Elongate, compressed. Golden above, with elongate white blotches; silvery below; upper pectoral fin base usually peppered with black speckles; front of anal fin often dark. *Snout long, pointed, upturned; tip of lower jaw projects beyond upper;* maxilla exposed. Dorsal fin short, with 7–10 spines, 13–17 rays, wide gap between end of fin and caudal fin; anal fin with 3 spines, 20–25 rays; caudal fin long, slightly forked.

Habitat: Among fronds in kelp beds from near surface to depths of about 100′ (30 m).

Range: Northern BC to Bahía Tortugas, Baja California.

Similar Species: Reef Perch *(Micrometrus aurora)* has 15–19 dorsal fin rays and series of half rings on scales just posterior to pectoral fin; occurs in tide pools and shallow waters over rocks. Dwarf Perch *(M. minimus)* has black area at pectoral fin base followed by dark stripes just below lateral line, horizontal mouth with jaws of equal length, and 12–16 dorsal fin rays; occurs in tide pools and shallow waters over rocks.

Comments: This species rarely occurs far from kelp, hence its common name; it is also known as Kelp Surfperch. It breeds in the fall and gives birth to fully developed young in the spring. Kelp Perch is a cleaner; much of its food consists of ectoparasites picked off other fishes. This perch is too small to be sought by anglers.

---

584 Shiner Perch
Cymatogaster aggregata

Description: To 7″ (18 cm), usually 4–5″ (10–12.5 cm). Elongate, compressed, depth one-third length; *distance from pectoral fin*

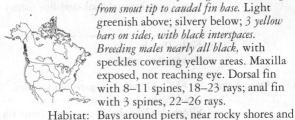

insertion to dorsal fin origin one-third length from snout tip to caudal fin base. Light greenish above; silvery below; *3 yellow bars on sides, with black interspaces. Breeding males nearly all black,* with speckles covering yellow areas. Maxilla exposed, not reaching eye. Dorsal fin with 8–11 spines, 18–23 rays; anal fin with 3 spines, 22–26 rays.

Habitat: Bays around piers, near rocky shores and kelp beds, and outer coastal waters over soft bottoms to depths of 480' (146 m).

Range: Wrangell, AK, to Bahía de San Quintín, Baja California.

Similar Species: Black Perch *(Embiotoca jacksoni)* has patch of enlarged scales below pectoral fin.

Comments: This species is also known as Shiner Surfperch. Anglers catch large numbers of this abundant perch from piers. A more slender ecological variant of this species was formerly recognized as Island Perch *(C. gracilis).*

---

586 Black Perch
Embiotoca jacksoni

Description: To 15½" (39 cm), usually to 12" (30 cm). Deep, very compressed. Usually dark brown to reddish brown above; yellowish below; dark bars on sides; *blue bar on anal fin base;* lips usually reddish brown to orange or yellow. Lips thick; frenum on lower lip; maxilla exposed. Dorsal fin with 9–11 spines, 18–22 rays, longest spines shorter than rays; anal fin with 3 spines, 23–27 rays. *Patch of enlarged scales adjacent to pectoral fin insertion; row of scales extends to pectoral fin insertion;* row of scales extends onto anal fin rays.

Habitat: Rocky shores and kelp beds, occasionally over sand; intertidal areas to depths of 150' (46 m), usually to 20' (6 m).

Range: Fort Bragg, CA, to Punta Abreojos, Baja California, including Isla de Guadalupe.

Similar Species: Barred Surfperch *(Amphistichus argenteus)* lacks enlarged scales below pectoral fin;

occurs in surf zone over sandy beaches and around rocks and pilings.

Comments: This species is also known as Black Surfperch or Butterlips. It feeds on worms, crustaceans, and mollusks; individuals occasionally act as cleaners, picking parasites off both their own and other species of fishes. The peak breeding season is in the summer, and most young are born in the spring. The annual catch by anglers fishing from shore and skiffs off southern California is about 125,000 fish.

592 Walleye Surfperch
Hyperprosopon argenteum

Description: To 12″ (30 cm). Deep, very compressed. Silvery to bluish above; back faintly dusky; *pelvic fin black-tipped; caudal fin black-edged. Eye very large, width equal to about one-third head length;* mouth oblique; no frenum on lower lip; maxilla exposed; 20–23 gill rakers on lower limb of first arch. Dorsal fin with 8–10 (usually 9) spines, 25–29 (usually 27) rays; anal fin with 3 spines, 30–35 (usually 32) rays.

Habitat: Surf zone over sand and around piers, rocky shores, and kelp beds; bays and outer coasts to depths of 60′ (18.5 m).

Range: Vancouver Island, BC, to Punta Rosarito, Baja California; abundant off s CA.

Similar Species: Spotfin Surfperch *(H. anale)* has black blotch on dorsal fin spines and on anal fin rays. Silver Surfperch *(H. ellipticum)* has pinkish caudal fin and tip of pelvic fin is not black.

Comments: Walleye Surfperch breeds from October to December, giving birth to five to 12 young in the spring. It feeds on small crustaceans. Shore anglers in southern California bays and on the outer coast take from 150,000 to 200,000 fish annually. This species is also part of the commercial surfperch catch.

591   Rainbow Seaperch
Hypsurus caryi

Description: To 12″ (30 cm). Deep, very compressed;
belly characteristically flat and long,
turning sharply upward at anal fin.
Reddish, with blue streaks and spots on
head; usually dark spot at rear of upper
jaw; about 10 reddish-brown bars on
upper body; *red and blue stripes on sides;
pelvic and anal fins usually reddish orange,
with blue edges;* dark blotch on soft dorsal
fin. Dorsal fin with 9–11 spines, 20–24
rays; anal fin with 3 spines, 20–24 rays,
*base shorter than distance from pelvic fin
insertion to anal fin origin.*

Habitat: Rocky shores, around piers, and kelp
beds; bays and outer coastal waters to
depths of 152′ (46 m).

Range: Cape Mendocino, CA, to Isla de San
Martín, Baja California.

Similar Species: Striped Seaperch *(Embiotoca lateralis)*
lacks bars on body, and has dusky pelvic
fin, 29–33 anal fin rays, and anal fin
base longer than distance from pelvic fin
insertion to anal fin origin; occurs to
depths of 70′ (21 m).

Comments: Rainbow Seaperch gathers in large
aggregations to breed in the fall; the
young are born the following summer.
Individuals occasionally act as cleaners,
picking parasites off both their own and
other species of fishes. Anglers along the
coast of California take from 10,000 to
20,000 fish annually.

593   Sharpnose Seaperch
Phanerodon atripes

Description: To 12″ (30 cm). Elongate, very
compressed. Silvery, usually with
reddish tint caused by reddish-brown
spot at base of each scale, combining to
form reddish streaks along scale rows;
scale edges often blue; *pelvic fin dusky,
black-tipped;* dark spot often on front of
anal fin. Maxilla exposed. Dorsal fin
with 10–11 spines, length of spines

increasing posteriorly, 22–24 rays; anal
fin with 3 spines, 27–30 rays; *caudal fin
deeply forked.*

Habitat: Rocky shores, around piers, and kelp
beds from shallow bays to depths of
150′ (46 m).

Range: Bodega Bay, CA, to Islas San Beníto,
Baja California. Formerly more
abundant; now common only in
Monterey Bay, CA.

Similar Species: White Seaperch *(P. furcatus)* lacks
reddish-brown marks on scales, has thin
black line at base of soft dorsal fin, and
tip of pelvic fin is not black.

Comments: This species is also known as Sharpnose
Surfperch. It obtains some of its food by
picking parasites off other fishes. It is
less common than White Seaperch, and
is seldom caught by anglers.

589 Rubberlip Seaperch
Rhacochilus toxotes

Description: To 18″ (46 cm). Deep, very compressed.
Brassy above; tan below; 1–2 dusky bars
on sides; occasionally with wide,
tapering, light bar below middle of
dorsal fin; lips pink; pelvic fin often
blackish; pectoral fin yellow or orange.
Young to 6″ (15 cm) long mostly
pinkish, with dark bar on mid-sides.
*Lips large, fleshy; lower lip has 2 fleshy
ventral lobes;* maxilla exposed. Pectoral
fin insertion below dorsal fin origin;
dorsal fin with 9–11 spines, 20–25 rays,
spines shorter than longest ray, first ray
shorter than third, base of spiny
segment shorter than soft segment; anal
fin with 3 spines, 27–30 rays.

Habitat: Usually rocky coasts or around piers and
kelp beds from shallow bays to depths of
150′ (46 m).

Range: Russian Gulch State Park, CA, to
Thurloe Head, Baja California; also
around Isla de Guadalupe, Baja
California.

Similar Species: Pile Perch *(R. vacca)* has lips not fleshy
or pink, black-tipped pelvic fin, dark

bar below middle of dorsal fin, and rays at front of soft dorsal fin segment much longer than dorsal fin itself.

Comments: This species is also known as Rubberlip Surfperch. A large female produces about 20 young each summer. Adults feed on shrimps, amphipods, small crabs, and other crustaceans. Often found in schools, Rubberlip Seaperch is an important sport and commercial species. Large numbers are caught by anglers in California, and commercial anglers take about 10 tons each year on hook and line and in gill nets.

DAMSELFISHES
Family Pomacentridae

28 genera and about 320 species worldwide; 5 genera and 19 species in North America (14 Atlantic, 5 Pacific), plus 11 species confined to Mexican Pacific waters. Damselfishes are mostly found in tropical seas, and the vast majority are associated with coral reefs; a few species occur in temperate waters. Most species are small, but a few attain lengths of more than 12″ (30 cm). These fishes usually have deep, moderately compressed bodies and are brightly colored, especially when young. The mouth is small, but the jaws are very protractile. There is usually a single nostril on each side of the snout (a small obscure second nostril is present in two genera), a characteristic that distinguishes this family from all similar ones except the mostly freshwater cichlids (family Cichlidae). The slightly notched dorsal fin has eight to 17 (usually 10 to 14) spines and 11 to 18 rays, and the base of the spiny segment is always longer than the soft-rayed segment. The anal fin almost always has two spines (rarely three) and nine to 16 rays. The scales are ctenoid, and the incomplete lateral line usually ends under the soft dorsal fin. Males assume parental care of the eggs. Included in this family are the brightly colored and distinctively patterned Indo-Pacific anemonefishes (genus *Amphiprion*), which have the unusual habit of living among the tentacles of poisonous sea anemones. Because of their interesting habits and attractive colors, members of this family are a common component of home and public marine aquariums. The taxonomy of certain genera is difficult, mainly because of pronounced color changes between the young and adults. All Atlantic and

eastern Pacific species formerly classified as members of the genera *Pomacentrus* and *Eupomacentrus* are now included in the genus *Stegastes*.

372 Sergeant Major
Abudefduf saxatilis

Description: To 7″ (18 cm). Oblong, deep, compressed. *Bluish white; back yellow or greenish yellow under spiny dorsal fin; 5 prominent dark bars on sides, with wider and lighter interspaces;* dark spot at pectoral fin base. 1 nostril on each side of snout; mouth small, terminal, slightly oblique. Dorsal fin with 13 spines, 13 rays, little or no notch between spiny and soft-rayed segments; anal fin with 2 spines, 12–13 rays; soft dorsal and anal fins pointed, similar in size and shape. Lateral line with 28–30 scales.

Habitat: Shallow reefs, sea-grass beds, and around pilings and rock jetties.

Range: RI to Uruguay, including Bermuda, Bahamas, Gulf of Mexico, and Caribbean; n records based on seasonal waifs. Also around Ascension Island and possibly other areas in mid–South Atlantic and e Atlantic.

Similar Species: Night Sergeant *(A. taurus)* has generally darker body, with pale interspaces narrower than dark bars, 9–10 anal fin rays, and noticeably less notched caudal fin.

Comments: Sergeant Major is apparently most abundant on shallow reefs in the Caribbean; far fewer occur north of Florida. Young are part of the sargassum fauna. Adults feed on plankton, deep-sea invertebrates, and plants. The common name presumably is derived from the dark bars that resemble the insignia of the military rank. Populations with a very similar pigmentation pattern are found in coral reef habitats throughout the world, and were once considered to be the same species.

384 Blacksmith
Chromis punctipinnis

Description: To 12″ (30 cm), usually smaller.
Deep, elongate, somewhat compressed.
*Back slate to dark blackish blue; sides
grayish blue* (males guarding eggs may
be quite pale); *black spots on posterior back
and on dorsal fin.* Young to lengths of
about 2″ (5 cm) purplish anteriorly,
yellowish orange posteriorly. Breeding
males have dark bar through eye. 1
nostril on each side of snout; mouth
slightly upturned; maxilla not reaching
eye. Dorsal fin with 11–13 spines,
15–17 rays; anal fin with 2 spines,
10–12 rays. Lateral line ends under soft
dorsal fin.

Habitat: Rocky areas and kelp beds to depths of
270′ (82 m).

Range: Monterey Bay, CA, to Punta San Pablo,
Baja California.

Similar Species: Blue Chromis *(C. cyanea)* is combination
of blue and black. Brown Chromis *(C.
multilineata)* has grayish to olive brown
body, white spot at base of last dorsal
fin ray, and yellow-tipped caudal fin.
Sunshinefish *(C. insolata)* has bright
yellowish-olive upper one-third of body.
Yellowtail Reeffish *(C. enchrysura)* has
yellowish caudal fin. Purple Reeffish
(C. scotti) has completely dark blue
body. All occur in open Atlantic waters
over coral reefs.

Comments: No other species of *Chromis* occurs in
North American Pacific waters,
although two other members of the
genus are found in Mexican Pacific
waters. Species of *Chromis* live in small
schools, and feed on small mid-water
organisms. Blacksmith spawns during
the summer; the male cleans the nesting
site, then herds a ripe female to it. After
spawning, the male guards the eggs
until they hatch. Because of its small
size, Blacksmith is not sought by
anglers, but it is occasionally caught on
small hooks and by spear fishers.

377 Garibaldi
Hypsypops rubicundus

Description: To 14″ (36 cm). Deep, compressed.
*Bright orange overall. Young have iridescent
blue markings on head, body, and fins.* 1
nostril on each side of snout. Dorsal fin
with 11–13 spines, 12–15 rays, extends
from above pectoral fin insertion to end
of anal fin base; anal fin with 2 spines,
1–12 rays; caudal fin forked, with
rounded tips. Lateral line ends under
soft dorsal fin.

Habitat: Rocky areas and kelp beds to depths of
100′ (30 m).

Range: Monterey Bay, CA, to Bahía Magdalena,
Baja California; rare north of Point
Conception, CA.

Comments: This is the largest North American
species of Pomacentridae and probably
one of the larger members of the family.
Garibaldi spawns from March to July.
The male prepares the nest and guards
the eggs for two or three weeks until
they hatch. It feeds on a variety of
invertebrates. This fish is protected by
law in California, and may not be taken
for either sport or commercial purposes.

381 Yellowtail Damselfish
Microspathodon chrysurus

Description: To 7½″ (19 cm). Robust, depth about
half of length. *Entire body and all fins
except caudal fin dark blue, becoming black in
large adults; cheek and breast bronze; caudal
fin bright yellow. Young have light blue spots
on back and dorsal fin,* disappearing with
increasing size and age; caudal fin
whitish. Profile of upper head steep,
slightly concave; 1 nostril on each side of
snout; eye small, relatively high on head;
mouth small, terminal; *teeth in upper jaw
flexible, brush-like;* deep notch next to
exposed maxilla anterior to eye;
preopercular bone smooth. Posterior
edges of soft dorsal and anal fin truncate.

Dorsal fin with 12 spines, 14–15 rays; anal fin with 2 spines, 12–13 rays. Lateral line ends under soft dorsal fin.

Habitat: Coral reefs in shallow to offshore waters.

Range: Northern FL to Venezuela, including Bahamas, Gulf of Mexico, and Caribbean.

Similar Species: Yellowtail Reeffish (*Chromis enchrysura*) also has yellow caudal fin, but reaches length of only 4″ (10 cm) and lacks brush-like teeth, notch anterior to eye, and blue spots on body; occurs at depths of 185–230′ (56–70 m).

Comments: This fish feeds on algae, organic debris, and certain corals. The young pick parasites from larger fishes. Records from the eastern Atlantic are based on a related species, *M. frontatus*.

378 Beaugregory
Stegastes leucostictus

Description: To 4″ (10 cm). Relatively slender, compressed, depth about two-fifths length. Dark gray to brownish, with paler olive scale centers; small black spot at pectoral fin base; *small black spot midway up side of dorsal fin at border between spiny and soft segments* (obscure in large, darkly colored individuals). Young are bluish on upper parts of head and body; scattered bright blue spots on head, upper half of body, and dorsal fin, often in horizontal rows; most of soft dorsal fin, caudal fin, and caudal peduncle bright yellow to orangish yellow; *no spot on upper edge of caudal peduncle.* Eye width greater than length of snout; 1 nostril on each side of snout; mouth small, terminal; *preopercle strongly serrate.* 17–19 (usually 18) pectoral fin rays; dorsal fin long, continuous, with 12 spines, 14–15 rays; dorsal and anal fin rays taper to acute points. Lateral line ends under soft dorsal fin.

Habitat: Shallow waters in rocky tide pools and over coral or sand; usually near bottom around coral heads or other objects.

Range: Bermuda; s FL to Brazil, including
Bahamas, s Gulf of Mexico, and
Caribbean. Possibly also in e Atlantic.

Similar Species: Cocoa Damselfish *(S. variabilis)* adults
also dark, nearly identical, but with
19–21 (usually 20) pectoral fin rays;
young have small dark spot on posterior
dorsal fin placed lower and closer to
back, and small distinct black spot on
top of caudal peduncle. Dusky
Damselfish *(S. adustus)* adults also turn
dark, but have shorter, more rounded
anal fin and 20–22 (usually 21) pectoral
fin rays; young slightly less colorful.

Comments: This highly territorial fish is one of the
most common damselfishes in shallow
reefs and rocky areas of the Bahamas and
the Caribbean. The western Atlantic and
eastern Pacific damselfish genus *Stegastes*
is superficially similar to the Indo-
Pacific genus *Pomacentrus,* and these
species were formerly classified under
the latter generic name.

379 Cocoa Damselfish
Stegastes variabilis

Description: To 4¼" (11 cm). Relatively slender,
compressed, depth slightly less than half
of length. Dark gray to brownish, with
paler olive scale centers; *small black spot
at pectoral fin base; small black spot on lower
part of dorsal fin at border between spiny and
soft segments* (obscure in large, darkly
colored individuals). Young bluish on
upper parts of head and body; scattered
bright blue spots on head, upper half of
body, and dorsal fin, often in horizontal
rows; most of soft dorsal fin, caudal fin,
and caudal peduncle bright yellow to
orangish yellow; *small distinct black spot
on upper edge of caudal peduncle.* Profile of
upper head slightly convex; snout
pointed; eye width greater than length
of snout; 1 nostril on each side of snout;
mouth small, terminal; *preopercle strongly
serrate. 19–21 (usually 20) pectoral fin
rays;* dorsal fin long, continuous, with

12 spines, 14–15 rays; soft dorsal and anal fins bluntly pointed posteriorly. Lateral line ends under soft dorsal fin.

Habitat: Shallow coral reefs, rocks, and around wrecks and oil platforms.

Range: NC to Brazil, including Bermuda, Bahamas, w FL, nw and se Gulf of Mexico, and Caribbean.

Similar Species: Beaugregory *(S. leucostictus)* adults also dark, nearly identical, but with 17–19 (usually 18) pectoral fin rays; young lack small dark spot on caudal peduncle. Dusky Damselfish *(S. adustus)* adults also turn dark, but have shorter and more rounded anal fin, 20–22 (usually 21) pectoral fin rays, and 10 gill rakers on lower limb of first arch; young slightly less colorful. Longfin Damselfish *(S. diencaeus)* is most similar to Dusky Damselfish, but has longer anal fin reaching well beyond caudal fin base and 11–12 gill rakers on lower limb of first arch. Bicolor Damselfish *(S. partitus)* is blackish anteriorly and whitish or creamy posteriorly. Threespot Damselfish *(S. planifrons)* has steeper dorsal profile, long and pointed anal fin, broader and more diffuse blotch at pectoral fin base, larger and more diffuse blotch on top of caudal peduncle, and adults are grayish.

Comments: The different species of *Stegastes* display interesting behavioral characteristics, and as such have been the subject of numerous studies.

WRASSES
Family Labridae

At least 60 genera and roughly 500 species worldwide; 13 genera and 25 species in North America (21 Atlantic, 4 Pacific), plus 2 genera and 15 species confined to Mexican Pacific waters. The second-largest marine fish family, Labridae is one of the most diverse in terms of shape, color, size, and temperature requirements. Most wrasses live in tropical or subtropical seas, but some occur in warm-temperate or even cold-temperate waters. The body shape ranges from pencil-like to deep and extremely compressed. Many species are highly colorful, making them popular aquarium fishes, and several color patterns (often sexually oriented) may exist within a single species. The mouth is terminal and protractile, with conspicuously thick lips. There are often strong canine teeth in the jaws and conical teeth on the pharyngeal bones, but none on the roof of the mouth; the jaw teeth are mostly separate and usually project outward. The dorsal fin has eight to 21 (usually fewer than 15) weak spines, lying low to the back, and six to 21 rays; the spiny and soft segments are not obviously separate. The anal fin has two to six (usually three) spines and seven to 18 rays. These fishes have medium to large cycloid scales; there are 25 to 80 scales in the lateral line, which follows the contour of the back. Some species reach a length of only 2″ (5 cm), whereas at least one Indo-Pacific species reaches a length of more than 7′ (2.1 m). Most small species are cleaners, picking ectoparasites off larger fishes. Wrasses propel themselves by sculling movements of the pectoral fins, and the majority bury themselves in sand at night. They are closely related to parrotfishes (family Scaridae), and display many of the same physical and behavioral characteristics.

---

411 Spanish Hogfish
Bodianus rufus

Description: To 24″ (61 cm), rarely more than 15″ (38 cm). Moderately deep, depth about one-third length. *Anterior two-thirds of body, including dorsal fin and upper part of head, deep red or bluish purple; posterior one-third of body and entire belly yellow; pectoral fin clear. Young lack red on anterior body;* dark blue spot between first 2 dorsal fin spines. Head pointed; profile of forehead not steep; maxilla reaches eye; jaws with canine teeth anteriorly; 1 large recurved canine tooth on each side of upper jaw; 17–19 gill rakers on first arch. Dorsal fin continuous, with 12 spines; upper and lower rays of caudal fin form short filaments. Lateral line complete.

Habitat: Around coral and rocky reefs to depths of about 100′ (30 m).

Range: NC to n Brazil, including Bermuda, Bahamas, and offshore reefs in Gulf of Mexico and Caribbean. Also around Ascension and St. Helena Islands in mid–South Atlantic.

Similar Species: Spotfin Hogfish *(B. pulchellus)* has
15–16 gill rakers on first arch, red body
with broad white band on sides from
chin to above middle of anal fin,
smudgy spot on upper edge of pectoral
fin tip, and yellow on posterior rays of
soft dorsal fin, upper half of caudal
peduncle, caudal fin base, and upper
caudal fin lobe; occurs in deeper waters.
Hogfish *(Lachnolaimus maximus)* reaches
length of 3′ (91 cm), has deep, strongly
compressed, usually reddish (never
bicolored) body, large blackish crescent
through base of caudal fin, black spot at
base of soft dorsal fin, and dorsal fin
with 14 spines, the first 3 elongate and
blade-like. Dwarf Wrasse *(Doratonotus
megalepis)* reaches length of only 3″ (7.5
cm), has greenish body and fins, first 3
dorsal fin spines moderately elongate,
and lateral line interrupted at front
of caudal peduncle; ocurs in shallow
turtle-grass beds. Rosy Razorfish
(Xyrichtys martinicensis), Pearly Razorfish
(X. novacula), and Green Razorfish *(X.
splendens)* have bizarre, extraordinarily
compressed body with very steeply
sloping forehead; all occur over open
sand.

Comments: As a defense mechanism, the bluish-
purple color of this fish becomes reddish
in deep water, which protects it from
predators because red is not visible at
great depths. The young pick parasitic
crustaceans off other fishes.

---

410 **Creole Wrasse**
Clepticus parrae

Description: To 12″ (30 cm). Moderately elongate,
depth about one-third length. *Mottled
and deep purple or violet above, becoming
lighter violet or purple below;* snout and
nape black; yellow area above anal fin
and on caudal peduncle; canine teeth
pale blue. *Snout blunt; mouth terminal,
small, very oblique;* lower jaw projects
beyond upper; canine teeth small, weak,

none in posterior part of jaws. Dorsal fin continuous, with 12 spines; caudal fin forked. Head and dorsal and anal fins scaled.

Habitat: Around outer reefs from mid-depths to 70′ (21 m).

Range: NC to n South America, including Bermuda, Bahamas, and Caribbean; also in Flower Garden Banks, nw Gulf of Mexico, and Yucatán.

Comments: Creole Wrasse is common on outer reefs, where it forms large feeding groups well off the bottom. It feeds on copepods, small jellyfishes, tunicates, and other invertebrates. Like most wrasses, this species is usually most active during the day, and at night may bury itself in the sand or hide in crevices of reefs.

417 Slippery Dick
Halichoeres bivittatus

Description: To 9″ (23 cm). Moderately slender, pencil-like. *Green above, becoming light greenish yellow or whitish on sides; 2 purplish or black stripes* overlaid with red extend on sides from eye to caudal peduncle, often broken into series of closely set spots toward rear; lower stripe sometimes yellow; sometimes pinkish markings on head; no spot at pectoral fin base; *small, sharply defined black spot at base of last dorsal fin ray and on dorsal fin just beyond midpoint (absent in large individuals);* upper and lower tips of caudal fins black, with irregular red bands. Head somewhat pointed; mouth terminal, not oblique; 2 large canine teeth anteriorly in upper jaw, 4 in lower jaw. Dorsal fin continuous, with 9 spines, 11 rays; caudal fin squarish. Lateral line complete, abruptly decurved below soft dorsal fin.

Habitat: Around shallow coral and rocky reefs and over nearby sand.

Range: NC to Brazil, including Bermuda, Bahamas, n Gulf of Mexico, Caribbean, and Central America.

Similar Species: The much less common Painted Wrasse
(H. pictus) is same size as a young
Slippery Dick, but lacks 2 black spots
on dorsal fin; occurs in deeper waters.
Yellowhead Wrasse *(H. garnoti)* adult
males have bright yellow head; young
have narrow, straight-edged blue stripe
on sides. Clown Wrasse *(H. maculipinna)*
usually has 1 much broader stripe and
only 2 large canine teeth in lower jaw.
Blackear Wrasse *(H. poeyi)* young have
green body with large dark blue spot
behind eye; occurs in sea-grass beds and
around reefs. Puddingwife *(H. radiatus)*
adults reach length of 20″ (51 cm);
young have 2 orange or yellow stripes on
sides separated by blue stripe. Rock
Wrasse *(H. semicinctus)* is yellow above,
lighter below, and has 12 anal fin rays;
males have dark blue bar behind
pectoral fin; females have large black
spots on scales adjacent to lateral line;
occurs in Pacific.

Comments: Slippery Dick is unusual among western
Atlantic species of *Halichoeres* in that it
undergoes little if any change in color
and pigmentation pattern throughout
its life. Along with Bluehead
(Thalassoma bifasciatum), this species is
perhaps the most common wrasse
around shallow western Atlantic reefs.
It is less fastidious than other wrasses
about its habitat and food selection.

418 Yellowhead Wrasse
Halichoeres garnoti

Description: To 7½″ (19 cm). Moderately slender,
depth about one-quarter length. *Males
bisected by oblique black girdle* extending
onto soft dorsal and caudal fins; *bright
yellow above and blue below in front of girdle;
bluish green behind girdle;* anal fin usually
reddish orange. Females reddish orange.
Young yellow, with narrow blue stripes
on sides. All have dark lines radiating
posteriorly from eye. Head somewhat
pointed; mouth terminal, not oblique; 2

canine teeth anteriorly in upper jaw, 4 in lower jaw. Dorsal fin continuous, with 9 spines, 11 rays; caudal fin slightly rounded. Lateral line complete, decurved below soft dorsal fin.

Habitat: Around coral and rocky reefs to depths of 162' (49 m).

Range: NC to se Brazil, including Bermuda, Bahamas, and nw Gulf of Mexico and Caribbean.

Comments: This wrasse is apparently common in the Bahama reefs, but it is rather rare in the peripheral areas of its range. The specific name, *garnoti,* honors Garnot, an early fish collector from Martinique.

409 Puddingwife
Halichoeres radiatus

Description: To 20" (51 cm). Depth about one-third length, deepest just in front of dorsal fin; dorsal and ventral profiles about equally rounded in smaller individuals. *Back olive yellow; sides yellowish orange, with round or crescent-shaped blue spots; blue lines on snout and through eye;* 3–5 blue bars on back (more conspicuous in young, becoming blotches in adults); *dark spot at upper part of pectoral fin base.* Young with 2 orange or yellow stripes on sides, separated by blue stripe. 2 canine teeth anteriorly in upper jaw, 4 in lower jaw. Dorsal fin continuous, with 9 spines, 11 rays; caudal fin truncate, with rounded corners. Lateral line abruptly decurved before beginning of caudal peduncle.

Habitat: Around coral and rocky reefs to depths of 180' (55 m). Young to 18' (5.5 m).

Range: NC to Brazil, including Bermuda, Bahamas, Gulf of Mexico, and Caribbean.

Comments: Puddingwife is one of the largest wrasses in North America and the largest western Altantic species in the genus *Halichoeres*. It has a deeper body than other *Halichoeres* wrasses. It feeds on mollusks and echinoderms.

416 Señorita
Oxyjulis californica

Description: To 10″ (25 cm). Elongate, pencil-like.
Dirty yellowish orange above; creamy
below; *large black area at caudal fin base.*
Young to 1″ (2.5 cm) long nearly
transparent, with large black spot on
dorsal and anal fins. Snout pointed;
mouth small; teeth small, protruding.
Dorsal fin continuous, elongate, with 10
spines, 13 rays; 13 anal fin rays; caudal
fin truncate to slightly rounded. Scales
large, cycloid.

Habitat: Rocky areas and kelp beds to depths of
330′ (101 m); usually to 75′ (23 m).

Range: Salt Point, Sonoma County, CA, to Isla
de Cedros, Baja California; common
in s CA.

Comments: Señorita occurs singly and in large
aggregations. It spawns from May to
August and feeds on small snails,
crustaceans, worms, and larval fishes.
Some individuals pick parasites from
other fishes; they are the most common
parasite cleaners off southern California.
Anglers catch this fish using very small
hooks, but few are retained, because they
are not considered edible.

413 California Sheephead
Semicossyphus pulcher

Description: To 3′ (91 cm). Fusiform, deep,
compressed. Males with black head,
posterior part of body, and caudal fin;
mid-body brick-red; *chin white;* large
individuals have fleshy lump on
forehead. Females reddish brown; chin
white. *Young brick-red, with white stripe on
sides; large black spots on pectoral, dorsal,
and caudal fins.* Forehead steeply slopes;
teeth large, canine. Dorsal fin
continuous, with 12 spines, 10 rays,
extends from pectoral fin insertion to
rear of anal fin base; anal fin with 3
spines, 10–12 rays; caudal fin almost
square.

Habitat: Kelp beds over rocks to depths of 180′
(55 m); usually at 10–100′ (3–30 m).

Range: Monterey Bay, CA, to Cabo San Lucas,
Baja California, and Gulf of California;
uncommon north of Point Conception,
CA.

Comments: California Sheephead is female until it is
seven or eight years old, when the ovaries
become testes; the fish then functions as
a male for the rest of its life. This species
spawns in the spring and summer and
feeds on crustaceans, echinoderms, and
mollusks. It is popular with anglers and
spear fishers; more than 50,000 fish are
taken annually in California. Southern
California populations have declined
because of fishing pressure and reduction
of kelp beds, and large males are
becoming increasingly rare.

---

415 **Tautog**
Tautoga onitis

Description: To 3′ (91 cm), usually to 18″ (46 cm);
22 lb (9.8 kg). Depth one-third length.
Coloration varies with background:
*mousy, chocolate gray, deep dusky green,
brownish, or dull black;* sides irregularly
mottled with paler shades; chin white in
large individuals. *Profile of head steep;
snout blunt; mouth terminal; lips thick;* jaws
stout, teeth conical anteriorly, molar-like
posteriorly. Dorsal fin long, notched,
with 16–17 spines, 10 rays; anal fin
with 3 spines, 7–8 rays; caudal fin
truncate, slightly rounded at corners.
Cheek unscaled, velvety to touch.

Habitat: Coastal waters to depths of 60′ (18.5
m); near wrecks, piers, docks, mussel
beds, and steep rocky shores.

Range: NS to SC; most abundant from Cape
Cod, MA, to DE.

Comments: Tautog feeds by crushing shelled
invertebrates with its strong teeth.
Although considered a good food and
sport fish, this species is not sufficiently
plentiful anywhere in its range to be of
great importance as either.

414 Cunner
Tautogolabrus adspersus

Description: To 10″ (25 cm). *Moderately slender.*
Reddish brown above, with bluish or
brownish tinge; mottled with blue,
brown, and red; coloration varies with
background: some individuals uniformly
brown, others deep sepia. *Snout bluntly
pointed; lips moderately thick;* teeth conical
anteriorly, molar-like posteriorly. Dorsal
fin long, notched, with 18 spines, 9–10
rays; anal fin with 3 spines, 9 rays. *Cheek
scaled.*

Habitat: Shallow coastal waters in eelgrass and
around pilings, piers, and rock piles.

Range: NF to NJ; occasionally south to
Chesapeake Bay.

Comments: This species is so variably colored that it
is difficult to describe. Individuals
living among red seaweed or in deep
water are reddish or rust-colored; those
living over sand are pale and speckled
with blackish dots. Cunner is
omnivorous. A good food fish, it is
popular with anglers.

412 Bluehead
Thalassoma bifasciatum

Description: To 6″ (15 cm). Elongate, depth about
one-quarter length. *Older adult males blue
anteriorly, green posteriorly; colors separated
by 2 broad black bands enclosing light area;*
soft dorsal and anal fins blue; upper and
lower caudal fin rays blackish. Younger
adult males, females, and young yellow;
usually with broad blackish lateral stripe
extending from opercle to caudal fin
base; red stripe extends from snout
through eye to end of opercle. Head
somewhat pointed; mouth terminal;
anterior teeth canine, progressively
longer toward front of jaws; no posterior
canine teeth. *Dorsal fin with 8 spines,*
12–13 rays; anal fin with 3 spines,
10–11 rays; caudal fin nearly square,
upper and lower lobes notably elongate

in older adult blue-headed males. Lateral line abruptly decurved below soft dorsal fin.

Habitat: Shallow coral and rocky reefs.

Range: NC to Brazil, including Bermuda, Bahamas, Gulf of Mexico, and Caribbean.

Similar Species: Wrasse Blenny *(Hemiemblemaria simula)*, in tube blenny family (Chaenopsidae), resembles younger adult male, female, and young Blueheads, but has more elongate body and more pointed snout.

Comments: Bluehead is sexually mature when it reaches a length of 1½″ (4 cm). Most individuals are yellow; the blue-headed older adult males are less common. In appearance and behavior, Wrasse Blenny mimics this species and thus can more easily approach potential prey, which probably assume that it, like Bluehead, is a parasite picker.

PARROTFISHES
Family Scaridae

9 genera and 83 species worldwide; 4 genera and 15 species in North America (14 Atlantic, 1 Pacific), plus 1 genus and 5 species confined to Mexican Pacific waters. These colorful, diurnal, herbivorous fishes abound on reefs of shallow tropical seas. The teeth are fused to form a pair of beak-like dental plates in each jaw (the basis for the family's common name), which are joined at the front of the jaws and in most genera are separated by a median groove; the groove is absent and the individual teeth fused together but distinguishable in a few of the more primitive genera. The paired upper and lower pharyngeal bones contain rows of molar-like teeth (the pharyngeal mill), which are used to grind up algae associated with the coral rock or sediment that is often ingested (parrotfishes thus are the primary producers of the coralline sand found around reefs). Most species have an oblong, moderately compressed body, with the head usually bluntly rounded anteriorly. All species have a continuous dorsal fin with nine flexible spines and 10 rays, and an anal fin with three spines and nine rays. All fins are unscaled. The scales on the body are large and cycloid. The lateral line usually has 22 to 24 scales and follows the contour of the back to below the rear portion of the dorsal fin. Sexual dimorphism is pronounced in many species,

which has led to past taxonomic confusion. The drab-colored young are male or female (the primary phase), with many maintaining this coloration into sexual maturity; some females apparently later change into brightly colored (with combinations of red, green, and blue) terminal males, which have been found to exhibit different reproductive behavior than primary-phase mature males. Parrotfishes are related to the wrasses (family Labridae) and exhibit many of the same physical and behavioral features. Slender-bodied parrotfish genera, such as *Cryptotomus,* so closely resemble wrasses in outward appearance that even specialists can be fooled. Both families are strongly diurnal and undergo a form of sleep at night, at which time some species may secrete a protective transparent mucal cocoon.

400 Blue Parrotfish
Scarus coeruleus

Description: To 4′ (1.2 m). Moderately deep, depth more than one-third length. *Large adults deep blue, smaller individuals light blue; top of head yellow (colored area diminishes with increasing body size); bases of scales yellowish pink; teeth white.* Young have 3 dark longitudinal stripes. Distinct hump on forehead in adults, visible in profile view; teeth form beak-like plates, individual teeth indistinguishable, *lower plate hidden by upper when mouth closed.* 13 pectoral fin rays; dorsal fin continuous, long; caudal fin truncate, with upper and lower lobes becoming longer as size increases. 3 rows of scales on cheek below eye; 6 predorsal scales.

Habitat: Shallow tropical coral reefs.

Range: MD to Rio de Janeiro, Brazil, including Bermuda, Bahamas, and Caribbean; n records based on seasonal waifs.

Similar Species: Midnight Parrotfish *(S. coelestinus)* has deep blue to blackish body, scales with bright blue centers, blue-green teeth, 2 scale rows on cheek below eye, and 14 pectoral fin rays. Rainbow Parrotfish *(S. guacamaia)* has bright green teeth and 14 pectoral fin rays, and adults lack distinct hump on forehead. Emerald Parrotfish *(Nicholsina usta)* is more slender and teeth are incompletely fused; occurs usually in sea-grass beds. The wrasse-like Bluelip Parrotfish *(Cryptotomus roseus)* is more slender and teeth are largely separate (thus sometimes called Manytooth Parrotfish); occurs in shallow waters with vegetation. Species in genus *Sparisoma* have small teeth that are less solidly fused together, upper jaw teeth hidden by lower when mouth closed, 1 row of scales below eye, and 4 predorsal scales.

Comments: Blue Parrotfish, like other parrotfishes, uses its molar-like teeth on the upper and lower pharyngeal bones to grind algae along with soft coral. The young, with alternating dark and white stripes, resemble Striped Parrotfish *(S. iseri)* and Princess Parrotfish *(S. taeniopterus).*

407, 408 Princess Parrotfish
Scarus taeniopterus

Description: To 13″ (33 cm). Moderately deep, depth about one-third length. *Terminal males blue-green and orange; 2 narrow blue-green stripes on head; broad pale yellow stripe above pectoral fin;* dorsal and anal fins blue, with orange band through middle; *caudal fin blue, edges orange.* Primary females and young have 3 alternating dark brown and white stripes; fins pale blue. Teeth form beak-like plates, individual teeth indistinguishable, *lower plate hidden by upper when mouth closed.* 12 pectoral fin rays; dorsal fin continuous, long; caudal fin truncate or slightly rounded. 3 rows of scales on cheek, first row with 7 scales; 7–8 (usually 7) predorsal scales.

Habitat: Shallow tropical coral reefs.
Range: Bermuda, Bahamas, s FL, Florida Keys, nw Gulf of Mexico, and throughout Caribbean to nw Brazil.
Similar Species: Striped Parrotfish *(S. iseri)* has white stripe usually ending above gill opening, yellow snout in primary phase, 12 pectoral fin rays, orange caudal fin (with blue edges in terminal phase), and 6 scales in first scale row below eye;

young similar, distinguished by number
of scales in first row below eye.

Comments: Female and young Princess and Striped
Parrotfishes are readily confused, both
having three brown stripes alternating
with white stripes on the sides.

---

406   Queen Parrotfish
Scarus vetula

Description: To 24″ (61 cm). Moderately deep, depth
one-third length. *Terminal males blue-
green; scale edges reddish orange; head green,
with alternating orange and blue-green stripes
on lower snout and chin; caudal fin green,
with orange stripe on upper and lower rays.*
Primary females dark reddish to purplish
brown, with broad whitish stripe on
lower sides. Young have 2 white stripes
and white belly. Teeth form beak-like
plates, individual teeth indistinguishable,
*lower plate hidden by upper when mouth
closed.* 12 pectoral fin rays; dorsal fin
continuous, long; caudal fin truncate,
lunate in adult males. 4 rows of scales on
cheek below eye; 7 predorsal scales.

Habitat: Shallow tropical coral reefs.
Range: Bermuda, Bahamas, and s FL to n South
America, including nw Gulf of Mexico
and Caribbean.

Similar Species: Princess Parrotfish *(S. taeniopterus)*
terminal males are blue-green and
orange, with 2 dark lines behind eye.

Comments: No other species of North American
parrotfish has dark gray young adults
with white stripes. This fish is one of the
most noticeable members of the coral
reef community. It and other
parrotfishes are believed to be the major
factor in reef attrition and sand
production in calm areas.

---

403   Redband Parrotfish
Sparisoma aurofrenatum

Description: To 11″ (28 cm). Moderately deep, depth
about two-fifths length. *Terminal males*

greenish gray above; sides and fins reddish, sometimes blue-tinged. Primary females brown to greenish brown, with deep bluish cast on sides; reddish below. *Small distinct spot behind base of soft dorsal fin in adults.* Young mottled grayish above, with broad white stripe along mid-sides, intensifying anteriorly into dark 4-sided blotch; no white spots on body. Fleshy tab at rim of anterior nostril not ribbon-like; teeth form beak-like plates, individual teeth distinguishable, *upper plate hidden by lower when mouth closed.* Dorsal fin continuous, long; caudal fin rounded in young, truncate at intermediate sizes, emarginate in adults. 1 row of scales on cheek below eye; 4 predorsal scales.

Habitat: Shallow tropical coral reefs.

Range: Bermuda, Bahamas, and s FL to Brazil, including nw Gulf of Mexico and Caribbean.

Similar Species: Redtail Parrotfish *(S. chrysopterum)* has large oblong spot on upper pectoral fin base and slightly emarginate to lunate caudal fin. Stoplight Parrotfish *(S. viride)* young have white spots in orderly vertical and horizontal rows.

Comments: Young Redband Parrotfishes feed over sea-grass beds near coral reefs.

---

404 **Bucktooth Parrotfish**
Sparisoma radians

Description: To 8″ (20 cm). Depth one-third length. Terminal males greenish brown, with pale dots and net-like markings; *some scale edges reddish; blue and orange stripe extends from mouth to eye; black bar at pectoral fin base; broad black border on posterior part of caudal fin.* Primary phases olive to yellowish brown, with many pale dots. *Fleshy tab at rim of anterior nostril ribbon-like;* teeth form beak-like plates, individual teeth distinguishable, *upper plate hidden by lower when mouth closed; canine teeth prominent.* Dorsal fin continuous, long; caudal fin slightly rounded. 1 row of scales on cheek below eye; 2 scales between pelvic fin bases; 4 median predorsal scales.

Habitat: Shallow tropical sea-grass beds.

Range: Bermuda, Bahamas, and s FL to n South America, including parts of Gulf of Mexico and Caribbean.

Similar Species: Greenblotch Parrotfish *(S. atomarium)* has black blotch above pectoral fin and 1 scale between pelvic fin bases.

Comments: This parrotfish can change colors rapidly to blend with its surroundings. The genus name, *Sparisoma,* is derived from the Greek words *spairo,* meaning "I gasp," and *soma,* meaning "body," and describes the viewer's reaction to these brightly colored fishes.

---

405 Yellowtail Parrotfish
Sparisoma rubripinne

Description: To 18″ (46 cm). Robust, depth about two-fifths length. Terminal males dull green, *with dark-edged scales; black spot on upper half of pectoral fin base.* Primary phases light greenish brown, with darker-edged scales; 2 pale stripes on chin; caudal peduncle and caudal fin yellowish. Fleshy tab at rim of anterior nostril not ribbon-like; teeth form beak-like plates, individual teeth distinguishable, *upper plate hidden by lower when mouth closed;* canine teeth not prominent. Dorsal fin continuous, long; caudal fin rounded in young, truncate at intermediate sizes, deeply emarginate in terminal males. 1 row of scales on cheek below eye; 4 median predorsal scales.

Habitat: Shallow tropical coral reefs.

Range: FL to Rio de Janeiro, Brazil, including Bermuda, Bahamas, and Caribbean; stragglers north to MA; apparently absent from Gulf of Mexico.

Similar Species: Redtail Parrotfish *(S. chrysopterum)* is similarly colored but lacks dark edges on scales, and has pectoral saddle in terminal males (young lack dark saddle), fleshy tab at rim of anterior nostril with only a few lobes, and yellow crescent on tail.

Comments: When pursued, Yellowtail Parrotfish can hide by rapidly changing its colors to match its surroundings. It was formerly known as Redfin Parrotfish.

401, 402 Stoplight Parrotfish
Sparisoma viride

Description: To 24″ (61 cm). Deep, depth about two-fifths length. Terminal males mostly green; *scale edges dull green; 3 diagonal yellowish-orange bands on head; opercle with orange edge and small bright spot on top; large yellow spot at caudal fin base.* Primary phases brown above and on head; lower one-third and fins bright red; scale centers lighter. Young have regular vertical and horizontal rows of white spots; dark blotch behind pectoral fin. Fleshy tab at rim of anterior nostril not ribbon-like; teeth form beak-like plates, individual teeth distinguishable, *upper plate hidden by lower when mouth closed.* Dorsal fin continuous, long; caudal fin truncate in young, emarginate at intermediate sizes, lunate in large males. 1 row of scales on cheek below eye; 4 median predorsal scales.

Habitat: Shallow tropical coral reefs and adjacent sea-grass beds.

Range: Bermuda, Bahamas, FL, Gulf of Mexico, and Caribbean to ne Brazil.

Similar Species: Redband Parrotfish *(S. aurofrenatum)* young have similar black blotch above pectoral fin base, but lack white spots on regular rows on body.

Comments: This rather large parrotfish is most abundant in the Florida Keys and in West Indian reefs. The specific name, *viride,* from the Latin *viridis,* refers to the fish's green coloration.

RONQUILS
Family Bathymasteridae

3 genera and at least 7 species world-wide; 3 genera and at least 6 species in North America. This

family is confined to cold-temperate inshore marine waters on both sides of the North Pacific. They are slender elongate fishes with large eyes; they reach lengths of up to 12″ (30 cm). Both the dorsal and anal fins are long, continuous, and uniformly parallel with the body, and neither is joined to the caudal fin. The dorsal and anal fins are composed almost entirely of rays (some species have a few weak spines at the front of the fins); there are 41 to 48 dorsal fin rays and 30 to 36 anal fin rays. The thoracic pelvic fins are just in front of the pectoral fins, and each has a single weak spine and five rays. The pectoral and caudal fins are rounded. The body is covered with numerous small, deeply embedded ctenoid scales. Ronquils have a straight lateral line, located high on the body and extending only to near the end of the dorsal fin.

---

504 Bluebanded Ronquil
Rathbunella hypoplecta

Description: To 8½″ (22 cm). Slender, elongate. Brown to purplish, with lighter areas; usually dark brown blotches on body, sometimes forming vague bars on upper sides and back; *blue stripe on anal fin;* outer edge of anal fin dark in males, white in females. Head and snout moderately blunt. Pectoral fin not extending back to front of anal fin; *dorsal fin long, low, not joined to caudal fin,* with about 46 rays, first 15 rays unbranched; *anal fin long, not joined to caudal fin,* with about 33 branched rays; caudal fin rounded.

Habitat: Exposed coasts over rocks or sand at depths of 20–300′ (6–91 m).

Range: San Francisco, CA, to n Baja California.

Similar Species: Stripefin Ronquil *(R. alleni)* lacks blue stripe on anal fin.

Comments: This species is also known as Smooth Ronquil, although other ronquils are actually smoother. Bluebanded Ronquil feeds on invertebrates. The male guards the eggs. This fish is rarely captured on small baited hooks, but is occasionally caught in trawls. Bluebanded and Stripefin Ronquils are so similar that they were long considered to be the same species.

EELPOUTS
Family Zoarcidae

About 46 genera and about 220 species worldwide; 10 genera and 34 species in North America (7 Atlantic, 20 Pacific, 7 shared), with additional species in deeper waters farther offshore. Eelpouts are mostly confined to cold-temperate to arctic waters of the North Pacific, North Atlantic, and Arctic Oceans; a few species inhabit seas of comparable temperatures around the southern continents, including Antarctica, but the family is absent from intervening tropical regions. North American eelpouts are found in shallow to moderately deep waters, usually to depths of 656′ (200 m). Most are bottom dwellers; a few are free-swimming mid-water fishes, as are the early-life stages of some bottom species. These fishes have an elongate tapering body with a relatively large head. The mouth is often big, with thick lips, and the upper jaw usually projects beyond the lower jaw. The long dorsal and anal fins are usually joined to the pointed caudal fin, extending unbroken around the end of the body. The pelvic fins, when present, are tiny and thoracic, just in front of the pectoral fins. Most species have fins without spines. When present, the scales are tiny and cycloid, embedded in the skin and difficult to see. Most species are oviparous, but a few are ovoviviparous. The concepts of the evolutionary relationships of this family to other fish families have changed greatly through time; prior to their current position in the order Perciformes, the eelpouts were thought to be closer to the codfishes (family Gadidae), cusk-eels (family Ophidiidae), and their relatives in the order Gadiformes.

---

505 Ocean Pout
Macrozoarces americanus

Description: To 3′6″ (1.1 m). Elongate, eel-like, depth about one-eighth length. Coloration variable: pinkish yellow, brownish, or reddish brown; mottled with darker hues above; dirty white or yellowish below. Head conical; eye small; teeth large, conical; maxilla reaches well beyond eye. *Pelvic fin small, not filamentous,* insertion in front of pectoral fin; pectoral fin broad-based, fan-like; *dorsal fin origin over posterior part of head above opercle,* about same height throughout, *not joined to caudal fin; anal fin long, low, joined to caudal fin.* Scales small. Flesh soft; skin slimy.

Habitat:	On bottom over sand, mud, rocks, or seaweed to depths of 630' (192 m).
Range:	Battle Harbor, Labrador, and Gulf of St. Lawrence to DE.
Similar Species:	Blackbelly Eelpout *(Lycodopsis pacifica)* has black belly and black spot on anterior part of dorsal fin; occurs over soft bottoms at depths of 30–1,310' (9–399 m) in Pacific.
Comments:	Though there is little demand for Ocean Pout as a food fish, the flesh is reputedly lean and wholesome. The dorsal fin of all other western Atlantic eelpouts is joined to the caudal fin, and all but one have the dorsal fin origin behind the head, above the pectoral fin.

PRICKLEBACKS
Family Stichaeidae

About 36 genera and about 65 species worldwide; 22 genera and 33 species in North America (3 Atlantic, 25 Pacific, 5 shared). This family is confined to cold-temperate waters of the North Pacific and Atlantic Oceans, with the greatest abundance in the Pacific. Most of these eel-like, elongate, compressed bottom fishes live in the tidal zone among rocks and vegetation. When present, the pelvic fins are small and thoracic, each with one spine and two to four rays. The dorsal and anal fins are long, extending almost to the tail, but they are joined to the caudal fin in only a few species. The dorsal fin origin is just behind the head. The anal fin, which consists of one to five small spines, begins at or before the mid-body. Some pricklebacks are unscaled; when present, the scales are tiny, cycloid, and deeply embedded. The lateral line is either faint, incomplete, or absent; when present, it occasionally has four main branches with vertical side branches. The gill membranes are sometimes medially joined. Pricklebacks have brown, red, or yellow coloring, and, in some species, faint bars or stripes. They are similar to the gunnels (family Pholidae), and are best distinguished by their longer anal fin.

509   High Cockscomb
Anoplarchus purpurescens

Description:	To 7¾" (20 cm). Elongate, eel-like, compressed; *fleshy crest on top of head.*

Coloration variable: blackish or purple to brown, often with darker and lighter mottling; usually 2 dark streaks on cheek. Males sometimes have orange fins. Gap between gill slits on underside of head usually more than three-fourths eye width. *No pelvic fins;* 54–60 dorsal fin spines; anal fin with 2 spines, 35–41 rays.

Habitat: Usually intertidal zone among rocks to depths of 100′ (30 m).

Range: Pribilof Islands, AK, to Santa Rosa Island, s CA.

Similar Species: Slender Cockscomb *(A. insignis)* also has fleshy crest on top of head and lacks pelvic fins, but gap is narrower between gill slits on underside of head. Monkeyface Prickleback *(Cebidichthys violaceus)* young have gill slits joined at throat and dorsal fin with both spines and rays. Black Prickleback *(Xiphister atropurpureus)* has much smaller pectoral fin (about same size as eye); occurs to depths of 25′ (7.5 m). Rock Prickleback *(X. mucosus)* has much smaller pectoral fin (about same size as eye); occurs to depths of 60′ (18.5 m). Gunnels (family Pholidae) have anal fin less than half of body length.

Comments: The many prickleback and gunnel species make up two of the most characteristic groups of small fishes living in tide pools and among weeds and rocks in the North Pacific.

---

508 Monkeyface Prickleback
Cebidichthys violaceus

Description: To 30″ (76 cm). Elongate, eel-like, compressed; *2 fleshy humps on head.* Coloration highly variable: generally light to dark brown; 2 dark bars below eye. Snout bluntly rounded; *lips fleshy, prominent;* gill membranes free of isthmus. No pelvic fins; dorsal fin with 22–25 spines, 40–43 rays, origin above gill openings; anal fin with 1–2 spines, 39–42 rays; dorsal and anal fins joined

to caudal fin, separated by deep notch.
Lateral line high, near dorsal fin base.

Habitat: Crevices and holes in shallow rocky areas
to depths of 80' (24 m).

Range: Brookings, s OR, to Bahía de San
Quintín, Baja California; rare south of
Point Conception, CA.

Similar Species: Black Prickleback *(Xiphister
atropurpureus)* has white band on caudal
peduncle and dorsal fin composed
entirely of spines, its origin about
halfway between snout and anal fin
origin; occurs to depths of 25' (7.5 m).
Rock Prickleback *(X. mucosus)* has dorsal
fin origin about one-third distance from
snout to anal fin origin; occurs to depths
of 60' (18.5 m). High Cockscomb
(Anoplarchus purpurescens) has gill
membranes attached to isthmus, dorsal
fin composed of 54–60 spines, and
lateral line at mid-side.

Comments: Monkeyface Prickleback is the target of
a specialized sport fishery called "poke
poling." Anglers use long cane poles
with a piece of wire 6" (15 cm) long
attached to the tip; a short leader and
hook are attached to the wire. The hook,
baited with a crustacean or worm, is
poked into crevices at low tide.

---

502 Snake Prickleback
Lumpenus sagitta

Description: To 20" (51 cm). Elongate; head length
almost one-tenth body length. Light
green above; creamy below; *greenish to
brown streaks on sides; dark spots at base of
dorsal fin rays and near edge of fin; about 5
narrow bars across caudal fin.* Snout
moderately long, rounded, not
overhanging mouth. Pelvic and pectoral
fin rays not elongate; 64–72 dorsal fin
spines; anal fin with 1 spine, 45–50
rays. Cheek unscaled.

Habitat: Shallow bays and offshore to depths of
about 680' (207 m).

Range: Bering Sea to Humboldt Bay, CA. Also
in Sea of Japan.

Similar Species: Daubed Shanny *(Lumpenus maculatus)* also has long snout, but lacks scales on most of head and pelvic fin is longer with elongate lower rays; occurs over sand to depths of about 200′ (61 m). Longsnout Prickleback *(Lumpenella longirostris)* has less elongate body, lacks bars on caudal fin, and anal fin has 3–5 spines; occurs at depths of 300–460′ (91–140 m).

Comments: Formal description of this species did not occur until 1956, in contrast to other members of the genus, which were all identified in the 18th and early 19th centuries. Snake Prickleback is one of the few prickleback species sometimes caught on a baited hook.

GUNNELS
Family Pholidae

4 genera and about 13 species worldwide; 4 genera and 10 species in North America (1 Atlantic, 8 Pacific, 1 shared). Gunnels are confined to cold-temperate marine waters of the North Pacific and Atlantic Oceans, with the greatest abundance in the Pacific. They are eel-like fishes with long, slender, compressed bodies; most species are less than 12″ (30 cm) long. The teeth are small and conical. The pelvic fins are rudimentary or absent; when present, they have a single spine and a single ray. When present, the pectoral fins are very small, with seven to 17 rays. The dorsal fin is twice as long as the anal fin; both fins are usually joined to the caudal fin. The dorsal fin consists of 75 to 100 flexible spines; the anal fin has one to two spines and usually 30 to 45 rays. The cycloid scales are usually inconspicuous and covered with thick mucus. The lateral line is short or absent altogether. Most gunnels live in the intertidal zone in shallow water, hiding among rocks and crevices near algae. They are very similar to the pricklebacks (family Stichaeidae), and are best distinguished by their shorter anal fin.

503 Penpoint Gunnel
Apodichthys flavidus

Description: To 18″ (46 cm). Elongate, eel-like, compressed. Green, yellow, light brown,

or red; dark streak extends down from eye, with second streak often radiating from upper posterior edge of eye. Head bluntly rounded; mouth terminal, small. No pelvic fins; *pectoral fin length about twice eye width;* dorsal fin extends from pectoral fin insertion to caudal peduncle, joined to caudal fin; *anal fin with 1 strong deeply grooved spine, 36–42 rays,* about one-third length of dorsal fin, origin about two-thirds back along length of body, joined to caudal fin.

Habitat: Intertidal zone among rocks and shallow eelgrass beds.

Range: Kodiak Island, AK, to Santa Barbara Island, s CA.

Similar Species: Saddleback Gunnel *(Pholis ornata)* has series of dark V- or U-shaped marks along dorsal fin base, small pelvic fin, and 34–38 anal fin rays. Red Gunnel *(P. schultzi)* has anal fin with bars and 40–44 rays. Rockweed Gunnel *(Xererpes fucorum)* has pectoral fin same length as eye width and anal fin spine without groove.

Comments: This rarely seen gunnel spawns in January. It feeds on small crustaceans and mollusks. The common name is derived from the strong grooved anal fin spine.

WOLFFISHES
Family Anarhichadidae

2 genera and 5 species worldwide; all found in North America (2 Atlantic, 2 Pacific, 1 shared). This family is confined to cold-temperate marine waters of the North Pacific and Atlantic Oceans. The largest of these eel-like fishes exceeds a length of 8′ (2.4 m). Pelvic fins are absent, and the pectoral fins are large. The dorsal fin is composed of numerous flexible spines. The anal fin has numerous rays and sometimes a single spine. The small caudal fin is usually pointed. The gill membranes are attached to the isthmus. Wolffishes are usually unscaled and lack a lateral line; when present, the scales are small and cycloid. They have strong jaws with large, peg-like canine teeth in the front and molar-like teeth in the rear, with which they can cause serious wounds.

507 Atlantic Wolffish
Anarhichas lupus

Description: To 5' (1.5 m). Elongate, greatest depth at nape, tapering to slender caudal peduncle. Coloration varies with substrate: purplish, brownish, bluish gray, olive, or combinations of these; 10 or more irregular bars on sides. Eye small; maxilla reaches beyond eye; *front of jaws with large canine teeth, back of jaws with molar-like teeth.* No pelvic fins; pectoral fin broad-based, fan-like; dorsal fin long, continuous, begins at nape, *with 69–77 flexible spines of equal length;* anal fin about half as long as dorsal fin, with 42–48 rays; dorsal and anal fins not joined to caudal fin.

Habitat: Over hard bottoms from near shore to depths of 510' (155 m).

Range: Greenland and Davis Strait to Cape Cod, MA; occasionally south to NJ.

Comments: The solitary Atlantic Wolffish is not abundant anywhere. Its large jaws, formidable teeth, and habit of attacking objects and people, in the water or when caught, make it a potentially dangerous species. It feeds on a variety of shelled mollusks, echinoderms, and crustaceans.

506 Wolf-Eel
Anarrhichthys ocellatus

Description: To 6'8" (2 m). Eel-like, elongate, compressed, tapering to pointed caudal fin. Light gray or grayish brown, with *dark mottling and spots surrounded by lighter areas.* Snout blunt; *front of jaws with large strong canine teeth partly exposed when mouth closed.* No pelvic fins; dorsal fin long, continuous, with 210–250 flexible spines; anal fin about two-thirds length of dorsal fin, sometimes with 1 spine, 180–233 rays.

Habitat: Rocky areas and around wrecks with large crevices to depths of 636' (194 m).

Range: Kodiak Island, AK, to Imperial Beach, San Diego County, CA.

Similar Species: California Moray (*Gymnothorax mordax*) lacks pelvic and pectoral fins.

Comments: Wolf-Eel spawns during the winter; the eggs are deposited in crevices or caves and are guarded by both parents. This large predator feeds on crabs taken from traps and on fishes, sea urchins, sea cucumbers, and snails. Anglers and spear fishers occasionally catch this fish; caution should be taken, as it may bite and can cause serious wounds. The large, tusk-like teeth are so distinctive that Wolf-Eel should never be confused with any other fish.

SAND LANCES
Family Ammodytidae

5 genera and about 18 species world-wide; 1 genus with 3 species in North America, plus 1 species confined to Mexican Pacific waters. This family is found in cool to tropical waters in the Arctic, Atlantic, Indian, and Pacific Oceans; species in tropical regions occur in deeper colder waters. These small, eel-like fishes are quite long, and swim with an undulating motion. Unlike eels, they have wide gill openings, a large opercle, a forked caudal fin, and small cycloid scales. Sand lances have long dorsal and anal fins, both without spines; the dorsal fin has 40 to 69 rays, and the anal fin has 14 to 36 rays. Pelvic fins are usually absent (present in one genus). The lateral line is high, close to the dorsal fin. Sand lances lack teeth, and the premaxillae are protractile in all but one genus.

American Sand Lance

American Sand Lance
Ammodytes americanus

Description: To 7″ (18 cm). Very elongate, depth less than one-tenth length from snout tip to caudal fin base. Bluish green to olive brown above; sides silvery, often with

steel blue iridescence; belly white. Head large; *snout sharply pointed;* mouth large; lower jaw projects well beyond upper jaw. *No pelvic fins;* pectoral fin insertion well below axis of body; dorsal fin long, low, with 51–62 rays, origin over pectoral fins, extends almost to caudal fin base; anal fin similar to dorsal fin but less than half as long, with 23–33 rays; caudal fin forked.

Habitat: Primarily sandy shores of continental shelf; rarely over mud and rocks or in deep waters.

Range: Northern Labrador to Cape Hatteras, NC.

Similar Species: Northern Sand Lance *(A. dubius)* has more slender body, 56–68 dorsal fin rays, and 27–35 anal fin rays (fin ray counts in both species subject to geographic variation); occurs farther offshore to depths of 120′ (37 m). Pacific Sand Lance *(A. hexapterus)* is metallic blue above; occurs in Bering Sea and Pacific.

Comments: American Sand Lance has in the past been considered the same species as Pacific Sand Lance. It often occurs in schools consisting of several thousand individuals. It swims with an undulating motion similar to that of eels. Sand lances are the primary prey of terns, and are often eaten by other seabirds, predatory fishes, and marine mammals; to escape predators they burrow rapidly into the sand.

STARGAZERS
Family Uranoscopidae

8 genera and about 50 species worldwide; 3 genera and 6 species in North America (4 Atlantic, 2 Pacific). This family is found in shallow to moderately deep tropical to temperate seas throughout the world, usually along continental shores with open bottoms. Stargazers are heavy-bodied fishes with flat to broadly rounded heads. The mouth is large and extremely oblique, with fringed lips. Some species have a small, worm-like filament extending from the floor of the mouth, which functions as a "lure."

Two large, double-grooved spines, each with a venom gland at the base, may be present just above the pectoral fin and behind the opercle. The small eyes project dorsally upward. The body is unscaled or covered with small scales. The pelvic fins each have a single spine and five rays, narrowly separated from one another, and are located under the throat well ahead of the large rounded pectoral fins. The dorsal fin in some species is composed entirely of rays; in others, there are usually four short, relatively low spines completely separated from the soft dorsal fin. In all stargazers, the soft dorsal fin is moderately long, usually containing 10 to 13 rays. The anal fin has 12 to 18 rays. Members of this family burrow, covering themselves with a layer of sand or silt, the eyes protruding just above the head; the fish ambushes its prey as it passes by or comes to investigate the worm-like "lure" in the floor of the mouth. Portions of the eye muscle in members of the genus *Astroscopus* are modified into weak electric organs; whether the electric organ is used as an aid in capturing prey is uncertain.

513 Southern Stargazer
Astroscopus y-graecum

Description: To 17½" (44 cm). Heavy-bodied; bones on top of head form Y. Bluish gray or brown, *with numerous uniform bright white spots on back and upper sides;* 2 large blackish areas on soft dorsal fin; prominent dark bars on pectoral and caudal fins; no blackish stripe on caudal peduncle. Head depressed, flat (especially in young) to broadly rounded; eye small, on upper side of head; no long spines on sides of back of head. *Dorsal fin with 4 spines,* 12–13 rays. Top of head unscaled where electric organs located.

Habitat: Coastal waters over sand or mud to depths of 100′ (30 m). Young often in water less than 12″ (30 cm) deep.

Range: NC to Yucatán.

Similar Species: Northern Stargazer (*A. guttatus*) has smaller light spots of variable size, smaller on back and larger on sides, and pale tan soft dorsal fin with 4 narrow blackish-brown areas. Lancer Stargazer (*Kathetostoma albigutta*) is reddish brown above and white below, without spots, and has long prominent spines projecting upward and backward from sides of back of head; occurs farther offshore at depths of 130–1,260′ (40–384 m).

Comments: The specific name, *y-graecum,* refers to the bones on the top of the head in the shape of a Y. The burrowing behavior, small upwardly directed eyes, and stalking habits of stargazers are shared by the much smaller sand stargazers (family Dactyloscopidae).

TRIPLEFINS
Family Tripterygiidae

20 genera and at least 115 species worldwide; 1 genus with 3 species in North America, plus 2 genera and 8 species confined to Mexican Pacific and Atlantic waters. This family occurs in shallow tropical to temperate seas, usually around coral reefs or rocks. The pelvic fins are located under the throat, in front of the well-developed pectoral fins. The dorsal fin is divided into three distinct and often completely separated segments. The first dorsal fin segment is shorter than the second, and both are composed entirely of spines: three to six in the first segment, and 11 to 23 (usually 16 or more) in the second. The third dorsal fin segment consists of seven to 14 rays. The anal fin is either spineless or has one to two (usually two) spines and 15 to 28 rays. There are no cirri on the nape. The gill membranes of triplefins are broadly attached across the isthmus. The premaxillae are protractile. The scales are usually ctenoid. The maximum length of these fishes is about 10″ (25 cm), but most species reach lengths of less than 2¼″ (6 cm). This family was once included in the wide-ranging family Clinidae (now known as the kelp blennies).

533 Redeye Triplefin
Enneanectes pectoralis

Description: To 1¼″ (3 cm). Terete, small, tapering. Grayish tan, often with red tint; dark bar on cheek below eye; 5 dark saddle-shaped bars on body; *last bar on caudal peduncle, wider and darker than others; no dark bars on anal fin; iris of eye red.* Head rather pointed; short spines on anterior rim of eye socket. Dorsal fin in 3 distinct segments, first segment with 3 spines, second with usually 12 spines, third with usually 7 rays; anal fin with 2 short spines, usually 15 rays. Belly and pectoral fin base scaled. Lateral line with usually 13 pored scales.

Habitat: Coral reefs to depths of 35′ (10.5 m).

Range: Bahamas, s FL, and throughout Caribbean to coasts of n Central America and South America; apparently absent from Gulf of Mexico.

Similar Species: Mimic Triplefin *(E. jordani)* also has scaled belly and spines on front rim of eye socket, but has 6–7 dark bars on anal fin.

Lofty Triplefin *(E. altivelis)* also has scaled belly, but has smooth front edge of eye socket and higher first dorsal fin. Roughhead Triplefin *(E. boehlkei)* has unscaled belly, blunter snout, and 15 pored scales in lateral line. Blackedge Triplefin *(E. atrorus)* has unscaled belly and 12–13 pored scales in lateral line.

Comments: The collective common name triplefin is derived from the separation of the dorsal fin into three distinct segments.

SAND STARGAZERS
Family Dactyloscopidae

9 genera and 41 species worldwide; 3 genera and 8 species in North America, plus 12 species confined to Mexican Pacific waters. This family is restricted to sandy shores and sandy areas around coral reefs or along coasts in tropical to warm-temperate seas from North to South America; it is one of only a few marine families confined to the Western Hemisphere. Sand stargazers are small fishes with moderately elongate, tapering bodies that are compressed posteriorly. The pelvic fins, each with a single spine and three rays, are located under the throat, in front of the well-developed pectoral fins. The dorsal fin is long and continuous, sometimes with one or two notches, and has seven to 23 spines and 12 to 36 rays. The long anal fin begins under the middle of the pectoral fin and has two spines and 21 to 41 rays. The dorsal and anal fins are not joined to the rounded caudal fin. The scales are cycloid, with 33 to 73 in the lateral line; the lateral line is high anteriorly, then arches abruptly downward near the pectoral fin and continues posteriorly on the mid-side of the body. These fishes have

extremely oblique mouths; many species have fringed lips, which permit a free flow of water over the gills and keep out sand particles. The eyes are high on the body, somewhat protruding, and often on a stalk. The upper edge of the gill cover is subdivided into finger-like protrusions, and the gill membranes are separate and free from the isthmus. Sand stargazers are never brightly colored, but the overall pigmentation varies from nearly pallid to strongly marked by broad crossbands. These fishes bury themselves in the sand, leaving only their eyes barely exposed, lying in wait for passing prey.

Sand Stargazer

Sand Stargazer
Dactyloscopus tridigitatus

Description: To 3½″ (9 cm). Slender, elongate, somewhat compressed posteriorly. *Dirty white to very pale tan; back dotted with small brown melanophores, sometimes forming 11–14 faint irregular bars. Eye small, at end of long stalk;* snout relatively blunt; lower jaw not projecting notably beyond upper; *upper part of gill cover with 10–16 finger-like protrusions.* Pectoral fin flat against body; dorsal fin long, continuous, not notched, with about 12 uniformly low spines, 27 rays, origin on nape; anal fin with 2 spines, 31–32 rays, origin behind dorsal fin origin. Arched part of lateral line short and abrupt, curving down to mid-side well before pectoral fin tip.

Habitat: Shallow waters over sand; often near coral reefs.

Range: Bermuda, Bahamas, and FL south throughout Caribbean to Brazil; absent from most of Gulf of Mexico.

Similar Species: Bigeye Stargazer *(D. crossotus)* has similar dorsal fin, but eyes are non-stalked;

occurs to depths of 25' (7.5 m).
Speckled Stargazer *(D. moorei)* has
similar dorsal fin, but eyes are on low
stalks; occurs at depths of 10–115'
(3–35 m). Masked Stargazer *(Gillellus
healae),* Arrow Stargazer *(G. greyae),*
Warteye Stargazer *(G. uranidea),* and
Saddle Stargazer *(Platygillellus
rubrocinctus)* have deeply notched
anterior spiny dorsal fin and non-stalked
eyes; all occur in shallow waters, Masked
Stargazer at depths of 70–240' (21–73 m)
and Arrow and Saddle Stargazers to
100' (30 m).

Comments: This fish has the smallest eyes, on the
longest stalks, of any species in the
family. Because of its secretive nature,
Sand Stargazer is never seen by the
casual observer. All specimens collected
have been garnered with fish narcotics or
heavily weighted beach seines.

LABRISOMID BLENNIES
Family Labrisomidae

14 genera and about 91 species world-
wide; 7 genera and 22 species in North America (19 Atlantic, 3 Pacific), plus 3 genera and 33 species confined to
Mexican Atlantic and Pacific waters. The Labrisomidae is
one of the very few marine families almost entirely confined
to the Western Hemisphere; the exceptions are two species
from western Africa (one of which is also found in the western Atlantic). These moderately elongate, usually tapering
fishes typically inhabit tropical to warm-temperate seas
from shallow waters to mid-depths around coral reefs or
rocky coasts. Labrisomid blennies are covered with large cycloid scales that are never embedded; as a group they are
sometimes known as scaly blennies. Fleshy cirri may be
present on the nape and near the eyes or nostrils. The dorsal fin is continuous; the relative number of dorsal fin spines
and rays is variable (some species have only spines), but
there are always more spines than rays. The long anal fin has
numerous rays, and the caudal fin is rounded. The pectoral
fins are large and located along the mid-sides; the thoracic
pelvic fins have two to three visible rays and are located just
in front of the pectoral fins. Most species have external fertilization, but males of the genus *Starksia* have the anteriormost anal fin ray modified into a long organ that serves as a

conduit for transmitting sperm. A few eastern Pacific species are viviparous. Previously included in the wide-ranging family Clinidae (now known as the kelp blennies), this group was only recently elevated to family status. Phylogenetic relationships of the labrisomid blennies are still under study, and two genera (*Stathmonotus* and *Neoclinus*) once included in this family were recently placed in the closely related tube blenny family (Chaenopsidae).

534 Island Kelpfish
Alloclinus holderi

Description: To 4″ (10 cm). Elongate, slender. Gray, with red stripes, iridescent blue spots, and 6–8 dark bars; *dorsal fin with green spot anteriorly, no ocelli.* Snout bluntly rounded; 2–3 small cirri above each eye. Pectoral fin long, reaching beyond anal fin origin; pelvic fin almost as long as pectoral fin; dorsal fin with 24–26 spines, first 4 spines flexible and longer than others, 9–11 rays, rays longer than spines; anal fin with 2 spines, 21–23 rays; caudal fin profile straight, with branched middle ray. *Abrupt arch in lateral line just behind pectoral fin tip.*

Habitat: Rocky coasts to depths of 162′ (49 m).
Range: Santa Cruz Island, s CA, to Punta San Pablo, Baja California.
Similar Species: Deepwater Blenny *(Cryptotrema corallinum)* has dorsal fin spines of about equal length and no abrupt arch in lateral line; occurs to depths of 300′ (91 m). Reef Finspot *(Paraclinus integripinnis)* has spot near end of dorsal fin.
Comments: Island Kelpfish is a good aquarium fish. Because it is easily approached, it is frequently photographed by divers.

535 Hairy Blenny
Labrisomus nuchipinnis

Description: To 8½″ (22 cm). Robust. Varies from pale to almost black, with darker bars on sides; *dark spot on preopercle and anterior dorsal fin.* Adult males have red chin, belly, and fins. Cirri around nasal flaps and over eye; *maxilla exposed, reaching almost to edge of eye; crosswise row of cirri on nape, widely separated into 2 sections.* Dorsal fin slightly notched. *Lateral line with 64–69 scales.*

Habitat: Shallow water over rocks and sand or in vegetation.

Range: Bermuda; s GA to Brazil, including Bahamas, w and ne Gulf of Mexico, and Caribbean. Also in e Atlantic.

Similar Species: Quillfin Blenny *(L. filamentosus),* Longfin Blenny *(L. haitiensis),* Mimic Blenny *(L. guppyi),* and Spotcheek Blenny *(L. nigricinctus)* also have large dark spot on preopercle; only Quillfin Blenny has more than 55 lateral line scales. Whitecheek Blenny *(L. albigenys),* Puffcheek Blenny *(L. bucciferus),* Palehead Blenny *(L. gobio),* and Downy Blenny *(L. kalisherae)* lack dark spot on preopercle and have fewer lateral line scales. All these *Labrisomus* blennies occur around coral reefs or over other rough bottoms.

Comments: Hairy Blenny is the largest and one of the most common blennies in the Atlantic. It feeds on a variety of invertebrates, including crustaceans, echinoderms, mollusks, and annelids.

536 Saddled Blenny
Malacoctenus triangulatus

Description: To 2½″ (6.5 cm). Moderately compressed, tapering. Males pale tan, with bright orange cast; females and young tan; *4 large, inverted, triangular saddles on back, purplish black in adult males, dark brown in females and young;* dark, often diamond-shaped marks on lower sides; dark spot at base of first dorsal fin spine; *band at caudal fin base.* Snout pointed; most of maxilla covered by preorbital bone when mouth closed; *crosswise row of cirri on nape, narrowly separated into 2 sections. 14 pectoral fin rays;* dorsal fin continuous, with 2 distinct notches, about 19 spines, 13 rays; anal fin with 2 spines, 18 rays. Lateral line with 52–61 scales.

Habitat: Shallow coral reefs and rocky shores; often in coral rubble.

Range: Bahamas, s FL, and Yucatán throughout Caribbean to Brazil.

Similar Species: Goldline Blenny *(M. aurolineatus),* Barfin Blenny *(M. versicolor),* and Dusky Blenny *(M. gilli)* also have 14 pectoral fin rays, but bars on sides do not form inverted triangles. Rosy Blenny *(M. macropus)* has nondescript color pattern. Imitator Blenny *(M. erdmani)* has broken bars along sides and well-defined dark spot just beneath posterior part of spiny dorsal fin.

Comments: In contrast to many of the smaller reef-dwelling fish species, Saddled Blenny is frequently observed on coral formations.

KELP BLENNIES
Family Clinidae

About 20 genera and 73 species worldwide; 2 genera and 4 species in North America (all Pacific). This family occurs mostly in cool-temperate waters in rocky habitats of both the Northern and Southern Hemispheres, but is absent from intervening tropical waters; no kelp blennies are found in the western North Atlantic, and only one Mediterranean species occurs in the eastern North Atlantic. These fishes have moderately to markedly elongate bodies that are compressed posteriorly. The long dorsal and anal fins are sometimes joined to the caudal fin. The continuous dorsal fin is sometimes slightly notched, containing a combination of spines and rays, but always with more spines than rays; the anal fin has two spines and numerous rays. The cycloid scales are usually small and embedded. Kelp blennies do not have cirri on the nape. The maximum length of these fishes is 24″ (61 cm); most species are much smaller. Ongoing studies have brought about radical changes in the classification of the Clinidae in recent years; several groups once included in the family have been recognized as distinct families, including the labrisomid blennies (Labrisomidae), the tube blennies (Chaenopsidae), and the triplefins (Tripterygiidae).

512 Giant Kelpfish
Heterostichus rostratus

Description: To 24″ (61 cm). Slender, elongate,
compressed. Coloration varies with
surroundings: greenish yellow, green,
or reddish brown, with silvery stripes.
Snout long; *lower jaw with pointed tip,
extends beyond upper jaw.* Dorsal fin with
33–38 spines, 11–13 rays; anal fin with
2 spines, 31–35 rays; *caudal fin forked.*

Habitat: Kelp beds and rocky areas with eelgrass,
leafy red algae, or jointed coralline algae
to depths of 132′ (40 m).

Range: BC to Cabo San Lucas, Baja California.

Similar Species: Scarlet Kelpfish (*Gibbonsia erythra*) lacks
scales on caudal fin. Striped Kelpfish (*G.
metzi*) has 7–10 equally spaced dorsal fin
rays and rounded caudal fin. Crevice
Kelpfish (*G. montereyensis*) lacks scales on
caudal peduncle and caudal fin.

Comments: Giant Kelpfish feeds on small
crustaceans, mollusks, and fishes. It is
occasionally caught by anglers but
seldom retained. This fish is probably
most familiar to scuba divers.

TUBE BLENNIES
Family Chaenopsidae

11 genera and at least 67 species world-
wide; 7 genera and 17 species in North America (13 Atlantic, 4 Pacific), plus 2 genera and 22 species confined to
Mexican Atlantic and Pacific waters. This family is almost
entirely confined to coral reef or rocky habitats in tropical
waters of North and South America. Tube blennies have a
slender elongate body that is not usually notably tapering
toward the tail. The body is usually unscaled and lacks a lateral line. Cirri are sometimes present above the eyes, on the
rim of the nostrils, and on the sides of the nape. The head is
often spiny or rough, with various types of bony protuberances in some species. The pectoral fins have 12 to 15 rays;
the pelvic fins are located on the throat, slightly ahead of
the pectoral fins. The continuous dorsal fin has 17 to 28
spines and 10 to 38 rays; in some species the anterior portion is much higher than the rest of the fin. The anal fin has
two spines and 19 to 38 rays. The rounded caudal fin is either separate or variously united with the dorsal and anal

fins. Classification of the family has changed considerably; until recently the group was included in the family Clinidae (now known as the kelp blennies), along with the related families Labrisomidae (labrisomid blennies) and Tripterygiidae (triplefins). More recently, two genera (*Stathmonotus* and *Neoclinus*) formerly included in the family Labrisomidae were transferred to the Chaenopsidae; this action resulted in the expansion of the range limits of the Chaenopsidae to include a limited area of the western North Pacific Ocean (Taiwan to Japan). Members of this family are sometimes collectively referred to as pikeblennies or flagblennies.

532 Sailfin Blenny
Emblemaria pandionis

Description: To 2″ (5 cm). Elongate, slightly compressed. Males dark anteriorly, with irregular mottling posteriorly; slightly lighter below. Females irregularly mottled. Young straw-colored, with scattered small spots and dark flecks. Head blunt; *no spines on top of head;* snout short; *cirrus above eye short, about same length as eye, often slightly forked;* cirrus at edge of nostril; lower jaw projects slightly beyond upper; lips thick. Pelvic fin long, with 3 obvious rays; 13 pectoral fin rays; dorsal fin with about 21 spines, 15 rays; *spiny dorsal fin elevated anteriorly and sail-like in adult males,* slightly elevated in females; anal fin with 2 spines, 23–24 rays. *Unscaled. No lateral line; no canals or tubes.*

Habitat: On bottom over coral rubble, sand, or shells.

Range: Bahamas, s FL, nw Gulf of Mexico, and Caribbean to coasts of Central and n South America.

Similar Species: Blackhead Blenny *(E. bahamensis)* lacks cirrus over eye, and lower jaw does not project beyond upper. Roughhead Blenny *(Acanthemblemaria aspera)* has spines and elongate fleshy papillae on top of head. Papillose Blenny *(A. chaplini)* has fleshy papillae.

Comments: Tube blennies are limited to tropical areas and are rarely found in U.S. waters except off Florida.

531 Wrasse Blenny
Hemiemblemaria simula

Description: To 4″ (10 cm). Slender, elongate. *Yellow; dark mid-lateral stripe extends from snout to caudal fin base,* sometimes broken into block-like segments; dark spot near edge of dorsal fin from fourth to sixth spines. Snout long, moderately sharply pointed; no cirri above eye; cirri on nostril rudimentary. *Dorsal fin long, continuous, with moderately deep notch between spines and rays,* about 22 spines, 19 rays; anal fin with about 24 rays, origin about midway below length of dorsal fin; caudal fin not joined to dorsal and anal fins. *Unscaled.*

Habitat: Around shallow coral reefs; often in abandoned holes of Christmas tree worms.

Range: Bahamas, s FL, Cuba, and w Caribbean off Belize and Honduras.

Similar Species: Bluehead *(Thalassoma bifasciatum),* in wrasse family (Labridae), has less elongate body and less pointed snout.

Comments: This species bears a remarkable resemblance to younger adult male, female, and young Blueheads. Bluehead sometimes acts as a cleaner, picking parasites off other fishes, and it is presumed that this resemblance allows Wrasse Blenny to approach and prey on fishes that normally would not flee a Bluehead. A key factor in this behavior pattern is that Wrasse Blenny is invariably present in far fewer numbers than Bluehead. Wrasse Blenny, in contrast to other tube blennies, swims off the bottom, mimicking the swimming behavior of Bluehead.

537 Onespot Fringehead
Neoclinus uninotatus

Description: To 9″ (23 cm). Elongate, slender, moderately compressed. Light to dark brown, with dark brown or red speckles; sometimes with dark stripe; *ocellus*

between first and second dorsal fin spines.
Snout bluntly rounded; several large
cirri over each eye, *1 pair very long and
forked at tip; jaw huge* (somewhat larger
in males); maxilla ends halfway between
snout and posterior edge of opercle; lips
prominent. Dorsal fin long, nearly
uniform in height; caudal fin rounded.

Habitat: Siltstone areas with crevices and holes or
over soft bottoms with debris at depths
of 10–90' (3–27 m).

Range: Bodega Bay, CA, to n Baja California.

Similar Species: Sarcastic Fringehead (*N. blanchardi*) has
maxilla extending almost to rear edge of
opercle and 2 ocelli on dorsal fin
(between first and second spines, and
fifth and ninth spines); occurs to depths
of 210' (64 m). Yellowfin Fringehead
(*N. stephensae*) has maxilla extending
almost halfway to rear edge of opercle
and lacks ocelli.

Comments: Species of the genus *Neoclinus,* until
recently included in the family Clinidae
(now known as the kelp blennies), are
also found in the tropical western North
Pacific, from Taiwan to Japan. This is
one of the most unusual distribution
patterns for a group of Pacific marine
fishes. Onespot Fringehead and the
closely related Sarcastic Fringehead are
by far the largest North American
members of the family. Onespot
Fringehead is very aggressive and
threatens intruders by opening its large
mouth or by lunging. Anglers who
occasionally catch it usually have trouble
removing the hook because the fish will
attempt to bite.

COMBTOOTH BLENNIES
Family Blenniidae

53 genera and about 345 species world-
wide; 9 genera and 22 species in North America, plus 3
species confined to Mexican Pacific waters. These bottom-
dwelling fishes occur mostly in shallow waters of temperate
to tropical seas, very rarely in fresh water but occasionally in

brackish water. They are small, unscaled, and usually drably colored. Robust and deep-bodied, they have a blunt snout and a steep head profile. Each jaw has a single row of comb-like incisor teeth, and some species also have canine teeth; the incisor teeth are either firmly set in the jaws or are freely movable. Feather-like cirri are present above the eyes and sometimes on the nape. The pelvic fins, each with only two to four visible rays, are inserted in front of the pectoral fins. The dorsal fin is long and continuous or slightly notched, with three to 17 flexible spines and nine to 19 rays (most species have fewer spines than rays); the base of the spiny segment is shorter than the soft-rayed segment. Combtooth blennies usually have two flexible anal fin spines.

538 Striped Blenny
Chasmodes bosquianus

Description: To 3″ (7.5 cm). Elongate, compressed. Brownish; dark blotches on sides, forming wide irregular bands; dark spots sometimes form wavy horizontal lines. Breeding males have blue spot or band on anterior dorsal fin, with orange streak extending posteriorly. *Snout pointed;* maxilla reaches beyond eye; usually 4 pores on lower jaw; teeth slender, recurved, in 1 row; *no large canine teeth in rear jaws.* 12 pectoral fin rays; dorsal fin long, continuous, not notched, spines slightly shorter than rays, *last ray attached to caudal fin by membrane;* usually 2 anal fin spines, with fleshy knobs at ends in males.

Habitat: Shallow grassy flats over sand; rarely to depths of 100′ (30 m).
Range: NY to ne FL; rare north of MD.
Similar Species: Florida Blenny *(C. saburrae)* has blunter snout, smaller mouth, and 6 pores on lower jaw. Longmouth Blenny *(C. longimaxilla)* has longer jaw.
Comments: Originally regarded as a subspecies of Striped Blenny, the disjunct population occurring from Pensacola, Florida, westward is now classified as a distinct species, Longmouth Blenny.

539 Barred Blenny
Hypleurochilus bermudensis

Description: To 3½″ (9 cm). Elongate, robust
anteriorly, depth greatest at dorsal fin
origin. Coloration sometimes highly
contrasted, varies with substrate: grayish,
olive, or reddish brown; 6 dark bars on
sides; males darker than females; no black
spot between anteriormost dorsal fin
spines; black spot at center of caudal fin
base. *Profile of head steep; snout blunt;* no
median row of cirri on top of head and
nape; relatively short cirrus over each eye;
mouth small, terminal, horizontal; *canine
teeth in rear jaws; gill openings restricted to
side of head, usually without connecting fold
or ridge.* 14 pectoral fin rays; dorsal fin
slightly notched, with 12 spines, 13 rays,
last ray attached to caudal peduncle;
anal fin with 2 spines, 14 rays.

Habitat: Rocky areas and jetties; less common
around coral reefs.

Range: Bermuda, Bahamas, FL, and Gulf of
Mexico.

Similar Species: Oyster Blenny *(H. pseudaequipinnis)* has
black spot at beginning of spiny dorsal
fin. Orangespotted Blenny *(H. springeri)*
lacks spot at caudal fin base. Crested
Blenny *(H. geminatus),* Zebratail Blenny
(H. caudovittatus), and Plumed Blenny
(H. multifilis) have 14–15 dorsal fin rays
and 16–17 anal fin rays. Redlip Blenny
(Ophioblennius macclurei), Pearl Blenny
(Entomacrodus nigricans), Molly Miller
(Scartella cristata), Seaweed Blenny
(Parablennius marmoreus), Mangrove
Blenny *(Lupinoblennius vinctus),* and
Highfin Blenny *(L. nicholsi)* have
distinct fold of skin between gill
openings across breast. Species of genus
Hypsoblennius lack canine teeth on
posterior jaws.

Comments: Blennies are frequently observed by
snorkelers around coral reefs and rock
jetties. They feed freely on animal and
plant materials, particularly algae, and
make good aquarium fishes.

540 Feather Blenny
Hypsoblennius hentz

Description: To 4″ (10 cm). Elongate, robust anteriorly. Brownish, with darker blotches or spots; fins variously spotted, pelvic fins darkest. Males have blue spot on anterior dorsal fin. Head short, with rounded profile; *cirrus over each eye, with many short side branches,* larger in males; mouth small, terminal; lips fleshy; *upper lip attached to snout, without free rim;* lower lip narrow; teeth incisor-like, *no canine teeth.* 14 pectoral fin rays; dorsal fin with usually 12 spines, 14 rays, last ray attached to caudal peduncle by membrane; anal fin with 2 spines, 16–17 rays.

Habitat: Grassy flats and oyster reefs over mud.

Range: NS to Yucatán.

Similar Species: Freckled Blenny *(H. ionthas)* has thick upper lip free of snout and cirrus over each eye without side branches. Tessellated Blenny *(H. invemar)* has black spot on side of head behind eye and bright orange spots on head and pectoral fin; occurs in old barnacle holes and shells. Longhorn Blenny *(H. extochilus)* has elongate posterior flap on lower lip and very long and branched cirrus over each eye; occurs around reefs.

Comments: Feather and Freckled Blennies lay their eggs in "oyster boxes," empty oyster shells with the hinge intact and the interior relatively clear of silt or mud. Both species are suitable for aquariums.

541 Molly Miller
Scartella cristata

Description: To 4¼″ (11 cm). Elongate, robust anteriorly, deepest at nape. Usually olive, with darker blotches often extending onto dorsal fin; pearly spots sometimes along dorsal fin base; lighter below, with almost no spots or blotches. Head short, blunt; *median row of cirri on top of head and nape;* mouth small, terminal; lips fleshy; teeth incisor-like, *canine teeth in rear jaws.*

14 pectoral fin rays; dorsal fin long,
continuous, with 12 spines, 14–15 rays;
anal fin with 2 spines, 16–17 rays.

Habitat: Nearshore rocky areas.

Range: Bermuda, w Gulf of Mexico, and
Bahamas to Brazil.

Comments: Molly Miller is the only blenny in North
America with a median row of cirri on
the top of the head. It is commonly
found in very shallow water around
rocks and jetties and in sandy tide pools.
It is primarily herbivorous.

CLINGFISHES
Family Gobiesocidae

About 36 genera and about 120 species
worldwide; 4 genera and 10 species in North America (3 Atlantic, 7 Pacific), plus 3 genera and 24 species confined to Mexican waters (including 3 freshwater species). Clingfishes are found mostly in tropical to warm- and cold-temperate seas throughout the world; four Mexican and Central American species are restricted to fresh water. The family has a peculiar distribution: The greatest diversity of genera and species worldwide is in cold-temperate waters, particular those of the Southern Hemisphere, yet in North America the greatest diversity is in the tropics, particularly in the Gulf of California. These small, unscaled, tadpole-shaped fishes have a complex sucker-like disk on the ventral surface composed of modified pelvic fins and parts of the pectoral fins. They use the disk mostly to attach themselves to rocky bottoms in the surf zone, but sometimes they cling to plants. The disk has patches of short papillae; the arrangement of these patches is useful for identification. The dorsal and anal fins are soft-rayed. Most clingfishes are less than 2″ (5 cm) long, but two species reach lengths of about 12″ (30 cm). Phylogenetic relationships of this family have long puzzled ichthyologists, and its placement within fish classifications has changed many times throughout the years.

350 Skilletfish
Gobiesox strumosus

Description: To 2¾″ (7 cm). Very broad, greatly
depressed anteriorly, tail section
becoming more compressed posteriorly.
Beige, with dark mottling on back and

sides; irregular dark brown spots on top of head; *6 faint lines radiate from eye.* Head length and width each about two-fifths body length; dermal flap on nostril; eye directed upward; mouth broad; lips with papillae. *Modified pelvic fins and broad, apron-like dermal flap form large adhesive disk; 2 widely separated patches of papillae on central part of disk;* pectoral fin very broad-based; caudal fin rounded.

Habitat: Usually over mud or among oyster shells.

Range: Mostly continental coastlines from NJ to sw Gulf of Mexico.

Comments: This distinctive little fish is common around oyster reefs, where it clings so tightly to shells and other objects that it continues to grip them even when it is lifted from the water. Skilletfish was once thought to occur in Bermuda, but that record is no longer considered valid. An unconfirmed record from St. Martin, Lesser Antilles, is most likely also erroneous, considering that it is the only insular record for the species and the only one from the West Indies.

DRAGONETS
Family Callionymidae

18 genera and about 130 species worldwide; 4 genera and 5 species in North America (4 Atlantic, 1 Pacific). Dragonets occur in tropical to warm-temperate seas; the great majority of species are found in the tropical Indo-Pacific region, from near shore to depths of 2,100' (641 m) or more. These benthic fishes live over soft to hard bottoms, and many are found around coral reefs. They have a tapering body with a slender caudal peduncle, and are usually brightly colored and strikingly pigmented, particularly those species inhabiting coral reefs. They reach lengths of about 10″ (25 cm). The pectoral and pelvic fins are well developed, the latter thoracic and in front of the pectoral fins; the inner ray of each pelvic fin is connected to the body by a membrane. The dorsal fin is divided into two distinct segments. The first dorsal fin has four flexible spines and is usually short-based, highly elevated, and brightly colored (especially in males); the second dorsal fin has six to 11 rays. The anal fin is composed of four to 10 rays. The caudal fin is rather elongate, with the middle rays sometimes greatly

extended in males. The head is triangular when viewed from above. The eyes are large and bulbous, situated near the top of the head and directed upward. The small terminal mouth has strongly protractile jaws. The small gill opening is on the upper side of the head. The preopercle is usually armed with a strong spine at the tip that sometimes has up to three forward-projecting, supplementary hooks on the inner edge; the opercle and subopercle lack spines. Dragonets have a complete lateral line that extends to the caudal fin base. Sexual dimorphism is usually apparent in these fishes, especially in regard to the size and development of the dorsal fin.

---

529 Spotfin Dragonet
Foetorepus agassizii

Description: To 6½" (16.5 cm). Slender, tapering. Orangish red, with yellow markings on fins; *ocellated black spot between third and fourth dorsal fin spines; black submarginal stripe on anal fin. Preopercular spine ends in 2 upturned points, no hooks on inner edge.* 19–22 pectoral fin rays; first dorsal fin relatively low, with 4 spines, slightly higher than second dorsal fin, *without long extension;* second dorsal fin convex in males, almost straight in females, with 8 rays, first ray branched, middle 2 rays projecting in males; *7 anal fin rays.*

Habitat: Level, open, soft to hard bottoms at depths of 300–2,100′ (91–641 m).

Range: NS nearly to Amazon River, Brazil, including Gulf of Mexico, Caribbean, and deeper waters around West Indies; not yet recorded from Bermuda or Bahamas.

Similar Species: Palefin Dragonet *(F. goodenbeani)* lacks black spot between dorsal fin spines and black submarginal stripe on anal fin, and first dorsal fin spine is long and filamentous; occurs at depths of 155–1,300′ (47–396 m). Spotted Dragonet *(Diplogrammus pauciradiatus)* has mottled body, row of dark spots on fleshy keel along lower sides, preopercular spine with 3 hooks on inner edge, including upturned tip, and 4 anal fin rays; occurs in shallow sea-grass beds. Lancer Dragonet (*Paradiplogrammus bairdi*) has mottled reddish body, preopercular spine with forward-projecting barb on outer edge and usually 3 hooks on inner edge, and 8 anal fin rays; occurs over coral reefs to depths of 300' (91 m).

Comments: Many early records of Spotfin Dragonet off the eastern United States were based on Palefin Dragonet, which has only recently been described. Certain shallow-water members of the family in the Indo-Pacific region are extremely attractive and are popular aquarium fish. The North American species are either too rare or occur in water too deep to be collected for this purpose.

SLEEPERS
Family Eleotridae

About 35 genera and at least 150 species worldwide; 5 genera and 8 species in North America (6 Atlantic, 2 Pacific), plus 3 species confined to Mexican waters. This family is found in tropical to temperate marine, brackish, and fresh waters; only one North American species appears to be entirely restricted to a marine habitat. These elongate robust fishes are drably colored and often have irregular mottling. The pelvic fins are inserted close to each other near the insertion of the pectoral fins but, unlike those of most gobies, are not united to form a disk. The distance from the end of the second dorsal fin to the base of the caudal fin rays is equal to or longer than the length of the second dorsal fin base. This group was once included in the family Gobiidae, primarily because of confusion over the significance of the separated pelvic fins found in certain gobies.

117, 419   Fat Sleeper
Dormitator maculatus

Description: To 15" (38 cm). Robust, depth one-fourth length. Dark brown; light bluish spots and row or dark spots forming inconspicuous stripes on sides; top of head to dorsal fin origin dark; large usually dark blue blotch above pectoral fin base; rusty spots on dorsal fin; anal fin

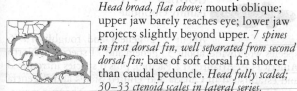

dusky; gill membranes dusky to black. *Head broad, flat above;* mouth oblique; upper jaw barely reaches eye; lower jaw projects slightly beyond upper. *7 spines in first dorsal fin, well separated from second dorsal fin;* base of soft dorsal fin shorter than caudal peduncle. *Head fully scaled; 30–33 ctenoid scales in lateral series.*

Habitat: Brackish ponds and ditches, saltwater marshes, and freshwater coastal streams.

Range: NY to Brazil, including Bermuda, Bahamas, Gulf of Mexico, and Caribbean; rare north of NC.

Similar Species: Largescale Spinycheek Sleeper *(Eleotris amblyopsis)* has more elongate body and 44–54 scales in lateral series. Smallscale Spinycheek Sleeper *(E. perniger)* has more elongate body and 59–68 scales in lateral series.

Comments: Fat Sleeper is used for food in some areas. It is locally common along the Gulf coast, where there is abundant dense growth of aquatic vegetation.

118, 420 Bigmouth Sleeper
Gobiomorus dormitor

Description: To 24″ (61 cm). Large, terete. *Dark yellowish to olive brown above; lighter below;* variously mottled and often spotted; dark lines radiate across cheek and opercle. *Lower jaw strongly projects;* no preopercular spines. 6 spines in first dorsal fin. About 60 ctenoid scales in lateral series.

Habitat: Coastal estuaries and lagoons; usually at freshwater interface and often ascending well into fresh water.

Range: Southeastern FL, w Gulf of Mexico, coastal Caribbean, and throughout larger islands of West Indies to e Brazil.

Comments: Bigmouth Sleeper is one of the largest members of the family. Other family members have jaws of equal length or with an only slightly projecting lower jaw. This species looks and behaves like a large darter of the freshwater family Percidae, and was once described as a new species in that family.

GOBIES
Family Gobiidae

About 212 genera and roughly 1,875 species worldwide; about 35 genera and 71 species in North America (59 Atlantic, 12 Pacific), plus 6 species introduced and established in Canada and United States and 7 genera and 51 species confined to Mexican waters. The vast majority of gobies are found around tropical reefs, but many live in warm- or cold-temperate marine waters, and some (including 11 North American species) permanently or occasionally occur in fresh water. The Gobiidae is one of the two largest families of fishes in the world, equaled or exceeded only by the freshwater family Cyprinidae (carps and minnows). These small fishes have elongate robust bodies and are variably colored and marked. The family includes some of the smallest fishes known; a number of gobies are less than ½″ (1.5 cm) long when fully grown. In most species, the inner rays of the pelvic fins are united by a membrane, forming a sucking disk with which the fish clings to the bottom. There may be another membrane (the frenum) across the front of the disk between the pelvic fin spines. In some species, the pelvic fins are separate. The broad-based pectoral fins are inserted just above the pelvic fins. The dorsal fin is either deeply notched or divided into two separate segments; North American gobies usually have six to seven dorsal fin spines. The distance between the end of the second dorsal fin and the caudal fin base is less than the length of the second dorsal fin base. The dorsal and anal fins are not joined to the caudal fin. The species now assigned to the sleeper family (Eleotridae) were once included with the Gobiidae, primarily because of confusion over the significance of the separated pelvic fins found in certain goby species.

528 Frillfin Goby
Bathygobius soporator

Description: To 3″ (7.5 cm). Robust, moderately tapering. Various shades of brown, usually dark and mottled; *5 black saddles across back, broadest saddle below first dorsal fin.* Tongue notched. Pectoral fin with 20–21 rays, *uppermost rays not connected by membrane to remainder of fin, so that fin appears fringed;* 6 dorsal fin spines. *Body scaled;* 37–41 scales in lateral series.

Habitat: Rocky tide pools and shallows; usually to depths of 10′ (3 m).

Range: NC to Brazil, including Bermuda, Bahamas, Gulf of Mexico, and Caribbean.

Similar Species:

Notchtongue Goby *(B. curacao)* has deep notch at front of tongue, 16–17 pectoral fin rays, and 31–34 (usually 33) scales in lateral series. Island Frillfin *(B. mystacium)* has blunter head, 19–20 pectoral fin rays, and 33–36 (usually 35) scales in lateral series.

Comments: This is one of the most abundant gobies in tide-pool and inshore habitats throughout its range.

524 Bridled Goby
Coryphopterus glaucofraenum

Description: To 2¼" (6 cm). Slender, tapering. Pale, sand-colored; *black spot on side of head above operculum; 3 rows of round to X-shaped dark spots on body* (often quite faint); branchiostegal membranes pale; *dark, often dumbbell-shaped bar on caudal fin base,* sometimes broken into 2 spots. *Pelvic fins united to form ventral sucking disk,* with well-developed frenum, inner rays branched, about as long as outer rays; first dorsal fin with 6 spines, no filamentous extension on second spine; second dorsal and anal fins each with 10 rays.

Habitat: Around sandy bases of coral reefs to depths of more than 80' (24 m).

Range: NC to Brazil, including Bermuda, Bahamas, e and s Gulf of Mexico, and Caribbean.

Similar Species: Pallid Goby *(C. eidolon)* lacks black spot above operculum, and has 2 pale stripes on side of head, with lower stripe outlined in black and extending from eye socket to above pectoral fin base. Bartail Goby *(C. thrix)* has spot at pectoral fin base, well-defined above and diffuse below, and second spine in first dorsal fin with extension; occurs at depths of 15–200' (4.6–61 m). Barfin Goby *(C. alloides)* has separate pelvic fins, faint or absent pigmentation at pectoral fin base, and black mark between second and third dorsal fin spines; occurs at depths of 35–100' (10.5–30 m). Colon Goby *(C. dicrus)* has separate pelvic fins, 2 conspicuous spots, one above the other, at pectoral fin base, and first dorsal fin without prominent pigmentation pattern; occurs to depths of 105' (32 m).

Comments: Pale Bridled Goby individuals are sometimes recognized as a separate species, Sand Goby *(C. tortugae).*

525 Masked Goby
Coryphopterus personatus

Description: To 1⅜" (3.5 cm). Slender, tapering. *Pale orangish red; dark mask from snout through eye;* row of white spots along backbone shows through almost transparent flesh; *black ring around anus.* 2 pores between eyes. *Pelvic fins nearly separate,* no frenum; first dorsal fin with 6 spines, second spine elongate; second dorsal and anal fins each with 11 rays.

Habitat: Over bottom in caves and shaded areas in reefs.

Range: Bermuda, Bahamas, FL, and Caribbean.

Similar Species: Glass Goby *(C. hyalinus)* is less brightly colored, with less extensive mask posteriorly, and anus is near front of black ring. Peppermint Goby *(C. lipernes)* is rich yellow with blue snout, and has 2 dusky stripes behind eye and dark ring around anus.

Comments: Both Masked and Glass Gobies both often occur in large schools, hovering over the bottom. Peppermint Goby is usually solitary.

522 Highfin Goby
Gobionellus oceanicus

Description: To 8" (20 cm). Very elongate, slender. Brown above, sides lighter; belly pale; opercle dusky; *distinct dark oval spot on sides below first dorsal fin; small dark spot* at caudal fin base; fins with dusky rays and pale membranes; paler overall in lighter surroundings. Head bluntly rounded; mouth terminal, oblique. *Pelvic fins united to form ventral sucking disk, connected to belly only anteriorly;* first dorsal fin high, with 6 spines reaching well beyond origin of second dorsal fin; second dorsal fin with 14 rays; 15 anal fin rays; *caudal fin very long, lanceolate.* Head unscaled; 60–92 scales in lateral series.

Habitat: Bays, sounds, and near shore over mud.

Range: NC south along coast to s Brazil.

Similar Species: Spotfin Goby *(Oxyurichthys stigmalophius)* has 4 large rounded spots on mid-sides, conspicuous black spot at rear of first dorsal fin, first dorsal fin with 6 spines, second dorsal fin with 13 rays, 14 anal fin rays, and small scales; occurs over open, soft to firm bottoms at depths of 6–200′ (1.8–61 m). Darter Goby *(Ctenogobius boleosoma),* Mexican Goby *(C. claytonii),* Blotchcheek Goby *(C. fasciatus),* Slashcheek Goby *(C. pseudofasciatus),* Dash Goby *(C. saepepallens),* Freshwater Goby *(C. shufeldti),* Emerald Goby *(C. smaragdus),* Marked Goby *(C. stigmaticus),* and Spottail Goby *(C. stigmaturus)* have first dorsal fin with 6 spines, second dorsal fin with 11–12 rays, 12–13 anal fin rays, and 28–45 scales in lateral series. All these *Ctenogobius* gobies (formerly placed in genus *Gobionellus*) occur in shallow waters, Dash Goby also around deeper coral reefs; Mexican, Blotchcheek, Slashcheek, and Freshwater Gobies enter fresh water.

Comments: Like many other gobies, Highfin Goby is tolerant of wide fluctuations in salinity, and seems to prefer mud bottoms strewn with shells and debris or sandy and silty areas with vegetation. This species is remarkably variable in number of scales in the lateral series, which has resulted in past recognition of several different species, including Sharptail Goby *(G. hastatus).*

527 Bluebanded Goby
Lythrypnus dalli

Description: To 2½" (6.5 cm). Elongate, compressed. *Bright orangish red, with 4–9 blue bands;* blue marks around eye. Snout rounded. *Pelvic fins united to form ventral sucking disk;* pectoral fin with 17–18 rays, tip reaches anal fin origin; first dorsal fin with 6 spines, ends of second and third spines free from membrane, longer than other spines; second dorsal fin about same length as anal fin, with 14 rays; 12–14 anal fin rays; caudal fin rounded.

Habitat: Shallow rocky areas with crevices to depths of 318' (97 m).

Range: Morro Bay, CA, to Gulf of California.

Similar Species: Zebra Goby *(L. zebra)* has red body with at least 10 slender light blue bands.

Comments: Bluebanded Goby spawns from around May to August. The male courts the female by darting at her several times in rapid succession, with his dorsal fin fully extended, before she deposits the eggs; the male then guards the eggs until they hatch. This species was thought to be rare before the advent of scuba diving; it is now known to be abundant around the islands off southern California. Bluebanded Goby makes an excellent aquarium fish. The numerous species of *Lythrypnus* known from tropical western Atlantic reefs are much smaller in size and more secretive in their habits.

523 Clown Goby
Microgobius gulosus

Description: To 2¾" (7 cm). Moderately elongate, tapering. Dark grayish, *with dark spots and blotches; no bright colors;* dark marginal stripe on second dorsal fin; dark marginal or submarginal stripe on anal fin. Females have dark spots on dorsal fins and upper caudal fin. No crest on nape; *mouth greatly enlarged in males. Pelvic fins united to form ventral sucking disk, reaching anal fin origin; first*

dorsal fin with 7 spines, second through
fifth spines extend as filaments in males;
second dorsal fin with 16 rays; 17 anal
fin rays; *caudal fin rather long, lanceolate.*

Habitat: Muddy estuaries, often with vegetation;
sometimes enters fresh water.

Range: Chesapeake Bay to TX.

Similar Species: Green Goby *(M. thalassinus)* has pale
green body. Seminole Goby *(M. carri)*
has bright orange stripe along body
extending onto caudal fin; occurs in
burrows and hovers above bottom.
Banner Goby *(M. microlepis)* is light
brown, lacks dark spots on fins and
body, and has fleshy crest on nape;
occurs in shallow waters over soft
calcareous bottoms. These species do
not enter fresh water.

Comments: Clown Goby and Naked Goby
(Gobiosoma bosc) are common inhabitants
of freshwater sections of Florida's St.
Johns River.

526 Blackeye Goby
Rhinogobiops nicholsii

Description: To 6″ (15 cm). Elongate, almost round
in cross section. Tan to olive, usually
with brown mottling and speckles;
*iridescent blue spot beneath each eye; first
dorsal fin black-edged.* Breeding males
have black sucking disk. Snout rounded.
*Pelvic fins united to form ventral sucking
disk;* pectoral fin tip reaches anus; second
dorsal fin long, almost reaching caudal
fin; anal fin almost one-third body
length; caudal fin rounded. *Scales large,*
cycloid; 25–28 scales in lateral series.

Habitat: Bays and off coast over sand or mud near
rocky reefs to depths of 420′ (128 m).

Range: Queen Charlotte Islands, BC, to Punta
Rompiente, Baja California.

Similar Species: Arrow Goby *(Clevelandia ios)* has mouth
reaching beyond eye, and distance
between dorsal fins is longer than width
of eye. Tidewater Goby *(Eucyclogobius
newberryi)* lacks black edging on first
dorsal fin and has 2 pores between eyes.

Longjaw Mudsucker (*Gillichthys mirabilis*) has huge maxilla reaching almost to posterior edge of opercle. Bay Goby (*Lepidogobius lepidus*) has pectoral fin extending halfway to anus and widely separated dorsal fins, the first black-edged.

Comments: Spawning occurs from April to October. The male lures the female into a cave, where she deposits the eggs, which are then guarded by the male. Blackeye Goby was until recently included in the genus *Coryphopterus;* that genus, as now constituted, consists entirely of tropical species living in or around coral reefs.

SPADEFISHES
Family Ephippidae

7 genera and about 20 species worldwide; 1 genus with 2 species in North America (1 Atlantic, 1 Pacific), plus 1 species confined to Mexican Pacific waters. Most members of this family are found in tropical marine or brackish waters. Spadefishes are similar to butterflyfishes (family Chaetodontidae) in that their bodies are very deep, disk-shaped, and compressed; this body shape allows them to make quick and easy lateral movements in confined places such as shipwrecks. The small mouth is not protractile, a feature that distinguishes spadefishes from butterflyfishes. The stout dorsal fin spines are separate from or slightly connected to the dorsal fin rays.

371 Atlantic Spadefish
Chaetodipterus faber

Description: To 3′ (91 cm), usually to 18″ (46 cm). *Short, very deep, disk-shaped, compressed. Bronze or silvery gray; 3–7 somewhat irregular dark bars on sides,* fading with age. Larger individuals more silvery; bars increasingly obscure. Young almost black. *Snout blunt;* mouth terminal, small, ending below nostrils; preopercle finely serrate, without spine at angle; *opercle ends in blunt point.* Pectoral fin shorter than head; dorsal fin with 9 stout spines, slightly connected to rays;

soft dorsal and anal fins similar in size and shape, *anterior rays of both long, falcate;* caudal fin emarginate. Dense scales on soft dorsal and anal fins.

Habitat: Shallow waters near rocks, pilings, and wrecks; occasionally around coral reefs.

Range: Cape Cod, MA, to Brazil, including Bahamas, Gulf of Mexico, and Caribbean; rare north of Chesapeake Bay; unsuccessfully introduced in Bermuda.

Similar Species: Pacific Spadefish (*C. zonatus*) has 6 dark bars, with first bar passing through eye; occurs in bays over sand or rubble in Pacific.

Comments: Atlantic Spadefish has tasty flesh, and it is popular with anglers and spear fishers. It feeds on a variety of invertebrates.

SURGEONFISHES
Family Acanthuridae

6 genera and about 72 species worldwide; 1 genus with 3 species in North America (all Atlantic), plus 1 genus and 5 species confined to Mexican Pacific waters. Surgeonfishes occur in tropical coral reefs. The body is deep and compressed, and the eyes are located high on the head. The small mouth has spatula-shaped, finely serrate teeth. These fishes have a continuous dorsal fin with nine spines. The caudal fin is emarginate. The collective common name is derived from the hinged scalpel-like spine that folds into a groove on either side of the caudal peduncle; these spines (each actually a modified scale) are present in most species. When the fish is moving, it can lash out the spines at other fishes, either to warn or injure. Surgeonfishes are not known to attack divers, but they should be handled carefully. All species are strictly herbivorous. Members of this family are also known as doctorfishes or tangs.

382 Ocean Surgeon
Acanthurus bahianus

Description: To 14″ (36 cm). Deep, compressed, depth half of length. *Grayish brown to yellow, with pale bluish- to greenish-gray lengthwise lines; opercular membrane purple or black;* pelvic fin rays pale blue; narrow alternating dull orange and light blue-green bands on dorsal fin; dark gray to grayish-blue bands on anal fin; caudal fin olive to yellowish brown to dark blue, with bluish-white posterior edge; *area around caudal peduncle spine edged in violet.* Mouth small, slightly inferior; 20–22 gill rakers. Dorsal fin continuous, not notched; *caudal fin emarginate or lunate.* Scalpel-like spine on each side of caudal peduncle.

Habitat: Shallow coral and rocky reefs.

Range: NC to Brazil, including Bermuda, Bahamas, parts of Gulf of Mexico, and Caribbean; summer waifs north to MA.

Similar Species: Doctorfish *(A. chirurgus)* has 10 narrow dark bars on sides, 16–19 gill rakers, and less emarginate caudal fin without whitish posterior edge.

Comments: Ocean Surgeon is a bottom dweller. The algae that it scrapes off hard substrates is ground in its gizzard-like stomach. Gulf Surgeonfish *(A. randalli),* thought to be restricted to the Gulf of Mexico, was until recently considered to be a fourth North American surgeonfish species, but it is now regarded as a variant of Ocean Surgeon.

385, 386 Blue Tang
Acanthurus coeruleus

Description: To 14″ (36 cm). Deep, almost disk-shaped, compressed, depth more than half of length. *Blue to purplish gray, often with narrow gray stripes;* narrow purplish-gray stripes on dorsal and anal fins; *sheath of caudal peduncle spine white.* Young lemon yellow; subadults sometimes partly yellow, partly blue, or blue, with yellow fins. Eye high on head; mouth small. Dorsal fin continuous, not notched; caudal fin distinctly concave in adults, emarginate in young. Scalpel-like spine on each side of caudal peduncle.

Habitat: Shallow coral and rocky reefs.

Range: NY to Brazil; most abundant in West Indies; stragglers in n and s parts of range; recorded in w Gulf of Mexico off TX (Flower Garden Banks) and LA.

Comments: Blue Tang and other surgeonfishes have three color phases: juvenile, subadult, and adult. They are active during the day and often occur in rather large groups. Their teeth are adapted for feeding on algae that grow on or among coral and rocks.

BARRACUDAS
Family Sphyraenidae

1 genus with 20 species worldwide; 6 species in North America (4 Atlantic, 2 Pacific), plus 1 species confined to Mexican Pacific waters. Barracudas are found in a variety of habitats, ranging from coral reefs to estuaries, in tropical and subtropical waters throughout the world. These elongate fishes have dark bars, chevrons, stripes, or dark blotches. The pelvic and pectoral fins are small; the pelvic fins are inserted more or less under the dorsal fin origin, and the pectoral fins are inserted in front of the pelvic fin bases. There are two widely separated dorsal fins; the first consists of five spines, the second has a spine in front of the rays. The second dorsal and anal fins are mirror images. Barracudas are voracious predators that feed mainly on other fishes. They may be solitary or gregarious, largely depending on the species and the size of the individual. Although they are good food fish, care should be taken in eating large individuals, as they have often been implicated in ciguatera poisoning. Barracudas have formidable teeth that are capable of inflicting serious wounds; in North America, only Great Barracuda *(Sphyraena barracuda)* reaches a sufficiently large size to be of any potential danger. In general, their danger to people has been greatly exaggerated, and the attacks that have occurred have been by accident. Once allied with the mullets (family Mugilidae), largely because of the similar positions of the widely separated dorsal fins, this family is now believed to have a closer relationship to the mackerels and tunas (family Scombridae).

670 **Pacific Barracuda**
Sphyraena argentea

Description: To 4' (1.2 m); 18 lb (8.2 kg). Very elongate, cylindrical, cigar-shaped. Bluish to brownish above; silvery below;

caudal fin yellow. Snout long, pointed; tip of lower jaw extends beyond upper; teeth large, canine. Pelvic fin insertion below origin of first dorsal fin; dorsal fins widely separated; first dorsal fin with 5 spines, second dorsal fin with 8–10 rays; anal fin with 1 spine, 8–10 rays, mirror image of second dorsal fin.

Habitat: Nearshore surface waters and around outer edges of kelp beds to depths of 60′ (18.5 m); migrates north in summer and south in fall. Young enter bays.

Range: Kodiak Island, AK, to Cabo San Lucas, Baja California.

Comments: This species is also known as California Barracuda. After it matures, at about two years of age, Pacific Barracuda spawns during the summer. It is deemed an excellent food fish, and is highly prized by anglers. This barracuda is often found in small schools. It is more abundant off southern California during warm-water years, and the annual sport catch has fluctuated from 100,000 to one million fish.

669 Great Barracuda
Sphyraena barracuda

Description: To 6′ (1.8 m); 84 lb (38 kg). Elongate, robust, torpedo-shaped. Coloration varies with surroundings: deep green to steel gray above, sometimes with purplish cast; sides silvery; white below; sometimes with 18–23 oblique bars on sides; dark irregular blotches on lower posterior sides; second dorsal, anal, and caudal fins violet to black, with whitish tips. Top of head flat or concave between eyes; mouth large; no distinct fleshy flap on jaws; teeth palatine, large, pointed, blade-like. Tip of pectoral fin reaches to or beyond pelvic fin origin; *vertical line drawn from dorsal fin origin would touch pectoral and pelvic fins. Lateral line with 75–78 scales.*

Habitat: Mostly shallow waters from mangrove areas and other turbid inshore waters to clear waters around coral reefs; individuals less than 24″ (61 cm) long in shallow inshore waters over sand, larger individuals more often offshore.

Range: NC to s Brazil, including Bermuda, Bahamas, Gulf of Mexico, and Caribbean; seasonal waifs north to MA.

Similar Species: Northern Sennet *(S. borealis)* and Southern Sennet *(S. picudilla),* often regarded as a single species, have pelvic and dorsal fins set farther back. Guaguanche *(S. guachancho)* has elongate last ray of second dorsal and anal fins and 108–114 lateral line scales.

Comments: Great Barracuda feeds chiefly on fishes and occasionally on squids and shrimps. Smaller individuals frequently occur in schools, whereas larger fish are usually solitary. Although the danger is probably exaggerated, this barracuda has been known to attack people. Its large, blade-like teeth are capable of cutting great lumps of flesh, and divers should be cautious. This species may cause ciguatera poisoning.

CUTLASSFISHES
Family Trichiuridae

16 genera and about 23 species worldwide; 4 genera and 7 species in North America (3 Atlantic, 4 Pacific). These silvery elongate fishes are found in tropical and subtropical seas, often in very deep water. Their long jaws are armed with large canine or lance-like teeth. When present, the pelvic fins are small. The long dorsal fin usually continues from behind the head to the tip of the tail.

Atlantic Cutlassfish
Trichiurus lepturus

Description: To 5′ (1.5 m). *Very elongate, ribbon-like, highly compressed; tail tapering to point.* Silver, with light blue iridescence; dorsal fin yellowish gray. Mouth large, terminal; lower jaw projects beyond upper; teeth large, fang-like. No pelvic fins; dorsal fin long, with 135 rays,

Atlantic Cutlassfish

begins at nape, continues to near tip of tail; *anal fin reduced to long series of very short, separate, inconspicuous spines;* no finlets; no caudal fin. Unscaled. Lateral line near ventral profile.

Habitat: Estuaries over mud or over continental shelf to depths of 1,150' (351 m).

Range: Gulf of Maine to Argentina, including Gulf of Mexico, Greater Antilles, and coasts of Central and South America; absent from Bermuda and Bahamas.

Similar Species: Pacific Cutlassfish *(T. nitens)* has eye larger relative to length of snout, shorter maxilla, and 118–128 dorsal fin rays; occurs from mid-depths to 1,260' (384 m) in Pacific. Snake Mackerel *(Gempylus serpens),* in closely related snake mackerel family (Gempylidae), has first dorsal fin with 28–32 spines, second dorsal fin with 1 spine and 11–14 rays, obvious anal fin, 5–6 finlets, and forked caudal fin; occurs from near surface to depths of 654' (199 m) in Atlantic and Pacific.

Comments: The occurrence in shallow water of both Atlantic and Pacific Cutlassfishes is unusual, since other family members are confined to deep water. Atlantic Cutlassfish is voracious, feeding on almost any kind of fish. Although it is edible, it is not often used as food in North America.

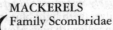

MACKERELS
Family Scombridae

15 genera and 49 species worldwide; 9 genera and 24 species in North America (9 Atlantic, 8 Pacific, 7 shared). Members of this family, which includes mackerels

and tunas, are found in tropical to cold-temperate seas throughout the world. These torpedo-shaped fishes are prized commercially and for sport. The pelvic fins are either beneath or slightly in front of the pectoral fins, and the pectoral fins are inserted above the mid-axis of the body. The dorsal fin is divided into two sometimes well-separated segments; when depressed, each segment fits into a groove. The first dorsal fin begins well behind the head, and has nine to 27 spines. There are five to 12 finlets between the second dorsal fin and the caudal fin, and between the anal fin and the caudal fin. Mackerels and tunas have two or three pairs of keels on the caudal peduncle. The scales are small and cycloid; some species have a corselet of large thick modified scales behind the head that encircles the back and extends along the lateral line. Some species are endothermic, with elevated body temperatures. Because mackerels and tunas are fast-swimming, schooling fishes occurring in open seas, some have cosmopolitan distributions.

---

671 Little Tunny
Euthynnus alletteratus

Description: To 4′ (1.2 m); 26 lb (12 kg). Fusiform, robust, slightly compressed. Dark blue to steel blue above; silvery below; dark wavy stripes on unscaled area above lateral line; *dark spots between pelvic and pectoral fin bases.* Snout shorter than rest of head; 37–45 gill rakers on first arch. Pelvic fin short, not reaching to end of first dorsal fin; *dorsal fins narrowly separated,* first dorsal fin with 15 spines, *first spine longest;* 8 dorsal finlets and 7 anal finlets. 1 large median keel between and anterior to 2 smaller keels on each side of caudal peduncle. Unscaled except for corselet of well-developed scales.

Habitat: Surface of tropical and subtropical open seas; turbid inshore waters over continental shelf.

Range: Bermuda, Bahamas, n and e Gulf of Mexico, and Caribbean to Brazil; seasonally north to Gulf of Maine; common off s FL in summer. Also in e Atlantic and Mediterranean.

Similar Species: Skipjack Tuna *(E. pelamis)* has conspicuous dark stripes on unscaled area below lateral line.

Comments: Abundant inshore in tropical and subtropical waters of the western Atlantic, Little Tunny is popular as an edible sport fish and is used as bait.

674 Skipjack Tuna
Euthynnus pelamis

Description: To 3'4" (1 m); 50 lb (23 kg). Fusiform, robust, slightly compressed. Dark blue above, with metallic reflections; silvery below; *4–6 broad dark lengthwise stripes on unscaled area below lateral line.* Snout shorter than rest of head; 53–63 gill rakers on first arch. *Dorsal fins narrowly separated, first dorsal fin with 15–16 spines, first spine longest;* 7–9 dorsal finlets and 7–8 anal finlets. 1 large and 2 small median keels on each side of caudal peduncle. Unscaled except for corselet of scales well-developed anteriorly.

Habitat: Surface of tropical to subtropical open seas; sometimes to depths of 680' (262 m).

Range: In Atlantic from Gulf of Maine to Argentina, including Bermuda, Bahamas, clear deep waters of Gulf of Mexico, and Caribbean. In Pacific from Vancouver Island, BC, to Peru.

Comments: This schooling tuna is found in tropical and warm-temperate waters worldwide. It is a popular sport fish and is of considerable commercial importance.

663 Atlantic Bonito
Sarda sarda

Description: To 3' (91 cm); 16½ lb (7.6 kg). Fusiform, elongate, somewhat compressed. Steel blue above; silvery below; *5–11 dark, slightly slanted stripes on upper sides.* Head large, compressed, tapering to pointed snout; maxilla reaches to or beyond posterior edge of eye; teeth in jaws slender, conical, slightly compressed. *First dorsal fin straight in profile,* with 20–23 spines,

second spine longest; 7–9 dorsal finlets and 6–8 anal finlets. 1 small keel above and 1 small keel below large median keel on each side of caudal peduncle. *Body fully scaled;* corselet of well-developed scales. *Lateral line distinctly wavy.*

Habitat: Surface of tropical to temperate open seas and inshore waters.

Range: NS to FL; n Gulf of Mexico; off Yucatán; disjunctly from central Brazil to Argentina; absent from Caribbean.

Similar Species: Pacific Bonito *(S. chiliensis)* is also fully scaled and has slanted lines on back; occurs near surface in Pacific.

Comments: This important commercial fish is often found in schools. It feeds on herrings and other fishes, including other mackerels.

658 Atlantic Chub Mackerel
Scomber colias

Description: To 25″ (64 cm); 6¼ lb (2.9 kg). Fusiform, elongate, slightly compressed. Dark green to bluish black above, with about 30 dark wavy streaks extending to just below lateral line; *silvery below, with numerous dusky blotches or spots.* Head pointed, depressed between eyes; snout conical, shorter than rest of head; *adipose eyelid present.* Dorsal fins well separated; *first dorsal fin triangular, with 8–10 spines;* second dorsal fin slightly concave; *5 dorsal finlets and 5 anal finlets. 2 small keels on each side of caudal peduncle; no large median keel.* Body fully scaled; largest scales around pectoral fins; no corselet.

Habitat: Mostly temperate to subtropical seas over continental shelf; usually offshore.

Range: NS to n Greater Antilles and e Gulf of Mexico, including Bermuda and Bahamas; disjunct population in sw Atlantic. Also widespread in e Atlantic.

Similar Species: Atlantic Mackerel *(S. scombrus)* has 20–23 nearly vertical blackish bands across back that end above lateral line, lacks spots below lateral line, and first dorsal fin has 11–12 spines.

Comments: This species was formerly considered to occur in the Pacific Ocean, but that population is now recognized as a separate species, Chub Mackerel (*S. japonicus*). Usually a schooling fish itself, Atlantic Chub Mackerel feeds on other schooling fishes, such as anchovies and herrings, and on invertebrates. It is an excellent food fish. The fishing industry makes no distinction between this species and Atlantic Mackerel.

661 Atlantic Mackerel
Scomber scombrus

Description: To 22″ (56 cm). Fusiform, elongate, slightly compressed. Dark bluish green to bluish black above; top of head darker; *silvery below, no blotches or spots; usually 20–23 dark, wavy, vertical, transverse bands extend down to just below lateral line.* Head large, pointed; maxilla reaches middle of eye; adipose eyelid present. *First dorsal fin triangular, with 11–12 spines,* depressible into groove; second dorsal fin slightly concave; 5 dorsal finlets and 5 anal finlets. *2 small keels on each side of caudal peduncle; no large median keel.* Scales minute, barely visible except around pectoral fin base; no corselet.

Habitat: Open seas and over continental shelf in cool-temperate waters to 68° F (20° C).

Range: NF to Cape Hatteras, NC.

Comments: Atlantic Mackerel is abundant and travels in large schools; it is important commercially as a food fish. The fishing industry makes no distinction between Atlantic Mackerel and Atlantic Chub Mackerel (*S. colias*).

662 King Mackerel
Scomberomorus cavalla

Description: To 5′ (1.5 m), usually 30″ (76 cm); 100 lb (45 kg), usually 50 lb (23 kg). Fusiform, elongate, moderately compressed. Iridescent bluish green or iron gray above; silvery below; *first dorsal fin pale, other fins dusky.* Young have spots on sides. Snout shorter than rest of head; maxilla exposed, extends to middle of eye; lower jaw projects beyond upper; 8–9 gill rakers on first arch. First dorsal fin with 14–16 weak spines; 8–9 dorsal finlets and 9–10 anal finlets. 3 keels on each side of caudal peduncle. Scales small; no corselet. *Lateral line abruptly decurved below second dorsal fin.*

Habitat: Open warm seas. Young in bays and near shore.

Range: Gulf of Maine to s Brazil, including Bermuda, Gulf of Mexico, and Caribbean; possibly in Bahamas.

Similar Species: Spanish Mackerel *(S. maculatus)* has evenly distributed yellowish-bronze spots on mid-sides, dorsal fin black anteriorly, and 13–15 gill rakers on first arch, and lacks abrupt curve in lateral line below second dorsal fin. Cero *(S. regalis)* has yellowish-bronze oval spots on sides below and above darker yellow mid-lateral stripe, and lateral line is not abruptly decurved. Wahoo *(Acanthocybium solandri)* has dark bars on sides and longer snout; occurs near surface of tropical to temperate open Atlantic and Pacific waters.

Comments: King Mackerel and Wahoo are highly esteemed sport fishes.

---

660 Spanish Mackerel
Scomberomorus maculatus

Description: To 3′ (91 cm); 11 lb (5 kg). Fusiform, elongate, strongly compressed. Iridescent bluish green or dark blue above; silvery below; *yellowish-brown or golden spots evenly distributed on mid-sides;* pectoral fin dusky, tinged with yellow and green; anterior one-third of first dorsal fin black; pelvic, second dorsal, and anal fins white. Snout shorter than rest of head; maxilla exposed posteriorly, reaching posterior edge of eye; 13–15 gill rakers on first arch.

Dorsal fins narrowly separated; first dorsal fin with 17–19 (usually 19) spines; 8–9 dorsal finlets and 8–9 anal finlets. Scales small; no corselet. *Lateral line not abruptly decurved; gradually undulating from opercle to caudal peduncle.*

Habitat: Surface of open seas and near shore in continental bays and estuaries.

Range: Atlantic and Gulf coasts from ME to Yucatán; absent from Bahamas and other insular areas.

Similar Species: King Mackerel (*S. cavalla*) lacks spots on sides, and has 8–9 gill rakers on first arch and abruptly decurved lateral line; young lack black pigment on dorsal fin. Cero (*S. regalis*) has yellow spots above and below darker yellow mid-lateral stripe and 15–18 gill rakers on first arch.

Comments: Spanish Mackerel is important commercially. It is caught with gill nets and purse seines, and anglers also troll with artificial lures. This fish swims in large schools; excited birds overhead are often an indication of the schools' presence. Spanish Mackerel feeds on schooling bait fishes, such as anchovies.

---

657 Cero
Scomberomorus regalis

Description: To 32″ (81 cm). Fusiform, elongate, strongly compressed. Bluish green to dark blue above; silvery below; *yellowish-bronze oval spots above and below darker yellow mid-lateral stripe;* anterior one-third of first dorsal fin black. Snout shorter than rest of head; maxilla exposed posteriorly, reaching almost to posterior edge of eye; 15–18 gill rakers on first arch. First dorsal fin with 17–19 spines; second dorsal and anal fins somewhat falcate; 8–9 dorsal finlets and 8–9 anal finlets; caudal fin deeply forked. 3 keels on each side of caudal peduncle. *Scales small, including those on pectoral fin;* no corselet. Lateral line gently decurved under second dorsal fin, undulating to caudal fin base.

Habitat:	Over reefs and turtle-grass beds and in shallow open waters.
Range:	MA to Brazil, including Bermuda, Bahamas, parts of Gulf of Mexico, Antilles, and e Caribbean; infrequent north of FL.
Similar Species:	Spanish Mackerel *(S. maculatus)* has evenly distributed yellowish-brown or golden spots on mid-sides.
Comments:	Cero, unlike Spanish Mackerel, tends to be found singly or in small groups.

677 Albacore
Thunnus alalunga

Description:	To 5′ (1.5 m); 95 lb (43 kg). Fusiform, compressed, depth greatest at pelvic fin insertion. Dark blue or gray above and on fins; light gray below; dorsal finlets yellowish; anal finlets silvery or dusky; rear edge of caudal fin white. Snout pointed; mouth terminal; teeth palatine; 25–31 gill rakers on first arch. *Pectoral fin very long, reaching beyond end of second dorsal fin and anal fin origin;* dorsal fins narrowly separated; 7–8 dorsal finlets and 7–8 anal finlets; caudal fin slender, lunate. Scales tiny; corselet indistinct. Lateral line straight.
Habitat:	Surface to mid-depths of open seas.
Range:	In Atlantic from NS to n Argentina, including Bermuda, Bahamas, and e Caribbean. In Pacific from se AK to Isla Clarion, Baja California.
Similar Species:	Yellowfin Tuna *(T. albacares)* has 26–34 gill rakers on first arch and pectoral fin not reaching beyond origin of second dorsal fin. The larger Bluefin Tuna *(T. thynnus)* has 32–43 gill rakers on first arch and much shorter pectoral fin. Blackfin Tuna *(T. atlanticus)* reaches length of only 3′ (91 cm), and has 19–25 gill rakers on first arch and moderately long pectoral fin; occurs to depths of 828′ (252 m) in Atlantic.
Comments:	Albacore is found worldwide in tropical seas. It feeds on small bait fishes, squids, and crustaceans. This is one of the most

prized fishes on the Pacific coast; the annual catch by anglers has totaled 230,000 fish. In the winter it migrates to the middle Pacific, and then returns to the California coast in the summer.

673 Yellowfin Tuna
Thunnus albacares

Description: To 6′ (1.8 m); 450 lb (208 kg). Fusiform, compressed. Dark blue above; gray below; fins tinged with yellow; finlets yellow, black-edged. Snout moderately pointed; eye relatively small; mouth terminal; 26–34 gill rakers on first arch. *Tip of pectoral fin not reaching beyond origin of second dorsal fin;* second dorsal fin very long in large individuals; 8–9 dorsal finlets and 7–9 anal finlets; caudal fin with slender lobes, rear profile lunate. Scales tiny; corselet indistinct.

Habitat: Surface to mid-depths of open seas.
Range: In Atlantic from s NS to Brazil, including Bermuda, Bahamas, Gulf of Mexico, and Caribbean. In Pacific from Point Buchon, CA, to Chile.
Similar Species: Albacore *(T. alalunga)* has pectoral fin reaching beyond anal fin origin. Bigeye Tuna *(T. obesus)* has shorter and blunter snout, larger eye, and 23–31 gill rakers on first arch.
Comments: Found worldwide in tropical seas, this is the most valuable of all tunas. Schools are pursued by fleets of purse-seine boats from around the world. Dolphins are frequently caught in large numbers with the tunas, and these large expensive boats have had to modify their nets and fishing methods to resolve this problem. Yellowfin Tuna is also a highly prized sport fish.

672 Bluefin Tuna
Thunnus thynnus

Description: To 14′ (4.3 m), usually 10′ (3 m); usually 200–300 lb (91–136 kg).

Fusiform, robust. *Dark blue or black above; silvery white below, with alternating pale lines and rows of light dots; first dorsal fin yellow or bluish;* second dorsal fin reddish brown; anal fin and all finlets dusky yellow, black-edged; *median keels on caudal peduncle black.* Snout conical, shorter than rest of head; maxilla reaches middle of eye; 32–43 gill rakers on first arch. *Tip of pectoral fin falls well short of second dorsal fin;* dorsal fins narrowly separated; first dorsal fin with 14 (rarely 12) spines; 8–10 dorsal finlets and 7–9 anal finlets. 1 large lateral keel and 2 smaller keels on each side of caudal peduncle. Scales tiny; corselet indistinct.

Habitat: Surface of open seas. Young in warm waters.

Range: Labrador to ne Brazil, including Bermuda, Bahamas, Gulf of Mexico, and Caribbean. Also in e Atlantic.

Comments: Bluefin Tuna is a very important part of the commercial longline fishery. The heaviest recorded individual, caught off Nova Scotia in 1979, weighed in at 1,496 lb (680 kg). Until recently, this species was formerly considered to have a worldwide distribution; recent studies have shown the Atlantic and Pacific populations to be taxonomically distinct, and the latter is now considered a separate species, Pacific Bluefin Tuna (*T. orientalis*). Although the two species are very similar in appearance, individuals from the eastern Pacific apparently reach a smaller maximum size; the largest on record was 6′2″ (1.9 m) long and weighed 297 lb (135 kg), but most weigh 10–44 lb (4.5–20 kg).

SWORDFISHES
Family Xiphiidae

1 species worldwide. This family occurs in tropical and temperate open seas throughout the world. These large distinctive fishes have a long snout; the anterior upper jaw and nasal bones are modified to form a sword,

and the jaws lack teeth. The gill membranes are free from the isthmus. Adult swordfishes lack pelvic fins. The two dorsal fins are widely separated, the first much larger than the second. The caudal peduncle has a single keel. Adults are unscaled. Although swordfishes superficially resemble the closely related billfishes (family Istiophoridae), a group that has sometimes been considered a subfamily of the Xiphiidae, the two families may be readily distinguished by the presence or absence of teeth, pelvic fins, keels on the caudal peduncle, and body scales.

---

664 Swordfish
Xiphias gladius

Description: To 15′ (4.6 m); 1,180 lb (536 kg). Fusiform, elongate, compressed, greatest depth near first dorsal fin. Dark gray or black above; gray or sometimes yellowish below. Snout very long, forming flat beak or sword; *no teeth in jaws.* No pelvic fins; pectoral fin length about equal to height of first dorsal fin; dorsal fins widely separated, rigid in adults, folding back in young; first dorsal fin large; caudal fin lunate, with very long lobes. 1 keel on caudal peduncle. *Adults unscaled; young have peculiar spiny scales.*

Habitat: At surface near shore and in open seas to depths of about 2,000′ (610 m); deeper waters in more tropical latitudes.

Range: In Atlantic from NF to Argentina, including Bermuda, Bahamas, Gulf of Mexico, and Caribbean. In Pacific from OR to Chile.

Comments: Swordfish feeds on squids, crustaceans, anchovies, hakes, mackerels, rockfishes, and other fishes. Although it is a highly prized sport fish, few are taken by anglers because of the great expense involved in the pursuit. The annual commercial catch off southern California has grown to more than 500 tons; most of the catch is now taken with gill nets, and a smaller portion with harpoons.

BILLFISHES
Family Istiophoridae

3 genera and about 11 species worldwide; 3 genera and 7 species in North America (2 Atlantic, 3 Pacific, 2 shared). Members of this family are found in tropical and temperate open seas throughout the world. They are closely related to swordfishes (family Xiphiidae), and until recently were included in that family. Billfishes and swordfishes have an elongate snout that forms a sword or spear and a deeply forked, lunate caudal fin. Billfishes differ from swordfishes in having the snout rounded rather than flat in cross section, teeth in the jaws, pelvic fins, scales, and, in adults, two keels on the caudal peduncle. The pectoral fins are on the lower mid-sides of the body, usually pointed backward but not downward. The dorsal fin is divided into two narrowly separated segments. The first dorsal fin is long-based, depressible into a groove, and is very high and fan-like in all individuals less than 3′ (91 cm) long; with the exception of the genus *Istiophorus,* all but the anteriormost rays become notably shorter in larger individuals. The anal fin is divided into two widely separated segments. There is usually one lateral line, but it may be branched to form a chain-like pattern.

665	Sailfish

Istiophorus platypterus

Description: To 10′9″ (3.3 m); 182 lb (83 kg). Elongate, tapering, compressed. Dark blue above; silvery below; adults have vertical rows of gold spots on sides; first dorsal fin dark blue, with darker spots. Snout elongate, forming sword; jaws with teeth; distance from nostril to rear edge of opercle less than sword length from nostril to tip and than pectoral fin length. Pelvic fin rod-like; first dorsal fin fan-like in all individuals, *middle rays longer than greatest body depth, longer than anterior rays.* 2 keels on caudal peduncle in adults. Body scaled.

Habitat: Surface to mid-depths of open seas.
Range: In Atlantic from RI to Brazil, including Bermuda, Bahamas, Gulf of Mexico, and Caribbean. In Pacific from San Diego, CA, to Chile.

Similar Species: Shortbill Spearfish *(Tetrapturus angustirostris)* has first dorsal fin with middle rays slightly shorter or about equal to greatest body depth, not fan-like; occurs in Pacific.

Comments: Sailfish is found almost worldwide in warm seas; the Atlantic and Pacific populations are sometimes considered to be separate species. This fish grows most during its first few years, and lives for only four or five years. It is rarely caught off southern California, but is a very popular sport fish off Mexico.

---

667 Blue Marlin
Makaira nigricans

Description: To 14'8" (4.5 m); usually 200–400 lb (91–182 kg). Deep, moderately compressed. Deep blue to rich brown above; silvery below; pale blue spots form 15 bars on sides; first dorsal fin bluish black, usually without spots; other fins brownish black. Profile of head steep; snout elongate, forming spear. Pelvic fin long, slender, shorter than pectoral fin; pectoral fin folds back against body (except in very large individuals); tips of pectoral, first dorsal, and anal fins pointed; first dorsal fin long, high anteriorly, rays becoming abruptly shorter in individuals more than 3' (91 cm) long, height less than body depth. *Scales dense, embedded, ending in 1–2 long spines. Lateral line branches into network of hexagons; no dominant central canal except in very large individuals.*

Habitat: Usually near surface of open seas.

Range: In Atlantic from New England to Uruguay, including Bermuda, Bahamas, Gulf of Mexico, and Caribbean; uncommon in Gulf of Maine. In Pacific from s CA to Chile; rare in n part of range.

Similar Species: Black Marlin *(M. indica)* has rigid pectoral fin, not folding against body and angled slightly downward; occurs in Pacific. Striped Marlin *(Tetrapturus audax)* has much longer pelvic fin than pectoral fin.

Comments: Found worldwide in tropical to warm-temperate seas, Blue Marlin is highly prized as a sport fish and is also caught in significant numbers on commercial longlines. The largest individual on record weighed 1,800 lb (818 kg). Females attain much larger sizes than males.

---

666 White Marlin
Tetrapturus albidus

Description: To 10′ (3 m); 188 lb (85 kg), usually 50 lb (23 kg). Elongate, compressed. Blue to rich brown above; silvery white below; *usually no bars or spots;* first dorsal fin bluish black; dorsal and anal fins covered with numerous small black spots; other fins brownish black. Snout elongate, forming spear; conspicuous hump between eyes and origin of first dorsal fin. Pelvic fin long, slender; *tips of pectoral, first dorsal, and anal fins rounded; first anal fin immediately behind anus.* Scales dense, embedded, *ending in point. Lateral line continuous, not creating net-like pattern.*

Habitat: Usually near surface of open seas.
Range: Gulf of Maine; Long Island, NY, to Brazil, including Bermuda, Bahamas, Gulf of Mexico, and Caribbean. Also in e Atlantic and Mediterranean.
Similar Species: Longbill Spearfish *(T. pfluegeri)* lacks spots on first dorsal and first anal fins, and first anal fin is well behind anus.
Comments: White Marlin feeds on squids and a variety of fishes, including herrings and jacks. This species is fished primarily between New Jersey and Cape Hatteras, North Carolina, and in the Gulf of Mexico. It is also often accidentally caught on commercial longlines.

668 Striped Marlin
Tetrapturus audax

Description: To 13'5" (4.1 m); 692 lb (315 kg). Slender, elongate, compressed posteriorly. Dark blue above; silvery below; *dark blue bars on sides.* Snout elongate, forming spear. *Pelvic fin much longer than pectoral fin;* pectoral fin folds back against body; first dorsal fin falcate, anterior height equal to or greater than body depth, anterior spines and rays much longer than posterior spines in individuals more than 3' (91 cm) long. Body scaled. Lateral line not creating net-like pattern.

Habitat: Surface to mid-depths of open seas.

Range: Point Conception, CA, to Chile; possibly north to OR. Also in w Pacific and Indian Oceans.

Similar Species: Shortbill Spearfish *(T. angustirostris)* has short spear, lower jaw more than two-thirds length of upper, and length of middle rays of dorsal fin about equal to body depth in individuals more than 3' (91 cm) long. Black Marlin *(Makaira indica)* has rigid pectoral fin. Blue Marlin *(M. nigricans)* has pelvic fin shorter than pectoral fin, dorsal fin height less than body depth, and lateral line creating net-like pattern.

Comments: Striped Marlin spawns from May to August in the North Pacific. This greatly prized sport and food fish feeds on other fishes and squids. A small, highly specialized sport fishery for Striped Marlin has existed off southern California since the early 1900s.

DRIFTFISHES
Family Nomeidae

3 genera and about 15 species worldwide; 3 genera and 7 species in North America (5 Atlantic, 1 Pacific, 1 shared), plus 1 species confined to Mexican Pacific waters. These fishes live near the surface of tropical and subtropical open seas, often in association with floating seaweed or other objects. The pelvic fins may be either large or

small. There are two joined dorsal fins, the first with nine to 12 spines, the second with up to three spines and 15 to 32 rays. The anal fin has one to three spines and 14 to 31 rays. The caudal fin is forked. The lateral line runs high on the side, along the dorsal fin base. Driftfishes also have a system of mucous canals along the side that is usually visible through the skin.

693   Man-of-War Fish
Nomeus gronovii

Description:
To 8″ (20 cm). Small, elongate. Dark blue above; *sides silvery, with dark blue patches; pelvic fin black.* Head deep; snout rounded, relatively short. *Pelvic fin large, with inner rays joined by membranes along entire length;* caudal fin deeply forked.

Habitat:
Open warm seas, among tentacles of Portuguese Man-of-War.

Range:
Bermuda, Bahamas, Gulf of Mexico, and Caribbean south to Brazil; occasionally north to New England.

Comments:

Other driftfishes have pelvic fins connected to the belly for less than half the length of the fin. Man-of-War Fish lives among the tentacles of Portuguese Man-of-War; the tentacles of this jellyfish are up to 60′ (18.5 m) long and armed with powerful stinging cells fatal to other fishes. Man-of-War Fish is not harmed by these cells, however, and is thus protected by its host.

BUTTERFISHES
Family Stromateidae

3 genera and about 13 species worldwide; 1 genus with 5 species in North America (3 Atlantic, 2 Pacific), plus 2 species confined to Mexican Pacific waters. This family is found in tropical to temperate coastal waters throughout the world. These fishes are short, deep, and compressed; the upper profile is a mirror image of the lower. Butterfishes are gray to blue or green above and have intense silvery reflections, especially on the lower sides and the belly. The mouth is small, not protractile, and located at the end of a blunt snout. Pelvic fins are absent in adults. The pectoral fins are long and pointed. The dorsal and anal

fins are long-based, and each has only two to six weak spines. The caudal peduncle is narrow and lacks keels. The scales are cycloid, and the lateral line is parallel to the dorsal profile. Until recently this family included species now placed in five other families, the Nomeidae (driftfishes), Centrolophidae (medusafishes), Ariommatidae (ariommatids), Tetragonuridae (squaretails), and Amarsipidae (which consists of a single Indo-Pacific species).

688 Harvestfish
Peprilus paru

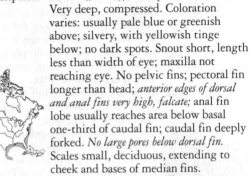

Description: To 12″ (30 cm), usually to 6″ (15 cm). Very deep, compressed. Coloration varies: usually pale blue or greenish above; silvery, with yellowish tinge below; no dark spots. Snout short, length less than width of eye; maxilla not reaching eye. No pelvic fins; pectoral fin longer than head; *anterior edges of dorsal and anal fins very high, falcate;* anal fin lobe usually reaches area below basal one-third of caudal fin; caudal fin deeply forked. *No large pores below dorsal fin.* Scales small, deciduous, extending to cheek and bases of median fins.

Habitat: Surface of inshore and offshore waters over continental shelf to depths of about 90′ (27 m).

Range: ME to Uruguay, including Gulf of Mexico and Greater Antilles; absent from Bermuda, Bahamas, and w Caribbean; infrequent north of Chesapeake Bay.

Similar Species: Butterfish *(P. triacanthus)* has usually irregular dark spots on body, only slightly elevated front lobes of dorsal and anal fins, and row of large pores below dorsal fin. Gulf Butterfish *(P. burti)* lacks dark spots on body, and has highly elevated front lobes of dorsal and anal fins and row of large pores below dorsal fin.

Comments: Harvestfish adults swim in large schools and feed on jellyfishes, crustaceans, worms, and small fishes. The young are plankton feeders and often live among floating weeds or large jellyfishes.

Order Pleuronectiformes

This order consists of 11 families, six of which are found in North America; it contains the flounders, halibuts, soles, and tonguefishes, which are collectively known as flatfishes due to their highly compressed bodies. When first hatched, flatfishes have one eye on each side of the head, like any other vertebrate, but as they develop one eye moves to the opposite side. In some families, the eyes are on the left side; other families have the eyes on the right side. (Rarely, however, an individual that would normally be left-eyed has eyes on the right side, or vice versa.) The eyed side is usually pigmented, and the blind side has very little pigment or is plain white. Some species have distinct spots or rings on the eyed side. The pelvic fins are usually asymmetrical in both size and position (the relative size and position of these fins are of considerable taxonomic importance). The pectoral fin on the blind side is often reduced or absent; occasionally both pectoral fins are absent. The dorsal and anal fins are long, continuous, and soft-rayed. Many species are capable of remarkable instantaneous color changes to match their environment. Flatfishes live on the ocean bottom, resting with the blind side downward; they swim on their side with the eyes facing upward. They usually lie partially buried on the seafloor and dart quickly upward to seize passing prey. All flatfishes are edible.

LEFTEYE FLOUNDERS
Family Bothidae

20 genera and at least 115 species worldwide; 5 genera and 9 species in North America (8 Atlantic, 1 Pacific), plus 2 species confined to Mexican Pacific waters. These highly compressed flatfishes are found over open bottoms in tropical to temperate seas throughout the world. The eyes and pigmentation are usually on the left side of the body. The pigmented side is usually brownish, often with markings, and the blind side is white; these fishes are capable of changing color patterns to match the substrate. The edge of the preopercle is visible and not hidden by skin. The pelvic fin base on the eyed side is longer than on the blind side. The dorsal fin base is long, beginning above or in front of the eyes and, like the anal fin, is not connected to the caudal fin. Some species exhibit sexual dimorphism, most notably in a greater distance between the eyes and longer pectoral fins in males. Many species formerly included in this family are now placed in the families Scophthalmidae (turbots) and Paralichthyidae (sand flounders); the most

obvious external differences by which these families may be distinguished pertain to the placement and relative lengths of the pelvic fin bases.

324 Eyed Flounder
Bothus ocellatus

Description: To 7″ (18 cm). Highly compressed, depth two-thirds length; eyes on left side. Eyed side light tan or gray, usually with bluish rings or blotches; 3 diffuse dark blotches along lateral line; *2 small vertically placed black dots on caudal fin.* Blind side white. Eyes well separated, more so in males; maxilla not reaching middle of lower eye; preopercle visible. *Pelvic fin base on eyed side twice as long as on blind side;* dorsal fin with 76–90 rays, anterior rays not branched, origin anterior to eyes; 58–68 anal fin rays. Lateral line distinctly arched over pectoral fin.

Habitat: Shallow waters in protected areas over sand; usually around coral reefs, less frequently over mud.

Range: Long Island, NY, to Rio de Janeiro, Brazil, including Bermuda, Bahamas, parts of e and s Gulf of Mexico, and Caribbean.

Similar Species: Twospot Flounder *(B. robinsi)* also has deep body and similar dorsal and anal fins, but caudal fin has 2 horizontally placed black spots. Peacock Flounder *(B. lunatus)* has shallower body with bright blue rings, concave anterior head profile, usually 9 gill rakers, usually 11 pectoral fin rays, 91–101 dorsal fin rays, and 71–79 anal fin rays, and lacks conspicuous spots on caudal fin. Maculated Flounder *(B. maculiferus)* has similar body and dorsal and anal fins to Peacock Flounder, but has convex anterior head profile, usually 7 gill rakers, and usually 9 pectoral fin rays.

Comments: Eyed, Twospot, and Peacock Flounders are all good food fishes, but they are of little commercial value due to their

small size and the fact that they are
infrequently caught by anglers. They
burrow into sand or mud, behavior
shared with other flatfishes.

TURBOTS
Family Scophthalmidae

5 genera and about 18 species worldwide; 1 species in North America. Tur-
bots are confined to temperate waters of the Atlantic and
the Mediterranean Sea. The eyes are usually on the left side
of the body. The mouth is large, with a prominent lower
jaw. These flatfishes were recently separated from the lefteye flounders (family Bothidae) as a distinct family; external morphological characteristics are virtually identical in
the two groups, the principal difference being that both
pelvic fin bases are elongate in turbots.

339 Windowpane
Scophthalmus aquosus

Description: To 18″ (46 cm). Highly compressed,
depth about two-thirds length; eyes on
left side. Eyed side olive, brownish,
reddish, or grayish, translucent, *mottled
with numerous small, irregular, light or
dark blotches on head, sides, and fins.* Blind
side white, sometimes with dusky
blotches. Mouth large; lower jaw
projects slightly beyond upper; maxilla
reaches middle of lower eye; preopercle
visible. *Pelvic fin base on each side very
long, extending toward head;* dorsal fin
with 63–73 rays, *first few rays without
connecting membranes, origin above snout;*
46–54 anal fin rays. Lateral line highly
arched anteriorly.
Habitat: Over sand from near shore to depths of
about 150′ (46 m).
Range: Gulf of St. Lawrence and NS to n FL.
Similar Species: Spotted Whiff *(Citharichthys macrops),*
the only other w Atlantic left-eyed
flounder with numerous small irregular
dark spots on body and fins, reaches
length of 6″ (15 cm), and has smaller
mouth, shorter pelvic fin bases, dorsal

fin with 80–85 rays and shorter anterior
rays, 56–64 anal fin rays, and straight
lateral line.

Comments: Windowpane is most common off the
coast of New England, where it is a year-
round resident. It is of little importance
as a food or sport fish.

SAND FLOUNDERS
Family Paralichthyidae

About 16 genera and at least 85 species
worldwide; 9 genera and 32 species in North America (24
Atlantic, 8 Pacific), plus 13 species confined to Mexican Atlantic and Pacific waters. Sand flounders are found mostly
in tropical to warm-temperate waters of the Atlantic, Pacific, and Indian Oceans; some species occasionally enter
fresh water. The eyes are usually on the left side of the body.
The size of the mouth varies from large to small, with teeth
ranging from large and strong to small and weak. These
fishes were recently separated from the lefteye flounders
(family Bothidae) as a distinct family; external morphological characteristics are virtually identical in both groups, the
principal differences being that sand flounders have pectoral
fins with branched rays and pelvic fins with short bases of
nearly equal length (the base on the eyed side is attached to
the ventral ridge).

340   Three-eye Flounder
Ancylopsetta dilecta

Description: To 7″ (18 cm). Highly compressed,
depth about half of length; eyes on left
side. Eyed side light brown, with
numerous small spots and blotches; *3
large ocelli form triangle with apex on
lateral line near caudal peduncle.* Blind
side white. Head long; lower jaw not
projecting; preopercle visible. *Pelvic fin
bases of about equal length;* pectoral fin on
each side; *dorsal fin with anterior rays
longer and with fleshy tips,* origin above
eyes. Lateral line highly arched
anteriorly.

Habitat: Over open bottoms of continental shelf
at depths of 192–1,200′ (59–366 m).

Range: NC to Yucatán.

Similar Species: Ocellated Flounder *(A. quadrocellata)* has 4 ocelli, fourth above arched part of lateral line; occurs usually to depths of 150' (46 m).

Comments: Three-eye Flounder feeds primarily on crustaceans and small fishes.

338 Spotted Whiff
Citharichthys macrops

Description: To 6" (15 cm). Highly compressed, depth half of length. Eyes on left side; *eyed side tan to dark brown, with numerous small spots or blotches on body and median fins.* Blind side white. Maxilla reaches middle of lower eye; 1 row of teeth in each jaw; front teeth larger than lateral teeth; preopercle visible. *Pelvic fin bases of about equal length;* dorsal fin with 80–85 rays, first ray longer than second or third, origin anterior to eyes; 56–64 anal fin rays. *Lateral line nearly straight.*

Habitat: Over hard sand or crushed shells from shoreline to depths of 60' (18.5 m); occasionally to 300' (91 m).

Range: NC to Honduras.

Similar Species: Horned Whiff *(C. cornutus)* males have spines on snout. Bay Whiff *(C. spilopterus)* lacks spots and blotches on body; enters fresh water.

Comments: Like most sand flounders, Spotted Whiff can move rapidly over short distances in pursuit of prey.

334 Pacific Sanddab
Citharichthys sordidus

Description: To 16" (41 cm). Extremely compressed, deep; eyes on left side. Eyed side brown, with darker brown mottling and sometimes dull orange spots. Blind side off-white to pale brown. Snout moderately sharp; *ridge between eyes concave; width of lower eye longer than snout;* preopercle visible; 18–25 gill rakers on outer arch. *Pelvic fin bases of about equal length, base on eyed side attached to ventral.*

ridge; dorsal fin with 86–102 rays, origin above eyes; anal fin with 67–81 rays, origin below pectoral fin; anal and dorsal fins extend almost to caudal fin. *Lateral line straight.*

Habitat: Over soft bottoms to depths of 1,800' (549 m).

Range: Bering Sea to Cabo San Lucas, Baja California.

Similar Species: Speckled Sanddab *(C. stigmaeus)* has 11–15 gill rakers on outer arch, short pectoral fin, 75–97 dorsal fin rays, and 58–77 anal fin rays. Longfin Sanddab *(C. xanthostigma)* has 16–19 gill rakers on outer arch, very long pectoral fin with upper rays longer than head, 79–89 dorsal fin rays, and 61–69 anal fin rays.

Comments: Pacific Sanddab spawns during the winter; some females may spawn twice in a season. Highly regarded as food, this flatfish is sought by anglers as well as commercial trawlers.

88, 331   **Gulf Flounder**
Paralichthys albigutta

Description: To 16½" (42 cm). Oval, depth less than half of length; eyes usually on left side, very rarely on right. Eyed side light to dark brown, olive brown, or dark gray; diffuse black, dark brown, or dusky spots and blotches (disappearing with age); *3 small distinct ocelli form triangle,* 2 placed at equal distances above and below lateral line at mid-body and 1 straddling lateral line anterior to caudal fin; 2 vertically placed spots just behind pectoral fin, 1 to rear of lateral line. Blind side white or dusky. No bony ridge between eyes; maxilla reaches beyond middle of lower eye; preopercle visible; usually 10–11 gill rakers on lower limb of outer arch. *Pelvic fins with bases of about equal length* and rays of equal length; pelvic fin on eyed side inserted off median line; pectoral fin on each side; dorsal fin with usually 75–81 rays, origin slightly anterior to eyes; anal fin with usually 56–61 rays, first ray shorter than second. Lateral line highly arched over pectoral fin.

Habitat: Over sand or slightly muddy bottoms in estuaries and coastal waters to depths of 420' (128 m).

Range: NC to ne Mexico, including w Bahamas; more common in e Gulf of Mexico than in w Gulf.

Similar Species:

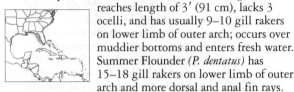

Southern Flounder *(P. lethostigma)* reaches length of 3' (91 cm), lacks 3 ocelli, and has usually 9–10 gill rakers on lower limb of outer arch; occurs over muddier bottoms and enters fresh water. Summer Flounder *(P. dentatus)* has 15–18 gill rakers on lower limb of outer arch and more dorsal and anal fin rays. Spotfin Flounder *(Cyclopsetta fimbriata)* has large black blotch on pectroal fin, 2 large spots on dorsal and anal fins, and large dark spot enclosing lightish area at center of caudal fin; occurs over open bottoms to depths of 750' (229 m).

Comments: Gulf Flounder is an important food and sport fish, but its relatively small size makes it less valuable than other flounders. It is a voracious predator and will take both live and artificial bait. Many are caught at night in shallow water by spear fishers.

---

325 California Halibut
Paralichthys californicus

Description: To 5' (1.5 m); 73 lb (33 kg). Elongate, deep, highly compressed; eyes usually on left side, rarely on right. Eyed side light to dark brown, with lighter mottling. Blind side lighter. Snout moderately sharp; mouth large; *maxilla reaches beyond posterior edge of lower eye;* numerous sharp teeth in jaws; preopercle visible. Dorsal fin with 66–76 rays, origin above eyes; 49–59 anal fin rays; caudal fin truncate or notched. *Lateral line highly arched over pectoral fin.*

Habitat: Over soft bottoms to depths of 600' (183 m).

Range: Quillayute River, WA, to Bahía
Magdalena, Baja California.

Similar Species: Bigmouth Sole *(Hippoglossina stomata)* has
eyes on left side, maxilla almost reaching
posterior edge of lower eye, 63–70 dorsal
fin rays, 47–55 anal fin rays, and rounded

caudal fin. Fantail Sole *(Xystreurys liolepis)*
has eyes on left side, small mouth with
maxilla not reaching posterior edge of
lower eye, pectoral fin longer than head,
73–80 dorsal fin rays, 57–62 anal fin
rays, and rounded caudal fin.

Comments: Other flatfishes with the common name
halibut are very large members of the
righteye flounder family (Pleuronectidae).
California Halibut, the largest species in
its family, probably received its name
because of its size. The annual sport
catch may exceed 300,000 fish. It also is
an important commercial species, with
annual landings of up to 1,000 tons.

---

328 Summer Flounder
Paralichthys dentatus

Description: To 3′1″ (94 cm). Relatively large,
robust, deep, highly compressed; eyes
usually on left side, very rarely on right.
Eyed side light to dark brown, with
lighter mottling and numerous obscure
ocelli; *5 larger, more obvious ocelli on
posterior half of body: 2 near dorsal fin base,
2 almost directly below near anal fin base, 1
straddling lateral line.* Blind side white.
Mouth large; upper jaw reaches to or
beyond posterior edge of lower eye;
teeth well developed; usually 15–18 gill
rakers on lower limb of outer arch. *Pelvic
fin bases of about equal length;* usually
85–90 dorsal fin rays; usually 66–70
anal fin rays. Lateral line with usually
62–70 scales in straight part; anterior
part loops upward over pectoral fin and
then extends straight back along
midline of body to caudal fin base.

Habitat: Over open, hard to soft bottoms on
continental shelf; usually to depths of
120′ (37 m).

Range:	Gulf of Maine to Sebastian Inlet, se FL.
Similar Species:	Southern Flounder *(P. lethostigma)* lacks ocelli, and has usually 9–10 gill rakers on lower limb of outer arch and 56–64 scales in straight part of lateral line. Gulf Flounder *(P. albigutta)* has 3 small but well-defined ocelli, 2 placed at equal distance above and below lateral line at mid-body and 1 straddling lateral line anterior to caudal fin, usually 10–11 gill rakers on lower limb of outer arch, usually 75–81 dorsal fin rays, and usually 56–61 anal fin rays.
Comments:	This species is an important commercial and sport fish, especially on the northern Atlantic coast of North America.

RIGHTEYE FLOUNDERS
Family Pleuronectidae

26 genera and about 59 species worldwide; 16 genera and 33 species in North America (6 Atlantic, 26 Pacific, 1 shared), plus 1 species confined to Mexican Pacific waters. This family is found in cold-temperate to arctic waters of the North Atlantic and Pacific; one eastern Pacific species commonly enters fresh water. Most righteye flounders are found over soft bottoms. They almost always have the eyes on the right side. These flatfishes have a deep, very compressed body. The pelvic fins are symmetrically placed. The dorsal fin origin is usually near the eyes, and the anal fin origin is below the pectoral fin; both are elongate, extending almost to the caudal fin base, and are composed of only rays. The caudal fin is truncate, rounded, pointed, or slightly notched. The scales are either ctenoid or cycloid; in some species, they are ctenoid on the eyed side and cycloid on the blind side. The lateral line is straight or highly arched over the pectoral fin, and some species have a dorsal branch off the lateral line. As a result of recent studies, the 20 species from cold-temperate oceans of the Southern Hemisphere formerly included in the Pleuronectidae have been placed in different families.

336 Pacific Halibut
Hippoglossus stenolepis

Description:	To 8′9″ (2.7 m); 800 lb (364 kg). Elongate, highly compressed, diamond-

shaped; eyes on right side. Eyed side dark brown, with fine mottling. Blind side lighter brown. Snout moderately sharp; teeth sharp, conical, in double row in upper jaw; *maxilla not reaching beyond anterior edge of lower eye.* Dorsal fin with 89–109 rays, origin above middle of eyes; 64–81 anal fin rays; *longest rays of dorsal and anal fins at about mid-body;* caudal fin slightly forked. Scales numerous, cycloid. Lateral line arched over pectoral fin.

Habitat: Over soft bottoms at depths of 18–1,800′ (5.5–549 m).

Range: Bering Sea to Santa Rosa Island, s CA. Also in Sea of Japan.

Similar Species: Arrowtooth Flounder *(Atheresthes stomias)* reaches length of 33″ (84 cm), and has unpigmented blind side, 2 rows of sharp strong teeth in each jaw, dorsal fin origin above middle of upper eye, 81–99 anal fin rays, and nearly straight lateral line. Greenland Halibut *(Reinhardtius hippoglossoides)* reaches length of 3′ (91 cm), is light to dark brown on blind side, and has maxilla reaching posterior edge of lower eye, jaws with 1 row of strong sharp teeth, dorsal fin with 83–105 rays, its origin behind upper eye, and straight lateral line; occurs in Atlantic and Pacific.

Comments: Pacific Halibut supports one of the oldest and most valuable fisheries on the Pacific coast. It is a highly desirable sport fish off Alaska, British Columbia, and Washington.

333 Rock Sole
Lepidopsetta bilineata

Description: To 24″ (61 cm). Moderately deep, compressed; eyes on right side. Eyed side dark brown or gray, mottled. Blind side whitish. Snout short, moderately sharp; maxilla not reaching middle of lower eye; teeth in both jaws, more developed on blind side. Dorsal fin with 67–82 rays, origin above eyes; 51–64 anal fin rays; caudal fin slightly rounded. Scales cycloid on blind side, ctenoid on eyed side, extending onto dorsal, anal, and caudal fin rays. *Lateral line arched over pectoral fin, with short dorsal branch not extending beyond posterior edge of opercle.*

Habitat: Over rocks or soft bottoms at depths of 12–1,200′ (3.7–366 m).

Range: Bering Sea to Tanner Bank, CA. Also in Sea of Japan.

Similar Species:

Petrale Sole *(Eopsetta jordani)* has maxilla reaching middle of lower eye, 82–103 dorsal fin rays, 62–80 anal fin rays, and lateral line not arching over pectoral fin. Butter Sole *(Isopsetta isolepis)* has maxilla not reaching middle of lower eye, dorsal and anal fins with yellow edges, 78–82 dorsal fin rays, 58–69 anal fin rays, and rough scales on body, head, and fins on eyed side. Yellowfin Sole *(Limanda aspera)* has 61–69 dorsal fin rays, 48–58 anal fin rays, scales on dorsal and anal fins, and lateral line arched over pectoral fin, without dorsal branch.

Comments: Each Rock Sole female releases from 400,000 to 1,300,000 eggs during the spawning period from February to April. Adults feed on clam siphons, polychaete worms, shrimps, small crabs, brittle stars, and sand lances, all of which can be used as bait by anglers.

326 English Sole
Parophrys vetulus

Description: To 22″ (56 cm). Deep, elongate, highly compressed, almost diamond-shaped; eyes on right side. Eyed side dark to light brown, occasionally with brown spots. Blind side pale yellow to white. Snout moderately long, sharp; *upper eye visible from blind side;* mouth small. Dorsal fin with 71–93 rays, longest rays at mid-body, origin above middle of upper eye; 52–70 anal fin rays; caudal fin notched. *Fins unscaled.* Lateral line almost straight, with short dorsal branch.

Habitat: Over soft bottoms to depths of 1,800′
(546 m).

Range: Bering Sea to Bahía de San Cristóbal,
Baja California.

Comments: The migratory English Sole may travel
up to 700 miles. Although very few are
caught for sport, this species ranks
among the top three flatfishes in terms
of pounds taken by commercial trawlers.
Other right-eyed flatfishes in the North
Pacific have at least one of the following
characteristics: a large mouth, a rounded
caudal fin, or an abrupt arch in the
lateral line.

89, 335 **Starry Flounder**
Platichthys stellatus

Description: To 3′ (91 cm). Deep, compressed,
almost diamond-shaped; eyes on either
left or right side. Eyed side dark brown
to nearly black, with vague blotches;
*distinctive black and white or black and
orange bars on dorsal, anal, and caudal fins.*
Blind side white to creamy white,
occasionally blotched. Mouth small.
52–64 dorsal fin rays; 38–47 anal fin
rays; dorsal and anal fins with longest
rays posterior to mid-body; caudal fin
straight or rounded. Scales star-shaped,
very rough to touch. Lateral line only
slightly arched over pectoral fin; no
dorsal branch.

Habitat: Over soft bottoms in bays and
estuaries and off open coasts to depths
of 900′ (274 m); frequently enters
fresh water.

Range: Arctic Ocean off AK to Santa Barbara,
CA. Also in Sea of Japan.

Comments: Starry Flounder feeds on crabs, shrimps,
worms, clams, and small fishes. It can
tolerate very low salinity and is often
found in major rivers, well away from
the open ocean. Small numbers are
taken by anglers and commercial
trawlers. Some populations have an
unusually high percentage of left-eyed
individuals.

329 C-O Sole
Pleuronichthys coenosus

Description: To 14″ (36 cm). Deep, highly
compressed; caudal peduncle about one-
fourth body depth; eyes on right side.
Eyed side brown, with darker mottling;
*prominent C- and O-shaped marks on caudal
fin.* Blind side creamy white. Snout
rounded; mouth small, almost hidden
by eyes when viewed from above. Dorsal
fin with 65–78 rays, *first 4–6 anterior
rays extend onto blind side but not beyond
mouth,* origin anterior to middle of upper
eye; 46–56 anal fin rays; caudal fin
rounded. Scales cycloid, on both sides of
body. Lateral line not abruptly arched
over pectoral fin, with dorsal branch
extending posteriorly to about mid-body.

Habitat: Over soft bottoms or rocks to depths of
1,146′ (350 m).

Range: Southeastern AK to Cabo Colnett, Baja
California.

Similar Species: Curlfin Sole *(P. decurrens)* has at least 9
dorsal fin rays reaching below mouth
and extending onto blind side. Spotted
Turbot *(P. ritteri)* has 1–2 black spots on
middle of lateral line, 61–70 dorsal fin
rays, 43–49 anal fin rays, and caudal
peduncle less than one-fourth body
depth. Hornyhead Turbot *(P. verticalis)*
has 2 prominent spines between eyes
and 44–51 anal fin rays. Diamond
Turbot *(P. guttulatus)* has numerous blue
spots on body.

Comments: This flatfish probably spawns in the late
winter and early spring; its eggs float
near the surface. Small numbers are
caught by anglers with hook and line
and by commercial trawlers. The
unusual common name is derived from
the markings on the caudal fin.

337 Diamond Turbot
Pleuronichthys guttulatus

Description: To 18″ (46 cm). Deep, *diamond-shaped,*
highly compressed; eyes on right side.

Eyed side dark gray, *with numerous blue spots;* area around mouth yellow. Blind side unpigmented. Snout short, moderately sharp. Dorsal fin with 66–75 rays, origin above eyes; 48–54 anal fin rays; middle rays of dorsal and anal fins longest; caudal fin rounded. *Lateral line with dorsal branch extending more than halfway to caudal fin.*

Habitat: Over soft bottoms at depths of 6–150′ (1.8–46 m).

Range: Cape Mendocino, CA, to Bahía Magdalena, Baja California.

Similar Species: Sand Sole *(Psettichthys melanostictus)* is usually right-eyed, lacks blue spots, and has 72–90 dorsal fin rays, with first 4–5 rays free of membrane, and 53–66 anal fin rays.

Comments: This distinctively shaped flatfish is commonly encountered by divers off southern California. In other eastern Pacific flatfishes, the dorsal branch of the lateral line is absent or much shorter. In addition, other eastern Pacific species of *Pleuronichthys* have at least the first four dorsal fin rays extending down on the blind side of body.

---

332 Winter Flounder
Pseudopleuronectes americanus

Description: To 23″ (58 cm). Highly compressed, elliptical; dorsal and ventral profiles evenly curved; eyes on right side. Coloration of eyed side varies with substrate: reddish brown to olive green to almost black, sometimes mottled; fins plain. Blind side white. *Head small; maxilla barely reaches anterior edge of lower eye;* preopercle visible. Dorsal fin with 60–76 rays, origin above anterior edge of upper eye; 44–58 anal fin rays; caudal fin rounded. Scales strongly ctenoid on eyed side, smoother on blind side; scales between eyes rough to touch. *Lateral line almost straight,* slightly arched over pectoral fin.

Habitat: Over mud or sand to depths of 120' (37 m) or more; sometimes with vegetation.

Range: Labrador to GA; most abundant in Gulf of Maine; rare south of Chesapeake Bay.

Similar Species: American Plaice *(Hippoglossoides platessoides)* has larger mouth, 75–107 dorsal fin rays, 64–84 anal fin rays, and moderately to strongly arched lateral line. Atlantic Halibut *(Hippoglossus hippoglossus)* has larger mouth, 75–107 dorsal fin rays, 64–84 anal fin rays, emarginate caudal fin, and moderately to strongly arched anterior lateral line. Greenland Halibut *(Reinhardtius hippoglossoides)* has larger mouth, 75–107 dorsal fin rays, 64–84 anal fin rays, and emarginate caudal fin; occurs in Atlantic and Pacific. Yellowtail Flounder *(Limanda ferruginea)* has smaller mouth, 73–91 dorsal fin rays, and lateral line notably arched over pectoral fin. Witch Flounder *(Glyptocephalus cynoglossus)* has circular depressions on lower side of head on blind side, smaller mouth, and at least 100 dorsal fin rays. Smooth Flounder *(Pleuronectes putnami)* lacks scales between eyes, and has smaller mouth, 53–59 dorsal fin rays, and 35–41 anal fin rays.

Comments: Winter Flounder has a thicker body and broader caudal peduncle than any other small flounder in its range. South of New York, it goes into deep water in the summer and reappears in shoal waters during the winter (hence its common name). It is an important food fish.

AMERICAN SOLES
Family Achiridae

9 genera and about 28 species world-wide; 3 genera and 6 species in North America (5 Atlantic, 1 Pacific), plus 7 species confined to Mexican waters. This family is found mostly in shallow coastal waters to depths of about 600' (183 m) on the Atlantic and Pacific coasts of the American continents; one Atlantic species regularly occurs in fresh water during the juvenile stage. Formerly included in the sole family (Soleidae), this group has only

recently been accorded family status; it is one of the few marine families restricted to the American continents. These flatfishes have a rounded or oval body, with tiny, closely set eyes on the right side. They are usually blackish brown, with blotches or bars. The head is rounded, and the snout is basically absent. The tiny mouth is oblique, and the lips are fleshy and usually fringed with dermal flaps. The edge of the preopercle is hidden by skin. All fins are soft-rayed. Pectoral fins are sometimes absent. The long dorsal and anal fins are not joined to the caudal fin. Tiny ctenoid scales are usually present, but are completely absent in the genus *Gymnachirus*. The lateral line is almost straight and often crossed with accessory branches or minute fleshy flaps.

330 Naked Sole
Gymnachirus melas

Description: To 6¼" (16 cm). Oval, depth one-half to three-fifths length; eyes on right side. Eyed side and caudal fin dark brown or black, *with 20–30 beige or brown zebra-like bars* extending onto median fins. Blind side whitish, with dusky-edged median fins. Head very small; mouth small, twisted; edge of preopercle hidden. Pelvic fin small, hidden under skin, continuous with anal fin on eyed side; pectoral fin on eyed side only, small, sometimes hidden under skin; dorsal and anal fins enclosed in loose skin. Lateral line with branches at right angles. Skin soft, fleshy. *Body unscaled.*

Habitat: Over sand on continental shelf to depths of 600′ (183 m).

Range: NC to n Gulf of Mexico.

Similar Species: Fringed Sole *(G. texae)* has more than 30 dark bars and long dermal cirri on eyed side; occurs over mud, usually at depths of 180–300′ (55–91 m).

Comments: Naked and Fringed Soles overlap in a very narrow zone east and west of Mobile Bay, Alabama. This is probably because of the difference in the seafloor, which is sandier east of the zone of overlap and muddier west of it. In the western Gulf of Mexico, Naked Sole is ecologically replaced by Fringed Sole.

87, 327 Hogchoker
Trinectes maculatus

Description: To 6″ (15 cm). Depth more than half of length; eyes on right side. *Eyed side dusky, with usually 7–8 narrow black bars; dark streaks or spots on fins (especially in young).* Blind side white, often partly pigmented. Head blunt; eyes and mouth very small; edge of preopercle hidden; right and left gill chambers separate, not connected by open interbranchial septum. Pelvic fin on eyed side continuous with anal fin; *no pectoral fins;* dorsal fin with short first ray, origin above snout. *Scales small,* strongly ctenoid. Lateral line nearly straight, narrow, dark; no dermal flaps.

Habitat: Shallow coastal waters over mud, silt, or sand in bays and estuaries. Young regularly enter fresh water and large rivers, particularly in s part of range.

Range: ME to Yucatán, including Gulf of Mexico.

Similar Species: Scrawled Sole *(T. inscriptus)* has network of thin dark lines on paler body, lacks interbranchial septum, and has pectoral fins; does not enter fresh water. Lined Sole *(Achirus lineatus)* has gill chambers connected by interbranchial septum, pectoral fins, and tufts or patches of dark hair-like cirri on body; does not enter fresh water.

Comments: Young Hogchokers ascend streams for distances of up to 150 miles. Spawning takes place in estuaries. This species is replaced in the south of its range, along the coasts of Central and South America, by the very similar Southern Hogchoker *(T. paulistanus).*

TONGUEFISHES
Family Cynoglossidae

3 genera and more than 110 species worldwide; 1 genus with 14 species in North America (13 Atlantic, 1 Pacific), plus 7 species confined to Mexican Pacific waters. Tonguefishes are found in tropical and

subtropical seas throughout the world. They are tongue-shaped flatfishes that posteriorly taper to a narrow point. The tiny, closely set eyes are on the left side of the body, which is brownish with darker bars or blotches. The mouth is quite small, and the edge of the preopercle is hidden by skin and scales. The scales are ctenoid. All fins are soft-rayed. Pectoral fins are absent. The long dorsal and anal fins are joined to the caudal fin. There are 10 to 14 caudal fin rays; the number of caudal fin rays can be an important diagnostic characteristic, which is very unusual among fishes. In the western Atlantic, and perhaps elsewhere, species have markedly distinct depth distributions, which also can be an aid in identification. These flatfishes exhibit an obvious relationship to the soles (family Soleidae) and American soles (family Achiridae), and have sometimes been placed in the family Soleidae.

323 Blackcheek Tonguefish
Symphurus plagiusa

Description: To 7½″ (19 cm). Elongate, rounded anteriorly, tapering to narrow point posteriorly; eyes on left side. Eyed side brownish, usually uniformly pigmented, sometimes with black blotches; *large blackish blotch on opercle;* no spots on dorsal and anal fins. Blind side light gray to white. Eyes and mouth small; edge of preopercle hidden. Pelvic fin on eyed side only; 84–86 dorsal fin rays; 69–70 anal fin rays; *10 caudal fin rays.* Lateral line with about 71–76 scales.

Habitat: Shallow coastal waters and estuaries.
Range: NY to Yucatán, including Bahamas and n Cuba.
Similar Species: Offshore Tonguefish *(S. civitatum),* Longtail Tonguefish *(S. pelicanus),* Deepwater Tonguefish *(S. piger),* Northern Tonguefish *(S. pusillus),* and Caribbean Tonguefish *(S. arawak)* have 12 caudal fin rays. Freckled Tonguefish *(S. nebulosus)* has elongate body with nearly parallel dorsal and ventral profiles, and is only Atlantic tonguefish with 14 caudal fin rays. Spottail Tonguefish *(S. urospilus)* has large black spot on tail, and is only Atlantic

tonguefish with 11 caudal fin rays. Spottedfin Tonguefish *(S. diomedeanus)* has large black spot at rear of dorsal and anal fins and 10 caudal fin rays. Largescale Tonguefish *(S. minor)* and Pygmy Tonguefish *(S. parvus)* have 10 caudal fin rays. Freckled and Largescale Tonguefishes occur in deeper waters.

Comments: Blackcheek Tonguefish is by far the most common western Atlantic tonguefish, and is the only one with a black patch on the cheek. As is true of other tonguefishes, it is too small to be of any value as a food fish.

Order Tetraodontiformes

This order contains nine families, seven of which are found in North America. These fishes exhibit greater diversity in size, body form, scalation, color, and habitat than virtually any other order of fishes in the world. Some have unscaled bodies; others are covered with spike-like processes, or even encased in immovable bony plates. When present, each pelvic fin is reduced to nothing more than a ventral spine.

TRIGGERFISHES
Family Balistidae

11 genera and about 40 species worldwide; 4 genera and 8 species in North America (5 Atlantic, 2 Pacific, 1 shared), plus 2 species confined to Mexican Pacific waters. This family is found in tropical to temperate seas throughout the world. Some family members are brightly colored fishes that live along rocky coasts or around coral reefs and surrounding sea-grass beds, usually in shallow water; others live in open seas. The young are pelagic; those of some species are a part of the floating sargassum community. Triggerfishes have an oval compressed body covered with large, thick, diamond-shaped scales in a regular series, resembling a coat of mail. The scales just above the pectoral fin base are usually enlarged and slightly separated to form a flexible tympanum that probably serves to transmit sound to the fish. When present, the pelvic fins are reduced to spiny projections of the pelvic bone. There are two well-separated dorsal fins. The first dorsal fin has three spines; the first spine can be locked into an upright position by the second,

and the third is often minute. (Only after the second dorsal fin spine has been depressed can the first be lowered; hence the collective common name triggerfish.) The upper jaw has an outer series of four strong teeth on each side; the premaxilla has an inner series of three teeth on each side, developed more for crushing than for nibbling. Some triggerfishes are good food fishes, but others are toxic. △

387 Queen Triggerfish
Balistes vetula

Description: To 20″ (51 cm). Oval, compressed. Greenish gray or bluish gray above; yellowish orange below; *blue lines, outlined in yellow, radiate from eye; 2 oblique bright blue stripes extend from mouth to pectoral fin base;* blue submarginal band on median fins; wide bluish band around caudal peduncle. First dorsal fin with 3 visible spines; second dorsal fin with 29–31 rays; 27–28 anal fin rays; second dorsal and anal fins notably elongate anteriorly; *caudal fin lunate in adults,* emarginate in young. Scales thick, diamond-shaped; *patch of enlarged scales above pectoral fin;* scales on posterior part of body without keels.

Habitat: Rocky and coral reefs, around pilings and stone jetties, and adjacent sandy and grassy areas.

Range: MA to Brazil, including Bermuda, Bahamas, Gulf of Mexico, and Caribbean; occasional summer stragglers north of Cape Hatteras, NC.

Similar Species: Gray Triggerfish *(B. capriscus)* is uniformly gray, lacks blue stripes on head, and has 26–29 dorsal fin rays and 23–26 anal fin rays. Sargassum Triggerfish *(Xanthichthys ringens),* Rough Triggerfish *(Canthidermis maculata),* and Ocean Triggerfish *(C. sufflamen)* lack patch of enlarged scales above pectoral fin; all occur over deep coral reefs or along deep rocky slopes. Black Durgon *(Melichthys niger)* is solid black with narrow pale blue stripes at bases of second dorsal and anal fins.

Comments: Queen Triggerfish feeds on sea urchins, which it turns over in order to eat the contents of the body. It is common, and is used as food throughout much of its range. This fish can change color in response to changes in the background and in light intensity; however, the bright blue stripes on the head persist.

388 Black Durgon
Melichthys niger

Description: To 20″ (51 cm). Oval, compressed. *Black, sometimes with dark greenish cast; pale blue stripes at bases of second dorsal and anal fins;* scale edges on front of head sometimes orange. First dorsal fin with 3 spines, small third spine not readily visible; second dorsal and anal fins not notably elongate anteriorly, edges more or less straight; upper and lower caudal fin rays slightly longer than rest of fin. Scales thick, diamond-shaped; *scales on posterior part of body with prominent keels forming lengthwise ridges.*

Habitat: Clear waters of outer reefs to depths of about 60′ (18.5 m); often near surface or at mid-depths.

Range: In Atlantic around Bermuda and se FL to Brazil, including Bahamas, nw Gulf of Mexico, and Caribbean. Also around islands in mid–South Atlantic. In e Pacific only around a few offshore islands.

Comments: Found worldwide in tropical seas, this triggerfish frequently forms loose schools. Black Durgon is omnivorous; it grazes on algae attached to rocks or coral, and will rise to the surface to feed on floating plants or planktonic invertebrates. Because it has been observed feeding on dead or dying fish or other animals, this species is erroneously considered to be dangerous. It is known as Blackfish around Ascension Island, in the South Atlantic.

FILEFISHES
Family Monacanthidae

About 31 genera and about 95 species worldwide; 4 genera and 10 species in North America (9 Atlantic, 1 Atlantic and Pacific), plus 1 species confined to Mexican Pacific waters. This family is found in tropical to warm-temperate waters of the Atlantic, Indian, and Pacific Oceans; the greatest abundance of species is found in Australia. Filefishes are small to medium, highly compressed fishes. They have two well-separated dorsal fins. In most species, the first dorsal fin has two spines (a few species have only one); the second spine is tiny and always less than one-third the length of the first. The first dorsal fin spine usually can be locked upright by the second. The body is covered with tiny, modified, bristle-like scales that are not discernible to the naked eye. Filefishes have a well-developed pelvic bone that is hinged to the pectoral girdle and supports a ventral flap of skin between its tip and the anus; the pelvic bone can be moved to expand or contract the ventral flap. In some species the flap is highly pigmented and probably used in courtship displays. When present, the pelvic fins are rudimentary, represented by a series of up to three scales covering the end of the pelvic bone. The young of certain species are components of pelagic sargassum communities. Filefishes are closely related to triggerfishes; in the past, the two groups have been lumped together in the family Balistidae and collectively called leatherjackets.

354   Orange Filefish
Aluterus schoepfii

Description: To 24″ (61 cm). Oblong, deep, strongly compressed. Grayish to brownish, with large irregular pale blotches; *head and body covered with numerous small orange to yellowish spots.* Snout pointed, upper profile straight to slightly concave in adults; mouth terminal; 6 outer teeth in each jaw; gill slits oblique. First dorsal fin spine prominent, long, weak; second dorsal fin spine barely visible; second dorsal fin with 32–39 rays; 35–41 anal fin spines. Scales minute, numerous.

Habitat: Over sand or mud with sea grasses from shallow waters to depths of 150′ (46 m).

Range: NS to Brazil, including Bermuda, Bahamas, Gulf of Mexico, and

Caribbean; n records based on seasonal waifs.

Comments: This is one of the largest filefishes. It feeds on a variety of plants, including algae and sea grasses. The young are often found on the surface of open seas in rafts of sargassum weed.

---

353 Scrawled Filefish
Aluterus scriptus

Description: To 3′ (91 cm). Elongate, strongly compressed. *Light bluish gray to olive or brown; blue or blue-green spots, irregular lines, and scattered small black spots on body and head. Snout very long, upper profile distinctly concave in adults;* lower jaw projects well beyond upper; 6 outer teeth in each jaw; gill slits oblique. First dorsal fin spine long, slender, often broken; second dorsal fin with 43–49 rays; 46–52 anal fin rays; caudal fin long, with rounded posterior profile. Caudal peduncle more deep than long. Scales numerous, minute.

Habitat: Sea-grass beds in tropical and subtropical seas.

Range: New England to Brazil, including Bermuda, Bahamas, Gulf of Mexico, and Caribbean; New England records based on seasonal waifs.

Similar Species: Unicorn Filefish *(A. monoceros)* has scattered brown spots on body, and

convex upper profile of snout in adults. Dotterel Filefish *(A. heudelotii)* reaches length of 12″ (30 cm), and has deeper body with blue spots and lines, concave upper profile of snout in adults, 36–41 dorsal fin rays, and 39–44 anal fin rays. Orange Filefish *(A. schoepfii)* reaches length of 24″ (61 cm), and has orange to yellowish spots on body, straight to slightly concave upper profile of snout in adults, 32–39 dorsal fin rays, and 35–41 anal fin rays.

Comments: This filefish often assumes a vertical head-down position, to mimic blades of grass and to survey the bottom for food.

355 Planehead Filefish
Stephanolepis hispidus

Description: To 9″ (23 cm). Very deep, greatly compressed. *Coloration varies with background: gray, tan, or brown, sometimes greenish, with irregular dark blotches or spots;* caudal fin dusky yellow, other fins yellow. 6 outer teeth in each jaw; gill slits almost vertical; pelvic bone has prominent external spine, disappearing in large individuals. First dorsal fin spine strong; second dorsal fin with 29–35 rays, second ray forming long filament in adult males; 30–35 anal fin rays; caudal fin roughly rounded. Modified, bristle-like scales on sides of caudal peduncle. Surface of body velvet-like.

Habitat: Over sand or mud around vegetation from near shore to open seas; usually in shallow waters, occasionally to depths of 265′ (81 m).

Range: NS (seasonally) to Brazil, including Bermuda, Bahamas, Gulf of Mexico, and Caribbean.

Similar Species: Pygmy Filefish *(S. setifer)* has rows of dark streaks on sides and usually 27–29 rays in each dorsal and anal fin. Fringed Filefish *(Monacanthus ciliatus)* has large ventral flap. Slender Filefish *(M. tuckeri)* reaches length of 3″ (7.5 cm), and has longer, more pointed head and large ventral flap; occurs usually around reefs.

Comments: Filefishes are often found in the open ocean among floating sargassum weed or inshore around sea-grass beds. Adults move seaward in winter. In the past, the species of *Stephanolepis* were included in the genus *Monacanthus.*

BOXFISHES
Family Ostraciidae

14 genera and about 33 species world-wide; 3 genera and 6 species in North America (5 Atlantic, 1 Pacific), plus 1 species confined to Mexican Pacific waters. Boxfishes occur in tropical to warm-temperate seas throughout the world, where they frequent shallow coral

reefs and rocky or sandy and grassy areas to depths of about 270′ (82 m). The family takes its common name from the immovable protective carapace (a shell formed of modified scales) that almost completely encloses these small, slow-moving fishes. The carapace has an opening for the mouth, eyes, gill slits, and fins, leaving only the caudal peduncle unprotected. In some species, the two sides of the carapace are completely joined along the dorsal midline behind the dorsal fin; in others, the carapace is incomplete behind the dorsal fin. Some species have horn-like spines on the head and on the rear undersides of the body. Those with a bony projection above each eye are often known as cowfishes. Pelvic fins are absent. Certain boxfishes are highly prized as food in the Caribbean; however, some species are toxic.

356 Scrawled Cowfish
Acanthostracion quadricornis

Description: To 19″ (48 cm). Deep, wide ventrally; immovable carapace complete behind dorsal fin; *spine projects posteriorly from rear ridge on lower side of body.* Grayish brown or grayish green, with numerous bright blue or blackish-blue irregular spots, bars, and short lines on back and sides; *3–4 distinct blue horizontal stripes on cheek.* Profile of head steep; eye on upper side; *forward-pointed, horn-like spine above each eye;* mouth small, ventral, terminal; lips fleshy; teeth conical. Pectoral, dorsal, and anal fins small, rounded; caudal fin larger.

Habitat: Shallow, grassy, sometimes turbid waters to depths of 240′ (73 m).

Range: MA to Brazil, including Bermuda, Bahamas, Gulf of Mexico, and Caribbean. Also in e Atlantic.

Similar Species: Honeycomb Cowfish *(A. polygonia),* the only other Atlantic member of family with horny projections both on front of head and lower back, has olive body and dark, net-like pattern on head; occurs around shallow reefs.

Comments: This cowfish is reported to be an excellent food fish. It feeds primarily on tunicates, gorgonians, sea anemones, and crustaceans. Scrawled and Honeycomb Cowfishes have sometimes been included in the genus *Lactophrys.*

358 Spotted Trunkfish
Lactophrys bicaudalis

Description: To 21″ (53 cm). Deep, wide ventrally;
immovable carapace complete behind
dorsal fin; *spine projects posteriorly from rear
ridge on lower side of body. Pale gray or
whitish, with numerous brown or blackish
spots;* 3 large white spots behind eye in
large individuals; lips whitish. Profile of
head steep, concave; snout blunt; eye on
upper side; *no horn-like spine above eye;*
mouth small, ventral, terminal; teeth
conical. Pectoral, dorsal, and anal fins
small, rounded; caudal fin larger.

Habitat: Shallow sea-grass beds or coral reefs to
depths of 165′ (50 m).

Range: Bermuda; FL to Brazil, including
Bahamas, s Gulf of Mexico, and
Caribbean.

Similar Species: Trunkfish *(L. trigonus)* lacks dark spots,
and has bony projections only on rear of
body and 2 large, poorly defined, chain-
like dark blotches on sides. Smooth
Trunkfish *(L. triqueter)* lacks bony
projections on both head and rear of
body. Scrawled Cowfish *(Acanthostracion
quadricornis)* and Honeycomb Cowfish
(A. polygonia) have horny projection in
front of each eye.

Comments: Spotted Trunkfish is suspected of
secreting a poison that kills other fishes.

359 Trunkfish
Lactophrys trigonus

Description: To 21″ (53 cm). Deep, wide ventrally;
immovable carapace incomplete behind
dorsal fin; *spine projects posteriorly from rear
ridge on lower side of body. Greenish, tan, or
olive, with small white spots; 2 dark,
blackish, diffuse, chain-like markings on
sides.* Profile of head steep, concave;
snout blunt; eye on upper side; *no horn-
like spine above eye;* mouth small, ventral,
terminal; teeth conical. Pectoral, dorsal,
and anal fins small, rounded; caudal fin
larger.

Habitat: Shallow sea-grass and sponge beds or coral reefs to depths of 165′ (50 m).

Range: NC to Brazil, including Bermuda, Bahamas, s Gulf of Mexico, and Caribbean; seasonally north to MA.

Comments: Trunkfish may cause ciguatera poisoning if not properly prepared.

---

357 Smooth Trunkfish
Lactophrys triqueter

Description: To 11″ (28 cm). Deep, wide ventrally; immovable carapace complete behind dorsal fin; *no spines on carapace. Blackish brown, with numerous white to golden yellow spots; lips and bases of fins blackish.* Profile of head steep; snout slightly protruding; eye on upper side; mouth small, ventral, terminal; lips fleshy; teeth conical. Pectoral fin large; dorsal, anal, and caudal fins small, rounded.

Habitat: Over sand near rocks or coral reefs.

Range: Bermuda; FL to Rio de Janeiro, Brazil, including Bahamas, nw Gulf of Mexico, and Caribbean; seasonally north to MA.

Comments: This is one of the smallest trunkfishes and the only one without spines on the carapace. It may secrete poison when excited and should not be kept with other fishes. It shoots water from its mouth into the sand to uncover the small invertebrates on which it feeds.

PUFFERS
Family Tetraodontidae

19 genera and about 121 species worldwide; 3 genera and 12 species in North America (9 Atlantic, 2 Pacific, 1 shared), plus 1 genus and 4 species confined to Mexican Pacific waters. Puffers are found in tropical to temperate marine and fresh waters throughout the world; the majority are marine. As the common name implies, these fishes are capable of rapidly inflating their bodies with either water or air. Most species are drably colored on the back, with various markings, and are silvery or white on the sides and the belly. The head is moderately pointed, with the eyes high on the sides. The mouth is terminal, and there

are two teeth in each jaw. Pelvic fins are absent; the broad
pectoral fins are well developed. The short-based dorsal and
anal fins are located posteriorly. Puffers are unscaled, but
some have spiny prickles, and some have small fleshy flaps
on the sides. Some species are toxic.

360 Sharpnose Puffer
Canthigaster rostrata

Description: To 3¾" (9.5 cm). Elongate, round in
cross section; nearly globular when
inflated; *ridge or keel on back anterior to
dorsal fin.* Orangish brown to purplish
brown on upper one-third; lower two-
thirds abruptly white to orange; blue
lines radiate from eye onto caudal
peduncle; lower part of caudal peduncle
slightly darker, with parallel narrow
blue bars; upper and lower caudal fin
rays dark, middle rays and all other fins
pale orange. 2 teeth in each jaw. Dorsal
fin opposite anal fin; 10 dorsal fin rays;
9 anal fin rays; caudal fin emarginate.
Prickles absent or greatly reduced; no
fleshy flaps.
Habitat: Coral reefs and sea-grass beds to depths
of 85′ (26 m); always in clear water.
Range: NC to n South America, including
Bermuda, Bahamas, nw Gulf of Mexico,
and Caribbean.
Similar Species: A second (as yet unnamed) species of
Canthigaster has more profuse spotting
on body; occurs in deeper waters.
Comments: In the United States, Sharpnose Puffer is
most abundant in southern Florida. It is
frequently found around sea fans and
stinging coral. This species, like other
puffers, feeds primarily on shellfishes.

361 Smooth Puffer
Lagocephalus laevigatus

Description: To 3′3″ (99 cm). Elongate, round in
cross section; globular when inflated.
Back gray, greenish, blue-green, or
bluish gray; sides silvery; dark saddle-
like bars sometimes across sides and

back; belly white. Head bluntly rounded; eye high on head; mouth terminal; 2 teeth in each jaw. 17–18 pectoral fin rays; 13–14 dorsal fin rays; 12–13 anal fin rays; dorsal and anal fins moderately pointed, anterior rays longest; *caudal fin concave,* lower lobe slightly longer than upper. *Prickles on belly; no fleshy flaps.*

Habitat: At and near shore over sand or mud to depths of about 60′ (18.5 m). Young common on coastal or offshore banks.

Range: New England to Argentina, including Gulf of Mexico and e Caribbean; absent from Bermuda and Bahamas. Also in e Atlantic.

Similar Species: Oceanic Puffer *(L. lagocephalus)* is darker, pectoral fin usually has 15–16 rays, and dorsal fin is farther back on body; occurs in open seas far from shore to depths of 210′ (64 m).

Comments: This is the largest puffer in North America. Unlike some other puffers, its flesh is apparently not toxic, and it is considered a good food fish.

364 Northern Puffer
Sphoeroides maculatus

Description: To 10″ (25 cm). Elongate, round in cross section; globular when inflated. Back gray to brown, with vague black spots or saddle-like blotches; belly yellow to white; *tiny black spots on back, sides, and cheek; series of bar-like markings on lower sides.* 2 teeth in each jaw. 16 pectoral fin rays; 8 dorsal fin rays; 7 anal fin rays; caudal fin slightly rounded. Covered with prickles; no fleshy flaps.

Habitat: Bays and estuaries over sand, silt, or mud to depths of about 180′ (55 m). Inshore in summer; offshore in winter.

Range: NF to ne FL.

Similar Species: Southern Puffer *(S. nephelus)* lacks tiny black spots on upper body, and has 14 pectoral fin rays and 9 dorsal fin rays. Least Puffer *(S. parvus)* lacks dark area at axil of pectoral fin; occurs in shallow, often turbid waters. Bandtail Puffer *(S. spengleri)* has row of distinct round or oval spots on lower sides, black bar on base and outer one-third of caudal fin, and fleshy flaps. Marbled Puffer *(S. dorsalis)* has snout and sides of head marbled with pale blue, and pair of small black fleshy tabs on back; occurs over open bottoms at depths of 60–300′ (18.5–91 m). Checkered Puffer *(S. testudineus)* has 1–2 distinct transverse bars between eyes and web-like pattern of white lines on back. Blunthead Puffer *(S. pachygaster)* is uniformly gray or brown and lacks prickles on body; occurs along continental coasts.

Comments: Northern Puffer is used as food and marketed as Sea Squab. Care should be taken not to confuse it with Bandtail Puffer, which is definitely toxic, and Southern Puffer, which is reported to be mildly toxic.

---

363 Bandtail Puffer
Sphoeroides spengleri

Description: To 6¾″ (17 cm). Elongate, round in cross section; globular when inflated. Back olive green to yellowish brown, with black blotches or spotting; *lengthwise row of distinct spots on lower sides;* belly white; *dark bar on base and outer one-third of caudal fin;* other fins very pale. 2 teeth in each jaw. Dorsal and anal fins similar in size and shape; 8 dorsal fin rays; 7 anal fin rays; caudal fin truncate, slightly rounded. Prickles on belly; fleshy flaps on back and sides.

Habitat: Usually in clear shallow waters; occasionally to depths of 240′ (73 m).
Range: MA to São Paulo, Brazil, including Bermuda, Bahamas, Gulf of Mexico, and Caribbean; most common in Bermuda, s FL, Bahamas, and Caribbean; n records based on summer strays.
Comments: This species is often associated with turtle grass in the tropical areas of its range. It feeds on small crabs,

echinoderms, and mollusks. It is definitely toxic and should not be eaten. Bandtail Puffer is represented in the eastern Atlantic by the closely related Guinean Puffer *(S. marmoratus),* which is sometimes considered to be a subspecies.

362 Checkered Puffer
Sphoeroides testudineus

Description: To 15″ (38 cm). Elongate, round in cross-section; globular when inflated. *Back dark, with diverse white lines and web-like patterns;* belly white; distinct spots on sides; *1–2 distinct transverse bars between eyes.* 2 teeth in each jaw. Dorsal fin with 8 rays, directly opposite anus; 7 anal fin rays; caudal fin straight to slightly rounded. Prickles on back and belly; no fleshy flaps.

Habitat: Over mud or sand to depths of 66′ (20 m).

Range: FL to Santos, Brazil, including Bahamas, s Gulf of Mexico, Caribbean, and Central American coast; absent from Bermuda; seasonally north to NJ.

Comments: This puffer sometimes occurs in nearly fresh water and often around mangroves, although there are no freshwater records from North America. Like all puffers, it is a poor swimmer and propels itself by flapping its little dorsal and anal fins.

PORCUPINEFISHES
Family Diodontidae

6 genera and 19 species worldwide; 2 genera and 7 species in North America (4 Atlantic, 1 Pacific, 2 shared). These small to medium fishes are found in tropical waters throughout the world. Like the members of the related puffer family (Tetraodontidae), porcupinefishes are capable of rapidly inflating their bodies with either water or air. They are quite robust and covered with spines. The spines either resemble erectile quills with two-rooted bases (genus *Diodon*), or they are stout and immovable with three-rooted bases (genus *Chilomycterus*); the bases are

visible only when the skin is removed. There is a single tooth in each jaw; the teeth are fused at the midline, forming a parrot-like beak. Pelvic fins are absent, and the pectoral and caudal fins are well developed. The dorsal and anal fins are short-based.

---

347 Striped Burrfish
Chilomycterus schoepfi

Description: To 10″ (25 cm). Oval, broad, slightly depressed; *covered with stout, 3-rooted, immovable spines.* Back green to olive green or brownish; *upper sides with irregular, oblique, narrow to wide, black or brown lines;* lower sides whitish; belly whitish or golden yellow; *dark blotches with light halos at dorsal and anal fin bases and above and behind pectoral fin base.* 1 tooth in each jaw, fused to form parrot-like beak. Pectoral and caudal fins well developed; dorsal and anal fins short-based.

Habitat: Shallow sea-grass beds in summer; to depths of 225′ (69 m) in winter.

Range: Cape Hatteras, NC, to Yucatán; occasional stragglers north to ME and NS; rare in Bahamas; possibly south to Caribbean and Brazil.

Similar Species: Web Burrfish *(C. antillarum)* has greenish to brown body, with network of fine dark lines enclosing roughly hexagonal areas, large black blotches on sides, and wide dark bar below eye; occurs to depths of 165′ (50 m). Bridled Burrfish *(C. antennatus)* is covered with small dark spots and has larger kidney-shaped spot above pectoral fin; occurs around coral reefs to depths of 30′ (9 m). Spotted Burrfish *(C. atinga)* has black spots and sometimes dark blotches on body, but lacks kidney-shaped spot above pectoral fin; occurs at depths of 15–138′ (4.6–42 m).

Comments: Striped Burrfish is often quite common, especially south of the Carolinas in the summer. Those under 3″ (7.5 cm) long make good aquarium fish and will readily inflate when rubbed on the belly. In an aquarium, this fish will feed on pieces of fishes, shrimps, or virtually any fleshy food offered.

348, 349 Balloonfish
Diodon holocanthus

Description: To 18″ (46 cm). Elongate, robust, slightly depressed; *covered with long, 2-rooted, erectile spines, longest on forehead. Back light brown, with scattered, medium, dark brown spots;* belly light yellow; 4 dark bars on back, 1 on forehead extending down through eye; no spots on fins. Snout blunt; mouth small; 1 tooth in each jaw, fused to form parrot-like beak. Dorsal and anal fins soft-rayed; rear profile of caudal fin rounded.

Habitat: Over shallow reefs and soft bottoms from mangrove shores to coral reefs.

Range: In Atlantic around Bermuda and from FL to Brazil, including Bahamas, nw and s Gulf of Mexico, and Caribbean. In Pacific from Gulf of California to Peru.

Similar Species: Porcupinefish *(D. hystrix)* is covered with small dark spots, but lacks dark bars on back, and longest spines are behind pectoral fin.

Comments: Balloonfish is found worldwide in tropical seas. This puffer inflates itself with water or air when molested, and a mild toxin is secreted from the skin that is probably distasteful to potential predators. It is slow moving and easy to approach, making it a favorite with divers. In some areas it is harvested and dried in its inflated state to be sold to tourists.

351, 352 Porcupinefish
Diodon hystrix

Description: To 3′ (91 cm). Wide, slightly depressed, cylindrical in cross section; *covered with 2-rooted, spike-like, erectile spines, and small evenly distributed dark brown or blackish spots same diameter as spines.* Back tannish, with greenish hue above; sides lighter; belly white; dusky bar below each eye, another in front of each gill slit. 1 tooth in each jaw, fused to form parrot-like beak. Pectoral and caudal fins well developed; dorsal and anal fins short-based.

Habitat: Shallow coastal waters and coral reefs to depths of about 50' (15 m).

Range: In Atlantic from NC to Brazil, including Bermuda, Bahamas, and Caribbean; seasonally north to MA. In Pacific from San Diego, CA, to Chile.

Similar Species: Balloonfish *(D. holocanthus)* has longer spines on forehead and spots are larger than diameter of spines. Pacific Burrfish *(Chilomycterus affinis)* has short immovable spines with 3-rooted bases; occurs in shallow Pacific coastal waters.

Comments: Porcupinefish occurs worldwide in tropical seas. Most individuals collected are 10″ (25 cm) or less in length (or diameter when inflated). It feeds mostly on gastropods, sea urchins, crabs, and other crustaceans, using its strong beak to crush mollusks and other hard-shelled invertebrates. This species is not ordinarily used as a food fish.

MOLAS
Family Molidae

3 genera and 3 species worldwide; all found in North America (1 Atlantic, 2 Atlantic and Pacific). These distinctive and unusual fishes occur in tropical to subtropical seas throughout the world. They have a very deep and compressed body; the posterior portion of the body looks as though it has been cut off. The snout is short and blunt, and the mouth is very small. The gill opening is reduced to a small, round to oblong pore. Molas have very short-based dorsal and anal fins, usually with extremely long rays. The caudal fin is reduced to a feathery flap, except in Sharptail Mola *(Mola lanceolata)*.

366 Ocean Sunfish
Mola mola

Description: To 13′ (4 m); 3,300 lb (1,500 kg).
Deep, almost round, highly compressed.
Back grayish blue; sides and belly
metallic silver. Snout short, rounded;
mouth small; gill opening small. *No
pelvic fins; dorsal and anal fins very long,*
soft-rayed, placed far back on body;
*caudal fin greatly reduced, rounded, flap-
like.* Unscaled; covered with thick
mucus.

Habitat: Surface of open seas; occasionally near
shore.

Range: In Atlantic from Gulf of St. Lawrence to
Argentina, including Bermuda, Gulf of
Mexico, and Caribbean; probably in
Bahamas. In Pacific from BC to South
America.

Similar Species: Sharptail Mola *(M. lanceolata)* has lobe-
like, blunt-tipped projection just above
mid-body and obvious caudal fin with
18–20 rays; occurs in Atlantic. Slender
Mola *(Ranzania laevis)* has long slender
body and lacks caudal fin; occurs in
Pacific.

Comments: Ocean Sunfish is found worldwide in
tropical to temperate seas. All members
of the family feed on jellyfishes,
ctenophores, and salps. They are not
sought by sport or commercial anglers,
but they are a familiar sight, drifting
lazily on the surface of the water during
the late summer.

GLOSSARY

Abdominal Located on the ventral surface of the body, usually between the pelvic and anal fins.

Adherent scale A usually deeply embedded scale that does not slough off.

Adipose eyelid A thick translucent membrane partially covering the eyeball.

Adipose fin A fleshy fin, usually without supporting rays, behind the dorsal fin.

Anadromous Migrating from marine waters into fresh water to spawn.

Anal Pertaining to the anus or the surrounding area.

Anal fin The fin on the underside of the body; typically just behind the anus.

Anterior Located toward the front.

Axil The inner angle at which the pelvic or pectoral fin is joined to the body.

Axillary scale An enlarged elongate scale at the insertion of the pelvic or pectoral fin.

Band A broad, pigmented, vertical or diagonal line.

Bar A short, pigmented, vertical or diagonal line of varying width.

Barbel A fleshy, often whisker-like or thread-like projection of fleshy tissue, usually found near the mouth, chin, or nostrils.

Base The part of a fin joined to the body.

Basibranchial teeth Very small teeth just behind the base of the tongue.

Batoids Collective term for the sawfishes, skates, and rays.

Benthic Living on or associated with the bottom of a body of water.

Bioluminescent Having the ability to organically emit light.

Brackish Water that is slightly less salty than seawater.

Branchial Pertaining to the gills or gill chamber.

Branchiostegal rays The long, slightly curved, ray-like bones that support the gill membranes along the lower edge of the operculum.

Buckler A highly modified scale, often with a projecting spine.

Canine teeth Long, pointed, conical or lance-shaped teeth; typically larger than surrounding teeth.

Cardiform teeth Sharp teeth that are closely set in rows and look like the bristles of a brush.

Caudal Pertaining to the tail.

Caudal fin The fin on the posteriormost part of the body; also often referred to as the tail.

Caudal spot A dark area or spot, usually with a sharply defined edge, at the caudal fin base.

Caudal peduncle The part of the body between the posterior end of the dorsal and anal fins and the caudal fin base.

Ciguatera poisoning An illness in people caused by eating fish with toxic flesh.

Cirrus (*plural* cirri) A finger-like protuberance, sometimes occurring in a fringe-like series; typically located on the head.

Clasper A modified part of a pelvic fin; used in copulation.

Coastal waters Inshore waters.

Cold-temperate Having an annual average temperature of 36–54° F (2–12° C).

Complete lateral line A lateral line that runs uninterrupted from opercle to caudal fin base.

Compressed Flattened from side to side; higher than wide.

Conical Cone-shaped.

Continental shelf The submerged, relatively flat, gently sloping part of a continent extending from shore to depths of about 656′ (200 m).

Continental waters Waters bordering the continents; i.e., not around islands.

Corselet A girdle of small scales on the anterior part of the body.

Ctenoid scale A scale with small spines on the exposed edge.

Cusp A pointed projection, as on a tooth.

Cycloid scale A smooth scale without spines.

Deciduous scale A loosely attached scale that easily sloughs off.

Decurved Curved downward.

Denticle A small serration or prickle on the skin.

Depressed Flattened from top to bottom; wider than high.

Dermal ridge A ridge of skin.

Disjunct Describes a geographical distribution of a species that is characterized by major gaps; discontinuous.

Distribution The range of a species or population.

Dorsal Pertaining to the back or upper surface of the body.

Dorsal fin The fin on the midline of the back, supported by rays; often notched or divided into separate fins.

Drainage An area drained by a system of streams that join and flow into a major river.

Elongate Length proportionally much greater than depth.

Emarginate Notched, but not deeply forked.

Estuary A semi-enclosed tidal body of water of variable salinity, with free connection to the sea; or the lower end of a freshwater river. *Adjective:* estuarine.

Falcate Strongly inwardly curved or lunate.

Family A subset of an order, containing one or more genera.

Filament A long, thread-like structure.

Filter feeder A fish that feeds by removing plankton from the water using gill rakers.

Finlet A short, isolated, separate fin segment behind the dorsal and/or anal fins.

"Fishing pole" A usually greatly elongate modified dorsal fin spine (illicium); often with a fleshy "lure" (esca) at the tip used to attract prey.

Frenum A bridge of tissue connecting the upper jaws to the snout; also the bridge of overlapping tissue on the anteriormost part of the sucking disk in some species of the family Gobiidae.

Fusiform Spindle-shaped; tapering at both ends.

Ganoid scale A thick, hard, diamond-shaped scale.

Genus (*plural* genera) A subset of a family, containing one or more species.

Gill arch A bony or cartilaginous structure bearing gill filaments and gill rakers, located inside the gill chamber.

Gill cover The operculum.

Gill filaments Finger-like projections along the posterior surface of a gill arch.

Gill membrane Tissue along the outer edge of the operculum that prevents water from entering the gill chamber through the gill openings during respiration.

Gill opening The opening at the posterior end of the head through which water used in respiration leaves the body; may be pore-like or slit-like.

Gill rakers Slender, bony or hardened projections along the inner side of a gill arch.

Gills Filamentous respiratory organs.

Gular plate A bony plate on the throat between the lower jaw bones.

Habitat The physical and chemical environment in which an organism lives; an organism's ecological support system.

Heterocercal Describes a caudal fin in which the upper lobe is considerably larger than the lower; the vertebral column extends into the upper lobe.

Humeral Pertaining to the area just behind the opercle and above the pectoral fin base.

Hybrid An offspring resulting from the interbreeding of two different species.

Ichthyology The scientific study of fishes.

Incisor teeth Flattened teeth at the front of the mouth, forming a cutting edge.

Incomplete lateral line A lateral line that does not reach the caudal fin base.

Inferior Describes a mouth that is located on the underside of the head, with the upper jaw projecting beyond the lower.

Insertion The point at which the front of a paired fin is joined to the body.

Inshore waters Relatively shallow waters, including around islands, to depths of 656' (200 m).

Insular Pertaining to the area around an island.

Isthmus The narrow extension of the breast between the gill openings.

Juvenile A young individual that has not yet reached the adult form, color pattern, or reproduction stage.

Keel A sharp, fleshy or bony ridge.

Labial furrow A groove that extends forward from the corner of the mouth.

Lamella (*plural* lamellae) One of a series of thick, plate-like subdivisions that increase the surface area for respiration.

Lanceolate Lance-shaped.

Larva (*plural* larvae) The early developmental stage following the emergence from the egg, preceding the transformation to the juvenile stage. *Adjective:* larval.

Lateral At, pertaining to, or in the direction of the side.

Lateral line A connected series of tubes or pored scales associated with the sensory canal system; usually extending on each side of the body from the opercle to the caudal fin base.

Lateral series The rows of scales along the midline of the body between the gill opening and the caudal fin base.

Leptocephalus (*plural* leptocephali) Translucent, ribbon-like, pelagic larva.

Lobe A rounded projection.

Lunate Crescent-shaped.

"Lure" A fleshy appendage (esca) at the tip of a modified dorsal fin spine (illicium); used to attract prey.

Maxilla (*plural* maxillae) The posterior and usually larger of the two bones forming the upper jaw. *Adjective:* maxillary.

Median fins The unpaired fins: dorsal, anal, and caudal.

Melanophore A cell containing dark pigment; when contracted, these cells appear as pepper-like dots; when expanded, they may form large dusky gray to black areas.

Molar teeth Broad flat teeth used for grinding or crushing.

Morphology The physical attributes of an individual.

Myomere A muscle segment, each of which is separated from the adjacent segment by a septum.

Nape The area on the back between the head and the dorsal fin.

Nasal Pertaining to the nostrils and the surrounding area.

Nictitating membrane A thin membrane at the inner angle or beneath the lower lid of the eye; capable of extending across the eyeball, providing a protective cover.

Oblique Neither perpendicular nor parallel; at an angle.

Occiput The posteriormost part of the top of the head, where the head joins the nape. *Adjective:* occipital.

Ocellated Having one or more ocelli.

Ocellus (*plural* ocelli) A pigmented eye-like spot, usually dark with a lighter border.

Offshore waters Waters beyond the limits of the continental shelf.

Open bottom Without rocks or other obstructions.

Opercle The uppermost and largest of the bones that form the operculum. *Adjective:* opercular.

Operculum A movable bony plate covering the gill chamber; also known as the gill cover.

Order A subset of a class, containing one or more families.

Origin The point at which the front of a fin is joined to the body.

Oviparous reproduction Laying eggs that hatch outside of the mother's body.

Ovoviviparous reproduction Giving birth to live young that have hatched from eggs held inside the mother's body without receiving nutrients from her.

Oxbow lake A lake that is formed when a bend of a stream is cut off and isolated from the main channel; usually located in the flood plain adjacent to the stream channel.

Paired fins The fins that occur in pairs: the pelvic and pectoral.

Palatine teeth The teeth on the palatine bones, a pair of bones on the back of the roof of the mouth.

Papilla (*plural* papillae) A small, nipple-like projection, often occurring in groups. *Adjective:* papillose.

Parasite An organism that lives symbiotically with, and at the expense of, a host organism.

Pectoral fin The fin attached to the pectoral girdle; one on each side of the body.

Pectoral girdle A paired series of bones that supports the pectoral fin; also known as the shoulder girdle.

Pelagic Pertaining to or living in open waters above the bottom.

Pelvic fin The fin on the lower part of the body; one on each side of the body, usually just below or behind the pectoral fin.

Peritoneum The membrane lining the abdominal cavity.

Persistent Not shed or lost as the fish matures.

Pharyngeal teeth The teeth on the bones of the pharynx, the passage between the mouth and the esophagus; vary from blade-like to molar-like.

Photophore A light-emitting organ or spot.

Phylogeny The pattern of evolutionary history shown by a group of organisms.

Placoid scale A bony, usually rough, flat-based scale with a very hard, enamel-like outer layer.

Plankton Microscopic plants and animals that drift near the surface of open waters.

Plicate Folded, grooved, or wrinkled.

Population The individuals of a species in a given locality, usually forming an interbreeding community.

Pored scale A scale with a small opening into a sensory canal system; usually in a series along the lateral line.

Posterior Located toward the rear.

Precaudal Pertaining to the area immediately anterior to the caudal fin.

Predorsal Pertaining to the area on the back in front of the dorsal fin.

Prehensile Adapted for seizing or grasping.

Premaxilla (*plural* premaxillae) The anterior and usually smaller of the two bones forming the upper jaw. *Adjective:* premaxillary.

Preopercle The anteriormost bone of the operculum, below and behind the eye. *Adjective:* preopercular.

Preorbital bone The large bone just anterior to the eye, the lower part of which borders the upper jaw.

Prickle A small, pointed, highly modified scale.

Protractile Capable of forward extension; usually pertaining to the mouth.

Range The geographical area in which a species is usually found.

Ray One of the supporting structures in the fin membranes; may be either flexible (soft ray) or stiff (spine).

Recurved Curved or bent backward.

Reef A formation of coral, rocks, or other hard substrate, usually at or near the surface. Coral reefs are complex ecological associations of bottom-dwelling and attached calcareous marine invertebrates found in warm clear waters.

Reticulation A chain-like or net-like pattern of lines. *Adjective:* reticulate.

Rhomboid Resembling a parallelogram with no right angles.

Riffle A shallow rapid or shoal in a stream where the surface water breaks into waves.

River basin A network of rivers, creeks, and other bodies of water that flow or drain into a particular bay or ocean.

River system A river and its network of feeder streams, rivers, and lakes.

Robust Describes a strong, sturdy, full-bodied fish.

Roe The eggs of a fish.

Rostral Pertaining to the snout and the surrounding area.

Saddle A blotch or patch of pigment extending across the midline of the back and onto the sides.

Sargassum A free-floating brown seaweed that occurs in warm marine environments.

Scale One of the many hard or bony plates that cover the skin.

School A group of fish.

Scute A modified scale, often large and shield-like, with one or more keel-like ridges.

Sensory pore A small opening leading to the lateral line canal system on the head and/or body.

Serrate Saw-toothed or jagged-edged.

Serration A formation resembling the toothed edge of a saw.

Sexual dimorphism When males and females of the same species differ in size, shape, color, or other characteristics; when one sex has distinctive secondary sexual characteristics.

Snout The part of the head in front of the eye.

Soft ray A flexible, usually segmented and branched fin ray.

Spawn To release eggs and sperm into the water; to breed.

Species A group of interbreeding populations that are reproductively isolated from other such groups; a subset of a genus, possibly containing one or more subspecies.

Spine An unbranched and usually rigid, unsegmented fin ray; also a sharp bony projection on the head or body.

Spiracle A respiratory opening, varying in size, on the back part of the head above and behind each eye.

Straggler An individual that occurs irregularly; also known as a stray.

Stray An individual that occurs irregularly; also known as a straggler.

Striations Narrow parallel grooves or lines.

Stripe A thin horizontal line or area of pigment.

Subabdominal Located on the anterior half of the belly.

Subadult An individual that has reached the adult form and color but has not reached the reproductive stage.

Submarginal Adjacent to the edge.

Subopercle The lower bone supporting the operculum.

Subrostral Pertaining to the underside of the snout.

Subspecies A subset of a species, completely or partly isolated geographically and showing differences in morphology or coloration compared to other members of the species.

Substrate The bottom of a body of water.

Subterminal Describes a mouth that is located just behind the tip of the snout, with the upper jaw slightly projecting beyond the lower.

Subtropical Having an annual average temperature of 55–68° F (13–20° C).

Sucking disk An adhesive structure; a disk formed by a jawless mouth, the union of paired fins, or a modification of the dorsal fin spines.

Suctorial Adapted for sucking or to adhere by suction.

Superior Describes a mouth in which the lower jaw projects beyond the upper.

Supramaxilla An additional bone or bones along the upper edge of the maxilla. *Adjective:* supramaxillary.

Swim bladder A gas- or fat-filled sac that provides buoyancy.

Tapering Describing a body that is deepest anteriorly and narrows toward the tail.

Taxonomy The theory and practice of classifying organisms. The highest level is the kingdom, which is broken down into subgroups called divisions (for plants) or phyla (for animals). Phyla are divided into classes, classes into orders, and orders into families. Within families, animals are grouped into other taxonomic levels, given here in sequence from larger to smaller: subfamily, genus, species, and subspecies.

Temperate Having an annual average temperature of 50–55° F (10–13° C).

Tentacle A fleshy appendage on the head and/or body.

Tenuis larval stage An extremely elongate, ribbon-like larva, characterized by a small head; typically found in demersal habitats (near the bottom).

Terete Slightly tapering at both ends and round in cross section.

Terminal Describes a mouth located at the tip of the snout.

Thoracic Describes a pelvic fin located on the breast (as opposed to the belly) area below or ahead of the pectoral fin.

Tide pool A depression within the intertidal zone that is alternately submerged and exposed with water remaining inside.

Toothband A row of basically parallel teeth on the roof of the mouth.

Tooth patch An isolated patch of teeth; usually on the roof of the mouth.

Tooth plate A group of tooth-like elements located on structures in the gill and pharyngeal areas.

Transverse To go from side to side across the long axis.

Tributary A creek or river that flows into a larger body of water.

Tropical Having an annual average temperature of more than 68° F (20° C).

Truncate With a straight vertical edge.

Tubercle One of a group of hardened conical projections that develop on the surface of the body, especially the head.

Turbid Water that has low transparency, normally due to large quantities of suspended silt or sediment particles.

Ventral Pertaining to the underside or lower part of the body.

Vermiculations Fine wavy lines.

Vexillifer larval stage A bizarre type of pelagic larva with an extremely long, deciduous, thread-like first dorsal fin ray with fleshy attachments.

Villiform teeth Minute slender teeth in compact patches or bands.

Viviparous reproduction Bearing live young that have received nutrients from the mother during embryonic development.

Vomer teeth The teeth on the vomer bone, located in the front part of the roof of the mouth behind the upper jaw.

Waif An individual that occurs on a somewhat regular basis, often seasonally.

Warm-temperate Having an annual average temperature of more than 54–68° F (12–20° C).

PHOTO CREDITS

The numbers in parentheses are plate numbers. Some photographers have pictures under agency names as well as their own. Agency names appear in boldface. Photographers hold copyrights to their works.

Rudolf G. Arndt (37, 124, 125, 205, 645, 653)

Tony Arruza (2)

Auscape
Yves Lanceau (43 inset, 486)
Neil McDaniel (333)
D. Parer & E. Parer-Cook (478)

Juan Miguel Artigas Azas (612)

Frank S. Balthis (3)

Robert E. Barber (377)

Bill Barss/Oregon Dept. of Fish & Wildlife (613)

Gray Bass/FWCC (44, 50, 60, 207, 237, 244, 250, 500)

Dick Biggins/U.S. Fish & Wildlife Service (281)

Susan E. Blanchet/Blanchet Photographics (369, 370, 375, 376)

Bob Bowdey (614)

Boyceimage.com (664, 666)

Tom Boyden (80, 160, 452, 480, 526, 590)

John Brill (25, 173, 177, 241, 282, 395, 477)

Wayne & Karen Brown/Brown & Co. (344, 383, 384, 388, 413, 416, 472, 476, 482, 497, 498, 585, 586, 604, 608, 615, 656)

Richard T. Bryant (53, 61, 63, 82, 142, 161, 162, 168, 192, 200, 233, 234, 291, 311, 323, 426, 474, 553, 652)

Frank Burek (99, 351, 470, 503, 581, 681, 682)

Joyce Burek (378, 379, 385, 405, 424, 443, 446, 447, 449, 463, 539, 606, 616, 618, 687, 689)

George H. Burgess (671)

Noel Burkhead (134)

B. M. Burr (41, 131, 229)

Francis E. Caldwell (557)

Francis & Donna Caldwell (552, 554, 555, 556)

Michael Cardwell (521, 595)

Marc Chamberlain (170)

Brandon D. Cole/brandoncole.com (435, 496, 704)

Bruce Coleman, Inc.
Gary Meszaros (52, 221)
Norman Tomalin (29, 639)

Mark Conlin (453, 461, 491, 580, 658, 676)

Gerald & Buff Corsi/Focus on Nature, Inc. (310, 527)

Bob Cranston (317, 320, 366, 637, 641, 670, 710)

E. R. Degginger/Color-Pic, Inc. (28, 36, 59, 77, 90, 546)

Renee DeMartin (86, 349)

Dembinsky Photo Associates
Susan E. Blanchet (358)
Gary Meszaros (46, 140, 187)

Kathy deWet-Oleson (632)

Andrew Drake (434)

John Elk III (9)

David J. Elliott (533)

Eric Engbretson (112)

Donald Flescher/NMFS (338, 361, 515, 519, 520, 529, 568, 663)

Jeff Foott (14, 457)

Richard Forbes (128, 135, 218, 421, 469, 489, 592)

Robert Fournier/The Wild Lensman (65)

Dennis Frates (5)

R. Bruce Gebhardt (96, 97, 151, 179, 198, 206, 209, 217, 225, 231, 269, 271)

John P. George (19)

Susan M. Glascock (98, 108, 239, 257, 263, 355, 391, 393, 540, 576, 588)

Daniel W. Gotshall (89, 307, 335, 337, 445, 451, 464, 534, 567, 593, 621)

Ken Graham Agency
David Hoffman (85)

Richard T. Grost (149)

Al Grotell (402)

Howard Hall/HHP (512, 668)

Thomas Hallstein/Outsight (21)

Chuck Haney (23)

Richard Herrmann (305, 329, 444, 466, 501, 683)

Michael Hubrich (10)

Joanne Huemoeller (591)

Paul H. Humann (343, 655, 660, 691)

Chris Huss (79, 81, 438, 440, 455, 456, 506, 550, 551)

Gregory C. Jensen (326, 336, 425, 483, 502)

Mike Johnson/earthwindow.com (696)

Breck P. Kent (43, 58, 150, 277, 485)

Kentucky Dept. of Fish & Wildlife Resources (155, 163, 679)

Ed King (13, 15)

Stephen Kirkpatrick (288)

David Liebman (145)

Bill Lindner Photography (35)

Milton Love (517, 566)

Ken Lucas Photo (133, 354)

Douglas F. Markle (132)

Andrew J. Martinez (1, 106, 365, 372, 410, 441, 505, 507, 544, 610)

Mittelhaeuser Photography (356, 381, 403, 418, 601)

Mondragonphoto.com
   Bradley Sheard (83)

C. Allan Morgan (116, 146, 174, 622)

Nebraska Game & Parks Commission/*NEBRASKAland Magazine* (104)

norbertwu.com
   Brandon D. Cole (488)
   Avi Klapter (665, 714)
   James D. Watt (667, 673)
   Norbert Wu (321, 672, 674, 699)

Patrick O'Neil (27, 56, 110, 147, 152, 191, 193, 202, 247, 296)

David Ostendorf/David Herzog/ Robert Hrabik (188, 224, 248)

Laurence Parent (18)

James F. Parnell (95, 180, 427)

John Pennington/Sea-Pen Photo (458, 459, 518, 698)

Photo Researchers, Inc.
   Charles V. Angelo (401, 407, 596)
   H. Berthoule/Jacana (74, 549)
   Collins (236)
   Joseph T. Collins (226)
   E. R. Degginger (94, 103, 259, 392)
   R. J. Erwin (57)
   David Hall (352)

John Lidington (475)

George Lower (562, 661)

Fred McConnaughey (380, 389, 400, 408, 409, 473, 531, 599, 600, 605, 657)

Tom McHugh (87, 327, 509, 558, 564, 577, 579, 589, 646, 675, 707)

Tom McHugh/Dallas Aquarium (115)

Tom McHugh/Steinhardt Aquarium (169, 341, 705, 720)

Gary Meszaros (54, 100, 109, 270)

Mohr (235)

G. Carleton Ray (624)

Bucky Reeves (439)

David T. Roberts (216, 251)

David M. Schleser (48, 144, 201, 238)

Mark Smith (183, 223, 261)

Alvin E. Staffan (51, 141, 167, 194, 195, 197, 284, 298, 303)

William E. Townsend (448)

Varin-Visage/Jacana (685)

Andrew G. Wood (345)

Harold Wes Pratt (339, 511)

ProPhoto
   James Beveridge (368)
   Mark Giovannetti (38, 73, 78, 84, 105, 547, 548)
   Doug Stamm (92, 119, 156)

John E. Randall (404, 429, 654)

Bruce Elliott Rasner (709)

Paul Rezendes (4, 8, 11, 12, 16, 17)

Joe Richard (627)

John Rinne (76, 130, 178, 182)

Eda Rogers (650)

Fred Rohde (55, 153, 278, 342, 494, 572, 688)

Steve W. Ross (186, 340, 516, 617, 649)

William Roston (75, 111, 139, 148, 172, 196, 210, 212, 213, 214, 215, 219, 227, 228, 243, 245, 249, 254, 262, 272, 275, 276, 283, 286, 287, 289, 290, 292, 293, 294, 295, 297, 299, 300, 302, 396, 398)

Jeff Rotman (308, 719)

Randal Sanders (88, 331)

David M. Schleser/Nature's Images, Inc. (91, 253)

W. D. Schmid (30, 39 inset, 39, 67, 138, 143, 157, 164, 189, 208, 267, 268, 678)

Konrad Schmidt/MN DNR (40, 154, 199, 211, 252)

Charles Seaborn/Odyssey, Chicago (619, 631)

Seapics.com
Daniel W. Gotshall (504)
Howard Hall (713)
Marilyn Kazmers (524)
Marilyn & Maris Kazmers (347)
Patrick O'Neil (536)
Doug Perrine (68, 306, 318, 319, 324, 353, 363, 374, 490, 492, 530, 543, 559, 587, 628, 662, 700, 701, 702, 708, 715)
James D. Watt (717, 718)

Herb Segars/gotosnapshot.com (313, 316, 328, 332, 367, 386, 414, 415, 462, 484, 514, 573, 602, 626, 633, 638, 706)

Marc Shargel/Lumigenic.com (659)

John G. Shedd Aquarium (32, 34, 45, 64, 93, 120, 121, 158, 159, 171, 175, 264, 315, 350, 433, 450, 495, 565, 569, 578, 582, 583, 609, 635, 640, 651)
Patrice Ceisel (49, 102, 137, 417)
Edward G. Lines, Jr. (71, 117, 304, 312, 419)

Allen Blake Sheldon (7, 20)

J. R. Shute/CFI (190, 273, 274)

Bill Silliker, Jr. (22)

Steve Simonsen (330, 346, 371, 387, 411, 468, 471, 525, 594, 597, 703)

Rob & Ann Simpson (101, 176, 280, 560)

Garold W. Sneegas (62, 66, 203)

David B. Snyder (362, 382, 406, 535, 541, 598, 630, 690, 712)

Richard A. Snyder (184, 397, 479, 644)

Alvin E. Staffan/Ohio Dept. of Natural Resources (41 inset)

Dr. Charles Steinmetz, Jr. (31, 69, 510, 563, 570, 574, 692)

Scot Stewart (72, 279)

Thomas L. Taylor (230)

Graeme Teague (322, 390, 460, 532)

Mark Turner (6)

Ursus Photography
Finn Larsen (42, 126, 487)

Visuals Unlimited
David S. Addison (26, 240, 394, 481, 523, 571, 634)
Hal Beral (373)
Patrice Ceisel (70, 181, 430)
Dave B. Fleetham (693)
R. J. Goldstein (118, 122, 123, 165, 420, 499, 528)
Daniel W. Gotshall (334, 454, 465, 677)
Bill Kamin (47)
Ken Lucas (107, 127, 256, 260, 364, 412, 428, 647, 648)
Gary Meszaros (185, 204, 220, 222, 242, 246, 265, 285, 166)
Glen M. Oliver (136, 258, 266, 399)
Patrice (114, 623)
Fred Rohde (113, 522, 538, 611)
Rob & Ann Simpson (33, 255, 636)
Robert C. Simpson (301)
David Wrobel (309, 314, 436, 467, 508, 537, 584)

Michele Warren (513)

WaterHouse Marine Images
Stephen Frink (348, 359, 360, 432, 442, 493, 561, 603, 607, 620, 625, 629, 642, 669, 684, 694, 716)
Marty Snyderman (325, 431)

Wildlife Collection
Chris Huss (357, 422, 423, 542, 643)

Krissy Wilson/Utah Division Wildlife Resources (129, 232)

Art Womack/art@awfoto.com (437)

George Wuerthner (24)

Robert Yin (695, 711)

INDEX

Numbers in boldface type refer to color plate numbers. Numbers in italic type refer to page numbers.

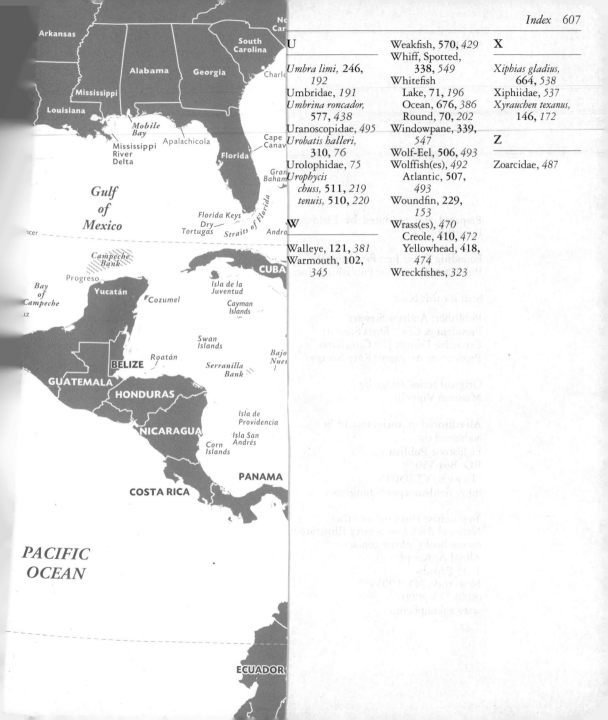

Arkansas

South
Carolina

Alabama Georgia

Mississippi

Louisiana

Mobile
Bay

Apalachicola

Mississippi
River
Delta

Florida

*Gulf
of
Mexico*

Florida Keys
Dry
Tortugas Straits of Florida

Campeche
Bank

Progreso

Bay
of
Campeche

Yucatán Cozumel

Isla de la
Juventud

Cayman
Islands

CUBA

Swan
Islands

BELIZE Roatán

Serranilla
Bank

GUATEMALA

HONDURAS

NICARAGUA

Corn
Islands

Isla de
Providencia

Isla San
Andrés

PANAMA

COSTA RICA

*PACIFIC
OCEAN*

ECUADOR

STAFF

Prepared and produced by Fieldstone Publishing Inc.

Founding Publisher: Paul Steiner
Publisher: Fieldstone Publishing, Inc.

Staff for this book:

Publisher: Andrew Stewart
President & CEO: Shyla Stewart
Executive Editor: Jim Cirigliano
Production Assistant: Katy Savage

Original series design by
Massimo Vignelli

All editorial inquiries should be
addressed to:
Fieldstone Publishing
P.O. Box 550
Norwich, VT 05055
info@fieldstonepublishing.com

To purchase this book or other
National Audubon Society illustrated
nature books, please contact:
Alfred A. Knopf
1745 Broadway
New York, NY 10019
(800) 733-3000
www.aaknopf.com